A HISTORY OF JAPAN
TO 1334

STANFORD STUDIES IN THE CIVILIZATIONS
OF EASTERN ASIA

Editors

ARTHUR F. WRIGHT   GEORGE SANSOM   JOHN D. GOHEEN
ROBERT H. BROWER   MARY CLABAUGH WRIGHT

A HISTORY OF JAPAN
TO 1334

George Sansom

STANFORD UNIVERSITY PRESS
STANFORD, CALIFORNIA

PREFACE

After the publication in 1931 of a volume on the cultural history of Japan and in 1950 of a study of the early impact of the West upon Far Eastern life, I planned for the future a complementary volume tracing the growth of Japanese civilization chiefly in its political and social aspects. I even contemplated an interpretative treatment, but I soon decided that this would be a rash venture, indeed a visionary task. I found that the mere collection and arrangement of facts would require not one volume but three, and would consume all the time and assiduity I could command. Consequently the thoughtful student will find in this book only a few matter-of-fact interpretations and here and there a comparison which may be useful although far-fetched.

Perhaps it is as well, for one who writes on the history of an Asian country for ordinary readers and not for professional scholars, to refrain from drawing any but the simplest conclusions from the material which he presents. A great deal has been written lately about philosophies of history, and it makes enjoyable reading. But it affords no practical guidance to the historian describing a living culture to which he does not belong and with which his readers are unfamiliar unless they happen to be specialists. The struggling Orientalist does not appear to come within the purview of the philosophers. He had better eschew theoretical assumptions about human societies and confine himself to a straightforward narrative.

That is what I have attempted here. I should add that throughout I have made use of the work of leading Japanese historians, both general and special studies, and I have also been careful to consult primary sources.

G. B. S.

ACKNOWLEDGMENTS

During the past three years I have been able to devote my time to the preparation of this work thanks to a generous grant from the Rockefeller Foundation. This grant was sponsored by Columbia University, New York; and I am much indebted to my former colleagues there for encouragement and help, especially the members of the East Asian Institute and the keepers of the East Asiatic Collections in the Library.

For valuable assistance I am indebted to Dr. Helen McCullough, who both in Japan and at the University of California helped me by furnishing translations, locating source material, checking references, and generally contributing to work in progress.

The East Asiatic Library of the University of California at Berkeley, under the direction of Dr. Elizabeth Huff, has provided exceptional facilities and a considerate treatment for which I shall always be thankful.

To my friends at Stanford University, and especially the staff of the Hoover Institution, I owe thanks every day for kind acts and good advice. I owe special thanks to Dr. Joseph Williams, Professor of Geography at Stanford, for preparing the maps and charts.

Dr. Arthur Waley gave me full permission to quote from his incomparable works and I am obliged to his publishers, George Allen and Unwin, Ltd. in England and the Houghton Mifflin Company in the United States, for authority to quote passages from *The Tale of Genji*. Edwin Arnold & Co. have kindly allowed me to quote briefly from *Japanese Buddhism* by Sir Charles Eliot.

Several Japanese scholars have given me precious help. I owe particular thanks to Professor Rikichiro Fukui, Professor Kenji Maki, Professor Katsumi Mori, and Mr. Masao Ishizawa, Curator of Research Materials at the Tokyo National Museum.

Last but not least among those whom I wish to thank are my friends at the School of Oriental and African Studies in the University of London, with which I was happily associated for several years.

CONTENTS

DESCRIPTIVE LIST OF PLATES

FRONTISPIECE

The upper part of a life-size standing figure in clay, originally painted. It represents a divine being. It is a superb example of the sculpture of the Tempyō period (720–810). In the Nara Tōdaiji.

1. The Hōryūji monastery from the air. The arrangement of buildings is that of the early eighth century, and much of the original work has survived, including the double-roofed Kondō (Golden Hall) and the Pagoda. The photograph is by Satō Tetsuzō, of Kyoto.

2. The handwriting of Kūkai. It is a portion of one of his letters to Saichō, known as the *Fūshin-chō*, from the opening words *Fūshin unsho*, "Tidings on the wind, writing of the clouds," by which he acknowledges the receipt of a message from Saichō. The original belongs to the Tōji in Kyoto.

3. Detail of a bronze lantern in the Tōdaiji, Nara. Eighth century.

4. Image of Bishamon (an Indian deity) subjugating evil. It is known as the Tobatsu Bishamon, and belongs to the ninth century, probably about 820. Bishamon is trampling upon two demons and is supported by a minor earth deity who has been converted to the Buddhist faith. The image may be regarded as an expression in art of the transition between Nara and Kyoto life which accompanied the move to a new capital just before A.D. 800.

5. Image (wood) of the Buddha Sâkya in the Muroji. Dated about A.D. 900, it is a fine example of the so-called Jōgan or Kōnin style, prevalent during the century after the move from Nara. It shows a departure from the gentle realism of Nara (Tempyō) sculpture and the growth of a formalism which, despite its technical excellence, tends to be solemn and at times heavy. The influence of the new Buddhist sects, and the loss of the fresh inspiration of the eighth century, are visible even in this excellent piece.

6. Portion of a scroll representing a ritual dance at the Festival of the Firstfruits (Niiname-Sai), performed late in the eleventh month in the courtyard of the Daigokuden, one of the palace buildings used for great public ceremonies. In the foreground are the musicians. Between them and the steps is a row of rice plants bearing ripe grain. From the Nenjūgyōji scroll.

7. Scene at the annual Archery Contest. Servants with staves driving back spectators intruding on the target area. From the Nenjūgyōji scroll.

8. Courtiers on duty in the royal apartments. From the Picture Scroll of Murasaki's Diary (Murasaki Shikibu Nikki Emaki) in the collection of the Hachisuka family.

NOTE ON THE NENJŪGYŌJI SCROLL

The first pictorial record of the annual Court ceremonies seems to have
been a scroll prepared for the Emperor Go-Shirakawa, about A.D. 1150. The
subsequent history of the scroll is not exactly known, but it seems to have
escaped loss or injury until 1350. It was carefully copied by court painters,
but original and copies went up in flames in the Ōnin war of 1467–68, except
for one copy which was kept in the house of the hereditary Court painters, the
Sumiyoshi family.

The scroll from which the illustrations in this book are taken is a version
of the Sumiyoshi copy (or of about twenty rolls of the original thirty). The
scenes which they portray may be taken as good evidence of the nature of
Court ceremonial in the middle ages from about 1200. A reproduction of
seventeen rolls was published in Kyoto in 1956 by Shichijō Kenzō.

LIST OF ILLUSTRATIONS IN TEXT

A HISTORY OF JAPAN
TO 1334

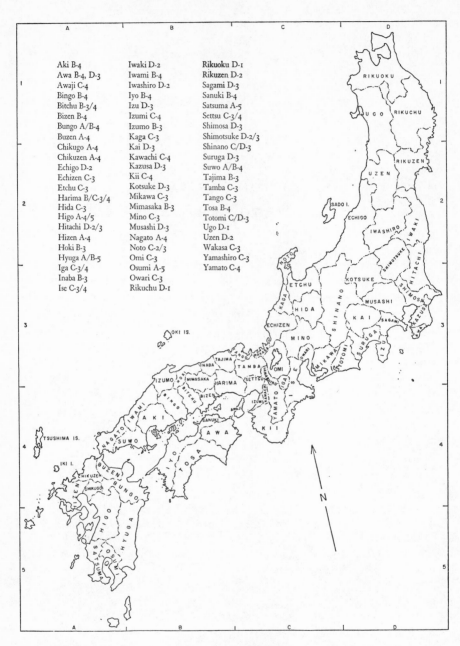

Aki B-4
Awa B-4, D-3
Awaji C-4
Bingo B-4
Bitchu B-3/4
Bizen B-4
Bungo A/B-4
Buzen A-4
Chikugo A-4
Chikuzen A-4
Echigo D-2
Echizen C-3
Etchu C-3
Harima B/C-3/4
Hida C-3
Higo A-4/5
Hitachi D-2/3
Hizen A-4
Hoki B-3
Hyuga A/B-5
Iga C-3/4
Inaba B-3
Ise C-3/4

Iwaki D-2
Iwami B-4
Iwashiro D-2
Iyo B-4
Izu D-3
Izumi C-4
Izumo B-3
Kaga C-3
Kai D-3
Kawachi C-4
Kazusa D-3
Kii C-4
Kotsuke D-3
Mikawa C-3
Mimasaka B-3
Mino C-3
Musashi D-3
Nagato A-4
Noto C-2/3
Omi C-3
Osumi A-5
Owari C-3
Rikuchu D-1

Rikuoku D-1
Rikuzen D-2
Sagami D-3
Sanuki B-4
Satsuma A-5
Settsu C-3/4
Shimosa D-3
Shimotsuke D-2/3
Shinano C/D-3
Suruga D-3
Suwo A/B-4
Tajima B-3
Tamba C-3
Tango C-3
Tosa B-4
Totomi C/D-3
Ugo D-1
Uzen D-2
Wakasa C-3
Yamashiro C-3
Yamato C-4

The provinces of Japan

The five northern provinces correspond to the earlier Mutsu and Dewa. There are two provinces named Awa; the names are written with different characters. The islands of Iki, Oki, Sado, and Tsushima are not provinces. A term commonly heard is "the Sixty-Six Provinces," that being the number about A.D. 1000. The number varied after that by two or three, following administrative changes.

CHAPTER I

THE LAND

S o m e millions of years ago, from the ocean floor at its greatest known depths, mighty volcanic convulsions thrust up above sea level the Japanese archipelago, which now stretches in an arc, bent away from the mainland of Asia, between the latitudes of 30° and 45° north. The highest peaks in Japan rise to some two miles above sea level. The great Tuscarora Deep, off the eastern flank of the islands, descends more than five miles below sea level. Geologists say that so immense a range of elevation within short lateral distances develops such stresses that this part of the earth's crust is a highly unstable area of numerous volcanoes and frequent earthquakes.

These are the circumstances which have determined the shape of the Japanese islands, the composition of their soil, and the behaviour of their inhabitants—what we loosely call the national character—in so far as behaviour is formed by the response of a people to its environment. The nature of that response is as important as the nature of the challenge; but a full understanding of the course of Japanese history cannot be gained without some knowledge of the physical characteristics of the land. These must be examined in some detail, but first it is necessary to place Japan in its wider setting as part of the region of Asia to which, despite its isolated position, it definitely belongs by geography as well as by culture. That is the vast monsoon area, which stretches from the Maritime Province of Siberia in the north to India in the southwest, and includes the great rice-producing regions of south China, Indochina, Indonesia, Siam, Burma, and the Philippine Islands.

A distinguishing feature of this area, a feature which gives it a certain organic unity, is the regularity of the seasonal winds. In summer they blow from the south over tropical seas and bring heavy rainfall to the heated land. In winter they blow from the northern parts of the Asian land mass towards the south, bringing lower temperatures and usually dry, sunny weather.

Dependence upon this constant rhythm produces a uniform character in the economic life of the inhabitants of eastern and southeastern Asia. It is true that in recent times intercourse with the industrial societies of the West has modified the agrarian societies of the East, but substantially they remain unchanged. Their life cannot escape the influence of the great epic of growth that is repeated year by year on an immense scale. The regular alternation of climatic phases in the monsoon area is most favourable to wet rice culture, and therefore great aggregations of sedentary peasant cultivators are found in those tracts of land that combine the best alluvial soil with the most dependable supply of water. Except in very favourable conditions they gain only a bare livelihood, and population is always pressing upon the limits of subsistence. They are the chief producers. The economy is mainly agrarian and there is little industry beyond what is needed for the manufacture of simple tools, household implements, and clothing. Because the economy is so predominantly agrarian, the common form of wealth is land, and the ruling class lives upon revenue from land, in the form of rent or tax. In these circumstances political institutions tend to despotism, for it is to the interest of the rulers to prevent change and to repress even the mildest forms of insubordination. Consequently the whole monsoon area is historically of a conservative character in social and political as well as economic life.

This aspect of Asian society is perhaps best appreciated by comparison with a typical European area, namely the Mediterranean, which has an organic unity of its own, in some respects not unlike the organic unity of the monsoon area. The summer climate of the Mediterranean countries is under the sway of the northeast trade winds, which originate in the Eurasian land mass and carry little moisture. In summer therefore the heat is great, but it is bearable because the atmosphere is dry. In winter there is a fairly heavy rainfall. It is irregular, but there are long bright intervals, so that the Mediterranean peoples are in general free from the depressing effects of both continuous cold and humid heat. By contrast with the monsoon area the really adverse feature of the Mediterranean climate is drought; and it is this which accounts for some of the important differences between life in the monsoon area and life in the southern parts of Europe.

Historically, in the home of European civilization—in the Greek archipelago—agriculture was severely limited by the configuration of the land and by the hot rainless summer. Here there was no possibility of increasing the area of arable land and from very early times the Greeks, for lack of grains, were obliged to seek subsistence in colonization and foreign trade. The history of ancient Greece is largely a history of seafaring, and Greek civilization was mainly the product of towns and cities with a maritime tradition. There has been, it is true, much sea travel between points in the monsoon area of Asia since very ancient times. Nevertheless, because of the great extent of cultivable soil and the abundance of water for irrigation, the great mass of the population remained at work on the land, and trading by sea was not felt to be of vital importance to the rice-growing peoples, since it dealt in luxuries rather than necessities.

In Greece and in general in the Mediterranean region there was no dominant land-revenue economy, but an economy dependent upon a carrying trade, which consisted largely of an exchange of wine and olive oil for corn grown in well-irrigated regions at a distance from the dry countries. Those who were engaged in this traffic were landless

men, but because they had capital resources in the form of special experience and skill the landlord did not enjoy in Greek territory that
virtual monopoly of economic and political power which was commonly
exercised by landowners as a class throughout the monsoon area.

Although Japan is situated on the edge of the monsoon area, it is
definitely under monsoon influence, and in respect of climate it partakes of the general character of the monsoon countries of eastern and
southeastern Asia. The following outline of the physical features of
the Japanese archipelago should therefore be read in the light of what
has been said of the whole area.

Because the arc formed by the Japanese islands stretches from high
latitudes not far from the Arctic zone down to subtropical latitudes,
it presents a variety of climates. But the most thickly populated and
most productive parts of Japan enjoy a climate that is genial and on
the whole stimulating. Summers are hot, winters are cold, but there
are no unbearable extremes. There is plenty of sunshine, plenty of rain.
The land is clothed with luxuriant vegetation, decorated with shapely
trees and lovely blossoms, enlivened by quick water. Nowhere in the
world are there more enchanting landscapes among the hills, across
the plains, and by the sea. It is a land suited to breed a vigorous race
of men and women happy in their surroundings. Yet it is a country
that hides poverty behind a smiling face. The very features that make
for natural beauty are often signs of infertile places. Three-fourths of
the land area is hill and mountain terrain unfit for the cultivation of
necessary food crops; and although much sloping ground is tilled thanks
to laborious terracing and embanking, the total area under cultivation
is less than one-sixth of the area of the whole country. Nor is all this
cultivable soil of high fertility, for (as is common in monsoon countries) abundant rains carry away soluble minerals which planted crops
need, and oblige the farmer to use great quantities of fertilizer. Furthermore, even the good cultivable soils, quite apart from these handicaps, are usually low in organic matter, because Japan, in common with
other countries in the area, has hardly any natural grasslands where
the matted roots turn into a rich humus and where herds or flocks at
pasture can furnish manure.

The richest soils in Japan occur only in certain alluvial plains, which
are not of very wide extent. The largest of these plains are on the
eastern (Pacific) side of the main island of Japan. They are only three
in number. One is the Kantō plain, at the head of Tokyo Bay, covering
about 5,000 square miles. The second is at the head of Ise Bay, covering
about 600 square miles. The third is the Kinai plain, covering 500 square
miles, at the head of Osaka Bay. These three plains between them
contain the greatest centres of population. They are of special importance in the history of Japan, because the growth of her social and
political institutions and the general nature of her culture have been

shaped in a large measure by rivalry for the possession of these, the main areas of food production and consequently the main sources of wealth and power. The earliest migrations of tribes from southwest to central and eastern Japan were doubtless movements in search of good land. The successive centres of political authority were the centres of rice culture in these fertile plains. Ise in remote antiquity was the home of the Food Goddess; the Kinai[1] plain includes Osaka, the great commercial centre, and Kyoto, the ancient capital city; and the Kantō plain includes Yedo (the modern Tokyo), long a place of strategic importance and after 1600 the main seat of feudal power.

The recurrent civil wars before 1600 were all in essence struggles for the possession of good rice lands, and feudal society was based primarily upon the conditions of the tenure of those lands. Though other grain crops (mostly unirrigated, such as barley, wheat, and millet), together with vegetables, mulberry, and tea, are grown in fair quantities in soil unsuited for wet rice culture, rice has always dominated the agrarian economy of Japan. This has been partly a matter of tradition, for rice has always been the preferred diet of the Japanese people, who do not willingly eat other cereals. This long-established taste is enough to explain why rice was grown almost to the exclusion of other food crops, but it must be added that physical conditions in all but the northern parts of Japan are favourable to its growth, and even in some regions allow of double cropping.

Subtropical warmth, abundant summer rains, easy irrigation, and strong sunshine in the ripening season continue to make rice the crop with the highest yield of grain for the space that it occupies. It requires intensive labour performed in tiny fields; and this fact has played a part in determining the character of peasant life. At the same time its position as the staple, almost the single, food crop has made the agrarian economy singularly vulnerable to abnormal weather conditions. Throughout the history of Japan fluctuations of population are recorded which are not easy to explain but seem to bear a direct relation to failures of the rice crop. Such failures have been recorded at intervals until recent times, when diversity of crops and the possibility of imports have removed the danger of famine.

The importance of agricultural products is heightened by the scarcity of other natural resources in Japan, for the land is poor in the materials of industry, even of such industry as existed before the machine age. Iron, copper, gold, silver, and mercury were mined in moderate quantities before the industrial age; but, for building and the making of utensils other than edged tools, wood from the upland forests together with the versatile bamboo served most purposes of use and ornament.

[1] The Kinai is a region consisting of the five provinces surrounding the capital: Yamashiro, Yamato, Kawachi, Izumi, and Settsu.

Thus from high antiquity the Japanese people were accustomed to a simple and frugal existence in surroundings agreeable to the eye. Thereby, it is pleasant to suppose, they learned the art of living without a multiplicity of possessions, and from such conditions there arose that love of natural beauty and that deeply rooted aesthetic tradition which seem to be their national heritage.

It was fortunate for them that they were able to cultivate the arts of peace free from the threat of invasion, for although Japan shares many characteristics with other countries in the monsoon region, her situation is somewhat remote. The most westerly point of the Japanese archipelago is distant some 120 miles from the nearest part of the mainland of Asia; and navigation of the China Sea is often dangerous for small craft. Moreover, approach to the mainland from Japan is made difficult for sailing vessels by the fact that the main ocean currents—the cold Oyashio or Okhotsk Current and the warm Kuroshio or Black Stream—flow from north and south respectively towards the shores of Japan. Further, the winter monsoon blows strongly away from northeast Asia in the direction of Japan and the summer monsoon is apt at its strongest to blow from southwest to northeast, and thus to discourage communication with China by direct sea routes. Communication by sea in both directions was of course possible and at chosen times not dangerous; but conditions in general were not such as to stimulate regular and continuous intercourse between Japan and other countries.

The contrast here between Japan and (say) Greece is very marked, since in the Mediterranean the prevalence of regular land and sea breezes, the clear atmosphere, the numerous harbours, and the distinct landmarks encouraged maritime traffic and therefore made for a degree of interdependence, political as well as economic, among Mediterranean countries. Japan's geographical situation, on the other hand, though it may have deprived her of some benefits, has by its remoteness resulted in a high degree of independence and has given a distinct, if not a unique, quality to Japanese civilization.

There are certain features of the geography of Japan which should be borne in mind as qualifying general statements about climatic conditions and their effect upon conditions of life. In the first place it must be reiterated that the Japanese archipelago has a very wide range of latitude which includes wide variations in climatic character. The crucial climatic division is at approximately latitude 38° north. Above this the winter weather is cold and the summer weather usually fine, but not hot, so that country north of the parallel must be regarded as marginal for rice culture and outside the monsoon area. South of the parallel the climate is humid and subtropical, and conditions are therefore favourable to wet rice culture.

Another division is morphological, and only indirectly climatic.

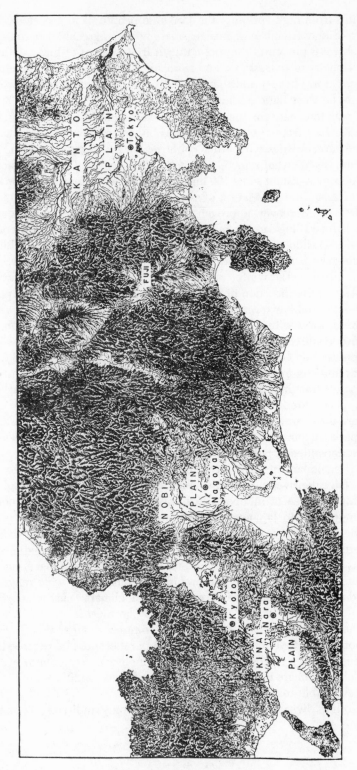

The three great alluvial plains

According to it Japan consists of two zones, Outer and Inner, parallel
to one another in the direction of the northeast-southwest axis of the
main island. The Outer Zone is on the Pacific side, and the Inner Zone
faces northeast Asia across the Japan Sea. The geological characters
of these zones differ in several respects.[2] They are too complex for
discussion here, but for broad historical purposes it is enough to point
out that such differences exist, and account for corresponding differences in habits, dress, speech, and other matters, especially where communities are separated from one another by difficulty of communication. Regional and local differences in Japan must not be overlooked,
though they are not such as to impair in any significant way the homo-
geneity which the people have presented since the formation of a centralized state in the seventh century.

Generally speaking, the population of the Inner Zone is isolated
from the population of the Outer Zone by mountains that form the
broad backbone of the main island. There is only one route which
affords easy access across country from the Asiatic to the Pacific side,
and that is from Wakasa Bay on the Japan Sea coast to the eastern end
of the Inland Sea. By contrast, land travel from the western extremity
of the main island to the ancient capital at Kyoto, following the northern shoreline of the Inland Sea, was always easy; and when the journey
was continued in the direction of the eastern provinces there was no
serious obstacle other than some fordable rivers and the Hakone Pass,
at an elevation of less than 3,000 feet. This whole journey comprised
the well-known Tōkaidō or Eastern Seaboard route. The Hakone Barrier, as it was called, was the key strategical point for the control of
traffic between the capital and the fertile area at the head of Tokyo Bay.

One result of the mountainous character of Japan was a familiarity
with high places which is in strong contrast to the fear of mountain
regions common in Europe until the end of the eighteenth century.[3]
It is not only a familiarity but also a liking for what is remote and, from
the point of view of both the religious recluse and the travelling poet,
beautiful and uncontaminated. Mountain places appear in Japanese
legend as the homes of gods and saints, not of evil spirits. In Japan and
also in China a peak or a high pass was thought to be a most suitable
site for a holy edifice, and the word *san* ("mountain") is often affixed
to the name of a monastery or a group of such buildings, as in Kōya-san
and Hiyei-san, two of the most famous monastic foundations in Japanese

[2] For details see G. T. Trewartha, *Geography of Japan*, a fascinating and indispensable work.

[3] Perhaps the English reader should be reminded that Gilpin, referring to the
English Lake District, wrote in 1772: "Here is Beauty indeed, lying in the lap of
Horrour." In the previous century, before ideas of the romantic and the picturesque
had developed, travellers admired classic landscapes, but were frightened by the
Alps.

history. The habit was perhaps borrowed from China, where such
religious establishments as Wutai-shan were often named after mountaintops.

The ascetic living in a lonely place is a common figure in the religious life of India, and in China and Japan Taoist sages and Buddhist
confraternities resorted to high places for the practice of their cults.
In Japan the love of wild scenery, of mountaintops and passes, is very
ancient and does not depend upon foreign example. The province of
Yamato in high antiquity was regarded as an especially holy land,
inhabited by great gods who protected its peaks and forests.

By contrast with this enjoyment of mountains Japan has suffered
from the turbulence of her rivers, because their descent from their
mountain sources to the narrow coastal plains is steep and rapid. There
are few really navigable rivers, and indeed one might say of most of
the streams that their swift currents, though pleasing to the romantic
eye, are obstacles rather than aids to travel. The names of rivers occur
in Japanese poetry, but they do not play a prominent part in legend
or in history. The difference here between Japan and other countries
is almost startling, for there is nothing in her folklore that plays such
a part in forming national sentiment as (let us say) the "sweet Thames,"
the quiet-flowing Don, the river of the Rhenish Symphony, the classic
Tiber, Danube, and Euphrates, to say nothing of the Indus, the Ganges,
and "China's sorrow," the mighty Yellow River. In such ways as these
a country's topography is an important element not only in its economy
but in the character of its art and letters.

There are other topographical and kindred features that should be
borne in mind. Earthquakes, of course, and volcanoes also, for no mountain has been more celebrated in art and literature than the now extinct
Fuji. But perhaps most important in furnishing ingredients of the
national temperament are the abundance of running water and the
rich vegetation of both plain and highland, luxuriant yet never so wild
as to become a jungle. The wealth of evergreens, the early blossoms
in the warm regions of the southern littoral; the cold and snows of the
north; the soft rains and the rough tempests; all these make an astonishing diversity of landscape and atmosphere. One thing is usually
missing in the rural scene, and that is the wide expanses of grassland
that elsewhere sustain flocks and herds. Except for an occasional pack-
horse or a few draft oxen the countryside is almost empty of domestic
animals; so that Japanese literature is lacking in pastoral themes and
cannot tell tales of flute-playing shepherds or neat-handed dairymaids.
But it can give us pictures of farmers' daughters planting out the young
rice, of mountain girls carrying heavy loads of brushwood on their heads,
of young women plucking the leaves of the tea plant or reeling silk
from the cocoons.

Rice and silk dominate country life, as against wheat and wool in European lands. A lack of good building stones and a wealth of forest trees together dictate the architecture of dwelling houses, churches, and palaces. The very nature of Japanese art, the techniques of sculpture and painting, are conditioned by the materials at hand and by the craftsmanship which their use has required. The hand of the carver of Buddhist images owes its cunning to the challenge of the hard wood and the exacting grain of the native camphor and cypress growing on the mountainsides.

CHAPTER II

THE PEOPLE

1. *Origins*

THE ORIGINS of the Japanese people are not known for certain, but most students of their history believe that they are of mixed ancestry which includes a strong strain of immigrants from northern parts of the Asian mainland and a perhaps less dominant strain from coastal regions of southeast Asia or, less probably, from Indonesia or Polynesia.

No palaeolithic remains have been discovered in the Japanese archipelago, and we may therefore assume that the islands were first inhabited in comparatively recent times—perhaps 5,000 years ago. A great deal of archaeological evidence has been brought together to show the nature of the Late Stone Age in Japan, and in that respect the picture is remarkably clear. Shell mounds, tombs, pottery, and other abundant remains testify to the existence of two distinct types of neolithic culture. They exhibit differences in kind and in distribution, justifying the belief that one type was much earlier than the other, by which it was eventually displaced. That is to say, the earlier culture (in its oldest remains mesolithic rather than neolithic) had spread over the whole archipelago and had probably reached its highest point long before the arrival of the later culture, of which the strongest traces are found in the western part of the country.

This earlier culture—of hunters and fishermen, and not of farmers—was probably developed by the descendants of migrants who arrived at different times from different parts of the mainland of Asia. Some of them, according to current archaeological findings, reached northern Japan from eastern Siberia, by way of Yezo (the Hokkaidō) and perhaps Sakhalin; and in course of time their culture spread to the centre of the main island (Honshū) and to the Kantō region. These people are thought by anthropologists to have been remote ancestors of the Ainu, a Caucasic people today surviving only in small numbers in the northern island of Japan and in Sakhalin.

Other currents of mesolithic or neolithic culture are thought to have reached Kyūshū and the western end of the main island from a coastal region in South China, by way of Formosa and the Ryukyu Islands.

In these statements about the earliest phase of neolithic culture in Japan there is a strong element of conjecture. But when we come to the later phase there is not much room for doubt. It is no longer a culture of hunters and fishermen, but it is essentially the product of a sedentary society engaged chiefly in the cultivation of rice in irrigated fields. It is therefore certainly of southern origin, so far as agricultural methods are concerned, and is likely to have reached Kyūshū (and perhaps southern Korea) from points in south China or Indochina and then moved to the main island. However, although stone implements predominate in most of the sites of this culture, bronze objects are also frequent, so that there is good reason for believing that what we call the later neolithic culture of Japan is, in so far as it includes bronze artifacts, an extension of an aeneolithic culture common to Manchuria, the Maritime Province of Siberia, and the Korean peninsula. Indeed throughout Japanese history, for obvious geographic reasons, relations with Korea have been of special importance. It was mainly by way of Korea that the later neolithic culture reached Japan, carried by migrants whose ancestral home was in northeastern Asia but who were not of the same stock as the men of the early neolithic phase already settled in Japan. They belonged to an ethnic group, or more correctly a linguistic group, which includes Finns, Huns, Tungusic tribes, and Mongols.[1] It cannot be said whether they entered Japan as invaders or as peaceful settlers; it seems likely, however, that there was no mass movement, but rather a series of immigrations on a small scale, by families and groups not satisfied with their life in Korea. There is no evidence to show that they tried to destroy or drive away the early inhabitants of those parts of western Japan in which they settled. On the contrary, it seems that there was some degree of fusion between the people whom we may call aboriginal and the later arrivals.

But such harmonious conditions, if they ever existed, did not last long, for with the passage of time the migrants during their sojourn in Korea came under the influence of a culture much superior to their own. This was the early metal culture of China, which can be dated with some accuracy. The bronze culture of north China (which had some Scytho-Siberian affinities) spread to south Manchuria and thence to Korea by about 300 B.C., and in course of time affected the neolithic culture of Korea. Migrants or other travellers passing from Korea to the western shores of Japan began to introduce things and processes belonging to a metal culture, and thus to modify the life of certain favourably situated Japanese communities, particularly those living in settlements on the coast of Kyūshū where it is nearest to southern Korea.

The influence of Chinese bronze culture no doubt reached Japan by about 200 B.C., if not earlier, and soon began to modify or displace the neolithic culture at its points of contact. But before this bronze culture could establish itself in Japan it was overtaken by the iron culture which China developed under the Han dynasty, say from about

---

[1] Philologists are not in agreement about the relationship between Finno-Ugric and Altaic languages; nor is there any certainty as to the origin of the Huns, generally equated with the Hsiung-nu. But there can be little doubt of the presence of Tungusic and Mongol elements in the ethnic composition of the Japanese people.

200 B.C., and which was presently passed on to Korea and thence to Japan.

The effect of Chinese culture upon Korea, and consequently upon Japan, was intensified by a great expansion of Chinese power under the Han emperors. This power was extended by conquest in 108 B.C. to the northern half of the Korean peninsula. Flourishing Chinese colonies were established in that region and thereafter certain tribal rulers in western Japan, impressed by the strength and rich variety of Chinese civilization, began to send missions to the colonial government established near the site of the present city of Pyongyang. Their purpose no doubt was to obtain useful objects and useful information, since those leaders who soonest adopted the material features of a superior culture were at a great advantage over their rivals. Of most immediate value to them were weapons and tools of iron, which helped them to increase their military strength and to improve their methods of cultivation, to reclaim land by felling trees and digging channels for drainage and irrigation, and to build better dwellings. Such work could be accomplished slowly and painfully with bronze tools, but it was the more efficient iron implements, particularly the edged tools, that enabled rapid advances to be made and gave their users a special position.

When, where, and how these changes came about can be deduced with a fair degree of certainty from archaeological remains, such as the contents of tombs, and from documentary evidence, such as early Chinese records. There is, for instance, good reason to believe that Chinese cultural influence, in the form of artifacts of both bronze and iron (such as mirrors and swords), began to reach Japan by way of the Han colony in Korea during the first century B.C.; and we can safely conclude that thereafter ambitious Japanese chieftains strove to open communication with the Chinese authorities and to trade with Chinese and Korean merchants. The first recorded instance of such connections is a report of the visit of a Japanese envoy not to the colonial government but to the metropolis of China. This is noted under the date A.D. 57, in the official dynastic chronicle, where it is stated that the envoy was given a gold seal with an inscription certifying his master as king of his country, which has been identified as a locality now known as Hakata, on the northwest coast of Kyūshū.[2]

This incident, besides showing that regular intercourse with China was already well established during the first century of our era, points to an important feature of the traffic between Japan and the mainland. On the Japanese side it was conducted almost exclusively by those tribes or communities most favourably situated for access to Korea.

---

[2] It should be noted that the gold seal found near Hakata and alleged to be the one in question was not discovered until 1784. It is regarded as spurious by some scholars. In any case the fact of intercourse in or about A.D. 57 can scarcely be disputed.

Thus Hakata, the place just mentioned, was a port from which it was not difficult to sail to southern Korea by a short, almost direct voyage, allowing of shelter in the lee of the islands of Iki and Tsushima. This was the shortest voyage, but other points on the northern coast of Kyūshū and on the coast of the Japanese main island facing towards Korea and Manchuria had a similar advantage of proximity to the continent and thus of close contact with its powerful culture.

It resulted naturally from these circumstances that the first important centre of economic and political power was in western Japan, and notably on the island of Kyūshū. It is there that we must look for the origins of the Japanese state as it developed in historic times; and it is interesting to note that, apart from its geographic position, the island of Kyūshū had little advantage, being poor in natural resources. As we shall see, once power was consolidated, it tended to move eastward to richer land and a more central situation. Meanwhile, the relationship between southern Korea and western Japan remained very close, and there was not much to distinguish them from one another.

There is some evidence in Chinese chronicles to show what kind of people the Japanese were in the first century of the Christian era, when they were visited by travellers from Han China. This was at a date when the people of Kyūshū had been open for some time to Chinese cultural influence of a material kind, so that what the travellers saw were tribes that had already emerged from neolithic life and had reached a point of social organization in which there were marked differences of rank and some degree of discipline. The Han records say that at this time there were more than one hundred "communities" in Japan, of which more than thirty had been in intercourse with China since the Chinese established colonies in Korea. Other Chinese chronicles, describing a later period, indicate that the number of "communities" diminished, and it appears that there was a tendency to amalgamation or federation among tribes or clans, from the first century onwards. This feature is brought out very clearly in the Wei records, which are the most detailed and the most reliable of the early Chinese notices of Japan. They were compiled (before the surviving chronicles of Han) not later than A.D. 292, and they give an almost contemporary account of conditions in western Japan in the third century. During the flourishing period of the Wei dynasty, which was paramount in north China from 220 to 265, embassies were sent from Japan to the Chinese governor in Korea, who resided near the present Seoul. This was between 238 and 247, and return visits were paid by the Chinese. It is the observations of the Chinese visitors that are embodied in the Wei account, and though the Wei travellers probably did not travel far by land in Kyūshū, they seem to have taken pains to learn what was afoot and on internal evidence their descriptions may be taken as exceptionally trustworthy.

They speak of "thirty countries" in Japan which were in some kind of tributary relation to China. These "countries" were evidently the territories of tribal chieftains, and they are described as under the rule of a queen. In fact Japan is described as the Queen Country, and a list is given of the countries forming the group over which she presided. The identification of this Queen and the situation of the several "countries" have been matters of dispute among Japanese scholars for many years, and the problem still gives food for thought and argument to historians. In the Wei account the Queen Country is said to be situated in a district called Yamato, and Yamato is a not uncommon place name which was later used for the region in central Japan where the reigning house of Japan was settled in the fifth century. Some authorities consider that this Yamato and the Yamato of the Wei records are the same; but recent research seems to support the view that the Queen Country was in the west and that with its associated countries it included most of the northern half of Kyūshū (the provinces later known as Buzen, Bungo, Chikuzen, Chikugo, Hizen, and Higo), part of Hyūga, and probably a part of the western end of the main island across the straits of Shimonoseki, which would correspond to parts of the provinces of Suwo and Nagato.

If the Wei evidence is carefully examined, it gives strong reason to believe that by the middle of the third century a number of Japanese tribes or clans living in Kyūshū had gone a long way towards unification under a single leadership. We do not know what circumstances favoured this movement, but it is most likely that the relations with Korea, which they seem to have shared, served as a bond of unity, distinguishing them from other tribes and increasing their power of attack and defense.

When the Wei dynasty fell (A.D. 265) Chinese power in Korea diminished, and before long it collapsed. There is no further mention of Japan in Chinese records for more than a century, but we know that Japanese leaders continued their intercourse with Korea, and as their strength grew they began to take part in struggles among Korean kingdoms. Details of these campaigns need not be given here. It is enough to say that by A.D. 369 Japanese forces were fighting with success for the control of southern Korea, and had established themselves in a small colony or permanent military base called Mimana, near the present Pusan.

These were enterprises which could not have been undertaken by a loose grouping of tribes, and it is therefore clear that the process of unification begun by the Queen Country had been carried towards completion on a large scale and in a durable form a generation or more before the invasion of Korea in 369. Indeed it is most likely that it was hastened by fear of the aggressive kingdom of Koguryö in northern Korea, which, as soon as Chinese power was withdrawn from the peninsula, began to threaten its southern neighbours and thus to cause anxiety to Japan. It was from this military base in Mimana in 391 that a strong Japanese force marched north and penetrated as far as Pyong-yang in an attack upon Koguryö.

But if the unification of Japan, or more accurately of a great part of Japan, under the rule of an established dynasty was complete by about A.D. 350, by whom and in what manner was it accomplished? This is one of the unsolved problems of Japanese history, and it is connected with the problem of locating the Yamato of the Wei chron-icles. It is the subject of much learned controversy, which need not detain us, though it is useful to know the main points at issue.

There is no doubt that by A.D. 400 there was a ruling family which had already for some time been exercising at least a general sovereignty over a number of powerful clans then residing in central Japan not far from Osaka and Nara, in the province now known as Yamato. The question is: What was the origin of this dynasty? It seems probable that it came from Kyūshū and that it owed its position to the superior strength and the prestige which its founders had acquired by the adop-tion of Chinese techniques and by their relations with Chinese rulers and officials. Kinship, or at any rate close association, with important chieftains in southern Korea may also have contributed to their influ-ence. That the sovereigns who ruled what was called the land of Yamato from their seat in central Japan were descendants or successors of the rulers of the Queen Country cannot be proved, but it is not rash to suppose that it was the matrilineal ruling house by which, in or about A.D. 250, the Wei travellers were impressed that later extended its authority so far as to have at its disposal a large military force capable of invading Korea in A.D. 369. Yet it is hard to believe that at this time there could have been two great centres of power in Japan, one of which claimed to rule the whole country from central Japan while the other could mount a successful invasion of Korea. We must assume that, as the strength and unity of the Queen Country increased, it began to expand towards the east, and that eventually, at some time between the fall of the Wei in 265 and the invasion of Korea in 369, it assimi-lated or subdued the inhabitants of western and central Japan as far as Yamato, and there set up an Imperial Court.

It was this Court that renewed political relations with China (which had lapsed with the fall of the Wei) by sending embassies to the Chinese court at Nanking. The arrival of such missions is recorded in the official chronicles of the Sung era under dates between 421 and 479.

While the circumstances in which political power thus moved away from Kyūshū can only be conjectured, it is not difficult to account for a great eastward migration. The island of Kyūshū is for the most part mountainous or hilly and has little space suitable for the cultivation of food crops by settled communities. It is on the whole poor country

(Hyūga in particular has always been an impoverished area), and it was natural that its bolder inhabitants should move on in search of better land. One group appears to have joined forces with people living across the straits, passed along the northern shore of the main island, and settled in the region later known as Izumo; but a greater number chose the way along the northern shore of the Inland Sea, which presents no great obstacles in the shape of high passes or unfordable streams. As knowledge of advanced methods of agriculture, especially of rice-growing, spread from China there would perhaps be a deliberate search for fertile soil, which in Japan is generally found in alluvial plains near the coast, and especially in river deltas. It may well be imagined that some of these migrants would stop at points along the shore, where they found small areas of cultivable rice land, but no extensive plains. The main body would push on until they reached the plain at the eastern end of the Inland Sea. There was no need to go further, for here is one of the three great alluvial tracts of all Japan. For many centuries this area remained the seat of the Ruling House and the home of Japanese civilization.

Though the foregoing evidence attests to the fact that an eastward migration from Kyūshū took place, there remains some doubt as to the scale and the time of a movement which seems to have ended in the settlement of a powerful group of tribes or clans in central Japan. The native chronicles compiled in the seventh century, in their account of early history, ascribe the foundation of the empire to the Emperor Kamu-Yamato-Iware-Biko (best known by his posthumous Chinese appellation of Jimmu Tennō), who is said to have set forth from Hyūga in Kyūshū in 667 B.C. and to have reached Yamato some years later. The legend as it stands is quite impossible to accept, though it certainly echoes well-based traditions of an eastward expedition of people from western Japan under a chosen leader supported by an armed force.

It tells how they embarked in ships and went by easy stages and a roundabout route into the Inland Sea. Then, either on land or by water, they continued eastward until they reached a point near the site of the present city of Okayama, where they stayed for three years collecting provisions (probably by sowing and harvesting rice) and preparing their ships and weapons. In the spring of 663, the record says, they reached Naniwa, at the mouth of the Yodo River, near the site of the present Osaka. There they began to meet resistance from local warriors. It was not until three years later that, with some divine assistance, opposition was overcome and the Emperor was enthroned at a place called Kashiwabara.

There are other versions of this legend, but they do not differ in essential features. They all show that there was a great expedition, that it encountered stubborn resistance at certain points, and that finally, by force of arms, it was able to establish a centre of power in Yamato, and the beginnings of a settled government. There is nothing to indicate the true date of these events, but it is hard to believe that they took place before the Kyūshū leaders had been under the influence of an advanced iron culture long enough to allow them to form a combination of clans and to equip a considerable fighting force with superior weapons. A likely date for the eastward migration appears to be about A.D. 350, or perhaps a generation sooner.

The legendary account describes the kind of resistance that the expedition met. It was negligible until central Japan was reached, but after that, in the Ōsaka plain, the Yamato plain, and the hills of Yoshino, there was stubborn opposition by local chieftains, who are referred to as bandits, brigands, earth-spiders, and "emishi." This last term, which seems to mean "barbarian" (in the Greek sense, of people whose speech is gibberish), is the name[3] by which the Ainu were subsequently known; and it is fairly safe to assume that the people who offered resistance to the men from Kyūshū were ancestors of the present-day Ainu, or at any rate an Ainoid people in an early neolithic phase, who were thinly spread over the greater part of Japan long before the later neolithic migrants arrived. These were not the only inhabitants whom the Yamato people had to pacify or absorb, for the chronicles of several reigns after that of Jimmu Tennō describe wars against people called "Kumaso." The 12th Emperor (Keikō) is reported to have led an expedition to Kyūshū to put down a rebellion of these tribes, who inhabited the southern part of the island. It is evident that they were fierce fighting men, who caused trouble to the Yamato rulers, for (if we follow the chronicles) we find that the Court was moved to Kyūshū for several years, and that three sovereigns in succession resided there in order to conduct operations against these Kumaso, but without complete success.

We cannot tell what was the origin of these people. It has been suggested that they came from the South Seas, by way perhaps of Formosa and the Ryukyu Islands, and that the Yamato people were of the same stock, but had the advantage of proximity to Korea; while the Izumo people were of Chinese origin and had gone direct from the mainland to Izumo. These are plausible theories, but the truth is that we have not enough evidence to form a valid opinion about the origins and composition of the Japanese people. We know that when the Yamato dynasty was established (let us say about A.D. 300) it was far from exercising power over the whole of the Japanese islands, and that campaigns against unreconciled tribes or other groups took place at intervals during the next five centuries.

Heavy fighting against aborigines was frequent in the north until after A.D. 800, and although the west was earlier pacified, as late as A.D.

---

[3] Cognate forms are *ebisu, emisu, ezo,* which by some scholars are said to be variants of the Ainu word for "man."

700 the official historians still found it necessary to invent or manipulate the records so as to justify the claims of a ruling house that stemmed from the distant island of Kyūshū. Indeed the most cursory study of Japanese history impresses one with the importance of the part played by gods and men in Kyūshū. It was upon the mountain called Taka-chiho that the divine ruler of Japan, Ninigi, descended. It was Kyūshū warriors whom the successive feudal dictators of Japan most feared. It was Kyūshū barons who led the movement that ended in the restoration of the imperial power in 1867 and who furnished many leaders thereafter.

We have traced as far as possible the origins of the Yamato rulers and dwelt perhaps too much upon the opposition they encountered. But although the process of ethnic and cultural fusion was rapid once a central power was established with command of superior resources, still the folklore of Japan shows that recollections of a long period of disorder were stored up in the national memory. This is well illustrated in the legend of Yamato-dake, the Brave of Yamato, who is the true folk hero, the embodiment of national ideals. He was a prince, an emperor's son, who spent his life subduing rebels east and west. A strong, handsome boy, at the age of fifteen he was sent to attack the Kumaso in Kyūshū. He achieved his purpose by dressing as a girl and entering the camp of the Kumaso chieftain, who became tipsy and amorous at a feast and was easily stabbed to death by his seductive guest. Having lost their leader, the insubordinate aborigines were easily defeated.

The western land being now pacified, Yamato-dake was called upon to subdue the Emishi in the east. He first went to the great shrine at Ise to worship the ancestral gods. Thence after saying farewell to his elder sister, the high priestess Yamato-hime (Princess of Yamato), who gave him the famous sword Kusanagi, a precious heirloom of the Imperial House that was in her keeping, he went to the province of Suruga, where by his resourcefulness he escaped from traps laid by the rebels and soon exterminated them. He then passed on farther to the east, meaning to cross to Kazusa by boat, but the sea was stormy and the boat was about to sink when his mistress, the Princess Orange-blossom, plunged into the waves and pacified them by sacrificing her own life. He subdued the Emishi in Shimosa, and then started on his return journey; but he learned that there were many Emishi who had not submitted in provinces to the north, and so went in search of them. There in high mountain country he lost his way, owing to the malignity of the mountain deity who appeared in the shape of a white deer, but he was saved by a white dog which came to his rescue. He then started on his journey back to Yamato, stopping to marry a lady on the way; but hearing of another wicked mountain deity he turned off and went unarmed to meet him. Worn out by fatigue and icy cold he fainted, and though he recovered, thanks to the water of a healing spring, he was ill of a mortal disease. He struggled to reach home, but presently lay down to die on a lonely moor. There he was buried in a great tomb by the Emperor's order, but taking the shape of a white bird he flew away and soared up to the heavens.

This legend is of some historical interest, as showing how wild and unsubdued were the regions east and west of Yamato as late as A.D. 400. But it is more precious as an early revelation of native sentiment, for it strikes the authentic note of Japanese romance. Here are all the elements that were to stir Japanese emotions in later times: the handsome young fighting man, the queller of evil, combining bravery with wily stratagems; the loyal mistresses; the magic sword; the wicked deities in animal disguise; the suffering, the self-sacrifice, and the pathetic early death.

2. Customs and Beliefs

It is an interesting if not very profitable historical exercise to try to discover what kind of life was lived by the people who inhabited Japan before the foundation of the Yamato state; or let us say before about A.D. 400, since by that time we may presume there was a high degree of ethnic fusion among the dominant clans or tribes and a fairly uniform culture throughout the parts of Japan over which the dynasty claimed to rule.

Some evidence is provided by the Chinese notices which have already been cited, and it is confirmed in some particulars by the research of archaeologists, who have discovered and investigated a great number of objects, such as tools, weapons, ornaments, and clay figures, that throw some light on the practices and beliefs of the people who had come under the influence of continental culture.

In the Wei accounts, which are the most reliable, it is social organization that interests the Chinese observers, and they do not make any direct statement about religious beliefs. What they single out for comment are such matters as gradations of rank, the signs of respect paid by inferiors to superiors, the severity of punishments, and in general the preservation of a strict discipline. Even making full allowance for the slightness of such evidence (for the Chinese travellers did not see very much and perhaps did not understand all they saw and heard), it is significant that the things which attracted their attention were those which many centuries later impressed other visitors to Japan, among them the Englishman Will Adams, who in 1611 described the people of that country as "very subject to their governors and superiors." Since throughout their history the Japanese have believed in firm government and a rigid social order, it is perhaps not too fanciful to detect the beginnings of this preference in their early tribal practices.

Other features noticed by the Chinese observers were certain taboos and ritual practices which suggest observances of a religious character. But there is no mention of worship in any form, except that the name of the Queen, Pimiku, seems to be an attempt to represent phonetically either Pimiko or Pimeko, which in archaic Japanese meant Sun Child or Sun Daughter. This points to a cult of a solar deity whom the tribal leaders claimed as an ancestor. Worship of the Sun Goddess is, as we know from later evidence, a leading feature of the Japanese myth recorded in support of the ruling dynasty, so that it is pretty safe to assume that a solar cult was practised before, perhaps long before, the date of the Chinese visits. But it is quite likely that this was a cult confined to the rulers, and there may have been other and more popular beliefs and practices of a religious nature, varying perhaps from tribe to tribe.

We cannot, however, hope to construct a complete picture of early Japanese society. Archaeology does not tell the whole story, and the literary documents available, though they no doubt embody much valuable tradition, are themselves attempts at reconstruction with a deliberate political purpose, so that they have to be used with great caution. Nor can we assume that the conditions observed by the Wei writers were common throughout Kyūshū, much less in other parts of Japan. It is highly probable that Kyūshū and the western part of the main island were inhabited by tribes of various origins. We have to account somehow for the "southern" element in Japanese culture, and we may perhaps suppose that some of the people south of the Queen Country were of southern origin. The wars mentioned by the Wei reporters may have been part of a process of unification, yet they may at the same time have been due to antagonism between groups of different ethnic origin or simply between aboriginals and latecomers. There may thus have been a variety of customs and beliefs, though as the advanced culture of the Chinese spread in Japan it would no doubt tend to reduce differences between tribes and create a substantial uniformity. Moreover, though each tribal community doubtless began with its own ancestral cult and a suitable ancestral myth, any process of unification under a powerful leadership would tend to promote a merging of cults.

This supposition seems to be confirmed by the contents of the great sepulchral mounds which are found, without any significant gaps in distribution, from Kyūshū to Kinai, and contain objects which show hardly any variation by locality. The age of sepulchral mounds is thought to have extended from the second century to its peak early in the fifth century. Unlike the earlier tombs, these no longer contain bronze weapons, but iron swords and body armour. They do contain bronze articles, but these are principally mirrors and ornaments, which are cult objects with a sacred or at least a ritual significance. Their presence and the general evenness of distribution suggest that there was a unity of cult throughout the whole area, and a degree of political unity also, by about A.D. 400 and perhaps much earlier.

It is true that the unity was not complete, as we know from the breach between those migrants who went from Kyūshū to Yamato and those who followed the northwestern coast of the main island and settled in Izumo. The earliest written chronicles attempt, with only partial success, to reconcile the legend cycles of these two groups; yet it does not appear that there was any fundamental difference in the nature of their beliefs, but only a claim to descent from different divine rulers, which bespoke political disagreement. In general, though different tribes no doubt worshipped different ancestral deities, they seem to have shared a common fund of beliefs and practices that together amount to a religion in its early form.

The information offered by the Wei account on these matters is not copious, but it stresses one important point, namely the practice of ritual cleanliness, which is achieved by lustrations and similar rites and by abstention from what is unclean. The exact text of the Wei record is worth quoting here:

When death occurs, mourning is observed for more than ten days. . . . When the funeral is over, all members of the whole family go into the water to cleanse themselves in a bath of purification. . . . When they go on voyages across the sea, they always select a man who does not comb his hair, does not rid himself of fleas, lets his clothing get dirty, does not eat meat, and does not approach women. This man behaves like a mourner and is called the fortune keeper.

It will be seen that the mourners cleanse themselves of the pollution of death by bathing, while the "fortune keeper" takes upon himself the impurities of the community and at the same time attains a positive purity by abstention from polluting acts. Similarly the most ancient Japanese myths abound in references to pollution and purification.

Here we see features of early Japanese society in which we can trace the origins of later religious beliefs and moral ideas. They appear to be free from Chinese influence, but they probably owe something to Korean and Mongol sources. In Japan, as elsewhere, the ritual requirements of purity become the starting point of ethical precepts, for from requiring that a man appealing to the unseen powers should have a clean body it is not a long step to requiring that he should have a pure mind.[4]

From these sources there is little more to be learned about the habits of the Japanese before they were subjected to a very strong Chinese

[4] On the transference of the notion of purity from the magical to the moral sphere, and in general on the origins of the idea of sin, see the comments of Professor E. R. Dodds in *The Greeks and the Irrational*, chap. ii, *passim*.

influence from about A.D. 400 onwards. The bronze objects from the
tombs suggest some kind of worship, but the tombs were those of kings
or chieftains, and the worship, if it was worship, may have been little
more than an expression of pious respect for the dead, paid to their
memory or to the cherished possessions which had been the symbols of
their power. These things do not necessarily throw light upon the beliefs
of the ordinary people of those times. We can only conjecture what
they were like by analogy with other cultures in similar circumstances
and by inference from later stages of development about which we have
some reliable information.

There is one thing about which we can be certain, and that is the
position of the most important settlements. They were almost without
exception in low-lying alluvial plains, and it is clear that the basis of
life was sedentary agriculture. A chart of the known centres of government after the establishment of the Yamato state shows that although,
owing to certain taboos, the ruler's palace was shifted at the end of each
reign, the new capitals were all within a narrow area of land favourable
to wet rice culture.[5]

Therefore we shall not be far out if we suppose that the customs
were of a kind common to most settled agrarian people, whose worship
is largely concerned with fertility and the preservation of crops and
therefore with propitiation of the powers of nature. Such a supposition
is amply borne out by a study of native beliefs and practices which survived the introduction of powerful foreign ideas. The fact that they so
survived goes far to prove that they were ancient and strong and deeply
rooted, so that a description of early Japanese society depending in
part upon inference from later conditions, though it may be at fault in
particulars, should be in general trustworthy as a guide to the history of
ideas and institutions.

The use of the word Shintō ("The Way of the Gods") to describe the
early beliefs of the Japanese is apt to be misleading in so far as it suggests

[5] The Yamato basin lies in the heart of the Kinki district. It is a small area,
perhaps twenty by ten miles, of which the floor is an extremely fertile alluvial plain.
It is one great paddy field, its yield per unit of area being one of the highest in all
Japan. In the centre is the city of Nara.

It has evidently been a centre of population since the earliest times, as is clear
from the great number of prehistoric sites throughout Yamato, notably the remains
of dwellings of hunters and fishermen upon rising ground just above the alluvial
tracts. The flatness of the alluvial tract and the relative ease of irrigation made it
most suitable to wet rice culture; and it is not surprising that Yamato became the
cradle of Japanese civilization. It is interesting to note that the present-day landscape shows signs of the distribution of allotment fields (handen) in the seventh
century, and it seems likely that the topography of this limited area was favourable
to the borrowed Chinese system, which called for the symmetrical division of land
into rectangles. It may even be that it was for such reasons that the Japanese persisted for so long in attempting to apply this artificial system, which never really
succeeded in its country of origin, and in the long run failed miserably in Japan.

an organized religion. To speak of a Way of the Gods is to presuppose a positive doctrine and a well-defined pantheon. But the objects of popular devotion were not those somewhat political abstractions that figure as the ancestral deities of the ruling class. They were the humbler but none the less powerful influences that determine the fortunes of men in an agricultural society, of the cultivator and his family no less than the territorial lord. They were the forces of nature in their divine embodiments as gods of mountain and valley, field and stream, fire and water, rain and wind.

Such features of pagan culture are not exceptional. They are to be found in most societies at the same early stages of growth; while the ancestral myth of the rulers, though not without counterparts elsewhere, seems to display some political ideas peculiar to Japan, and therefore invites special study. But before considering the chronicle of the Age of the Gods, which is a prelude to the legendary account of the foundation of the empire, it is best to examine the popular cult, because it gives a clue to early Japanese ideas about life and society, about family life, tribal life, and man's relations to the world around him. It seems to present the first elements of national character, for unlike such great religions as Buddhism or Christianity it was not something which added to or contributed to national life, but was rather an expression of the most intimate and vital sentiments of the Japanese people. In that sense it somewhat resembles the pagan cults of Greece and Rome, in their archaic strata. It is not a religion whose principles demonstrably arise from historical events. It it not the product of a revolution in ideas. Unlike Buddhism or Christianity or Islam, it has no founder, no inspired sacred book, no teachers, no martyrs, and no saints.

It may be described as a form of nature worship, based upon a feeling that all things are animate and in their degree partake of sentient existence. Thus the manifestations of nature, great and small, are thought of, perceived, as harbouring a kind of divine presence and worshipped accordingly. Much misunderstanding of Japanese thought in modern as well as ancient times has been caused by the word *kami*, which is usually rendered as "god" or "spirit" in Western languages. This word carries the general sense of "upper" or "superior," and a thing or person is called kami if it is felt to possess some superior quality or power. The same idea is expressed in Polynesian countries by the term *mana*, which stands for a special power or influence possessed by certain persons, things, or places, something above their everyday quality. The same or a similar idea appears in Roman beliefs, where the special quality is called *numen*. That which has mana or numen is in Japanese a kami. The great ancestors and the great heroes have it. So have certain objects, like rocks and trees, and certain places like groves and springs, and certain important things like tools and weapons and boundary stones between fields. The quality may be conferred by rarity, or by beauty, or by exceptional shape or size, or by great utility, or by past history, or only by the feelings of a worshipper.

If there is a difference between the Greek and Roman ideas and those of Japan, it is perhaps in the tendency of the classical myths to give a human likeness to the spirit that inhabits the exceptional things or places singled out as having a superior essence. In Japanese mythology there is nothing to correspond to the nymphs, dryads, and oreads which are the spirits of streams, woods, and hills in our classical lands. The Japanese custom was to pay respect to the kami of such useful or beautiful things, but not to think of them as in the shape of men or women. Thus in the countryside where tradition lingers, the traveller will still find at the summit of a hill a stone bearing the carved inscription "Yama no Kami," the Spirit of the Hill, but he will not usually find a picture of the imagined form of that or any other of the many kami to which the Japanese countryman pays reverence.

Allowing for this difference, there are many points of similarity between Japanese beliefs and those of other early societies, as for instance the Japanese care to propitiate the kami of the kitchen, which is like the deference paid by the Romans to their Penates, the little gods of the pantry. Such analogies should not be pressed too far, though they ought to be noticed as showing that what we call primitive Shintō was by no means an exceptional cult. That it differs from other cults in its comparative weakness in visual imaginative power is a point of interest in the light of the dominance of the plastic arts in later Japanese history. By contrast with the vivid pictorial imagination of the Greeks, the Japanese vision of the world of gods and spirits is in general rather dim. The figures of the Japanese myth are very shadowy by comparison with the vigorous gods and goddesses, the lively nymphs and satyrs, of Mediterranean folklore.

On the other hand, the Japanese, no doubt because they were not anthropocentric in their outlook, seem to have nourished a strong feeling of community, almost of identity, with all of nature; and we might say that their view of life as it was expressed in pagan customs was, if weaker in poetic fancy, perhaps stronger in sentiment than the Greek view. The Roman view is perhaps nearer to the Japanese in some ways, the Romans being more matter-of-fact, less lively-minded, organizers rather than inventors.

We have already noticed the place of ritual purity in the Japanese cult, as it was described by Chinese observers; here again there are resemblances to Greek and Roman paganism, where lustrations and ceremonial cleanliness were necessary practices. The avoidance of pollution is of high importance, and in the earliest recorded customs of Japan, as in other tribal cults, there was an "abstainer," whose duty it was to fast, to observe certain prescribed taboos, and in other ways to maintain ceremonial purity on behalf of the community. This is the "fortune keeper" of the Wei records, and in later Japanese history we hear of a family of hereditary abstainers, called Imibe, where *imi* means abstention, and *be* a closed occupational group.

These features of the early Japanese cult are almost universal. There are, for instance, points of resemblance to Mosaic law in regard to what is unclean, and in general outline the popular mythology of early Shintō is what is found among most peoples at a like stage of development. Is there anything distinctive, anything that can be looked upon as uncommon and characteristically Japanese? It is a difficult question; but one may say that, perhaps because of the climate of Japan, its wealth of trees and flowers and its genial landscapes, there seems to be a special element of enjoyment and gratitude in the early forms of worship as they are known to us and as they were practised in the fertile regions where the early migrants settled. Their observances were of course directed to safeguarding their food supply or warding off calamities, but the unseen powers seem to be addressed with trust rather than fear, and to judge from such prayers as have been preserved by tradition they were not regarded as jealous gods, or as stern, cruel judges inflicting punishment and suffering upon men.

Doubtless the cult was not uniform throughout Japan, yet there must have been an increasing body of common belief as political unity was approached. We can see dimly the beginning of a process by which the simple customs of individuals and families developed into an organized religion of the state. Its origins may be traced to the importance of the family in an agrarian society. The early cult is concerned with the welfare of the household, extends to the larger local community, then to the tribe or clan, and finally to the nation as a whole. The framework of all these variations of the cult is the worship of an ancestor, a founder who represents and ensures the continuity of the family, the clan, or the ruling house. Here the first and second steps are natural developments, for they arise from a universal sense of the sacredness of fertility which is instinctive in mankind. In that sense all gods alike are fertility gods, because the yield of crops, the life of the family, the perpetuation of the tribe, are together matters of birth and growth which are felt to be indivisible.

It is not possible to trace the growth of the idea of collaboration, for it also arises from a natural instinct for survival; but the student of early Japanese history, on the scanty evidence at his disposal, is impressed by the strength of community feeling, of which reverence for the ancestor is both cause and effect. Family feeling as displayed in the cult is very strong, and so is the feeling of membership in the clan— the *uji*, which corresponds to the Roman *gens*, a society of freemen with the same surname. The leader of the clan is obeyed and respected as "uji no kami," the chief of the clan, while the object of its corporate veneration is the "ujigami" (ujikami), the clan god, who may be a departed leader, a forefather, or a local tutelary deity worshipped as the apotheosis of a remote ancestor. Family and communal effort, promoted by communal worship, evidently fostered a feeling of loyalty to the larger as well as the smaller group, a feeling which may be called piety, in the sense of the Latin *pietas* when it is used to signify a sense of obligation that partakes of religious sentiment or emotion.

One interesting point of difference between Chinese and Japanese customs lies in the attitude towards mourning. In China mourning involved prolonged austerities, and adherence to a strict rule by the surviving relatives, whereas in Japan the family, from early times, while not denying respect and consolatory rites to the departed, seem to have hastened to resume normal life as soon as possible.

Perhaps it is not proper to compare the customs of a highly developed society like that of China, a society held together by ritual, with the more primitive, or less regulated, behaviour of the Japanese. But the difference, such as it is, does give a clue to Japanese temperament. We are after all looking for differences that will explain the reaction of Japanese to Chinese teaching or example in social and political life.

It is difficult to say how much the indigenous cult was, in respect of family observances, influenced by Chinese ancestor worship. No doubt the earliest forms in both countries were similar, but ancestor worship in Japan never became so all-pervading an institution as it did in China, where long before the Japanese developed as a nation it was an intensely regulated and essential feature of the social system. In Japan the observances of the family and the tribal cult were extremely simple, and indeed simplicity, even austerity, remained a characteristic of the more highly developed Shintō of later times. They consisted of plain words or gestures of invocation following a simple purifying ritual, such as sprinkling with water (*misogi*) or waving evergreen branches (*sakaki*) or wands (*nusa*). This ceremony was performed out of doors, and there were no shrines or other permanent sacred edifices, but only a small plot of ground either purified for the occasion or having some traditional importance—for example, the site of an ancestral tomb or of some tree or stone thought to have a special quality of holiness.

There are traces of human sacrifice in the early myths and legends, and certain clay figures found in tombs are explained as substitutes for the burial of servants with their deceased master, an old custom that was abolished, according to the chronicles, about A.D. 3, though the Chinese dynastic records mention the practice as late as A.D. 247 in Japan. The sacrificing of animals (as a rule oxen) is recorded in the chronicles as late as the seventh century, but it seems by then to have been regarded as an abnormal practice; moreover, of course, it was contrary to Buddhist teaching. Certainly the usual (and, it would seem, the orthodox) practice was to present as offerings grains, fruits, and vegetables, and at times uncooked fish and fowl. Nothing showing blood was permitted, since blood was polluting; and therefore sacrificing live animals by cutting or stabbing was inconsistent with strict Shintō ideals of purity.

In the earliest written accounts we have descriptions of public ceremonies on something approaching a national scale, such as the Spring Prayer for good crops, the Autumn Harvest Thanksgiving, and the Great Purification exercises of summer and winter. These involved an elaborate ritual performed in the name of the sovereign by celebrants who had attained purity by fasting and other forms of abstinence. They recited a prayer in language prescribed for each occasion. Some, if not all, of these festivals must have arisen from popular worship, and those which had to do with sowing and harvest no doubt originated in simple rites performed by farmers and their families; but the liturgies as we know them from official records of a later period are highly elaborate versions of primitive themes.

This is true also of the two national chronicles which together record the genesis of the Japanese islands, the life of the gods, the foundation of the Imperial House, and the history of the empire up to the year 701. These are the *Kojiki*, or Record of Ancient Matters, and the *Nihon-shoki* (known also as *Nihongi*), or Chronicles of Japan. They have of necessity an artificial, literary quality, since they were modelled upon Chinese chronicles and the very script in which they were written was Chinese, as was part of their vocabulary. They were moreover compiled in part at least for the purpose of justifying and glorifying the reigning dynasty. Consequently they include a great deal of invention or manipulation of both myth and history, and they are full of inconsistencies, so that on a cursory reading they seem to be of little value. But it would be a mistake to dismiss them as unreliable, for the ingredients of which they are composed include much genuine tradition, and even where they are recognizably confused or wanting in veracity the expedients to which they resort throw light, if not upon the sequence of events, at least upon the ideas and purposes by which the compilers were animated. The two works together are therefore a valuable mine of evidence about the nature of Japanese society and the development of Japanese thought before the country was exposed to the full force of the high civilization of China—let us say approximately before the year 500.

Despite their shortcomings, both as literature and as history, they are very remarkable monuments for their times. They are episodic rather than epic, but they are not wanting in a certain "Biblical" character. The credibility of the *Nihon-shoki* after about A.D. 600 is fairly high, since its compilers (who were at work from 672 onwards) could draw upon written records going back a hundred years or more.

A thoroughgoing analysis of these two documents is work for spe-

cialists, and there are still innumerable points of interpretation upon
which Japanese scholars disagree. The general outline, however, is
clear, and the story is one of great interest to the historian of ideas. It
begins with an account of the beginning of things, telling how Heaven
and Earth were formed from chaos. There is no mention of a Creator,
and the ideas presented look as if they were borrowed from Chinese
cosmology. Then follows the myth of the birth of the gods, which seems
to be the expression, or rather perhaps the elaboration, of an indigenous
tradition that is possibly of Polynesian origin.

The first generations of gods are nameless abstractions, until the
arrival of the god Izanagi and the goddess Izanami. This heavenly
couple are the parents of the islands of the Japanese archipelago, to
which Izanami gave birth, as well as to their surrounding waters and
their rivers, mountains, rocks, grass, and trees. Then according to one
version she produced the wondrous Sun Goddess and the Moon God,
who were sent up to Heaven. She also bore many other gods and goddesses, her last child being a son, the Fire or the Fire God (Ho-musubi),
by whom she was burned as he emerged from her body, so that she died.

There follows what is perhaps the most notable part of the whole
legend, for now Izanagi goes to seek his wife in the Land of Darkness
(Yomi no kuni), but finds her a mass of putrefaction in that polluted
world.

This myth of Izanagi's search for his wife in the underworld is sometimes compared to the story of Orpheus and Eurydice; but a closer
parallel is that of Persephone condemned to remain in Pluto's kingdom
because she had eaten there. Izanami tells Izanagi that he is too late,
because she has eaten from the cooking pot of Yomi. In the Japanese
myth the tragedy of Izanami is related in a rather matter-of-fact way.
Contrast the poetic value given to the Greek myth in Milton's reference:

> Not that fair field
> Of Enna, where Proserpin gathering flowers,
> Herself a fairer flower, by gloomy Dis
> Was gather'd, which cost Ceres all that pain
> To seek her through the world . . .

It would seem that the failure of the Japanese to develop the tragedy
of the Persephone (or Eurydice) myth betokens some essential difference in outlook. In Europe these classical themes (and also similar
themes from the Bible) have been the stuff of tragedy for centuries. But
Japanese imagination does not seem to have been stirred in the same
way, although the material is there in their national scriptures.

Yet there is some resemblance between the attitude of the Japanese
towards their native legends and that of Western European peoples
towards theirs. Greek and Roman mythology was carried to the West
by Christianity, as a by-product of knowledge of classical languages, and

among educated people it displaced or thrust into the background the simpler and less artificial beliefs of an earlier age. In Japan the powerful influence of Confucian thought and Buddhist teaching similarly tended to diminish the currency of the myth of the native gods, or at least to force it to some compromise with the new kinds of teaching brought over from the mainland. It must be admitted, however, that the parallel is not exact, since Greek and Roman myths not only were borrowed under Christian influence but were also selected and adapted to meet the taste of Christian societies or to suit the ideas of Christian leaders.

Izanagi returns to Japan—to southwestern Japan, to be precise—where he purifies himself by bathing in a stream. This passage is of importance as giving a kind of scriptural authority to the abhorrence of impurity and the practice of lustration, which we have already noticed as being at the core of the Shintō cult, and at the root of ideas of morality. The part played by the idea of purity in legend as well as in ceremonial is of the greatest significance. It is fundamental from the earliest stages (observed by the Wei travellers) and has displayed a remarkable power of survival until modern times.

The things which pollute are various. Chief among them are uncleanness of the person or of clothing, menstruation, sexual intercourse, childbirth, disease, wounds, and death. These are not thought of in terms of guilt, but as impurities that must be removed before a man or woman can resume a full part in the life of the community. Certain acts such as murder, wounding, incest, bestiality, are looked upon as offences which create impurity and pollute the person who performs them. Such acts must therefore be expiated by ceremonial cleansing, at times accompanied by purgation in the form of a fine or some other punishment.[6]

Notice that drawing blood is polluting. The word *kega*, which means a wound, is the original word for defilement, and in the modern language the words *kegare, kegare-ru,* and *kegasu* are used for "stain," "to be stained," and "to stain." There is a close analogy to ancient Greek ideas of purity, though water was not always thought sufficient to wash off blood guilt in Athens. Sometimes the blood of a sacrificial animal was used. Blood can be washed away only with blood in the Greek view, as expressed in the *Oresteia* of Aeschylus. There is nothing comparable in early Japanese beliefs.

To revert to the myth of the gods, an alternative version relates that when Izanagi bathed in the stream he threw down his garments on the river bank, and from each piece of cloth and each part of his body there was born a deity. From his left eye came the Sun Goddess (Amaterasu-ōmikami), from his right eye the Moon God, and from his nose the Storm God (Susanowo). The Sun Goddess and the Moon God retired

[6] "Offence and pollution are inseparable ideas," says Dr. K. Florenz in his *Ancient Japanese Rituals.*

to Heaven, but the Storm God remained upon earth and travelled about behaving in an extremely violent fashion. It is an interesting point that Susanowo, the Destroyer, is the only God in the whole myth who is presented as a being with definite, positive character. The other deities have their attributes, but are rather shadowy creatures, little more than abstractions to which a name but not a personality is given. Susanowo's exploits as related are not all easy to explain, though some of them are clearly symbolic versions of ancient history. His quarrel with the Sun Goddess, his sister, must surely be an echo of quarrels between a woman ruler in a matrilineal society and a vigorous brother or other male relative jealous of her power. In the *Nihon-shoki,* when the Sun Goddess hears that Susanowo is coming to Heaven to say farewell she suspects that he means to rob her of her kingdom. She arms herself, "puts forth her manly valour," and utters a mighty cry of defiance. The discord between Amaterasu and Susanowo evidently reflects an ancient historical event, probably the clash referred to in the Wei-chih account of the Queen Country; and this provides a clue to many other stories of the age of the gods, which are designed to show that their descendants, in their acts and their customs, were following divine precedent, or even divine commands.

In the course of this quarrel the Impetuous Male (for that is what Susanowo's name is thought by some scholars to mean), after having destroyed the banks of his sister's paddy fields and performed other impieties abhorrent to an agricultural society, intruded violently upon her as she sat weaving with her maidens, and by rough and unseemly conduct polluted her palace in Heaven. The outraged Sun Goddess withdrew into a cave, the light of the world went out. The eight hundred myriad gods were in despair and with difficulty persuaded her to come out again. It must be remembered here that the later life of men on earth is conceived of as following, even as dictated by, the pattern of the life of the gods, and this may account for the immense number of lesser divine persons so frequently mentioned in the myth. They are the subjects, so to speak, of the heavenly realm, and the great gods like Amaterasu-ōmikami are the sovereigns and their ministers.

This legend, or rather the whole cycle of which it is a part, was no doubt intended to show that although Susanowo was a powerful and ingenious god, he committed offences which must in the long run bring upon him a deserved punishment. We are told that he and his descendants had been entrusted with the rule of the earth—that is to say, of Japan, and in particular of the province of Izumo—but at length, after remarkable adventures and numerous misdemeanours, he vanishes. He reappears later as the "filthy and capricious deity of Hades," though he appoints one of his descendants to be the ruler of Japan.

This confused but lively story, here much abridged, evidently reflects some ancient political strife, in the course of which the Izumo chieftains, whom we have seen leading their people along the north-western coast of the main island, at last had to abandon their claim to sovereignty of all Japan. Plainly we are here at a point where the myth of the divine ancestors begins to merge into the legend of the early sovereigns, first (it would appear) those who ruled in Kyūshū and then those who ruled in Yamato.

The story of the dispute for the sovereignty of Japan (which at that time meant the land from Kyūshū eastward to Yamato) is given so much prominence in this mythology, and the actions of Susanowo are so pro-fusely described, that we may safely conclude that the chroniclers thought it of the highest importance to support the claim of the Yamato sovereigns by basing it upon the supreme will of the Sun Goddess, at the same time showing that Susanowo was not worthy of such an in-heritance. He is in fact reported to have gone back to the lower regions, thus by reason of his pollution making it impossible to renew his own claim. He was induced to resign by the promise of a great shrine where he could be worshipped, and this is the origin of the Great Shrine of Izumo, at Kizuki, dedicated to his descendant Ō-kuni-nushi (Master of the Great Land). It is the second most holy place in Japan, the first being the shrine of the Sun Goddess at Ise.

It is clear enough from this legend that the process of unification begun by the Queen Country in Kyūshū was attended by great difficul-ties, not least of which was the strong character of the Izumo leader, whose mythical counterpart is the Storm God. Evidently the Yamato rulers felt obliged to share the sacred if not the secular authority with Izumo; and it is noticeable that in the legend the God of Miwa, who is identified as the deposed Izumo sovereign, continues to reappear and has to be placated. The material strength of Izumo was not great, since it is a region relatively poor in productive land and not favoured by a good climate, though in upland areas of volcanic ash there is pasture for cattle and horses, and some silver, tin, and copper have been produced since ancient times. It may be that the people who settled there had special prestige because they were closely related to Korean rulers and more culturally advanced than their rivals. In some versions of the legend Susanowo is said to have visited Korea, and to have dis-played an interest in metals and in timber for shipbuilding. Evidence of a traditional connexion with Korea is furnished by the farmhouses in parts of Izumo, which closely resemble the buildings of southern Korea.

This, and much other evidence, points to a very close connexion, in fact an intermingling, of the inhabitants of southern Korea and those of western Japan. There is much in the folklore of Japan which is demonstrably of Korean origin. For example, in a work called *Izumo Fūdoki* (a topographical survey compiled in 733) there is a legendary account of the origins of the people of Izumo. It relates that a god,

observing that there was too much land in southern Korea, tore off a
part of the country of Silla, dragged it across the sea, and fastened it
on to the land of Izumo. This is obviously a folklore version of emigra-
tion, what was dragged across being not surplus land but surplus people.
It should be added that there are many elements in the *Kojiki* and
Nihon-shoki which can definitely be traced to Tungusic origins.

3. *The System of Government*

A general survey of the mythological portions of the early chronicles
in the light of recent knowledge seems to justify a somewhat more
favourable view of their value as historical material than was held by
the first Western translators of the *Kojiki* and *Nihongi*. The great pioneer scholars (Chamberlain, Aston, and Murdoch) were inclined to
dwell upon the manifest shortcomings of those works. They were
looking for exact dates and veracious reporting, and were naturally
disappointed by the inconsistencies and defective chronology of the
compilers. But those very weaknesses are significant, because they
reveal something of Japanese thought in the seventh century. The
chronicles were compiled (ca. 700) at a time when the influence of
foreign ideas (both Confucian and Buddhist) was growing rapidly in
Japan. Yet they show that traditional beliefs were still powerful and
that the indigenous cult retained much of its vitality. Since those days
not only have many of the legends remained part of the nation's folklore, but also the principles of monarchy and the theory of government
which the two works were designed to uphold have for centuries entered into political thought despite great events that in logic would seem
to shatter them. This persistence of an ancient pattern in the face of
contradictions is a characteristic phenomenon; time after time a new
political situation arises and yet is somehow made to square with early
doctrine. Perhaps it is due to the lack of a really positive, constructive
character in the national cult called Shintō, for it is in reality not a religion or a system of thought but an expression of national temperament.

Why this ancient ceremonial paganism should have survived without making good its obvious deficiencies cannot be more clearly explained than in these words of Sir Charles Eliot, from his *Japanese
Buddhism*, here quoted in piam memoriam:

> It has no moral code; its prayers and sacrifices aim at obtaining
> temporal prosperity and indicate no desire for moral or spiritual
> blessings. Yet these strange lacunae are somehow filled by its in-
> tensely patriotic spirit. For it Japan is the land of the Gods; the
> greater preside over the Empire, the lesser over towns or hamlets;
> the noble or the humble dead have their due place in the cult of
> the State, city or family. So primitive is the thought of Shintō that
> it is hardly correct to say that natural features or individuals are

deified. They are simply accepted as important facts in the continuous national life and addresses or appeals are made to them about such things as concern them. This sense of community in national life, though expressed in almost childlike language, is really equivalent to saying that the individual exists only as a member of the family and the family as a member of the State: that the present must sacrifice itself to the traditions of the past and the needs of the future. And thus the heroism of Japan grows naturally out of a religion which if considered unsympathetically in the light of pure reason is as foolish as a fairy tale.

Although we have little direct and positive evidence of the nature of the Yamato state as it developed in the first few centuries after its formation, it can be reconstructed without much difficulty from material furnished by the chronicles and from vestiges of early institutions that survived the process of reform which took place as the reigning dynasty strove to consolidate its power.

The mythological narrative and the legends of the early sovereigns present the emperors as absolute monarchs, but it is clear that they describe ideal, not real, conditions, and that the federation of the clans which led to the establishment of a central power in Yamato was by no means complete or stable, even as late as the end of the seventh century, when the chronicles were being composed. The imperial clan was able, for reasons which are not entirely clear, to exercise some degree of authority over the other powerful clans, but it could not deprive them of their independence, and they retained for centuries their control over their own land and their own people.

The great clans, descendants of those tribes which migrated eastward from Kyūshū, paid deference to the leader of the imperial clan chiefly because he was the intermediary between the people and their gods. His power was religious rather than political, because where there is a cult of divine ancestors, and therefore of divine kingship, it is the function of the acknowledged sovereign to perform the ceremonies upon which the welfare of the whole community, all the clans and all their leaders, is firmly believed to depend. He is high priest and chief among chieftains, but he is not directly concerned with matters of administration. The ancient Japanese word usually translated as "government" is *matsurigoto*, which means literally the business of worship, or ceremonial observances. It was in this capacity that the early emperors presided over the state, and of course their sacred function gave them a certain political advantage; but otherwise the autonomy of the leaders of the other great clans was not diminished. Moreover, it must be remembered that those leaders themselves claimed descent from their own clan gods, divinities only a degree less sublime than the imperial ancestors. The tribal cults and the communal life of the clans had great vitality and power of resistance to change.

Among the great, though not the highest, officers of state were the heads of such families as the Nakatomi and the Imibe. As well as being influential landholders they had hereditary priestly functions, being Court ritualists who led in the performance of the national ceremonies. It was the Nakatomi who recited twice a year the litany of the Great Purification ("Ō-harai"), calling upon the gods to cleanse the people from the pollution of their offences. It was the Imibe who performed or supervised the rites of abstention, the observance of taboos, on behalf of the whole community, so as to ensure the ceremonial purity of worship. These two priestly families came close to the imperial family in prestige, and had great influence at Court, so much indeed that by the middle of the seventh century, though other clans had outstripped them in material strength, the leader of the Nakatomi was the most powerful man in Japan. But until then the Nakatomi were opposed by other ambitious families, rivals for dominance and even at times contenders for the throne.

These rivals were descendants of the tribal chieftains who had shared with the imperial clan in the founding of the Empire. They also derived importance from their hereditary functions, and they were distinguished one from another, nominally at least, by their occupation. Thus the Ōtomo clan were the hereditary bodyguards of the emperor, the Mononobe were responsible for the supply of weapons, and lesser clans or families had a monopoly of other professions or trades. In such cases the necessary labour was supplied not by the freemen of the clan but by organizations of workers attached to and controlled by the clan. These were the occupational groups known as *be* or *tomo*, a peculiar institution which is not thoroughly understood in all its complexities, but can best be described as resembling the hereditary association of workers, the *corporati*, of the later Roman empire. Membership in the Japanese corporations was hereditary, the son pursuing the trade of his father and unable to leave it; but the members of a particular corporation were not related by any blood tie, nor were they members of the clan or other group to which the corporation was attached.

A corporation was in fact, for the clan or family or person that controlled it, an important form of property, a continuous source of wealth, especially if it was engaged in making some valuable product or if its members were skilled in some essential craft. Perhaps the most common form of corporation was that of agricultural workers, for the ownership of land was useless without men to cultivate it.

The chiefs of the great clans (the "uji no kami") were not the only owners or controllers of corporations. There were many middling and small landholders who exercised authority over groups of their own workers, and there were also corporations which enjoyed a substantial autonomy under their own hereditary leaders, descendants in many cases of men appointed by a former sovereign. The Mononobe family, for example, constituted a corporation, the Corporation of Arms, as their name shows. Where the function of a corporation was of great importance, its titular head might rival the great territorial chieftains in power. Thus there were some inconsistencies between the social and economic systems; and the development of agricultural and industrial groups as the economy of the country expanded had consequences which are too complex for discussion here. But the following list of corporations (*tomo* and *be*) may serve to give an idea of their wide ramification. It should be explained that some of the corporations, notably those which exercised their functions at Court, were on a national scale, and others were only local organizations. Thus the Imbe (Imibe) were Court ritualists, and they were established in the seat of government. Though it is true that there were Imbe in the provinces, they were not members of the Imbe family, but dependent bodies which furnished clothing, food, and other requirements to the ritualists. In other words, they formed country estates owned by the metropolitan Imbe and provided them with income. Different from these were local corporations of workers who performed services for the local landholder to whom they were attached.

A generic description of these groups was "Momoyaso no Tomo," which literally means "One-hundred-eighty Corporations" but actually is a comprehensive title, meaning simply all the numerous groups. Among them were:

Imibe	Ritualists	Fubitobe	Scribes
(Imbe)	(Abstainers)	Osabe	Interpreters
Mononobe	Armorers	Urabe	Diviners
Kumebe	Soldiers	Kataribe	Reciters
Tanabe	Ricefield	Umakaibe	Grooms
(or Tabe)	workers	Sakabe	Brewers
Amabe	Fishermen		(of rice wine)
Oribe	Weavers	Yugebe	Bowyers
Ayabe	Brocade workers	Kajibe	Smiths
Hasebe	Potters	Kibe	Woodcutters

It is clear that, since these were occupations necessary for the maintenance of the national economy, there must have been severe competition for the control of the most essential resources. The records show that the Imperial House took vigorous measures to extend its power by creating new corporations of land workers, thus increasing its revenues, or by appointing to the headship of key corporations men upon whom it could depend for support. At the same time the clan leaders and other territorial magnates of various degrees, however willingly they acknowledged the sacerdotal supremacy of the Emperor, were the real rulers of their own domains, controlled their own groups of workers, and could count upon the loyalty of all their clansmen, to whom they were united by the bond of clan worship.

These independent leaders were thus a great obstacle to the formation of a centralized state; and the history of the fifth and sixth centuries is largely a record of struggle between the Sovereign and the great lords, the Omi and Muraji, whose pedigree was as noble as his own, and who stood in a relation to him not unlike that of the unruly barons to the king of England, whom they accompanied rather than followed on his campaigns. The Great Omi was the head of all the Omi or Grandees, the Chief of Chieftains, one might say; and they were of high ancestry. The Great Muraji was head of all the Muraji, clan leaders of somewhat less distinguished origin but nevertheless powerful. Among them were the families of Nakatomi, Ōtomo, and Mononobe, whom we have already noticed as holders of high office. These grand nobles were in a position to challenge, if they wished, the authority of the Throne, by virtue of their wealth as well as their descent. Of lower rank were the country gentry ("Kunitsuko" or "Kuni no miyatsuko"), local landholders of various origins, some possessing large estates, others only a modest area of farm land. They may in theory have been tenants of Crown land, but in fact they were the owners of the soil which their dependents tilled.

The total holdings of these great landowners and provincial gentry, together with their control of important corporations of workers, threatened to endanger the position of the Imperial House and obliged or rather encouraged it to extend its own possessions as rapidly as possible. This it did by creating new corporations and forcing or persuading local chieftains to set aside land labour for their support. Probably most effective in this field was the policy of creating new corporations of highly skilled workers or specialists. At first such persons could be recruited only from the refugees who began to cross over from Korea about A.D. 400, when conditions on the mainland were disturbed by dynastic upheavals. Among them were men of good birth with their families, former officials, scholars, and artists, who were made welcome at Court, where their service as scribes, secretaries, and accountants was invaluable. Equally useful were craftsmen of various kinds, masters of processes with which Japanese workmen were not yet familiar.

Such people entered Japan in large numbers, if we are to believe the native chronicles, which record the arrival of hundreds of households of "men of Ts'in" and "men of Han," who were Chinese, or at any rate Koreans claiming descent from well-known Chinese families. These important émigrés, who continued to arrive during the fifth and sixth centuries, were usually settled in areas under the control of the Crown, and formed into corporations under their own leaders. Thus, for instance, the makers of patterned silk stuffs were formed into the "Ayabe" or corporation of brocade workers, and their leader was given the rank and style of a nobleman of good standing. Similar treatment was accorded to other groups, and presently we find members of the old nobility betraying jealousy of the privileges which these aliens enjoyed. However, by the sixth century they were firmly established and were without doubt a most important, perhaps the most important, element in the composition of the Japanese people, if we exclude the mass of agricultural workers. Their contribution to the growth of civilized life was indispensable, for whatever virtues the Japanese possessed, prior to the fifth century their leaders were very backward in comparison with the exponents of the great cultures of the Asian mainland. They had courage in war, and a sense of loyalty in their communal life, but the early chronicles give glimpses of a really barbaric condition.

It may be appropriate to observe that, in studying early Japanese society, one is impressed by its late development. We are accustomed to think of the history of Asian cultures as reaching far back into an enlightened antiquity; but this is by no means true of Japan. Compared even with the experience of a benighted country like early Britain, similarly situated off the shores of a great continent, Japan's was one of isolation and late development. Britain was in relationship with Rome well before the Roman conquest, Latin-speaking merchants visited her towns, and British exports of corn and minerals were familiar in Europe. After the conquest a large part, perhaps half, of what is now England enjoyed (if not continuously, at least for long periods) the material benefits of Roman civilization and the beata tranquillitas of Roman peace, until the legions were withdrawn in 407. During that period Christianity was gaining ground, especially in the years of Constantine the Great, and British bishops sat in the Councils of the Christian Church. This was a time when Japan had only just begun to imbibe the essence of Chinese culture and had not yet come under the influence of Buddhism.

So the civilization of Japan is not of great antiquity, and the reason is not far to seek. The Japanese islands were not so near to the mainland as Britain was to Europe; and therefore communication was not easy. This obstacle might have been overcome by a determined invader, just as after the Roman withdrawal Britain was repeatedly overrun by seafaring people from parts of northern Europe as far distant as was the China coast from Kyūshū. But historically the Chinese felt no great urge for expansion across the sea, because they were principally occupied in extending and protecting their land frontiers and in settling their own gigantic domestic problems. Nor did Japan offer lucrative opportunities for trade, or strategic advantages, or tempting prizes of any kind such as attracted the Romans and later conquerors to swoop down in their galleys upon the English shore. Consequently once Japan was settled by the Late Stone Age and Bronze Age migrants, who appear to have arrived in small contingents and not in mass, she could accept or reject foreign influence at choice. Although she was now and again alarmed by Chinese expansion into Korea in the seventh century, she never was in serious danger. Nothing was imposed upon her by force. She was spared the experience of peoples on the edge of the Roman Empire, who were obliged to submit first to Roman influence, and then, when Roman protection was withdrawn, to sack and pillage by barbarians.

Whether the peaceful or the violent kind of cultural change is more salutary in the long run is a matter of opinion, but there can be little doubt that the most characteristic features of Japanese civilization are due to its development in comparative seclusion, which favoured the continuity of tradition and the survival of original elements of strength, and perhaps also of weakness, in the nation's life.

CHAPTER III

THE YAMATO STATE

1. *The Early Sovereigns and the Great Nobles*

THE SUCCESSFUL military expeditions to Korea which took place in the fourth century were soon followed by an increasingly close intercourse between southern Korean kingdoms and Japan, and a more rapid absorption of continental culture by Japanese leaders.

The most powerful influence after the introduction of iron tools and weapons was the introduction into Japan of the Chinese script, which made it possible for the Japanese, until then unlettered in the fullest sense, to keep records and accounts, to send written orders, and, in due course, to read Chinese books.

This second great step in the development of Japanese civilization was taken about the year 400, when scholars were sent to Japan as a thank offering by the King of Paikche, whose country had been saved by the Japanese expedition of 391 against his enemy the King of Koguryö.[1] These scholars are said to have carried with them some learned works (possibly a copy of the *Analects*) and a kind of copybook, the well-known *Thousand Character Classic*.

From this date onwards we enter into the period of recorded history, and can place some trust in the national chronicles. They are not entirely reliable for the first century or so after 400, but what they tell us about the events after 600 is on the whole credible, if we make allowance for the circumstances in which they were written. The following description is based principally upon these sources.

The names of sovereigns ruling during the fourth and fifth centuries, and approximate dates of their reigns, derived by conjecture from Japanese chronicles, are as follows:

Ōjin	[270–310?]	Yūryaku	456–479
Nintoku	313–399	Seinei	480–484
Richū	400–405	Kensō	485–487
Hanshō	406–410	Ninken	488–498
Ingyō	411–453	Buretsu	498–506
Ankō	453–456		

When these dates[2] are checked with references to Japan in Chinese dynastic chronicles several discrepancies appear. There are, for instance, some good reasons for placing the death of Ōjin much later than

---

[1] See p. 16.

[2] They are those in the *Nihonshi Jiten* ("Dictionary of Japanese History") published by Kyoto University in 1954.

310, and this involves adding several decades to the dates which follow, or diminishing the length of some of the reigns. The point is not of great importance. It will be noticed that, apart from the long reigns ascribed to Nintoku and Ingyō, the periods of rule are short, and there can hardly be any doubt that this chronology, though inexact, reflects an unstable dynastic situation, and some manipulation by the chroniclers.

The sixteen sovereigns up to Nintoku lived, according to the chronicles, between 711 B.C. and A.D. 399, a period of 1,110 years. By placing so far back in history the first Emperor, Jimmu, who is credited with leading the expedition from Kyūshū to found the state in Yamato, the chroniclers were obliged to allot to those sixteen sovereigns an average life of over 100 years. This is a device not uncommon in early historiography, when so many legends have to be fitted in that it becomes necessary either to lengthen the lives, or to increase the number, of personages described. Obviously not only is the chronology until A.D. 399 unacceptable, but the occurrences related, though something like them may have happened at some time, belong to the province of myth or even of deliberate fiction. Therefore this portion of the narrative is of interest as part of the history of literature rather than the history of events; and this is true, though to a less degree, of the record of the years after 400.

There are several reasons for this lack of authenticity. In the first place the records available to the compilers were scanty, and they had to draw upon oral traditions which preserved fragments of old memories, fanciful legends, and folk tales from various and often conflicting sources. Further these first essays in national history came from the enthusiastic but unpractised pens of scholars who were under the influence of the Chinese historical classics and felt on grounds of national pride that what they set down should not be an unvarnished tale, but must be provided with ample embellishment. They can scarcely be blamed for this, since their Chinese models were by no means free from bold invention and artful glosses. Nor had they ever heard that historians must describe an event "wie es eigentlich gewesen." Indeed it was their duty not to recite the bare facts of history but to present them in such a way as to magnify the reigning house and to uphold the institutions that had developed under its government.

Some check upon the chronology of the *Nihon-shoki* is provided by Chinese notices of Japan in which the arrival of Japanese envoys is recorded. The "King of Japan" is said to have sent a memorial to the Court of the Wei emperors in 478, in which he describes himself as Supreme Director of Military Affairs in Japan and Korea.[3] The Chinese emperor confirms the Japanese king in those titles, and the account adds

[3] This information is from the *History of the Liu Sung Dynasty*, which was compiled ca. 513 and covers the years 420–79. See Appendix I for full quotation.

that the king's four predecessors had made similar requests. Now the year 478 almost certainly falls within the reign of the Emperor Yūryaku, and his four predecessors cover the years from 400, or perhaps earlier. These dates square with the known military position of Japan in Korea after the establishment of the base in Mimana, which was prior to 400. We may therefore take the dates of the *Nihon-shoki* to be not far out from 400 onwards, and consider that we have left the age of legendary sovereigns and entered upon a period of authentic history. But the native chronicles still pursue their imaginative course, as may be seen from their description of the behaviour of the emperor about the year 500. He is vividly portrayed as given to debauchery, as taking a dreadful pleasure in cruelty, torturing his subjects, ripping open the bellies of pregnant women, and committing other unspeakable atrocities. This is very puzzling in a work designed to uphold the imperial dignity, and one can only guess that some problem of succession arose in or not long after Yūryaku's time, so that it became desirable to show that the line of Yūryaku had forfeited its claim to the throne by reason of its lack of virtue. That the story of these crimes is fabricated there can be hardly any doubt, for they are ascribed to Buretsu, the 25th Emperor, a probably imaginary collateral of Yūryaku; and they correspond almost exactly in their barbarous detail to offences ascribed in the *Book of History* and later works to the Tyrant Chou of the Yin dynasty of China (1200 B.C.). This King Chou had falsely held that nothing could deprive him of his divine kingship, and it may be that the Japanese historians, writing in about A.D. 700, under the influence of Chinese theories of government then current among scholars in Japan, thought it appropriate to borrow the Chou legend as an argument in favour of a new line of succession.

The particular issue of legitimacy is of no great importance, but the treatment of the episode by the chroniclers shows that in practice succession disputes were usually raised and settled by the great nobles; and it is their assumption of power and their fierce rivalries that dominate the political scene in the fifth, sixth, and seventh centuries. The ruling dynasty was in real danger, the principle of legitimacy was at stake, and the unification of Japan under a hereditary line of monarchs had clearly not proceeded so smoothly as official historians were to pretend at a later date. The great chieftains, the Ō-omi and the Ō-muraji, whom we have already seen enlarging their economic power by adding to their lands and people in competition with the imperial clan, assumed offices at Court as Great Ministers advising the Throne. It was they who chose the heir, at times in defiance of the sovereign's testament, and the position of legitimate heirs was often dangerous, for more than one of them fled to a distant province to escape assassination. Thus we are told that when, after Yūryaku's death, the line of the Emperor Ninken became extinct (apparently because of the murder of proper claimants), the Ō-muraji Ōtomo no Kanamura sent for a certain prince, who hastily fled when he saw an armed escort coming to fetch him, and was never heard of again. Upon this another prince was found, who took the risk and accepted the offer of the ministers. This was Keitai, the 26th Emperor, who reigned according to the official chronology from 507 to 531.

We do not hear much of his doings or of the five emperors who succeeded him:

	Nihon-shoki dates
Ankan	531–36
Senkwa	536–39
Kimmei	540–71
Bidatsu	572–85
Yōmei	585–87

Some of their reigns are suspiciously short as compared with those of the legendary emperors, but they seem to have died natural deaths, and the Great Ministers had reached such heights of power that now they could usually gain their ends without violence, chiefly by means of matrimonial connexions with the imperial family. Thus the Emperor Kimmei had many children by a daughter of the senior Great Minister of his time, Soga no Iname, who claimed descent from one of the legendary emperors and was the head of the Soga, one of the great clans of Yamato. It was a daughter of Kimmei by a Soga mother who married the Emperor Bidatsu, and later became the Empress Suikō, while the Emperor Yōmei, who was her full brother, married a daughter of Kimmei by another Soga lady; so that at his death in 588 there was a very strong admixture of Soga blood in all likely successors to the throne.

Soga Iname (who died in 570 and was succeeded by Soga Umako) had become Great Minister in 536. He was not the first of the great nobles to attempt to control the Imperial House. Before his time we have the example, just referred to, of Ōtomo Kanamura, who had in 498 crushed the rising of another grandee, Heguri no Matori. But it was the Soga clan that carried to extreme lengths the domination of the Throne by the nobility. Here again, the point of historical interest is not in the details of intrigue and bloodshed, which are commonplaces in the history of all states at a comparable stage of development. What deserves attention is the survival, the continuity, of the founding dynasty in spite of its seeming helplessness in checking the ambitions of the great clans. To discover how this came about is one of the leading problems in Japanese political history, for the sentiment of loyalty to the Throne outlasted many vicissitudes, weathered many storms.

The imperial clan was not without certain advantages. The purpose of the other clan leaders was to obtain real power, and this they could achieve not by usurping the throne but rather by standing as its protector. Soga no Iname saw this, and decided that he could most easily

gain his ends by destroying or at least weakening his rivals and exercising influence over the titular head of the state by building up family
connexions through the marriage of Soga women to imperial princes.

Consequently, in the long run and after some sanguinary struggles,
the Soga clan made a valuable contribution to the system of imperial
rule as a political institution, by diminishing the actual power of the
emperor to govern while upholding and perpetuating his right to reign
as a symbol of national unity. This seemingly paradoxical situation is
of course not uncommon in the history of monarchy. In Japan as elsewhere it arose from the action of powerful nobles, but it could hardly
have come about in Japan if there had been no strong and ancient tradition of reverence for the sovereign. It was undoubtedly the authority
of the emperor, as the high priest interceding with the gods on their
behalf, that united the people in a bond of religion more permanent than
conventional political ties. It should be added that the imperial clan
had, moreover, certain secular advantages, among which were its accumulated wealth, its possession of the Regalia, its function (however
nominal) as an arbiter among the other clans, and its position as representative of the whole Yamato people in campaigning against rebellious
tribes and in dealing with other peoples and countries, in particular
China, where importance was attached to dynastic claims, or at least
to the appearance of legitimacy. The mystic power of the sovereign
was recognized from the earliest times, as we see from the Wei records,
which say of the Queen Pimiku that she bewitched her people with
magic and sorcery. The history of the Age of the Gods, as it is related
in the native chronicles, does not merely assign divinity to the ruler,
but starts from the assumption that he possesses it.

European kings might call themselves sovereign "by the grace of
God," but the emperors of Japan described themselves as "manifest
gods," ruling the kingdom upon earth. It is important to understand that
the divinity of the sovereign, as it is conceived of throughout Japanese
history, is not something which is claimed, but is a basic assumption, a
historical growth from primitive sources. It is not like the "divine right
of kings," which is a political theory, remotely derived no doubt from
very early ideas of kingship but developed into a coherent doctrine
in modern times in support of absolutism. In Europe the very idea of
national sovereignty was vague until it grew out of the struggle for
independence from papal and imperial supremacy. The conditions in
which the European doctrine developed—the claims of the papacy in
particular and the general theological character of politics in the middle
ages—had no counterpart in Japan.

2. Relations with Korean Kingdoms

Domestic politics in Japan in the fifth and sixth centuries were closely
related to the position of Japan in the Korean peninsula. At the time

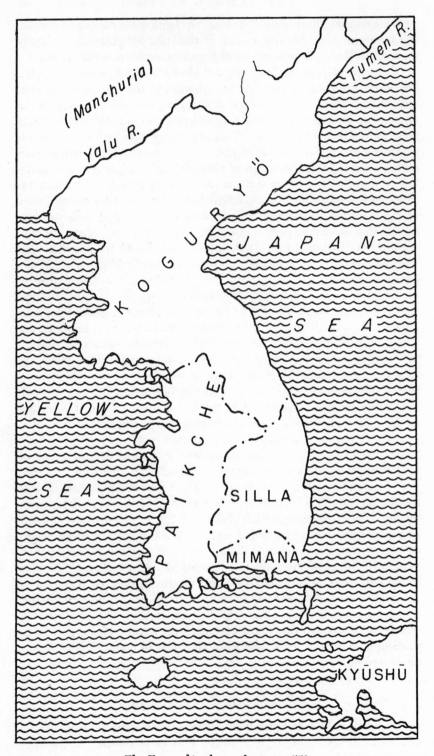

The Korean kingdoms, about A.D. *550*

when the great clans were asserting their authority and the chieftain of the Ōtomo clan, Kanamura, had placed the Emperor Keitai on the throne (ca. 507), the Japanese enclave of Mimana was being threatened by the rulers of adjacent Korean kingdoms, Silla and Paikche (known to the Japanese as Shiragi and Kudara), and also by the powerful northern state of Koguryö. Certain Japanese, or half-Japanese, warriors in Korea and certain chieftains in Kyūshū were conspiring with one or other of those kingdoms, taking bribes and actually transferring portions of Mimana to them. Kanamura himself was suspected of this kind of treachery; and when an expeditionary force was sent to Korea in 527 to put things right it was held up for more than a year by a Kyūshū chieftain named Iwai, who was in league with the kingdom of Silla. After the defeat of Iwai in 528–29 a new Resident was sent to Mimana, but he failed and was recalled. Another officer was sent in 530, a member of the Ōtomo clan, and he came to terms with the King of Paikche. Paikche was then struggling with Silla and, in order to prevent the expansion of its enemy, was prepared to see Mimana restored (to Japan) by the recovery of territory which Silla had annexed.

Paikche was at this juncture in a dangerous position, for she was threatened not only by the expansion of Silla but also by the growing power of Koguryö. She turned to Japan for help, and support was promised by the Yamato rulers. But there were many delays and difficulties, arising from treachery of the Japanese in Mimana, who were more than half Korean in sympathy if not by birth. A force was sent in 552, but in 554 Silla defeated Paikche, despite some very hard knocks given to Silla forces by the Japanese. There was a truce in 555, but Silla was now in a strong position and in 562 occupied and annexed Mimana. The Japanese made repeated efforts to get it back, but they failed; and so from that year Japan lost her foothold upon the continent.

Two interesting facts emerge from the history of this continental adventure. The first is that the Japanese excelled as fighting men in a fighting age. The second is that their policy failed not for want of military competence, but because the central government in Yamato could not depend upon the obedience of the great territorial chieftains in western Japan, especially in Kyūshū, or upon the loyalty of its representatives in Korea, or indeed upon the integrity of its Great Ministers at Court.

The hard-pressed King of Paikche constantly appealed for Japanese help, underlining his prayers by gifts of many kinds. In the year 552, when he was at his wits' end for means of defence against his enemies, he sent to the Court of Japan a bronze image of the Buddha, some volumes of Buddhist scriptures, and other presents, together with a letter praising the new faith, which (he said) had now spread eastward from its home in India as far as the land of Korea. This is generally regarded as the occasion of the introduction of Buddhism in Japan. There is some doubt about the chronology here, and in any case it is difficult to assign an exact date to an indefinite process. We know that Buddhism was making headway in the Tartar countries of north China during the fourth century, and had been brought to Korea in that same century. Some knowledge of it must have been taken to Japan by Korean scholars not long after that, but the strongest impetus to the spread of Buddhism in Korea and thence to Japan was the favour which it enjoyed under the Northern Wei and Liang rulers in the sixth century. Consequently the influence of Buddhism was felt in Korea and Japan somewhat later than the date of its arrival in central Asia and in south China. The reason for this delay is of course the remote peripheral situation of Korea and Japan, but endemic warfare in north China during the fourth century and most of the fifth was also an obstacle to the spread of the faith. It was adopted officially by the King of Silla not before 515, though Paikche seems to have accepted it a good deal earlier (in 384, according to some sources).

The results of the introduction of Buddhism in Japan were far-reaching and profound. They must be discussed in detail in any history of Japanese civilization. But the immediate effects of the gifts of the Korean king first deserve some brief attention, because they throw light upon the political scene in Japan as a struggle between the great clans and the Imperial House developed during the latter half of the sixth century.

The new religion which was recommended by the Korean king to the Japanese Court in glowing language—he said it was of all doctrines the most excellent—caused much dissension. It was naturally opposed by the leaders of the clans whose functions were concerned with the practices of the native cult. Chief among these were the Nakatomi family, priestly mouthpieces of the emperor in his prayers to the divine ancestors. But the real matter in dispute was not the truth of the new doctrine. It was a conflict between conservative forces and a growing desire for political reform.

Here again was a situation in domestic politics growing out of Japanese relations with Korea. The wisest among the leaders of Yamato were impressed by the power of the rising Korean kingdoms, which they rightly attributed to superior organization. The failure of Japanese arms and the threat to the base in Mimana had brought home to them the fact that their country was backward in everything but sheer fighting spirit. The rivalry between clans, the lack of unity, the intrigue and bickering, the treachery even, that had bedevilled policy in Korea were sources of weakness, and indeed of danger, for a coalition of Koguryö and Silla against Japan would be hard to resist. There was an urgent need for reform, by the adoption of such features of Chinese civilization as had, so it seemed, enabled the Korean states to develop their strength to the detriment of Japanese interests.

It is therefore not surprising that, when the mission from Paikche put to the Japanese Court the case for adopting a new creed which offered spiritual and material benefits, the proponents of reform took the side of Buddhism and the conservatives cried that it threatened the very foundations of the life of the Japanese people, the benevolence of their ancestral gods. The underlying conflict, it need hardly be said, was a clash of political interests; though it would be a mistake to assume that no genuine religious feelings were involved. The Nakatomi clan naturally stood for the indigenous faith. The Mononobe, a military clan, joined, and indeed led, the resistance to Buddhism, not so much on religious grounds as on what today we should describe as nationalistic grounds. They did not approve of foreign ideas, and they believed in the use of armed force as the proper instrument of policy. Opposed to this conservative school was the Soga clan, whose leader, the Great Minister Iname, was convinced of the need for a new system of government which would break the autonomy of the clans and assert the authority of the Crown and its appointed ministers. This was a line which the Soga family could afford to take, since (as we have seen) they had already established their own position by means of marriage relationships with the imperial family.

The strife between the two factions lasted a long time—some fifty years from first to last. Soga took the holy image and installed it in a pure shrine. The Mononobe and the Nakatomi protested that to do this was to incur the anger of the gods. So the fortunes of Buddhism rose as its benefits appeared credible and fell as current evils like sickness and drought were ascribed to its adoption. In one phase of doubt the image was mutilated and thrown into a canal. Shortly after that a plague of sores afflicted the people, and there was a reaction in favour of Buddhism. Soga Umako, the son of Iname (the Great Minister whom he succeeded in 570), obtained the emperor's permission to worship the Buddha, and built a small chapel. This was for his private devotions; but on the death of the Emperor Bidatsu (585) religious strife was merged in fierce succession quarrels in which the adoption of Buddhism was a subsidiary though important issue. The Emperor Yōmei, who succeeded Bidatsu, died suddenly in 587 after a very short reign, having declared himself in favour of the new religion. The Mononobe chieftain, Moriya, and his allies tried to put a prince of their own choice upon the throne, but Soga Umako supported the claim of a son of the Emperor Kimmei by a Soga lady. For the Soga the situation was now crucial, since opposition was mounting. Umako collected a great number of adherents from clans hostile to the Mononobe, and attacked Moriya in a decisive battle at Shigisen, where he annihilated the Mononobe family. This was in 587, and in the following year the prince chosen by Umako ascended the throne as the Emperor Sujun. The most powerful opponent of Buddhism had been destroyed; the Nakatomi offered no threat as a belligerent clan; and the Ōtomo, once a powerful military family, were reduced in importance, partly (it seems) because of their failures in Korea and partly because of their voluntary subordination to the political power of the Soga, now at its zenith.

Thus the fortunes of Buddhism rose quickly, thanks to the protection of the Soga clan, and by the end of the sixth century it was well established in Yamato, at Court and in a large number of noble families. It might therefore be thought that political reforms would now proceed apace, concurrently with the spread of both religious and secular learning from the continent. But there can be no doubt that conditions in Japan were still far more disturbed and civil government far less developed than the Chronicles would have us believe. The political record of Soga no Umako does not match his pious efforts to promote religion, for he proceeded to consolidate his power by acts of outrageous treachery. He caused the Emperor Sujun to be assassinated, and raised to the throne as the Empress Suiko his own niece, the widow of the Emperor Bidatsu. This was a flagrant departure from precedent, seeing that there had been no reigning empress since legendary matriarchal times. It will be clear from the genealogical table below that it was not for lack of male issue from Bidatsu that this lady—then thirty-nine years old and the mother of seven sons—was selected to succeed the murdered emperor. But Umako was following the policy of his father Iname by putting on the throne the child of a Soga mother.

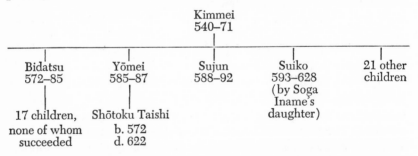

Once the Empress Suiko was on the throne Umako nominated as Heir Apparent and Regent not one of her sons but the second son of Yōmei, the Prince Umayado, known in Japanese history as Shōtoku Taishi, the Crown Prince Shōtoku. It is not quite clear why Umako selected this young man, but it must be that he recognized his great qualities, and knowing his zeal for Buddhism thought it prudent to have him on the Soga side. Though far from saintly himself, Umako was quite earnest in his desire to extend the Buddhist faith, because he was wise enough to see the importance to Japan of new knowledge from China, whether sacred or profane. In this he was moreover right from his own personal standpoint, for he was obliged to oppose the views of his enemies, the conservative clans with a vested interest in traditional

ideas. It was plain to him that the monks, scholars, artists, and craftsmen who were now making their way to Japan in increasing numbers
represented a kind of civilization far in advance of anything hitherto
known in Japan, and could teach principles of government that would
be of great advantage to any statesman aspiring to sovereign power.
Umako seems to have been content to stay in the background during
Shōtoku Taishi's regency, and to have devoted himself to the new learning, showing himself from time to time at Court ceremonies as the Great
Minister and no doubt quietly arranging marriages for Soga daughters.
He was still the power behind the Throne, but he saw no need to interfere while things were going his way. He and his kind wanted to see
a well-organized state, unified and therefore easier for them to control
than a loose association of unruly chieftains.

It is a notable testimony to the interest in problems of government
which Japanese leaders were feeling at this time—and which they have
continued to display ever since—that Buddhism should have commended
itself to the ruling class as a system of belief beneficial to the state. It
must be remembered, of course, that the introduction of the arts and
sciences of China into Japan was closely connected, or one might say
identified, in Japanese minds with the work of evangelization performed
by Buddhist missionaries from the mainland. By A.D. 601, when the
Sui dynasty had succeeded in uniting China and had declared in favour
of Buddhism, it had a powerful appeal not only as a great teaching but
as an essential feature of civilized life.

3. Prelude to Reform

There is no doubt that the Crown Prince Shōtoku was a most important figure in the history of his times. He is credited with many notable
achievements, in promoting the growth of Buddhism, in developing
relations with China, in encouraging learning, and in laying down the
lines for political reform in Japan. It is clear from what is recorded of
him in the Chronicles (which were compiled within a century after his
death) that he was admired and beloved as a great and good man.

But the condition of Japan at the time when he came into power
as Regent, being then only twenty-one years of age, was scarcely such
that he could in his short life have achieved all the political and social
reforms and engaged in all the profound studies that are ascribed to
him. According to the Chronicles, he issued in 604 a document known
as the Constitution of Seventeen Articles. This celebrated work is not
a constitution in any strict sense, but a set of moral and political principles which he is said to have regarded as essential conditions of reform. It is an important document and one of considerable historical
interest, but it is today not generally accepted by Japanese scholars as
Shōtoku Taishi's own work. It was most probably written as a tribute

to his memory a generation or more after his death, when some of the reforms which he desired had at last been introduced; and this was a not unnatural act of piety, since he did beyond doubt play a leading part in the importation of ideas and things from China, thus leading the way towards an enrichment of Japanese life. But before any genuine reform could be accomplished it was necessary to overcome stubborn opposition from the clans; and it was not possible to concentrate all energies upon that task, since Japan was not yet reconciled to the loss of Mimana, and made repeated efforts to regain her position in Korea. Missions were exchanged with the Korean kingdoms, but to no useful purpose, except for the receipt of presents of books, pictures, images, and men skilled in various arts and crafts, notably from the friendly state of Paikche.

In 602 troops were assembled for an invasion of Silla, but the commander-in-chief, Prince Kume, died and the project was abandoned. An attack on Silla was again discussed in 622, but again the project came to nothing. The situation was developing in a way quite unfavourable to Japan, for a united China was now seeking to expand into the Korean peninsula. Already in 612 the Sui emperor had sent an army against Koguryö, the northern kingdom, but his troops were defeated. For some time after that the Korean kingdoms were continuously at war among themselves, and the situation of Paikche grew desperate. Silla was gaining strength, owing to an understanding with China, now under the powerful rule of the T'ang dynasts, while Japan, immersed in succession struggles at home, could make no great effort abroad. A large T'ang force invaded northern Korea in 646, and was beaten by Koguryö; but Chinese pressure on Korea was not abandoned. In 659 a very large T'ang force was transported by sea to attack the Paikche coast. In 660 Paikche was invaded and occupied. By 663 it was made into a colony and placed under a Chinese viceroy. All this was naturally alarming to the Japanese, who made an effort to help Paikche to regain freedom. A fairly large Japanese expedition said to have numbered 27,000 had been sent across the straits from Kyūshū in 662, but it was met and almost entirely destroyed by a Chinese naval force. From that time Japan turned from an offensive to a defensive policy, concentrating upon protective works on the islands of Iki and Tsushima, in Kyūshū, and at Yashima and Sanuki in Shikoku. The special importance of the Kyūshū Defence Headquarters at Dazaifu dates from this period. Perhaps the immediate danger was exaggerated, but once the T'ang empire began to assert itself and to maintain a coalition with Silla the position was awkward. It is understandable that no very drastic changes in the clan system could be undertaken so long as men and material had to be ready for national defence.

It is curious, in the light of the Prince Shōtoku's posthumous fame, that we have very little exact information about his activities. His chief interest seems to have been the study of Buddhist literature and the Chinese classics. His intellectual prowess is described as miraculous; we are told that he could speak as soon as he was born, and when he grew up could attend to the claims of ten men at once and decide them all without mistake. It is clear that he was exceptionally gifted and virtuous, and that he did much to raise the level of learning and piety in his own country. The early monasteries in the environs of Nara, notably the Hōryūji, and the treasures from his day which they still enshrine, bear witness to his achievement, if not in actual authorship at least in encouragement and inspiration.

But of his secular activities in domestic affairs there is not much trace. If his "Constitution" is dismissed as a pious counterfeit, then his only recorded contribution to political reform is the institution of "cap ranks," that is to say ranks assigned to ministers and other officers, the order of precedence being marked by caps of prescribed pattern and colour. Here was no doubt a preliminary to the conversion of titles of nobility into official grades of Court rank. The purpose of this regulation, which was copied from current Chinese practice at the Sui Court, was of course to show that offices were held not as of right but at the will of the sovereign. Apart from being a first step towards forming a bureaucracy to carry out the policy of a central government, this measure is of interest as showing a traditional Japanese feeling for distinctions of rank, which had already been noticed by the Wei travellers of the third century.

It is not even certain that Shōtoku Taishi introduced this system, though it seems probable. Where he was most active was in the despatch of missions to China, and these were indeed essential to any plan of reform, as we shall see, for it was the knowledge acquired in China, knowledge of Chinese political theory and practice, that was applied in Japan to the organization of a central government and a well-defined administrative system. The first official envoy to represent the sovereign of a united Japan was Ono no Imoko, who left Japan in 607 and returned with a Chinese envoy in the following year. Apart from purely diplomatic missions, scholars were sent singly or in groups to China for study, while learned monks and laymen from Korea and China crossed to Japan, many of them taking refuge from the disorder of regions overrun by contending armies.

While these studies were in progress the Prince Shōtoku died, at the age of forty-nine, in 622, and shortly after that the Great Minister Soga Umako died also. He was succeeded as head of the Soga clan and as Great Minister by his son Yemishi. This Soga, on the death of the Empress Suiko in 628, assumed the right to choose her successor. The usual bitter dispute took place, and after much intrigue and some brutal murders was settled by the appointment of a grandson of Bidatsu in 629. Shōtoku's son, Prince Yamashiro no Ōye, was set aside, though his

claim was strong. He also had much Soga blood in his veins, and Yemishi did not think it prudent to have him put out of the way. The new
Emperor, Jomei, died in 641, and again the Soga clan decided the succession, choosing a granddaughter of Bidatsu (who, it will be recalled,
had married a Soga daughter).

Soga Yemishi now began to put on sovereign airs. He built himself
a tomb of imperial dimensions and conferred high ranks upon his son
Iruka and his other children, thus usurping the prerogative of the
Throne. He was nearly all-powerful, but not quite. The influence of
Yamashiro no Ōye was strong, and Yemishi at length decided to do away
with him. He was treacherously captured by Iruka, with his family.
They all committed suicide or were put to death. Yemishi and Iruka
continued to exercise a tyrannical power. They lived in fortified palaces
and bullied the members of princely and noble houses. All opposition
seemed to have been overcome, and the Soga were protected by a strong
bodyguard of hard fighting men. They also had gained the support of
a number of immigrant groups, Korean or Chinese, who could give
them valuable aid, and they seem to have made themselves popular
among the Ainu in eastern Japan. There is little doubt that, rejecting
the prudence of the great Soga Iname, who was content to stand behind
the Throne, they aimed at the destruction of the reigning dynasty. Iruka,
in particular, was a violent, blundering man, for he not only offended
princes and nobles, but also flouted the interests and hurt the pride of
junior branches of the Soga clan.

The inevitable trial of strength came in 644, when the head of the
Nakatomi family (which had been deprived of its importance by the
successes of the Soga and by the rise of Buddhism) conspired with the
Prince Naka no Ōye and an aggrieved member of the Soga clan to
destroy the power of Yemishi and Iruka. By a treacherous stratagem
no less reprehensible than those to which the Soga commonly resorted,
Iruka, after some bungling by assassins sweating with fright, was murdered at Court in front of the empress he had put on the throne. Naka
no Ōye and his party then withdrew to a monastery, where they prepared for a struggle. The adherents of Yemishi dispersed without putting up a fight and soon many of them were put to death. Next morning
the Empress Kōgyoku abdicated and the Imperial Prince Karu was enthroned as the Emperor Kōtoku (645), Naka no Ōye being named Heir
Apparent. Kurayamada, the Soga who had joined in the plot against
Yemishi and Iruka, was named Great Minister. Naka no Ōye had married Kurayamada's daughter—that was part of the plot—and thus the
Soga clan, or an important part of it, was now on the side of the Throne.
There was one recalcitrant member, however, in the person of Prince
Furubito no Ōye, who had been favoured by Iruka. He led an abortive
rising in 646 and was killed by Naka no Ōye's men, while his womenfolk
took their own lives to avoid capture and slavery.

These cruel and sordid episodes have no peculiar interest as samples of human behaviour. The history of any country, East or West, will furnish a wealth of incidents no less revolting. But the circumstances related in this chapter have an especial bearing upon two important problems in Japanese history. The first of these is to account for the survival of the Imperial House, despite its weakness and the strength of the great clans. The second is to ascertain the nature of Japanese society prior to the reforms which began after the death of the Soga kingmakers.

The Imperial House seems to have weathered its many storms because the sovereigns reigned but did not govern—an excellent recipe for dynastic stability. But it is also true that the Soga family, despite the excesses of Yemishi and Iruka, in the long run served as protectors of the Throne. They had a special interest in its safety because so much Soga blood circulated in imperial veins.

As for the condition of Japan before 645, it is clear that it was not by any means as well organized, as civilized, as the language of the official historians would suggest. It must be remembered that the chroniclers could not have written a line of history without knowing the Chinese language and its script. They are therefore inevitably anachronistic, for when they describe even purely Japanese things they are bound, for lack of a suitable vocabulary, to use Chinese terms which stand for Chinese things. Thus the *Nihon-shoki* uses the term "provincial governor" of a period before such posts were created, simply because there was no comprehensive term in Japanese to describe great territorial magnates who had power over their own land and their own people. In general Chinese influence is visible throughout the Chronicles. It appears where it is least to be expected, for example in folk songs which are quoted as being of great antiquity. It has been shown by Japanese scholars that many of the poems in the *Kojiki* as well as the *Nihon-shoki*, though older than the narratives in which they occur, have been, so to speak, polished and brought up to date according to the requirements of Chinese prosody. This is an interesting testimony to the prestige of Chinese culture in the seventh century, and at the same time a warning that nothing in the Chronicles can safely be assumed to be purely Japanese. Yet the sentiment of the poems seems to be purely Japanese, and the fact that poetry is recorded so freely in the course of a dry official narrative shows a native love of expression in verse. From this point of view, perhaps one of the most interesting poems in the *Shoki* is a love poem, or rather duet, attributed to Prince Magari and his bride the Princess Kasuga. It is a kind of epithalamium. We are told how through the moonlit night the couple held sweet converse until the dawn came on them unawares. Of a sudden the grace of elegant style was embodied in the speech of the Prince, who broke into song, describing the betrothal and then saying:

Arm embraced and twined with arm
In sweet slumber we lay.
'Tis the bird of the courtyard
The cock that is crowing.
'Tis the bird of the moorland
The pheasant a-calling.
Ere I have uttered
All my mind fully
The dawn has come, O my beloved.

Then the Princess replied, with much metaphor and simile, that if she were to ascend and stand on a hilltop proclaiming this sad news of the untimely daybreak,

The very fishes
That pass under the water
Would come to the surface and lament.

.   .   .   .

Not a man is there whoever he may be
Who would not rise and lament.

But the prosaic chronicle goes on to relate that the bride of this ecstatic occasion declares a few months later that she is barren, and asks for the grant of an estate to keep her name from becoming extinct.

4. *The Reform Movement, 645–701: Early Stages*

After the defeat of the Soga clan and the accession of the Emperor Kōtoku in 645, the sovereign and his advisers were able to proceed with their plans of reform free from any present danger of further succession quarrels and, what was of as much importance, fortified by some knowledge of Chinese theory and practice in matters of government. They lost no time in starting to carry out their intentions, taking the first steps only a few days after the death of Iruka, for this was a moment when success had given them great authority.

Their problem was how to induce the territorial nobility and gentry (the Omi, the Muraji, the Miyatsuko, the Kunitsuko, and other, smaller landholders) to surrender their autonomy and to regard themselves as servants of the Crown and tenants, not owners, of their estates. The necessary formula was not difficult to devise, since there were plenty of Chinese precedents to cite. It was easy enough to proclaim that "a sovereign cannot permit two governments, and a subject cannot serve two masters." What was not easy was to persuade the great private landowners that under a new central government they would not lose the substance of their hereditary positions. It was a question of land and of men to work upon the land; so that short of suppressing the great clans by force (a solution beyond the resources of the imperial clan), it was necessary to find a basis of allegiance that the territorial nobles could accept without losing possession of their lands and control over their people.

This problem had been discussed and considered by the Crown Prince Naka no Ōye and his adviser, the leader of the Nakatomi clan, which was now in eclipse. This was Nakatomi Kamako, who had taken part in the events that led to the Soga downfall. Known later as Fujiwara Kamatari, he was one of the greatest figures in Japanese history and the founder of a family, the Fujiwara, which was to play a leading part for several centuries, reaching heights of power and wealth far greater than those of the Soga in their prime. It was Kamatari who, having applied himself to Chinese studies, worked out with the Crown Prince a gradual introduction of measures of reform by announcing them as matters of principle and securing the agreement of the clan leaders to a practical arrangement which would not deprive them of their privileges.

Early in the year 645, after the enthronement of the Emperor Kōtoku, the great nobles were summoned to Court and the doctrine of absolute monarchy was proclaimed. Then followed certain practical measures, such as registration of households, the survey of arable land, the supervision of monks and nuns, and some procedure for settling claims. Not much is known about these preliminaries, which seem to have been of an experimental nature, and were perhaps mainly designed to test the feeling of the clans and prepare the way for more extensive changes. No doubt to help in providing a suitable atmosphere of optimism, the new era, beginning with the reign of Kōtoku, was given the name Taikwa, which means Great Reform; and in the second year of Taikwa (646) the celebrated Reform Edict (Kaishin no Chō) was pronounced. It consisted of four simple articles, which are easily summarized. Article I abolished private title to land and workers acquired by the formation of "namesake" or "succession" estates or by other means of appropriation. Article II established a metropolitan region, called the Kinai or Inner Provinces, to include the centre of government in a capital city; communications with the outer provinces were to be improved, and governors of provinces and districts within the Kinai were to be appointed. Article III ordered the institution of registers of population, with a view to the allotment of rice land to cultivators on an equitable basis, and provided for the appointment of rural headmen. Article IV abolished old taxes and contributions of forced labour and introduced a new system of taxation.

This was a bold attempt to apply the systems of land tenure, provincial and local government, and taxation which were then in operation in China, or if not in full operation were laid down in the T'ang codes.

To set an example to the nobles, the Crown Prince, at an assembly which he summoned in the third month of the new era, having first announced the appointment of governors and other officers to the eastern provinces, surrendered his own private estates (*miyake*) to the public domain. At the same time the building of great mausoleums was forbidden, new funeral regulations were issued, and the former workers of corporations were released, so becoming public and not private property. Finally a new administrative system was set up, in which appointments to office were made by the Crown on a fixed scale of ranks to which fixed emoluments pertained.

These changes taken together constituted a very far-reaching reform, which would indeed have been revolutionary had it succeeded, since it aimed at the concentration of all administrative and fiscal power in the hands of the sovereign. In a country dominated by a land-revenue economy characteristic of the monsoon area of eastern Asia, it is evident that the landlords, great and small, however smoothly the first stages were passed, would not surrender what they deemed to be their property rights without a desperate struggle. They must somehow be reconciled to the new order, and this was possible only if they were allowed to retain the substance of their privileges. Consequently the reformers confined themselves in practice to appointing to new posts men who would have performed similar duties under the former system. Thus great landowners were made provincial governors and given appropriate Court rank with corresponding emoluments. Landed gentry of less consequence were given posts as district governors, while a permanent staff of minor officials, such as secretaries, accountants, and tax collectors, was created where possible from men of the locality who could read and write and do sums. These arrangements evoked little active opposition, because the official salaries and allowances compensated the landowners and the minor functionaries for the loss of direct income which they had previously enjoyed. For such reasons the early phases of reform encountered no very great obstacles, and the principles of central power and state ownership appear to have been accepted without much argument.

The central government was in any case not strong enough to impose its new rules irrespective of all circumstances, and it is fairly certain that the degree of compliance with its orders varied from place to place with local conditions and the temper of the local notables. Furthermore, apart from those landowners who might be aggrieved at loss of independence, many people in country districts must have found their position improved, since they obtained a regular income, an added prestige, and an extended authority as government office holders. The ordinary free householder supporting himself by farming was now to receive an allotment of land based upon the number of "mouths" in his household, so that his family's subsistence was ensured; moreover, in theory at least, he paid only a fixed amount of tax to the local collector and was no longer subject to arbitrary demands from private dignitaries.

This was the position in 646, and we must presently trace the working of the new system as practical experience was gained. But first we should return to the events which rose out of the situation in Korea, because it is important to understand to what a great degree domestic affairs in Japan were affected by the trend of politics on the mainland.

We have seen that Chinese pressure on Korea caused anxiety to Japan from an early date in the seventh century. When the Japanese expedition to assist Paikche was defeated by T'ang forces, the Crown Prince Naka no Ōye (who was de facto sovereign from 655 to 662 and then succeeded as the Emperor Tenchi) withdrew his army from Korean soil. That was in 662, when the Reform Edict had been in force for some fifteen years. The Prince and his advisers had seen that they could not successfully challenge the enormous strength of the T'ang empire; and now, following the intentions of Shōtoku Taishi, they determined that their best course was to abandon all commitments in Korea and to concentrate upon friendly intercourse with China, a country from which they had so much to learn. Consequently, while taking precautionary measures of defence, they sought to renew friendly relations with the T'ang government.

The Chinese viceroy of the former state of Paikche was approached by Japanese emissaries, and in 664 that officer (his name was Liu Jen-yüan) sent an envoy to Japan carrying a letter and some presents, presumably return gifts, though the chronicle does not say so. The next year the same envoy conducted a T'ang ambassador to Japan; and after cordial entertainment at the Japanese Court (which included a kind of military review) the T'ang mission was escorted back to China by Japanese ambassadors. All this was in 665. During the reign of Suiko there had been some trouble between the two Courts, owing to the use of undiplomatic language in a letter from the Japanese sovereign, who describes herself as the ruler of the Land of the Rising Sun and addresses the Chinese sovereign (Yang Ti of the Sui dynasty) as the emperor of the Land of the Setting Sun. When the Japanese ambassador presented his credentials at Ch'ang-an in 607, the Chinese, who in their superb way regarded the Japanese as eastern barbarians ruled by petty kings, took offence at the assumption that a Japanese monarch was equal to a Chinese emperor. The difficulty was somehow got over, though formal relations between the two Courts remained delicate for some time. It was thought desirable to dispense with written exchanges while maintaining official relations on a personal footing. Ambassadors were sent from Japan at irregular intervals, only four missions to the T'ang Court being recorded from 630 to 665, the last of these being that despatched by the Emperor Tenchi.

The unofficial or private visits to China were far more important in the minds of the Japanese leaders than the formal diplomatic journeys. So important were sea communications at this time that the capital was moved from inland (Asuka) to Toyosaki, at the mouth of the Yodo River, in the reign of the Emperor Kōtoku, which began in the first year of the Great Reform. It was the students, teachers, novices and monks, artists, craftsmen, and men learned in the law who, passing to and fro between the mainland and Japan, provided the flow of useful knowledge upon which the reform party based its plans. These travellers not only brought precious books with them, but also were able to describe the institutions of a highly organized state and to report upon what they themselves had observed of the administrative methods of the T'ang government, its carefully graded civil service, and its far-reaching power. They were no mere transient visitors, but earnest students who usually stayed in China for long periods, immersed in their studies. Of the companions of Ono no Imoko on his voyage in 607, two remained abroad for more than thirty years. These were the lay student Taka-muku no Ayabito and the Buddhist priest Bin. In 645, on the eve of the Great Reform, they were invested with the rank and style of Kuni-no-hakase or National Scholar, an honour which indicates what impor-tance was attached to their services.

It is as well to mention here that, while the reforms were in progress, the reform leaders, as well as having to deal with a difficult situation in Korea, were by no means free from anxiety at home. A little more than twenty-five years after the issue of the Reform Edict there was a serious revolt, following upon the death of the Emperor Tenchi in 671. A violent succession dispute broke out. Tenchi's son, who had succeeded him, was killed during a civil war that lasted for some months, and the vic-torious rebel claimant, a younger brother of Tenchi, was enthroned as the Emperor Temmu in 672. This factional struggle was no doubt wel-comed, if not actually fostered, as a check to the reform movement, by some of the unreconciled nobles.

5. *The Rise of Buddhism*

Since the influence of Buddhism upon Japanese life is an important feature in Japanese history, it may be useful to give here a short account of Buddhist doctrine for the benefit of those who are not familiar with its elements.

From simple beginnings in the sermons of the Blessed One (the first being the Sermon at Benares) Buddhism in the course of time de-veloped a vast canon and a most comprehensive range of metaphysics, but its fundamental doctrine is short and not very difficult to under-stand. The Buddha taught that all clinging to life involves suffering; that the cause of suffering is craving for pleasure and rebirth; that suf-fering can be ended because its cause is known and can be removed;

and that the way to end suffering is to follow the Eightfold Path. These are the Four Holy Truths.

The Eightfold Path is right views, right aims, right speech, right action, right living, right effort, right mindfulness, and right rapture. These eight paths seem only to lead towards a simple morality, but taken together they are more than that; they are the necessary steps to complete enlightenment, since the last path, right rapture, means the ecstasy of perfect knowledge, from which comes the end of craving for pleasure and rebirth, and therefore deliverance from suffering. To these precepts are added the idea, which the Buddha described as the essence of his teaching, of the Chain of Causation, the inevitable sequence of events. "If that is, this comes to pass. On account of that arising this arises. If that is not, this does not come to pass."

The metaphysical elaboration of this Law is difficult to understand, but it was not hard for the ordinary man to grasp the idea that the whole universe is a process of birth and death and rebirth, involving suffering from which he can escape by reaching a goal (called nirvana) which is not annihilation but the absence of all causes of suffering.

This goal cannot be reached so long as a man thinks in terms of his own identity. So long as he believes that he has a self he must continue through an indefinite series of reincarnations. In other terms this is the doctrine of Karma, of which the essence is that a life is not complete in itself, but is both a sequel and a prelude, conditioned by past lives and conditioning future lives. In this chain there may be existences of many kinds, animal, human, and godlike, so that a man's actions may raise him towards deliverance or lower him to incarnation as an unhappy human, or a beast, or a bird, or an insect.

There are here admittedly points that require close argument, but in most Asiatic countries the main line of doctrine could be appreciated in a general way by any thoughtful convert anxious to learn. The Chinese, when they first encountered Indian thought, were already a highly literate people, accustomed to philosophical enquiry and interested in cosmology; so that before long they had mastered and translated some of the leading scriptures. The Japanese were less advanced. Their interest was first attracted by the magic power which they saw in this new religion and by its imposing ritual. But they soon began to understand its main principles, and thereafter what most impressed them was its understanding of the human heart, its mercy and compassion.

In declaring that all earthly goods and pleasures are illusory and that all existence involves suffering, Buddhism was not stating a truth entirely repugnant to the minds of the Japanese, for what we know of their temperament from their earliest poetry leads to the belief that they were often depressed by a sense of the transitory nature of the very things that they most admired, beauty and splendour and power. Consequently the Buddhist concept of an interminable procession of change made a strong impression on their minds, while the doctrine of Karma was perhaps the strongest and most durable of all influences brought to bear upon Japanese life from abroad.

In its earliest phases, as we shall see, Buddhism was never a popular religion. It was sponsored and promoted by the ruling hierarchy for their own purposes, both as a vehicle of culture and as an instrument of power, and the provision of sacred edifices and images was regarded as a prerogative of the state. But Buddhism grew and spread throughout the nation, and though it never succeeded in dominating Japanese life as Christianity can be said to have dominated European life, it stamped its imprint upon many aspects of Japanese culture, notably the fine arts but also the habits and customs of the people, their language, and their proverbial wisdom.

While the political development of Japan in the seventh century was, as we have just seen, dominated by Chinese political ideas and practices, still deeply rooted native customs offered stubborn resistance to changes which the reformers endeavoured to impose upon Japanese life. Although the reformers did succeed in constructing a new and elaborate machinery of government, it never worked smoothly, and in the long run it broke down, or at least had to undergo such alterations and repairs that it lost most of its original systematic character. Indeed the history of the seventh, eighth, and ninth centuries in Japan might well be written as a description of the building up of institutions after a Chinese model and then their gradual decay as they were displaced or smothered by a luxuriant growth of indigenous devices. It may be said that the political reforms were premature, that the reformers were too zealous and in too great a hurry. This is probably true in many particular instances, but in a wider historical perspective the failure of Chinese ideas to take root in Japan may be seen as an example of what Vico called the fallacy of scholastic succession. In other words Japan in the seventh century was not ripe for the adoption of a complex system that arose out of centuries of Chinese experience. There was a limit to Japan's power of absorbing new ideas in the political field, partly because they did not grow naturally in Japanese soil, and partly because change was distasteful to a powerful minority who were well satisfied with their present condition.

As for religious ideas, however, Buddhism as it was presented to the Japanese did not seem to bring any threat to cherished institutions. It offered rather an enlargement of life to the many, if only through its imposing ceremonial, and a career of learning and dignity to the few. Buddhism in Japan met with some resistance in its early phases, but its enemies or its rivals had no strong weapons to use against it. The old priestly clans, such as the Nakatomi and the Imbe, had lost most of their influence in the civil strife of the first half of the seventh century and were no longer powerful enough to bring political pressure to bear against the new religion, which was finding more and more favour in high places and brought with it certain visible and tangible benefits that the simple cult of the native gods could not offer. Moreover, the Buddhist Church—for by about 650 Buddhism had almost the character of a national institution and enjoyed imperial patronage—was tolerant, and it was not difficult, with a little good will, to work out a reasonable compromise between the two religions which, so it turned out, worked to the advantage of both.

The most striking and important feature of Buddhism in Japan is the fact that it spread so rapidly. Perhaps the reason is that it had nothing to fear and nothing to destroy. In China it had to contend with power- ful schools of philosophy and with the vested interests of an official class, whose function it was to govern in accordance with the tenets of one or other of those schools. Buddhism therefore, in spite of its strong appeal, at certain times met with strict prohibitions and even with severe persecution. Nothing of this kind happened in Japan, for the good reason that there was no native system of thought to challenge a new religion, and no highly developed ethical code to which the ruling class was committed. In the intellectual field Japan offered a tabula rasa to the evangelists of Buddhism. Further, Buddhism as it first appeared to the leading spirits among the Japanese was more than a new form of worship; it was a comprehensive system of profound beliefs and splendid ritual. It was as if a great magic bird, flying on strong pinions across the ocean, had brought to Japan all the elements of a new life—a new morality, learning of all kinds, literature, the arts and crafts, and subtle metaphysics which had no counterpart in the native tradition. Bud- dhism, in short, was the vehicle of an advanced culture and was therefore doubly welcome in a country zealously seeking to improve itself, as a poor but ambitious man strives to get on in the world by studying to develop his natural gifts.

The early phase of the spread of Buddhism in Japan began in about 550, or a decade or so earlier, with the gift of images and scriptures from the kingdom of Paikche, and continued for a generation or more to depend upon teachers from that country. These men were treated with great consideration in Japan, but it cannot be said that Buddhism as a religion made a great impression on Japanese minds at this time, for it seems to have been regarded only as one of several doctrines brought from China and was appreciated more for its material than its spiritual benefits. It was not until the dynastic quarrels ceased for a time with the enthronement of the Empress Suiko and the regency of the Crown Prince Shōtoku (ca. 600) that Buddhism began to make real and rapid progress in Japan. It was now not from Paikche but from the northern kingdom of Kōrai that the doctrine was brought, and Kōrai was in close touch with the Sui empire of China, which greatly favoured Buddhism. Shōtoku's teacher was a monk from Kōrai, and doubtless he was able to give the prince valuable advice on secular as well as religious matters. It should be noted that the prince had also a Confucian tutor, and in this respect the Regent represented his country as a whole, for Japan was now beginning a long course of study in many unfamiliar arts and sciences.

The Prince Shōtoku is reported to have studied and expounded several sutras and to have exerted himself to promote the new faith in many other ways. Apart from numerous private shrines and chapels, several important monasteries were built, beginning in 593 with the Shitennōji (Shrine of the Four Devaraja or Heavenly Kings), and the Hōkōji, which was completed in 596. In 607 the great monastery and seminary of Hōryūji was founded, and in its precincts the Regent built his residence and a chapel for his meditations, named Yumedono or the Hall of Dreams. By the end of 624 (three years after his death) there were in Japan forty-six monasteries, 816 monks, and 569 nuns.

It is difficult to describe in exact terms the progress made by Buddhist teaching in this period. The principal monasteries were seats of learning rather than places of public worship, and it is most probable that, while Buddhist studies flourished in such establishments, the ordinary man had little understanding of the new faith; nor is there any evidence to show that a persistent missionary effort was made, either by holy men from Korea or China or by Japanese monks, to spread their gospel among the people. But if the people were slow to perceive the spiritual excellence of Buddhism, they could not fail to be impressed by the material beauty by which it was accompanied. It satisfied the aesthetic cravings of a people whose native religion was simple to the point of austerity. The monasteries, the images which they enshrined, and the ceremonies that filled their precincts with colour and movement were works of art of a perfection beyond all former experience. Of this fact there is ample evidence in survivals from the age of Shōtoku Taishi, such as those parts of the Hōryūji buildings that belong to the seventh century, superb sculptures like the Sâkya-muni triad (623), and the Kwannon of the Chūgūji nunnery. These are works of the highest order, and they show that Japanese art owes a great debt to Buddhism. All the earliest manifestations of art in Japan (if we except certain prehistoric objects and some pre-Buddhist metal work) in building, sculpture, painting, embroidery, and calligraphy, were due directly or indirectly to the introduction of Buddhism. Indeed it is scarcely possible to imagine Japanese civilization without the influence of Buddhism, for its aesthetic quality is one of its essential characteristics.

It is a truly remarkable fact that it was to those beautiful things rather than to sermons or scriptures that the Japanese people owed their first direct knowledge of the culture which they were about to adopt. The simplest of them may well have felt, as they gazed at the serene figures standing in their holy edifices, that here was a glimpse of paradise. Even today a sceptical Western traveller, considering such an image as the lovely Kwannon of the Chūgūji, cannot but find it moving to the point of tears, so deep and strong is the impression of love and sweet understanding, of sheer goodness and peace. Speculating upon the past, he cannot help thinking that some poor peasant, some "lean unwashed artificer," coming upon such a figure unawares, must also have seen in those lineaments of grace and wisdom hints of a calm life of the spirit, an inward bliss, hitherto beyond his imagination.

The influence of Buddhist thought upon morality in Japan is less easy to trace in these early phases. The new religion was, after its first trials, adopted with enthusiasm by the Court, and no doubt the favour which it thus enjoyed contributed in some measure to the spread of its moral tenets. The Regent was a devout and virtuous man, who did his best to promote reverence for the Three Treasures—the Buddha, the Law, and the Order of Monks—saying that this was the way in which the evil in men could be diminished, "their crookedness made straight." But it would be difficult to show that in the seventh century the official recognition of Buddhism brought about any substantial change in the customary behaviour of the people. Even the most enthusiastic believers at Court did not as a rule allow their conversion to Buddhism to prevent their observance of the native cult. Some emperors, it is true, tended to neglect the performance of prescribed Shintō ceremonies, and indeed Kōtoku was said to have "despised the Way of the Gods"; but in general it is fair to say that the worship of the imperial ancestors and the regular rituals of thanksgiving and purification were duly performed. The Empress Jitō (686–97), to take an example late in the seventh century, was impartial in her devotions and gave liberally to both Buddhist and Shintō establishments.

Perhaps the first material sign of a spread of Buddhism beyond the capital city is an order issued in 685 by which all the provinces were instructed that in every house a small Buddhist shrine should be provided and an image of the Buddha with some Buddhist scriptures placed therein. This presumably applied only to official houses, but at any rate it shows an intention to make the performance of Buddhist rites a regular practice throughout the land. The most striking feature of early Japanese Buddhism is the enthusiasm with which members of the ruling class devoted their energies and their wealth to building monasteries and chapels, to filling them with precious objects, and to indulging a strong taste for imposing ceremonies performed by numerous monks in the richest of vestments. It was a common practice for the heads of great families to endow shrines for the benefit of their parents, living or dead; while less important people dedicated images, or made votive offerings, with prayers for the happiness of their relatives in this life and the next. It may be that here was a link between old and new ideas, for family feeling was a powerful element in the life of the Japanese people, and it was natural that they should seize upon those aspects of Buddhist teaching that seemed to echo their sense of piety. Thence it was not a difficult step to some understanding of the Buddhist view of human existence as a continuity in which every event is related to past causes and future effects.

The devout acts recorded in the early days of Buddhism in Japan, such as those offerings just mentioned, were mostly expressions of sentiments already embodied in the ancient creed. There were also certain practices arising from the Buddhist injunction to spare life and diminish suffering, and these no doubt encouraged gentleness of behaviour. In each province land free from tax was set aside as a kind of sanctuary, where animal food must not be taken and where on special occasions caged birds and animals were liberated as part of a religious ceremony.

These are mere speculations about the foundations of religious belief in Japan. There can be no doubt, however, about the material progress of Buddhism as an institution. By the year 692 the forty-six monasteries and shrines of 624 had increased to 545, and the study of Buddhist doctrine had made enormous strides, thanks to the labours of learned monks from China and also to the patient research of Japanese scholars. The great monasteries enjoyed the favour of the Court, and throve on lavish donations, to such a point that Buddhism was near to becoming the state religion. It did not in fact reach that position, but because it was the religion of the most powerful families it had very great political influence and economic strength.

CHAPTER IV

THE IMPACT OF CHINESE CULTURE

1. *The New Administrative System*

THE FIRST phase of the reforms initiated in 646 by the edict of Taikwa was concerned mainly with the establishment of certain general principles designed to uphold the authority of the central government, to deny all private ownership of land and labour, and to assert the right of the Crown to allot land to cultivators and to collect tax upon their product. It was, of course, essential in a land-revenue economy that the central power should have full control of the source of wealth. But in order to exercise in practice the rights thus claimed in theory it was necessary not only to consolidate the strength of the Throne but to build up an efficient system of administration; and here, as in almost every department of public life, the reformers turned for their models to the system then in force in China. This was inevitable, since there was no precedent to follow in the past history of Japan, while in China the success of the Sui and T'ang dynasties in unifying the empire was a strong argument in favour of the methods of government which they had developed.

To the reform party in Japan the reports which they received from their emissaries were entirely convincing, as well they might be, for China in the seventh century, especially after the foundation of the T'ang empire in 618, stood on a peak of power and magnificence, and was without doubt the most extensive and the most firmly governed state in the whole world.

By the Reform Edict of 646 the system of land tenure and taxation then in force in China had been adopted with very little change in Japan, and in the following decades steps were taken to make that system work by strengthening the position of the provincial and district officers, perfecting arrangements for the collection of taxes, and in general making necessary adaptations to local conditions. The next matter to engage the attention of the reformers was the structure of the central government, and an order to establish departments of state and a number of official bureaus was issued in 647. But, probably because the government was preoccupied with affairs in Korea until 662, and then with the serious succession war of 671–72, the preparation of a complete new system was delayed. Work was begun on codes of law in 662, and these were under revision from 672 to 686, probably because experience showed that they followed the T'ang codes too closely. In 689 the new codes (which dealt mainly with the functions of ministries and the duties of officials) were distributed to government offices, so

that there must already have existed the framework of a central administration. But it was not until the spring of 702 that a further revision
of the codes was concluded and a full organization of administrative
bodies was proclaimed in the *Taihōryō* or code of Taihō—Taihō being
an era name, meaning Great Treasure, which was meant to introduce
the new measures under good auspices.

By this new system[1] the central government consisted of two parts,
the Department of Worship (Jingi-kan) and the Department of State
(Dajō-kan). The Department of Worship took precedence over the
Department of State. It was concerned with the performance of the
great religious ceremonies (such as the rites of enthronement and
national purification, and the festivals of the first-fruits and harvest
thanksgiving), the upkeep of shrines, the discipline of shrine wardens,
and the recording and observance of oracles and divinations. It presided over the worship of the national divinities, and had nothing to
do with Buddhism. The Department of State was concerned with all
secular aspects of government. Its organization is described below:

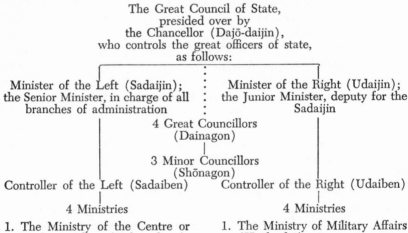

The Great Council of State,
presided over by
the Chancellor (Dajō-daijin),
who controls the great officers of state,
as follows:

Minister of the Left (Sadaijin);   :   Minister of the Right (Udaijin);
the Senior Minister, in charge of all   :   the Junior Minister, deputy for the
branches of administration   :   Sadaijin

4 Great Councillors
(Dainagon)

3 Minor Councillors
(Shōnagon)

Controller of the Left (Sadaiben)   Controller of the Right (Udaiben)

4 Ministries   4 Ministries

1. The Ministry of the Centre or
   Mediate Office (Nakatsukasa),
   forming the channel from the
   Throne to the administration
2. The Ministry of Ceremonial
   (Shikibushō)
3. The Ministry of Civil Affairs (Ji-
   bushō)
4. The Ministry of People's Affairs
   (Minbushō)

1. The Ministry of Military Affairs
   (Hyōbushō)
2. The Ministry of Justice (Gyō-
   bushō)
3. The Ministry of the Treasury
   (Ōkurashō)
4. The Ministry of the Imperial
   Household (Kunaishō)

The country was divided into provinces (Kuni) administered by
governors (Kami) appointed by the central authority, usually from the

[1] Details of the system of central and provincial government are given in my
paper entitled *Early Japanese Law and Administration* in the Transactions of the
Asiatic Society of Japan, Vol. IX, 1932.

official class in the metropolis. The provinces were divided into districts (Gun, or Kōri), under district governors (Gunshi) who were usually locally appointed from the rural gentry. The number of provinces increased as new land was developed. At the beginning of the eighth century there were sixty-six provinces comprising 592 districts.

The principal duty of provincial and district officials was to see to the collection of taxes, to recruit labour for the corvée, and to keep the peace. They were also responsible for registers of population and land allotment. The smallest unit of rural government was the "township" of fifty households, under a headman answerable to the district governor.

The new system was very near to a faithful copy of the T'ang system, but there were certain points in which it differed from the Chinese original, notably the precedence of the Department of Worship over the Council of State. The fact that special recognition was accorded to the priestly functions of the sovereign shows that, despite an almost slavish adherence to the Chinese pattern in other respects, the Japanese reformers were not willing to abandon their national tradition of kingship, according to which the sovereign is in theory sacred and inviolable. Even when Chinese political thought exercised its greatest influence upon their minds the Japanese leaders did not accept any Chinese doctrine[2] which held that the mandate of Heaven could not be exercised by a sovereign without virtue, since in the Japanese tradition the claim to the throne is based upon descent alone.

In one other feature the Japanese system of official grades differed, in practice perhaps more than in theory, from the Chinese system: the hierarchy in Japan was based upon birth and not upon talent. Japanese society was definitely aristocratic, and Japanese history consistently displays a deep interest in pedigree, rank, and title. The matter is put quite bluntly in an edict of 682, which provides that in selecting men for office the considerations are to be first birth, then character, and then capacity.

Apart from these exceptions—which are important—a general survey of the codes shows that Japan accepted the current Chinese theory of government and the ethical principles on which it was said to be based. These were, specifically, the principles of Confucianism of the Han dynasty, which are not, like the teaching of the *Analects*, a system of ethics in the shape of positive rules and injunctions, but postulate a natural order of things—of the universe, in fact—which must be respected by the ruler and his subjects. This concept of a moral law is not easy to understand, though it is not without its counterparts in Western

[2] Not all Chinese theory requires a celestial mandate. But Mencius, for example (V (2)lx), says that a ruler who has great faults should be admonished by his chief ministers, and that if he continues to neglect their advice, they may dethrone him.

history. Its influence upon Japanese thought is perhaps best explained by reference to certain features in the new (702) administrative system which are clearly of Confucian origin.

The senior Ministry of State was the Nakatsukasa or Mediate Office, the channel of communication between the sovereign and the ministers. One of its most important subdivisions was devoted to the study of natural phenomena for the purposes of government. It was called the Ommyō-ryō, or Bureau of Yin-Yang, those two principles, positive and negative, active and passive, dark and light, which according to Chinese cosmology by their interaction produce and control events. Its staff consisted of Doctors and Masters of Divination and Doctors of Astrology, Chronology, and Calendar-Making. The Director of the Bureau reported under seal to the Court any unusual phenomenon, for the guidance of the ruler. He was in charge of astrology, calendar-making, and the study of clouds and rain; and it should be noted that the functions of the Chancellor of the Empire are defined as "ordering the state and deliberating on the (Confucian) Way" and "harmonizing Yin and Yang."

The adoption of this Yin-Yang philosophy is a striking example of the working of Chinese cultural influence, for it was difficult, if not impossible, for the Japanese to take over Chinese institutions without at the same time admitting into their intellectual system some of the concepts to which the borrowed institutions gave expression. The admission of Yin-Yang is a simple and rather clear example; but of course all the political institutions of Sui and T'ang China have the support of an imposing body of doctrine which, for convenience, is called Confucianism. The title is somewhat misleading, because the Confucianism of the Han period presented to the Japanese in the seventh century contained much more than the social ethics taught by Confucius and his early disciples. It had developed, by both conflict and coalescence with other schools of thought—the incorporation of Yin-Yang being one example—into a comprehensive philosophical system; and when the Japanese, on somewhat utilitarian grounds, enthusiastically adopted the Chinese practices of astrology, divination, and so forth as aids to government, they could not help absorbing at the same time some of the fundamental moral ideas that regulated Chinese conduct. It must be remembered also that Chinese literature was the source and the Chinese language the medium of all the higher learning in Japan. Chinese history and philosophy were the classical studies in the University from its foundation in 702 until very recent times.

Thus it was impossible for the leaders of Japan, or for any persons of even modest education, to be free from the influence of Confucian ideas. But to estimate the effect of those ideas upon Japanese thought it is necessary to consider a little further the nature of Confucianism as it was known in Japan during the period of reform, let us say in about the year 700, when Chinese influence was very strong and direct. Confucianism in its early phases is a statement of ancient Chinese usages and ceremonial, prominent among them being such practices as those demanded by the rules of filial piety which many past generations had felt—instinctively, one might say—to be right. This body of beliefs and practices was called Li by the Chinese. This is a difficult notion to define, but it may be taken to mean something like Propriety, or a natural moral order. At any rate, the essential part of Li is a statement of what is proper behaviour in given circumstances. Han Confucianism was rather broader in its scope; and in so far as it was speculative, and not a simple code of social ethics, its cosmology is based upon the hypothesis that the universe is a harmonious whole, in which Man and Nature or Heaven and Earth constantly interact in all aspects of existence.

It will be observed that this is not an anthropocentric world view, as popular Western philosophies tend to be, but the expression of a feeling for natural order on a cosmic scale as seen in relation to human affairs. This deep interest in phenomena as guides to understanding events is not unique, for in Greek ideas of nature and destiny there was also a conviction of the unity of ethical and cosmic orders. The simple word "disaster" hints at that kind of philosophy in Western life, and so does the line: "There was a star danced and under that I was born." The solemn words from *Julius Caesar*:

When poor men die there are no comets seen.
The heavens themselves blaze forth the death of princes,

testify to a belief that there is a link between terrestrial and celestial events. The universe is composed of magic elements, different in their nature and function like stars and stones, trees and insects, but all related and combined.

The Chinese (Confucianists and professors of other schools of thought also) have tended to the belief that the behaviour of men, and especially of men in commanding positions, can affect the natural order, which is sensitive to the good or bad (that is, the ethical) quality of their acts. Consequently aberrations, departures from the normal course of nature—not only storms, famines, and lesser calamities, but uncommon phenomena such as eclipses or comets—could be directly related to the conduct of men. Thus to take recorded examples, excessive rain or floods might be attributed to the injustice of a ruler; prolonged drought to his incompetence; and intense heat to his neglect.

In conformity with this world view the misdeeds of individuals were looked upon not as offences against human law but as "ominous disturbances in a complex network of filaments of cause and effect by which mankind was connected on all sides with surrounding nature." Consequently it was felt to be wrong to depart from natural principles, from ancient usages and traditional sentiment about what was proper and seemly—in a word, from what was summarized as Li—and to establish legal standards of right and wrong with graduated punishments. Thus we find in Far Eastern societies a reluctance to engage in detailed penal legislation and a preference for arbitration and compromise. In the earliest extant Japanese code, which follows the T'ang model, only one of thirty chapters deals with penalties, the remainder being concerned chiefly with administrative matters and with ceremonial. Indeed the preface to the T'ang code itself states the position succinctly by saying that it is dangerous to "leave Li and enter upon punishments." It results from this deliberate avoidance of sanctions that, as there is a reluctance to give a strict legal definition of a man's duties, so there is no disposition to guarantee his rights. In fact the concept of individual rights is rarely encountered in Far Eastern thought, and certainly rights are never emphasized at the expense of duties. Chinese thought sees "only duties and mutual compromises governed by ideas of order, responsibility, hierarchy, and harmony." (Escarra: *Le Droit chinois.*)

It is unlikely that the Japanese of the seventh century fully understood the nature of Chinese society, since they had not gone through Chinese experience; but when they adopted the T'ang system of government they were obliged to accept (if only formally) the leading assumptions upon which it was based. These are summarized in a combination of the ideas of Yin-Yang and the highly schematic Five Elements analysis of the universe which is familiar to all students of Chinese philosophy, and which has profoundly influenced Far Eastern thought, in the sense that it has provided ready-made categories that are not difficult to understand and together make a plausible cosmology. It ·sees the universe in such terms as the following:

> One original principle at the root of existence
> Two poles, negative and positive, male and female
> Three manifestations, Heaven, Earth and Man
> Four motions—in space the four cardinal points,
>   in time the four seasons
> Five elements—wood, fire, earth, metal, water, which
>   control the rhythm of life
> Six kinships—ruler and subject, father and child,
>   husband and wife,

and so forth on a diagrammatic basis which assumes that the course of nature and the course of human events are interrelated. With regard to the Five Elements (*wu hsing, gokō,* 五行) it is important to note that these are not "elements" in the full Greek sense, but dynamic concepts, as the character 行 shows. It is the movement, rhythm, of life that is concerned here, not the composition of matter.

Of the same diagrammatic character are the categories used in divination which form the substance of the *I-ching* or Book of Changes—the eight trigrams and their combinations of sixty-four hexagrams. These figures, devised to simulate the cracks in tortoise shells previously used for divination, formed the basis of an elaborate symbolism of the universal order.

This was the first kind of organized, systematic teaching about the order of the universe that came to the knowledge of the Japanese. It opened a new kingdom of thought to them, for what strikes one in studying both *Kojiki* and *Nihongi* is the confusion, the number of fragmentary, naïve, and inconsistent world views which they present. This was of course to be expected in an attempt to synthesize legends of different origins; and Chinese cosmology when it became known to the Japanese undoubtedly impressed them by its range and its coherence. It had great influence upon their minds, an influence which still endures. Even today, baffled by their modern problems, Far Eastern people are apt to hark back to this ancient theory and think in terms of its catalogue for the guidance of their lives. Indeed the student of history will find that the stability of the great civilizations of Asia has depended in no small degree upon the prevalence of a coherent view of the universe. Such a view may appear, to those who do not hold it, mistaken and even absurd, but so long as it offers a plausible description of the pattern of existence a man who adopts it is free from the pains of doubt and uncertainty. He can accept with equanimity or resignation his place in the grand order of nature. The world view of Confucianism is one such system, and its contribution to the strength of Chinese civilization is beyond doubt. It is no wonder that it had an appeal to the Japanese, whose own indigenous theology did not supply all their needs.

The document known as the Constitution of Shōtoku Taishi (ascribed to 604 but probably drawn up some decades later) reveals something of the effect of Chinese ideas upon Japanese minds during the seventh century. It owes nothing to indigenous thought. Of its seventeen articles some draw upon Buddhist teaching, and others upon different Chinese schools, because the author was citing foreign authority whenever he could find support for the principles that he recommended. Where it lays down political rules it draws freely upon Confucian doctrine. Thus in the opening article it calls for Harmony among the different classes in a community, and this is pure Confucian morality from the *Analects*. It contains the idea of compromise, of reaching agreement on what Li (the orderly principle) demands in any case under dispute. Indeed the ideal of harmony is fundamental in Chinese social thought. The third article sets forth a Chinese theory of sovereignty. It contains a reference to the cosmic order in the words "Heaven shelters, Earth upbears." Here the argument is that, as the processes of nature follow their appointed course, so in government the natural order must be preserved. The proper relationship between superior and inferior must be maintained, and while inferiors must obey, superiors must follow the dictates of Li. Any interruption of cosmic harmony is morally bad and therefore politically wrong.

It may be appropriate here to ask if there has been any prevailing world view in the Western world with which this "phenomenal" world view can be compared. The comparable Western view must, at any time after Constantine, surely be the Christian view. In modern times (that is to say post-Renaissance times) the issue, as seen by such typical modern men as Hobbes and Machiavelli, is the "secular" issue, whether God or Man is the centre of the universe. But mediaeval Western thought about the "laws" of nature is represented by Hooker, who said: "Of Law there can be no less acknowledged than that her seat is in the bosom of God. All things in heaven and earth do her homage . . . both angels and men and creatures of what condition soever." Chinese thought does not seem to have seen a fixed natural order, a law of nature which can be studied and understood whether it is a law laid down by a divine lawgiver, or whether its source is unknown or unknowable.

It seems to me that Hooker's statement gives the fundamental difference between the Western and the Far Eastern view of life.

2. *Theories of Sovereignty*

One of the difficulties in early Japanese history is to establish the extent to which Japanese ideas about sovereignty were definitely influenced by Chinese political theory. It can scarcely be said that the Japanese had any political theory, since the claim of divine ancestry for the Ruling House was part of the indigenous cult and sprang from tribal practices. The only available evidence on this point is furnished by the two national chronicles, which, as we have seen, were written on the model of Chinese historical works; so that it cannot be said of any statement in either work (but particularly the *Nihon-shoki*) that it describes native institutions in their purity.

There are, however, certain documents of the seventh and eighth centuries which suggest that divine origin and absolute power were claimed for the Japanese sovereign in imitation of Chinese practice. These are the edicts recorded as having been proclaimed by the sovereign on important national occasions. The first edict after the reform of 646 instructs governors of provinces that hereafter all provinces will be governed according to the commands of the heavenly gods, and it refers to the emperor simply as the ruler of the people. But when envoys from Koguryö and Paikche visited Japan shortly after this, the message granted to them refers to the emperor as "the heavenly sovereign" who as a manifest god rules over "the land under heaven." The characters used here for "heavenly sovereign" and "land under heaven" are those which would have been used in China; and there can be little doubt that the secretary who drafted this edict—he was probably a Chinese or Korean scholar—when he described a small country like Yamato as coextensive with the heaven above and its ruler as the heavenly emperor, was influenced by Chinese terminology, if not by Chinese ideas about sovereignty. In subsequent edicts, throughout the eighth century, the same formula is used, always with a stress upon the quasi-divine character of the emperor, who is a "manifest god," a visible deity performing his task of ruling the land in due succession to his divine predecessors, themselves the offspring of the Sun Goddess.

It is appropriate here to consider briefly some other aspects of sovereignty as they are revealed in the edicts that followed the reform of Taikwa. There is, for example, an edict of 697, pronounced when the Emperor Mommu succeeded to the throne, in which he declares that it is his divine purpose to bring peace and order to the country and to cherish and soothe the people. In another edict (of 708) the Empress Gemmyō uses similar language, saying that it has always been the desire of the sovereigns to cherish and love their people as parents foster and nourish their children. In both these edicts the nobles and officials are enjoined to labour with "bright, pure and true hearts." Here we have simple moral ideas that belong to an early form of government by worship, but are now applied in a "modern" political context. There are traces of Chinese influence, though it is rather thin. But in subsequent edicts there is a marked change. The preamble is briefer, there is little or no recital of the legendary aspects of sovereignty, but an emphasis upon the laws, primarily the laws of succession laid down by previous emperors; and soon this becomes the usual practice. Some groping for a juridical basis of kingship can be detected here, and it can probably be ascribed to Chinese influence. In later edicts there are textual points which tend to confirm that impression, as for instance an edict of 724, which mentions auspicious signs as justifying succession to the throne; a description of the ruler as a "sage" in 729; and in 743 a reference to Ritual and Music as essential to the tranquil government of the realm. These are direct recognitions of Chinese political philosophy.

In general in the first half of the eighth century Chinese influence appears to be very strong, though this was a time when Buddhism had gained a remarkable position. The Japanese found no great difficulty in reconciling apparent conflicts of ideas by an ingenious method of selection. There is an interesting example of this habit in the decade from 732 to 741, years during which storms, earthquakes, floods, and drought were widespread and frequent, much property was destroyed, crops were ruined, and the country was afflicted by famine and plague. In 721 the Emperor had issued an edict in which he accepted such disasters as a punishment for his own lack of virtue. They were manifestations of Heaven's displeasure at his bad government. This was pure Chinese doctrine, and did not square very easily with the native cult.

When misfortunes fell upon the country again in 732, again an edict went forth in which the Emperor declared that the people were not at fault, but that he himself lacked virtue. He ordered prayers to be said at each provincial (Shintō) shrine, addressed to the "Gods of Heaven and Earth, to famous mountains and to great rivers." Buddhist prayers were ordered at the same time. On this occasion and in following bad years relief was given to the people by gifts, loans, remission of taxes, and an amnesty for offenders. This also was an act of Virtuous Rule in accordance with Chinese principles of government, which required that the ruler should display benevolence and help his people in distress. The influence of Chinese political ideas here is very strong. But it is interesting to find that in 741, when a very good harvest had relieved the government of anxiety, it was taken as a response to prayer; in that year an order went out that a Buddhist monastery for twenty monks, a nunnery for ten nuns, and a seven-storeyed pagoda should be built in each province, no doubt because it was felt that local prayers had been effective, perhaps even more effective than the imperial declaration. Shortly afterwards valuable gifts, which included copies of Buddhist scriptures, were presented to the shrine of Hachiman, the Shinto God of Battle.

This mixture of Confucian and Buddhist doctrine, combined with a belief in the good will of the national gods, is characteristic of the age; and indeed such a spirit of tolerance or compromise in matters of faith is visible throughout the history of religion in Japan. It should be borne in mind, when considering this question of tolerance, that a comprehensive religion like Buddhism can make compromises that are not possible for a monotheistic creed.

It is doubtful whether the moral vocabulary used in the edicts cited above owes anything to direct Chinese influence. It seems rather to show a phase in the evolution of ethical ideas from early notions of ritual purity. There is a constant repetition of such epithets as "clean," "pure," and "bright" to denote good thoughts and acts, and perhaps these simple descriptions were suggested by Buddhist rather than Confucian sentiment. But in considering foreign influences at this time it would be wrong to suppose that there was a conflict between the religious and the secular learning brought from China. There was in fact no contradiction between the two philosophies, or at least no contradiction that obliged the Japanese to make a choice. They were taking over a whole new world of ideas, and it was not for them to exercise a severe discrimination while they were, so to speak, still at school.

3. *The Strength of the Native Cult*

In some respects the introduction of foreign ideas and methods served to strengthen rather than to weaken native tradition, since the use of the Chinese script permitted the Japanese to record their own history and to give literary expression to their inherited ideas about life and society. It was Chinese learning and Chinese addiction to historical study that enabled and encouraged them to compile the two great national chronicles from which our knowledge of early Japanese customs is derived. The *Kojiki* and the *Nihon-shoki,* completed in 710 and 720, respectively, although admittedly written under the influence of Chinese canons and containing much that is artificial and anachronistic, are nevertheless remarkable monuments of literature and repositories of an ancient tradition which they served to perpetuate, not to destroy. It is true that for beauty and majesty they do not rank with sacred writings like the Bible and the Vedas, or epics like the Ramayana and the Mahabharata, but they are in the class of great national scriptures.

Similarly the introduction of Buddhism and Confucianism served to stimulate in some ways the ancient cult, and persuaded its adherents to regard what had hitherto been an anonymous body of religious practices as a system comparable to those two organized beliefs. It was not until the Japanese knew of "Butsudō," the Way of the Buddhas, that they began to think and speak of "Shintō," the Way of the Gods; and if we survey the literature of the seventh and eighth centuries we find that it includes, as well as the two Chronicles, quite copious records of native religious usages which are precious sources for the history of ideas in the Far East.

We cannot study these in detail here, but it is worth while to glance at the edicts from which passages have already been quoted (see pp. 74-75) to show the persistence of the legend of the divine origin of the ruling dynasty. It is because the Chinese script makes it possible to reconstruct them as they were pronounced in Japanese that we have some exact knowledge of very early views about the nature of sovereignty and the duties of sovereigns. Though they are in Chinese dress they are clearly not fabricated but represent, however imperfectly, a long-standing oral tradition which, had it not been put into writing, might have been submerged under the pressure of Chinese thought.

Similarly we have certain collections of ancient liturgies, which throw light on the beliefs held and the rites practised by the Japanese people before the introduction of foreign religious and philosophic ideas from China. They too are recorded in Chinese script, but are certainly based upon a reliable oral tradition going back many generations. Like most recorded speech, they were no doubt given a literary polish by the scholars who wrote them down, but we can be fairly sure that they preserved ideas and language of the sixth century if not a good deal earlier, in a form handed on by ritualists of the priestly families, the Nakatomi and the Imibe, whose business it was to follow the most ancient precedents—the Nakatomi in pronouncing the words, the Imibe in furnishing the utensils and preparing the offerings.

Important among such documents are those which preserve the

language of the Prayer for Harvest and the Great Purification service, for these are liturgies stamped with an imprint of the oldest religious ideas of the Japanese people, and they seem to go back to an early phase of tribal life. The first, as its name suggests, is permeated with a strong concern for the production of food, and reveals the feelings of the ruling class about the importance of agriculture to the state. The second expresses a deep sense of the value of ritual cleanliness. It dwells on the need to avoid actions that result in pollution, of the body in the first place, but also, by implication, of the mind.

The Prayer for Harvest was celebrated in the early spring, approximately at the vernal equinox, in the capital city. Originally the ceremonies were performed in or near the palace of the ruler, but after the establishment of central administrative offices in 702 the prayer was intoned by the ritualists in the courtyard of the Department of Worship, in the presence of the ministers of state, the officials of the department, and a great number of priests and priestesses of the shrines dedicated to the deities to which the prayer was addressed. At the same time in the provinces the governors presided over a similar service, the prayer being addressed to the gods worshipped in country shrines. The first account of the ritual observed on such occasions belongs to the year 871, or thereabouts, by which time the Chinese system of government was firmly established and Chinese influence had reached its peak. It is therefore interesting to observe that this ancient and thoroughly Japanese ceremony was performed on official premises under the supervision of officers of state whose titles and functions were borrowed from Chinese practice. It is evident that foreign influence had not succeeded in diminishing the position of the sovereign as the intermediary between the nation and the gods, or in weakening the religious faith of the people. The performance of this great ritual both in the capital and in the provinces was definitely an act of government as well as an act of worship, and it is significant that over three thousand shrines throughout the country received offerings on this occasion. The indigenous cult was by no means in eclipse.

A full study of the text of the Prayer for Harvest brings out much detail of interest to the student of religious history, but here it is enough to state that it is addressed not only to the Gods of the Harvest (who are not identified), but also to other groups of gods, such as the Gods of Growth ("Musubi"), the Gods of the Wells, the Gods of the Gateways, the Gods of the Islands, the Gods of the Farms, the Uplands, and the Streams, and finally to the Great-deity-shining-in-heaven, the Sun Goddess worshipped at Ise, the holiest place in the land. The language is appropriate to the solemn occasion. It is powerful in its impact and by its impressive recital of names of persons and things it evokes a vivid picture. When the ritualist says, on behalf of the emperor, that he will fulfill the praises of the gods by many offerings, "if they will bestow in many-bundled and luxuriant ears the late-ripening harvest, which will be produced by the dripping of foam from the arms and by pressing the mud between the thighs" the listener can see in his mind's eye men and women standing knee-deep or kneeling in mud as they transplant the young rice in the flooded paddy field. There is the toil and sweat of generation after generation of peasants, the labour on which the civilizations of the monsoon regions of Asia are founded.

The Great Purification Liturgy, though the surviving texts belong to the ninth century, certainly contains material of great antiquity. The service was performed in the imperial palace, in the presence of princes, nobles, and all ministers, secretaries, clerks, and metropolitan officials, civil and military. Its purpose was by prayer and offerings to purge the whole nation of offences which had been committed or might be committed, deliberately or inadvertently. The list of offences recited in the course of the service is of great interest. They are divided into heavenly offences and earthly offences. The heavenly offences are in general those attributed to the stormy god Susanowo, who figures in the myth of the age of the gods as a kind of scapegoat. They are offences especially reprobated in an agricultural society, either because they endanger its food supply, like damaging irrigation ditches or sowing tares; or because they offend against ritual purity, like polluting a dwelling place by filthy acts. These appear to be styled "heavenly" offences because they are especially abhorrent to the gods who preside over the destinies of the nation. The "earthly" offences are disturbances of the social order, actions which are repugnant because they affect the welfare of individuals in a community. They include killing and wounding, incest, bestiality, witchcraft, sorcery, and loathsome diseases, which are seen as causes of pollution and defilement rather than breaches of a moral law.

The language of this liturgy is of real beauty, perhaps because it expresses strong and intimate feelings inherited from distant ancestors. There is no doubt that a strong desire for cleanliness, a fear of contamination, have been characteristic of Japanese life since the earliest times, and have shaped the Japanese attitude towards questions of morality and of taste.

Particularly striking is the language telling how the gods in answer to prayer will dispel the offences named. The heavenly gods, on hearing the invocation, will thrust through the clouds to listen, and the earthly gods will ascend to the tops of mountains and hills and push aside the mists to listen. "Then in answer to prayers we believe that all offences will disappear and no offences will remain, as the breath of the Wind God blows apart the manifold clouds, as the morning breeze and the evening breeze blow away the thick morning mist and the thick evening mist, as the great ships lying in the harbour, their bow moorings and their stern moorings being unloosed, are pushed into the ocean; as the dense growth is cleared with the sharp-tempered sickle." Then the offences are carried from the mountaintops and the hilltops down rapid currents to the sea, where they are swallowed with a gurgle in the whirlpool meeting of the briny currents, then utterly blown away to the lower regions, and there for ever banished.

This prayer in particular raises the difficult question of the nature of moral ideas in Japan before the influence of Buddhist and Confucian ethical teachings made itself felt. The word translated "offences" or "sins" is the Japanese word *tsumi*, which etymologically has the meaning of something covered up or concealed. This seems to show that what was reprobated was what was socially undesirable rather than morally wrong, an act or a state that aroused feelings of shame, but not of guilt. Perhaps this is a stage in the life of a people like that in our life as children, when

> we knew not
> The doctrine of ill-doing, no nor dreamed
> That any did.

There appears to be some hygienic purpose in the catalogue of offences, especially those which concern defilement and thus resemble certain parts of the Mosaic code. But it is perhaps wrong to analyze early notions of behaviour in terms of modern thought. It is useful, however, to notice that the beginnings of a moral consciousness can be traced in the earliest mythological narratives, in the words represented by the Chinese characters standing for "good" and "bad." The native words are *yoki* and *ashiki*, "good" and "bad" in the sense of agreeable and disagreeable. But we also find, parallel with yoki and ashiki, pairs like *uruwashiki* and *kitanaki* ("clean" and "dirty"), and yoki and ashiki themselves used for "lucky" and "unlucky."

More interesting and significant are groups of words used to describe the disposition (*kokoro*, the heart) of man. A good heart is *akaki* ("bright") or *kiyoki* ("pure, clean"), a bad heart *kuraki* ("dark") or *kitanaki* ("dirty"). Some Japanese scholars argue that the terms used in the myth to describe the attributes of the gods are expressions of what was felt to be right behaviour in men. The gods are spoken of as gentle and loving, and the divine sovereigns also are said to love and cherish the people. This may be so, for it is a marked feature of the myth that there are no jealous gods who punish men for wrongdoing. Even the so-called bad gods (Akugami) are conciliated, because they are mischievous rather than wicked. Indeed the myth does not include any satanic spirit of evil. This reluctance to recognize the existence of evil seems to have a counterpart in the Japanese attitude towards positive law. The penal code plays only a minor part in the legislation of T'ang China and of Japan under Chinese influence, because punishment of an individual does not rectify a disturbance of the natural order.

But we must remember that if Zeus and Jehovah rebuke and punish unrighteousness, it is from their attitude towards wrongdoing that the abstract idea of Justice arises. There appears to be no close Chinese or Japanese analogy to that concept.

4. *The Growth of an Organized State*

In the foregoing pages the gradual absorption of new ideas, both religious and secular, has been described in some detail. But in the political sphere the transition from a tribal society to an organized state may seem abrupt. The truth is that reliable data are not available for an exact description of the political developments that took place during the years following the adoption of Buddhism. Indeed it would seem that it was the development of the great Buddhist foundations as much as the work of political reformers that fostered the growth of a national state with a relatively stable government. If we cannot trace all the steps by which this goal was reached, we can at least recognize that they led to an important new situation when the reigning dynasty established a permanent seat in the province of Yamato.

CHAPTER V

THE CAPITAL CITY, 710–774

1. *The Founding of Nara*

UNDER the influence of an ancient belief that a dwelling place was polluted by death, it was customary upon the demise of a sovereign for his successor to move into a new palace, and therefore we find the centre of government transferred from place to place in Yamato and neighbouring provinces at intervals from the earliest recorded reigns until a time when the reforms of Taikwa were substantially completed. Then, following the intention of the edict of 646 to regulate the capital, the Court moved from Asuka to Nara, though not until the year 710.

Nara, like other seats of the dynasty since its establishment in central Japan, was situated in the Yamato Basin, one of the basins of the alluvial tract of the home provinces—an appropriate position for the heart of an agrarian society. The reasons for its selection are not entirely clear, since at the height of intercourse with T'ang China the coastal district of Naniwa, a previous capital, would have been more convenient for communications by sea. But the choice of Nara was probably dictated by the presence in the neighbourhood of several important Buddhist establishments, including the Hōryūji, founded in 607, and the Yaku-shiji, founded in 680. There were other considerations also, chief among them being the need to select a position which would satisfy the requirements of the Chinese geomancy which was then in high esteem. The "Air and Water" (what the Chinese call Fengshui) of the situation were satisfactory, the configuration of the surrounding hills and streams auspicious; and after some years of planning and building before the move in 710 the new city became the metropolis, the centre of administration, the home of the arts, and the Holy See of Buddhism. Its charming natural surroundings and its imposing architecture gave it a style and a perfume which it retained for over a millennium, and has not yet entirely lost. Its beauty and its multiple character have been a frequent theme of Japanese poetry. They are well summarized in a short poetical epigram by Bashō, a master of the seventeenth century:

Nara nanae	Nara the Sevenfold
Shichidō garan[1]	Seven sacred buildings
Yaezakura	Many-petalled (lit. eight-fold) cherry blossoms

---

[1] The garan is the whole enclosure of a monastery. In Nara it usually consisted of seven separate buildings—pagoda, oratory, lecture hall, library, belfry, refectory, dormitory.

This gives a swift impression of the dual system, the palaces encircled by many walls, the monasteries each composed of seven edifices, and the rich natural beauty of which the double cherry blossom is a symbol.

2. Church and State and Land

This dual nature, as the headquarters of government and the stronghold of religion, reflects the history of the era, for the two outstanding features of the eighth century in Japan are the efforts of the state to exercise a close control throughout the country, and the efforts of the Buddhist Church to extend its own power in rivalry with the secular authority. It is a fair summary of the political development of the period to say that the economic measures upon which the reform depended failed because of the stubbornly aristocratic sentiment of the ruling class and the fiscal immunities of the great religious establishments. There were of course contributory causes, but the privilege of the nobility and the ambition of the clergy were together an obstacle to change which the Throne was unable to surmount.

Much has been written about the religious fervour and the artistic abundance of the period during which the Court remained at Nara, and it is scarcely possible to exaggerate the achievement of learned monks expounding the scriptures, the fruitful work of practitioners of all the arts, the sudden ripening of a rich and varied culture, in those few crowded decades from 710 to 790. Such eagerness, such almost magical growth of taste and skill, can rarely have been excelled or even equalled in any other country.

But in contrast to those brilliant successes, the economic history of the same years is of a peculiar and melancholy interest. The chief task of the reformers, once settled in a permanent capital, was to see to the proper execution of those portions of the Taihō codes which dealt with the revenue from land, for it was upon its effective control of the exclusively agrarian economy of the country that the new system of government depended. The power of the great clans could be broken only if they were deprived in fact, and not only in name, of their control over the land and the people in their former domains. The new system of land tenure and taxation was designed to spread the ownership of land very widely by granting allotments. Its purpose was to give a fair share of land and a real security of tenure to the ordinary cultivator and his family; and the allotment was made on a basis of so much rice land for each member of a household, on a scale adjusted for sex, age, and status, a distinction being made between free men and slaves or serfs. Such allotments were subject to review at the end of five years, when a new census had to be taken and necessary changes made in respect of increases or decreases in the number of persons in a household.

The area of rice land allotted to a household was at the rate of two *tan* for each male over five years of age, and two-thirds of that amount for each female over five years of age; so that a family of three males and three females would hold ten *tan*, which is about three acres. The plots were not necessarily or even usually all together, or of the same size. The average was perhaps as much as one acre, the smallest as low as one-tenth of an acre. The grant for slaves was two-thirds of the amount allotted to free men and women respectively. The holders of allotment land were liable to a tax, assessed on the normal yield of rice for the area, which may be regarded as land rent. There was also a produce tax levied on the output of produce other than rice; and finally there was a labour tax. The latter imposts were levied on male individuals only, and bore no relation to the occupation of land. The produce tax was payable in kind in local produce, such as silk, or fish, or timber, and it was graded according to the age and physical capacity of the taxpayer. The labour tax was payable in actual service, or in kind at a fixed rate of commutation.

Of these taxes the land tax was not excessive, the standard rate being about five sheaves of rice to the acre, or not more than five per cent of the crop in a normal year. The produce tax was burdensome enough, but the most dreaded of all was the labour tax, the corvée, especially when it took the form of military service, by which the household might be deprived of strong young men for two or three years. The temptation to avoid these two levies was accordingly very strong, and the breakdown of the allotment system is partly to be ascribed to the harshness of the labour tax, which produced evasion of many kinds.

The tax burden, including forced labour for public works and military service, was so heavy that farmers at times lacked seed rice in spring. They were obliged to borrow, for repayment at harvest, at ruinous rates of interest. This system, known as *suiko*, caused more and more debt and consequent absconding by peasants. The government introduced some palliative measures by advancing rice at reduced interest, but even this public rate ranged from 30 to 50 per cent, while private rates reached exorbitant levels near 100 per cent. The system set up a progressive decline in rural economies, because the more the tax evasions and desertions of land, the greater the local authorities' need to resort to harsh measures for enforcing repayment of rice loans.

Clearly this elaborate system of taxable allotments could not be operated without full preparation on the basis of accurate registers. A careful procedure was devised by the officials at the capital, in order to prevent abuses, but difficulties were encountered from the beginning, partly because of defects inherent in the scheme and partly because of a lack of capable and reliable officials in the provinces. It is doubtful whether it was ever uniformly applied over the whole country. It worked somehow or other for a time and in some areas, especially where the authority of the central government was strongest, but it was after

1

2

3

all a copy of a system laid down in the Sui and T'ang codes, suitable
no doubt to Chinese conditions, but not to Japanese needs without drastic modifications.[2] It did in fact undergo frequent revision, but it failed
in the long run, perhaps as much from defects in its character as from
the inability of the government to enforce its provisions. For though the
professed aim of all legislation since 646 was to bring all the land and all
the people into the domain of the Crown, in practice exceptions were
made which in the aggregate defeated the purpose of the law, and at
length brought about the collapse of the new system.

It would be tedious to describe in detail the numerous disguises
under which private ownership of land was allowed to continue. It is
enough to say that tracts of land were granted to nobles and officials
according to their rank, their office, or their meritorious service. These
grants carried with them certain personal immunities from tax, and
they gave the grantees control amounting almost to ownership of workers on the land. These important exceptions made on behalf of members of the ruling class, while legally authorized, were contrary to the
spirit of the land laws, though perhaps there was something to say in
favour of handsome emoluments for ministers of state and other loyal
public servants whose efforts supported the Throne against the great
territorial lords.

The withdrawal of valuable land from the public domain was bound
to cause a serious loss of revenue and at the same time to diminish the
authority of the government, since it created areas of immunity from
the jurisdiction of the state. It had further a serious disadvantage in
that the allotment system favoured households where there was a large
family with a number of slaves, since the allotment was on a per capita
basis. The small cultivator with a small family and no slaves was badly
off, because he felt the heavy burden of tax, to say nothing of the danger
of aggression by stronger neighbours. Many such poor men felt that
their situation was not improved by the new arrangement, and some preferred to transfer their services to a great private landowner rather than
face the growing exactions of the state. Some hints of this condition
appear in the official records, where we find mention of absconding
cultivators as early as 670, 677, 679; and later, in 731, we learn of bands
of vagrants numerous enough to cause great concern to the authorities.
Other early indications of distress among farmers are an edict of 685

---

[2] The land registers and tax receipts preserved in the Shōsōin at Nara are almost identical in form and language with contemporary Chinese registers found in
Tun-huang. In any discussion of the system of land allotments (Kubunden) and
its failure in Japan, it must be remembered that the Chinese system from which
it was derived (the Chün-t'ien or "equal plot" system) failed in China. It seems
to have been working imperfectly during the seventh century, but to have become
inoperative in the eighth. In China as in Japan the system was meant to keep
peasants on the land, and to prevent them from absconding owing to oppression by
landlords. It could only succeed where there was spare land (out of cultivation or
unreclaimed) to distribute. It was not intended as a large-scale measure of redistribution of farm land.

remitting their debts, and reference to the planned migration of large numbers of peasants to new settlements.

Such contradictions and inconsistencies in the working of the land laws, though not yet catastrophic, began to cause misgiving in the days of Nara at its most prosperous. The leading administrators saw the need for action, and since they could not hope to unravel the tangled laws, they endeavoured to increase the total area of rice fields. To that end they encouraged the reclamation of undeveloped land as a matter of national policy, and in 722 ordered three million acres of new land to be brought under cultivation. From the point of view of agriculture as a whole, of rapid increase of total productive capacity, they were remarkably successful. But such an increase was obtained—it could be obtained—only by excluding reclaimed land from the allotment system. Nobody was willing to undertake the labour and the cost of reclaiming waste land if it had to be handed over to the state; and therefore the government, to encourage the cultivation of new land, declared such land when developed to be private property for one generation, a period later extended to two and then to three generations and later in some cases to perpetuity.

The government seems to have been unable to make a firm decision on the policy of opening up new land. Its high officers were aware that the heavy calls upon peasant labour were at the root of the failure of Japanese agriculture to develop in the eighth century, but the alleviations which they introduced did not result in any basic improvement. The loans of seed rice (already mentioned) and the establishment of "charitable granaries" (gisō), two measures devised to keep peasants on the land, failed owing to maladministration and the illegal acts of local landowners. The edict of 722 was an attempt to offset the encroachment of private ownership by decreeing a national undertaking. But in the following year the task of developing new land was shifted to private hands by a promise of three generations of private ownership. At the same time the tendency to claim and defend outright and hereditary ownership was growing stronger everywhere, and in 743, when newly opened lands were granted in perpetuity, the government was obviously recognizing a situation which it could not prevent.

It was tempting for a great landowner or religious institution to get hold of reclaimed land as soon as it was ready, and in 711 and 713 the appropriation of *konden* (reclaimed rice land) by princes, nobles, gentry, and monasteries was forbidden by ordinance. The government asserted the right to determine what land should be reclaimed, and by whom, an essential condition of eminent domain. But in 749 the pious Emperor Shōmu, on the occasion of the dedication of the Great Buddha of Nara, decreed that konden should be allowed to the various Buddhist establishments throughout the country, and in a subsequent edict declared the amounts of land which might be reclaimed by the great monasteries of Nara and the official provincial churches which had been

LEFT: *Seal of the Emperor (Tennō Gyoji)*, A.D. 749. CENTRE: *Seal of the Chancellor's Office*, A.D. 783. RIGHT: *Seal of the Treasury*, A.D. 745. *The originals are about 3¾, 2¾, and 2½ inches square, respectively.*

founded in the year 741. The Tōdaiji, at that time the principal Buddhist establishment of the empire, was allowed the greatest share, some 12,000 acres, and it was left to the local governments in each province to decide what land should be occupied under this grant.

It was not the intention of the law that reclaimed land should be permanently immune from tax. In principle, where reclamation was sanctioned by the local authorities, the regular taxes were to become payable as soon as the land was in full and regular cultivation. But an important exception was made in respect of the Buddhist Church, for though the taxes were duly collected by the proper officials, they were then remitted to the monastery in question. This qualified immunity soon developed into almost complete immunity, creating such valuable interests that the monasteries or other religious bodies which held large areas of land in the provinces began to send their own representatives to reside on the spot and deal with the local government. Presently the local officers appear to have handed over to the agents of the churches the duty of collecting and delivering the taxes, and finally the complete fiscal immunity thus acquired was recognized officially. Before long the secular holders of reclaimed land would begin to claim a similar privilege. The loss of revenue to the state was not the only result of these immunities, for they enabled the holders of reclaimed land to reduce or otherwise change the rates of tax and rent so as to attract outside farmers, who found it worth while to donate or commend their holdings to the monastery or to a secular domanial lord.

The effect of these measures was to heighten the contradiction between the principles and the practice of land tenure throughout the country. Before long even the small cultivator, whom reclamation was supposed to benefit, found himself carrying an increasing load, because the proportion of private land was increasing and the tax on public land had to be raised. Sometimes, as we have seen, a poor peasant would abscond, leaving his fields to go to waste, or he would sell or mortgage his land to a wealthy farmer or a monastery, becoming himself a landless man, little better off than a slave, though he would retain his status as a freeman. Deeds have been preserved in which a freeman, desperately anxious to keep his small plot, mortgages his allotment, pledging the women of his house as security, so that in case of default they would be taken as servants. There are signs of such practices soon after the institution of the allotment system.

Such poor men could not as a rule improve their position by bringing new land under cultivation. Wet rice land depends upon irrigation requiring the careful construction of dams, dykes, and embankments. This calls for a high degree of skill and much labour, for the ground must be thoroughly cleared and perfectly levelled. Differences of water level between fields must be expertly contrived so that adjustments can be made to changes of weather and season; and if the source of water supply is distant, long canals must be constructed. Therefore to reclaim land for rice fields requires experienced direction, corporate labour, and the expenditure of capital resources on tools and workers drawn from adjoining places. In practice most reclamation work had to be carried out by large farming households, or by wealthy persons or institutions; so that here also the rich landowners and the great monasteries and shrines profited at the expense of the small cultivator. Some poor peasants endeavoured to scratch a living from land not suited to rice-growing, but there again they were at a disadvantage, for powerful families found it profitable to gain possession by purchase, force, or threat, of arable uplands, forest lands, river deltas, lakes, ponds, and swamps, which they could bring into use and retain as private property upon which little or no tax was levied.

Thus the distribution of good farm land grew more and more inequitable. Yet it is probable that the increase in food production was needed by a growing population, and it may well be that the rapid progress of reclamation, though it involved harsh methods, was on balance advantageous to the country. But a desirable economic result was achieved at the expense of the authority of the central government, and in course of time the failure of the land laws led to the decay of the administrative system and the growth of feudal institutions in its place.

It should be added that such great religious establishments as the Tōdaiji Monastery of Nara played an important part in the work of reclamation by advancing funds, providing tools, or offering protection to small farmers who would donate a share of areas reclaimed with their help. The development of large areas of uncultivated land was at this time not possible without a rudimentary form of capitalism. There was no true money economy, but the great monasteries and the most powerful landowners had at their disposal not only a number of workers but also an accumulation of iron tools, which were essential for reclamation work. There was a little copper currency in circulation after 708, but the most important form of mobile wealth was the iron spade or hoe, without which a man's labour would hardly produce more than he consumed. The records of the late seventh and early eighth centuries contain entries of gifts by the Crown of several thousand iron spades

and hoes, or quantities of unworked iron, to monasteries and great officers; and there is no doubt that reclamation on a large scale could not
have been carried out otherwise, nor could large bodies of men have
been suitably armed for frontier duty as reclamation work advanced.

In the registers of land owned by the monasteries and nobles entries
of large areas in different localities, showing aggregate holdings ranging
from 1,000 to 10,000 acres, are not uncommon—and these are very considerable areas of land for the intensive culture of rice. Nor were these
the only continuous sources of income for the monasteries, since they
received frequent donations of land and labour from the Throne and
from pious nobles at the Court. So it came about that the Buddhist
foundations in Nara attained a position of considerable political power,
which seemed at times to threaten the Imperial House.

3. Nara Politics: Dynastic Problems and Frontier Fighting

In the history of the monarchy in Japan the eighth century is remarkable for the number of female sovereigns. The Empress Gemmyō,
sister of a former ruling empress, succeeded in 708, shortly before the
move to Nara. She was followed by her daughter in 715; and the next
ruler, the Emperor Shōmu, after a reign of twenty-four years abdicated
in August 749 in favour of his unmarried daughter, who reigned first
as the Empress Kōken from 749 to 758, and then (having deposed the
Emperor Junnin, in whose favour she had abdicated) as the Empress
Shōtoku from 764 to 770.

These were years when the power of Buddhism was growing fast,
and it is highly probable that the palace intrigues of ambitious Buddhist
prelates had much to do with the succession of princesses who could
be counted upon for pious contributions to the welfare of the clergy. The
tale of favours accorded to the Buddhist Church by the Court is well
epitomized in the history of the Tōdaiji, the Eastern Great Monastery,
which was founded in 738 and within a brief space of time grew into the
wealthiest and most influential of all religious foundations in Japan. In
737—the Chinese theory of government would say because of some
blunder committed by the sovereign—an epidemic of smallpox ravaged
the country and carried off many persons of importance. The Gods and
the Buddhas were implored to grant relief to the sovereign and his
people. It was planned as a measure of persuasion to construct a colossal
bronze image of the Buddha; and (so the legend has it) the Sun Goddess, having been consulted by a messenger sent to her shrine at Ise,
gave her consent to the project. It was not carried out for some years,
partly for want of funds and partly for lack of the necessary skill; but
at length, after many disappointments, a bronze seated figure, fifty-three
feet high, was completed in 749. Gold had meanwhile been found in
the remote province of Mutsu, and sent to Nara for use in gilding the
image. Then there took place a remarkable religious ceremony, attended

by the Emperor Shōmu and all the princes, princesses, nobles, dignitaries, and civil and military functionaries.

The Emperor stood in the Hall of the Great Image (Daibutsuden), facing north in the position of a subject seeking audience with his sovereign; and a great Minister of State was sent forward to address the Buddha image in the ruler's name, using humble language and declaring that he, the Emperor, was the servant of the Three Precious Things "whose name is to be spoken with awe," that is of the Buddhist religion. There is no reference to the divine ancestry of the Imperial House in this proclamation; but shortly afterwards, at a ceremony of thanksgiving, there was pronounced an edict in which the sovereign refers to himself as a Manifest God, and goes on to say: "Of all the various Laws the Great Word of the Buddha is the most excellent for protecting the state." Then, through the ritualist who is his mouthpiece, he gives thanks for the gift of gold and affirms that "the great sign of the Word" was vouchsafed by the Buddhist religion; but he is careful to add that "this is a thing manifested by the guidance and grace of the Gods that dwell in heaven and the Gods that dwell on earth," by which he means all the divinities worshipped in the native cult. He next makes gifts of rice land to shrines of the gods, and gives permission to Buddhist monasteries to hold land for reclamation, while bestowing favours upon monks and nuns.

It will be seen that by this action Buddhism was virtually adopted as the religion of the Court, although worship of the national gods as a customary rite was not disavowed. In such circumstances the power of the leading Buddhist ecclesiastics was naturally very great, and so we learn of bold attempts by priests to exert undue influence upon ladies of the palace. The most celebrated story of this kind is that of a vigorous and handsome monk named Dōkyō, who made such an impression upon the ex-Empress Kōken that before long he became Chancellor of the Realm, and nearly succeeded in having himself named as her successor on the throne.

Such pretensions naturally angered the members of the government and other influential people at Court. Among those outraged by this troublesome priest were the Fujiwara family. Descended from that Kamatari who had been the chief author of the reform of 645, they had acquired a strong political position thanks to their native ability and their practice of marrying Fujiwara girls to imperial princes. Kamatari's son Fubito was a great figure in his day (659–720), but the family suffered a check by the death of his four sons in the smallpox epidemic of 737, so that the monk Dōkyō was able for some years to outwit the leading Fujiwara, Nakamaro, better known by his later title as the Minister Oshikatsu, who was in high favour with the Emperor Junnin but not with the ex-Empress. In a civil disturbance that took place in 764–65 Oshikatsu was captured and killed, while the young Emperor was deposed and exiled in 765 and presumably strangled. The ex-Empress reascended the throne as the Empress Shōtoku, and Dōkyō was all-powerful until she died without issue in 770. Then the Fujiwara family saw to it that he was banished, and an amiable grandson of Tenchi succeeded as the Emperor Kōnin (770–81). On his death the council of ministers refused to allow a woman to take the throne, thereby creating a precedent which was followed consistently in later times.[3] They selected Kōnin's eldest son, the Prince Yamabe, who ruled as the Emperor Kammu, and figures in history as one of the ablest sovereigns in the long imperial line. It was during his reign that the seat of government was moved away from Nara, partly—it is generally supposed—to evade the influence of the Buddhist Church.

Though the chronicle of the period after the accomplishment of the the reforms is disfigured by the succession disputes which we have already noticed, it must be said that those disputes were mainly the work of disaffected nobles who were hostile to the new measures, and that the administration, in the face of great difficulties, seems to have done its best to carry out a constructive policy in many fields.

Efforts had been made in previous reigns to push the frontier further north and east, and to pacify or subdue the Ainu, who were a constant source of trouble and a hindrance to the opening up of new land, which became necessary as population grew and the available rice fields in the home provinces (the Yamato plain) proved insufficient. Risings of the Ainu in the first decades of the eighth century much embarrassed the central government, whose control over the outer provinces was far from complete. In 720 they proved so irreconcilable that troops had to be raised from nine provinces for an offensive against them, and it was only after hard fighting that a frontier post was established at Taga, near the present Sendai, where a heavy garrison was stationed to hold them in check. The ambitious Fujiwara Nakamaro, then known as Oshikatsu, was not inactive when he came to power. He paid particular attention to military matters, and while he was Chancellor he planned a line of forts at points in the northern provinces of Mutsu and Dewa, which were to be bases of operations against the rebellious aborigines. His project did not succeed, however, for the Emishi were stubborn fighters, and for years after Oshikatsu's time there were continued risings and incursions. In 776 the garrison at Taga was destroyed by raiders, who kept the offensive until 790, from time to time inflicting heavy losses upon the Japanese frontier forces. Oshikatsu was no more fortunate in another undertaking, which was to send a large expedition against Korea. He set up commissions to equip some five hundred ships, which were to transport an army of 40,000 men across the straits. It seems that only moderate progress had been made when the project was abandoned upon his death in 765, and no doubt the failure of these bold undertakings contributed to his downfall.

[3] Except for two unimportant instances after 1600, when the Throne was powerless.

Under the Emperor Kōnin (770–81) came a settlement of accounts. He weeded out bad characters, got rid of superfluous officials, and introduced a policy of retrenchment. He (or his ministers) paid close attention to matters of local administration and to communications with the outer provinces, while in all but a few provinces the military divisions provided for by the codes were disbanded, thus relieving the farmers of a crushing burden. The system of forced military service had proved ruinous since its establishment and it was now replaced by a system of regular forces, composed of men trained in the use of arms. This was the beginning of a distinction between peasants and soldiers which may be regarded as the germ of the warrior class that reached its maturity in feudal times.

4. Cultural Progress

Although the political life of Nara, marred by conspiracy and bloodshed, does not present an edifying spectacle, it should not be supposed that all the leading men were misguided and their labours fruitless. Within its limitations as a bureaucracy functioning on behalf of an aristocratic society, the government strove earnestly enough to carry out the reform policy. It paid close attention to the operation of the administrative and penal codes, which were from time to time reviewed in the light of experience. The revision of the Taihō code of 701, completed in 718, was a careful piece of work, and in some respects took into account special conditions arising out of native customs. There were occasions when respect for Chinese precedent was carried to absurd lengths; but on the whole an effort was made to adjust the laws to actual requirements, by amending them or by creating special organs to supplement their working. An imposing body of detailed legislation, of case law and commentary, was built up little by little, and Japanese jurists in this period laid the foundations of a system which survived many vicissitudes in later times and was not without influence on the feudal laws which ultimately displaced it.

In general there was, outside the field of government, a notable advance in scholarship of all kinds. The development of Buddhist learning requires special study, but here we should notice two important literary achievements. The first is the compilation of the two national chronicles, which have already been described as remarkable works, inspired by Chinese example; and with them might be coupled the important *Fudoki*, topographical surveys of the provinces, with lists of their products. The second notable literary monument is the great anthology of poetry known as the *Manyōshū*, a collection of verse from the earliest times to the year 760. It contains some 4,000 poems, short and long, and it can be taken as reflecting Japanese sentiment in the seventh and eighth centuries, with perhaps some hint of earlier or at any rate simpler life in the so-called "Azuma-uta," or Eastern Songs.

No history of Japanese thought would be complete if it neglected the evidence which this classical work provides. The very fact that the first important literary achievement, apart from historical records, is a collection of native verse testifies to the singular eminence of poetry in the national tradition.

Here speaks the authentic voice of Japanese poetry. It shows some signs of foreign influence, but most of it (especially the work of such great poets as Hitomaro) betokens a fresh and spontaneous outpouring of the native spirit, no doubt stimulated by the invigorating atmosphere of the period of reform that followed the Taikwa edicts. Japanese poetry never recaptured the quality of those early masterpieces.

Looking through the subjects that the poets most usually treated, one finds that there is not a great deal about Buddhism. There are scattered allusions to Buddhist themes, but in general the poems cannot be described as penetrated by Buddhist sentiment or a Buddhist view of life. What at first sight seems like the influence of Buddhist ideas is a tendency of the poets to dwell upon the emptiness of human life, the evanescence of beauty and pleasure. Such figures of speech as the fading flower, the vanishing dew, and the bursting bubble are very common. Here are some examples, taken almost at random:

Shōji no	Loathing both seas, of Life and
Futatsu no umi wo	Death, how I long for an upland
Itowashimi	free from tides.
Shiohi no yama wo	
Shinobitsuru ka mo.	

This is an interesting reference to nirvana, the state beyond life and death. It is evidence of a knowledge of the elements of Buddhist doctrine. Indeed it is said to have been written on a musical instrument found in a monastery, and may have been composed by a monk. But the turn of phrase, the vision of life, death, and eternity in terms of landscape, is perhaps characteristically Japanese.

Utsusemi wa	This mortal life is brief
Kazunaki mi nari	of span. Let me
Yamakawa no	seek the Way, contemplating
Sayakeki mitsutsu	the pure hills and streams.
Michi wo tazune na.	

This too has a Buddhist flavour, but again the sentiment is expressed in terms of the beauties of nature.

Yo no naka wo	To what shall I compare
Nani ni tatoen	this life? It is like a
Asabiraki	boat rowed away at dawn,
Kogi-inishi fune no	leaving no trace.
Ato naki gotoshi.	

'This again treats of evanescence, with a simile from visual memory, and it is not especially Buddhist in sentiment.

> Kono yo ni shi   If I can have pleasure in
> Tanoshiku araba   this life, then what matter
> Kon yo ni wa   if in the next I am an
> Mushi ni mo tori ni mo   insect or a bird!
> Ware wa narinan!

This is a direct reference to the doctrine of Karma, but clearly not very devout. It is by Tabito, a courtier who left this life in 731. It shows the influence of Chinese poetry, of the school of the bibulous Seven Wise Men of the Bamboo Grove.

Apart from such examples, which do not reveal any very deep religious feeling but only a poetic melancholy, love poems are the most numerous—sometimes passionate, but as a rule warm and tender, rather simple and natural. There is a great deal about separation, thwarted love, the loneliness of husbands or wives who have lost their partners through death. Perhaps the stress on conjugal love is a special feature. There is much also about parental love and in general about affection within the family. All kinds of natural human feelings are expressed, but there is a notable stress upon family ties, and it is extended to ancestors as well as to living relatives.

Loyalty to the sovereign or to a clan leader is a favourite theme. A classic statement of a warrior's duty is the well-known stanza (part of a long poem of 749, celebrating the discovery of gold for the great Buddha Image of the Tōdaiji) which refers to the Ōtomo clan, the hereditary bodyguard, in these words:

> Umi yukaba mizuku kabane   By the sea our corpses shall steep
> Yama yukaba kusamusu kabane   in the water. On the hills our
> Ō-Kimi no he ni koso shiname   corpses shall rot in the grass. We
> Kaerimi wa seji.   will die by the side of our sover-
>   eign, we will never look back.

The warrior's honour must be unstained; he must preserve "masurao no kiyoki sono na," the pure name of the man of courage. But apart from expressions of loyal duty there is surprisingly little about battles or military ardour. Bravery as such is not praised, but only bravery as an aspect of loyalty.

Throughout the whole anthology, irrespective of theme, runs a strong current of enjoyment of the beauties of nature. Here already you find the perennial topics of Japanese poetry—plum blossom, cherry blossom, snow, moonlight, clouds, hills, and streams. It seems already a trifle artificial at times, but it does betoken a naturally aesthetic inclination— anima naturaliter poetica. It is difficult to judge in what measure poetry of this kind was influenced by Chinese originals, but it was certainly not enough to obscure the native quality of both feeling and expression. Yet it is probably true that the great vogue of poetry in T'ang China (as represented by Li Po, Tu Fu, and other masters) encouraged the poetic spirit in Japan. In this context it should be noted that of the Japanese poets cited in the *Manyōshū*, twenty or more (belonging to the eighth century) are known as accomplished in Chinese verse; and it is significant that before the *Manyōshū* there was issued an anthology called *Kaifūsō*, containing only poems in Chinese by Japanese. It was of course impossible that Japanese verse should escape entirely from Chinese influence. The *Manyōshū* owes its very existence to the Chinese script, which was used for the phonetic notation of Japanese words; and no man of taste at the Court or in a monkish seminary could afford to be ignorant of the work of Chinese poets then in fashion.

Whatever may have been the effect of foreign ideas, it is significant that the *Manyōshū* contains many poems (composed, it is true, by courtiers) expressing reverence for the national deities. Indeed most aspects of the ancient cult are referred to, and there is even an occasional hint of a feeling about life after death, in which it is possible to discern the foundation of a religious belief which is not Buddhist in character. There is an interesting poem composed upon the death of a Prince Yuge (ca. 680). It runs:

Yasumishishi	waga ōkimi	Our lord and prince
Takahikaru	Hi no miko	Child of the Bright one above
Hisakata no	amatsumiya ni	God as he is, has taken
Soko wo shimo	ayani kashikomi	His divine seat in the Heavenly
Hiru wa mo	hi no kotogoto	Palace
Yoru wa mo	yo no kotogoto	Far above. We, awe stricken
Fushi-i nagekedo		Lie prostrate and weep
Akitaranu ka mo		Day after day and night after
Ōkimi wa	kami ni shi maseba	night
Amagumo no	io-e ga shita ni	And to our weeping there is
Kakuretamainu.		no end.
		Our lord and prince
		Because he is a god
		Has gone to dwell unseen
		In the five-hundred-fold clouds
		of heaven.

This is by Okisome no Azumabito, and there are similar poems on the death of Prince Kusakabe, also a son of the Emperor Temmu. It gives a picture of worship of a departed prince, who is thought of as dwelling in a Heavenly Palace (Amatsumiya) beyond a five-hundred-fold layer of cloud. Far below the mourners weep, but can never fully express their grief. This certainly shows no Buddhist influence. A God dwelling beyond the clouds is a rather Jovian concept, and seems to belong to a pagan creed.

There are some undoubted touches of Taoism in other poems. This is to be expected, since the magic and the other fanciful parts of Taoism naturally appeal to a lively poetic mind. One poem in particular is worth quoting because it reveals Taoist influence, and also because to modern taste it has an almost surrealist charm. It is about a traveller who comes across some girls fishing in a mountain stream. They say they are a fisherman's daughters. "Their spirits soared above the clouds and their gracefulness was not of this world."

"Will you pledge yourself to us for life?" they ask, and he says "Yes, gladly I will." Then he expresses his feelings in a gay poetical dialogue, speaking both for himself and for the girls:

> HE: But a fisherman's daughters
> You say of yourselves?
> Yet your looks reveal
> That you are of noble birth.

> THEY: On the Tamashima River
> Here by its upper stream stands our home.
> But from bashfulness
> We did not tell you where.

> HE: In the river of Matsura
> You stand fishing for *ayu*.
> Brightening up the shallows
> Your skirts are drenched.

> THEY: When spring comes round
> Through the ford near our home
> The little fish will dart
> Impatient to see you!

Of course they were not real girls, but fairy-like creatures, imagined by the poet in a Taoist trance. It was the poet Tabito, already mentioned as an admirer of bibulous Chinese men of letters. He was governor of Kyūshū, then regarded as an important frontier province. To be in such employment was to be deprived of the pleasures of good society, and so the *Manyōshū* (like many Chinese poems) contains much nostalgic verse expressing the solitude of exiled officials and frontier guards. When these plaints were written the eastern provinces, which are now the most populous region of Japan, were still unsettled, and remote from Yamato.

This is one of the poems of the Frontier Guards—a dialogue:

> If I leave you behind
> I shall miss you.
> O that you were
> The grip of the birchwood bow
> That I am taking with me.

If I stay behind
I must suffer
The pains of longing.
Rather I'd be the bow
You carry on your morning hunts.

Here is a picture of clandestine village love:

Come to me, my sweetheart
Parting the bamboo blinds!
Should my mother ask me
I'll say 'twas but a gust of wind.

This is described as "an old poem" and probably comes from an earlier collection.

Confucian studies played a leading part in eighth-century Japan, comprising almost the entire curriculum of the University, which was a government bureau under the Board of Rites. This was inevitable in view of the prestige of Chinese culture, since apart from poetry most of the classical literature of China that became known to the Japanese was in some way concerned with the exposition, or the refutation, of Confucian doctrine. The senior members of the Board of Rites were Confucian scholars of high rank, whose offices became hereditary in certain families. The head of the University was responsible for the examination of students and the celebration of festivals in honour of Confucius and his chief disciples.

We have already noticed the general character of the Confucian world view as it affected Japanese life, and seen how it supplied the theoretical, or rather the conceptual, basis of the system of government, while giving a special authority to certain practices of divination and geomancy. Moreover Chinese ideas of piety and loyalty fitted in well enough with the current requirements of the leaders of Japan and also with traditional sentiment about the family and the clan. Organized ancestor worship in Japan probably owes a great deal to Chinese precept as set forth in the Classic of Filial Piety.

But it is doubtful whether Confucian thought had much creative influence outside the institutional field from about A.D. 600 to the end of the middle ages. Later (a thousand years later) in Japanese history, it is true, Confucian teaching dominated the intellectual life of Japan; but that was a new form of Confucianism, rethought and restated by Sung philosophers with a strong metaphysical bias. From the eighth century onwards for an indefinite period—even as late as 1500, perhaps—the dominating foreign influence on Japanese thought was Buddhism; not the subtleties of the learned sects, but a general aura of worship and holiness, of belief in sublime and powerful essences, which (combined with the beauties of religious art) appealed more to the Japanese temperament than the conservative agnosticism of the Chinese sage. Indeed there is some ground for thinking that Taoism found a more ready response among Japanese of a speculative turn of mind.

Seeing that Confucianism is a coherent system of social ethics which has shown great durability for centuries and was once accepted throughout eastern Asia (in Korea, Japan, Annam, Siam, and even parts of Burma) its power of survival might well be attributed to the strength and truth of its moral teaching. In one sense this must be true, for Chinese society has depended for its permanence upon its rules of behaviour. But it can be argued that what distinguishes Confucian morality in its effect upon Japan is the fact that it is a social morality, and contributes very little to individual judgments as to Good and Evil. In the Chinese view, it seems, what conformed to the natural order—let us call it Li—was good and what did not conform was evil. This is a view which neglects the ethical problems of the individual, or at any rate makes of them a matter not of conscience but of convention. Perhaps this is going too far; but it is safe to say that Chinese thought contributed in Japan more to the organization of society than to the spiritual development of the individual. It is, in any case, a plausible conclusion that the impact of Li upon Japanese minds and hearts has not been so great as the impact of such Buddhist notions as karma and rebirth, for they have a profundity and at the same time a simplicity and emotional appeal which is wanting in the rational outlook of Chinese teachers.

There is, however, one important feature of Confucian thought which met with ready response in Japanese minds, or at least in the minds of the governing class. This is its elevation of duties above rights. Chinese thought is hostile to departures from Li, the prescribed order of behaviour; it sees only duties, ritual and social, and in case of conflict it dwells upon the need for harmony and compromise. The adoption of Confucianism as standard teaching was part of a deliberate policy of the founders of the Han empire. Its purpose was conformity; and it was to be expected that its effect upon Japanese thought should be to encourage conservatism in political and social life.

In that respect, it might be argued, the influence of Confucianism was unfortunate, for once the main elements of Chinese culture had been appropriated Japan entered upon a phase of expansion which called for experiment by trial and error, and not for adherence to a prescribed pattern. In fact a distinguishing feature of the history of the following period is the decay of borrowed institutions.

CHAPTER VI

THE NEW CAPITAL, 794–894

1. *The Move from Nara*

I N N A R A the monasteries had made important contributions to the study of Buddhist doctrine and had laid solid foundations for future enquiry, both historical and metaphysical—to say nothing of future sectarian controversies. The influence of Buddhism as a religion was benign, for it not only promoted learning and enlarged the aesthetic experience of the Japanese people, but also served as an instrument of material progress, because it encouraged useful handicrafts, building, road-making, and the improvement of agriculture. As an institution, however, Buddhism exercised an influence in many respects harmful to the state. The favours bestowed upon the great monasteries by the Throne and the leading noble houses served so to increase the political power of the Church that (as we have seen from the career of the monk Dōkyō) the authority of the Imperial House was, or seemed to be, endangered. Perhaps this is sufficient to explain the decision of the Emperor Kammu to move the capital; and though other reasons have been suggested, it is safe to conclude from the history of the previous decades that the civil government felt that such reforms as they had in mind could not be carried out unless there were a complete change of atmosphere. A further reason, if such were needed, was the distance of Nara from the sea. It was important for the centre of government to be on or near a navigable river; and since the harbour of Naniwa was already being developed, it was natural to select a position by the Yodo River, on the delta of which Naniwa stood.

The Court was first moved to a place called Nagaoka, some thirty miles from Nara, in the province of Yamashiro. This was in 784, but after ten years the work at Nagaoka, which was being carried out on a grand scale and at vast expense, was suddenly stopped and a new site was chosen only a few miles away. The reasons for this change are not entirely clear; but since misfortunes attacked the Emperor's family soon after the Court moved to Nagaoka, it is probable that these calamities were ascribed to some evil influence which could not be dispelled so long as the work at Nagaoka continued. Certainly superstitious dread had a great part in the decision to change to a new site; and after diviners and geomancers had been consulted and notice given to the Sun Goddess, to the Emperor's ascendants, and to the tutelary deities of the locality, work was begun on a new capital early in 793.

The place chosen was the site of the present city of Kyoto, and there the imperial capital remained until 1868. The Emperor moved into his

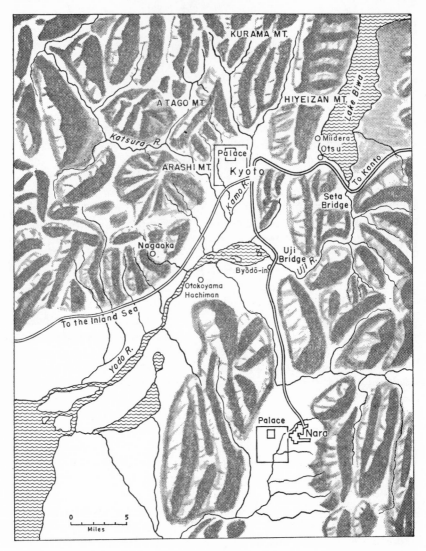

The capital city and its surroundings, about A.D. 900

new palace in 794, but work on other buildings continued for some years more. This was the city styled Heian-kyō, the Capital of Peace and Tranquillity. It was built on the same lines as the Chinese capital at Ch'ang-an under the Sui dynasty, which had also been the model for Nara. Its situation accorded with all the requirements of Chinese geomancy; for the Minister for Home Affairs, Wake no Kiyomaro, a very loyal servant of the Crown, had made sure that it was protected against evil by the guardian deities of the four cardinal points—who were, it may be remarked, known by Chinese names.

It was a great city, an example of planning on a grand scale. It was laid out symmetrically, with wide avenues running north and south and east and west, and numerous narrower intersecting streets and lanes.[1] Within it was a rectangular walled enclosure of considerable dimensions containing the palace buildings, the government offices, and the halls and pavilions in which assemblies were held and state ceremonies performed. All was formal and regulated. The influence of Chinese secular thought was strong and Chinese ceremonial and ritual precedents were scrupulously observed, except on those occasions when the sovereign communicated with the national deities, as in the Prayer for Harvest and the Great Purification.

The new capital was less than thirty miles from Nara, but that was a fair distance in those days of difficult travel. Moreover, the topographical features of the region around Kyoto were much more varied than those of the flat Nara basin. Consequently the old capital seemed more remote in feeling than it was in fact. The difference in character between the two places was marked. Nara stood for antiquity, Kyoto for what was lively and new.

Now that the seven great monasteries of Nara had been left behind, it seemed as if the power of the Buddhist Church was no longer to be feared; moreover, soon after his accession the Emperor Kammu had issued an edict which was intended to cut down the building of new Buddhist edifices, to limit entries into the monastic order, and to prevent the sale or donation of land to religious institutions. This was sound policy, if it could be executed, for it was the ironic truth that the Buddhist Church, which had given to Japan so much that was good and gracious, threatened the stability of government by reason of the political ambitions of its leaders and the fiscal immunities which they abused. The absorption of public lands into ecclesiastical domains deprived the state of revenue which it badly needed for the development of the country as a whole.

The misbehaviour of the clergy, however, was no more than the proximate cause of the financial troubles of the government. Their real origin was the failure of the ruling class as a whole to grasp the problems raised by an expanding agrarian economy.

2. The Political Scene, 794–891

EMPERORS REIGNING IN KYOTO, 781–876

Kammu	781–806	Junna	823–833	Montoku	850–858
Heizei	806–809	Nimmyō	833–850	Seiwa	858–876
Saga	809–823				

The dynastic history of the century or so after the move from Nara is not of great interest or importance. It consists, in the usual propor-

---

[1] See partial street plan of Kyoto in Appendix II.

tions, of succession disputes and rivalries for influence at Court. On the whole it may be regarded as a period in which the imperial authority was at first well maintained but presently, little by little, was encroached upon by leaders of the great clans, notably members of the Fujiwara family, which had been founded by Nakatomi in the seventh century.

The Emperor Kammu (who had succeeded in 781) ruled firmly, relying upon his own judgment; and it is generally agreed among Japanese historians that the power and prestige of the Throne were at their highest during his reign. He died in 806, and his immediate successors were less able to resist the influence of the great nobles. The Fujiwara family continued to pursue its policy of gaining political power by providing Fujiwara ladies as imperial consorts or concubines, so that Fujiwara nobles, through their connection by marriage with the sovereign, were able to secure all the commanding offices in the government, from that of Chancellor or Regent to more modest but still important posts in ministries and bureaus. For some time the heads of the Fujiwara clan used their powers with discretion, and proved on the whole capable administrators.

Fujiwara Yoshifusa served from 857 to 872 as Chancellor and then Regent. He was succeeded by Fujiwara Mototsune, who held the highest offices from 873 to 891. During approximately a century (from the move to Kyoto in 794 to the death of Mototsune in 891) a good deal of earnest if not always useful administrative work was accomplished under direct orders from the Throne, as one emperor after another attempted to check the dominance of the Fujiwara clan in affairs of state. The Fujiwara themselves, owing to dissension among various branches of their clan, could not present such a solid front to their adversaries as they did at a later period; so that statesmen from other families were able occasionally to assist the sovereign in maintaining the imperial prerogative. An effort to break the Fujiwara power was made by the Emperor Daigo, who wished to govern as well as reign. But it was only partly successful, and on Daigo's death in 930 a Fujiwara Regent was appointed. Thereafter the sovereigns never regained full authority. They were traditionally respected, even venerated, as the heads of the nation, but they were not permitted to exercise supreme political rights. Not all of them were capable of imperial rule, and some abdicated under pressure or threat at an early age. Others devoted themselves to literary pursuits, or to painting or calligraphy, and some became devout followers of Buddhism.

During this century the chief political issues to occupy the attention of the government were, first, the prosecution of campaigns against unreconciled aborigines in the eastern and northern provinces, who were hindering the opening up of new farm land; second, the reform of the system of land tenure and taxation, whose breakdown was destroying the authority of the central administration and its provincial officers as well as impairing its financial stability; and finally, the reorganization of the whole administrative system borrowed from China, which was proving unworkable.

In order to furnish a background for the description of social and religious life in the ninth and tenth centuries, let us take these three questions in turn, beginning with the settlement of the eastern and northern provinces.

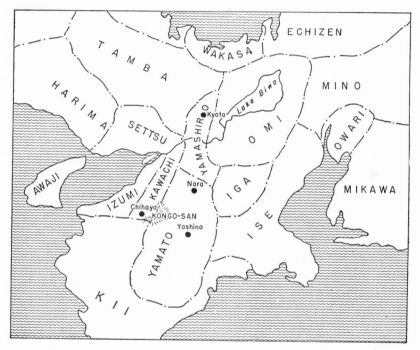

The five home provinces and neighbouring provinces, about A.D. *900*

(a) Land settlement and frontier problems

After the reform of 645 the general condition of the country had gradually improved. In spite of frequent succession disputes and sporadic disorder, a relatively settled life brought about some increase of population and a general movement of expansion. The Kinai plain, fertile as it was, could not support many more people on a rising standard of living; so that enterprising persons began to migrate eastward in search of new cultivable land. They naturally moved east and north in the general direction of the Kantō plain, the largest area of rich alluvial soil suitable for wet rice culture. There had been sparse settlements in the provinces east of the Hakone mountain barrier for a long time past, since such good land had always attracted the most vigorous and adventurous type of farmer. They had acquired their holdings by pushing back the aboriginal settlers, the Yezo (or as they were later called, the Ainu), whose ancestors had inhabited the Kantō area in great numbers since neolithic times. By 720 the frontier was as far north as Taga, a few miles from the present city of Sendai. But, although many of the Ainu had been pacified and lived amicably alongside their Japanese neighbours, there remained — especially in the northern provinces of Mutsu and Dewa—a very large number of turbulent people, including Japanese who had thrown in their lot with the Ainu. These irreconcilables made frequent raids upon settlements to the south of their own encampments. They were stubborn fighters, and the military forces sent to help the settlers were unable to hold them in check.

The reason for this failure was that the military provisions of the Taihō code were quite inadequate. They had introduced a scheme of national military service under which all males from twenty to sixty years of age were liable to be called up for military duty, either in the provincial forces or in the guard regiments stationed at the capital, or in special frontier forces formed to operate against the Emishi ("barbarians") or against attacks from the mainland, which at that time were not thought impossible. But surprisingly for a people with so belligerent a tradition, the ruling class in the eighth century was predominantly civilian in outlook, preferring compromise to violence and, no doubt owing to the influence of Buddhism, averse to bloodshed. In 701 the possession of weapons by private persons had been forbidden, the uniform of the officers of state included no deadly implements to symbolize their powers, and the profession of arms was not respected. This state of affairs was due in part to Chinese ideas; it was inherent in the administrative structure, which gave little importance to military arrangements except for purposes of parade and display. But its immediate cause was the inefficient working of the system of recruiting.

Military service was a very great burden on the small farming families, and their young men did all they could to evade it, either by running away or by working on the estates of rich landowners or officials, sometimes as domestic servants. The system was most oppressive. Each conscript had to furnish his own provisions and weapons, together with footgear, cooking utensils, and other necessaries. Further, each file of ten men had to supply and feed six horses as well as bring spades, axes, sickles, and other tools. The households to which these men belonged were excused certain labour taxes, but not the ordinary levies on rice and other produce. So great was the burden that, according to a popular saying, when one man was called up his family was ruined. Middle-class and upper-class families were able to evade military duty by various claims and pretexts.

During the eighth century the shortage of trained men was such that the frontier forces were unable to hold back the Ainu raiders, and the government was obliged to introduce new military measures. In 792, under the Emperor Kammu, the principle of universal military service (which had never been fully applied) was dropped and the government of each province was left to form its own force by conscripting able-bodied young men, selected by lot not from the ordinary run of farming households but from the families of district officers and other members of the landed gentry who held an order of merit from the Court.[2] In other words the responsibility for defence and the preservation of order was placed in the hands of a class of well-to-do landowners, locally powerful but preserving an association with the central government, who had a strong interest in the protection of private property.

But this system never really came into force, and there was no organization responsible for keeping the peace in the name of the Crown. Indeed, by this time (ca. 800) the private domains (the shōen) had so developed in size and so promoted local separatism that the authority of the government in the remoter provinces had almost collapsed. Contemporary accounts give a picture of disorder and violence, of the depredations of armed bands, so threatening that the farmers were obliged to arm in their own defence, and to attach themselves to powerful landlords for protection. Some of the wealthier magnates even kept their own soldiery, which they did not hesitate to use for attack upon rivals or even for the invasion of public domains.

It was in such conditions that there began to arise a class of private warriors which in course of time was to dominate the whole country. Long before the Reform period it had been usual to recruit men from the eastern provinces for expeditions against Korea, and their reputation was high because they were practised in warfare against the aborigines. They were known as Azumabito or Men of the East, and their praises were sung in early Japanese literature. The regular government forces in the eastern provinces were not of this mettle. Their commanders were so notably unsuccessful that in 783 the Emperor publicly rebuked them for cowardice and ordered a new campaign to be undertaken under competent leadership.

A "General of the East" was appointed, but he died in 786 without having taken the offensive, and it was not until 789 that a well-equipped force under a new commander advanced from Taga into the province of Mutsu, there to be ignominiously routed by the Ainu near the site of the present town of Morioka. The commanding general, a courtier

---

[2] Special arrangements were made for coastal defence in strategic areas, particularly in Kyūshū. Able-bodied young men were recruited for special service for a term of three years, and it was found that youths from the eastern provinces made the best soldiers for this purpose, having been brought up in warlike surroundings. The coast guards called Saki-mori ("cape wardens") are a frequent subject of nostalgic verse in the Heian era, owing to their lonely life far from home. The system was modified in 757, and men were recruited in the western provinces.

rather than a soldier, was recalled, tried, and lightly punished, and a new campaign was planned on a more thoroughgoing scale. At length in 791 a commander was appointed, and given the title of Seitō Taishi, or Envoy for the Pacification of the East; his deputy was one Sakanouye Tamura Maro, celebrated in Japanese history as a paragon of military virtues. Tamura Maro preceded his superior officer to the front in 793, and in 795 they both returned to the capital in triumph. But for a decade or more it was necessary to keep up the pressure against the Ainu and to encourage farmers to settle near the effective frontier so as to provide a permanent defence against raids and sallies, which Tamura Maro's successes had not entirely checked. In order to finish the affair he was given a new commission in 800 and sent off again. In a series of campaigns lasting until 803 he finally accomplished his purpose, and was able to push the frontier as far north as Izawa and Shiba (see map, p. 250), where strongholds were built and garrisoned. So important was his task in the eyes of the Court that the title of Sei-i Tai-Shōgun or Barbarian-subduing Generalissimo, which he was the first to hold, was sought after by the highest military officers in the land for the next thousand years.

The expense of these campaigns was very heavy. The burden fell mainly upon the small cultivator. A further claim upon the taxpayer was the provision of labour and materials for the new capital. In 805 we find advisers to the Throne discussing the question of an Act of Grace which should cancel outstanding tax and private debts, and agreeing that the people were suffering from the cost of war and public building. No doubt they were right, but these were not the only causes of agrarian distress and the failure of provincial authority.

Despite Tamura Maro's resounding successes the Ainu continued their incursions, though on a lessening scale, until about 811, if not later. Thus they had held out for more than twenty years since the first large-scale expedition was sent against them; and there is little doubt that their resistance was due not only to their own stubborn character, but also to the neutrality, if not the positive assistance, of a number of pioneer settlers who resented the intrusion of the central government in the affairs of a border country where they were free from taxation, and other attacks upon their liberty. Some of them were probably themselves Ainu, or the offspring of mixed marriages; and it was perhaps on that account that the government presently transferred several thousand people from the more developed eastern provinces to the newly opened land in the north. These new settlers were assured that land which they brought under cultivation would be exempt from tax; and from these pioneers descended some of the hardiest and most intractable military families in the history of Japan, families with a long and cherished tradition of disregarding orders from the capital.

These were extreme cases, but in general, as the process of reclamation begun in the eighth century extended the area of cultivation, there arose a conflict between rural and metropolitan interests, which in its varied manifestations is the main feature of the history of the next three centuries. In the ninth century the expenditure of the central government increased rapidly as it undertook, in addition to military measures and palace architecture, such public works as the building of roads and bridges. The more taxes it was obliged to levy, the more determined were the great landowners to evade them; and it would not be far from the truth to say that the major issue of the conflict in question was a continuous struggle between the administration and the provincial notables for the effective control of agricultural land.

(b) Failure of the land laws

Less specifically, but perhaps more correctly, we may say that political history from the time of the Taihō reform (701) is essentially a record of the gradual breakdown of the elaborate, logical, symmetrical system of government that had been borrowed from China by ardent admirers without adequate experience of the problems of civil administration. It was a system which soon proved unsuited to conditions in Japan, where ancient habits were still strong and where the method of rice culture made the Chinese regulations unworkable in practice. The scheme for the distribution of land in allotments to each household began to break down in the eighth century, as we have seen, and though painstaking efforts were made to restore it by the Heian government they did not succeed. The records, which are fairly copious, show that the procedure was extremely cumbersome, requiring examination, registration, inspection, accounting, and reporting, so onerous and vexatious that it would have been hard for a modern highly trained civil service to make it work. It is not surprising that the provincial and local officials were unable, and often unwilling, to follow the rules. Grants of land were made at irregular intervals, and in an arbitrary fashion, and though the allotment (handen) system was never officially abandoned it gradually collapsed, as we know from an edict of 902, which said that it had been in disuse for a long time, and ordered it to be resumed. In some parts of the country there had been no allotment since 850, or even before; and there is no record of any allotment after 902. Within a decade or so we find the government concerned not about granting land, but about the tax or tribute from vacated allotments, whose tenants had either died or gone to work on private estates, in some cases after leasing or selling their plots with the connivance of local officers.

The fugitives were known as ukarebito or as rōnin, a term used in later, feudal times to denote men who had left the service of their lords. The situation was not new, for (as we have seen in Chapter V) the records mention absconding farmers as early as 670. In 780, according to an official proclamation, there were so many absentees in the province of Ise that no public works could be undertaken. Inspecting officers found that persons entered in the registers as "dead" or "absconded" were in fact taking refuge in neighbouring manors, and could not be forced out on corvée because provincial authorities dared not challenge great domanial lords.

The failure of the allotment system was due in the first place to its unsuitability. It was not appropriate to rice land in a country where the cultivator was deeply attached to the small plot which he himself cultivated and, irrespective of title, regarded as his own. It was not capable of close enforcement in the existing state of communications by provincial officials who put local sentiment before legal claims. Its sponsors, for their part, had not foreseen the sequels of the reclamation programme and of the heavy burden of tax, forced labour, and military service which combined to drive the holders of allotments either to sell or lease their fields with the connivance of local officials, or merely to abscond and seek a livelihood elsewhere. Some at least of these abuses might have been removed had the central government been able to control its representatives in the provinces, but the hierarchical character of the Chinese administrative system had been transmitted to Japan only in form and not in substance, since powerful persons and institutions refused to submit to the orders of a new bureaucracy. Moreover, there is no good ground for assuming that the Chinese system, as laid down in the Sui and T'ang codes, worked well in practice in its country of origin. Indeed the available evidence goes to show that it worked rather badly and that the survival of a strong central administration in China was due not to the wisdom of the legislators but to certain economic and topographic conditions, such as the need for a large-scale irrigation policy, which favoured and even required the concentration of power in the hands of highly trained officials.

(c) Unsuitability of the codes

The breakdown of the administrative system in Japan cannot be ascribed to one single cause. In fact, it is scarcely correct to say that it broke down, seeing that hardly any of the provisions of the codes which dealt with land ownership and land revenue had been fully observed since they were promulgated. In a general way this can be accounted for by saying that the Chinese system was unsuited to Japan, that it was premature to impose upon an unregulated and expanding society a complicated procedure which could not possibly work where communications were poor and where there were not enough competent and reliable local officials to enforce the law impartially. But the true cause was something more deep-seated than a mere shortage of capable functionaries. It was the self-regarding and insubordinate conduct of great nobles at the capital, who by their influence were able to corrupt or defy provincial authorities, from provincial governors down to minor tax collectors. In other words, it was the power of the hereditary principle which set at naught the provisions of the law. A few officials struggled against this pressure, but most were in league either with the great men themselves or with their local representatives; and, it should be remembered, most of the officials below the rank of governor were locally appointed and thought first in terms of local benefits and local interests.

It would be superfluous to describe in detail the many forms of peculation to which the country officials resorted; but it is worth while to mention some of the abuses which the bureaucracy in the capital tried in vain to correct by positive rules and regulations, since it was the flouting of central authority that created those independent country magnates whose descendants were to be the founders of a feudal state.

One of the commonest abuses of official power was the falsification of tax registers, so that the provincial officers could retain for their own use a portion of the tax (in rice or other produce) due to the government. Another deplorable offence was the misappropriation of interest (in kind) paid by farmers on official loans of seed rice, or the seizure of stocks of grain held in reserve against short crops. In general public land was liable to seizure for private use under various pretenses, and men liable for labour tax were put to work on private estates.

So common was peculation of various kinds that great difficulties arose when a newly appointed governor arrived at his post. The law required that he should give a release or clearance to his predecessor, so that no claim could be brought against a retired official. But the newcomer, knowing that illegal acts were likely to have been committed, was always very cautious; and often it was many months or even several years before agreement could be reached. At last the Chancellor's office was obliged (ca. 790) to set up a special commission to decide upon the conditions of transfer; and in 802 there was drawn up a code of procedure to be applied to transfers at all posts. It was revised at intervals and reached its final form in 867. The Release Commissioners, known as Kageyushi, formed a kind of board of audit which was characteristic of the numerous extra-legal organs that developed as the weaknesses of the early system became apparent in matters of government, both central and provincial.

However one may choose to explain the failure of the central government to enforce its own administrative code, it is quite clear that immediately it arose from the stubborn resistance exercised by local landowners. Rural interests were in the hands of rural settlers, who in matters of land tenure and taxation could count upon the protection of great nobles residing in the capital but holding extensive property in the country. These were powerful men whom only the boldest of provincial governors would dare to offend. In other words, the Taikwa reforms, though they had given nominal control of land and people to the sovereign and his ministers, had not in reality broken the power of the great territorial lords.

The truth is that the real source of power in Japanese life was the land, and the apparatus of government in the capital city was an artificial growth. The stream of edicts and rules from the metropolis did not succeed in changing the character of agrarian society. It was the law that had to be adjusted to the society, not the society to the law, as is shown by the growth of extra-legal institutions which we have just noticed. Chief among them was the form of landed property known as the shōen or manor, which was an estate enjoying fiscal immunities entirely contrary to the intention of the land laws, but acquired in practice during the eighth and ninth centuries and thereafter fully if reluctantly recognized. Its growth is characteristic of the refusal of rural life to follow a pattern prescribed by urban authority.

The shōen in Japan has much in common with the manor in Europe, though the European development is earlier in date and somewhat different in its origin.

The manorial system in England was substantially the same as that which prevailed in northern France and western Germany. That system in its turn was a continuation of conditions which had prevailed under Roman rule. In England before the withdrawal of the Roman legions (say about A.D. 360), hundreds of vessels used to carry corn from Britain to cities on the Rhine. This corn was grown on great private estates which surrounded the villas and granaries of the landowners. The land was cultivated not by free men, but by coloni, freedmen, and slaves. Of these workers, the first two categories might be nominally free, but in fact they were bound to the soil. These conditions of agricultural labour continued through the eighth century. Documents of that period recording the transfer of land by sale or bequest would run "farms, with buildings, lands, woods, and meadows . . . and the slaves dwelling thereon."[3] Grants by the Crown usually would specify the land of so many families and the persons and property of all its inhabitants.

Similar conditions obtained in Japan during the same period. The shōen consisted of a villa (shō), cultivated land (en), granaries and other buildings, together with free workers (ryōmin) and "base people" (semmin) and their families. The ryōmin were nominally free, but were often so situated that they had no land of their own to cultivate, either because they had absconded from their allotments to avoid tax or because their holding had been confiscated. They were therefore in practice bound to the soil.

The semmin were praedial serfs. The number of serfs is not known,

[3] The language used was: mansi cum aedificiis una cum terris, silvis, pratis . . . . mancipiis commanentibus.

but to judge from household registers of the eighth century they formed less than 5 per cent of the farm population. An interesting parallel is furnished by a gift of land to a churchman (Wilfrid) in Saxon times, recorded by the Venerable Bede.[4] The people went with the land, and there were eighty-seven families, owning together 250 slaves, or less than three slaves for a household. These slaves were emancipated by Wilfrid on religious grounds. It does not appear that the great Buddhist foundations in Japan freed the slaves in their manors; but it is evident that as new land was brought into cultivation the demand for farm labour increased and the treatment of slaves improved, so that the distinction between free and unfree tended to disappear.

3. *Institutional Change*

From the point of view of institutional history the century or so after the move from Nara may be described as a period of reaction against the codes as they stood about A.D. 800, when such revisions as had been made had not substantially altered their Chinese character. The reaction was due to the practical failure or unsuitability of many of the earlier provisions, and (it may be added) to a germinating desire for freedom from Chinese influence. The codes consisted of two parts: the *ryō*, which included both an administrative code and a civil code; and the *ritsu*, which were prohibitive and disciplinary regulations of a penal character, but not, strictly speaking, a penal code. The administrative code laid down the names, divisions, functions, and precedence of all departments of state and their functionaries; the civil code regulated the status of subjects from the nobility down to the slaves, their duties, obligations, rewards, and punishments, together with such matters as marriage, succession, taxation, civil and military services, arrest, imprisonment, ceremonial, costume, mourning, funerals, and religious exercises.

The whole life of the individual as well as the character of the administration was thus fixed by law; but the society to which this law applied was changing rapidly, and therefore the law was in constant need of revision. Continuous revision did in fact take place, in the form of amendments, deletions, and additions known as *kyaku* and *shiki*. Indeed the ninth century might be described in the history of Japanese law as the age of legislation by official order. The kyaku were regulations issued ad hoc to meet changing conditions, and they modified or replaced laws or provisions thereof which were no longer appropriate. The shiki were detailed rules and forms supplementing the codes and necessary for their practical operation. The distinction between kyaku and shiki (which was fairly clear in the T'ang legislation) tended to disappear in Japan. Often the enforcement of rules in either class was

[4] Cited by Gibbon, *Decline and Fall*, Chapter 38.

in effect a means of amending or even overriding the provisions of the codes, so that Japanese writers sometimes say that the "ritsuryō" period was followed by the "kyakushiki" period in Japanese legal history.

There were three important compilations of these amending rules and regulations, following upon some minor revisions before 800. They were: the Kōnin-kyaku and Kōnin-shiki (both 820); the Jōgan-kyaku (869) and the Jōgan-shiki (871); the Engi-kyaku (909) and the Engi-shiki (967). The Kōnin-kyakushiki was a compilation of rules, regulations, and precedents covering the 119 years since the issue of the Taihō code in 702. The Jōgan-kyakushiki supplemented the Kōnin compilation, and the two together had the force of statutory law, alongside of the original codes and at times superseding them.

The Engi-kyaku added to the two previous collections of kyaku but did not supersede them. The Engi-shiki included all shiki that had been in the two previous collections, which it therefore superseded. Only fragments of the collections of kyaku exist, but the Engi-shiki has been preserved with little loss. This is the classical collection, a precious source of information about the evolution of juridical ideas and practices in ninth-century Japan. It fixed administrative principles and procedure in such permanent form that a number of the offices which it set up, both high and low, became hereditary in certain families. Soon after the promulgation of the Engi institutes and formularies the law was to become fossilized and neglected, its place being taken by the arbitrary commands of the Fujiwara family or by the decisions of certain extra-legal or extra-constitutional offices which had developed alongside of the kyaku and shiki and for similar reasons.

One of these offices we have already noticed in the Kageyushi, or Release Commissioners, a special body set up to remedy deficiencies in the method of making and terminating appointments to official posts. This was in 790, but changes in the title and function of officials as well as the creation of new offices had begun to take place quite soon after the promulgation of the Taihō code in 702. These we need regard only as normal revisions made in the light of practical experience; but the free creation of new offices which the code had never contemplated, still less authorized, is a matter of historical importance, deserving some attention because it shows the practical reaction of Japanese minds to difficulties arising from a too logical, schematic treatment of problems of administration. It is in fact a rejection of the Chinese habit of setting up rigid classifications and categories in human and celestial affairs. It is a preference for the practical, empiric solution of difficulties.

Such extra-legal offices were as a rule created out of practical necessity, and it is true to say that in general they were more influential and more effective than the offices prescribed by the codes. It does not follow that they produced better results, only that they worked more easily. Perhaps the most important of them was the office of Kampaku or Regent. The Regent for a sovereign during his minority, or for a female sovereign, was called Sesshō, and although this title does not appear in the codes, the office was traditionally accepted as proper and necessary. However, certain powerful ministers of state continued to act as Regent even after the sovereign came of age, and they now assumed the title of Kampaku, a great officer who was in theory the adviser and spokesman of the Throne, but in practice a dictator. Analogies to this irregular office are not uncommon. In European history the Merovingian Mayors of the Palace and in Asiatic history the Ranas of Nepal closely resemble the Fujiwara Regents who in practice usurped the imperial prerogative.[5]

The first instance of this kind of usurpation is that of the Fujiwara statesman Mototsune, who was Regent (Sesshō) during the reign of a child emperor (Yōzei, 877–84), and assumed the style of Kampaku in 880. This office, with all its dictatorial powers, was soon to become hereditary in the Fujiwara family and was often held in addition to such appointments as Chancellor, Prime Minister, and Great Counsellor.

The effect of such special offices was of course to take power away from the regular ministerial organs, the departments and bureaus formed under the Taihō code, and to permit decisions to be made arbitrarily by the most powerful men at Court. On a lower level than the Regent, but still very influential and cutting across the functions of the heads of departments and the counsellors, was an institution called the Kurando-dokoro, which began as a palace secretariat dealing with the emperor's confidential affairs and what might be called his privy purse. The Kurando (the word means something like "treasury officers") originally had charge of the emperor's private property and his personal archives, but were without any administrative powers. In 810, however, when an abdicated sovereign (Heizei) was conspiring to regain the throne, the reigning sovereign (Saga), for purposes of secrecy and as a temporary measure, issued orders and made arrangements not through the usual channels but through trusted friends whom he appointed for that purpose to the secretariat.

It was from these beginnings that the Kurando-dokoro became perhaps the most important single organ of government, assuming most of the functions of the Nakatsukasa, or Mediate Office, which under the Taihō code was the senior of the eight ministries of state, especially

---

[5] There is, however, an important point of difference. Some Mayors of the Palace, as their office grew in importance, sought to exercise power in their own name and to assume the title and office of king. Thus the Merovingian mayors Charles Martel and Pepin le Bref became kings in the eighth century, Pepin establishing the Carolingian dynasty by deposing the Merovingian King Childeric III. In Japan neither the Fujiwara Regents nor, later, the Shōguns, ever claimed to displace the legitimate sovereign. The office of emperor was regarded as something separate and inviolable, to which no subject could aspire. In the feudal period, when the warrior class had deprived the emperors of all governing authority, still a mystic power was ascribed to the reigning sovereign.

charged with relations between the sovereign and the purely executive offices. Its minister's duties included the scrutiny of imperial rescripts and edicts, and involved intimate knowledge of the emperor's ideas and intentions. But by the end of the ninth century the Kurando-dokoro had become a permanent institution, much favoured by the Fujiwara dictators because it enabled them to dispense with departmental routine and to govern at will. The influence of the new organ was such that it attracted the most talented persons, who could be sure of attaining high office. It came to be known in the official world as Tōryūmon, the Gateway of the Ascending Dragon.

Another and equally characteristic growth was that of the Kebiishi-chō, which began as a special metropolitan police office, attached to the Guards' Headquarters (Emon-fu) about 810, when disturbed conditions in the capital and its environs made special police work necessary. As we have seen, this was the year in which the ex-Emperor Heizei's conspiracy gave rise to the special power of the Kurando-dokoro. The new police force proved effective, and presently developed into a larger and independent office, charged with tracking down and arresting offenders. The official appointment of Kebiishi (Police Commissioners) with regular functions was made in 816; and thereafter, owing to its prompt and effective action, the new organ grew in importance. Soon it was carrying out most of the police duties which the Ministry of Justice and its regular organs had failed to perform to public satisfaction. The chief of the Kebiishi-chō was usually a high official, and specially qualified assistants from other posts, military and civil, were seconded to work under him. The work was carried out so efficiently, from the point of view of the inner ring at the palace, that the operations of the Kebiishi-chō were extended to the provinces. At the same time it began to assume judicial functions, taking in men with legal training. In some provinces the Kebiishi are said to have taken excessive powers, flouting the governors and invading the jurisdiction of local authorities, as well as oppressing the people. Rural disorder seems in many regions to have called for drastic measures, and to have justified some extension of their original constabulary functions. In certain more remote provinces conditions of banditry and piracy were so grave that it proved necessary to recruit local forces, a kind of gendarmerie to assist the regular police officers. These adjuncts were meant to be temporary but in the most disturbed areas they were not disbanded. They were in close touch with the Kebiishi and so assumed an importance and authority which had not been foreseen. Here also we have an extra-legal emergency organ developing permanent and important functions because of the failure of the official system. The offices of Ōryoshi and Tsuibushi—let us call them Sheriffs and Chief Constables—continued into the feudal period as the means of keeping order in the country, long after the Ministry of Justice had become an ineffective survival.

These examples will have sufficed to show the nature of the extra-legal offices and the circumstances in which they arose. There were many others, but of them we need only say that in the aggregate they came near to destroying, or reducing to impotence, the elaborate administrative system of the Taihō code.

One interesting point emerges from a broad survey of the legal history of Japan. It is that members of the Fujiwara family were responsible for most of the important developments in the first five centuries of legislation, beginning with the Reform Edict of 645. Most of the announcements constituting the Reform were the work of Kamatari, the founder of the clan. The Taihō code of 701 was drawn up by a committee headed by Fujiwara Fubito, and revised by him in 718. Further amendments, including the successive issues of kyaku and shiki, were made under the superintendence of Fujiwara ministers, Tokihira in particular, while Fujiwara statesmen and officials played a leading part in the development of most of the extra-legal offices which in the ninth and tenth centuries supplemented or replaced provisions of the administrative code. This interest of the Fujiwara may be explained as arising from the mere fact that they exercised supreme political power continuously; but their part in legislation was very positive. They did not confine themselves to approving what their subordinates had proposed.

An instructive sidelight on the evolution of administrative forms is provided by the development, parallel to the growth of extra-legal bodies, of a simplified official procedure which, by no means accidentally, contributed to the effective power of the Fujiwara Regents. The matter is too complicated for full description here, but it is worth while to trace the main lines of development.

The original practice, arising out of the codes and consonant with the absolute authority of the sovereign, was for him to issue commands by means of edicts and ordinances under his imperial seal. The process of drafting and promulgating these documents (which of course had the force of law) was very cumbrous and slow. Naturally in course of time simpler forms were preferred. These were gradually devised and introduced in growing numbers, until they came into general use. Of this character were notices issued by the Kurando-dokoro, simple statements of the royal wish, usually drafted by officers of the Bureau. Then, as the Fujiwara family gained power, its leaders seized upon this legislative device and developed a most convenient practice of issuing orders on behalf of the sovereign in a semi-official style, the so-called Mi-Kyō-sho, or Letter of Instruction, which His Majesty was supposed to have authorized on the advice of his Ministers. Further simplification soon followed. The intermediate stages need not be set forth here, since the final stage was the issue not by the sovereign but by departmental officials of orders to subordinates, called "kudashi-bumi," which were supposed to represent the will of higher authorities. These often replaced the full-dress directions of the Chancellor, known as Dajōkan-fu or Dajōkan-chō, and were simply styled Office Notifications ("kansen"). It goes without saying that all such short steps favoured a system of government by which sovereign power was delegated to great nobles and exercised in their interest.

4. Metropolitan Life: Religion and Scholarship

The first clear signs of the failure of the borrowed Chinese system were to be seen where it was put to the severest test, namely in that conflict of interests and purposes between the central government and a firmly entrenched land-owning class, which has just been described. But the weakness of the administration is also revealed in other matters, which it is necessary to examine so as to understand why eventually it had to give way to forms of pressure other than the intransigence of rural magnates.

For that purpose it is best to gain some general impression of the nature of metropolitan life as it evolved after the move from Nara, because the gap between capital and country, between Court and people, grew wider and wider as the society of aristocrats and high officers of state that dominated the capital became more and more refined and sophisticated and aloof from common concerns. Its interests were chiefly matters of taste and feeling; its chief modes of expression were in ceremonial, in the niceties of deportment, and in the elegancies of literary style. The age was one of immense literary activity, not only in the issue of the stream of edicts, orders, and injunctions, the official documents and paperasseries which we have already noticed, but also in the composition of historical records and poetical anthologies.

It was an artificial society, remote from the harsh realities of the life of ordinary men in town or country; but it was on the whole peaceful, averse to violence, and deeply interested in all the arts. It was not an intellectual society, not much—hardly at all—given to speculation; but it respected learning and it was open to the appeal of Buddhism, especially though not exclusively on its emotional or sensual side. If the faithful did not suffer from a restless desire to penetrate the secrets of the universe, they knew the pleasures of tranquil meditation.

Buddhism indeed was for centuries the vehicle of the continental culture that transformed Japanese life, and no true history of Japan can be written that leaves out the study of Buddhist influence in all its departments.

The most striking feature of the early part of the new regime is the change which took place in the character of Buddhism as it developed free from the influence of the Nara sects. Those sects were of much importance in the intellectual life of Japan, since it was through study of the works of the great Indian and Chinese thinkers that the Japanese people became aware of philosophical problems. But their doctrine was remote from common understanding, and their monasteries had little to do with the daily life of the people. If they were not scholastic, their chief concern was with matters of organization and Church property, or with the performance of impressive ritual on official occasions. In general their connexion was with the Court and not with a public congregation of believers. There were, it is true, provincial churches, but these too had an official character, so that on the whole they made no deep impression upon the ordinary countryman, who continued in his ancient beliefs.

Although the capital city had been moved away from Nara so as to escape ecclesiastical influence, the Court was by no means hostile to Buddhism. On the contrary it was committed to Buddhism in several ways, since religious observances had become an important part of the business of government and also of the social, if not the spiritual, life of the aristocracy. In all but the strictest sense Buddhism was now a state religion; but the Nara sects had served their purpose and a new feeling filled the air of a new capital. There was a need for a form of Buddhism more in harmony with the native temperament, and it was satisfied at length by two remarkable religious leaders, Saichō (whose posthumous title was Dengyō Daishi) and Kūkai (whose posthumous title was Kōbō Daishi). They founded two sects which, although derived from China, acquired a certain Japanese flavour once they had been transplanted. The history of Japanese Buddhism in this phase can be told by relating their biographies.

Saichō (767–822) as a young man had studied under Chinese teachers in Nara, and as he grew up he was impressed by the degradation of the leading religious communities and turned over in his mind plans of reform. His reaction against the formal and conservative rules of his order (he belonged to a sect which paid special attention to Church discipline and apostolic succession) drove him to leave Nara and live as a recluse in mountain country near his birthplace. Hitherto Japanese Buddhism had been almost entirely urban; thus Saichō may be regarded as the originator of a habit of seeking solitude in mountain places, where monks or laymen could meditate or practise austerities alone or in small communities. The development of mountain confraternities is a special feature of Japanese Buddhism. The recluse, whether Buddhist or Taoist, living in a mountain retreat is a common figure in the pictorial art of both China and Japan. This feeling of the sanctity of high ground led also to the building of small shrines or modest chapels on eminences remote from towns, and it followed that most of the important monasteries of the ninth century were situated on rising ground or at any rate in sequestered surroundings, unlike the Nara monasteries which were mostly on level ground and within the city limits. This difference in elevation corresponded to a difference in outlook, for the new sects, though their inner doctrine was subtle and difficult, expressed a freer and bolder spirit than the old. Saichō believed firmly in rigorous training and austere life—a true monastic discipline in contrast to the ease of urban Buddhism and its intimate association with the Court. His rule was that aspirants should for years remain secluded in the mountains before admission into the monastic order.

The small shrine that Saichō built—in 788, before the move from Nagaoka—was on Mount Hiyei, an eminence which looked down from the northeast upon the site of the future capital; and when the move was made this position assumed a special importance, because the northeast was what is called the Kimon, or Demon Entrance, that is to say the quarter from which, according to Chinese geomancy, malign influences could attack the new city. Furthermore, because in the native cult all high places in the land of the gods, and notably in the imperial province of Yamato, were thought to be sanctified by the presence of mountain deities, Saichō was careful to pay reverence to the god or gods of Hiyei, whom he addressed as Sannō, or King of the Mountain. Thus, by the friendly collaboration of Indian Buddhism, indigenous Shintō, and Chinese geomancy, the protection of the city was assured.

It was owing to these fortunate circumstances that Saichō attracted the attention of the Emperor Kammu and was sent to China for study in 804. There he paid most attention to the T'ient'ai sect, having already learned something of its teaching from a monk under whom he had studied in Nara. He stayed on Mount T'ient'ai (notice that this was a mountain monastery, and its name means Celestial Platform), receiving instruction from Chinese masters and collecting scriptures to take back to Japan. He reached home in 805 and received from the Court a license to found a "Tendai Lotus Sect" (Tendai being the Japanese version of T'ient'ai). His monastery on Mount Hiyei was enlarged; it grew steadily in size and power, maintaining a close connexion with the palace; and the Tendai school thereafter played a leading part in Japanese Buddhism, following the course of the parent sect in China, which had set out to reconcile all forms of Buddhist doctrine in one grand comprehensive statement of quintessential truth.

This is not the place for a discussion of Tendai principles; but it is interesting to notice here that from a purely historical viewpoint the importance of the T'ient'ai school is that it was not of Indian origin, but was developed in China as a reaction, almost a protest, against the pretensions of older sects, which each emphasized a different aspect of the way to salvation. The success of the Tendai school in Japan is due to a similar attitude—an impatience, let us say, with the metaphysical excesses and the scholastic aridities of most of the Nara schools, which erred by a complexity of doctrine or an elaboration of ritual that offered no consolation to the ordinary man. Both T'ient'ai and Tendai may therefore be regarded as displaying a certain national character and as expressing the somewhat matter-of-fact response of Far Eastern minds to the everlasting discussions of theologians, who (it seemed) only planted impenetrable thickets of argument in the way of poor men looking for guidance towards paradise. It was, after all, absurd to teach, as did the Nara schools, that paradise was unattainable by the ignorant layman. That was a repugnant thought to a people whose worldly life was made coherent by the ties of family affection. Why, they might ask, should our fathers, brothers, wives, sons and daughters, be punished for not understanding what a monk takes a lifetime to study?

This kind of practical attitude had much to do with the later developments of Buddhism in Japan, for although the Japanese have always been sensitive to new impressions, they have never in their history—so long as they had freedom—surrendered the inmost stronghold of their own tradition.

The Tendai school grew and prospered, attaining great power and prosperity. It owed its success to its accommodating character, for it was so comprehensive in its scope that all later varieties of Japanese Buddhism, whatever their remoter origin, arose from within the Enryakuji, the monastery which in course of time comprised some 3,000 buildings on the summit and flanks of Mount Hiyei. It is true that by its multiplication of doctrines Tendai seems to have departed from its earlier broad principles; but it retained its influence and its eclectic character until it was struck down by the secular arm on political rather than religious grounds, in the sixteenth century.

In point of time the second great ecclesiastical figure of the ninth century was a man who takes a higher place than Saichō, or any other great religious leader, in the history of Japan. This was the monk Kūkai, whose posthumous title was Kōbō Daishi. Like Saichō, he went to China for study, and he spent more than two years (804-6) at Ch'ang-an, where he is said to have worked at Sanskrit under an Indian teacher and to have been attracted by a form of Buddhism then popular in China. It was, unlike the Tendai brought back by Saichō, not of Chinese origin, but a late form of Indian Buddhism known as Mantrayana or Tantric Buddhism, which had spread and flourished in China as Chenyen, and after its introduction by Kūkai took a high place in Japan as Shingon (meaning True Word). Shingon, though its doctrinal system was extremely complex and highly esoteric, had a less philosophical, and more practical, popular side which had to do with spells and magical formulae (*mantra*) in general.

In China for a time, and in Tibet, and indeed in India also, this superstitious side of Buddhism was carried to extreme lengths, resulting in a degenerate phase of religion given to extravagant and at times immoral practices. In Japan, however, although the spells, charms, and incantations of Shingon were seized upon by most believers, the pure taste of the Japanese people rejected—or better, did not permit—the growth of the excesses which had disfigured the Mantrayana in other parts of Asia. Thus Shingon, like Tendai, is of general historical interest as showing the reaction of Japanese sentiment to what is monstrous or extravagant. Perhaps, on a broad and general view, the importance of Shingon Buddhism in the development of Japanese civilization lies in its remarkable power to inspire the fine arts. Its doctrine was one of lofty ideas, but also of deep mysteries difficult to explain in simple language; so that it was obliged to resort to a free use of symbolism and to depend upon pictorial expression. Its influence upon Japanese religious art has been very powerful and beneficial, and it made a valuable contribution to the arts in general. But it must also be said that its philosophical principles found a response in Japanese minds and an expression in certain practical fields. There is no doubt that the character of Shingon as it developed in Japan owed much to the tolerant and constructive spirit of Kōbō Daishi himself.

The full doctrine of Shingon, in all its complexities, is not easy to explain, but its fundamental principle is simple enough to state, if not to apprehend. It sees the whole universe as a manifestation of the Supreme Buddha Vairocana. The Supreme Buddha is present everywhere and in everything, in every thought, every act, every word; so that all Buddhas and Bodhisattvas are parts of the Supreme Buddha. From this point it was easy to argue that the Shintō deities were of the same order as other manifestations of the Supreme Buddha.

The comprehensive and hospitable character of Shingon had thus an interesting result, in that it gave a high doctrinal authority to the idea of identifying Shintō deities with Buddhas or Bodhisattvas. Previously, as we have noticed, identification had not been complete, for the practice (as stated in an imperial edict of 765) had been to regard the Shintō deities as protectors of the Buddhas and Buddhism. But under the influence of the two new sects (for both Saichō and Kūkai were anxious not to quarrel with Shintō) the process of amalgamation was encouraged, and it ended, though not until the close of the tenth century, in what was called Ryōbu Shintō, or Dual Shintō, a mature syncretic form. It was to the advantage of the native cult to favour such identifications, since it lost nothing by sharing the benefits of Buddhism as the faith of the most powerful and enlightened people in the country. This harmony between Buddhism and Shintō is in significant contrast to the hostility between Buddhism and Confucianism or Buddhism and Taoism in China, or for that matter the struggle of paganism with Christianity in Europe.

In Japan, although Buddhism brought about some changes in Shintō practices, the indigenous faith did not succumb to its influence, but retained a considerable measure of strength within a diminished sphere. For one thing, Buddhism in the ninth and tenth centuries was not yet a popular religion. It was a vehicle of high learning and the professed faith of the Court and nobility, for there was a Shingon chapel in the palace and the courtiers regularly attended services at the leading monasteries near the city. But the country people remained pagan at heart, cherishing their old beliefs and paying reverence to their accustomed gods. Kōbō Daishi himself, though a man of universal interests and sympathies, was not primarily an evangelist with an ardent desire to spread his gospel among the people. Indeed it has been said of Shingon that though universal in its scope, it yet failed to provide for universal salvation.

In a society dominated by the Court and the leading members of the official hierarchy, this great teacher's object was to gain for his system the support of the ruling caste. He was not given to controversy, for his whole outlook was tolerant and conciliatory, his life's purpose being to construct an all-embracing system able to accommodate every pantheon and any version of truth. It was on that account that Shingon cosmology took the gods of old Japan to its capacious bosom. But Kōbō Daishi was not very actively concerned in the movement, except in so far as he was active in almost every direction. His genius was displayed not only in the architecture of a great theological edifice, but also in secular learning, in the arts, in literature and linguistics, in public works and charity, and notably in details of the mystic ceremonies of his sect. He may be regarded as the supreme exponent of that eclectic approach to philosophy which seems to be characteristic of Japanese thought.

There is nothing to show that Kōbō Daishi had political ambitions. He was on good terms with the Court but not a favourite with the Emperor Kammu. His influence on the aristocracy was great, because the rich and elaborate ritual of Shingon was a dominant feature in the life of the nobility, affording them social satisfactions and aesthetic enjoyment. But he did not attempt to use his position for secular ends. He was above such intrigue.

After his return from China he had in 816 founded a monastery on Mount Kōya, a lonely and beautiful site, fifty miles from the capital and not easy of access. There, after a busy life spent chiefly in the city, he was buried in 835. And there, in the belief of his followers, he lies not dead but peacefully awaiting the coming of the Buddha of the future. He had known the hills and streams of the Kōya region since early youth, when he was happy in these beautiful surroundings; and he is said to have fixed upon Kōya for his sepulture already in those days when, proceeding south from Yoshino and then turning eastwards, he had first come upon this perfect conjunction of peace and enchantment.

Quite apart from their religious importance, both Tendai and Shingon affected the history of secular ideas in Japan, in so far as the writings of Saichō and Kūkai encouraged a habit of systematic thought. The philosophical basis of the earlier Nara sects had been profound, but they transmitted Indian or Chinese thought only within a narrow pro-

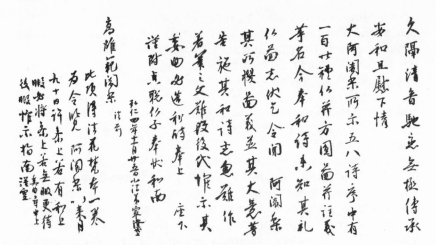

Letter from Saichō to a disciple, Yasunori, then staying with Kūkai. Decem-
ber 813. Original in the collection of Mr. Hara Tomitaro.

fessional circle, whereas these two leaders sought a wider audience.
Kūkai in particular wrote original treatises setting forth the Shingon
teaching in a well-articulated schematic fashion which must have influenced subsequent exegetical studies in Japan.

Some Japanese scholars think that Kūkai in his system endeavoured
to reconcile Mahayana Buddhism with the Chinese Yin-Yang—Five Elements cosmology. Though it seems doubtful whether he went out of his
way to make such a specific accommodation, there is some basis for
supposing that he was well aware of the difference between the Chinese
system and his own account of the body of the Supreme Buddha (that
is, of ultimate truth) as composed of six elements, which are the five
elements of Chinese cosmology together with the element of consciousness, thus adding a spiritual element to the phenomenal world with
which alone the Confucian analysis is concerned. In this respect there
is a conflict between Buddhism and Confucianism, which perhaps
Kūkai was trying to resolve.

The question is one of great interest in the history of Japanese
thought, since it bears on the means by which at length so many seemingly disparate elements were fused in the national ethos. But it is a
most difficult question, striking at the root of what we call national
character; and perhaps it is best to say that since both Tendai and Shingon were comprehensive sects aiming at some kind of universality, they
preferred to dwell upon resemblances rather than differences in their
attitude towards Confucian thought. Putting it more cautiously, one
may suggest that Buddhism did not meet with strong resistance from
Confucianism in Japan because Confucianism was not firmly established
there and was not an expression of indigenous Japanese sentiment.

In his earliest work, *Sankyō Shiki*, a treatise on Three Doctrines,
Kūkai discussed Buddhism, Taoism, and Confucianism, and his desires

to bring them together. In the course of his argument he says that Tao-ism more than Confucianism, and Buddhism more than Taoism, is suited to the great principles of loyalty and filial piety. He was of course think-ing in terms of Japanese principles of behaviour, and it seems clear that he felt the Confucian system to be lacking in moral guidance for the in-dividual. As a Buddhist, however tolerant, he could not admit that evil is a mere temporary disturbance of the natural order. He was bound to believe that a man can free himself from the chains of the phenomenal world and become a Buddha by his own will.

Whatever may have been the harmony or the conflict between dif-ferent schools of thought in learned circles, the leisured aristocratic society in the capital city succumbed to the influence of Chinese litera-ture, and under imperial patronage Chinese studies flourished among the Court nobles and high functionaries. This trend was favoured by the history of the early part of the ninth century, which was quiet and un-eventful enough to encourage the arts of peace.

The dynastic picture was as follows:

Saga	809–823	abdicated in favour of younger brother
Junna	823–833	abdicated at age of 48
Nimmyō	833–850	died 850
Montoku	850–858	died 858
Seiwa	858	succeeded at age of 9; Yoshifusa, the Fujiwara minister, governed as Regent (Sesshō), though not formally appointed until 866

With the accession of the Emperor Saga and the failure of the ill-judged conspiracy against him in 810, there was a pause in dynastic quarrels, and for the next two or three decades the sovereign was able to exercise his power to govern free from the restraint of great nobles like the Fujiwara, who contented themselves with a relatively modest part as advisers.

Some measures of reform were attempted, designed chiefly to relieve taxpayers from their excessive burdens and to correct abuses in local government. These had only moderate success, for the tide was running very strongly against official intervention in the affairs of country mag-nates; and the careful revision of the law by means of the kyaku and shiki, while it testified to a reforming spirit and to the growth of juristic studies, cannot be said to have produced any really beneficial changes in the agrarian situation.

Perhaps the keynote to political history at this juncture is provided not by the Emperor Saga's order of 811 reducing the rate of interest on rice loans, but rather by his pronouncement of 813 to the effect that good government depended upon literature and progress depended upon learning. It was in accordance with these principles, since China was the source of both, that the atmosphere of society at the Heian capi-tal became more and more Chinese.

There is at this point in the development of Japanese life an interesting contrast between the trend of Court society, which submitted
more and more to the influence of Chinese models of social behaviour
and of literary taste, and the trend of political practice, which was increasingly directed to modifying and even rejecting the administrative
patterns laid down in the T'ang code. We must examine the reasons
for this seeming contradiction; but for the present we may confine ourselves to the metropolitan scene as it appears in the early ninth century,
a generation after the move from Nara.

The prestige of Chinese studies was immense. This was natural
enough seeing that Japan had scarcely any literature of her own, if we
except the remarkable poems of the *Manyōshū*, cumbrously recorded
by the use of Chinese characters as phonetic symbols, and a few other
fragments of folklore in verse or prose. We have already noticed the
place of classical studies, that is to say of Chinese studies, under the system of education laid down in the code of 702; and we have seen how the
ruling class adopted Chinese political and philosophical ideas that were
expressed in Confucian teaching and in the Yin-Yang interpretation of
phenomena. Pure scholarship made great strides in Japan as the ninth
century unfolded, and the names of many great men of letters are recorded in the chronicles of the time, among them such celebrated figures
as Miyoshi, soaked in classical lore; and Shigeno Sadanushi, a jurist and
an encyclopaedist; to say nothing of such learned abbots and monks as
Saichō and Kūkai, who were familiar with Chinese secular literature as
well as with the Chinese versions of Buddhist scriptures. Among Kūkai's
celebrated works is a treatise called *Bunkyō Hifuron*, which is a survey
of early (pre-T'ang) Chinese prosody, based upon the views of Chinese
critics.

There is extant a catalogue entitled *Nihon Genzaisho Mokuroku*,
"A List of Books at Present in Japan." It was compiled about 890, and
records 1,579 titles and 16,790 volumes. A fire in the palace had destroyed a great number of books in 875, so that the total number of
volumes imported from China during the ninth century must have
reached an impressive figure.

Thus the Confucian studies which already in the eighth century
held first place in the official curriculum continued in their commanding position, and the new sects of Buddhism gave an impetus to profane as well as sacred learning. The work of specialists in several fields,
such as the jurists who wrote commentaries on the codes and the officials who drafted government documents, reached a high professional
standard, which was maintained as a matter of official duty and also
of family pride. The family names of the scholars of the ninth century
tend to recur in the chronicles of subsequent generations.

In such a studious atmosphere the elegant Court society tended to
follow at a respectful distance in the steps of the earnest scholars, and
to set up standards of taste and accomplishment for ladies and gentle-

men of leisure, who were now expected to have a little knowledge of the outlines of Chinese history and to be able to make an apt quotation now and then from Chinese masterpieces.

It is clear that there was in the capital a serious-minded highly literate class, devoting itself to scholarly pursuits. It is, however, doubtful whether even with reference to its highest level of accomplishment this society can properly be described as intellectual in the strictest sense, for it seems to have been lacking in speculative curiosity. The jurists, for example, though meticulous in their treatment of individual legal problems, do not in their commentaries include any discussion of the nature of justice; and in general there is little evidence of original thought or a critical spirit or a desire to formulate theories and principles. It may be that the weight of Chinese intellectual achievement was overwhelming, but whatever the reason, the cerebral activities of the learned men of Japan in the ninth and tenth centuries seem to have been directed to the study of Chinese literature in all its branches, or to the exposition of Buddhist scriptures, and not to creative work. There is a possible exception here in the development of the two new Buddhist sects, but it can be argued that this also was a work of arrangement and adaptation rather than a discovery of new religious or metaphysical principles. Certainly Japanese civilization at this stage shows nothing of the originality, the amazing inventiveness, of Chinese life. The difference is very marked; it is as clear as the distinction between talent and genius.

How to account for it is a puzzling and provoking question; perhaps part of the answer is to be found in the nature of the Japanese idiom, which was ill-suited to the expression of abstract ideas and therefore surrendered to the Chinese language, which forced thought into Chinese channels. The effect of Confucian and Buddhist terminology must have been prodigious in shaping and directing the action of the mind.

However this may be, a special feature of Japanese metropolitan culture in the ninth century is the attitude of the Throne towards learning, as revealed in the edict of the Emperor Saga mentioned above, for when he recommends literature he means Chinese literature and when he recommends learning he means Chinese studies. The history of Japan is not in Court society regarded as important or interesting. The statesman and the lawyer must know about Chinese methods of government, past and present. The man of taste and breeding must be familiar with Chinese masterpieces of verse and prose. Most remarkable is the interest of the ruling class in Chinese poetry, which was part of their general interest in literature of all kinds. This is especially true of the Emperors Saga and Junna, for it must be understood that all important literary activities depended upon the approval and encouragement of the sovereign or his spokesman. In the dynastic history of Japan, though the emperor was often stripped of power, the Throne remained throughout the centuries the arbiter of elegance in literature and deportment. It was for such reasons that the compilation of national histories as well as codes of law was looked upon as an essential part of government, performed at the imperial command.

Anthologies of Chinese verse by Japanese poets were not commanded until the time of the Emperor Saga, when we have three celebrated collections: the *Ryōun-shū* (815), the *Bunka shūrei-shū* (ca. 818), and the *Keikoku-shū* (827). No more Chinese collections were made by imperial command after these three. They were followed in 922 by the important *Kokinshū*, which is an anthology of Japanese verse, and it is significant that the greatest of all collections of native poetry, the *Manyōshū*, was completed some time after 750, so that for the space of a century the taste for Chinese poetry seems to have dominated the literary scene. There seems to be no doubt that it was the personal taste of the Emperors Saga and Junna that led to this new kind of fashionable poetical activity. The *Ryōun-shū* was put together at the command of Saga by a group of scholars and connoisseurs, the pieces chosen being submitted to him for final approval. Such collections had been made in China by imperial command from the Six Dynasties onward, and Saga was probably following Chinese precedent. The name Ryōun means "cloud-topping," and it stands for the idea of excellence, as of a dragon rising into the sky. In this work the order of pieces was by the Court rank of the poet, and the collection includes several poems by the Emperor Heizei, as well as by Saga and his younger brother Junna. Then follow verses by the leader of the Fujiwara family and a score of other noble persons.

The two collections that followed were of the same kind. The poems were classified according to subject, and the list (which follows) gives an interesting picture of the range and nature of poetical sentiment:

Banquets	Music
History	Religion (Buddhist ideas)
Partings	Regrets
Sightseeing	Love
Grief	Sending and receiving gifts

This is very like the classification in the great Chinese anthology *Wen Hsüan*, which (as *Monzen*) was well known in Japan in the eighth century and played an important part in the formation of Japanese taste. These three collections of verse in Chinese by Japanese poets arranged by social rank symbolize in a graphic way the contemporary mood of the ruling class, a small group dominated by Chinese standards in literature and philosophy but stubbornly adhering to their own aristocratic outlook.

Signs of luxury and extravagance are visible early in the ninth century and they were offensive to the stern moralists who were guided by Confucian principles but were, as a rule, not powerful enough to impose their purity of conduct upon an idle and pleasure-loving upper class.

Yet it is true that learning was in these days highly respected, as it has been ever since in Japan. In addition to the poetical gifts recorded above, the Emperor Saga was a great calligrapher, Junna was good at cursive script in particular, while the Crown Prince Tsunesada followed in their inky tracks, as well as being a voracious reader. These monarchs were also musicians. They insisted upon careful education for their sons, as we know from the curriculum of the Crown Prince, which included history, Buddhism (both open and mystic), classical Chinese literature, calligraphy, and music, all under the greatest professors of the day. We even have a record of the way in which the Crown Prince formed his script. His brush strokes had the "muscle" of Saga and the "flesh" of Junna.

Courtly historians no doubt exaggerate, but it is clear that the sovereigns set an example which was followed by their Court nobles, who thought it the thing to study Confucianism or Buddhism, or a little of both, with handwriting and music as indispensable graces. Much of their enthusiasm was a matter of fashion, but apart from the compulsion of social rivalry there was plainly a feeling for learning in the air. The tide was flowing in favour of the kind of learning and accomplishment that was prized among the leaders of T'ang society. The system of education laid down in the codes provided for one central college (*daigaku*), which we may call the University, in the capital, with not more than 400 students, and one provincial college (*kokugaku*) in each province, with from twenty to fifty students. The students were to be bright boys of from thirteen to sixteen years of age, from the families of princes and nobles of the fifth rank and upwards, and places were also allotted to members of families of scholars who had traditionally served the state. In the provinces entry was confined to the relatives of district governors (*gunshi*).[6]

There was thus no opportunity here for sons of men of the lowest rank, and though efforts to found private schools were made (by Kūkai and other Buddhist leaders), they had little success. The truth is that, despite much encouragement, there were not enough capable men to teach in the provincial schools; and we learn of men appointed Kuni no Hakase (head of a provincial college) who have reached the age of thirty without taking a degree, some of them nominated after taking a simple reading test. Sometimes men were appointed to provincial colleges, but did not proceed, preferring to draw their salary and stay at home.

But in the capital there was a general enthusiasm. The great clans founded colleges for their young men, in which they resided while attending the University. Thus the Fujiwara (Fuyutsugu) built the Kangaku-in, furnished it with books, and endowed it liberally. In general the treatment of scholars improved and their importance was recognized. We hear of a Great Minister (Fujiwara Otsugu) who resigned

[6] See Appendix III.

because he had not sufficient knowledge of Yin-Yang for the proper performance of his duties. There is even a story that another Fujiwara minister when on horseback dismounted if he met students on the road. Such anecdotes at least show that learning was respected, and (although it can be argued that much of Confucian doctrine was not to Japanese taste) there is no doubt that certain members of the ruling class had persuaded themselves or were persuaded that government must be guided by Confucian principles, and that in private life the law of filial piety must be regarded as the foundation of all morality. This latter belief was so strong that the Emperor Nimmyō paid daily obeisance to his mother, facing north as a subject faces the throne.

The compilation and revision of laws, the writing of commentaries, even the composition of prose and verse, were tasks inspired by Confucian training. The great names of the period include (as well as the poets already mentioned) such jurists as Kiyowara Natsuno, the author of the great Commentary on the Codes (*Ryō no Gige*), and the scholar-statesman Miyoshi Kiyotsura (847–918), who was inspired by Chinese classical learning and antagonistic to Buddhism. Miyoshi is the author of a celebrated memorial calling the attention of the Emperor to current abuses, many of which he ascribes to the greed of the Buddhist clergy, though he does not spare the Court officers or the Shintō priests. He is a good example of the stern, high-minded Confucianist, who is to be found throughout Japanese history calling in Chinese prose for political or social reform.

In estimating the importance of Chinese learning in Japan it must not be overlooked that it was a passport to office. The administrative code (of Yōrō, enforced from 757), in the chapter dealing with appointments and promotions, prescribes as subjects for the qualifying examinations parts of such classical works as the *Chou Li*, the *Tso Chuan*, the *Shih Ching*, the *Analects*, and the *Classic of Filial Piety*. This is the examination for the highest degree. For the ordinary "pass" (*shinshi*) a familiarity with the *Wen Hsüan* is essential, the candidate being required to recite and construe passages from certain set chapters. These rules were similar to those of the Chinese codes, and it is interesting to observe the importance attached to Chinese verse. It appears that the emphasis on the *Wen Hsüan* was such that in both countries a student who had a good knowledge of its contents was said to be halfway to success in the examination.

Although by the time of the *Keikoku-shū* (the last of the three official anthologies of verse in Chinese) the *Wen Hsüan* type of poetry was falling out of favour and the Japanese were beginning to copy the style of contemporary Chinese poets—the great ones of the T'ang era—still the influence of the *Wen Hsüan* lingered. Its antithetical pattern and its conventional ornaments were still admired by the less lively men of letters, and its general flavour even crept into official prose.

CHAPTER VII

REACTION AGAINST CHINESE INFLUENCE

1. *Literature*

A CERTAIN reaction against the influence of Chinese ideas and methods is visible in the revisions of the administrative codes, and the parallel growth of irregular organs, that took place (as we have seen)[1] in the light of practical experience. It was natural that in matters of government the Japanese should wish to solve their own problems in their own way, and without too great a strain upon traditional social habits, which could not be changed by proclamation or ordinance. They did not deliberately cut themselves off from Chinese influence, but a feeling of independence grew as they digested and assimilated the knowledge that they had acquired through intercourse with the mainland. The trend of feeling is well displayed by the history of official missions to China. The first of these was under the leadership of Ono no Imoko, who went to China (to the capital of the Sui emperor) in 607. They continued at fairly regular intervals until 838, when an official (Ono Takamura) refused to take up his appointment as deputy leader of the party then due to leave. There was a growing dislike of these voyages, which were always arduous and often dangerous, to such a point that the poetry of the *Manyōshū* contains many references to the perils which the envoys faced, and prayers for their safe return. It is clear that by 838 the need for these official exchanges had begun to be questioned. The mission of 838 returned in the following year and Takamura, who had been sent into exile as a punishment, was allowed to return to the capital. From that date the missions ceased. In 894, after a lapse of over fifty years, it was proposed to renew them, but the man chosen as ambassador (Sugawara Michizane, one of the great ministers and a celebrated man of letters) asked to be excused, on the ground that conditions in China were most disturbed. This was true; the T'ang dynasty was in decline and its collapse came soon afterwards, in 907.

There were thus good political reasons for ceasing official relations, especially since the private interchange of visits, by monks, scholars, and merchants, was not interrupted. But political reasons were not the only reasons why the Japanese wished to free themselves from Chinese dominance in matters of learning, thought, and taste. Their own culture—thanks, of course, to Chinese example—was now taking shape and gaining substance. It was combining native and borrowed elements in such a way as to form its own distinct character. Perhaps the best

[1] Chapter VI, 3.

illustration of this process is to be found in the field of literature. The importance of Chinese studies did not decline, since the Chinese language remained the key to all treasures of secular and religious learning. But the literary fashion changed, and not long after the issue of the three anthologies of verse in Chinese, which had enjoyed such lofty patronage, taste in high circles began to turn towards the appreciation of poetry in Japanese.

For this development there were some interesting practical, as well as artistic, reasons. Representing Japanese sounds by Chinese characters was very cumbrous, since often a character of many strokes was needed to represent a single syllable. Thanks to a happy invention—simple, like most valuable devices—the Japanese developed an easy and practical syllabary by abbreviating Chinese characters selected to stand for separate Japanese sounds. This syllabary, in its cursive form known as *hiragana*, made it possible to write Japanese words in a running hand that was both intelligible and pleasing to the eye. The encouragement and stimulation thus given to Japanese literature was truly remarkable. Tales and poems and intimate letters could now be written in Japanese, in a style near to everyday speech, by those who had no great knowledge of Chinese, and especially women, whose education was not supposed to include the classics. It is to these circumstances that we owe such important works as *Taketori Monogatari*, a kind of fairy tale that appeared not long after the cessation of missions to China, and the *Kokin-shū*, or "Ancient and Modern Collection," the great anthology of native verse that followed the *Manyōshū*.

It would be a mistake to look for very clear-cut causes for this new movement. It was a natural thing that in course of time there should appear signs of a reaction against Chinese superiority. The new syllabary did not create the new trend, but made a native literature possible, and indeed inevitable, by furnishing a necessary medium of expression. Yet it should not be supposed that Chinese literature went out of favour. There were, it is true, no more collections of verse in Chinese by Japanese poets; but Chinese poetry remained popular, and Po Chü-i in particular was most warmly appreciated in Japan for his easy, flowing, natural style. Indeed Japanese literature contains many references to a collection of his works known as *Hakushi Monjū*. In the classical *Tale of Genji*, when Genji goes into exile, he chooses a few books to take with him; and this is the one which he regards as indispensable. It was the book of verse most admired by men of discrimination and also, it must be added, by men of fashion. Po was widely imitated, and one Japanese writer of the day suggested that enthusiasm for Chinese masters led Japanese poets to copy their weaknesses without their merits, thus revealing in their own work the "lightness" of Yüan Chen and the "commonness" of Po Chü-i, but the talent of neither.

There is something in this charge, but there is no doubt that the great

Chinese poets, and especially those of the T'ang era, exercised a far-reaching and beneficial effect upon Japanese literature, giving it depth and a wider range than it had before. In much Japanese poetry echoes of Chinese masters can be heard, and most critics are agreed that Japanese prose owes something to the sentiment and manner of the Chinese masters whose work was known in Japan in the ninth and tenth centuries. The language of parts of the great romance, the *Tale of Genji*, seems to have been inspired by certain poems of Po Chü-i that were highly esteemed in Japan, notably the well-known "Chōgonka" or "Everlasting Sorrow," which is referred to in the first chapter. It is even said that the whole episode of the Emperor's grief at the death of his beloved mistress Kiritsubo is based upon Po's work, which treats of the death of the beautiful Yang Kuei-fei, mistress of the Emperor of China. At any rate, the writer of the *Genji* likes to show her acquaintance with Chinese literature, though at times she speaks up—who better qualified?—in favour of the native speech, and makes fun of what is pretentious and "Chinesy."

The following passage will give some idea of the movement of her own prose:

Kono goro ake-kure goranzuru Chōgonka no on-ye, Teiji-in no kakashitamaite Ise, Tsurayuki no yomasetamaeru Yamato kotonoha wo mo Morokoshi-uta wo mo tada sono suji wo zo makuragoto ni nasasetamau.

At this time it was His Majesty's wont to examine morning and evening a picture of the Everlasting Sorrow, the text written by Teiji no In with poems by Ise and Tsurayuki, both in Yamato language and in that of the men beyond the sea; and the story of this poem was the common matter of his talk.

(Arthur Waley's translation)

It will be noticed that this passage contains no Chinese words, except for two proper names.

As to such tales as the *Taketori Monogatari* and the *Ise Monogatari*, it is easy to find Chinese works to which they bear some resemblance and from which they perhaps derived. Literary historians work hard at detecting sources, and it should not be difficult for them to prove that all early Japanese prose works owe something to Chinese originals. But the important point here is that the beginnings of a national literature are plainly visible by the end of the ninth century, and thereafter progress is rapid. The classical authors of China retain their immense prestige, and any man of taste and breeding must have at least a superficial acquaintance with their works; but in those slight pieces and in the *Kokinshū* the "Yamato language" has already begun to prove in skilful hands a delicate sensitive instrument for the expression of the native turn of mind.

It is to anticipate a little, but it is convenient to notice here that by the year 1000, when Murasaki was writing her masterpiece, Japanese prose style had come to a classical maturity. It was a style well suited for romances, for intimate diaries and letters, because it was a polished form of contemporary speech in which words of Chinese origin had been naturalized. But it was not adequate for serious practical business and the Chinese language had to be used in official papers, laws and regulations, and works dealing with religious or philosophical matters. To turn from a page of the *Genji* to a collection of historical documents of the same time—such as monastery records, contracts, and inventories—is to enter another world of language, stiff, formal, intelligible only to the eye and not the ear—something quite Chinesy, as Murasaki might say.

Thus the native language had to struggle against a powerful enemy or rival, and its successes testify to the strength of a reaction against Chinese learning, or rather against the pretensions of Chinese scholarship—a reaction that was gathering strength during the ninth century, and reached a climax at its close. It was in belles-lettres that "the Yamato language" was best able to assert its qualities. Chinese, or a blend of Chinese and Japanese in which Chinese elements predominated, continued in use for learned purposes, and its effect upon the intellectual life of Japan was very great. Whether on balance it was beneficial is a moot question; but there can be no doubt that it tended to confine the flow of Japanese intellectual activity within a somewhat narrow channel.

2. *Political and Commercial Relations*

The development of political forms throughout the ninth, tenth, and eleventh centuries may be regarded, from one point of view, as a gradual departure from Chinese models, and the political history of that long period may be summarized by saying that practically all the leading features of the system of government borrowed from China gradually became obsolete, to be displaced by new methods designed to meet new conditions, and at length survived only as empty forms in a feudal society which differed in all its fundamental characteristics from the unworkable scheme of centralized monarchy.

It would not be correct to say that this process of institutional change arose from a conscious and deliberate reaction against Chinese influence. It was rather a natural and inevitable reassertion of Japanese traditional habits of thought and sentiment, which became stronger and stronger as the leaders of Japan gained confidence in their own capacity to conduct their own affairs with the help of the new knowledge and the material benefits which they had obtained through intercourse with China. What was new was their attitude towards China, now moving from the deferential to the respectful and even occasionally critical. One encounters in the literature of this period frequent references to a distinction between "Kara-jie" and "Yamato-damashii," or (one might say) Chinese knowledge and Japanese sense, the latter being a Far Eastern counterpart of esprit gaulois. There is also a celebrated scroll, portraying the adventures in China of one of the early Japanese envoys, the great Kibi no Mabi. The scroll belongs to the thirteenth century, but it evidently rests on a well-based tradition, for it shows how time after time the Japanese with his practical wisdom and his courage and his sharp wits defeats the tricks of the Chinese officials who are trying to humiliate him. He emerges triumphant from this ordeal, having upheld the dignity of his own country at every point.

It must not be supposed, however, that relations with China ceased or diminished in importance. They continued and grew, though with some change of character; and the private and public intercourse of Japanese travellers with T'ang officials, monks, scholars, and merchants is a special feature of Japanese history.

A brief account of diplomatic relations with China, and of the private intercourse of traders and scholars, will serve to make clear the change in the nature of Chinese influence upon Japanese life that took place as time went on from those early days when the leaders of Japan were sitting at the feet of Chinese masters and, naturally enough, were learning with more zeal than discrimination.

Leaving out the pioneer missions of men like Ono no Imoko (607), we may begin with the first embassy after the Taihō reform. This was an official approach to the T'ang emperor in 702; and thereafter a mission left in every reign until the accession of Kammu in 781. In that year the previous mission, which had left in 779, returned to Japan. The despatch of a new mission was delayed for over twenty years owing to the government's preoccupation with the move away from Nara; but missions were resumed in 803, when Fujiwara Kadonomaro was appointed ambassador. He was given a farewell banquet at the palace, where the Emperor (Kammu) drank a toast and recited a verse of his own composition, in which he spoke of

> tairaka ni   the wine in which we drink
> kaerikimase to   to your safe return.
> iwaitaru sake

The envoy and his party were in need of such good wishes, for their voyage began with misfortunes. They set sail in May, but met with storms, in which their four ships were badly damaged and some members were drowned. The damage was repaired and the ships made a new start in 804, carrying among their passengers the two great religious leaders, Saichō and Kūkai, who were then young men of promise. This mission was blown off its course, and two vessels fell out. The other two reached China, but separately. The first, the envoy's ship, reached the coast of Fukien instead of the Yangtze estuary as had been intended.

After some trouble and delay its passengers were escorted overland to the capital at Ch'ang-an, where they were met by a Chinese ambassador early in 805.

This was the last year of the T'ang Emperor Te-tsung, who died shortly after receiving Kadonomaro. Because of Court mourning the Japanese mission withdrew and sailed for home in 805. Kadonomaro's vessel reached Tsushima safely, and the companion vessel found its way to Matsuura in Kyūshū, but was lost on the next stage of its voyage. From Tsushima Kadonomaro sent news of conditions in China, where the T'ang dynasty was showing signs of weakness in the face of risings by border people and the insubordination of high military officers. In the year of Kadonomaro's return a special mission was despatched to the Court of the new emperor, with orders to return without delay.

The years following these missions—the reigns of Heizei, Saga, and Junna—were times of a feeling of friendship for China and a great enthusiasm for Chinese literature; but there were no more missions, doubtless because the reports of both official and private travellers described insurrections against the T'ang rulers, and these were amply confirmed by Chinese refugees coming to Japan by way of Silla.

After the accession of Nimmyō in 833 a new envoy was appointed, in the person of Fujiwara Tsunetsugu, with Ono Takamura as deputy. This was twenty-nine years after the previous mission, and it appears that its purpose was not to promote amity but to acquire Chinese books, pictures, and articles of luxury like perfumes, since the new emperor had a taste for good things, and his near predecessors were still alive, enjoying an elegant retirement. But they were to be disappointed, for despite elaborate preparations this mission also met with misfortunes.

A full mission usually included the ambassador, his deputy, an official staff of secretaries, interpreters and shipwrights, a number of returning Chinese (monks as a rule), and also Japanese going to China to study medicine, divination (yin-yang), writing, music, astronomy, calendar-making, and kindred matters. The total number of persons carried was— as on this occasion—as high as 600. The expedition was not ready to sail until 836; and before this the Court ordered prayers at the Kitano shrine to all the national gods without exception. Promotion in rank was notified to the tombs of officials who had lost their lives on previous missions, in an effort to dissuade their spirits from any thought of vengeful action.

But this mission also met with severe losses, and had to return to Japan to re-equip its surviving vessels. Repeated efforts were made to induce the leaders to sail again, but they were reluctant and quarrelsome; and it was not until the summer of 838, nearly five years after the appointment of Tsunetsugu, that he sailed from Kyūshū for China, then under the rule of the Emperor Wen Tsung. His deputy Ono Takamura, who felt that he had been badly treated by Tsunetsugu, stayed behind and wrote a satirical poem about missions to China. The Emperor an-

grily ordered him to be strangled for disobedience to the imperial command, but he was let off with a sentence of exile. Tsunetsugu for his
part had a difficult time getting back from China. He travelled by way
of Korea, and chartered Korean vessels, which he thought more sea-
worthy than those of Japanese build, no doubt with good reasons, for
the Koreans seem always to have been more skilled in maritime matters
than the Japanese. Tsunetsugu reached Japan in 839, and died in the
following year.

These calamities made the missions so unpopular that there was no
great opposition when it was decided to cease sending them; and Takamura was pardoned and returned to the capital. From 630 to 838 there
had been nineteen appointments to the post of envoy to China, but in
that period only twelve missions entered China.

The chief impulse towards communication with China was the desire
for knowledge, religious, philosophical, and, in a lesser degree, technical.
The demand for Chinese goods was limited. The Court was much interested in certain Chinese products, and in 874–75 sent a special trade
mission to China to purchase incense, perfumes, and medicines. The
government endeavoured to exercise some control over the disposal of
articles imported from China. The trading ships frequently touched
first at a point in Kyūshū on their return voyage. They were not permitted to sell their cargo to the first comer; for it was laid down under
severe penalties in the codes—in that portion dealing with markets' and
barriers (octroi)—that officials must have first choice before private
buyers. In practice, however, these rules were not obeyed. As soon as
news of the arrival of a ship at the Kyūshū port of entry reached the
capital, nobles and other rich persons sent emissaries who bought what
they wanted at auction, before the arrival of government officials. The
desire for Chinese goods and curiosities, including books, was so great
that the officials were helpless. The chief objects of trade were scrolls
(of sutras or classical Chinese works), Buddhist images and paintings,
temple furnishings, books of verse and prose, drugs, incense, and perfume.

It was mainly a luxury trade, stimulated by the fashion for Chinese
things of all kinds. It involved close relations with traders from Silla,
but the Japanese were loth to open diplomatic relations with that country. They suspected it of sinister designs and they knew that the defences of Kyūshū were weak, because the system of military service was
a hopeless failure. It is difficult to understand the unconcerned attitude
of the Court, for although it is not likely that Silla (then on the point
of collapse as a state) had any thought of invading Japan, there were
continuous piratical raids on the Japanese coast, and the countermeas-
ures taken were absurdly inadequate. One is continually surprised in
studying the records of this period to find how soft and unwarlike the
metropolitan ruling class had become. In 870, for instance, there is a

public announcement that, although the defences are poor, Japan is the country of the Gods, and that if prayers are addressed to them pirates will be deterred from approaching her shores. Even a proposal to exclude Koreans from Japan was not approved, because it was the "kingly attitude" to treat refugees and castaways with compassion.

When in 894 it was proposed to resume diplomatic relations with China and to send Sugawara Michizane and Ki Haseo as envoys, the plan was dropped on the ground that conditions in China were disturbed. There were other reasons, of a personal nature, why these two men did not wish to leave Japan at that time; but it was true that the T'ang dynasty was declining and this was a genuine cause for alarm, for despite the remote situation of Japan and the somewhat tenuous nature of her relations with the mainland, political vicissitudes in China have always exercised an influence upon the course of events in Japan, if only in an indirect fashion.

The T'ang dynasty had already begun to show some signs of weakness by the middle of the eighth century, in the face of pressure from frontier peoples (such as the Uighurs and Khitans) and disloyalty at home; but these troubles were overcome and the great structure remained stable and impressive for another hundred years or more. It was not until about 900 that it collapsed, and from the fall of the T'ang it was another fifty years until China was again unified, under the Sung dynasty. In this interval disorder prevailed in the border states—Manchuria and Korea to the north—and Chinese power ebbed. When order was being established, advances were made by the Chinese, and official envoys arrived in Japan from Chekiang in 945; they were reluctantly received, and not encouraged. Even when the Sung dynasty was established and made advances to Japan, the Japanese Court remained suspicious and responded only with reluctance.

Chinese prestige had no doubt fallen in Japan and Japanese self-confidence had grown; so that while intercourse with China did not diminish and Chinese influence in matters of learning and religion continued strong, by the close of the ninth century the leaders of Japan were exercising a degree of critical discrimination in their attitude to the culture of the mainland.

It is interesting that it was the Chinese who took the initiative in the renewal of official relations. In trade also it was the Chinese who approached Japan. There was much going and coming of Sung ships; some captains pretended that they had been blown towards Japan by strong winds. Japanese subjects were forbidden to leave, but an exception was made for certain monks sent to China for study.

Thus Chōnen, a Fujiwara, a monk of the Kōfukuji, was given gold by the Court, and by the retired Emperor Uda, so that he could travel to China for study at Wutaishan and then make a pilgrimage to India to follow the traces of the Buddha. He had an audience with the Sung

Emperor T'ai Tsung in 984, and presented His Majesty with valuable books, including a genealogy of the Japanese imperial family. According to the Chinese chronicles the Emperor was much impressed by the stability of the Japanese government, and expressed a liking for the hereditary principle—a not unnatural preference in one of the founders of a dynasty.

Chinese monks visiting Japan were also well treated by the Japanese Court, and in general it may be said that, even when political relations between the two countries were uneasy, cultural intercourse was not interrupted. For example, although no official envoys were sent to the Chinese Court after 838, many merchants and monks travelled to China and a fair number of Chinese laymen and monks, especially of the Tendai sect, crossed over to Japan. Thus in one ship in 848 a Chinese traveller named Chang Yu-hsin took passage to Japan with thirty others. In general there was more going and coming than heretofore, since conditions of travel by sea to China had much improved by the middle of the ninth century and trading vessels from China now made frequent visits to Japanese harbours.[2] Better ships were being built in China. Conditions of sea travel improved, partly because more had been learned about seasonal winds and partly because relations with Silla were now such that Japanese could take advantage of Korean ships, which were better built and better handled than their own, and made regular voyages to China on behalf of Silla merchants residing there. The Japanese recognized the superiority of Korean shipbuilding, as we know from Tsunetsugu's choice and also from orders sent in 839 by the Court instructing Kyūshū to build a "Silla ship" to stand up to storms.

It is evident that the Japanese were backward in maritime knowledge. Experienced navigators agree that there is no regularity in the direction of the winds off the coasts of Japan, and this would explain why, unable to rely upon known "prevailing" winds, the ships which took the direct route from Kyūshū to central China made the land at many different points, from the Yangtze estuary southwards as far as the Fukien coast and even the vicinity of Canton. But apart from these difficulties there was a definite lag in the technology of building, rigging, and navigating sailing craft, which can perhaps be explained by the location of the central government in the middle of farmlands and away from the seacoast. Interest in overseas trade was secondary, and not a matter of vital importance to an agrarian society occupied in develop-

[2] Early Japanese embassies had gone along the west coast of Korea and then across to Shantung. But with the embassy of 702 they began to cross direct from Kyūshū to central China, this being the shortest route and also the most convenient, because upon arrival it offered better communication with inland destinations, thanks to the Grand Canal system. At that time it was a very dangerous route, and was only taken because of the hostility of the kingdom of Silla, which dominated the west coast of Korea after the withdrawal of Japanese forces in 662. By the ninth century the picture had changed.

ing its own soil. The early developments of shipbuilding in Japan seem to have been governed by the needs of coastal traffic in fairly sheltered waters and of piratical raids rather than regular trade.

It is perhaps significant that for our knowledge of conditions on voyages to China in the ninth century we depend largely upon the work of a celebrated Buddhist monk, Ennin (later known as Jikaku Daishi), whose *Nittō Gubō Junreiki* ("Record of Pilgrimage to China in Search of the Holy Law") is full of fascinating detail of his adventures, from 838, when he sailed from Japan as a member of Tsunetsugu's embassy, until 847, when he returned to Japan after much travel and hardship on sea and land.

CHAPTER VIII

THE FUJIWARA REGENTS

1. *Political Rivalries—The Throne and the Clans, 794–967*

THE DEVELOPMENT of a form of government in which full sovereign power is exercised on a virtually hereditary basis by members of a great family acting as Regents is characteristic of Japanese political evolution during the three centuries under review. It therefore deserves some study as an aspect of the general history of institutions, and it also is of great interest because of the nature of the society which came into being under the dominance of successive leaders of the Fujiwara clan.

Their rise was gradual. Although members of the Fujiwara family were influential during the reigns of the early sovereigns after the move to the new capital in 794, they did not attain a truly commanding position in the state until they had settled differences within their own clan (which had several branches), and had disposed of possible rivals in the person of leaders of other prominent families, notably the Kiyowara, Tachibana, Ki, and Miyoshi, families that could claim distinguished ancestry and even, in some cases, imperial connexions.

There were four branches of the Fujiwara clan, founded by the four sons of Fubito (659–720), son of the Great Minister Kamatari, who had been given the name of Fujiwara in 669, the year of his death. By the middle of the ninth century the Northern Branch (Hokke) had outstripped the others in political power and wealth. Members of the other branches either moved to the provinces, where they became warriors, or remained in the capital as minor bureaucrats. Fujiwara daughters were married into the royal family already in the Nara period. The empress was in antiquity supposed to be of royal blood, but the Emperor Shōmu was married to Fubito's third daughter, who became in her turn the Empress Kōmyō.

As a rule the Fujiwara achieved their ends not by violence but by the relentless use of political pressure, which they were able to apply because of their matrimonial relations with the Throne or by means of their great wealth and consequent influence in the provinces, where their estates multiplied rapidly. They were very well aware of the importance of land as the foundation of power; and their domains grew because they could afford protection to small landowning families who would "commend" their fields to Fujiwara manorial lords. Land is the key to political history in Japan, at almost every point.

The first Fujiwara to act as Regent was Yoshifusa, who married a daughter of the Emperor Saga. He conducted affairs of state from 858 to 872 as "Sesshō" (a term equivalent to Regent for a minor), the sovereign at that time being Seiwa, who was enthroned at the age of nine.

Seiwa, it should be noted, was the first child emperor, and the first male sovereign to be placed under the tutelage of a Regent. Moreover, Yoshifusa was the first Regent not of the blood royal.

Yoshifusa was succeeded by his nephew Mototsune, who was Regent during the minority of Yōzei, and continued as Kampaku, or Civil Dictator, until his death in 891. This was an office which, unlike the true Regency (the office of Sesshō), was not confined to periods of minority or other incapacity. It was a real dictatorship, the Kampaku issuing commands as if he were the emperor, on whose behalf he was supposed to speak. Mototsune was a man of considerable talent and strength of character. He may be regarded as the first of the great Fujiwara autocrats. His rise was rapid. It is interesting to note that he was secretary of the Kurando-dokoro when the young Emperor Seiwa was enthroned in 858, for this was a post which gave great political advantage to its holder. In 877, on the accession of Yōzei, a minor, the abdicating Emperor Seiwa ordered Mototsune to continue as Regent.[1]

Mototsune had difficulties with Yōzei, who was insane and criminal. He withdrew as a gesture of disapproval but presently returned to office and endeavoured to purge the Court of some of its most undesirable elements. Yōzei was forced to abdicate in 884, at the age of seventeen, and was succeeded by an elderly monarch who left all acts of government to Mototsune. In 887 this Emperor died, and for want of other issue was succeeded by a prince who, very exceptionally, was not the son of a Fujiwara mother. He reigned as the Emperor Uda from 887 to 897. He did not like Mototsune's high-handed conduct. Mototsune had been made Kampaku in 880, and Uda, while "ordering" him to continue in that office, resented the Fujiwara dictatorship and manoeuvred against him in various ways. But Mototsune was a master of political and social strategy, and the Emperor Uda had to give way. Mototsune retained his title and power as Kampaku until his death in 891. This trial of strength was necessary for the prestige of the Fujiwara house, since the Emperor Uda had obtained the support of certain families which resented the dominance of the Regent's clan. These included a Tachibana, a Minamoto, and the celebrated Sugawara Michizane, whose downfall became necessary to the Fujiwara cause.

After Mototsune's death no new appointment to the post of Kampaku was made, his eldest son Tokihira being then in his twenty-first year; and for a short time it looked as if the imperial family had driven out the dictators.

---

[1] In the following text, "Regent" is used to indicate both Sesshō and Kampaku, a distinction being made only when it seems necessary.

Reigns of Titular Emperors during Period of Fujiwara Regents
Yoshifusa to Michinaga, 858–1016

Seiwa	858–876	Murakami	946–967
Yōzei	877–884	Reizei	967–969
Kōkō	884–887	Enyū	969–984
Uda	887–897	Kazan	984–986
Daigo	897–930	Ichijō	986–1011
Suzaku	930–946	Sanjō	1011–1016

List of Fujiwara Regents, 858–1184

	Sesshō	Kampaku
Yoshifusa (804–872)	857–872	—
Mototsune (836–891)	873–880	880–891
Tadahira (880–949)	930–941	941–949
Saneyori (900–970)	969–970	967–969
Koretada (924–972)	970–972	—
Kanemichi (925–977)	—	972–977
Yoritada (924–989)	—	977–986
Kaneiye (929–990)	986–990	990
Michitaka (957–995)	990–993	993–995
Michikane (961–995)	—	995
Michinaga (966–1027)	1016–1017	[996–1017]*
Yorimichi (992–1074)	1017–1019	1019–1068
Norimichi (996–1075)	—	1068–1075
Morozane (1042–1101)	1086–1090	1075–1086; 1090–1094
Moromichi (1062–1099)	—	1094–1099
Tadazane (1078–1162)	1107–1113	1105–1107; 1113–1121
Tadamichi (1097–1164)	1123–1129; 1141–1150	1121–1123; 1129–1141; 1150–1158
Motozane (1143–1166)	1165–1166	1158–1165
Motofusa (1144–1230)	1166–1172	1172–1179
Motomichi (1160–1233)	1180–1183; 1184–1186	1179–1180
Moroiye (1172–1238)	1183–1184	—

* Michinaga began to hold high ministerial posts in 995. He was never appointed Kampaku, but by 996 he was so firmly established in power that he was Regent in everything but name. He was confidential adviser to the sovereign, with the honorary title of Nairan; and he was Chieftain of the Fujiwara clan.

The young Emperor managed to rule alone, with the advice of men like Miyoshi and Sugawara. He abdicated in 897, at the early age of thirty-one, to be succeeded by his son, the thirteen-year-old Emperor Daigo, who also managed to rule for a time without appointing a Regent or a Kampaku, depending upon the advice of Michizane and others. But these men were not strong enough, or capable enough, to keep the Fujiwara family out of the key posts in government. In 899 Fujiwara Tokihira was appointed Minister of the Left (Sadaijin), and Michizane had to be content with the junior post of Minister of the Right (Udaijin). Before long Michizane was in exile in Kyūshū, where he is said to have died of a broken heart in 903. Ki Haseo was awarded a sinecure at the Tōdaiji monastery in Nara, while Miyoshi gave lectures on Chinese history and otherwise devoted himself to scholastic rather than political activity.

Tokihira did not assume the title of Regent, but he ruled the country. Thereafter the Fujiwara were firmly established, and successive Fujiwara dictators, usually the Chieftains of the clan (Uji no Chōja), were to be the real rulers of Japan until about 1068, when their power began to decline. Some of them were really talented men, and all of them could rely upon the solid backing of the most powerful family in the empire.

There was no Regent or Dictator after Mototsune's death in 891 until 930, when Tokihira's brother Tadahira succeeded him and was first Sesshō and then Kampaku until 949. There was a short space during which neither office was filled, but Fujiwara dominance was not in fact interrupted. In the centuries from about 850 to the final collapse of the political authority of the clan in 1167 all the important offices of state were held by bearers of the Fujiwara name; and in the list of ministers and high Court functionaries only by exception does there appear here and there the name of a Minamoto or some other historical patronym.

It is not easy to account fully for the success of this family. It is true that they held a position of great advantage in that their daughters regularly married into the imperial family, and as a rule a Regent was uncle or father-in-law or grandfather to the occupant of the throne, or father of the sovereign's second consort or favourite. Yet they (or many of them) appear not to have been moved solely by vain personal ambition, but to have truly wished to guide the monarchy in the interest of the state. Their feeling of solidarity was strong (despite some internecine quarrels) and family pride gave them a powerful weapon and shield in dealing with a divided and inexperienced opposition. It may be added that, whether by natural or by artificial selection, they seem generally to have produced the kind of capable man the times demanded. The political tradition followed, or one might say created, by the Fujiwara Regents—the clan loyalty, the patronage, the devotion to persons rather than principles—played an important part in later history, and therefore, though their power and riches in the course of time declined and came to dust, it seems proper to discuss their successes and their failures at some length. Japanese political thought has been formed by habit rather than by reasoning, and some study of the sentiment of a ruling caste will perhaps be profitable.

There is an interesting document, known as the Kampyō Testament (*Kampyō Go-Yuikai*) which was composed during the Kampyō era (889–98) by the Emperor Uda. It is a paper of advice addressed to his successor, in whose favour he abdicated. It includes an appreciation of the talents of such statesmen as Fujiwara Tokihira, Sugawara Michizane, Ki Haseo, and Miyoshi Kiyotsura, who frequently figure in the history of his reign. He tells where he went wrong in his policy and expresses some resentment at Mototsune's harshness; but though he clearly wished to promote Michizane so as to counteract Fujiwara influence, he gives praise, perhaps a little grudgingly, to Tokihira, whom he recommends to the young Emperor Daigo as an adviser of great wisdom in political matters. At the same time he speaks highly of the loyalty of Michizane, the scholarship of Ki, and the virtues of other supporters of the Imperial House.

In a general account of the problems which will confront his successor, he pays most attention to the appointment of officials at Court and in government; their rewards and promotions; the collection of revenue from tax; the proper scale of living for the Vestals of Ise and Kamo, the two great Shintō shrines most closely connected with the Ruling House; the care of palace property; and certain questions of ceremonial and the conduct of palace affairs, including the rank and precedence of officers of the Guards.

Most of what he says is concerned with the private affairs of the sovereign. He enjoins caution upon his successor on occasions when the emperor appears in public, recommends that he display neither pleasure nor anger in the expression of his face, and in general sets up a strict standard of personal conduct. There is nothing about problems of government as seen from a national point of view; and it is therefore not surprising that the leaders of great clans like the Fujiwara should have thought it right to intervene on a large scale in state business, and should have come to believe that their private interest and the public interest were identical.

Nevertheless the whole document displays a strong sense of the importance of right behaviour, of the moral duties of a prince. In general it enjoins simplicity, a modest rule of life, strict attention to affairs of state, and consultation with loyal and capable ministers. In his turn, the Emperor Daigo, to whom this advice was given, left behind him certain rules of conduct which show that he also had a high standard of behaviour. They include such rules as:

—Do not drink much wine

—In conversation confine your speech to what is necessary for your purpose

—In your household do not discuss before others private affairs, questions of right and wrong conduct, money matters, etc.

—Control your temper

—Avoid bad company; do not make friends of noisy, turbulent people

—In all matters, from your dress to your carriage and horses, seek what is of practical value and not what is ornamental.

Documents of this kind are not exceptional, for it was the custom of testators to bequeath advice.

The chronicles and diaries of the time do not on the whole confirm the impression of a frivolous, loose-living society of aristocrats which may be gained from too exclusive a study of the romantic literature of the tenth and eleventh centuries. No doubt there were a great many gay young courtiers addicted to amorous adventures; but there seem to have been a compensating number of grave and industrious officials, men who were diligent in performing their ceremonial duties, scribbling their memoranda, issuing their orders and despatches, men steeped in official routine. As for the great ministers who presided over the departments of state, they were as a rule hard-working men. Typical of this kind was the Senior Minister (Sadaijin) Fujiwara Otsugu, who died in 843 at the age of seventy, after a long official career. He had served longest in the arduous post of Inspector of the Northern Provinces, in which capacity he was energetic in measures designed to increase production and reduce expenditure.

Tokihira in popular historical accounts figures as a ruthless dictator, who drove his rival Michizane to exile and misery; but he was in point of fact a vigorous, practical administrator who saw very clearly the need for a reform of provincial government, which was without doubt the most urgent task of the day.[2] He was not a man of elegant literary accomplishments, but an energetic statesman who stirred things up and made enemies, both at Court, where he tried to enforce a simpler habit of life, and in the countryside, where he endeavoured to curb the power of the great landowners. When he was the senior statesman under Daigo, from 897 to 909, he was extremely well-informed about local conditions. He caused the issue of a series of edicts which, had they been enforced, would have struck a death blow at the privileges of great nobles and monasteries as lords of tax-free domains. They are proof that he saw clearly the nature of the troubles that were eroding the power of the central government and destroying its financial strength.

---

[2] The legend of Michizane's ill treatment and his unhappiness in exile is one which appeals to Japanese sentiment. He is still regarded as a kind of martyr and worshipped as the god of calligraphy. But it is doubtful whether his banishment was so unjust or such a loss to the state as is usually supposed.

His efforts were not in general successful, but there are traces of his reforms in certain temporary improvements, such as a partial revival of the system of allotment lands and some diminution in the confiscations of public land by private notables.

The successors of Tokihira, his brothers Tadahira (as Regent) and Nakahira (as Senior Minister) lacked his strength of character. They were unable to cope with the disasters which seemed to threaten the state from all quarters. Indeed it is doubtful whether the most resolute statesman could have found remedies for the troubles of the time. The country was in a most disturbed state, rebellion threatening in the provinces and banditry rife everywhere. The capital itself was in a sad condition, for robbers even entered the Imperial Palace and the Guards were obliged to patrol the whole city at night.

Chief among the rebels was Masakado, a chieftain of the Taira family, holding large estates in the eastern provinces of Shimōsa and Hitachi. Greedy for land and power, he struggled with his kinsfolk from 935; but he had greater ambitions and in 940 even declared himself Emperor in a letter to the Prime Minister Tokihira. For a time he had virtual control of eight eastern provinces; but after a struggle that lasted for about five years he was defeated on the Shimōsa border in 940, when the forces of his allies (said to number 8,000) failed to come to his support.

At about the same time a warrior chieftain in western Japan named Sumitomo got together a thousand or more small craft and plundered all along the shores of the Inland Sea, especially in the province of Iyo, where he had once been governor, and where he chose to settle rather than return to the capital at the end of his term. His depredations extended to Sanuki, Suwo, and northern Kyūshū; and it may be noticed here that local disturbances were common in all provinces, especially those whose governors were weak and unable to settle disputes about property.

Sumitomo was finally defeated in 941. At about this time there was also trouble in Dewa province, in the north, an uprising of "pacified" Emishi, who did much damage to the property of Japanese settlers. All these calamities caused great distress to the government; and when Sumitomo was at length subdued, the Emperor proceeded in person to the Kamo shrine for thanksgiving. Prayers for the dead, both loyal troops and rebels, were also offered at a great service in the Enryakuji monastery, which was now spreading over the flanks of Mount Hiyei, the mountain that overlooks the capital city. The text of some of these prayers has been preserved. One of them says that both loyal and rebel warriors were subjects of His Majesty, who wished all feelings of hatred to be sunk in a common desire for the well-being of all sufferers.

The Emperor was right to pray for harmony among his people, who were given to violence and insubordinate behaviour. But neither he nor his Fujiwara advisers could foresee that the loyal provincial warriors who had suppressed such rebels as Masakado and Sumitomo were one day to develop, as guardians of the peace, a degree of military strength that could be used as a threat to the civil power. It was the greatest leaders of those warrior families who, as the civil power weakened, were to save the country from anarchy, by the founding of a strong feudal dynasty committed to firm government and the suppression of disorder. This was to come only as the termination of a long process, during which the Fujiwara family was to rise and fall as the warrior clans struggled among themselves to inherit its wealth and its political authority. For a century or more after the suppression of Masakado the Fujiwara remained supreme. The warriors were content for the time being to be the "claws and teeth" of the civil autocrats, under whose rule and patronage the metropolitan culture of the eleventh century, and part of the twelfth, grew in elegance and refinement, nourished the fine arts, and saw remarkable developments in religious life.

It may well be asked how such capable men as these Fujiwara dictators could rest content with dominating a small society of Court nobles when the affairs of the whole nation so clearly called for the efforts of experienced and determined statesmen. The early Fujiwara were, as we have seen, hard-working public men; but once the clan had broken the power of its great rivals its leaders evidently found that to dominate emperors, to manipulate and coerce a jealous aristocracy, and so to further Fujiwara private interests was more interesting, more absorbing, and more profitable than the commonplace routine of government business.

Their general aim and purpose was to increase the wealth of their family. This they might have achieved by administrative competence; but the refinement of intrigue, the weighing and balancing of character and motive, the constant interplay of personality, the game of skill with living pieces, is to a certain temperament a more fascinating exercise of talent than is called for by passing laws and supervising a herd of civil servants. It requires a delicacy of perception, a sensitiveness to fine shades of behaviour, and a superb confidence, which, when used for deliberate ends, can be a source of aesthetic pleasure, of epicurean delight. Indeed it is in this feeling for the most subtle points of human relations that one can perhaps find a key to that unique society of which we get a glimpse, or rather a partial revelation, in the diaries and romances of the early eleventh century, notably the *Makura no Sōshi* and the *Tale of Genji*. It is a society governed less by a rule of conduct than by a rule of taste.

Of all the phenomena in the social history of Japan this is perhaps the one which most deserves attention, for it has no very close counterpart in other times or places.

An account in general terms of the political background may help to place this society in its proper setting. Reading descriptions of life at the capital, one might suppose that with the suppression of such rebellions as those of Masakado and Sumitomo the country had entered upon an era of peace. And it is true that the chronicles of a subsequent era refer to the periods of Engi and Tenryaku, say from 900 to 950, as a kind of golden age. But it seems that it was golden only by contrast with the more debased and delinquent society of the later part of the century.

Our evidence is rather strong. It consists of a great number of edicts and orders which, since they are repeated at brief intervals, show that the government was struggling in vain to correct the manifest evils of the day. There are also two celebrated documents, preserved as masterpieces of style and monuments of failure, in which two statesmen implore the Throne to reform a number of current abuses which they describe in lofty language. The first is the Memorial or Statement of Opinion ("Iken Fūji") of 914 by a distinguished Confucian scholar, Miyoshi Kiyotsura,[3] who after a career as professor of literature, provincial governor, Rector of the University, and then State Counsellor died in 919 at the age of seventy-one while still in office. He was evidently a man of great attainments and high character, who held very strong views and did not hesitate to express them. His memorial is a rather long and detailed account of the gradual deterioration of public finances and the decay of morality among the ruling class which, he alleges, has been continuous since the introduction of Buddhism. He deplores the growth of luxury and the extravagance of expenditure, and in balanced prose he describes the growing poverty of the whole nation, which he ascribes to a capricious taste for luxuries. "Each day brought a change in costume, each month a change in fashion. Bedrooms and nightdresses were more beautiful, banquets and dancing more frequent, than ever before. In this way half the entire revenue was expended. And so the treasury became empty and taxes were increased."

This kind of all-round condemnation leaves out part of the picture, no doubt. It does not describe the life of the virtuous and diligent citizen; and indeed Kiyotsura himself admits that he is as one looking at a leopard through a tube, who can see only one spot and not the whole animal. But there is plenty to substantiate the picture which he paints, and there is a special interest in his Confucian contempt for the corrupt and lazy lives of Buddhist priests, Shintō functionaries, and certain Court officers. In his recommendations he entreats the sovereign to regulate dress in accordance with the rank of the wearer, and to order the metropolitan police headquarters to see to it that his edicts are enforced. He also has some interesting things to say about education. He explains how the University has lost revenue by being deprived of its rice lands, and shows that the standard of learning is very low. Average

---

[3] Also called Kiyoyuki.

students have no chance, and in the country you find "snowy-haired students starving on the green banks of a river," so that the University has come to be looked upon as a place of disappointment, the birthplace of hunger and poverty. Parents do not any longer want their sons to enroll, the quadrangles are overrun with wild grass, the lecture halls are silent. The professors do not trouble to read the papers of candidates, but make recommendations merely by glancing at a list of students.

The second memorial to the Throne, that of Sugawara Fumitoki, is shorter. It is dated 954, but it attacks the same abuses as those which had distressed Kiyotsura forty years before. He criticizes lower-class as well as upper-class people for wasting their money building palaces and monasteries, or acquiring extravagant costumes and rare and costly objects of luxury. He pleads that people of high rank should lead the way to simplicity. He deplores the sale of offices, and other kinds of disloyal and dishonest conduct. He does not, as Kiyotsura did, make definite suggestions for suppressing the bad behaviour of which he complains, though in a general way he recommends the encouragement of learning as a means toward spreading virtuous ideas. Some positive steps were taken by the government, such as the issue of a number of sumptuary rules which the police were told to enforce. Thus when Kiyotsura begged the Court to see that its rules about the use of pattern and colour in garments were obeyed, an order was promptly issued limiting the use of certain dyes, notably the scarlet "beni," a very expensive vegetable colour; and nobody paid attention to the embargo.

The interest of these documents lies not so much in their importance as evidence of economic conditions—there is plenty of exact detail in more matter-of-fact records of taxation, prices, land rents, currency, and so forth—but in the conflict between a soft view of life and a hard view of life which is brought out by a comparison between the pleasure-loving society of Court nobles and the earnest Confucian doctors, given to high learning and frugal living.

And it is also of interest to notice that, as the central government finds itself less and less able to preserve order, the occupant of the throne, while remaining the fountain of honour, becomes less and less the upholder of law and the source of armed authority. He is looked upon as the protector of learning, the guardian of a ceremonial tradition that is wearing thin. The sovereigns during the tenth century were principally concerned with the promotion of great literary undertakings, including compilations of laws and precedents (such as the kyaku and shiki already mentioned), compilations of history (notably the Sandai Jitsuroku, the last of the six national chronicles), and anthologies, of which the most celebrated is the Kokin Wakashū, or collection of Ancient and Modern Poems, the second of the great treasuries of verse. One of the important literary monuments of Japan, it was compiled at

5

the command of the Throne by a board including Ki Tsurayuki, himself a distinguished writer, who contributed a translation in Japanese of a preface (by Yakamochi) in Chinese discussing the nature of poetry and the style of different poets. The Japanese version is still regarded as a masterpiece.

These were days indeed when the Imperial City was crowded with culture, as is shown by a series of memorials to the Throne by a scholar named Ōye Masahira (952–1012). Born in a distinguished family of scholars, he was the most learned Confucianist of his day, and a poet of more than usual felicity. A child prodigy, after a brilliant career at the university, he passed the highest examinations and was given a modest appointment in the civil service. He lectured on Chinese classics to the Emperor and was tutor to the Heir Apparent. He was appointed (1010) Court Chamberlain and named deputy governor of several provinces in turn. At his death he had reached the senior grade of the lower fourth rank, an unusual honour for a man of his class. Indeed his record was exceptionally fortunate for a literatus not of Fujiwara birth. But he was dissatisfied, and he has left a poem which reveals his sense of grievance. It runs:

Kawafune ni	In the river boat
Norite kokoro no	I ride along
Yuku toki wa	With mind at ease.
Shizumeru mi to mo	Who would think of me
Omoenu ka na?	As a man of sunken hopes?

His frequent memorials set forth the disappointments, the thwarted ambitions, to which these lines refer. He cites Chinese and Japanese precedents for promoting scholars to high official posts and urges that his obscurity is a slur upon Chinese learning and Confucian principles. He goes on to say: "Our present government conforms in all respects to the ancient usages of the Engi period. Letters flourish, rewards and punishments are discriminating, and the sovereign is joyously admired by his subjects. Yet Masahira, who has made literature his vocation, is impoverished and old, although the positions in which he has served qualify him for promotion to a governorship," and so forth, as is the habit of aggrieved civil servants.

His failure to rise to higher office may have been due to lack of support from Fujiwara ministers. But he seems to have been an odd character, crotchety and friendless. A small ray of light is thrown upon his behaviour by an incident recorded in a contemporary diary under a date in January 985, which tells us that he had a finger cut off by an enemy who attacked him with a sword. It was discovered that the assailant was an officer of the palace guard, a Fujiwara named Nariaki. Nothing more is known of the affair, except that Nariaki is said to have been arrested and executed some weeks after the event. No explanation has been offered of this attack, though it has been suggested that some question of gallantry was involved, since Masahira's poems include many stanzas addressed to different ladies. This would not be inconsistent with the social manners of the day, for the life of many members of the educated class seems to have been almost equally divided between literature and love.

The point of historical interest in this anecdote is the reason for Nariaki's punishment. He seems to have been executed not because he attacked a respectable official, but on the more general ground that the Fujiwara leaders were firmly opposed to bloodshed of any kind. They did not believe in violent solutions. They achieved their own ends by planning and persuasion, and here they were prudent as well as moderate, for once they admitted the argument of force their own supremacy would be shattered. They favoured civilian virtues and were impressed by scholarship so long as scholars did not seek political advancement.

It is hardly necessary to add that two of the greatest classical works in the whole history of Japanese literature belong to this period, this fin-de-siècle when the arts flourished and government declined; for Murasaki Shikibu was gathering material for her *Tale of Genji* at the close of the tenth century, and her contemporary Sei Shōnagon was also observing life from the point of view of a lady-in-waiting at the Imperial Court, and preparing to make pungent observations about people she knew and things they did.

2. *The Decline of Imperial Authority*

So far we have not examined the economic or, more specifically, the fiscal aspects of the decline in the authority of the Throne which is the most prominent feature of the political history of the middle ages in Japan—let us say of the stretch of time from 900 to 1200, by which date the effective governing power had been usurped and exercised by military dictators. It will be necessary to treat this question in some detail if we are to understand the history of Japan during those difficult and eventful three centuries. For the moment, however, it will be enough to give a bare outline of the process by which during the eleventh century the Crown lost its revenues, and in consequence its power, to the great landowning families who dominated provincial as distinct from metropolitan life.

Of course it might be argued that the failure of the Crown to keep an efficient standing army was one of the chief reasons for its decline. But historically the sovereign had always depended upon one or other of the clans for military support; and systems of conscription for military service seem never to have succeeded. This state of affairs can scarcely be attributed to lack of revenue, since it already existed quite early in the Heian period, when there was no serious financial stringency.

The fact is that after the decline of Silla and the beginning of friendly intercourse with the T'ang empire Japan entered upon a period of peace and freedom from fear of foreign invasion or domestic uprising. It is true that there was in the eighth century and the early ninth century a good deal of hard fighting against the Emishi in the north, but this did not affect life except at the frontier, which was far away from the home provinces. In the western part of Japan there was no longer any real danger of attack from the mainland, and we learn that the defence force in Kyūshū, at one time composed of stout fighters from the eastern provinces, was now made up of lazy coast guards who spent their time fishing and sleeping, and were presently disbanded.

There seemed to be no need for maintaining a regular army, since all was well at home and abroad. Much new land was being reclaimed, production was increasing, city life was luxurious, the Buddhist Church was flourishing, and the new system of administration seemed to be working well, while friendly intercourse with China was fruitful of both material and spiritual benefits. In short the capital seemed to deserve its name of the City of Peace, where the only military officers were members of the Bodyguard, whose duties were ceremonial and whose purpose was ornamental. In the light of Japan's subsequent history, it is interesting and important that signs of the growth of a military spirit and the emergence of a strong military caste are not clearly visible until the close of the ninth century at the earliest. The civil authority, however illegitimate and voracious, remained supreme for another hundred years, and contrived to hold its position without bloodshed, though with increasing difficulty, for a century to follow.

The suppression of the revolts of Masakado and Sumitomo may be taken as showing that midway in the tenth century the Throne had still enough prestige to command the loyal services of provincial magnates. But it brought home to the people of the capital the great and growing influence of those leading country families, for it was their military strength that had saved the day, and not the armed forces recruited by the central government, which were scanty and hopelessly inefficient.

From about this time there is a steady decline in the political power of the sovereign. The chronicles relate fascinating stories of intrigue, of palace conspiracies and succession disputes, but from the point of view of the exercise of political power the reigns after Uda (887–97) show a transfer of strength from the Throne to the great families, which have either wealth or military force, or both, at their disposal at a time when the revenues of the Crown are dwindling. The work called *Gukanshō* (ca. 1223), which is the first Japanese historical study to attempt a reasoned interpretation of the past, expresses the view that the old regime, the true imperial government, came to an end with the Kampyō period in 898, and that thereafter began the "middle" age, lasting until about 950, during which the Throne continued to flourish as the centre of learning and literature, but was in an increasingly shaky position. The full transfer of power to the Fujiwara Regents may be placed at 967, when Saneyori was made Regent (Kampaku) for the Emperor Reizei.

There can be little doubt that one of the chief proximate causes of the decline of the authority of the Crown was the failure of its reve-nues, which in turn arose from the inability of the central government to control the landowners in the provinces. The measures of economy which the government tried to introduce failed of their purpose. In 902 the Emperor Daigo, who managed for a time to keep free from Fujiwara control, made attempts to deal with the land problem, issuing orders intended to arrest the process of confiscation and defaulting which was drying up the sources of revenue. But the domanial lords— the owners and the managers of the shōen, the manors which enjoyed various degrees of immunity—could not be constrained to surrender their privileges, however unlawful, since the local governors had not as a rule the strength to impose their discipline upon the landowners, who were themselves, or had at their back, nobles powerful at Court. In-deed the revenue of most of the important members of the Court society was derived from country estates enjoying a high degree of immunity. When Prince Genji goes into exile, he makes arrangements for the care of his property, handing over to a trusted friend the deeds and certifi-cates pertaining to his *misō, mimaki, mikuramachi,* that is to say his rice lands, pasture lands, granaries, and rows of warehouses.

One of the last attempts by the Crown to assert its rights of eminent domain was made in 985, when an imperial ordinance was issued saying that the manors were to be "adjusted." In the spirit of this ordinance the Governor of the province of Bizen endeavoured to impound a manor which belonged to the Fujiwara family, and of which the income was reserved for the Kōfukuji monastery and the shrine of Kasuga, both religious foundations devoted to the interests of the clan. The steward of the estate appealed to the Clan Chieftain, at that time Yoritada, the Regent (Kampaku), who sent an official to look into the case on the spot. The Governor—according to the story told by the steward—sent secretly to the capital complaining of the behaviour of the official, who was thereupon deprived of his post by the Court, while the Governor was ordered to arrest the steward. Acting on these orders the Governor, with several hundred soldiers, broke into the estate, opened its store-houses and took out some thousand bushels of tax rice, seized property from the houses of other residents on the estate, and then arrested both the inspecting officer and the steward.

The Abbot of the Kōfukuji next appealed directly to the Regent, and the Court sent more officers to ascertain the facts. They were however Fujiwara adherents, and the Governor reported that, far from investi-gating, they were trying to profit by their mission to ill-treat the farmers and to confiscate large amounts of rice on the pretense that it was due as tax. Further enquiry was made in the Chancellor's office in the capital, and the case dragged on. The records do not show what were the rights and wrongs of the case, but it is clear that the steward of the estate and his colleagues sought to defy the authority of the governor of the province and to take shelter behind the Regent. We do know that it was the Regent who had the last word, for he told the Governor (who was a Fujiwara) that he was a disgrace to his clan, a worm in the wood, and must be expelled for having dared to make forcible entry into a Fujiwara domain. This anecdote is one of many that reveal the attitude of the Fujiwara clan towards the laws and edicts of the Crown. They could be flouted when Fujiwara property was at stake. The great Regent Michinaga (995–1017) was said to possess immune estates throughout the country, and a kinsman at that time in office said of them: "All the land in the Empire belongs to the First Family ("Ichi no Iye"— the senior house—here means Michinaga's branch of the clan), and there is not a pin-point where they are not owners. What miserable times we live in!" It is symbolic of the dominant position of the clan that their monastery, the Kōfukuji, was so powerful that for a time no governor was appointed to Yamato province, because this would have interfered with the almost plenary power of the Abbot of the Kōfukuji.

Further efforts to arrest the process of decay of the land laws were made in 1032 by the Emperor Go-Ichijō, who secretly approached a minister for help in resisting the Fujiwara claims and was told to "talk to the Regent"; and again in 1040 by the Emperor Suzaku, only to find that the orders of the Court were no longer respected by local authorities.

In 1056 the Court, abandoning hope of cancelling existing titles to immune domains, made a modest effort to prevent the formation of new shōen, but with little success, since while Fujiwara strength was declining other land-hungry clans were rising to power. Finally the Emperor Go-Sanjō (1068–72) made a last desperate effort to reform the whole system, by setting up a Record Office (Kiroku-jo) and instituting close enquiry into title and other measures of scrutiny and control. It had some effect, and caused alarm to the Fujiwara and to some of the great monasteries, who said that the examination might proceed but that for their part they had no documents to produce. The main result of this step was to cause the domanial lords to obtain some kind of permit for immunities which they subsequently acquired or claimed.

Thus, though the immunity of many estates was challenged, the central government was in general obliged to recognize de facto immunities, even when they depended upon inadequate certificates or merely upon prescription. Indeed one of the most remarkable features of the shōen system disclosed by these enquiries is that hardly any of the estates recognized as immune could produce valid orders from the

imperial Court, or from a minister of state, as evidence of title. At best
they could rely upon a certificate under seal of local authorities. Such
certificates were as a rule issued by a governor or his deputy at the request, which amounted to a command, of the Fujiwara or other powerful
family concerned. Thus despite all attempts at reform the number of
immune estates increased throughout the eleventh century. This failure
of the authority of the Throne was manifest not only in matters of land
tenure, but also in every sphere of government, except that of ceremonial observances.

The Emperor Shirakawa (1072–86) made an effort after his abdication to restore the authority of the Imperial House by instituting the
remarkable Insei system—the system of cloistered emperors who, although abdicated, continued to exercise sovereign power, and by disregarding the high officers of state (Regent and Chancellor) contributed
to the decline of the Fujiwara. In this struggle, however, Shirakawa
alienated much public land in order to raise funds for his own purposes;
and he thus defeated the object of Go-Sanjō's edicts by increasing the
number of immune private estates.[4]

3. Hereditary Dictators

For an understanding of the role played by the Fujiwara Regents
it would be superfluous to recite in order and detail the activities of
those who follow Tadahira. Their individual successes and failures in
matters of government are not of great importance, and their careers
are of interest mainly as illustrating the rapid rise of their clan to a
position of arbitrary and absolute power. Briefly, they were Saneyori,
the son of Tadahira; Koretada, the son of Saneyori's brother Morosuke;
Kanemichi, Yoritada, and Kaneiye, sons of Koretada; and Michitaka,
Michikane, and Michinaga, sons of Kaneiye. With Michinaga the Fujiwara family (the so-called Northern Branch) reached the summit of its
power and renown, having established a complete dominance over the
Ruling House.

We do not know very well what kind of men they were, because
contemporary chroniclers usually flattered them and because for the
most part they had no constructive public services to their credit but

---

[4] The Record Office (Kiroku-jo) did not attempt to confiscate estates that
could not show a valid title, but such estates could not claim protection against third
parties. The method of enquiry is well described in the archives of some of the
great monasteries. An interesting example is to be found in the archives of the
Iwashimizu Hachiman shrine, which describe the examination of title to thirty-four
estates belonging to the shrine, some of them comprising several thousands of acres
of rice land. It was found that only twenty-one of these could claim some immunity,
while for the remaining thirteen no evidence of title was forthcoming.

Even the Fujiwara leaders, after at first saying that they had no documents, did
upon pressure produce some evidence of title, after the death of Yorimichi.

only an assiduous, even relentless, pursuit of the private interests of their clan. Indeed it might be said with truth that the history of the Fujiwara Regents is not part of the history of political thought, but rather a record of the development, and the application to political matters, of that hereditary principle which was already so firmly entrenched in Japanese life, so widely approved in Japanese society.

The true basis of Fujiwara power was not the rank or the ability of Fujiwara men, but the matrimonial success of Fujiwara women. The Fujiwara who could claim the highest office under the Crown was not necessarily the most senior or the most talented member of the clan, but the person who could claim to be the closest relative by marriage of the sovereign or his heir—a father-in-law, a brother-in-law, or a maternal grandfather. Thus the Minister of State Fujiwara Morosuke had a daughter Yasuko, who became consort of the Emperor Murakami, a relationship which gave special prestige to Morosuke and his descendants. When she gave birth to a Crown Prince, who succeeded to the throne as the Emperor Reizei in 967, Morosuke's position as maternal grandfather of the sovereign gave him almost unlimited authority, although he did not choose to leave his own comparatively modest official post.

On the death of the Regent Koretada in 972 his third son Kaneiye, an ambitious and ruthless man, thought to succeed him. But his elder brother Kanemichi had taken care to get a written promise from the Empress Yasuko, and when he showed this to the reigning emperor, who was Yasuko's son, the Emperor, though he disliked Kanemichi, felt obliged to carry out the wishes of his mother, who had declared: "Succession to the office of Kampaku must go by order of age. There must on no account be any exception to this rule."

So we find that it is a Fujiwara dowager empress and not the ruling emperor whose wishes determine the succession to the high post of Regent and Dictator, because this appointment is regarded not as an affair of state but as family business of the Fujiwara clan. Many such instances could be quoted, where the wishes of the emperor were disregarded and the choice of Regent settled by strife or by agreement among Fujiwara claimants.

When Kanemichi was at the point of death in 977, he denounced Kaneiye and named his eldest brother Yoritada as Kampaku. Here again the wish of the Emperor was disregarded, and all His Majesty could do was to quote a consoling poem to Kaneiye, whose appointment he had favoured. Now both Yoritada and Kaneiye offered a daughter to the Emperor, but Yoritada's daughter proved barren and therefore he could not exercise authority as Regent when in 984 the Emperor Kazan (Hanayama) succeeded to the throne.

High office and high rank were not enough to qualify for the exercise of the highest power, for although a Fujiwara might become Regent, he could not make final decisions on behalf of the sovereign if he were not also a close maternal relative within certain accepted degrees. It was the close maternal relative who had the last word in all affairs of state.

There is a singularly interesting example of this rule at work in the reign of the Emperor Kazan. Kaneiye, then the senior Fujiwara Minister of State, wished to become Regent at the new emperor's accession, but he agreed that he had no right to the office, since he was "neither father-in-law nor grandfather" of the Emperor ("gaiso shūto ni mo arazu"). Accordingly no Regent was appointed until the Emperor Ichijō succeeded in 986, when Kaneiye became Regent (Sesshō), because he was then maternal grandfather of the sovereign. The Regent Yoritada, who had been appointed in 977, thereupon resigned. He had exercised no special powers under the Emperor Kazan, and now he said that he could not stay in office as he was "not of the family," but *yosobito*, an outsider.

Once Kaneiye became Regent (having tricked Kazan into abdicating), his position was very strong. He followed his own bent and took no pains to show respect to the Throne. He would appear at Court improperly dressed, even stripped to his undershirt in hot weather. He was head of the clan; he had three sons to follow him, and three fruitful daughters well married in the Palace. He, perhaps more than any other Regent, may be said to have consolidated the power of the Fujiwara family, for it was his descendants, generation after generation, who succeeded to the highest rank and the greatest power, as Sesshō or Kampaku.

His three sons succeeded him in turn, the third being the great Michinaga. By now the office of Chancellor (Dajō Daijin) was no longer of real authority, although according to the codes it was so important that it could be filled only by one of the highest capacity and must otherwise be left vacant. When Yorimichi, who succeeded Michinaga in 1017, was made Regent he was in the junior rank of Naidaijin, the lowest of the state ministers; but he was given preference over his colleagues by an edict which made him Ichi no Hito (The First Subject), with a place at Court next to the throne.

The importance of these marriages of their daughters was so vital to the Fujiwara grandees that, if a Fujiwara girl did not upon marriage in the Palace produce a child, her parents, brothers, and sisters felt that they were disgraced and without prospects. Yoritada's daughter Nobuko, who married the Emperor Enyū, was known as the Barren Consort, and it was on her account that he resigned from the Regency as an "outsider."

Two important points arise from this institution of regency. The first is that it was in the interest of the leaders of the Fujiwara family to preserve the Imperial House and to protect the Throne. The second is that, as they were sensible enough to recognize, the prestige and power of their clan derived not only from their own talents but also from their blood connexion with the reigning house. Both were factors tending to perpetuate the monarchy despite its political impotence.

Michinaga, the greatest of the Regents, said: "Great as are our power and prestige, nevertheless they are those of the Sovereign, for we derive them from the majesty of the Throne."

No doubt in his cynical moments Michinaga thought otherwise, but he was a man of understanding, quite likely to have had a certain feeling for the mystic virtues of kingship; and although many Regents treated the sovereign with scant respect and at times with positive rudeness, they were naturally careful not to do lasting damage to the tradition of sublime descent by which they themselves profited. For if they desired rank and title, there must be an undisputed fountain of honour; and this, in their eyes, was the great purpose and function of a royal house. What a statesman cannot do in his own name he can often achieve in the name of his sovereign.

This peculiar monopoly of power by maternal relatives of the sovereign is of importance in the study of Japanese political ideas, especially with reference to the contradiction between the legend of the divine origin of the Imperial House and the history of its treatment at the hands of the great nobles.

The mansions of the leading members of the Fujiwara clan were more splendid than the palace of the emperors, which owing to frequent conflagrations as well as to neglect tended to grow smaller and less imposing as the houses of the nobility grew larger and more pretentious. The reigning emperor and his empress would stay for long periods in the mansions of the Fujiwara chieftain. Pregnant empresses and princesses used to return to their parental homes for their confinement, and often left their offspring there to be brought up. Succession to the throne was very much a family affair—a Fujiwara family affair—and it was said that affairs of state in general were discussed and decided in the Fujiwara *mandokoro,* which was in the nature of an estate office where the business of a great family is transacted by stewards, lawyers, accountants, and clerks.

It is interesting to note that, in subsequent Japanese history, the power of the Throne was repeatedly usurped by dictators who, from their mandokoro, governed the whole country in the interest of their own clan, as if it were an immense family estate. Indeed it might easily be argued that what in the long run destroyed central government under a monarchy was not, except as a proximate cause, the failure of the fiscal policy of the Crown or its lack of a standing army to enforce its authority, but the absence of any genuine national feeling strong enough to resist clan solidarity and the presence of a firm belief in the principle of heredity.

As might be expected of a family so powerful, so rich, so proud, and so prolific, the chronicles of the Fujiwara contain much that is scandalous, and this is an aspect of the life of the upper classes during the tenth and eleventh centuries which, though it need not be stressed, should not be neglected.

Some of the less edifying anecdotes relate the behaviour of Kaneiye, whose efforts to capture the post of Regent have already been mentioned. When he wanted to get rid of the Emperor Kazan (to whom he was not related) he told that unfortunate young man that he had better enter religion, seeing that the Imperial Regalia were already in the hands of the Heir Apparent, a child of seven, son of Kaneiye's daughter Akiko, presently to be set upon the throne as the Emperor Ichijō.

At this suggestion Kazan demurred, but under pressure he went to the Gangō-ji monastery with Michikane, Kaneiye's second son, who was to take the tonsure at the same time. But upon arrival at the monastery Michikane said that he would like his parents to see him for the last time as a layman, excused himself, and went home. He did not return, for he had never intended to take orders. This was in 986. Kazan (as we shall see) never settled down to religious life. He had irretrievably lost his crown, but he did not abandon secular pleasures.

Kaneiye had two daughters and three sons by his principal wife Toki-hime. The daughters were Akiko and Yukiko; and the sons were Michitaka (957–95), Michikane (961–95), and Michinaga (966–1027), each of whom in turn became Regent, Michinaga being the greatest, or at any rate the most celebrated, of all the Fujiwara dictators. Kaneiye had intimate relationships with many ladies of varying degree, and one of these, a secondary wife, in 955 gave birth to a boy, named Michitsuna, who was recognized as Kaneiye's son but was not in line for succession to the Regency. He is a minor historical figure only because his name appears in a work called *Kagerō Nikki*, or the *Gossamer Diary*, in which his mother wrote a description of her life with Kaneiye.

This diary, which is one of the most important literary works of its kind and period, not only is a touching document, expressing deep emotion and frequent melancholy, but also throws much light upon the manners and morals of the times. The writer, whose name is unknown, was the daughter of Fujiwara Tomoyasu, governor of the distant northern province of Mutsu. She is said to have been one of the reigning beauties of her day. She describes Kaneiye's courtship, quoting the many poems they exchanged. This was in 954, and she then tells of the birth of her son in 955, followed by a growing coolness on the side of her lover and her own mounting grief as she learns of his numerous liaisons with other women. There is never a complete breach between them, but Kaneiye, though he pays her occasional visits, is only sometimes affectionate, often neglectful, and always absorbed in his own ambitions. He is a boisterous, euphoric extrovert. She for her part nurses her own distress and rejoices in his rapid rise in the world. She lives near the Palace, and lies awake listening for his deliberate cough as he passes by at dawn and at dusk on his way to and from his duties. She is romantic and lachrymose; he is vigorous, lively, practical. She threatens suicide. He enjoys the world.

There is no question of any moral reprobation of his very catholic love-making, which was in accord with contemporary standards of behaviour in the upper classes, nor did any stigma of illegitimacy spoil the life of the issue of such adventures. In this and other respects the *Gossamer Diary* is a precious source of knowledge about the aristocratic society of the tenth century. It seems to strike an authentic note, unlike most of the old romances which, as the diarist herself observes, were fabrications pretending to describe from intimate knowledge the high life of which their authors had no experience. What she herself wrote was obviously truthful, and what she saw was observed with a keen perception heightened by jealousy.

The diary comes to an end in 974, by which time Kaneiye was well on the way to the highest office in the land. His daughter Akiko (also known as Senshi), then twelve years old, was a concubine of the Emperor Enyū, and as soon as she was nubile she conceived a son, who ascended the throne in 986, at the age of seven. It was at this point that Kaneiye became Regent (Sesshō) and Akiko received the title of Kō-taigō or Dowager Empress. Her life is perhaps the best illustration of the power of women in the age of the Fujiwara Regents. Akiko was so influential that it was she who had the last word on questions of succession, and she was quite ruthless in her treatment of opposition. When Michitaka died (995) he named his son Korechika to succeed him as Kampaku. Korechika was a popular young man, of lively character, the favourite brother of the Empress Sadako and well-liked by the Emperor Ichijō himself. Despite these claims the Dowager Empress Akiko, who disliked him, was able to force the Emperor to confer upon Michinaga the title of Nairan, which he assumed in 995.[5] Her prestige was enormous, her character formidable. In 991 she had retired from Court life and, as the Buddhist phrase went, she had "discarded her finery" (*raku-shoku*) and entered religion. She was given the unprecedented title of Higashi Sanjō no In, "In" being a style previously reserved for cloistered emperors. She did not, however, allow religious duty to interfere with her participation in state affairs but resided in Michinaga's own mansion, the very centre of political life, headquarters of political manoeuvre.

Her name occurs in a celebrated "chronique scandaleuse" in which the leading figure is the young Korechika, whose ambition she was determined to thwart. Like many stories of this nature, it is worth relating

---

[5] Nairan was a title of honour. Its holder was supposed to have access to all the sovereign's secret papers and to be his most trusted adviser.

in some detail, for it gives a description of Court intrigues which, taken together with such evidence as is contained in the *Gossamer Diary,* provides for us a good picture of high society in its more scabrous aspects.

Korechika's father, Michitaka, is celebrated as a great drinker, and it is related of him (and no doubt of other distinguished inebriates) that on his deathbed, when urged to pray to Amida for admission to Paradise, he asked whether he could be sure of meeting his old drinking companions there. He lasted only a few years as Regent (990–95) and was succeeded by his brother Michikane, who enjoyed office for only seven days and then passed away, to be known in history as Nanuka Kampaku, or the Seven Day Dictator.

There now followed a struggle for primacy between Michinaga and his nephew Korechika, Michitaka's favourite son. Korechika was twenty-two in 995, and he had been made Sangi (Counsellor of State) at the age of eighteen and Naidaijin at twenty-one. Michinaga, his uncle, was now thirty, and a vigorous claimant, but Korechika was popular at Court, where he had influential friends. When his father was still alive Korechika, as a handsome lad of eighteen, made a great impression upon Sei Shōnagon, a lady-in-waiting to his sister the Empress Sadako. He quoted poetry with great facility and his charm was such that once, when he came up and talked to her, she almost fainted. He used to give out themes for poetry contests among the Palace ladies, and Sei more than once in her *Pillow Book* refers to his splendid costumes, his graceful manner, his learning, and his literary taste. In one entry she tells how once at evening he came to the Palace and sat talking literature to the Emperor until nearly dawn. All the courtiers stole away, except Sei herself, and His Majesty fell asleep leaning against a pillar. He was awakened by the squawks of a cock which was being chased by a dog along a gallery outside the apartment. Here is a curious, intimate glimpse of simple, untidy, uncomfortable life in the Palace, and at the same time of courtly elegance, revealed when Korechika most appositely quotes a line of Chinese verse (from the *Rōyeishu*) which runs: "His voice surprises the enlightened Monarch plunged in sleep."

But such accomplishments were not enough to defend the splendid young man against the designs of the Dowager Empress Akiko and her brother Michinaga. The sovereign and his close companions might lead a sheltered life deep in the Palace, but this was a time of confusion and calamity in the capital city. There were violent quarrels at Court between rival families, and street fighting between factions, as of Montagues against Capulets. Fires were frequent, robbery was common, epidemics rampant. There were intrigues, plots, and conspiracies of all kinds, not excluding clandestine courtships in which the highest personages were implicated. In this kind of gallantry Korechika was not behindhand. As was the fashion among young nobles of the period he used in secret (it was an open secret) to visit a young lady late at night. The object of his wooing lived with her sisters in the Ichijō Palace, one of the Fujiwara mansions. It was rumoured that the retired Emperor Kazan—whom we have seen unwillingly taking the tonsure—frequently visited the same mansion in the small hours; and Korechika, supposing that it was his own mistress with whom Kazan was intimate, hid in the garden with an accomplice (his brother Takaiye), and when the ex-Emperor appeared making his way to an assignation they shot at him. One arrow touched the Imperial sleeve; there was a great uproar, of course, for it was a grave offence to do violence to a monk, and an ex-emperor had been put in an ignominious position. Michinaga's party, profiting from this incident (which they had probably arranged), pressed a charge of lèse-majesté against the two young men. This was early in the year 996.

The case was considered by the leading jurists ("Myōbō Hakase") of the day, who decided that the fault lay with the servants of the parties, and not with the principals; but Michinaga trumped up other charges, and Korechika was appointed Vice-Governor of Kyūshū, while his brother Takaiye was posted to the provincial government of Izumo.[6] These were polite sentences of banishment, which both culprits tried to evade. This was at a time when the position of the Empress Sadako, Korechika's sister, was growing difficult, owing to various bedchamber intrigues by other consorts of the Emperor and their respective supporters. In the spring of 996 Sadako moved from the Imperial Palace to the Nijō mansion, where at the end of the year she gave birth to a princess, Osako. Meanwhile the Princess Yoshiko, and other favourites of the Emperor, were promoted and Sadako found herself almost deserted. The Dowager Empress Akiko disliked her, she had lost her closest relatives, and Michinaga took care that no courtiers should take her side.

The Emperor did not neglect her. He visited her in her confinement and in due course she returned to the Palace with her baby. She had another child, a boy, in 999, and early in the following year she was raised to the true position of Empress (Kōgō), having hitherto been only a Consort (Chūgū) and not strictly speaking of imperial rank. It was at this time (999) that Michinaga's daughter Akiko,[7] then a girl of eleven, entered the Palace as a prospective concubine (nyōgo), presently to become the Emperor's favourite.

There was noise and laughter in the Emperor's apartments at the end of the year 1000, but the Empress Sadako lay ill in her bedchamber. For her confinement on this occasion she moved to the house of Taira Narimasa, who was Intendant of the Chūgūshiki, the office administering the apartments of the Imperial Consorts.

[6] Korechika was accused of laying a spell upon his uncle Michikane, and later of putting a curse upon the Dowager Empress Akiko.
[7] Not to be confused with the Dowager Empress.

This was the beginning of Sadako's downfall—nobody saw her off from Koichijō-In, where she was living with the Emperor, and thanks to Michinaga's "precautions" nobody of importance welcomed her at Narimasa's mansion.

The poor lady died in childbirth, being then only twenty-five years old. Judging from the references to her in the *Pillow Book* of her lady-in-waiting Sei Shōnagon (who was not easily pleased), she must have been of a sweet and gay disposition, much beloved by those around her. Sei evidently fell in love with the child consort when she first went to Court. She describes a charming scene, where Sadako, herself only fifteen, is showing pictures to the shy young woman of twenty-five, hoping to put her at her ease. "It was cold and I could just see her hand as it peeped out of her sleeve. It was of a lovely light pink and I found it most beautiful. I was all eyes for her and I asked myself with amazement, being just up from a provincial home, how such adorable people could exist in this world."

It is a really delightful picture of life in the private apartments of the sovereign that one derives from Sei Shōnagon's little sketches. There are discussions about books and pictures, much innocent fun and a little mild mischief. As Sei adds stroke after stroke to her description we see the Empress portrayed as clever, sensitive, gentle, and delicious. She would enjoy a harmless joke against one of her ladies or the Emperor's gentlemen, but was quick to reprimand ill-natured words or deeds. Even her reproaches were agreeable, said Shōnagon; she disliked cruelty in any form, and had delicate ways of doing kindnesses to those around her. She was well-educated, and her mind was equal to her heart. She was pious and modest. When somebody spoke in obsequious respect of the Regent, she said that it was a more splendid thing to attain Buddahood than to reach the pinnacle of earthly ambition.

While there was much cruelty and empty display in the society over which the Fujiwara family held sway, there can be no doubt that it produced many remarkable women, and founded a tradition of beauty, grace, and devotion of which their country may well be proud.

Though Michinaga turned out to be the most powerful of the Fujiwara Regents, on grounds of birth and Court rank his claim to the highest office was not strong. He was fortunate in that his elder brothers died young, and that he had several clever and good-looking daughters. But apart from his good luck, he was a very adroit statesman who knew how to deal with both friends and enemies. Being alive to the changes that were taking place in the country he foresaw the rise of the military families who were beginning to dominate provincial life, and early in his career he made up his mind to get on his side the leading warriors, whom he could trust to support him in case of need, in return for benefits which he could confer. He chose certain members of the Minamoto clan, by whose talents he was impressed, and it was their presence in the background that enabled him in the early days of his rise to power to defeat or intimidate his rivals. There was at that time no other force that he could use, and none that he need fear, for the Imperial Guards were useless, being composed of lazy peasants who had come to the capital to avoid hard work on the farm and commanded by ornamental young men who had no intention of practising the military arts.

As to his title, he was given the supreme style of Nairan but his office was only that of Udaijin, or Minister of the Right, a modest post. He never took the title of Kampaku, nor did he even become Dajō Daijin, or Chancellor of the Realm, which was the highest place in the purely official hierarchy. He did not depend upon rank, for he was satisfied with his own strength of character and his extremely close family connexion with the Throne.

When he became Nairan in 995 he had no valid claim to the Regency as a "maternal relative," and it became desirable for him to create one. His daughter Akiko was then only a child of seven, but in 999, though too young for marriage, she became an imperial lady (nyōgo) and in the following year she was promoted to the rank of Chūgū, or Second Consort, of the Emperor Ichijō (reigned 986–1011). She is mentioned frequently in the history of those times, especially by the name she bore after the Emperor's death, Jōtōmon-In. She was the Empress in whose service a favourite lady-in-waiting, the novelist Murasaki Shikibu, acquired the insight into Court life that was turned to good use in her great romance, the *Tale of Genji*.

Michinaga struck the keynote of his relations with the Imperial House by an enormous entertainment to celebrate Akiko's entry into the inner palace. Her apartments were furnished in a most lavish manner, and embellished with paintings by great artists (such as Kose Hirotaka); and she had forty lady attendants, chosen from the best-looking and the cleverest of many aristocratic candidates. She soon became the Emperor Ichijō's favourite, and when she bore him a son he named that child the Heir Apparent, because his position as Emperor depended upon the support of a powerful man like Michinaga. He did in fact appeal to Michinaga in favour of his first son, by his first wife, promising that in due course Akiko's boy should succeed. But Michinaga would not listen. This was in 1008, and Akiko's son later became the Emperor Go-Ichijō. His father, Ichijō, was so ill and so worried by the weakness of his position that he abdicated in 1011, and died a few weeks later at the early age of thirty-one, having reigned since he was five years old. He was succeeded by the Emperor Sanjō (1011–16), who was the son of the Emperor Reizei; and then followed Akiko's two children, Go-Ichijō (1016–36) and Go-Suzaku (1036–45), a son born in 1009. Such was the pressure upon the emperors to marry Fujiwara women selected for them by the leaders of the clan that Sanjō married Michinaga's second daughter; Go-Ichijō married the third, who was his aunt; his brother Go-Suzaku married the fourth, also an aunt; and the fifth and last daughter was given to a son of Sanjō, an Heir Presumptive who was already married.[8]

It must be admitted that Michinaga's policy of forming connexions by marriage with the Imperial House was carried out in a thorough-going way. He was indeed a man who thought and acted on a generous scale. It is unfortunate that we have no really satisfactory knowledge of his character, for whatever may be thought of his morals he must be recognized as a man of parts, the leading statesman of his age and one of the great figures in Japanese history. That he was a man of re-markable power and exceptional gifts is clear from the mere fact that in an age when the imperial authority was at a low ebb and the power of provincial warlords was rapidly growing, he was able not only to hold subversive forces in check but to carry the Fujiwara family to heights of power and glory by sheer political virtuosity.

Although accounts of his character are conflicting, there is no doubt that he had the kind of judgment, the knowledge of human nature, needed by a ruler of men. Most records seem to agree that he was courageous, and had a firm hold on his own temper. He was a skilful archer and a good horseman, and his poetry was much praised by his friends. He knew how to use friends and win over enemies, for he had, so says one of his chroniclers, a deep understanding of the human heart. He knew what was going on in the minds of all kinds of people, from the highest to the lowest. He liked to do things on a grand scale and he was unscrupulous in working for the interests of his own family and of his own clan. He had a good conceit of himself, for he said that he was flawless, like the full moon riding the skies. It really is a pity that we do not know more about his inner life. He loved ostentation, luxury, and, of course, the exercise of power, but in his later years he spent much time upon prayers and pious undertakings. Whether his religious feeling was deep or not we cannot tell.

We know that he squandered great sums on building shrines and chapels and on Buddhist services in which thousands of monks took part. He is said to have been an ardent believer in the Lotus Sutra, which he copied out in letters of gold; and he appears to have invoked the Buddha Amida on his death bed, begging for admission to Para-

---

[8] The complex relationship of Michinaga with the Throne through his daughters may be made clearer by the following diagram:

Michinaga's Daughters

1 (Akiko)	2	3	4	5
m. Ichijō	m. Sanjō	m. Go-Ichijō (son of Akiko)	m. Go-Suzaku (son of Akiko)	m. Son of Sanjō by second daughter

The prefix "Go," of course, means "the Second."

dise. He is also recorded as having rebuked officials for neglecting Shintō rites, and as Chieftain of his clan he promoted ceremonial at the Kasuga and other Shintō shrines. But where religious observances flourish religious fervour is often wanting, and it may be that Michinaga, like many of his contemporaries, was more superstitious than devout.

4. *The Power and the Glory, 966–1027*

The ascendency of the Fujiwara Regents was carried to its highest point by Michinaga. His times are described in a work called *Eiga Monogatari*, a title which by a little stretch might be translated as "Tales of Power and Glory." It is favourable to the Fujiwara clan, but we have also a chronicle known as *Ō-Kagami*, or the *Great Mirror*, which is more critical of Michinaga. There is in addition to these major works a large corpus of literature of a special sort, in the form of diaries and similar notebooks kept during the period of Fujiwara supremacy. As sources of information about events they are apt to be dismissed as of little value, for they are concerned with what at first sight seems to be most trivial detail of Court life, points of ceremonial and the niceties of etiquette. But their very existence bears witness to a significant feature of metropolitan life under the rule of the Fujiwara; and therefore a brief description of their contents may properly serve as an introduction to the study of Japanese society, or more correctly the society of the governing classes, in the capital city during the period of Fujiwara dominance, which may be put roughly at the two centuries between 950 and 1150, though towards the end of that time the great clan was in a steep decline.

The principal journals of this kind and of this period are:

Shōyūki, the diary of Fujiwara Sanesuke, Minister of the Right (Udaijin), a man favourably mentioned in her miscellany by Murasaki Shikibu. He covers the years 957–1023.

Gonki, the diary of Fujiwara Yukinari, an acting Grand Counsellor (Dainagon), covering the years 991–1017.

Sakeiki, the diary of Minamoto Tsuneyori, Controller of the Left (Sa-Daiben), covering the years 1016–35.

Shunki, the diary of Fujiwara Sukefusa, Council Member (Sangi), consisting of fragments only, covering the years 1038–42.

Chūyūki, the diary of Fujiwara Munetada, Minister of the Right (Udaijin), covering the years 1087–1131.

Sankaiki, the diary of Fujiwara Tadachika, a minister of state who died in 1195 at the age of sixty-five. It covers the years 1151–94.

Gyokuyō, a very careful daily record (also known as *Gyokkai*) kept by the Regent Fujiwara Kanezane. He went to Court as a youth in 1158, and thus did not belong to the time of Fujiwara dominance. But he reached the highest rank and office and was a regular attendant at all discussions at the Palace. He was not in the good graces of the powerful cloistered Emperor Go-Shirakawa In, and therefore not in his inner councils. Nor of course was he consulted by the leaders of the Taira clan, who dominated the political scene from 1156 to their downfall in 1185. He was, however, a good observer, and always spoke his mind. His journal is probably the most valuable single source of evidence for the politics of the twelfth century. It is most carefully written and is of great length, the standard printed edition containing 2,139 pages of print. In his daily entries he is careful to distinguish fact from rumour, and his sober work is therefore a useful check upon the contemporary chronicles and romances, which are frequently prejudiced and highly coloured. He was an observer of the leading events from 1163 to 1200, and records interesting conversations with colleagues and friends, as well as his dealings with Yoritomo after the downfall of the Taira.

Taiki, another voluminous journal, kept by the ill-fated Yorinaga, who lost his life in the rebellion, or rather the abortive coup d'état, of 1156. It covers principally the years 1142–55 in the parts which are extant, but much has been lost. It gives an extremely detailed and interesting picture of the life of a remarkable man in a position of authority, and throws light on standards of scholarship and religious beliefs.

There are other works of this kind, but those cited give a fair impression of a remarkable, perhaps unique literary form and reveal an interesting social phenomenon. They are almost without exception minute day-to-day records kept by officials of high rank, and they deal principally with Court business, whether administrative, ritual, or social. They seem on cursory examination to pay excessive attention to matters of ceremonial. In the *Shōyūki* are to be found descriptions of a wrestling match, a poetry contest, prayers for harvest, and the correct form of documents. The *Gonki* deals largely with etiquette and ceremonies. The *Chūyūki* treats of rules for Court dress, for the conduct of horse races as part of religious festivals, for precedence at official functions, and similar matters. The *Sakeiki* reports on certain religious services. But on closer scrutiny these works are found to contain much valuable historical information. They are not written by men with a sense of history. Their writers record things carefully, but without any guiding principle, so that one entry is as important as another. But they do in fact furnish reports of conversations, summaries of discussions, and items of news as they came to the knowledge of the writer or his friends. General ideas are not touched upon, and separate administrative acts or political events are usually recorded without consideration of their political significance.

At first sight the apparent neglect of questions of high policy is surprising, but it must be remembered that it is good Confucian doctrine to look upon rites and ceremonies as an essential part of good government. What is of special historical interest here is the fact (to which these diaries amply testify) that although the general trend of Japanese life was in some respects running counter to Chinese influence already during the tenth century, the Chinese theory of government and Chinese principles of cosmology still carried great weight and determined the forms if not the spirit of official business at the highest levels. So long as the cosmic harmony was preserved by correct ritual behaviour, or at least was not disturbed by errors of conduct, then the duty of the sovereign and his great ministers was fulfilled. Administrative details might be left to subordinate officers in the capital or the provinces, but laissez faire was the rule in high matters.

In these authoritarian times of ours it appears laughable that great officers of state should concern themselves with correct usage in speech and deportment when they might be instructing the people in categorical terms. We are inclined to think that the more we are governed the better we behave, though the truer proposition might be that the better we behave the less we need to be governed; and there is much to be said in favour of an ideal condition of philosophical anarchy, where the state does not attempt to regulate conduct by legislation but depends upon the beneficence of natural law and the virtue of the sovereign. The issue here is not the rightness or wrongness of the Confucian view. What is important for the student of Asian history is that he should not assume his own views about life and society to have some universal warranty. It must also be remembered, in considering Japan under the Fujiwara Dictators, that actual administrative action was decided upon and taken by men who did not trouble to work through the prescribed official channels.

With this proviso in mind, we may examine some sample entries in the diaries. Perhaps one of the most interesting is an entry in the *Shō-yūki*, describing an annual Court ceremony at which official reports of crop failures and farm lands fallen out of cultivation were read, and the Chancellor requested approval of a remission of taxes. As the diarist describes it, the participants in the ceremony were but little interested in the substance of the reports, in such points as the area, position, and nature of the rice lands in question. What mattered was the form in which the reports were drawn up, the exact language used in presenting them, the correct placing of signatures and seals, and even the deportment of the officials. It seems also that, to the distress of the courtiers, the provincial officers who forwarded the reports were careless about formalities. Thus in one entry in the diary Sanesuke says: "I then untied the cord to look at the acreage reports of land in cultivation in each province. For five or six provinces the reports gave the names of the inspecting commissioners, but did not state the area. . . . I pointed out to the Controller (Daiben) that the reports from many provinces did not give the commissioners' names. Thus, although the province of Ōmi takes up two pages, the name of the commissioner is not stated. . . .

Further, I said, the report from Bizen does not bear the signature of the Governor of the province, nor has it a seal. It ought to be returned."

It is clear from such documents that decisions made at the imperial Court in councils of this nature had little to do with the practical issues which were raised; and it is safe to assume that as a rule the more urgent matters were dealt with either by direct orders from a deputy of the Regent or by provincial officers on their own responsibility. The real authority of the Court, never very great or very well defined, grew less and less and its addiction to ceremonial increased. As an example of the triumph of form over substance, the surrender of facts to rules, an event of the year 1019 may be cited. In that year pirates (? Jurchen) from northern Korea attacked the province of Chikuzen, and the Court offered rewards to the soldiers in adjoining provinces if they could drive off the invaders. Before news of this offer reached the local commanders (under Takaiye, whom Michinaga hated) they had already defeated the Jurchen; but the Court refused to pay rewards because the victory had preceded their promise. On another such occasion the Court refused to deal with an urgent military question until the choice of an auspicious time for action had been discussed for ten days. In 1028, when it became necessary to send an expedition to put down an uprising by Taira Tadatsune, there was a delay of forty days until an auspicious day for the departure of the commanding officers could be agreed upon. Yorimichi said: Short journeys don't matter, but difficult enterprises must be treated with all precautions.

One result of this emphasis upon the ceremonial duties of the high officers of state was the practice of making appointments upon a basis of birth, and not capacity, since the ability of a functionary was of less importance than his pedigree and his knowledge of etiquette. Consequently, we find, from about A.D. 1000, as the real executive power came to be exercised in the Fujiwara mandokoro, that posts in the various ministries tended to lose importance but retained prestige in Court circles, and were filled by the formal appointment of members of a family or group that claimed hereditary rights. Among the more striking examples of this practice was a monopoly of the office of head (Haku) of the Ministry of Religion (Jingi-kan) by members of the Shirakawa family. Similarly certain secretarial posts were held in regular succession for centuries thereafter by members of the Nakawara, Kiyowara, and Ōye families.

What counted now in official appointments was family connexion. This had always been true in some measure, but under the Fujiwara it became the rule, and merit alone gave no advantage to candidates. The result of this system was a decline in the morale of the ordinary applicants for office, since even for posts that were not hereditary they had to find a patron, and accordingly the search for work or sinecures led to all kinds of unworthy devices and intrigues, accompanied by flattery and obsequious behaviour. Even members of the Imperial House, not excluding empresses and crown princes, were in a very unfortunate position if they did not enjoy the protection of the Chieftain of the Fujiwara clan. Indeed the condition of the emperor and his Court was often most humiliating. Deprived of real authority, the sovereigns suffered from the incompetence of those around them, who were chosen for their posts on almost any ground but suitability. The very safety of the Palace, indeed of the whole imperial city, was endangered by the irresponsibility of those charged with its protection. The Commander (Bettō) of the Metropolitan Police Bureau (Kebiishi-chō), whose duty it was to seek out and arrest offenders, was always chosen for his pedigree. In 1025 a young man of seventeen years of age was appointed to this key post; and the Emperor Toba, soon after his accession in 1107, laid down the qualifications for this appointment as: good family, good sense, knowledge of precedent, good looks, high Court rank, and wealth.

It is not surprising that conditions in the capital were extremely dangerous. Fires, accompanied by robbery, were very frequent. A glance at the chronicles from 990 to 1010, a space of twenty years, shows a destructive fire in or near the city almost every year, with frequent mention of the loss by fire or theft of valuable property and precious books. Palaces and rich monasteries seem to have suffered most, and there can be no doubt that deliberate incendiarism was common.

The failure of the metropolitan police to preserve order may seem to be a matter of no great historical importance. But in fact the collapse of the Kebiishi was the collapse of the only force which might have preserved the authority of the Crown, since it had no standing army for its support. On the other hand the Regents, who depended upon political skill and did not readily use violence, saw the need for some military backing upon which they could rely in emergency, and accordingly they favoured and rewarded certain warriors of the Minamoto or the Taira clan, who were willing to fight in the Fujiwara cause, thereby increasing their own influence at Court as well as in the provinces, where their families were important landowners. Thanks largely to the aid of these warriors Michinaga had some success in restoring order in the capital, but in the provinces the powerful warrior families did not submit to his rule unless it suited their convenience.

Apart from the unique institutional character of the Fujiwara Regency, there is a singular interest in the social aspects of the metropolitan scene over which the leaders of the great clan presided, for they were dictators of taste and fashion as well as of political behaviour. It is not easy to describe in precise and ordered terms the nature of the small society—a few thousand at most—of great officers of state, Court nobles, functionaries of high rank, and some leading churchmen, who constituted the ruling class and whose daily existence was so remote from that of the common people that we find a contemporary Court lady (early in the eleventh century) describing some country folk whom she saw while on a pilgrimage to a monastery as "a parcel of common people in queer clothes, unpleasant to look at, like a swarm of caterpillars." And within this favoured group, so insulated from the vulgar, there were the most rigid distinctions of class and gradations of rank. The diaries from which we have already quoted reveal the preoccupation of the ladies and gentlemen of the age with questions of protocol and precedent, with standards of deportment, costume, and language, and with canons of taste. Hierarchical sentiment is prominent, almost obtrusive, in the history of the Japanese people from the times before Chinese influence was powerful; and one of the first borrowings from China was, as we have seen, a system of Court ranks distinguished by caps of different colours.

Later very detailed laws based upon Chinese practice but adapted in some respects to native social tradition laid down a comprehensive scale of Court and official ranks, with appropriate duties and privileges. These at all times played an important part in the life of members of the ruling class, being the object of ambition and the cause of intrigue; but under the rule of the Fujiwara Regents, as the political power of the sovereign withered away, his purely ritual functions assumed more and more importance, so that the life not only of courtiers but also of many administrative officers was dominated by questions of rank and title and the correct performance of ceremonial duties.

Some knowledge of the main features of this system is therefore necessary for an understanding of Heian society; and for this it is best to begin with the Court ranks, which were set forth in detail in the earliest codes of law and remained without substantial change until the reforms of 1868, when some parts of the system were abolished or fell into disuse.

In the Heian period there were nine Court ranks, each rank being divided into two categories, senior and junior. The senior first rank was the highest, the junior ninth rank the lowest. Each of the lower six ranks was again divided into an upper and a lower class, so that a full description of a man's Court rank would be of the type Senior Fourth Rank, Upper Class, or Junior Eighth Rank, Lower Class, and so on.

The very highest rank, the senior first (Shō Ichi-i), was very rarely granted, even to the most powerful subjects, except posthumously; the junior first rank was usually awarded on appointment to the holder of the highest office under the Crown, the Dajō Daijin or Chancellor; and with that exception the senior second rank was reserved for men of the noblest birth or the highest distinction. Following Chinese practice, ranks were at times bestowed upon deities or spirits who were thought to need praise or gratitude for their favours, and vengeful ghosts were pacified by similar grants of terrestrial honours. Each rank carried with it certain emoluments, usually in the form of appropriate areas of rice

land and workers for its cultivation, on a scale corresponding to gradations of rank. At Court the most important distinction of all was the line
drawn between *denjō bito,* those admitted to the level of the emperor
in his audience chamber, and *chige,* those who remained on a lower
level, the groundlings, so to speak.

Alongside of the Court ranks were the official ranks, which were laid
down in the administrative codes. Since the Fujiwara Regents frequently held posts in the official hierarchy that did not correspond to
their Court rank or to their actual political eminence, it is worth while
to take note here of the principal appointments. Indeed it is essential
seeing that all literature of the Heian period, and indeed of any period
of Japanese history, whether romances or plain chronicles, is so full of
references to ranks, offices, and titles that it is barely intelligible without
some knowledge of the terminology of order and precedence. It is the
more necessary in so far as it was a common habit to refer to persons
not by their names, but by their posts or their places of residence.
Michinaga, for instance, was known as Midō Kampaku after his Palace and as Hōjōji Kampaku or the Regent of the Hōjōji (his family
monastery); and the Empress Akiko after entering religion was called
Jōtōmon-In, which means the Imperial Nun of the Upper East Gate. In
general there was a tendency to avoid direct use of family and personal names, and to prefer such appellations as the Third Avenue Counsellor or the Minister of Fortune Lane (Tomi no kōji no Sadaijin), or
the Mistress of the Wardrobe (Mikushige-dono, title of a Fujiwara
daughter who was the lady attending to the hairdressing of the Empress
Sadako—so styled by Sei Shōnagon). The importance attached to name
taboos at Court was doubtless due to Chinese influence.

From the end of the reign of Murakami (967) emperors were not
known by personal (or posthumous) names but by the name of some
locality or building with which they were associated. Thus Reizei was
the name of a palace apartment; Ichijō, of a street; Tsuchi-Mikado, of
a gate. This practice was due to the rise of Fujiwara power and the
Regent's policy of suppressing the personal prestige of the sovereigns.

The two great departments of government were (as shown in the
diagram on p. 68) the Department of Religion (Jingi-kan) and the
Department of State (Dajō-kan). The former, though of great importance as the organ responsible for the proper performance of the great
national ceremonies and the maintenance of shrines, was small in size,
and its prestige was greater than its power. The Department of State
was the office or council that controlled and supervised the whole administrative apparatus. It was rather a council of state than a cabinet
office, since the heads of the eight ministries were not members of it,
but were responsible to it. It was composed of

> The President or Chancellor (Dajō Daijin)
> The Minister of the Left (Sadaijin)

The Minister of the Right (Udaijin)
The Minister of the Centre (Naidaijin),

and below these four great officers of the Crown, in order of precedence,

Three Great Counsellors (Dainagon)
Three Middle Counsellors (Chūnagon)
Three Minor Counsellors (Shōnagon)
Eight Members of Council (Sangi)
One Controller, of the Left (Sadaiben)
One Controller, of the Right (Udaiben).

The eight executive departments were controlled by ministers (Kyō) and their deputies. Each department or ministry consisted of a number of bureaus, at the head of which were chiefs called Kami and vice-chiefs called Suke. The ministers at the head of departments were of lower rank and less political importance than the members of the Council of State.

Apart from the administrative offices, the Imperial Bodyguard played an important part in the life of the capital, though its functions were more ceremonial and ornamental than military. The officers of the various regiments of guards were usually men of noble family, whose social position was very high. Readers of the *Tale of Genji* will remember that one of the young aristocrats who figures as a smart and popular man about town in the most exclusive society is Tō no Chūjō (the Captain), son of an emperor's sister. If he had any military duties, they are not mentioned.

All ranks in the capital were one grade higher than the corresponding ranks in the provinces. The leading man in each province was the Governor (Kami); and the Court rank of governors varied with the importance of the territories under their rule, rich provinces and those nearest to the capital having precedence over poorer and remoter places. The attitude of the courtiers towards officials serving in country posts is well revealed by a brief aside in the *Tale of Genji*, where it is said of a highborn lady that she had "come down in the world and married a deputy governor [*zuryō*]."[9]

As the power of the Fujiwara Regents increased, the functions of the ministries diminished in importance, since the Regents preferred direct action to administrative routine, or at most made use of the extra-legal organs which had replaced some of the conventional departments and offices. Therefore, as we have seen, the posts of departmental ministers and higher civil servants took on more and more a formal character, and

[9] The word *zuryō* means literally a receiver of land rent. Its use to stand for the office of provincial governor shows how that functionary was regarded by the Court—as a superior kind of tax collector, residing in the province while a titular governor remained in the capital and enjoyed his emoluments.

many appointments became empty honours, conferring rank and title but not executive authority. Even the highest office in the regular official hierarchy, that of Chancellor, gave no real authority to its holder unless he was a Fujiwara Regent or a person approved by the Fujiwara clan; so that from time to time the post was not filled, or the Regent was satisfied with the office of Minister of the Left (Sadaijin), which was the next highest office and a convenient channel for the issue of executive orders. Thus the Regent Tadahira, when he died in 949, held the office of Chancellor; his first son, Saneyori, was Minister of the Left; and his second son, Morosuke, was Minister of the Right. After Tadahira's death there was no appointment as Regent (either Sesshō or Kampaku) or as Chancellor until 967; but government was in the hands of Saneyori and Morosuke, who retained their comparatively modest ministerial posts. Morosuke died in 960 and Saneyori was not promoted until after he became Kampaku in 967. He was made Chancellor in the first month of 968, and it is in that year that the full autocracy of the Fujiwara was reached. By Michinaga's day the power of the Regents was so firmly established that they scarcely troubled to assume any other office. Michinaga retained the post of Minister of the Left from 996 until 1017, and was never named Kampaku. He was given the style of Nairan, a title of honour but not of office, which nominally gave him access to all confidential palace documents. He was Regent (Sesshō) for a little over one year beginning in 1016, and he accepted promotion to the office of Chancellor just before resigning in favour of Yorimichi, who became Sesshō in 1017 and Kampaku in 1019.

In such cimcumstances as these it was to be expected that the life of many high officers of state as well as of Court nobles would be devoted to pleasure rather than to the performance of administrative duties which had lost most of their meaning and effect; and it is to the social habits of the aristocracy, their pastimes and ceremonies, their books and paintings, their sentiments and beliefs, that we must now turn. We shall find that while the search for pleasure did, if we are to judge from romantic literature, lead many of the young gallants and some of their elders into foolish, not to say licentious, courses, in general the atmosphere of the Court was serious; and in the upper levels of Heian society behaviour was ruled by strict canons or, if moral principles were neglected, at least by a strong feeling for style.

Even the extravagance of Michinaga, which was in contrast to the frugal habits of his early predecessors, did not lead him into truly reprehensible errors of taste. He aimed at splendour, but he did observe standards which he thought proper, and he did encourage the arts by his expenditure on the decoration of monasteries and palaces. Seeing that the main purpose of government as it was conducted by the Fujiwara Regents was to maintain their dominance over the Imperial House, it is not to be wondered at that they chose to display their own magnificence and minister to their family pride. One of Michinaga's great enterprises devoted to those ends was the building of the monastery called Hōjōji, which he dedicated to the repose of his own soul when he resigned from office and took the tonsure. This, however, was not the end of his career, for although his son Yorimichi became Regent in 1017, Michinaga kept power in his own hands, dictating the succession to the throne and (as we have noticed) boasting, in a poem attributed to him, that he was the master of his world, like the flawless full moon riding the skies.

The dedication of the Golden Hall of the Hōjōji is described in some detail in the *Eiga Monogatari*. The following abridged version of part of the text may serve to give an impression of the pomp and splendour with which the retired statesman signified his entry into the religious life:

*

The logs floated downstream for the Hōjōji buildings and covered the entire surface of the Kamo River; the gifts from provincial governors had far exceeded expectations. Michinaga selected the fourteenth day of the seventh month of the second year of Chian (1022) for the dedication of the Golden Hall.

Because the Emperor was to attend the service, extraordinary attention was devoted to the preparations. The most careful thought was given even to the courtiers' allowances and the vestments to be presented to the priests. The monks themselves, young and old alike, hurried excitedly about arranging their costumes, and dance rehearsals were held for two or three days, drawing crowds of spectators who could not hope to be present at the dedication ceremony.

The noble guests began to arrive on the night of the thirteenth. Michinaga's Empress daughters, his son the Regent Yorimichi, and all the other important members of the Court circle were assigned quarters in the various buildings of the monastery.

The next day was fine. Behind curtains of choice fabrics bearing pictures executed in gold and silver, the ladies put on dresses of dazzling splendour. "How auspicious it was! The adornments of heavenly beings must certainly be thus." The Emperor arrived to the accompaniment of a great burst of music from reeds, strings, and drums. "When the Supreme Highness went before the Buddha to bow, His Eminence the Novice [Michinaga] wept without restraint." Soon the Heir Apparent also came.

"The sand in the garden glittered like crystal, and on the fresh, clear water of the pond innumerable lotus blossoms rose from the ripples. Each of them bore a Buddha, its figure mirrored in the surface of the pond. The buildings on the east, west, south, and north were reflected, even to the Library and Bell Tower, presenting the appearance of a Buddhist world. Jewelled nets were suspended from the branches of the plants fringing the pond. . . . Boats adorned with gems idled in the shade of trees, and peacocks strutted on the island in the middle. . . . The shining tiles of the Golden Hall reflected the sky. Its pillars rested upon masonry supports shaped like huge elephants, the roof ridge was of gold and silver, the door was of a golden hue, and the foundations were of rock crystal. The hall was magnificently adorned with jewels of many kinds." Inside, there were pictures depicting the life of the Buddha Sâkya and the accomplishment of bodhisattva vows. Gold, silver, and lapis lazuli were spread over the floor. The main image of Vairocana Buddha and other images and appointments were all executed in the most elaborate manner, with lavish use of gold and precious stones.

The officiating monks, who were the most important Buddhist prelates in Japan, were borne in palanquins in a solemn procession. As at a Buddhist ceremony at Court, high-ranking officials accompanied them on foot. The monks' vestments had been especially imported from China for this occasion. Costly incenses perfumed the air of the courtyard, and the skill of the musicians and dancers made it seem that Paradise must certainly be like this. When the prayers were recited by the Tendai chief abbot, it was a moving sight.

After the services, the members of the imperial family bestowed exceedingly generous gifts upon all the participants.

Michinaga's daughters spent the night at the Hōjōji. On the following day, the courtiers all returned, looking much more attractive in ordinary clothing than in the ceremonial robes of the previous day. Fruit and wine were served, and the guests, becoming intoxicated, recited Chinese poems. It was much more enjoyable than the stiff formality of the dedication.

✿

Michinaga's taste was inherited by his son, the Regent Yorimichi, who gave a lavish entertainment on the twentieth day of January in the year 1025, which so aroused the envy of his sister, the Dowager Empress Yoshi-ko, that she resolved to outshine her brother, and arranged a great New Year celebration for the twenty-third day of the same month. This gathering was thought worthy of description by the chroniclers, whose enthusiastic account is here given in an abridged version:

✿

By the night of the twenty-second, the young people who had been eagerly awaiting the occasion were full of anxiety about how they would fare in the competition of colours and scents. There was a great bustle of preparation in the palace apartments, where the ladies paired off to sew, fret about their hair, and blacken their teeth. Some ladies, thinking that the fans supplied by Yoshi-ko might not be good enough, had ordered specially painted ones, which they feared would not be ready in time. "Those who had been given permission to dress in [forbidden] colours wore satisfied expressions and behaved in a condescending manner; those who had not were chagrined." When dawn came, they rushed about carrying large bundles, dressing their hair, applying cosmetics, and so on. "One also saw pairs of them bearing amazing piles of folded things on the lids of large boxes. Those who beheld them laughed, saying 'How many garments can a single person wear?'" When the sun rose, their attendants urged them to eat so that they would be strong enough to support the weight of their clothes, but they were too excited to listen. At eight o'clock, Yoshi-ko summoned them to come to her at once, but they remained in their rooms adding extra touches to their toilettes. After repeated orders, they went, taking servants to support their skirts. "Unable even to hold up a fan because of the great thickness of their silks, they were completely lacking in grace."

Early in the afternoon Yorimichi and the other noble guests arrived, dressed in brilliant colours, fashionably perfumed, and attended by impressive retinues. Taking up seats according to the rules of precedence, they were dazzled by the ladies' costumes, but some of them commented to one another on the impropriety of such excessive numbers of skirts.

"Now as the lords enjoyed themselves in the most agreeable manner, night drew on. . . . When something which might have been either a blossom or a snowflake fell into his cup, the Master of the Empress's Household recited,

> 'Plum blossoms blent with snow
> Fly down upon the lute;
> The willow's colour through the smoke
> Is mirrored in the wine.'"

When the guests finally left, the ladies dropped exhausted wherever they could find room to sleep.

The next day, Michinaga summoned Yorimichi and questioned him in detail about the entertainment. When he learned that Yoshi-ko had violated his rule that palace ladies were not to wear more than six skirts at once, he reprimanded Yorimichi sharply for not reproving her.

❋

From such reports it will be seen how the life of these royal and noble persons was filled with ostentation, and what care they spent upon details of dress and deportment. It should be added that most entertainments included some religious element, which made an impressive addition to any occasion, by reason of both the beauty of vestments and the solemnity of such ritual as was performed. All contemporary historical sources combine to show that religious exercises usually served a double purpose, of pious devotion combined with aesthetic pleasure. There were popular monks, known for their good looks as well as their preaching, and there were fashionable churchmen well received at Court.

Although most of the ceremonial in the royal palaces and shrines was plain and simple, the great buildings of the Fujiwara nobles—their palaces, mansions, villas, tutelary shrines, and chapels—were very fine and costly, and such entertainments as those just described, together with frequent masses and religious festivals and contributions to the Church, must have involved enormous outlays. Yet while this lavish expenditure had to be kept up in order to maintain their power, it was on the other hand their power that enabled them to accumulate great wealth throughout the country by acquiring manorial rights over land "commended" to them for protection. Only the boldest of provincial officials would dare to challenge any claim to immunity from tax that might be put forward by tenants of so powerful a domanial lord as a Fujiwara nobleman, with all the strength of his clan behind him.

There was thus a close connexion between the expenditure of the Fujiwara Regents and the breakdown of land laws. It was not a connexion of cause and effect, for both phenomena were expressions of a failure of the fiscal system adopted centuries before. The Regents, or at least the most competent of them, and Michinaga in particular, tried to bring about order and security in the capital, and there they had some success. But in the provinces they could not succeed, because their private interests were not consistent with a just administration of the affairs of the countryside. Thus as the provincial gentry grew more and more conscious of their own strength, the power of the Fujiwara began to wane in a sort of autumnal splendour. Meanwhile in the metropolis there flourished a society devoted to elegant pursuits and happily insulated from the shocks of common life.

For all its shortcomings it was a society devoted to the pursuit of beauty, and being without close parallel in the history of other civilizations it deserves some separate consideration.

CHAPTER IX

THE RULE OF TASTE

THE MOST striking feature of the aristocratic society of the Heian capital is its aesthetic quality. It is true that it was a society composed of a small number of especially favoured people, but it is none the less remarkable that, even in its emptiest follies, it was moved by considerations of refinement and governed by a rule of taste. It is in the period of the Fujiwara Regents that there were formed among upper-class men and women in privileged situations certain standards of personal behaviour and certain canons of aesthetic judgment which are the source, or it might be better to say the foundation, of Japanese social life as it developed in later centuries. It is not an exaggeration to suggest that traces of the manners of the Heian era are to be detected long after the decay of its political institutions, and are still visible in some departments of modern life. It is worth while, therefore, if we wish to discover what were the springs of behaviour, what were the distinguishing characteristics of the ruling class in Japan in the middle ages, to examine their acts and thoughts and feelings in the light of such evidence as is available. What is this evidence?

In quantity it is copious enough, for we have plentiful literary remains in the shape of chronicles, diaries, romances, and poems which, though not always known to us in their original form, are useful sources of information when circumspectly used. Of these the most important is the great classical romance, the *Tale of Genji*. It is a work of imagination, a masterpiece of fiction, but it is based upon the writer's own experience, and enlivened by her sensibility, so that in itself it is a most penetrating study of Court society. It is more than that, however, for like most great works of art it discloses much that does not appear elsewhere—the unconscious forces, the unspoken ideas, the silent motives of the period. Something of the same kind is true of other than the literary arts, for to convey the impalpable spirit of an age, pictorial representation is often the best resource, and, to be sure, the paintings and sculptures of the Fujiwara period speak very plainly of its character.

If those plastic arts are for the most part of religious origin or purpose, that is an indication of the part played by Buddhism, or at least by Buddhist observances, in the life of the Court and of other great patrons. Of course enquiry into the place of religion, into the authority and influence of the Church, must be an important feature in any study of the national history at any time. But it is mostly in its external features that the Buddhism of the Heian period is relevant to the nature of the metropolitan society, so that its fuller significance may properly be left for separate treatment. What is especially interesting in the so-to-speak philosophical aspects of Heian life is an ability to reconcile such seemingly incompatible beliefs as those of Buddhism, Confucianism, and the indigenous Shintō cult. It is not difficult to explain, and in itself it provides a strong hint of the nature of the society with which we are here concerned, for if we recognize that the courtiers and officials of the capital city constituted an élite in which the principles of taste were extravagantly honoured, we must also agree that they were conspicuously undisturbed by spiritual and intellectual needs. The prevalent mood, it seems fair to say, was one of sentimentality, or at best of sensibility, and not of anxious speculation about good and evil and the nature of being.

These opinions are perhaps too bold, but they rest upon conclusions which can fairly be drawn from the romances of the period, notably the *Tale of Genji,* or from miscellanies like the *Pillow Book* of Sei Shōnagon; and it is doubtful whether the manners of any ancient period have been more fully reported in the contemporary literature of any other country. Of course such writings must not be taken as an exact and realistic account of fashionable doings in the metropolis and its suburbs, for they are confessedly literary, romantic, and sentimental. But they need not be dismissed as unreliable evidence, since a work of genius is the best kind of social history. These two brilliant observers both directly and by implication give a very credible picture of a small aristocratic coterie devoted to pleasure but guided by certain feelings of propriety and a definite rule of taste.

It is true that most of the incidents related in the *Tale of Genji* have to do with gallantry. Courtship and seduction and their varied consequences provide the central theme, and it might be supposed that these were the chief interest and occupation of the highborn men and women living in or near the imperial city. But in fact this long romance is astonishingly free from erotic passages. The novelist accepts the conventions of her day, which allowed a certain degree of sexual freedom; but she is a lady of birth and breeding, with a discriminating and delicate taste, and a deep understanding of the motions of the human heart. She is interested not in the details of her hero's conquests, but in the subtlest refinements of human intercourse; not in the lovers' embraces, but in their longings and their regrets. It is as well to appreciate this quality of Murasaki's romance, and indeed of most of the romantic literature in which the times were so rich, for it is just to say that though the topic common to them all is relationships between the sexes, its treatment is not coarse or even merely sensual. Its keynote is refinement, and at times a refinement that merges into the ascetic, and is tinged with melancholy.

The ascetic motive, the feeling for simplicity, purity, frugality, is as characteristic of Heian taste as is the strong sense of form and colour expressed by contrast in brilliant costume and elaborate ceremonial.

It is an integral part of the great aesthetic tradition, which is perhaps rooted in early ideas of ritual purity. It is certainly an aspect of Japanese social ideals which should not be overlooked, and we may therefore leave the warm world of amorous adventure and turn for a little while to the chillier circles of high-minded statesmen and severe moralists. Their standards of propriety are set forth in many diaries and injunctions to posterity, notably of the tenth century, some of which have already been cited. It is significant that one of the most important of these is a document known as *Kujō-den no Goyuikai*, the Testamentary Admonitions of Kujō-den, who was none other than the great Fujiwara leader Morosuke, Minister of the Right at his death in 960. Though it is too long for full quotation here, the following extracts will give a fair idea of its quality. It must be read as setting forth a rule of life followed by Morosuke and recommended by him to his heirs and successors.

*

"Upon arising, first of all repeat seven times in a low voice the name of the star for the year. [There are seven—the seven stars of the Great Bear.] Take up a mirror and look at your face, to scrutinize changes in your appearance. Then look at the calendar and see whether the day is one of good or evil omen. Next use your toothbrush and then, facing West [i.e., in the direction of Paradise], wash your hands. Chant the name of the Buddha and invoke those gods and divinities whom we ought always to revere and worship. Next make a record of the events of the previous day. [Throughout the document much stress is laid on the careful use of the calendar for noting engagements and on the accurate recording of the day's business as soon as possible after the event.]

"Now break your fast with rice gruel. Comb your hair once every three days, not every day. Cut your fingernails on a day of the Ox, your toenails on a day of the Tiger. If the day is auspicious, now bathe, but only once every fifth day. There are favourable and unfavourable days for bathing.

"Now if there is any business upon which you must go abroad, put on your clothes and cap. Do not be sluggish in attending to your duties.

"When you meet people do not talk a great deal. And do not discuss your personal affairs. State your opinion, and say what is necessary, but do not repeat what others have said. The disasters of mankind proceed from the mouth. Beware, be on your guard. [Note that most works of this kind emphasize the importance of reserve, of circumspection in speech and gesture.] And when you read documents concerned with state affairs always treat them with discretion.

"At the morning and evening meals you must not make a habit of eating and drinking to excess. Nor should you eat except at proper times. [This rule is supported by a slightly garbled quotation from the Odes.]

"Careful planning can secure the future. In general as you get on in years and become well-acquainted with affairs, you should read classical literature in the morning, next practise handwriting, and only after this indulge in games or sports. But an excessive addiction to hawking and hunting is positively wrong.

"After receiving your manly robes [this refers to the ceremony called "genbuku," the donning of the toga virilis] and before you embark on an official career, conduct yourself in this manner: Early in life select a divinity as the object of your devotion and chant his holy name, after cleansing your hands in a basin of water. One may judge how near a man is to salvation from the frequency with which he recites the mantra [the invocations and spells of the mystic sects].

"There are many warning examples close at hand of disaster and calamity overtaking our irreligious colleagues. Thus the Third Regent, the Lord Tadahira [Morosuke's father], has told us: 'In the eighth year of Enchō (930) when a thunderbolt struck the Pure Cool Hall, the courtiers went pale. I, having taken refuge in the Three Treasures [the Buddhist faith], found in this event nothing to be frightened about. But the Great Counsellor Kiyoyuki and the Vice-Controller Mareyo, who had never paid homage to the Law of the Buddha—these two were struck dead.' From this we may draw our lesson, that the grace bestowed upon us by our faith in the mantra will save us from misfortune. Moreover, many of the clergy, men of faith, purity, and wisdom, can according to their spiritual power bear witness to similar events. But faith is not of help only in this life, for it will indeed ensure for us the life to come.

"If you would learn something of literature, let your attention be devoted especially to the histories and chronicles of our native land.

"In all things render always the utmost loyalty and upright service to your Lord. Always devote the fullest degree of filial piety to your parents. Let your deference to your elder brother be like that which you pay to your father, and your love for your younger brother like that which you feel for your child; so that in all things great or small your hearts may be all one, and the aspirations of all [members of the family] so united that they do not differ by a hair's breadth.

"Cherish your defenceless sisters with all care.

"Whatever you see and hear, tell it to your parent at your morning or evening interview with him. If there should be any person who, though agreeable to you, is displeasing to your parent, give up such company at once.

"Even though a person is offhand with you, so long as he is courteous to your parent always act in a sociable way towards him.

"In general, so long as you are not ill, you should always wait upon your father once every day. Should there be some obstacle, send word and enquire whether it would be suitable to call in the evening. The son and heir of King Wen will serve exceedingly well as a model of filial behaviour. [This is the celebrated Duke of Chou, regarded by Confucius as the paragon of all virtues.]

"It always becomes a man to pay the greatest respect to others, and not to allow a spirit of self-assertion to arise. While you are in society, let this be your attitude. Should anybody in your presence say something offensive, though not legally slanderous, always leave the place at once. If you are unable to leave, watch your language and take care not to get involved in the disagreement. We should not speak of others, even to praise their good deeds. How then should we speak evil of them? This is what the men of old meant when they said 'Let your mouth be like your nose' [meaning Be Silent].

"Unless it is on public business, or for some unavoidable private affair, do not frequent the houses of others. Social intercourse unless on a strictly formal footing is to be regarded as dangerous, leading to jealousy, quarrels, and slander. You must keep yourself to yourself and so preserve your dignity.

"Reflect three times before you say anything to anyone. Never do anything lightly. Take a pride in your person, spend your days as recommended, and be not unmindful of your past errors. Always keep in mind the acts of the sages, and do nothing for which there is no precedent.

"Never discourse on your own poverty or riches. In general personal and domestic matters must be positively avoided as topics of conversation.

"From your garments and your caps up to your carriages, use these things only so far as necessity demands, and do not seek for beauty and display.

"Never borrow the property of another. Only in the case of public business may an exception be made, and then the borrowed thing must be returned promptly by the promised date.

"When you hear of the actions of worthy men, plan and resolve to emulate them, however difficult that may be.

"One who has an official position ought to spur on those under his direction, in each case carrying out his own duties in detail, thus inviting the approbation of his colleagues.

"When making appointments remember that even though a person has talent he is not thereby qualified for preferment unless he is also diligent; while a man who is not precisely a sage but is nevertheless eager and industrious is suitable for promotion.

"At Court it is desirable for you to prize gravity and solemnity. In private you should be relaxed, with humanity and love. Never take offence at small things. If someone has committed a wrong, even while deciding the matter strictly, exercise forbearance. Never give way to great anger.

"Let neither your joy nor your anger be excessive. Let the actions of each day be such as will serve as an improving example for ten thousand years to come.

"Let the income of your house as it is received be divided first into ten parts, and let one part be devoted to alms.

"Make complete plans beforehand for the conduct of your affairs after your death. . . . When this is not done you invite all manner of inconvenience for your wife, your children, and your servants, who then must ask favours of those from whom they ought not to expect them, or will lose that which they ought not to lose, thus leading to the ruin of your house and to censure by others.

"Always put by a portion of your income to provide for the Seven Requiem Masses, for the repose of your spirit, beginning with the cost of the funeral itself.

. . .

"Do you who come after me reflect fervently on these things, and always devote yourselves to public and private affairs with the utmost diligence."

❀

These cold injunctions to posterity do not sound like the sentiments of a great noble presiding over an extravagant and dissolute aristocracy. They are more akin to the utterances of a prophet deploring the evils of his day. But they are not really moral principles. Rather they are rules for success in life, calling for extreme self-control, and the observances of a very strict code of behaviour exacted by Buddhist faith and Confucian piety. Perhaps their most notable feature is the great weight given to filial duty, together with a disapproval of all social intercourse beyond what is required for the due performance of public obligations. The family is the unit, the means, and the purpose of life. It is self-contained and independent of, if not hostile to, other families. In public what is to be prized is gravity and solemnity. Only in the bosom of the family may one abandon something of the reserve which distinguishes a man of breeding, and relax in an atmosphere of humanity and love.

What seems at first sight surprising is the repeated stress upon frugality and simplicity. It is, of course, in part of Confucian origin, for the Sage must always avoid excess of any kind; but it comes also from a persistent strain in the Japanese character which finds expression in the earliest Shintō ritual and is visible throughout Japanese social history. It is interesting to note that the passage recommending simple clothing and furniture and condemning display is quoted in later literature as a classical dictum on frugality. One of the most familiar instances occurs in the fourteenth-century miscellany called *Tsuredzure Gusa,* where the writer, dwelling upon the importance of a simple, frugal life, says: "In Kujō-den's admonitions to his descendants it is written that they should not seek for elegance and splendour."

A predilection for what is simple and pure shows itself in many forms of artistic expression, and sometimes in surprising places. The *Tale of Genji* is not at first sight a source to which the historian of morals would turn for a description of austere pleasures and frugal habits, seeing that it is devoted principally to the love affairs of a handsome young prince and to their extremely complicated sequels. But it is rich in sage comment upon human affairs in general, and it contains certain passages that throw light upon questions of style as they were seen in the Heian era. One of these, known as the "Shina-sadame" ("Judgment of Quality"), reports an argument among Genji's friends about what makes the perfect woman. The debaters are four young noblemen, in their quarters at the royal palace, as officers of the Guard. They agree that there are three classes of women, upper, middle, and lower, but they find it hard to decide whether birth or beauty or character is the essential quality in a wife. Uma no Kami, an officer of the Horse Guards, described as "a great lover and a good talker," concludes that it is with women as it is with the works of craftsmen; there is the man who makes things to suit a passing fashion, and there is the sober artist who strives to give beauty to things which men actually use, in the shapes which tradition has ordained.

It is characteristic of the contemporary habit of mind that human problems should have been considered by analogy with the fine arts. Uma no Kami talks of painters who are most proficient, yet whose purpose is to astonish the eye of the beholder by their skill and riotous fancy. "But," he goes on, "ordinary hills and rivers just as they are, houses such as you may see anywhere with all their real beauty and harmony of form—quietly to draw such scenes as these . . . and all this with befitting care for composition and proportion—such works demand the highest master's utmost skill."

This is high discourse, one might think, for guardsmen in their leisure hours, and it shows that (in Murasaki's view at least) the young men of fashion were inclined to pride themselves on avoiding what was obvious and gross, and seeking what was refined and delicate in matters of appreciation. Not only in painting or calligraphy, for Uma no Kami continues: "So it is in these trifling matters. And how much more in judging the human heart should we distrust all fashionable airs and graces, all tricks and smartness learned only to please the outward gaze. . . . Let me tell you a story."

Having so spoken, this garrulous gentleman came and sat nearer to his friends. The Prince Genji had begun to doze. "Dressed in white silk with a rough cloak carelessly flung over his shoulders . . . in the light of the lamp he looked so lovely that one might have wished he were a girl. Tō no Chūjo [a Captain of the Guard and Genji's brother-in-law] was sitting with his cheek propped upon his hand. Genji woke up. Uma no Kami's speech that night was very much like a preacher's sermon about the ways of the world, and was a little absurd. 'It happened while I was young,' he continued. 'I was in love with a girl. . . .'"

In such conversations they passed the night. Here is an intimate scene, revealed as it were in a flash, evoked and illumined by Murasaki's vision. It is an imaginary scene, but it helps towards an understanding of the nature of Heian life, at least in aristocratic circles and in respect of those features which are of interest in the history of taste.

What is peculiarly interesting about the reminiscences of these young gallants is that, far from boasting of their conquests, they tell rather dismal stories of failure and regret. They are disillusioned but in their search for the ideal mistress they appear to be indefatigable. Genji, so Murasaki's narrative continues, on the following morning returned to his own mansion to visit his wife, the Princess Aoi, whom he had not seen during his long term of attendance at the Palace. He was oppressed by her perfection of beauty and character, her scornful dignity which seemed to make intimacy impossible.

The remainder of this long romance is devoted to an account of Genji's love affairs as a young man, and then his relations with his wives, his mistresses, and his children, and finally the lives of his descendants after his death. He is represented as the embodiment of masculine excellence. He is of noble birth, of great wealth, of exceptional beauty of person; wise and witty, kind and generous, debonair and ingratiating. He is almost irresistible and he is always in trouble. It is perhaps significant that the one quality not specifically attributed to him is courage. Most of the romances of the period are silent on this aspect of a hero's character, no doubt because a Fujiwara gentleman regards warlike accomplishment as the business of professionals.

At first Genji appears as an incorrigible voluptuary, and his reckless entanglements at times lead to tragic consequences. He nearly breaks the heart of the wife of a provincial governor, who is dazzled by his high rank. The beautiful girl Yugao dies in the middle of the night, bewitched or possessed by a demon. An intrigue with the Lady Fujitsubo, who was then the Emperor's consort, brings him near to ruin when her child is seen to resemble Genji himself and not the Emperor.

But as the story proceeds, and as Genji grows older—he is a youth of seventeen in the early episodes—his conduct becomes less scandalous. He is wiser and more compassionate, more truly affectionate. Indeed, behind all his thoughtless conduct there appears a real tenderness, so that this great work, which starts as if it were to be a dreary epic of seduction, gradually develops a note of sadness and becomes a long and fascinating study of the subtleties of human intercourse, a chronicle of melancholy and fatalism relieved by a deep sense of beauty. Tears flow easily. The irresistible amorist is a pessimist at heart, weighed down by a sense of misfortune, by the weight of an unhappy karma. At the age of thirty we find him haunted by the impermanence of worldly things, and on the point of embracing a monastic life.

These extracts from the *Tale of Genji* are adduced here as historical evidence, for the whole work is a treasure house of the materials of social history. Some historians, both Japanese and foreign, are inclined to use very harsh language about the ruling class in the Heian capital, as when the courtiers and officials are described as "an ever-pullulating brood of greedy, needy frivolous dilettanti, as often as not foully licentious, utterly effeminate, incapable of worthy achievement." Certainly it was a polygamous society, and pleasure-seeking too; but it can scarcely be condemned as degraded. It was elegant and artistic, given to pious exercises, and it had a puritanical side, as Kujō-den's admonitions show. Even the loose behaviour that was permitted, let us say even encouraged, had to keep within a rule of moderation, as we can tell from a rebuke administered to Genji by the old Emperor (his father). "In future," said His Majesty, "you must be careful to avoid indiscreet behaviour. You will find yourself an object of unfriendly criticism if you give way to your slightest amorous inclinations. Love affairs must be so managed that the woman, whoever she may be, is treated fairly and not put into a humiliating position. You must be at pains to give her no cause for bitter resentment."

Genji listened to this rebuke in silence. He was miserably conscious of a misspent life. But he said to himself—and here is a clue to the essence of the emotional life of his kind—"I know that even at this moment the sight of something very beautiful, were it only a common flower or tree, might in an instant make life again seem full of meaning and reality." Throughout the story, even in its saddest episodes, there runs a thread of delight in beauty. All the love talk is interspersed with enjoyment of colour, shape, and perfume, and with a continual exchange of poetic messages. Calligraphy plays almost as great a part as the tones of a lover's voice in arousing tender emotion. When Genji's young wife Murasaki sees no more than the superscription of a letter which he has received from another woman, she recognizes that it is in "a flawless hand, such as the greatest lady in the country would have no cause to disown." From that moment she knows what is in store for her. *This* could assuredly be no fleeting fancy! Handwriting, it was the general belief, revealed (or rather it expressed) character, breeding, distinction, and other qualities more clearly than speech, and it ranked high among the fine arts.

Though life at the Palace may appear as an empty round of ceremonies and entertainments, it would not be right to say that the Court was corrupt and dissolute. It would be nearer the truth to say that most royal and noble personages lived a life that was refined, but far from luxurious, in untidy and uncomfortable surroundings. Indeed much leisure was spent by the sovereigns and their courtiers in most innocent, simple pastimes. Such was the charming music party described by another gifted writer, the lady-in-waiting Sei Shōnagon, as taking place on a spring day in the year 1000. "The sun shone splendidly in a pure calm sky. The Emperor was playing the flute, in a room near the Western Gallery. The Deputy Governor of Kyūshū, Fujiwara Takatō, who is a clever flautist, was at his side. They played the air *Takasago* several times, and their music had a charm that banal words cannot express. Takatō, posing as a professor of the flute, showed His Majesty how he should play. It was really superb. The other ladies-in-waiting and I pressed up to the curtain in a crowd, and while we watched them it seemed to me that I had never gathered parsley [had never had any troubles]. All my troubles had vanished."

She goes on to tell of one Suketada, an upstart official, a chamberlain whom the Court ladies disliked and nicknamed "The Violent Crocodile." They made a rather detrimental song about him, and the Emperor played the tune on his flute, but very, very softly, so that Suketada should not hear. Presently His Majesty went out to consult the Empress, and came back, saying "It's all right. He's not there." And he blew away on his flute. "How pretty it all was!"

While the leisure hours of the Empress Sadako's ladies were filled with childish pleasures and frivolity, service in the Empress Akiko's apartments was a rather serious occupation. Life for her ladies was far from being dissipated, seeing that Her Majesty had very strict views on behaviour and thought that learning was more important than finery and flirtation. Her senior ladies-in-waiting were dowdy and not at all playful. No doubt some of the younger ones had their gay occasions, but in general the daughters of the aristocracy were given an education to prepare them for a strict society in which calligraphy, music, and poetry were necessary accomplishments. Reading contemporary literature one gains the impression that there was more talk of handsome men than of beautiful women in Court circles; but perhaps this is because we depend chiefly on the works of women writers of diaries and novels.

Yet even in the serious journals kept by men we find descriptions of ceremonies, horse races, archery contests, and even religious services in which the good looks of men are carefully recorded, as matters of prime importance. In descriptions of women little is said about their features, perhaps because Court ladies were supposed to be hidden from the gaze of men behind screens or curtains, and not to show more than their eyes and brows as they peered over a fan. But women prided themselves on their hair, which must be glossy black, straight, and very long, and that is how it is lovingly depicted in the scrolls of the day. It was usually worn uncut, without any arrangement other than a parting, and it was thought right that the hair of a beautiful woman should reach the ground.

Though teeth were blackened, a white skin was much prized, the ideal for a young girl being a skin "white as the down on the breast of the young of a wild goose," and not only white but having a sweet scent. For a woman's complexion white combined with a rosy tint was most desirable, and the make-up of the day was of this kind. Men also used cosmetics, and even soldiers of the guard put powder on their faces, which sometimes rubbed off as they marched, leaving their dark skin exposed, "like the ground where snow has melted." Perhaps the most surprising thing about standards of female beauty is that the Court ladies were horrified by nakedness; and in Japanese art the nude has rarely been portrayed. Nor has Japanese poetry much to say about particulars of feminine charms, whether of face or figure, while even in the tenderest love passages in the *Tale of Genji* it is rare to find anything more outspoken than such a phrase as "using her limbs with subtle grace."

While separate passages in the *Tale of Genji* can be used as evidence of the nature of the society in which its characters move, the romance

Detail from a twelfth-century scroll

itself, as a complete work of art, is a superb example of the contemporary standard of taste. This is not the place for literary appraisal, but it is not foreign to our theme—which is the aesthetic quality of Heian life— to single out some special beauties.

In the chapter called "Hotaru" ("Fire-Fly") there is a well-known passage in which the authoress puts her views about the novel into the mouth of Genji, who says: "History books such as the *Chronicles of Japan* show only one small corner of life, whereas these diaries and romances contain, I am sure, the most minute information about all sorts of people's private affairs. . . . But I have a theory of my own about what this art of the novel is, and how it came into being. To begin with it does not simply consist in the author's telling a story about the adventures of some other person. On the contrary it happens because the storyteller's own experience of men and things, whether for good or for evil—not only what he has passed through himself but even events which he has only witnessed or been told of—has moved him to an emotion so passionate that he can no longer keep it shut up in his heart. . . . Clearly it is no part of the storyteller's craft to describe only what is good or beautiful. Sometimes virtue will be his theme, but he is just as likely to have been struck by numerous examples of vice and folly around him, and about these he has exactly the same feelings as about the preeminently good deeds which he encounters. They are important and must be garnered in."

All this confirms the impression that there is a solid basis of truth for most of the incidents related by Murasaki, and certainly she regarded her work as a serious form of fiction, an elaborated version of her experience, but not a light and frivolous fabrication. Many of her characters are historical personages, whom she knew during her long service at Court. Among them are the Emperors Suzaku and Ryōzen (Reizei), Vestal Princesses, Fujiwara noblemen (she was a Fujiwara herself), great officers of state, and lesser people about the Court. The monk Yogawa, described in the chapter called "Tenarai," is thought to be based upon the great Buddhist teacher Eshin, who was one of the leaders of popular Amida worship in Japan and wrote the "Essentials of Salvation" (*Ōjō Yōshū*) in 985. Genji himself is thought to be modelled mainly upon Korechika, but also in part upon Michinaga. The lively descriptions of the first part of the romance seem to suggest a cheerful life at Court, whereas the later chapters express a mood of disillusionment, a desire to escape from the world of appearances. This change of atmosphere assuredly reflects the fluctuating sentiment of the times, for there is much evidence to show that later Heian life was touched with pessimism. The characters in that part of the narrative concerned with the generation after Genji's death seem neurotic and complex compared with the gay companions of his youth.

So much for the matter of Murasaki's book. There is little indication of her views about style, but that she had a subtle feeling for beauty of expression is evident on every page. Her lapses are very rare. Much vanishes even in the most faithful translation, but the reader can discern, as through a veil, her mastery of the arts of suggestion, her power of creating an effect by seemingly simple touches. Here is one of several passages selected for praise by a modern Japanese novelist, who was a considerable virtuoso himself, and admired ornamental prose:

Living in solitude in her house in the woods a forlorn lady receives one of her lover's rare visits. "In her narrow life it was as if the light of a star in the wide heavens were by chance reflected in a basin of water."[1]

Another charming turn of phrase is in a description of flowering trees in spring: "Among them it was the plum trees that gave the surest promise, for already their blossoms were uncurling, like lips parted in a faint smile."

Some light is thrown upon questions of taste by most literary works of the Heian age, whether in verse or prose. Perhaps the most valuable guide to feeling in such matters is the *Pillow Book* of Sei Shōnagon, who was a lady-in-waiting to the Empress Sadako during the ten years at the close of the tenth century. It is not strictly speaking a work of imagination, but a miscellany recording incidents and ideas, often in a witty and somewhat astringent manner. Its descriptions are more direct, but no less penetrating, than those of Murasaki, for Sei Shōnagon was gifted with a poetic eye, a perceptive mind, and a fastidious sense of beauty, so that what she has to say is the best possible kind of evidence about the aesthetic standards of her time. Her love affairs appear to have been numerous, and she refers to them quite frankly and without any sense of guilt or even indiscretion. This is of no great importance, except in so far as it reflects the conventions of the day; but it is perhaps a useful indication that in the society which she adorned matters of taste were not governed by ethical principles. Here is a point which should be considered when basing any theory of aesthetics upon descriptions of Heian society.

Sei Shōnagon, as we have seen, was much loved by the Empress, whom she in turn adored, and she consequently had a most intimate knowledge of Court life, which she describes with a sophisticated delicacy of understanding and a flash of humour like summer lightning. She deplores ugliness and rebukes stupidity, but she refrains from moral judgments. The life of which she gives a picture includes not only a round of ceremonies and religious exercises, but also many hours of leisure passed in desultory talk and simple recreations. Poetry as usual plays a leading part, and so does letter-writing, both being necessary accomplishments contributing to the art of social relations. Calligraphy,

---

[1] The critic was the novelist Ozaki Kōyō (1867–1903).

quite apart from its value in tender missives, is so important that Nori-
tsune, assistant secretary in the Board of Rites, is laughed at by the Court
ladies because he writes such an atrocious hand; and a man of fashion
who cannot woo a lady with a well-turned verse has little hope of conquests, while a young woman unable to respond in kind to poetical
advances is unlikely to attract suitors. Correct costume is a matter of
the highest importance, as a display of rank and consequence but also
as a sign of good taste. Both men's and women's garments are examined with a very critical eye. Poor or ill-matched colours, a false
note in the choice of shade or texture, these are as painful to the eye as
a dissonance to the ear of a musician. They are to be pointed out by
arbiters of elegance in the disparaging terms called for by any grave
social blunder.

The same exacting criticism is applied to ritual movements and the
conduct of ceremonial. The great Buddhist services are regarded as
displays of rich vestments and handsome uniforms and correct posture
rather than as the performance of pious exercises. There are experienced
connoisseurs of such matters, eager to discuss the aesthetic merits of
different clerics whose sermons and scripture readings they have heard.
Sei Shōnagon herself says that a preacher must be good-looking, because if he is ugly your eyes stray and your mind wanders, but if he is
handsome you keep your eyes fixed upon his face, and thus you feel the
sanctity of the truth which he expounds. In this world of the senses
the words for good and beautiful are almost interchangeable.

Sei Shōnagon, like most of the ladies of the Court, enjoyed these
spectacles and watched them with an almost breathless interest, while
keeping her wits about her. One of them she described as follows:

"There was a superb ceremony at the residence of the Commander
of the Bodyguard, who lives at the Little Palace of the Fifth Avenue,
when the Eight Lectures were read under the auspices of the great officers. Everybody came to listen to these sermons, and as we had been
warned that carriages arriving late would not be able to get near, we
rose very early with the morning dew, and found them all closely
packed. . . . It was midsummer and the heat was extraordinary, and
only those of us who could look at the lotus blossoms in the pond could
feel that we were enjoying a little freshness. All were present except
the Ministers of the Left and Right. All wore laced trousers [sashinuki,
a divided skirt], and violet Court mantles which did not conceal their
bright yellow underdresses. The youngest among them, mere youths,
had blue-gray laced trousers or cool-looking white trousers. The State
Counsellor Yasuchika himself was there, dressed like a young man,
which was scarcely in keeping with the sacred character of the ceremony. What an odd sight! The blinds had been rolled up high, and
the great dignitaries were seated in long rows across the room. Below

them on the outer verandah the courtiers and the young lords, very elegant in their hunting uniforms or in their Court mantles, had not yet taken their seats, but walked about, talking and joking. It was a pretty sight. . . . As the sun rose near the zenith the Captain of the Third Rank arrived—that is what one called the then Regent. [This was Michi-taka, the father of the Empress Sadako.] He came in wearing a summer tunic of light colour, a violet mantle, laced trousers of the same colour worn over underdrawers of deep red, and over all a stiff unlined gar-ment, brilliantly white. He might be thought too warmly dressed, but he was nevertheless of a marvellous elegance. . . . All the gentlemen carried fans of which the thin ribs were lacquered in various colours, but of each fan the paper was a brilliant red. It looked like a bed of pinks superbly flowering."

In summing up the affair, Sei writes that the great variety of subtle shades, each enhancing the effect of the others, formed a splendid pic-ture, wonderfully pleasing; and throughout in her descriptions of such scenes she dwells lovingly upon details of colour. She belongs to a society in which the enjoyment of visual beauty is almost passionate. At times on reading such accounts one feels that the strongest emotions of these connoisseurs are aroused not by their love affairs, which seem to proceed according to rule with a kind of gentle amiability, but by well-chosen colours, unfaltering strokes of the writing brush, and an apt manipulation of syllables.

Here is another passage revealing a deep interest in fine points of male apparel: "The Lord Vice-Chamberlain . . . came forward, mag-nificent in his Court mantle of a superb cherry colour, with a lining of which the hue and lustre had an inexpressible charm. His divided skirt was of the shade of wineberry, very deep, and it was embroidered with branches of wistaria, larger than life. The colour and brilliance of his scarlet underdress were splendid, and beneath it he had put on other garments of white and light violet, one after another. . . . He seemed in truth to be one of those personages who are painted by artists or cele-brated by writers of romance."

In Murasaki's Diary (an interesting record of her life and her opin-ions) there is a well-known passage on the question of colour. At Court a lady-in-waiting appeared beautifully attired, but there was a little fault in the combination of colours at her wrist, where the edges of the sleeves of her numerous undergarments showed. This was noticed by the nobles present and it rather upset Murasaki's friend, the Lady Saishō, who said, however, "It was not really very bad—only one colour was a little too pale." This, I should think, is the classic statement about Japanese taste, and not only taste in regard to colour.

Even in love affairs costume seems to play a predominant part, and the dress of the man is as important as that of the woman. Sei recalls or imagines a scene where a man appears unexpectedly at her bedside, when the dawn landscape is covered by a heavy mist. She does not describe his features, but notes that he is wearing violet trousers and a hunting jacket of a shade of dove-colour so light that it scarcely looks as if it had been dyed, and an unlined tunic of stiff white silk under a cloak of brilliant scarlet.

Besides illuminating Japanese taste in form and colour the works of women writers like Murasaki and Sei are of interest in the study of the peculiar linguistic history of Japan. The fortunate invention of a syllabic script which served excellently for the notation of Japanese speech made it possible for those gifted ladies to write their masterpieces in their own tongue and so to escape from the domination of the Chinese classics, which had threatened to stifle the growth of a truly native style. The beginnings of a native literature may be traced to the *Manyōshū* and the Shintō liturgies, which were recorded, however clumsily, in something like their original accents. If we take these early phases as a starting point, we may conclude that writings in pure Japanese go back to about A.D. 800, which is a very early date compared with, say, that of the first important vernacular literature in England and France. French verse began to contend with Latin in the time of Ronsard and the Pléiade, some of whom still wrote only in Greek or Latin. Even *Paradise Lost* might have been written in Latin, and on the continent Milton was known not as a master of English but as a Latin pamphleteer. Of course in Europe Latin served as an international medium, to the great benefit of European culture, and Greek studies were promoted by the fact that early Christian literature was in Greek. There was no English New Testament until after the Greek editio princeps of Erasmus came out in 1516.

The parallel is admittedly far-fetched, for it is true that circumstances in East and West are not fully comparable; and it cannot be said that the need for Japanese versions of Buddhist scriptures hastened the growth of a native literature. But even if we put its beginnings at the time of the *Taketori Monogatari* and Tsurayuki's preface to the *Kokinshū*, say about A.D. 900, that is a difference of over five hundred years. All things considered, it is remarkable that the prestige of the Chinese classics should have proved less powerful than Greek and Latin works in delaying the rise of a vernacular literature; or, to put it in another way, it is remarkable that a not very highly developed language like Japanese should have offered such effective resistance to the monumental strength of Chinese. Surely this was mainly due to such writers as Sei and Murasaki, women of genius whose passion for expression brooked no denial.

There is a further question to be considered here, and that is whether in fact the Chinese language could ever have reflected the Japanese temperament. It is not easy to imagine the true Japanese spirit—if the use of such controversial terms may be allowed—expressing itself in a curt monosyllabic tongue. It seems fair to suppose that, whatever practical use was later made of Chinese, the essence of Japanese culture was best revealed by the native idiom, and Japanese taste throve upon the flavour and rhythm of Japanese speech. No doubt the Japanese aesthetic tradition was formed chiefly in the practice of the visual arts, but the contribution of the vernacular literature cannot be neglected.

Perhaps this is a suitable place in which to speculate about the part of the *waka*, the short Japanese poem, in the development of the Japanese language as an instrument for the expression of sentiment rather than the statement of facts. I do not think there can be any doubt that the difficulty of expression with a limited number of sounds (fifty open syllables only, to be exact) forced the Japanese poet to resort to certain enigmatic cadences, certain delicate, almost imperceptible harmonies that give to poetry, and to some kinds of prose, a subtle flavour that a Western student does not easily appreciate. The paronomasia, the play upon words, that offends the taste of one brought up to dislike puns, in this poetic medium falls into place as a conventional ornament having a function not unlike that of rhyme.

An attempt, such as that made in the foregoing pages, to describe in words an aesthetic society is bound to give a false or at best an inadequate impression, for such a lively, irrational, eccentric, and specialized organism does not submit to simple definition. In some regards the behaviour of the Heian exquisites reached extremes of silliness, and the fatuity of their sentiments is at times quite hard to believe. Yet it is no small achievement to have succeeded in developing a mode of existence dedicated to the acute perception of beauty and the refinement of personal relations to such a point that ideas and feelings could be conveyed by the merest shadow of a hint.

There is one aspect of the love of beauty which is not usually considered, and that is its bearing upon the intellectual history of the Japanese people up to the end of the middle ages. Can it be said of them that before all else they were lovers of the beautiful? This has often been said of the Greeks, but on the other side a distinguished classical scholar, H. J. Garrod, while not challenging the power with which the Greeks developed and illustrated a specially Greek conception of the beautiful, has argued that this conception has influenced the modern world far less than we pretend, and that our real debt to Greece is elsewhere. He thinks that what makes the Greeks a race apart is the logicality and honesty of their minds. "They like what is rational, like to get to the bottom of things. It is much easier to love the beautiful than to love the true and the sensible. The Greeks did both."

It is very doubtful whether this could be said of the Japanese as a people at any time before the modern age. Everything in their early history points to love of beauty, little or nothing to exceptional logicality and honesty. On the other hand, there seems to be a warmth and depth in their love of beauty which qualifies them as a race apart, or at least distinguishes them from the Greeks, as the features of a Buddhist image expressing love and mercy differ from the cold marble countenances of an Apollo or an Artemis.

We must remember, of course, in discussing standards of taste in the early part of the eleventh century that we can draw conclusions only from the life of a chosen few as it is described in their writings and their pictures. We know very little about the clerks, the shopkeepers, the peasants, the footmen, and the grooms, except as they appear in some contemporary drawings. It is only the upper class, the Court nobles, the high officials, and the leading churchmen whose manners and ideas are recorded in literature. The artists and craftsmen are for the most part mute and anonymous, though it is thanks to them that we happen to know some details of the outward appearance of life as it was lived by members of the aristocratic society in the capital city.

In numbers it must have been a very limited society, already on the decline at the turn of the century and destined by 1100 to lose its exclusive character by the admission of new men without much claim to birth and breeding. As a society its importance lies not in its size but in its quality; and it no doubt owed much of its distinctive character to its isolation from the disagreeable realities of the times, for in the eleventh century a sense of foreboding filled the common air even if misgivings had not yet reached the nine-times-encircled penetralia of the Court. It is a curious fact that the royal city, laid out on a lavish scale, was already showing signs of decay long before the Fujiwara Regency reached its heights of ostentation. It was planned at the end of the eighth century on ambitious lines, no doubt looking forward to a great increase of population. By the end of the tenth century no such increase had taken place. Migration from country to town certainly was common during that interval, but there is also evidence of a considerable movement away from the city to rural areas where conditions were more promising.

Originally the capital had covered about eight square miles, but by Michinaga's day the western half (Nishi no Kyō) had practically fallen into ruin for lack of habitation. Walls and embankments had collapsed, tiles had dropped from the roofs, and there were left only a few mansions or smaller houses uncared for in deserted fields. In the eastern part, by as early as 850 most of the great halls and government offices had been destroyed by fire or allowed to get into a hopeless state of dilapidation. By 900 the official building of the Chancellor had centipedes in the ceiling and wasps' nests hanging from the roof, and parts of other ruined edifices were used by Michinaga in building his own Hōjōji monastery early in the eleventh century. After 850 some government offices were rebuilt on a smaller scale, but still there were constant fires, and frequent epidemics laying waste whole quarters of the city.

Thus it seems that the population of the capital and its suburbs must have increased very slowly, if it increased at all, for in addition to these calamities there was a tendency for enterprising people to move to the eastern provinces, where land was more plentiful and opportunity greater. At a guess, the true aristocratic society, with its close dependents, can scarcely have numbered more than two or three thousand in Michinaga's time; or if we include the courtiers of lower ranks, the lesser officials of the ministries, and a small number of leading ecclesiastics, perhaps five thousand. One is much struck, in reading accounts of Heian life, by the impression that nearly all the people mentioned are somehow related to one another.

There is a temptation for the reader of the *Tale of Genji* to regard it as an exact depiction of Heian society. That it certainly is not, for it is a romantic tale and not a historical study; but it reveals the essence of life at the Heian Court in a convincing way. It is an idealized version by a brilliant witness of what people did and said in Kyoto in the year 1000. If Sei's *Pillow Book* is used as a sort of corrective, we cannot be far from the truth.

While this metropolitan culture is an important element in the history of Japan, it should be remembered that only a small proportion of the people were directly affected by urban life. By A.D. 900 the rural population, not alone in numbers but also in productive capacity and military competence, had already begun to outstrip the city-dwelling aristocrats in real power. An account of the growth of a strong rural society is given in Chapter XII; for the present it is enough to bear in mind that the strength and independence of the leading provincial families were gradually increasing, and that great military houses were coming into prominence. During the tenth century they were still subordinate to the aristocratic leaders of society in the capital, especially so long as the Fujiwara Regents were able to select the sovereign and manipulate the Court. The heyday of the aesthetic society may be said to coincide with the supremacy of the Fujiwara, which ended towards the year 1150.

It is not easy to find a parallel to the aristocratic society of the Heian capital. Islamic life in Persia offers some analogies, but perhaps the closest resemblance is to be found in life at the court of Akbar, as it is described in the so-called "Memoirs of Akbar," or *Akbar Nāmah*.[2]

---

[2] This was pointed out to me a long time ago by Dr. Arthur Waley, who also told me that the novel of Leo Myers, *The Root and the Flower*, was much influenced by the *Tale of Genji*. Myers's is a fascinating work, describing an aesthetic society similar to that of Akbar's court, and it can be read with profit and pleasure by students of Japanese culture. There is a translation from the Persian of *Akbar Nāmah* by H. Beveridge, in three volumes of Bibliotheca Indica, published by the Asiatic Society of Bengal (Calcutta, 1907, 1912, and 1939).

CHAPTER X

GOVERNMENT BY CLOISTERED
EMPERORS

As we have seen, the Fujiwara Regents are sometimes described as a Far Eastern counterpart of the eighth-century Frankish Mayors of the Palace. The comparison is useful, but it is not exact, since some of the Mayors of the Palace went on to acquire sovereignty, whereas the Fujiwara Regents never assumed royal titles or claimed royal prerogative even when in fact they exercised royal power. Nor did they enjoy that power for long after the death of Michinaga in 1027.

The successor of Michinaga was Yorimichi, who held the office of Kampaku for fifty years, during the reigns of Go-Ichijō (1016–36), Go-Suzaku (1036–45), and Go-Reizei (1045–68). These monarchs were still under the influence of their Fujiwara connexions, so that during their reigns the power of the Regents was not very obviously declining. But it was in truth on the wane, partly because the conduct of affairs since Michinaga's day had been both ruthless and self-seeking and partly because rival clans were beginning to feel their own strength. At this juncture, when (in sentiment, if not in action) opposition to the Regents was gathering, the Emperor Go-Sanjō succeeded on the death of Go-Reizei in 1068. That is an important (though not crucial) date in Japanese history, for although the collapse of the Fujiwara was no doubt inevitable, it is probable that the character of the new Emperor Go-Sanjō was what precipitated their downfall.

This monarch was the second son of Go-Suzaku, and his mother was the Princess Yōmeimon-In, so that he had no direct connexion with the Fujiwara family and owed them no debt of piety or gratitude. He was determined to govern in person. His determination was no doubt strengthened and his dislike of the Fujiwara increased by the unhappy experience of his youth, for although he had been named by his father as the Crown Prince who was to follow Go-Reizei (his elder half-brother), the Regent Yorimichi was antagonistic to him. For the twenty years and more that elapsed between his father's death and his own accession in 1068 he was continuously slandered and threatened. He was for example accused of trying to cause the death of Go-Reizei by spells, and he himself lived in dread of violence. It is not surprising that when at last he came to the Throne he should have shown a strong desire to govern without interference, and accordingly embarked without hesitation upon policies highly unfavourable to the interests of the leaders of the Fujiwara clan. It was not long before the Regents began to lose ground, for when Yorimichi's younger brother took on the post

Heian Emperors

EMPEROR	BIRTH	ACCESSION	ABDICATION	DEATH
Kammu	737	781	—	806
Heizei	774	806	809	824
Saga	786	809	823	842
Junna	786	823	833	840
Nimmyō	810	833	—	850
Montoku	827	850	—	858
Seiwa	850	858	876	880
Yōzei	868	877	884	949
Kōkō	830	884	—	887
Uda	867	887	897	937
Daigo	885	897	—	930
Suzaku	923	930	946	952
Murakami	926	946	—	967
Reizei	950	967	969	1011
Enyū	959	969	984	991
Kazan	968	984	986	1008
Ichijō	980	986	—	1011
Sanjō	976	1011	1016	1017
Go-Ichijō	1008	1016	—	1036
Go-Suzaku	1009	1036	—	1045
Go-Reizei	1025	1045	—	1068
Go-Sanjō	1034	1068	1072	1073
Shirakawa	1053	1072	1086	1129
Horikawa	1079	1086	—	1107
Toba	1103	1107	1123	1156
Sutoku	1119	1123	1141	1164
Konoye	1139	1141	—	1155
Go-Shirakawa	1127	1155	1158	1192
Nijō	1143	1158	—	1165
Rokujō	1164	1165	1168	1176
Takakura	1161	1168	1180	1181
Antoku	1178	1180	(deposed)	1185
Go-Toba	1180	1184	1198	1239

of Kampaku in 1069 he is reported to have said that his title was a useless ornament. This trend continued as Go-Sanjō, encouraged and aided by good advisers, took the lead in an attempt to restore the administrative authority of the Crown, which had been either usurped or flouted by the Fujiwara nobles. One of his first acts of major policy was the establishment of a Land Record Office (Kirokujo) which is described elsewhere.[1] This was a bold effort to deal with the estates (shōen) that by their claims to fiscal and judicial immunity were destroying the centralized administrative system and creating a very great number of quasi-autonomous domains throughout the country.

The Emperor Go-Sanjō unfortunately died in the year 1073, at the early age of thirty-nine, after only four years on the throne. There were many difficult problems of government still to solve, but at last the Fujiwara grip was broken. The rule of the dictators was now to be replaced not, as one might suppose, by the direct rule of enthroned monarchs but by a curious political device known as Insei, a term usually translated into English as "Cloister Government." Under this system the titular sovereign would at his own pleasure abdicate, placing a suitably docile heir, usually a minor, upon the throne, and (generally after taking the tonsure) he would continue to direct affairs of state from the palace or mansion or other retreat to which he had moved. This dwelling place, because of his now religious life, was known as his "In," that being a customary affix to the name of a secluded monastic apartment. By a practice very usual in Japan, the name of the residence was applied to the resident, so that once the reigning monarch Go-Sanjō had abdicated and put his son upon the throne (as he did in 1072, not long before his death) he moved to his In or Cloister, and was known by the style of Go-Sanjō In. He had intended to govern through his son, the Emperor Shirakawa, who, as it turned out, was both titular and actual sovereign from 1072 to 1086, then abdicated, entered holy orders, and continued to govern until his death in 1129, after ruling as a cloistered emperor for forty-three years. During this period three titular emperors in succession occupied the throne, but without the exercise of any real authority.

Although the practice of cloister government strictly speaking began with the abdication of the Emperor Shirakawa in 1086, it arose naturally from certain long-standing habits in Japanese life. The demands of ceremonial and family duty lay heavy not only on the sovereign but also on most men of rank. They were so exacting that it was common for the head of a great institution or a great house to retire at an early age, so as to spend his late years, if not in peace, at least free from the burden of social obligation. This custom, known as Inkyo (which means a sheltered or passive life) has not entirely disappeared, even in modern

---

[1] Chapter VIII, p. 153.

times. In the dynastic history of Japan the frequency of abdication is very marked, as will be seen from the table of Heian emperors (p. 198), which shows that of thirty-three sovereigns thirteen died while on the throne, one was deposed, and nineteen abdicated. No doubt there were occasions when abdication was forced, but it is certain that some of the most capable emperors abdicated so as to rid themselves of the load of ritual duties or the danger of palace conspiracies and to devote their talents to the business and pleasure of exercising real power.

Most of them "entered religion" and were given the appellation of Hō-ō, or Sacred Ruler. This was not an essential feature of the system of cloister government, but it was common for men of rank who wished for freedom of action to "take the tonsure" and assume a holy office which gave them some protection against secular dangers.

The confused situation which resulted from these practices is represented in the following table:

DATE	TITULAR EMPEROR	SENIOR CLOISTERED EMPEROR	OTHER RETIRED EMPEROR
1067–1072	Go-Sanjō	——	——
1072–1073	Shirakawa	Go-Sanjō	——
1073–1086	Shirakawa	——	——
1086–1107	Horikawa	Shirakawa	——
1107–1123	Toba	Shirakawa	——
1123–1129	Sutoku	Shirakawa	Toba
1129–1141	Sutoku	Toba	——
1141–1155	Konoye	Toba	Sutoku
1155–1156	Go-Shirakawa	Toba	Sutoku
1156–1158	Go-Shirakawa	——	Sutoku
1158–1165	Nijō	Go-Shirakawa	——
1165–1168	Rokujō	Go-Shirakawa	——
1168–1180	Takakura	Go-Shirakawa	Rokujō (to 1176)
1180–1185	Antoku	Go-Shirakawa	Takakura (to 1181)
1184–1192	Go-Toba	Go-Shirakawa	——
1192–1198	Go-Toba	——	——

The anomalies of the Insei system, or negation of a system, are well illustrated here, for Toba had abdicated and himself became Cloistered Emperor in 1123, so that for a time there were two retired sovereigns and one titular emperor (Sutoku). It may be imagined that such a state of affairs was pregnant with dynastic and jurisdictional quarrels. When Shirakawa died (in 1129) his grandson Toba succeeded to his position and as sole cloistered emperor governed the country until 1156. Thus the Insei system lasted altogether for seventy years, from 1086 to 1156, ending with Toba's death. It survived in form for a little longer, but after 1156 it had lost much of its real significance, for almost the last shreds of power had been torn from both titular and cloistered emperors by the rising warrior clans.

These clans in turn made use of the cloistered Emperor Go-Shirakawa in their struggle for supremacy. Each claimed to be the protector of the Throne, and Go-Shirakawa stood as the symbol of a sovereign power that he was unable to wield. He survived from his abdication in 1158 until his death in 1192 thanks to the prestige of the Imperial House and to his own uncanny agility in playing one faction off against another. But though in that sense he reigned, he did not govern.

The rise and fall of such an unusual political arrangement calls for some explanation. Though there was something accidental in its growth, its main purpose was no doubt to break away from the Fujiwara Regents and restore the Imperial House by creating a source of authority independent of the maternal relatives of the occupant of the throne. In fact, under this new system the emphasis moves from the maternal relative to the paternal relative, so that whereas a Regent had been able to influence the reigning emperor because his empress was a Fujiwara daughter, now an abdicated emperor could govern because the reigning emperor was his own son. It is true that this device might not have succeeded had the Fujiwara clan preserved their solidarity and their determination; but the inherent wrongness of their dictatorship was bound to be a source of weakness in the long run, and a simple explanation of the new system is that the Fujiwara "mandokoro" was transferred to the office or council chamber of the retired sovereign. Chance also favoured the enemies of the Fujiwara, since after Michinaga's day it happened that Fujiwara ladies either died young, or had only girl babies or none at all. The feminine source of power seemed to have dried up. Finally there were rivalries within the clan, or rather within the northern branch from which the Regents came; and it was this weakness that put a finishing touch to their downfall, for when Go-Sanjō claimed the throne because his brother's empress was barren, he had the powerful support of a Fujiwara noble (Yoshinobu) who, though a kinsman of the Regent Yorimichi, took sides against his chieftain.

These dynastic minutiae are tedious and of only remote historical importance, except to the extent that they show the stages of development of an unusual political form. This form, because of its own anomalous character, endured only a little while, to give way of necessity to an entirely new method of government administered by a new class, relying not upon birth or reputation but upon sheer military power. All political history subsequent to the Reform of 645 may be interpreted as a series of attempts to perpetuate, by one device after another, a

complex system of centralized administration with no real power behind it, a system that seemed to work in the metropolis but was quite
unsuited to actual conditions in the country and to the temper of the
rural magnates. It was the new rulers, the leaders of the warlike provincial families, who as a class were to control the destinies of Japan
for the better part of a millennium.

But they did not acquire their position by the mere collapse of the
Regency. They had first to settle the question of supremacy among
themselves in a protracted series of civil conflicts. Meanwhile, the political form which replaced the Regency—the anomaly, the one-sided dual-
ism, called cloister government—survived and in some measure even
prospered for a few decades as the great House of Fujiwara lost first
its power to rule and then its eminence. For a time members of the clan
continued to hold office as Regent or Chancellor or Minister of State,
but they served the titular sovereign only, while the cloistered emperor—
the Hō-ō or Sacred Ruler—kept his own Court and governed through his
own administrative and judicial officers. These were for the most part
new men, a new type of statesman, adviser, and official of lesser social
standing than the Fujiwara favourites whom they displaced.

Among them were certain scholars, such as members of the Ōye
family, hereditary Confucian literati who had been in positions of
minor importance under the Regents. Ōye Masafusa, distinguished as
a man who knew politics and could give sound advice to the sovereign,
is a good representative of the class of learned and loyal servants of the
Throne who owed their advancement to their talents rather than to their
birth. His official title was Gon-Chūnagon, or Acting Middle Counsellor,
a modest rank. A celebrated scholar, he was tutor to the emperors
Shirakawa, Horikawa, and Toba. He is known to posterity chiefly as
the author of a work called *Kōke Shidai*, which is one of the most valuable historical sources of detailed information about state ceremonial
and public functions in the eleventh century. It is particularly valuable
in that it records changes which took place during his own lifetime,
using earlier chronicles for comparison. He died in 1111, in his seventy-
first year.

Members of the Fujiwara clan were not denied employment if they
were thought trustworthy, and members of the Minamoto clan (in a
branch descended from the Emperor Murakami and known therefore
as Murakami Genji) were gradually taken into important posts. In the
year 1027, of twenty-four appointments of the highest rank twenty-two
were held by Fujiwara nobles, but by about 1100, that is to say some
twenty-five years after the death of Go-Sanjō, more than half of those
posts were filled by members of the Minamoto family, and those retained
by the Fujiwara were junior to the offices of Chancellor and Minister of
the Left, which were in Minamoto hands. In general the Fujiwara were
displaced by a new class, consisting in part of courtiers who were close

to the abdicated sovereign (the In) and owned no allegiance to the line of Regents. Also appointed to office were a number of wealthy persons who were of lower rank than those whom they displaced. These were men who owned lucrative estates, and their growing influence is shown by the fact that the Kampaku Yorimichi (1019–68) sent his son to be adopted by a rich man of this kind, with the intention that he should presently marry an adopted sister. The decline in the fortunes of the Fujiwara was such that some members of the Regent's family had to obtain help from wealthy friends, and by 1150 we learn of Yorinaga, the Fujiwara Minister of the Left, complaining that although he had served the Crown in high positions he had not been granted so much as a single farm or fief.

But the Fujiwara still clung to their traditional offices, which at least carried with them high social standing and moreover gave opportunities to conspire against the cloistered emperors. Those who did not choose to plot for a revival of the Regency are reported, in some contemporary records, to have abandoned their gentility and taken to dissolute or eccentric courses, thereby hastening the disintegration of that aristocratic culture which had hitherto adorned the metropolis.

The *Imakagami* recounts how Fujiwara Koremichi (who was Chancellor from 1160 to 1165), when at the age of thirty-three he was passed over for promotion, flew into a rage at the insult, burned his official carriage in the street outside his house, mounted his horse, and wearing very gay garments of crimson and blue, galloped off to the house of a well-known courtesan. Koremichi (1097–1165) was father-in-law of the Emperor Konoye, who reigned from 1141 to 1155, a space of years during which there were two ex-emperors. It is understandable that Koremichi should have been angered by "the system" by which cloistered monarchs governed while the legitimate emperor merely reigned. In such circumstances the quality of the Fujiwara Regents and ministers naturally began to diminish as their authority waned, until in 1180 we find it recorded by a diarist that the then Regent was utterly ignorant of the literature and history of Japan and China. That was certainly a grave complaint to bring against a statesman at the Heian Court, where learning had always been prized and encouraged.

Although the development of the system of cloister government deprived the Fujiwara clan of its privileges, there was at work a rising influence beyond the control of the Court and the Regents which before long was to overcome them both, and to bring the abdicated emperors down with them. To explain the origin of this subversive trend—subversive, that is, from the point of view of the established government or governments—it will be necessary to go back and trace the development of the forces, the men and the ideas, that were to dominate the political scene from about 1100 onwards. But first we should follow the course of palace politics, which is both interesting in itself as a study of human behaviour and useful as an explanation of the growth of a military society in its very early phases, on the way to evolving a dictatorship more powerful, more efficient, and far more durable than the Fujiwara Regency at its zenith.

In considering the political changes that took place at this time we should not overlook the influence of individuals, members of the old regime who suffered because of the reckless and self-seeking policy of the latter-day Regents. Thus the agrarian policy of the Emperor Go-Sanjō, which has been amply treated by scholars from the point of view of legislative and economic history, had also a bearing upon the personal life of many courtiers, who depended for a livelihood not upon official emoluments but upon income from manorial rights or even upon support from rich landowning families, some of whom were warriors. The "national" aspect of the problem of the immune estates (shōen) is well illustrated in such records as the Zoku Hōkanshū, which notes that in the one province of Kii from eight- to nine-tenths of the arable land was absorbed by such estates, and that in the whole province there was practically no Crown land (i.e., land in the public domain) left except in one district. Such a condition was not of course peculiar to Kii province, but this single instance shows how great must have been the vested interest opposed to any reform of the manorial system.

Those officials who had no income from the land were usually in distress, if we may judge from a kind of entry common in journals and other records of daily life. Thus a diary or notebook known as Shunki contains under a date as early as 1039 the following entry: "Today at noon Kaga no Kami and Mikawa no Kami and others came to call. They were all well disposed. I told them I could not make ends meet since I had no salary and not a single rice field to cultivate."

It is not certain whether the Emperor Go-Sanjō and his advisers intended the system of cloister government to be permanent. There is evidence that he devised the system himself, since he is reported in a serious historical work to have held the view that it was wrong for an emperor in his last years to become a simple subject, and to live a life of calm and refined elegance "on the borders of the unknown." Since he himself became In during the last year of his life, and continued to govern actively, it may be inferred that he was the inventor of the scheme, though it is not certain how he expected it to work out. However that may be, it was certainly a departure that demanded and produced a new type of adviser and supporter, who naturally displaced the family upholders of the Fujiwara, just as the In displaced the reigning monarch.

The appearance of such new figures on the political stage was not the direct result of the establishment of cloister government, for a class of wealthy men of modest family origins had begun to develop at an earlier date, as the profits from country estates increased. Some recent

Japanese historians distinguish what they call a middle class, others suggest a class composed mainly of *zuryō*, men who were or had been governors or deputy governors of rich provinces and, either by transactions on the spot or by their receipts as absentee officials, had made a respectable fortune and then looked round for posts at Court. As the system of cloister government developed, especially under Go-Sanjō and Shirakawa, their services were found very useful and timely. The cloistered sovereigns were short of funds to uphold their high position. They had no recognized claim upon the Treasury, depending (in theory at least) upon the revenue from their own manors. They were therefore usually alert to find useful supporters, especially when, like Shirakawa, they had luxurious and expensive tastes. These were conditions favourable to the wealthy candidates for office, and their rise is a symptom of a general social change that was taking place at the close of the eleventh century, a gradual relaxation of the strict hierarchical rule that had formerly governed the distribution of honours and offices.

Among these Court favourites were such men as Fujiwara Akisuye (1055–1123), known as Rokujō no Shūri Tayū, or the Sixth Avenue Commissioner of Works. He had held appointments as provincial governor. He posed as a poet, though he was an ignorant man, but his money and his practical wisdom were useful to Shirakawa-In his patron. Another favourite of Shirakawa-In was Minamoto Toshiaki (1044–1114), who had attracted attention by his presence of mind in emergency and rose to posts of considerable importance, almost dominating the cloistered Emperor and being feared by the Fujiwara Regent of the day. Another favourite was Fujiwara Akitaka (1079–1129), who began as a minor adviser to Horikawa, Toba, and Sutoku and was later highly esteemed by Shirakawa-In. He was on such familiar terms with the cloistered sovereign that his advice was usually taken, and he was always in attendance at night, because the In liked his company so much. He was even known in the capital as Yoru Kampaku, or the Night Regent.

Apart from their personal qualities men like these had an importance out of proportion to their rank and office. Their wealth was of course advantageous because it enabled them to minister to the luxurious tastes of their patrons, but perhaps more important was their ability to aid and encourage the sovereign, notably the cloistered sovereign, to stand up to the pressure of the Fujiwara Regents and later the Taira dictators. Not being dependent upon official emoluments or title, they could afford to indulge in a freedom that would have brought punishment to men in regular official life.

An account of these palace favourites would not be complete without reference to a notorious character named Fujiwara Iyenari. He came from a family not of the highest rank but of some consequence, which usually furnished deputy governors to the province of Ōmi; and because he had good connexions at Court through his uncle, a Middle Counsellor (Chūnagon), he made rapid progress. By the year 1145 we find the powerful Yorinaga complaining of his arrogant behaviour, but he retained his position because he was a wealthy man, thanks to his family's accumulations, and could give great pleasure to the Emperor Toba, his patron, to whom he made extravagant presents from time to time. He spent lavishly on the building of sacred edifices and on the performance of most elaborate Buddhist festivals and ceremonies, which highly delighted his devout master. He cannot be placed in the same category as ignorant familiars like Akisuye and Akitaka, for he belonged to the traditional ruling class and dealt on a footing of equality with such statesmen as Yorinaga, who hated him and thought that he and his associates were leading the country to ruin. Nevertheless he was a "new man," a palace hanger-on relying upon money and a vulgar display that horrified his sober contemporaries.

Though there were doubtless some exceptions, the new form of government seems to have been served mostly by men lacking competence and integrity. But more significant of the political aura of the day is the fact that most of the new men were, as compared with the highborn Fujiwara nobles, of a lower class. By strict standards of efficiency, not to say benevolence, in government there was perhaps not much to be said for the Regents and their methods. But they had certain standards of taste if not of morals, and they did foster and protect learning. In any estimate or balance of the merits and faults of Fujiwara dictatorship, this is something that ought to stand to its credit, and perhaps it is appropriate here to allude to the importance of scholarship in the life of a nation as it is expressed in the standards of the governing class.

Even when organized government was breaking down and old standards were no longer being maintained, the necessity for learning was still recognized. The cloistered Emperor Shirakawa would not promote his most powerful favourites if they were illiterate. The influential Akisuye, on being asked why he had not been made Prime Minister, sounded the Emperor for reasons. He was told flatly by His Majesty that such appointments were reserved for people who could write (that is, compose official documents). Both Akisuye and Akitaka were very close to the Throne, but both were unlearned and therefore neither reached high office.

Any perusal of the literature of the tenth, eleventh, and twelfth centuries in Japan must impress the reader with the importance attached to learning even in the most exalted and fashionable circles, where one might suppose that scholarship would be regarded with polite indifference. In Europe of the same period scholarship was primarily the business of the clergy, and a learned layman, that is to say a layman having more than a gentlemanly acquaintance with some branch of knowledge, was regarded as exceptional and strange. But in China and in Japan (though perhaps to a less extent in Japan), although there is a wide region of religious learning, beyond this all scholarship is the scholarship of the secular aristocracy and its dependents. All lay persons claiming eminence in social life, or even only in political life, are or profess to be scholars, and perhaps one of the features that most distinguishes Eastern from Western cultures is the respect paid to learning by the humblest person. In China and Japan in particular the relation of master and pupil is almost as sacred as the closest family tie.

Consequently one of the peculiar features of the decline of government in the age which we are surveying is a struggle between the tradition of learning and the demands of a new society. Perhaps the clearest evidence on this point is furnished by the characters of members of the party which most powerfully resisted the rise of the new men. Among them were certain Fujiwara nobles, such as Gonijō Moromichi and Fujiwara Yorinaga, together with certain members of the Minamoto clan. Before describing them and their deeds it is necessary to go back a little, so as to place them in their historical setting.

The Emperor Go-Sanjō, as we have seen, had some modest successes in agrarian reform, and he might have done better if he had lived longer. Shirakawa, though a strong-willed, passionate man, was without real wisdom and had no interest in reforms. He treated the titular Emperor (his son, Horikawa) with scant courtesy, and the relationship between the two Courts grew cool and distant. More serious perhaps than this breach, and certainly more damaging to the material welfare of the titular sovereign, was the behaviour of the cloistered Emperor in regard to his revenues. Whereas Go-Sanjō had tried to check the growth of immune estates, Shirakawa alienated great areas of public land in order to raise funds for his own expenditure upon building and adorning monasteries and for some less venial extravagances. He is said to have had carved more than one hundred large Buddhist images and to have gone to fantastic extremes in other pious undertakings. Every acre of rice land that gained immunity for such purposes reduced the revenues of the Crown and so worsened the condition of the titular emperor. Other devices, such as the sale of public offices, added to the decline of fiscal probity and hastened the breakdown of what administrative efficiency had been preserved in their own interests by the Fujiwara dictators.

There is an anecdote (recorded in the *Kojidan*) which throws some light upon the stubbornly civilian outlook of the Emperor Shirakawa and his Court at a time when the power of the military families was rising with inexorable speed. After he had abdicated and was leading a life of ostensibly pious contemplation and refined pleasure, he was listening one day to a very old and infirm warrior whom he had summoned to the Palace to tell the story of his campaigns. The old soldier began, "Once when Yoshiiye had left the Defence Headquarters for the fortress at Akita, a light snow was falling and the men . . . ," at which point His Majesty broke in and said: "Stop there! It is a most elegant and striking picture. Nothing more is needed." He gave the old man a handsome present and sent him away. His aesthetic sense was satisfied by the vision of soldiers in a thin flurry of snow, and he did not want any details of the hardships suffered by military men.

Thus, though the power of the Regents was destroyed, the rise of the cloistered emperors proved even more harmful to the state. It created wide fissures in the ruling class and invited reprisals from those whose welfare, or whose very subsistence, was endangered.

The titular Emperor Toba, born in 1103, succeeded his father Horikawa in 1107, and he abdicated in 1123 in favour of his son Sutoku. Upon the death of the cloistered Emperor Shirakawa in 1129 Toba reassumed power, this time as a cloistered emperor himself. Toba had been ill-disposed towards Sutoku, and now the breach widened. There were also quarrels between Sutoku and the Fujiwara Regent Tadazane, mostly it seems about the choice and treatment of concubines. These sordid affairs are not worth further description, for their only interest is as testimony to the poverty of the system which brought them about. It is at this point that there begins to develop the clash between the "new men" and those defenders of the tradition of the Regency to whom we have just referred, men like Moromichi and Yorinaga, representatives of a class of aristocratic statesmen which for all its shortcomings retained certain standards of competence and dignity.

We do not know much about Moromichi, beyond the fact that he was firmly and actively opposed to the new trend of cloister government and all its concomitants. It is unfortunate for the reader of the chronicles of this interesting era in Japanese history that we get no very detailed picture of its eminent figures. There are entries in journals or similar documents which tell us something of contemporary opinion about them, but these are usually brief and colourless. Japanese literature is not given to elaborate character study; it prefers a lapidary description, hinting at remarkable personalities and arousing curiosity that it fails to satisfy, so that much of Japanese history as recorded seems to be wanting in human interest. This fault may be attributed in part to the terse Chinese style in which it was the fashion for gentlemen to write, but it seems also to betoken a lack of active desire to probe into the nature of one's fellow men. Thus all that we are told about Moromichi in the historical work *Honchō Seiki* is that in 1094 he became Kampaku and Chieftain of the Fujiwara clan; that he had the virtue and the strength of character necessary in a ruler; that he was good and kind; that from 1069 to 1099, while he was in public life, the country was at peace; that in his leisure hours he was an ardent student; and that there was no great book he had not read.

This may be taken to mean that he was an aristocrat with a high sense of duty, a great pride in his own family, and a strong dislike for the system of cloister government. He upheld Fujiwara prestige in difficult times, and it is perhaps in keeping with those times that the account of his death is the most interesting passage in his story as it is told in the history books. His mortal illness was ascribed to the vengeance of monks, against whom he was the first to take action when they descended from their mountain shrines upon the capital in armed bands and committed flagrant breaches of the peace in the name of their deities, hoping thus to terrorize the Court. Nobody had shown courage enough to deal with this scourge until Moromichi, by his firmness, had alarmed the ringleaders. In an effort to deter him a Shintō ritualist had been carried by the rioters into the oratory of the Hachiōji shrine there to pronounce a solemn curse "to hear which made the hair stand on end." After that the Regent, awake or in his dreams, felt with such dread the spell of the mountain gods that boils broke out on his skin. They healed for a little while and then appeared again, and shortly afterwards he died, in the sixth month of 1099. It was said that after his death, groans could be heard on rainy nights from under a stone midway between the shrines of Hachiōji and Sannomiya. This fragment does not tell us much about Moromichi, but it shows how incapable of keeping order in the capital the civil officers of the Crown had become and how dependent they were upon the help of warrior families.

A more prominent figure was Fujiwara Yorinaga, whose career was longer and more full of incident. About him we know more from his own memoirs, in which he is revealed as an exceptional character.

As a youth Yorinaga was dissolute and turbulent. In his own words: "In my early years I followed no advice from my preceptors but spent my time with a hawk on my wrist and a whip in my hand, galloping up and down the fields and the hills. I risked my life but I was protected by Gods and Buddhas. My body was safe, though it bears the scars to this day." Despite his early excesses he settled down and took to study. He became an enthusiastic reader of the Chinese classics, but was little interested in the native literature. Some Japanese historians suggest that his failure as a statesman was due to his ignorance of truly Japanese sentiment, which in the metropolitan region at least was gentle, tolerant, and fatalistic. This seems to be a well-founded conjecture, for what we have been examining is the slow decay of a cultivated, easygoing, and somewhat fatigued society, with little spirit of self-defence. It was such exceptional men as Yorinaga who were firm and active in their resistance; and he left behind him a reputation for rash conduct. One work (*Gukanshō*) says: "He was the finest scholar in Japan and he was richly endowed with both Chinese wisdom and Japanese sense. But he was of a hasty temperament and in all things inclined to take risks." Perhaps the most remarkable thing about him is the fact that he never composed a poem in Japanese.

He was the favourite son of the Fujiwara Regent Tadazane, who held office from 1105 to 1121 and then retired in favour of his eldest son Tadamichi. Yorinaga was born in 1120. He rose rapidly in official life, becoming Naidaijin at the age of seventeen and reaching the highest rank under the Regent in 1150, when, on his appointment as Minister of the Left, in true Fujiwara fashion he married his daughter to the Emperor Konoye, then eleven years of age. His ambition, like that of Moromichi, was to restore and reform the Fujiwara Regency, but he was more than a mere traditionalist. His memoirs (one of the most important and interesting documents of the age) testify to his wide range of interest, for as well as being a good classical Confucian scholar he studied Indian logic under a learned monk, while his subsequent political actions show that he was a man of high courage.

On assuming office as Minister of the Left he addressed himself to reviving certain practices and observances that had fallen into disuse, and thereby in his view had brought about a laxity in official discipline of which he highly disapproved. He was of course the kind of man to make enemies, and he was not in favour with the young Emperor Konoye, still less with the cloistered Toba. He was so strong and determined in his actions that he was known as "Aku Safu" or the Wicked Minister of the Left, but this nickname was probably given to him by adversaries who feared his reforming zeal. When the Emperor Konoye died in 1155 a most bitter succession dispute arose, and this is the point at which Yorinaga's fate was determined, in a clash of interests which also settled the political future of Japan for several hundred years.

At one point in this succession dispute Konoye's mother, the Lady Bifukumon-In, pressed the claim of one of her daughters, but without success because feeling in Japan had long ago hardened against empresses in their own right. The quarrel divided the already unfriendly brothers Tadamichi and Yorinaga; but Tadamichi's faction won and the old Emperor Toba's favourite son succeeded as Go-Shirakawa. Yorinaga then asked to be made tutor to the Heir Apparent, a post for which he was well fitted, but he was refused, and after this slight he took the side of Sutoku, who had been most contemptuously treated by Go-Shirakawa's party. He collected troops in the nearby provinces for a march upon the capital, where with Sutoku he established himself in a palace which he put into a state of defence.

The importance of this rising in the history of twelfth-century Japan is cardinal. Known as the Hōgen Insurrection (Hōgen no Ran) from the name of the era (Hōgen, 1156–58), it was a turning point in Japan's political development, for it led to the first stages in the evolution of a feudal state. But here, for the present, we are concerned only with the fate of Yorinaga, who may be looked upon as the most prominent and most stubborn defender of the old regime of autocratic regents and submissive emperors. The struggle was on a small scale, so far as the numbers engaged were concerned. Yorinaga could assemble only a few hundred warriors, while Go-Shirakawa had the support of leading captains of both warrior clans, the Minamoto and the Taira; and though the warriors took sides for reasons of their own and not for principles, the balance was in favour of the Court and against the insurgents. The clash took place at night; the position held by Sutoku's party was attacked and after stubborn fighting destroyed by fire. Yorinaga was killed and his chief comrades surrendered. We need not enter into further details of this encounter; but it is important to remember that it marked the end of the direct political power of the Imperial House and the beginning of a long strife for supremacy between the two great military clans, the Taira and the Minamoto. It was Yorinaga's determination, the last effort of the Fujiwara, that brought about not the restoration for which he fought but the defeat of an outworn autocracy of which he was the last champion. He was thus the agent of destiny as well as the brave defender of a lost cause. Perhaps because he failed he does not appear as an important figure in most conventional histories of Japan, but he was nevertheless a remarkable man whose memory ought to be preserved.

CHAPTER XI

HEIAN SOCIETY. ITS BELIEFS

1. *Divination and Exorcism*

THE DEFEAT of the conservative movement led by Yorinaga was a
turning point in Japanese political history. Its effect was to bring an
end to the rule of the Imperial House, whether exercised directly by its
members or by the Fujiwara clan, and to put in its place a new system
in which effective power came into the hands of a military class. This
class had slowly but inexorably grown in strength during the eleventh
century and by the middle of the twelfth century had become the dominant element in political life.

Our next task therefore should be to trace the growth of this new
element in mediaeval society; but before addressing ourselves to that
interesting problem it is necessary to survey the general scene, to observe the main currents of the national life, as it developed after the
move from Nara, when the Japanese people settled down to assimilate
and adapt the rich store of knowledge they had acquired from China.
We have already taken note of the lapse of official relations with China,
dating in effect from the return of the embassy which set out to visit
the T'ang Court in 838. This might be considered a datum line, but in
fact, despite these diplomatic failures, the influence of China upon Japanese religious and general intellectual life was but little diminished,
for in those fields intercourse was not broken off, and indeed it continued
with little difference. Such change as took place was in the attitude of
the Japanese leaders who, by about A.D. 900, though still respecting the
Chinese intellectual tradition, were no longer dependent upon Chinese
example. The change was one of practical necessity rather than of
principle or deliberate policy, since internal conditions in Japan had
by that time developed a pattern to which imported ideas had to be
adjusted. Yet, while the age of indiscriminate borrowing was now past,
there were features of Japanese life which, though of Chinese origin,
had become permanently embodied in the social structure.

Perhaps the most striking example of this power of Chinese thought
over Japanese minds is the almost universal belief of the governing
class in the Yin-Yang cosmology. Scarcely any action could be taken
by a Fujiwara nobleman in his public or private life without consulting
the oracles—the verdicts of astrologers or geomancers or necromancers
or other practitioners of the science of divination and prophecy. The
"Admonitions" of Kujō-den, which were cited at length in Chapter IX,
furnish illuminating examples of the rules that guided the daily conduct of a nobleman of the tenth century. He must follow particular

procedures and choose auspicious times for all his activities, from his personal toilet to the highest affairs of state. He must arrange his engagements so that he will never proceed to a destination by an inauspicious route, or undertake an important task on an inauspicious day.

This latter demand of the rules of divination is so frequent that it is almost a commonplace in the literature of the era. In the *Tale of Genji* we constantly come across references to geomantic or astrological conditions by which the hero's freedom of movement is restricted or which he welcomes as an excuse for choosing or avoiding a certain direction in his nocturnal wanderings. Thus, on one occasion when he was thinking of returning from his wife's mansion to the Palace, he was told that owing to the position of Saturn it would be unlucky. He therefore set out in another direction, to the house of one of his suite, knowing that his wife might suspect that he was using the stars as an excuse for leaving her.

The daily life of Heian men and women in the middle and upper classes was governed by such considerations to an astonishing degree. In late Heian society, in particular, belief in evil influences and an urge to propitiate or avert them was without doubt a source of the anxiety that seems to have been a characteristic feature of the epoch. A full description of the great body of prevailing superstition is beyond the scope of this study, and indeed it would be impossible to find any logic or to discern any order in the mass of proscriptions and taboos which regulated the conduct of even the most sophisticated people in those days. It must therefore suffice to mention here only a few of the methods by which they endeavoured to defeat the calamitous influences that seemed to beset mankind at every turn.

In general the precautions which a man must take against misfortune are described as *monoimi*, which roughly speaking means avoidance or abstention. One very simple form of abstention was to stay at home, doing no duties, seeing no guests, entering into no discussions. This method of keeping aloof from unfavourable influences was rational enough in the light of the cosmology of the times; and it had the further advantage that it provided busy statesmen or fatigued voluptuaries with an unanswerable excuse for solitude.

More troublesome than a mere retreat into seclusion was the avoidance of a wrong direction by those who could not stay in the safety of their own bedchamber but were obliged to walk or ride abroad. Here there came into operation various grave considerations, subsumed under the heading of *katatagae*, which might be translated "change of direction." It was necessary at certain times to take precautions against calamity which might arise from crossing the path of certain gods or spirits whose movements were regular and could be exactly predicted by professors of astrology or similar sciences. Thus the god Hitohimeguri moved in one of the eight directions every day, and it was unfor-

tunate (nefas) for a man or a woman to move in that direction on that
day, and so to interfere with the regular motion of the deity in question.

There were other deities who stayed for different periods at different points of the compass, and these also had to be carefully avoided.
Perhaps the most dangerous of all these powers was one that had to
be guarded against on one day in every sixty of the calendar, namely
the Day of the Monkey in the sexagenary cycle. This could be done
only by keeping awake all night and not staying at home, that is by going in no direction at all and remaining in a "neutral" place.[1] A singularly apt example of this particular form of superstition is described in
an entry in a courtier's diary under the date of March 3, 1104. It reads
as follows: "This evening His Majesty [the cloistered Emperor Shira-
kawa] had to observe change of direction [*katatagae*]. Accordingly
he went to the vicinity of the Gojō Gate, to stay there in his carriage
until cock-crow, and then to return to his Palace. . . . This was because
on the following morning he had to go to worship in the direction of
Hitohimeguri." Thus it will be seen that the Emperor, though himself
of divine origin, was constrained to defer to minor deities, products of
a fanciful Chinese theogony.

The choice of propitious times for ceremonies, and indeed for simpler and more ordinary acts, was a matter of great importance, requiring careful consultation with experts. The senior Ministry of State, the
Nakatsukasa, included a special department, the Ommyō-ryō or Bureau
of Yin-Yang, with a select staff of masters and doctors of divination and
astrology. These were at the service of the Court, while the ordinary
citizen could refer to private practitioners of the occult arts when planning a journey or some other enterprise, or wishing to arrange a wedding
celebration. Edicts of very early date call attention to the excesses of
such men, who deceive the common people by their claims to magic
power; and there is no doubt that the prevalence of such superstitions
lay like a heavy cloud over mediaeval life.

Akin to the precautionary measures just described was the very
common practice of calling in exorcists to cure disease. These were
generally, though not necessarily, Buddhist monks of a tantric sect, and
the exorcism usually took a religious form. But it belonged to a tradition of magic and sorcery that went back to a remote past, long before
the influence of Buddhism had touched Japan, and if it is Chinese it is
by the accretion of elements of later continental origin. The basis of
the cult is indigenous, or perhaps it would be more correct to say Sha-
manistic; and it takes according to circumstances a Confucian or a
Buddhist or a Shintō form. But it is very ancient and very deep-rooted,

---

[1] A curious footnote to the history of these practices is furnished by accounts of
robberies committed by criminals who knew when a householder would have to spend
a night away from home.

for the earliest Chinese accounts of life in Japan tell us of the magic powers of the Queen of the Wa, who was a great sorceress.

Among the Heian aristocrats a belief that disease was caused by evil spirits was very strongly held, and it was common for them, unless they were very rigid Confucianists, to resort to incantations and prayers, or even to long retreats when they would recite scriptural texts in the hope of curing sickness or otherwise promoting their own well-being. There is a very interesting account of the habits of a Fujiwara nobleman, one Sanesuke, Minister of the Right, who is praised as being "out of the ordinary" by Murasaki Shikibu in her Diary. In his note-book he describes how, on feeling ill in body and disturbed in mind, he summoned as exorcists several *ajari* (a name derived from the Sanskrit *ācārya*, a holy man) to pray by his bedside all that night. He fasted, and the next day the ajari again prayed by his pillow. After a few days of this treatment he felt better and consulted a diviner. He was told that his illness was due to a hungry spirit who must be appeased. This was· done by exorcism, and on the following day gongs and drums were beaten at a hundred monasteries or shrines by two ambulant monks, each of whom visited fifty establishments. On another occasion Sanesuke, disturbed by bad dreams, paid children to beat gongs at ten monasteries every day for ten days, one hundred monasteries in all.

Although these practices seem to have a strong Buddhist flavour, and are to that extent due to the Chinese influence that brought Buddhism to Japan, they belong to an amalgam of beliefs from several sources. The myth of the Gods, as related in the national chronicles, reveals traces of a strong belief that certain deities and the spirits of the dead could lay a curse upon living men; and there are records of great rituals of exorcism designed to rid the community of pestilence or some other form of disaster. The idea of possession by a vengeful spirit, which was very prevalent in the Heian era, thus appears to have been of native growth; but certainly Chinese learning and Chinese example did nothing to diminish or change it. Rather, it would seem, the powerful apparatus of more elaborate forms of magic was brought in to reinforce the simple incantations of earlier times. Thus great Buddhist masses were held from time to time to pacify offended spirits who were thought to have brought about calamities, as in the well-known case of Sugawara Michizane, the statesman who was disgraced and exiled by jealous Fujiwara leaders. Soon after he died in banishment (903), the Great Audience Hall (Shishin-den) of the Palace was struck by lightning, and week after week the capital city was drenched by rainstorms and shaken by thunderbolts. More disasters followed, notably the violent death of prominent men and the constant outbreak of fires. These and other misfortunes continued for so long and were of such magnitude and frequency that they could be ascribed only to the vengeful spirit of Michizane. He was therefore restored to the office and rank which he had held in his lifetime, and all official documents bearing upon his sentence of exile were destroyed. Still the calamities continued, and members of the Fujiwara family anxiously caused masses to be said in the hope of removing the curse. At length in 942 an oracle was said to have decreed that a shrine should be erected, where Michizane was to be worshipped as a deity. This is the Kitano Temmangu, a shrine which soon became popular and where he has been prayed to by many generations of worshippers as Tenjin, the Heavenly Deity, a title conferred upon him by a royal decree of 986, which led to his being regarded as the god of learning, and especially of calligraphy.

Although belief in particular forms of magic may have diminished with the progress of time, in general the members of Heian society at its highest levels continued to resort to occult practices of invocation and incantation in order to defeat the forces of evil, which were supposed to be extremely active. Such practices were encouraged both by the cosmology of Yin-Yang and by the teaching of tantric forms of Buddhism such as those of the Shingon sect, which was powerful in the Heian era; nor is this surprising, for it will be recollected that both Chinese philosophy, whether Confucianist or Taoist, and the Buddhist religion first commended themselves to the Japanese by the superior magic powers they were supposed to offer to believers.

The diviners and exorcists who were practitioners of Yin-Yang, as well as the Buddhist adepts, the ajari, claimed to heal the sick in mind and body by expelling evil spirits. Their method was to use special formulas and to sprinkle the patient with cold water. The formulas were taken from the Book of Changes, so that we have here a very clear example of Chinese influence working upon an ancient indigenous cult. This influence is displayed in a convincing way by the application of the Yin-Yang theory of auspicious and inauspicious days (fas and nefas). On inauspicious days it was necessary to abstain from all but the most essential acts and functions. No business could be transacted, no letter read or answered, no visitors seen. This condition was called *imi*, or abstinence. It originally meant the state of ritual purity exacted for sacred purposes by the earliest Japanese religion; but it came also to be used in a Chinese sense. A man who was in retreat in his own house would hang a wooden label (called *imifuda*) outside his door, and if he was obliged to go out he would carry a similar ticket in his hat, so that nobody would approach him or ask him for any service. There are other examples of the penetration of the indigenous cult by Chinese ideas, but this will suffice, for it was to be expected that the fundamental concepts of magic would be nearly identical throughout eastern Asia.

As for details of the method favoured in Japan for driving out the demon by which a sick person is possessed, there is a classical passage in the *Tale of Genji* relating the death of the Princess Aoi, who died possessed by the jealous spirit of her rival the Princess Rokujō. The rituals of exorcism and divination were assiduously performed by the greatest adepts, and the Abbot of the Tendai with other high ecclesiastics prayed ardently by her bedside, but with no success. The "living spirit" (*ikiryō*) which possessed her could not be identified or cast out.

Some details of method are given in a vivid description in Murasaki Shikibu's Diary of the delivery of one of the Empress Akiko's children in 1025. She was thought to be in danger, because the afterbirth was stubborn, and a number of exorcists were summoned to her bedchamber, where she lay in pain. Their duty was by shouts and objurgations to conjure the evil spirits to enter certain Court ladies present, in whose bodies they could do no harm. The Diary says:

"It was terrible to hear their voices as they cursed. The Ajari Shinyō took the Lady Gen, the Ajari Sōso took the Lady Hyōe, the Risshi of the Hōjūji took the Lady Ukon, and the Lady Miya no Naishi was assigned to the care of the Ajari Chisō. But this last exorcist was overcome by the evil spirit, and fell in a faint. He was in a pitiable state, but the Ajari Nengaku was called to conjure in his place. It was not that his exorcism was weak but that the evil spirit in possession [of Her Majesty] was very strong. The Lady Saishō's spirit [she was acting as a surrogate for the Empress] was being conjured by the monk Eikō, who cried aloud all through the night until he became quite hoarse. The ladies who had been summoned to receive the evil spirit remained unaffected, and were much perturbed. But by midday the sky was clear and it was as if the sun had at last come out. . . . Her Majesty was at ease and all was well. It was a beautiful boy."

Next came the bathing of the infant, carried out with great ceremony in the presence of the Regent, who held the child in his arms, while Court ladies in beautiful garments prepared the ablutions. Here also great care was taken to keep away all evil influences. Twenty archers of the Bodyguard loudly twanged their bowstrings to frighten evil spirits, and Doctors of Literature read aloud improving passages from the Chinese classics. It is characteristic of the manners of the period that Murasaki describes with loving care the dresses worn by the ladies at all the ceremonies and festivities connected with the birth. Their costumes were of great beauty and splendour, and their deportment passed the severest tests.

These quotations will have served to give some notion of the belief in spirits and magic that all but dominated the minds of the nobility and the commonalty of those days. It was tempered by an enjoyment of ceremonies and a delight in beautiful colour and shape. This combination of superstition with aesthetic judgment is well illustrated by a passage in Sei Shōnagon's *Pillow Book*, where she describes great Buddhist services at a monastery, which were attended by certain retired ministers of state, some wearing a taboo ticket (*imifuda*) in

Detail from a twelfth-century scroll

their hats. They ought really to have stayed at home, but they had come to enjoy the occasion as a spectacle and a social gathering without paying any attention to the sermon. The holiness of the place (they pretended) justified their presence, and the ticket discouraged criticism by strangers.

2. Buddhist Faith

We have already considered briefly the formation in Japan of the schools of Tendai and Shingon, during the early years of the Heian era. The history of Buddhism in Japan thereafter is mainly the development of those two systems and of certain dissident sects that more or less directly arose from them. The Tendai sect, or rather school, was more embracing, more catholic, and less exclusive than the Shingon, and indeed it was the parent of almost every version or sect of Buddhism that subsequently developed in Japan. Shingon, on the other hand, owing principally to its mystic character, its free use of spells and magic formulas of all kinds, was popular in Court circles, because it was well adapted to those ritual and ceremonial occasions of an imposing, rather ostentatious kind that so frequently ministered to the pride of the Fujiwara nobles.

The Tendai teaching, though it can scarcely be described as popular, for much of it was recondite, grew in influence thanks to the position of its many monastic establishments, chapels, and seminaries on the flanks of Mount Hiyei overlooking the capital. It owed much to the energy and learning of some of its professors, and by the end of the tenth century its more ambitious prelates were even interfering in politics and using armed force against the government.

The doctrinal features of these two schools need not be treated here, but it is useful to note that the Buddhist Church was very active in this era, perhaps because it attracted men of great learning or strong character who had no prospect of rising in any other career so long as the Fujiwara family dominated the government. Buddhism, after the move from Nara, became what is called "praying Buddhism" to distinguish it from the "teaching Buddhism" of the older sects and fraternities. Thus it spread more widely throughout the country. The mere size of its establishments and the numbers of its clergy increased rapidly, and by about 900, or one hundred years after the foundation of the Heian capital, Buddhism was playing a very considerable part in almost every aspect of the national life. It met with no opposition from a powerful official class—none of the official hostility, proscription, and even persecution that it encountered in China.

What we have already seen of the aristocratic society under the Fujiwara Regents will have shown that both the Crown and the nobility were patrons of the Church. They spent lavishly on the maintenance and decoration of chapels and shrines; they attended religious services which were held frequently to celebrate high occasions or to pray for intercession in times of distress. A knowledge of some sacred texts was required of any well-bred man, and many Buddhist terms were used in everyday speech, where they became thoroughly naturalized. A broad survey of the position of Buddhism in the heyday of the Fujiwara gives the first impression that it was primarily a social force; but closer study shows that it was a spiritual force as well, especially in the early part of the Heian era. At its best it not only inspired much that was finest in the arts and in certain branches of literature, it also encouraged practical virtues (like temperance and charity) and demanded at least the semblance of piety in regular observances. There were believers who led devout lives as well as fashionable worshippers; and as for prelates, monks, and nuns, the chronicles of Buddhism in Japan report in copious detail their holy labours. Yet as a popular faith it cannot be said to have been effective among the mass of the people, whose condition was generally wretched and who could not understand its abstruse doctrine. What it contributed to raising the standard of rural life is hard to measure, though on balance its influence was probably benign even where existence was burdensome and charity rare, for at least it revealed the possibility of a better world. So far as concerns the upper classes, it must be said that the Fujiwara nobleman was at times most unrestrained in his behaviour, so that both the discipline of the Church and the fear of divine retribution were needed to serve as a check upon his grosser delinquencies.

However much the prestige of the Church contributed to morality, it is clear that among the laity there was little sign of a deep understanding of the fundamental truths of Buddhist teaching, its emphasis upon selflessness, its insistence upon the folly of craving for pleasure and rebirth. What did most powerfully affect the religious sentiment of the times was the doctrine of Karma.

There were few Japanese in the Heian era who did not think that their life was a link between past and future lives, and that in the chain of causation each link, each life, was conditioned by deeds done in previous existences. The earliest Japanese literature from which we can draw some modest inferences about the beliefs of the times, notably the poetry of the *Manyōshū*, does not seem to reveal any particular interest in the idea of reincarnation. It is recognized, but only in a rather light-hearted way. Yet it is clear that after the eighth century it gained ground rapidly, and by the tenth century, if not much sooner, the idea of karma, of the inevitable consequences of a man's actions whether good or bad, had become a commonplace of Japanese belief. Tenth-century literature is scattered with references to *sukuse*, which is a thoroughly naturalized colloquial form of the technical religious term *shukusei*, a Sinico-Japanese word denoting a previous existence that has harboured or conditioned the character of the present existence. There is hardly a romance or a poem but contains some passage deploring the sukuse, the destiny, that has produced sickness or unrequited love or some other calamity. Another fully naturalized word is *inga*, literally "cause-and-effect." "To what inga," cries an unhappy man, "do I owe this suffering?" In other words, what offence or error committed in a past life has resulted in his present misery? It should be noted here that the issue is not one of punishment for sin, but only of the inevitable sequence of cause and effect, for which the victim deserves sympathy rather than rebuke.

Whatever argument there may be about the place of Buddhism in Japanese life, there can be no doubt that the adoption of this one idea, which is entirely foreign and has no indigenous counterpart, brought about a truly revolutionary change in the moral outlook of the Japanese people. It was perhaps more an addition than a change, since neither the native cult nor the Confucian ethical creed has anything to say about past or future lives, or about the spiritual needs of the individual or his view of human destiny.

Nevertheless, despite this important contribution to the national culture, the Buddhism of the two great Heian schools could not satisfy the religious needs of the ordinary man. Both Tendai and Shingon were suitable to the educated class but even for the learned their doctrines were difficult to understand, and there was a pressing need for some simpler faith, easy to explain, easy to practise, and offering some consolation in troubled times. For the times were troubled even in those days when, the country being at peace, the life of the fortunate ones seemed to be at its most shining and prosperous. As early as the late tenth century there are clear signs of distress and disorder in the capital city, abuses which the government was incompetent to remedy. There were, in addition to the fruits of human fallibility, constant plagues and pestilences which, as in most mediaeval societies, were utterly beyond the control of the civil power. The chronicles and diaries of the time record occasion after occasion when great services of intercession were held, and amnesties granted, in an attempt to avert or moderate natural disasters. The quarrelsome monks on Mount Hiyei did little to promote the exercise of those qualities of gentleness and tolerance which their religion enjoined; on the contrary they—and the members of other sects—grew so overbearing that they formed armies of their own, with which they endeavoured, often with success, to hold the Court to ransom by demonstrations in force in the streets of the capital and in general by playing upon the fears of superstitious believers. The Enryakuji of Mount Hiyei, an immense monastery, could put thousands of men into the field, and other monasteries had at their disposal similar forces. One of the famous Nara monasteries, the Kōfukuji, is said to have sent a force of 20,000 men against the Enryakuji in 1113.

These belligerent activities may seem to have little to do with the history of religious faith, but the circumstances that led to them offer an extremely interesting commentary on both the failure of the central government to exercise its authority and the character of early Heian, or let us say Fujiwara, Buddhism, and the reasons for its decadence. A study of this process, by which a rise in material strength was accompanied by a decline in moral force, goes far to explain the success of more popular gospels, which began to make themselves heard by about A.D. 1000.

After the great innovator Saichō had founded the Tendai headquarters in 805 he was succeeded by a line of abbots, bearing the proud designation of Tendai Zasu (Chief Abbot). Partly because of its proximity to the capital and partly because of the character of its leaders the Tendai outstripped the Shingon in influence, and was in 827 made a seat of ordination (Kaidan) on the same footing as the Tōdaiji of Nara. Eminent among its abbots were the celebrated Ennin, whose pilgrimage to China has already been described, and his successor, Enchin. Ennin stayed on Mount Hiyei as Zasu for more than twenty years, and during his ministry he founded the monastery called Onjōji (more usually known as Miidera) which lay at the foot of Mount Hiyei on the shore of Lake Biwa. Enchin was named abbot of that branch in 873, at a time when Ennin was much favoured by the Throne and enjoyed the support of the Fujiwara family. The prestige of the Tendai sect was thus very high. But in course of time there developed differences of opinion between the followers of Ennin and those of Enchin, leading to a split in the sect, which was now divided into two parties, the Sammon or Mountain Order at the Enryakuji and the Jimon or Church Order at Miidera. The names are topographical, and do not relate to sectarian differences. In fact there does not appear to have been any genuine division on a point of doctrine, but only an unseemly jealous rivalry, perhaps intensified by a conflict over the degree of emphasis to be placed upon the mystic side of Buddhism, which it was Ennin's purpose to introduce into the Tendai teaching and practice. Whatever its nature, the disagreement led after Enchin's death in 891 to an open breach between the two orders, with an occasional resort to force. It was at this point that the great monasteries began the regular use of guards or bullies known as Akusō or Bad Monks, a habit which was later to expand into the maintenance of monastic armies on a large scale.

The special interest of this phenomenon lies in the intensity of an ecclesiastical rivalry that ended in open warfare among the great monastic foundations. Most students of Japanese history have been impressed by the tolerant and catholic attitude of the Japanese toward questions of religious faith. As a people they seem to have been spared the bitterness of sectarian strife, and to have usually shown a disposition to compromise. Certainly there has been little in their history of the cruel bigotry that stains our Western chronicles, and nothing to correspond to the great wars of religion, not only between Christian and heathen, but between Christian and Christian as well. The breach between the two Tendai branches, the Sammon and the Jimon, if it really began as a sharp division upon a point of doctrine, would seem to indicate that Japan was not free from purely religious animosities. But it is a doubtful case, and at most a rare exception to the general habit of tolerance.

It was about 970 that a religious body first recruited mercenaries for its protection. This was when the Tendai Zasu of the day, Ryōgen (Jie Daishi), who had found it necessary to use force in a dispute with the Gion shrine, an important Shintō establishment in the capital, decided to maintain a permanent body of fighting men. This practice grew and spread during the eleventh century, until by 1100 or thereabouts all the great monasteries of the Tendai and some of the leading Shintō shrines, among them Gion, Kumano, Kitano, and Hiyoshi, had large standing armies. In 1081 the Kōfukuji of Nara (the *ujidera* or family church of the Fujiwara) combined with another monastery to attack both Mount Hiyei and Miidera, burning the latter and making off with much loot.

Although these armed bands were at first used chiefly in disputes between monasteries, it was not long until they began to descend upon the capital, making demonstrations of force with the object of influencing the Court or the government. The most troublesome of all was the Tendai monastery on Mount Hiyei, whose troops, numbering several thousand, time after time between 981 and 1185 swarmed into the city in support of their usually unreasonable claims. As a rule the Court was helpless, giving way in despair and even dismissing high officers of state so as to placate the monks. On one occasion the Sacred Emperor said in an edict: "Because our faith is fervent we have at last granted this petition, making right of wrong."

It is clear that, although the seed of these disgraceful episodes may have been some genuine argument on a point of doctrine, the motive of the subsequent conflicts was greed for power and property. They had no religious character whatever beyond the names of the contending parties. Often the clashes arose from disputes about title to land, without any pretence that sacred issues were at stake. It is not surprising that these gross abuses of ecclesiastical power evoked a dissenting movement which appealed far more strongly to the majority of believers than the abstruse teaching and the vainglory of the older sects. The Shingon sect, being remote on Mount Kōya, kept out of the strife, except for an offshoot at Negoro, in the province of Kii, which raised levies like the Tendai troops and developed such wealth and strength that it became a menace to the civil power, by which (in common with other such bodies) it was in the end ruthlessly destroyed. That, however, was late in the sixteenth century when the civil power was in most competent and determined hands, and this fact suggests that the main reason for the overbearing conduct of the Church in the eleventh century was the weakness of the State. Here was another example of the failure of the central government to deal with subversive movements. It failed because it had no armed force at its own command, and depended for its very existence upon the voluntary support of military leaders who could exact their own price. But the weakness of government does not excuse the delinquencies of the ecclesiastical body, and any impartial study of Buddhism during the Fujiwara period, or let us say from 950 to 1150, is bound to lead to the conclusion that as an institution it failed miserably to provide the moral force that the times demanded, since the influence of the sects with the greatest power and the greatest responsibility in mediaeval Japan was on the whole an evil influence, breeding disorder, corruption, and bloodshed. Allowance should of course be made for the work of those good and learned monks who, in the seclusion of their seminaries or of remote country temples, maintained the tradition of piety and scholarship. But the remarkable spread of popular, dissident sects that began about 1000 and swept the country in the following centuries is in itself strong testimony to the failure of the older schools in both precept and example.

It is evident that the times demanded a simple and comforting faith that would hold out to the ordinary man some prospect of salvation, and this was forthcoming in the worship of the compassionate Buddha Amida, which was preached by new religious leaders in a gospel that was easy to understand and offered consolation for the miseries of this world as well as hope for bliss in the next. The miseries of the age were not imaginary, for as we have already seen natural calamities were frequent, life was precarious, and political conditions were unstable. Already in the eleventh century disorder was rife, while civil tumult grew worse and more frequent in the twelfth century, culminating in the revolt called the Hōgen Insurrection. We need not enter into details of the common causes of discontent, though it is worth noting that the turbulence and greed of the great Buddhist sects were enough to make the ordinary worshipper feel doubtful and disconsolate. There is ample evidence in contemporary books that a spirit of pessimism was abroad. It might be said that, for all but members of the rising military class, anxiety was the keynote of the times. This sentiment, in most studies of the Heian period, is related to certain prophecies about the decline of Buddhism in what was called the Latter Day of the Holy Law (Mappō); but this seems a far-fetched and superfluous explanation of an uneasy phase of regret for the past and fear for the future such as all societies pass through during periods of change and growth. It is possible, however, that some of the evangelists were influenced by the idea of a degenerate age, for the Buddha Sâkya is recorded to have said that in the period of the decline of the Law, the Holy Path which he himself preached could no longer be followed. But the motives of teachers are not necessarily what inspires their pupils.

The nature of this new form of Buddhism, apart from its importance in the study of religions, is of singular interest because of the light it throws upon the Japanese temperament. Amida worship had a long history in China and Japan as a late-developing feature of Buddhist teaching and practice which was adopted or recognized in most of the older sects; but it began to attract special attention only towards the end of the tenth century. The cult, with special emphasis upon rebirth in Amida's paradise, was brought to popular notice by a learned monk named Genshin (afterwards styled Eshin), who wrote a celebrated work, the Ōjōyōshū or "Essentials of Salvation," which did much to encourage the kind of invocation known as Nembutsu or "Buddha-calling." The purpose of Nembutsu is, merely by the utterance of the name of the Buddha, to express complete faith in the power of Amida out of his infinite compassion to grant salvation to the suppliant. All that is needed is the repetition of the formula "Namu Amida Butsu." There is no need now to understand the subtleties of the great sects, to take part in their elaborate ritual, or to practise any of their austerities. Trust in the Buddha is the only necessary thing.

This very simple creed developed on different lines at different times, and there arose several versions of the Pure Land teaching—"Pure Land" being the appellation of Amida's Paradise. But the divisions or sects were not quarrelsome, and all kept to the central point of doctrine, namely the efficacy of calling the name of the Buddha, of depending upon faith and not upon works. Nothing, it will be seen, could be in greater contrast to the complexity of Tendai and Shingon and to the magnificence of their institutions. It is no wonder that the invocation of Amida spread through the country in a powerful flood. Pure Land teaching naturally had a special appeal to the poor and the wretched, but evidently it was congenial to the native temperament, for it was eagerly accepted by many whose temporal situation was high and fortunate. Among these was Michinaga, who called to Amida on his death bed. Later came Yorinaga, the brilliant but ill-fated Fujiwara statesman who in the diary from which we have already quoted wrote: "From tonight I begin one million invocations of Amida."

This was halfway through the twelfth century, but already long before that the Nembutsu teaching had made great progress in schools which grew as branches within Tendai or Shingon establishments. At first they did not arouse antagonism in the parent sects, but later (as we shall see) they broke away, increasing and prospering until they developed into extremely powerful organizations, rivalling all other sects in the number of their adherents. To this day the Amidist sects can claim more members than any other religious body in Japan.

Evidently, then, there was something in the Pure Land teaching that harmonized with the emotional needs of the people not only in those disturbed times when it began to make headway but in subsequent periods of relative calm, when great political and social changes had taken place. To account for this phenomenon in the religious life of the Japanese people is an extremely difficult task; but one thing is clear enough, and that is their lack of interest in metaphysical argument or theological subtleties, and their preference for an emotional rather than a systematic approach to religious matters. True, the great seminaries had their learned monks, studying and commenting upon the sacred books and the exegetical literature in which Buddhism is so rich. But these were exceptional men, scholars and thinkers by vocation, of whose studies the ordinary layman had no comprehension. Nor indeed did such learned monks, whether by brilliant interpretation or by persuasive arts, contribute in any important measure to propagating among the unlearned the teaching of Buddhism in its more difficult aspects.

The great churchmen of Japan, the leaders and innovators, were those who took some cardinal feature of Buddhism as it had been received from India or China and gave it a shape or an emphasis that would recommend it to the popular mind. Thus two of the greatest figures in the religious history of Japan, Saichō and Kūkai, though leaders in a true sense, made no original contribution to doctrine, but, thanks more to character and statesmanlike gifts than to truly great intellectual power, were able to adapt borrowed systems to conditions in their own country and in their own times. That, of course, was a very important function because it was a necessary prelude to the further spread of Buddhism in Japan. But the nature of Japanese Buddhism as it subsequently developed was due to evangelists whose teaching was notable only in its departure from accepted tradition. This is not to disparage their labours, but to point out that what was original in their work was the native character with which they endowed their version of the truths of Buddhism. The growth of Pure Land Buddhism is an excellent example of this trend, since from the simple beginnings which we have noted it grew, thanks to the genius of two great ecclesiastics, Hōnen and Shinran, into a popular religion which, in its latest form, was scarcely recognizable as Buddhism at all, so far had it disregarded the conventions of the older schools. The truth is that these two (together with Nichiren, who belongs to a later period) owed their successes only partly to their depth and strength of character, and most of all to their understanding of popular psychology.

Although it is rash to make categorical statements about popular psychology, it is safe to say that the natural bent of the Japanese mind is (or was in the period here considered) averse to analytical or speculative exercises. It leans rather to a simple trust in the senses. If one were to venture a judgment about the national temperament, one might feel justified in concluding, from the poetry and romantic literature of the day, that it was on the whole sentimental, emotional even, and inclined to pessimism. Most of the poets and most of the heroes and heroines of romance (who may be taken as representing contemporary ideals) dwell upon the transitory nature of human existence and the illusory character of worldly pleasures. The mood of the time, if such language may be allowed, is not the fresh and innocent spirit that pervades the early poetry of Nara. At the end of the tenth century, it tends to melancholy. The poets no longer celebrate the joys of love, but prefer to bewail the inconstancy of lovers or to deplore the unkindness of fate. Spring blossoms and the autumn moon arouse only melancholy reflections upon *mono no aware*, or lacrimae rerum, the "pity of things"; and this somewhat overworked phrase might almost be taken as the keynote of the age.

Articulate persons, especially those who keep diaries, are fond of expressing world-weariness. They must, they tell us, give up the vain search for pleasure and retire to a monastery or to some mountain retreat where they can lead a holy life and attend to their own salvation. Yet they are not quite convincing, and the true votaries look askance at such confessions, observing sourly that they are made not out of faith but only from an urge to be in the fashion.[2] What these people really wanted was pleasure in this world and bliss in the next; and such being the prevailing sentiment it is not surprising that the Pure Land teaching met with so warm a response. It offered a prospect of Paradise

---

[2] In the *Tale of Genji*, in the book called "Tenarai," when the hero says that he wishes to escape from worldly vanities, a nun pungently remarks that this yearning for a mountain retreat is very up-to-date!

without arduous spiritual exercise, and in effect it said to its converts that they need not trouble much about sin, for the Buddha Amida was of infinite compassion and mercy. There was here no question of the continual watch of a "Great Forbidder, safe with all his Spies around him." Faith was needed, not works. Moreover, this new Amida worship not only promised salvation but held out prospects of bliss in this life also. It was a gospel that could not fail to attract the ordinary man of the day, superstitious, sentimental, quick to respond to hopes as well as fears.

Later developments of the Amidist sects are rather closely connected with political changes, and we must study them in due course. Here we need add only that the theological reasoning upon which the Nembutsu doctrine was based is by no means as simple and direct as the formula in which it was presented to the common run of aspirants. On the contrary, it is subtle and appealing, and it raises complex issues of faith and grace. It was attacked by the older sects as encouraging evildoers, but there can be no doubt that the Pure Land sects were well suited to their times, in which most men were thirsty for the consolations of religion.

As for the effect of faith in Amida upon the minds of people of high rank in Court society, it should be enough to quote a passage from the Diary of Murasaki Shikibu which explains the religious feelings of a clever, experienced woman. The original is somewhat obscure and scholars disagree as to its exact meaning, but its intention is clear enough:

"In any event," says Murasaki discussing her religious beliefs, "I shall now abandon my old reliance upon prayers and abstinence. I shall simply recite fervently the invocation to Amida Buddha. I no longer feel the least attachment to any odious worldly things, yet I shall doubtless vacillate until I ascend to the clouds. Thus I hesitate. I am nearing the right age for taking vows, and if I grow much older there will be nothing unusual about my not reading sacred texts. My mind too will probably become more and more alive. Now, though I seem to be imitating some very devout person, the truth is that I really do think of nothing but my devotions. Moreover it is not at all certain that a person like me, who has sinned gravely in earlier life, could succeed in becoming a nun. Now that I have learned of my wrongdoing in a previous life, I am filled with sadness."

She means that she is still too lively for a nunnery, but is so conscious of past sins that only the mercy of Amida can release her from the unhappiness to which they condemn her. The grace of Amida will help her to escape her *sukuse*, the destiny which she harbours, her karma. This was written about 1000, during the lifetime of the celebrated Eshin, forerunner of the great Pure Land evangelists who were to play a leading part in the religious history of Japan. Already he had many followers in high places. A work of about 980, contemporary with Eshin's book, gives accounts of the lives of a number of persons who had been reborn in Amida's Paradise, beginning with Prince Shōtoku and ending with distinguished monks and Court officials. A later work, compiled by the great scholar Ōye Masafusa about 1085, gives biographies of believers in salvation by Amida, including the emperors Ichijō and Go-Sanjō, high ministers of state and courtiers, and the great warrior Minamoto Yoriyoshi, who (it should be noted) founded the shrine of Hachiman, the War God, near Kamakura in 1073.

Such were the religious beliefs and practices common in high society during the eleventh century. Somewhat less important than the Amidist gospel was a belief in the Paradise of Maitreya, the Tusita Heaven of Indian Buddhism. It was encouraged not by great churchmen but by certain monks who paid men to march the streets beating drums and calling for admission to the Saviour Maitreya's Paradise, where the faithful would be welcomed and attended by beautiful nymphs. This was a somewhat popular form of Buddhism, depending upon repentance rather than faith, and it declined as the Amidist creed flourished and spread.

Some curious superstitions were fostered by the growth of the belief in Paradise which was a central feature of doctrines like Amidism. In the Heian age, especially in its later pessimistic phase, there were many who felt that they could not hope to be reborn at once in Paradise. They therefore prayed to be born in their next existence as a demon or even as a serpent, both of these being long-lived creatures. It was their hope that in a protracted life they might await a later opportunity to merit salvation. Such beliefs no doubt arose under the influence of some ancient cult which had no relation to Buddhist thought, and was perhaps of Chinese origin; but the sinner's desire to postpone judgment on his conduct is universal.

3. The Pagan Cult

One of the most interesting aspects of the religious history of Japan is the relationship that grew up between Buddhism and the ancient cult, the worship of the gods of old Japan. No serious difficulty was found in reaching a compromise, even a loose alliance, between these two so disparate faiths, one a great, splendid, all-embracing system, the other a simple pagan creed finding expression in a somewhat austere ritual.

It might be supposed that such a magnificent intellectual edifice as the highly developed Mahayana Buddhism of the Heian period would find no room for those rudimentary beliefs that together formed the Way of the Gods. But Buddhism had many mansions, and its very size and hospitality made it easy to accommodate the whole Shintō pantheon without any surrender on points of doctrine. There was a brief period of hostility when Buddhism was first introduced to Japan but this was political rather than religious in character, and before long the native divinities began to be recognized as avatars or manifestations of Buddhas and Bodhisattvas. Even the mighty cosmic Vairocana, presiding over a luminous Buddha-world, could be identified with Amaterasu, the Japanese Sun Goddess and Ancestress of the Royal House. Shintō shrines were often put under the charge of Buddhist monks, and Buddhist emblems often found their way into Shintō precincts. There was no conflict here, since Shintō had no sacred images and its apparatus was of the simplest kind. Consequently it offered no positive resistance to Buddhism, nor did it appear to Buddhism as an obstacle.

The details of this process of amalgamation are matters for the specialist in religious history, but its broad general features deserve some study here, in so far as they throw light upon the religious ideas of the Japanese people. The outstanding fact is the survival of a seemingly weak and primitive cult. Since Buddhism was a great force, material as well as spiritual, it seems natural to ascribe the survival of the simple ideas and institutions of Shintō to a special tolerance and magnanimity on the part of Buddhism. But it would be equally correct to say that Buddhism in Japanese hands found no great difficulty in reaching an understanding with Shintō, because Japanese thought in religious matters was inclined towards compromise. Japanese religious leaders have usually looked for points of agreement and not of dissent. This may be regarded as an expression of indifference rather than tolerance; and it does seem to be true that as a rule religious questions do not arouse bitter antagonism in Japanese minds. But a desire to find common ground, a disposition to regard different views as different aspects of one truth, is a positive characteristic which cannot be dismissed as a mere lack of interest.

Whatever the reasons, the facts are that as an institution Shintō displayed remarkable powers of self-preservation. It did not actively resist Buddhism, but by passively adhering to its own character it escaped being swamped or submerged by the sheer weight of Buddhism. Indeed in some respects it was Shintō that imposed changes, not very great changes but significant nevertheless, upon Buddhism as it developed in a Japanese environment. There can be no doubt that certain preconceptions of Shintō belief were adopted by the Buddhists, particularly in such matters as the veneration of ancestors, which was so vital a part of Shintō that Japanese Buddhism was compelled to provide for it.

Ultimately, beginning with the admission that the native gods were "protectors" of Buddhism, a fairly complete understanding between Buddhism and Shintō was reached. The process took several centuries to complete, and meanwhile Shintō retained a considerable territory of its own in the national life. Despite the influence of Buddhism, it was still the state religion. The traditional rites were regularly performed at Court, while the great shrines of Ise and Kamo were served by Vestal Princesses. The Fujiwara Regents, though almost fanatical in their Buddhist devotions, did not neglect their family shrines of Kasuga, Yoshida, and Ōharano, while the festivals of Kamo, Iwashimizu, and other leading Shintō places were celebrated with great splendour and sometimes attended by the sovereign in state. Indeed these observances were sometimes on so lavish a scale that the government tried to curb their excesses, ordering the Kebiishi-chō to intervene. But this office was reluctant to become involved in matters of worship, and took no action or issued only a mild oral reproof.

It would be wrong to suggest that the Shintō religion actually grew and flourished throughout the Heian period, for it had its ups and downs and had to make some large concessions to Buddhism. There was a decline in faith among the more sophisticated members of urban society as knowledge of Chinese philosophy and the practice of Yin-Yang tended to displace older beliefs. Provincial governors were at times accused of neglecting the proper rites, and courtiers in the mid-tenth century used to find excuses for absence from Shintō ceremonies. In documents of the time there are to be found edicts threatening such offenders with a reduction of salary. In another work the great Michinaga is reported to have rebuked officials for neglect of the same kind. Perhaps an even more startling piece of evidence is a passage in the Sarashina Diary (ca. 1060) in which the writer pretends not to know who Amaterasu Ōmikami was—the Sun Goddess! There is a clue to this kind of sentiment in a statement attributed to a daughter of the Emperor Murakami (946–67), who, though she was Vestal Princess at the Kamo shrine, regretted that in her position she could not invoke the name of a Buddha. She was a worshipper of Amida, and it seems that a growing faith in Pure Land teachings had some influence throughout the country in diminishing faith in other cults.

Such a reaction was of course natural. It was analogous to the reaction of educated or especially devout people against paganism in Europe after the adoption of Christianity. It was a popular religion which had this effect, or at least one may say that the effect was hastened by the spread of Pure Land teaching, which, though not hostile, was essentially unfavourable to other beliefs.

The degree of collaboration between Buddhist and Shintō clergy is shown in the practice of sending Buddhist monks, in times of calamity, to recite passages from Buddhist scriptures at great Shintō shrines near the capital. But despite these signs of weakness Shintō as an institution, though it took colour from Buddhism and even imitated certain Buddhist practices, did not fade away; and when, much later in Japanese history, institutional Buddhism fell out of favour, Shintō was able to reassert itself and claim the support of powerful political leaders. It served from time to time as a bulwark of authority, a conservative force arrayed against disturbing foreign ideas.

Even when the power of Buddhism in Japan was at its height, in any time of national danger the country would appeal to the national gods; and although in untroubled times the minor deities and their shrines might be neglected, the worship of the Sun Goddess never lapsed. Her shrine at Ise was the holiest place in the land. It was inviolable and its precincts were scrupulously guarded against Buddhist influence.

Shintō as an institution could not oppose the wealth and strength of Buddhism, nor could it match the depth and range of Buddhist thought. The very simplicity of Shintō observances and beliefs was such that it did not appear as a rival to Buddhism, whereas Buddhism for its part saw no difficulty in admitting Shintō deities to its pantheon. These two features combined to protect the indigenous religion against any attempt at control or suppression which might otherwise have been made. Buddhism was large and tolerant; Shintō was accommodating so long as it was able to preserve its identity and its function as the state religion for ceremonial purposes. Indeed, until the late sixteenth century, the history of the relations between the two religions is, with trifling exceptions, a history of conciliation; and although Shintō made concessions, such as admitting Buddhist emblems to Shintō shrines, Buddhism as it developed in Japan did not hesitate to make adjustments to certain native beliefs and customs.

One example will be enough to show that at times the Buddhist prelates took the initiative in conciliating the national cult. In 887 two monks from the Enryakuji monastery were assigned to serve in the shrines of the great gods of Mount Hiyei as a result of representations made to the Throne by the distinguished Tendai cleric Enchin, who in the course of his memorial said: "For a nation to be a nation depends primarily on the exposition of Li [Propriety]. For men to be men also depends upon the practice of Li. That is why the Book says, 'If men have Li there is safety. If they lack Li there is danger.'"

After this interesting passage in approval of Confucian doctrine, Enchin continued as follows: ". . . the reason for the Western Court's esteem of our country was that Japan was regarded as the home of Li and Yi [Righteousness]. When Dengyō Daishi founded the Enryakuji he relied upon the principal gods of Hiyeizan. Had he not done so, he could not have ensured the national safety for so long. At present, however, though there are monks to ensure safety in the East and West and also at Kamo and Kasuga, no such officiating monks are provided for the main deities of the mountain. This is certainly a breach of Li. There ought to be two monks to worship the two gods."

Besides illustrating the attitude of Japanese Buddhism towards native religion, this document reveals very clearly the eclectic nature of Japanese thought. Enchin justifies, or rather demands, homage to native deities on ethical grounds, since he invokes the moral principles of a code of behaviour which has none of the characteristics of a revealed religion. The whole passage is a very neat piece of evidence of a desire to harmonize all kinds of good teaching, such as had been expressed by Kūkai, who said that Buddhism, Confucianism, and Taoism were three legs of a philosophical tripod. Each needed the others for stability.

These facts bear witness to the breadth of view of the Japanese people in regard to freedom of religious belief. Neither in Japan nor in China was it thought wrong to believe or to pay respect to more than one religion, for it is a commonplace in those countries that all doctrines are expressions of one truth. The only forbidden doctrine is one that is politically subversive. As for the general attitude of Buddhism towards other religions, it should be remembered that the earliest Buddhist texts recognize the existence of the Hindu Devas and regard them as deserving of honour because they are protectors of the faithful. There was wisdom in this attitude towards the traditional beliefs of Japan, for however weak Shintō might be as an institution, the pagan sentiment upon which it was founded was ancient, deeply rooted, and tenacious. It was not something added to Japanese life, it was that life itself. It was not so much an articulated creed as the expression of deep feelings about man and society shared by all members of a nation. Such feelings included a love of their own land and a sense of continuity, expressed in veneration for ancestors and strong family affection, together with a worship of the powers of nature.

The sentiment of kinship or community with nature is very strong, and it has great powers of survival. It has fostered that enjoyment of natural beauty which is one of the most engaging features of Japanese life. The simple nature worship of early Japan no doubt suffered to some degree from the dominance of Buddhist and Confucian ideas. But it certainly struggled against these intruders and it probably found much support in the poetic tradition of Japan, which is closely linked to paganism. In all countries the pagan tradition, though it may be overlaid, is never wholly destroyed, for it expresses the most intimate and enduring feelings of a people. The words *Nymphs and shepherds dance no more!* sound like the death knell of a happy pagan life, but they evoke resistance even in the modern mind. The feeling of loss is beautifully described in the well-known lines from Coleridge (adapting Schiller):

> The intelligible forms of ancient poets,
> The fair humanities of old religion,
> The power, the beauty and the majesty
> That had their haunts in dale or piny mountain
> Or forest by slow stream or pebbly spring
> Or chasms or watery depths. All these have vanished,
> They live no longer in the faith of reason
> But still the heart doth need a language. Still
> Doth instinct bring back the old names.

This might almost have been written about Japan under the pressure of alien philosophies. True Shintō, as I understand it, is not a religion as defined by Matthew Arnold, morality touched with emotion, but perhaps it is not far from poetic emotion touched with ritual.

Some confusion has been caused by recent Western writers on "Shintō" who treat it as if it were nothing but an invention of nationalistic propaganda. Certainly it has been put to base uses, as have other creeds, but "the fair humanities" of the old religion have not entirely vanished. Examined from a historical viewpoint Shintō may perhaps be taken as revealing the natural bent of the Japanese mind, until fairly recent times, as simple, not metaphysical or resolutely rational; not upset by what is illogical; and definitely not monotheistic, even in its most popular Amidist beliefs.

CHAPTER XII

THE GROWTH OF A WARRIOR CLASS

1. *The Economic Basis*

WE HAVE SEEN that the gradual collapse of the civil power after
the decline of the Fujiwara dictators was accompanied by a rise in the
influence of the warrior clans. Once a cloistered emperor had been
obliged to depend upon those clans for his protection, as in the Hōgen
disturbance of 1156, effective control in all but purely ceremonial matters of government was certain to be grasped by military leaders. Yet
since those leaders were not united, but separated by family pride and
jealousy, the complete dominance of the military class could not be
achieved until the great clans themselves had settled their differences.

For several decades after 1156, therefore, the political history of
Japan is dominated by struggles between the two greatest military
clans, the Taira and the Minamoto. The fortunes of war and intrigue
favoured first one and then another, but in the end the Minamoto clan
gained the upper hand (1185). The Taira clan was destroyed, its lands
confiscated. The leader of the Minamoto established de facto control
over the whole country, and in due course built up a feudal hierarchy
more powerful and stable than any previous ruling class.

For an understanding of the events that led to Japanese feudalism
it is necessary to go far back and study the origins of the warrior class,
the chief component of feudal society; and in particular its economic
basis, because like all the leading phenomena in Japanese history it is
closely connected with the ownership of land and the production of the
staple foodstuff, rice. The decay of government administered by a
metropolitan aristocracy began with departures from the system of land
tenure based upon the number of consumers in a household, a system
upon which the survival of such a kind of government depended, since
it was designed to furnish the Crown with revenues and military service, while reducing the strength of those clans that rivalled the Imperial
House in prestige and ambition.

This equalitarian division of the means of production broke down
(for reasons explained in Chapters V and VI) and was little by little
displaced by a manorial system, in which estates of considerable size
were held by great landlords, whether individuals or institutions, enjoying fiscal and juridical immunity in varying degrees. In fact, though
not in name, these persons under different disguises exercised rights of
private ownership over land and jurisdiction over people which were
legally the sole prerogative of the Crown.

Such incursions into the public domain remained on a modest scale until the demand for foodstuffs grew with the increase of population in the home provinces and it became necessary to bring more land under cultivation. This situation was met by the central government's order of 722 that three million acres of new rice land should be developed, and that, to encourage the progress of the scheme, those who carried out such work were to receive substantial remissions of tax in respect of the land reclaimed. The interpretation of "reclaiming" given to the new law by local landowners was conveniently broad. They took over not only land suitable for rice-growing, but upland fields, forest tracks, swamps, rivers, and ponds which were already in partial use by poor cultivators. Since such property was only lightly taxable or even immune, their estates increased steeply in value because the incidence of tax over the whole area became very light.

On the other hand poor cultivators, finding themselves surrounded by predatory neighbours, were moved to "donate" or "commend" their own plots of allotted or reclaimed land to greater landowners. By so doing, while keeping the land in their own possession and farming it as before, they obtained the protection of a landlord. In return, the landlord, having incorporated the plots in his manor, took a part of their yield as a fee.

As a result of these practices influential persons gained control of very large areas of land. But this did not always result in their occupying great estates. To be sure, rights of ownership, that is to say manorial rights extracted (legally or otherwise) from the public domain, were acquired on a large scale throughout the country, but at the same time the right of possession by the real cultivator was firmly established. The main reason why a weak, practically defenceless cultivator was able to retain the right of possession was that, as the cultivable area increased, the great landowners could not find slave labour for their new farms and were therefore obliged to depend upon the services of freemen, many of whom were already in possession of small plots of their own. Furthermore—and this is an important fact in shaping the character and status of the Japanese peasant in later generations—the intensive cultivation of rice in small irrigated fields was best carried out by individual enterprise, so that the feeling of attachment to his own plot and the sense of permanent occupancy were very strong in the small farmer. This sentiment was a big factor in the development of agriculture and the growth of a traditional form of land tenure. It is a feature that must always be borne in mind when considering the agrarian economy of the country and the nature of its institutions.

There was another type of land tenure, which developed principally from the occupancy of reclaimed land that remained outside the control of a domanial lord or of the officers of the Crown. This kind of holding gradually spread, and by about A.D. 1000 its occupancy was assimilated to ownership to such a degree that the lands occupied were commonly

known as "name fields" (*myōden*), because the name of the original occupant served as a title of ownership, and he was known as the *myōshu*
or *nanushi*, which means "name master."[1] Such holdings were usually of
modest size, since they were farmed by members of the owner's household, with little or no hired labour. They ranged from less than one
acre to as much as twenty-five acres, but about ten acres was probably
the average size, fair dimensions for the intensive culture of rice.

It may seem that these technical details have little to do with the
growth of a class of private warriors; but it was the need for protection
felt by small and middling farmers that caused them to seek means of
self-defence in the insecure conditions of frontier life. They were as a
rule hardy men, used to bearing arms, but their individual effort was
not enough and they were not slow to form combinations with others
of their own standing, or if necessary to claim the support of a more
powerful landowner, preferably a local magnate rather than an absentee nobleman. These were the men whose descendants were to form
the bulk of the warrior class in later times. They were independent, but
where their title to land was not firm the officers of the central government might challenge them, or exercise a right of entry, or levy tax, or
otherwise embarrass them. In such cases it was prudent even for a
well-to-do private owner to commend his land to some stronger personage who could not be coerced by the civil authorities.

The first clear signs of the rise of a separate military class of provincial landowners appear about the year 900; and it is no coincidence
that this is a crucial date in the development of the immune estates,
the shōen (which for convenience we here call manors, though the two
are not identical either in origin or in character). By the end of the
ninth century these manors had so developed in size and strength and
so promoted local separatism that the authority of the central government in most provinces had virtually collapsed. This was a state of
affairs for which the Fujiwara clan, as the owners of more extensive
manorial rights than any other family or institution, were very largely
to blame. Indeed, since their political power in the capital depended
mainly upon their wealth in the country, they were in fact the chief
agents of the destruction of the central authority which they had
usurped. It was of course the failure of the central government to keep
order, in town as well as country, that brought the warriors into prominence. Contemporary accounts give a picture of confusion and violence so widespread that the commoners were obliged to arm in self-
defence, and to attach themselves to stronger people for defence of their
persons as well as their property. Some of the wealthiest provincial
notables kept their own private armed forces, partly for defence but
often for use against their rivals or even for the invasion of public lands.

---

[1] Even long after the land had passed into other hands it usually continued to
be known by the name of its earlier "master."

In such conditions the provincial governors, who were civilian officials, found themselves obliged to assume military functions—something quite contrary to their tradition—and to organize a military police force. Such organs were not contemplated in the codes (the early administrative laws), and since the central government had no effective police authority it was necessary to appoint a capable man in each province to command its police. These officers were styled Tsuibushi (Constable) and Ōryōshi (a kind of High Sheriff empowered to seize both the person and the property of an offender). The effect of such measures was to take the preservation of order throughout the country out of the hands of the officials of the central government and to transfer it to local magnates who were themselves important landowners. Even in the capital city the police force was very feeble, and the Chief Commissioner had to send to the provinces to recruit armed men, who were brought to the capital by leaders belonging to the class of private warriors. Some noblemen also sent for men from their own estates, to protect their private property in the city against marauding bands. Thus we find members of the rising military class serving in the capital in a semi-public capacity, and beginning to encroach in various ways upon the civil authority.

The chronology of the rise of the new warrior class, with all the social changes that it involved, is not very clear. Most historians are inclined to measure it by the decline of the system (the constitution, one might say) embodied in the codes, the ryō and ritsu of the eighth century. This is understandable, because instances of failure get recorded, whereas successes do not as a rule call for contemporary praise. By and large, we know that the power of the provincial and local landed gentry increased as the opening up of new land continued, because this was a process by which they grew wealthier and at the same time more capable of defending their property and their privileges by force. But it was a gradual process, and perhaps the best evidence that it was reaching a well-defined stage from about the year 900 is furnished by the numerous orders and prohibitions issued by the government in the Kampyō era, from 889 to 897, but never obeyed.

These documents point out that people of all ranks (notice the importance attached to social gradations) are settling on the land, oppressing poor farmers, resisting the officers of the Crown, and in general obstructing the administration. Characteristically these documents dwell in Confucian fashion upon the ethical aspect of the case, and deplore the corruption of public morals which follows such behaviour. But what they are really condemning is the rise of a military class, which had already begun to exercise real power at an even earlier date, when provincial governors on the expiry of their term of office would elect to remain in the country, there to found country families living on large estates and always, as their households grew, looking out for more land. By the middle of the Heian era (say 950) the Court could no longer keep the peace in the capital, nor could the aristocratic absentee landlords, whether nobles or abbots, protect their own property without the assistance of armed forces maintained by local magnates, who did not fail to exact a price for their services. This was the position soon after the era known as Engi (901–22), which gave its name to an imposing body of legislation that the central government was less and less able to enforce.

The greatest and most characteristic development of the warrior class took place in the district known as Kantō or "East of the Barrier," the barrier being a military post at the pass across the Hakone mountains by which travellers from western or central Japan approached the alluvial tract forming the greatest single area of fertile rice land in all the provinces of Japan. It was remote from the capital and it was settled much later than Yamato (except that in neolithic times it was the greatest centre of population). East and north of this again was wild territory, where life was hard and called for courage and endurance.

2. The Rival Clans. Their Family History

It was natural that in those days of border fighting the private warriors should form bands or leagues for attack or defence. Nominally many of those warriors were subject to the control of some great noble or important monastery in whose manor (shōen) their land was incorporated, in particular when they held the post of steward or manager for the manorial lord. At times, unless the manor was entirely immune, they might also be subject to the authority of the provincial governor in some respects. But as their influence extended, by virtue of their common interests or for other reasons they gradually thrust aside the authority of the absentee lords of the manor and the provincial and local authorities of their own areas; so that by about 950 we find the orders of the central powers and its provincial representatives flouted by wealthy landowners established at a distance from the capital. This strong trend is well illustrated by the revolts of Masakado and Sumitomo (described in Chapter VIII). It was disobedience on a large scale, but in other ways it was not exceptional, for throughout the country the warrior class as a whole was striving to free itself from the restrictions of the land laws and the control of officers of the Crown. One of the most obvious ways of achieving those aims was for individuals to combine against the representatives of government, and the formation of leagues or alliances for that purpose was an important stage in the development of a military class by coalescence. Thus such factions or parties as the "Bandō Hachi Heishi" (the Eight Taira Groups of the East) or the "Musashi Shichitō" (the Seven Parties of Musashi) began to appear in the eastern provinces, forming a more or less homogeneous class of warrior, at the centre or head of which were the chieftains of the great clans, the Taira and the Minamoto. It was the rivalry between those two clans for leadership of the warriors which ended in the formation of a strong and united military society.

It should not, however, be supposed that the rise of the soldiers was brought about by a class struggle in which the poor farmers revolted against the rich landowning aristocrats. Both the clans were led by men of aristocratic origin—of royal blood, in fact—and although both had their base and stronghold in the provinces, both had family connexions in the capital. Most of the local magnates, whether of Taira or Minamoto descent, had at one time been established as governors or deputy governors, or as domanial lords or less important officials and landholders, and both clans had promoted the formation of a warrior class by gaining the adherence of smaller settlers on the land. It may be taken for granted that, especially in the provinces remote from the capital, almost every farmer was a warrior.

Originally both these great clans were in the service of· the Fujiwara, a clan which was politically supreme in the capital and very powerful in the provinces through the influence of its rich manors and their stewards and managers. But in the course of time the warrior houses were able to put pressure on the Fujiwara and, while themselves becoming great landowners, to grasp political power. There is nothing exceptional in such a history of feudal barons. What is perhaps remarkable is the fact that despite their real power they did not repudiate the authority of the Imperial House, but rather professed to see in the divine character of the sovereign the moral basis of their exercise of supreme political authority as his deputy. This was the special character of the mutual relationship between a developing feudal system and an ancient monarchical constitution laid down in written codes of law.

The Minamoto family were descended from the Emperor Seiwa (858–76) and they obtained the name because the Taihō code, foreseeing the proliferation of imperial offspring, had decreed that in the sixth generation from an imperial sire his descendants were to be deprived of princely rank and title and assigned family names and ordinary titles of nobility. Towards the close of the ninth century this law had come into operation. The revenues of the Crown, already diminished by the fiscal immunity of the manors, were not sufficient for the support of all members of the imperial family, and the former princes were as a rule obliged to seek paid employment. The number of official posts available for persons of the highest rank was limited by law, so that it was prudent for these young men to divest themselves of privilege and enter official life wherever a post was available, or to take up farming themselves. Of these ex-princes those who bore the name of Taira or Minamoto were most numerous.

The Minamoto family in the tenth century included descendants of emperors from the Emperor Saga (d. 842) to the Emperor Kōkō

(d. 887). They were divided into branches known by the name of the ancestor, so that there were Saga Genji (Genji means Minamoto family),[2] Seiwa Genji, and about a dozen others; but the Seiwa branch were the most successful. Not all of them founded military houses, since many took service at Court, attracted by the pleasures of city life. It was the Seiwa Minamoto and the Kammu Taira who were the true leaders of the military caste, exceeding all others in strength and renown. The story of their rise is an instructive epitome of the development of the warrior class.

The Seiwa Genji sprang from a grandson of the Emperor Seiwa, a certain Tsunemoto, whom we have already noticed as the deputy governor of Musashi (Musashi no Suke) who resisted the rebellious Taira Masakado in 940. He went through the ordinary career of a nobleman, holding official appointments in the provinces, ending as governor of one important province after another. His sons all served at Court as military officers, and their descendants spread and flourished. Of them Mitsunaka was the most successful, holding the office of provincial governor in eastern and northern provinces. He was much trusted by the Fujiwara Regents, and it was in fact the Fujiwara clan that founded the fortunes of the Minamoto.

The bond between the warlike Minamoto and their Fujiwara masters was already close in the middle of the tenth century. Minamoto Mitsunaka is said to have denounced a kinsman (Takaaki) for conspiring to revolt in the year 968, which bore the era name Anna in the Japanese calendar. This was the so-called Anna Plot, which failed thanks to Mitsunaka's warning. Mitsunaka's family was important in the provinces. They had rich manors in Settsu, Yamato, Mino, and other provinces near the capital, and were therefore both wealthy and influential. The great names in the Minamoto clan as it rose to power in the eleventh and twelfth centuries are those of the descendants of Mitsunaka, as the accompanying tables show.

1. *The Seiwa Genji*

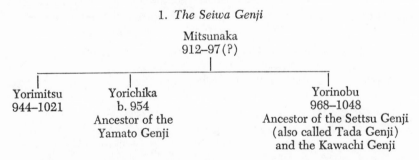

Mitsunaka
912–97(?)

Yorimitsu
944–1021

Yorichika
b. 954
Ancestor of the
Yamato Genji

Yorinobu
968–1048
Ancestor of the Settsu Genji
(also called Tada Genji)
and the Kawachi Genji

[2] "Genji" (the same name as in the *Tale of Genji*) is the Sino-Japanese reading of the characters meaning Minamoto family. Similarly, the Taira family are also known as Heiji, the same character being read alternatively as "Taira" and "Hei." ("Uji" or "Ji" means a family or clan name.) Nomenclature of this sort is explained in my *Historical Grammar of Japanese*.

2. *The Kawachi Genji*

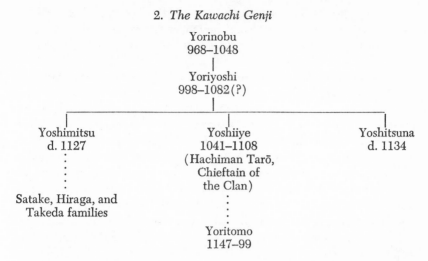

Yorinobu
968–1048
|
Yoriyoshi
998–1082(?)
|

Yoshimitsu	Yoshiiye	Yoshitsuna
d. 1127	1041–1108	d. 1134
:	(Hachiman Tarō,	
:	Chieftain of	
:	the Clan)	
Satake, Hiraga, and	:	
Takeda families	:	
	Yoritomo	
	1147–99	

Mitsunaka himself was popular at Court, because of his own gifts and the favour of the Fujiwara leaders which he enjoyed. He was at home in Court society, and was a poet of some distinction. Several of the early Minamoto of the highest rank were indeed elegant and accomplished men of letters, as well as being members of a family that bred successful military leaders. The great Michinaga saw clearly that he could not carry out his dynastic schemes unless he could be sure of support from one of the leading military clans whose chieftains had strong connexions at Court. It was the Seiwa Genji who best fulfilled this requirement, and became well entrenched in the capital, to the advantage of their provincial kinsmen. Michinaga depended upon Mitsunaka's two sons, Yorimitsu and Yorinobu, to take the violent measures which the Fujiwara themselves were too fastidious to adopt. These two were described by their enemies as "running dogs" of the Fujiwara family. But they were good soldiers as well as courtiers. Yorinobu is reported as saying that if his master told him to kill the Regent, he would rush to the Regent's quarters with drawn sword and spear, "and who would stop him?"

It is relevant to point out here, in this account of the rise of a military spirit, that bloodshed was distasteful to the civilian statesmen who administered the codes. In accordance with Chinese theory penal legislation was regarded not as an essential instrument of government, but rather as something to fall back upon when other measures failed. Thus in the Heian period, which for all its shortcomings was civilized and peacefully inclined, the laws were administered in a mild manner and there was great reluctance to inflict the death penalty or indeed any drastic punishment. Amnesties were common, and perhaps for that very reason crime flourished. Some of the hesitation to take life, or even to wound, no doubt arose from Buddhist sentiment and perhaps from superstitious fear of vengeful spirits. But the Minamoto and the Taira (in their early days at least) had no such scruples, and were quite ready to take life in order to preserve order and to further their own interests.

Consequently men like Yorimitsu and Yorinobu were very well placed for receiving favours from the Fujiwara and obtaining good posts in the capital and in the provinces. Yorimitsu held the lucrative posts of governor of Izu, Kōzuke, and other provinces in succession, and was in command of one of the Guard regiments as well as being a secretary in the Ministry of War. His daughter married a Fujiwara of high rank. On the whole the Genji in the early part of the eleventh century were strengthening their position in the central provinces (including the home provinces), while the Taira were gaining land and influence in the east. Thus Yorinobu and Yorimitsu were based upon the home provinces. Yorimitsu succeeded to his father's estates in Settsu, while Yorinobu was able to found a manor in Kawachi. In the capital at the beginning of the eleventh century (1017) there were in high official posts twenty-four Fujiwara nobles and only four Minamoto. But towards the end of the century, when the Fujiwara supremacy was at an end, there were Minamoto holding office as Minister of the Right and Minister of the Left, and serving in most of the high military posts at Court. These appointments carried no real authority, it is true, but they gave rank and prestige to their holders.

The Taira were of similar origin to the Minamoto, their ancestor being a grandson of the Emperor Kammu, named Takamochi. He was deprived of his princely rank and style in 824 and given the surname of Taira. He was made Governor of Kazusa province. This Takamochi had five sons, all of whom settled in the east. The third of these was Taira Yoshimochi, who had twelve sons, one of whom was Masakado, the insurgent of 935. Such people as these did not cut themselves off from the Court. They sent their sons to serve in the sovereign's body-guard or as gentlemen-at-arms in great Fujiwara houses. Masakado was in the capital looking for such employment in the year 930. He wanted to be Police Commissioner, and it was after (but not because) he returned disappointed to the east that he rose against the Imperial House and even claimed imperial dignity himself. These sons and grandsons of Takamochi, and their descendants, all owned property and generally held offices in the eastern provinces. Many of them were appointed to command troops sent against the Emishi (the aborigines) in the north, and within a generation or so most of the leading families in the east claimed Taira descent, though not always legitimately, naming their noble forebears on the field of battle.

There were other influential warrior houses, not so well-connected perhaps as the Taira, but as a rule of aristocratic origin. They included, it is true, the offspring of earlier settlers whose pedigree was not so long and noble, but family feeling and pride of ancestry were important elements in the growth of a warlike spirit and a tradition of loyalty. In fact it is very doubtful whether the ordinary farmers, armed for their own protection against rivals or tribal enemies, could have created a unified military society without aristocratic leadership. Nor could they have developed a real military prowess without the discipline of danger and hardship in very severe campaigns. It is an interesting feature of the development of the Taira and the Minamoto that both clans suffered at first from internal dissension, because their captains were passionate and unruly men, full of pride and easily offended. It was not until they had gone through some very hard experiences in fighting against a third warlike family that at length they learned the value of obedience and good faith.

The distribution of land between the two clans was not in accordance with their military strength in all localities. In the number of their adherents the Taira exceeded the Minamoto in eastern Japan and the northern provinces.[3] Yet it was in western Japan that the Taira rose to power, through official service and military success. On the other hand, though the Minamoto had great holdings of land in the home provinces, their most reliable adherents were in the north, where they had no great manors but had acquired what was to prove more valuable, a tough spirit and great experience in fighting against crafty enemies.

The real founders of the warlike reputation of the Minamoto clan were Yoriyoshi, the son of the Yorinobu whom the Regent Michinaga favoured, and Yoriyoshi's own son, Yoshiiye. Yorinobu had put down a rising led by Tadatsune, a rebellious deputy governor of Kazusa province, thus opening the way for Minamoto influence in the east. Yoriyoshi went with him, thereby gaining useful experience and a fine reputation. He had a large following among eastern landowners, and this was increased and strengthened by his notable successes in two frontier campaigns in northern Japan, known as the Early Nine Years War and the Later Three Years War, which were fought at intervals between the years 1050 and 1089.

Some details of these campaigns will serve to show the nature of warfare in those days, and to explain how the fighting, while consolidating the position of the Minamoto clansmen in the eastern and northern provinces, contributed to the formation of a strong tradition of military virtue, based upon mutual trust between leaders and men.

[3] During the eleventh century the respective centres of influence of Minamoto and Taira were, according to one account, as follows:

	Minamoto	Taira
Home Provinces	24	9
East	136	161
West	64	65

3. Rebel Chieftains

After the establishment of the government in Kyoto the first open revolt of a warrior chieftain against the authority of the Crown was the rising of Taira Masakado in the years 935–40. This has already been touched upon (in Chapter VIII), but it deserves some further attention.for the light it throws upon relations between the central government and the great landowners in the provinces. It also reveals some interesting aspects of the growth, in its early phases, of a peculiar military ethos which was to colour Japanese life for centuries to come.

The most valuable documentary source for enquirers into these matters is a work called *Masakado-ki*, thought to have been first compiled in the year 940, only a few months after the defeat and destruction of Masakado. In the version now extant the narrative has been dressed up in very high-flown language, with frequent allusions to Chinese history or even to Buddhist legend, and other ornamental features. But good authorities regard it as a substantially accurate recital of events based upon authentic contemporary records.

It is clear from this account that the greater provincial magnates had already in the early part of the tenth century firmly established themselves in their own spheres of influence and were exercising powers that gave them almost a regional sovereignty. They were nominally subject to the orders of the central government, but they enjoyed a virtual independence and were obeyed and respected by most of the warrior households in their territory. Their independence was in some respects recognized by the Crown, for they were as a rule given appointments as vice-governor (*suke*) of the province in which their estates were situated, and that office tended to become hereditary in the family of its early holders. This post was a valuable one. Its holder was in direct control of local administration, especially as the substantive governor was usually an absentee, living an agreeable life in the capital. Consequently much of the fighting in the more distant provinces arose from quarrels between warrior chieftains, often members of the same family, about succession to property or to offices in the provincial government. This is an important fact in the history of the growth of a warrior caste in Japan.

Masakado's short but violent fighting career began early in 930 with attacks upon his uncles and other members of the Taira clan, descendants like himself of a royal prince who was the founder of the Taira lordship in the province of Hitachi. In these internecine struggles several important leaders lost their lives resisting Masakado's onslaughts, some of them close relatives by blood or by marriage. Among these were Taira Kunika, father of Taira Sadamori, who was to rise to prominence later, and Minamoto Mamoru, who lost his three sons in one of Masakado's attacks. They were unable to stand up to Masakado, who in 935 attacked Minamoto Mamoru in his own province of Hitachi;

6

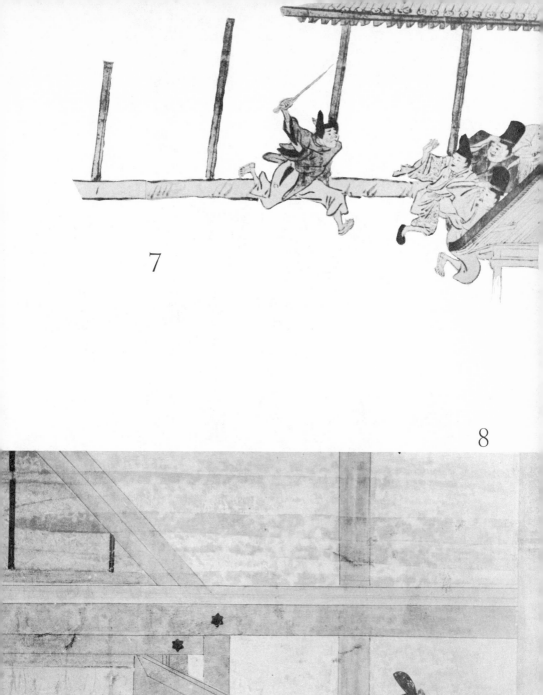

7

8

9

10

and after repeated defeats Mamoru determined to proceed to Kyoto and denounce Masakado as a rebel.

Masakado was summoned to the capital and examined, but it happened fortunately for him that a general amnesty was proclaimed on New Year's Day of 937, when the Emperor Suzaku came of age. Masakado was pardoned and returned home. In a manifesto which he issued later he said that he had settled down peacefully, forgetting all thoughts of warfare and living with a loose bowstring, when he was attacked by his uncle Yoshikane with a force of several thousand. This statement seems to refer to a battle which he fought on behalf of an unruly landowner, Fujiwara Haruaki by name, who lived in Hitachi and was known as a rebel and an oppressor of the people, whose crops he stole and whose taxes he did not remit to the capital. In general, so the official records said, "he behaved worse than barbarians or beasts."

The provincial authorities proceeded against Haruaki, but he escaped with his family to Shimosa (the neighbouring province), robbing official granaries on his way. Then the authorities of Shimosa, headed by Masakado as Tsuibushi (Constable) of the region, were instructed to arrest him. But they reported that he had escaped and they took no steps to pursue him, while he and his followers boasted that they had robbed the government and the people. When he appealed to Masakado for help, Masakado imprudently agreed to join forces with him, alleging that it was his chivalrous duty to support the weak against the strong. The government now sent a force of three thousand men against Masakado, but it was defeated by his smaller force of about one thousand. The government officers surrendered, and Masakado and Haruaki gained great booty.

Encouraged by these successes, Masakado was urged by a certain Prince Okiyo to extend his conquest to all the eastern provinces, on the ground that Masakado might as well be condemned for revolt in eight provinces as for resistance in one. Okiyo, it should be mentioned, was of royal descent, and was at this time serving as acting governor of Musashi. Masakado agreed with Okiyo, and stated that, being descended in the third generation from the Emperor Kammu, he had a clear title to the throne, and he meant to take the eight provinces as a first step to ruling the whole country. Thereupon he proceeded to attack the province of Shimotsuke, and in the elevated language of the *Masakado-ki* his horsemen, "riding on chargers like dragons, leading clouds of followers, raising their whips, pressing down their stirrups, advanced as if to cross ten thousand leagues of mountain, each man's heart afire, his spirits high, ready to conquer one hundred thousand foes."

The leading men in the province, seeing no hope of resistance, bowed to him and offered up their seals of office. Then Masakado, relying upon a timely oracle, proclaimed himself Emperor, and began to set up a government. To justify his action he wrote a long letter to the Regent, Fujiwara Tadahira, whose service he had entered when a youth in Kyoto. It is a curious document, couched in respectful language, and seems to show that Tadahira was still in touch with him. The letter was dated in January 940. At this time Masakado was sure enough of his strength to appoint governors to all the eight eastern provinces.

This was more than the long-suffering Court could bear. An edict was issued appointing new governors or vice-governors to four of those provinces and an order was issued by the Chancellor to pursue and capture Masakado. It was sent to all governors of eastern provinces in both circuits (Tōkaidō and Tōsandō), promising great rewards in rank and land and saying that there had never been such a revolt since the foundation of the Empire. This was in February 940. There was at this time much alarm and consternation among the courtiers and offiicals at the capital, for news from the front was not at all pleasing. At the beginning of the year 940 elaborate services and prayers for divine help had been ordered by the Court in the principal religious establishments, while throughout the country rituals of commination were performed by adepts of the mystic cults in the hope of destroying Masakado by the magic arts.

Meanwhile the commanders already in the field were struggling against Masakado and Okiyo with but little success. The Court thought that they needed encouragement and perhaps felt that without it they might go over to the rebel side. However that may be, promotion in rank was accorded to Minamoto Tsunemoto, the Vice-Governor of Musashi; Taira Sadamori, the Governor of Hitachi; and Fujiwara Hide-sato, the Constable of Shimotsuke. This was in April 940, and not long after this the confidence of the Court was justified, for both Masakado and Okiyo were defeated and killed before the generalissimo appointed to command the new levies had reached his post. Masakado's last stand was on March 25, 940, and Okiyo was captured and killed a few days later. But it was a month before news of the victory reached the Court, so that the promotion of Hidesato and Sadamori took place after the exploits which it was intended to encourage. Masakado's head was taken to the capital, where it was exposed in June 940 as a warning to rebels. Okiyo's followed soon after.

Although Masakado was the greatest rebel, and caused the Court most anxiety, it must be remembered that insubordinate and violent conduct was rife throughout the eastern provinces and also in many parts of the country westward of the home provinces. Risings led by Masakado and Sumitomo had been put down by provincial forces in 940 and 941, respectively, showing that the central government could still rely upon the loyalty of a number of military leaders who were themselves important landowners, usually members of the Taira or the Minamoto family. Less than a century later, in 1028, there took place another serious revolt, which was suppressed by Minamoto generals. This was the revolt of Tadatsune, an influential Taira chieftain, of a branch descended from the Prince Takamochi. His career deserves some further attention, since it helps to an understanding of conditions in the provinces early in the eleventh century, at a time when the Fujiwara Regents were beginning to decline in power and the system of dual government, by a titular emperor and an abdicated sovereign in holy orders, was developing. These conditions did not make for prompt and decisive action by the central power in times of emergency, and therefore any sign of disloyalty was alarming.

The Taira families descended from Prince Takamochi had a virtual monopoly of the governorships of Kazusa and Shimosa, where they had long been settled. From an early date they had spread from the neighbourhood of Chiba (which some of them took for a family name), and one branch acquired and developed a rich estate in a locality called Soma near the confluence of the two rivers, Tonegawa and Kogaigawa. This valuable and well-situated property they commended for protection to the Great Shrine of Ise, and thereafter it was always a member of the Chiba branch of the Taira who managed it on behalf of the Great Shrine. In due course that office was held by Tadatsune, who was in fact if not in law hereditary vice-governor of Shimosa and at times of Kazusa. His total holding of land was considerable and he had great influence in his own and adjacent provinces. Desiring to extend his territory he resigned his post as Vice-Governor of Kazusa, and in 1028 he raised a force in his own province of Shimosa and attacked the seat of government of Kazusa and the southern province of Awa, which is at the foot of the peninsula that encloses Tokyo Bay on the eastern side.

The Court on hearing of this attempt ordered him to be attacked, nominating to the command of the expedition Minamoto Yorinobu, a former governor of Ise and a man of high reputation. For private reasons Yorinobu could not comply and the Court had to despatch two Police Commissioners (Taira Naokata and Nakahara Narimichi) to the front in command of troops from the Eastern Circuits, while at the same time an order was sent to the northern province to raise levies there. It is evident that the government took a serious view of Tadatsune's action, and this was soon confirmed by events, for in the spring of 1030 the Governor of Awa threw away his seals and escaped from the province to make his way to Kyoto. Thus Naokata and his colleagues could make no headway, and presently they were recalled.

The government now called again upon Minamoto Yorinobu, made him governor of the province of Kai, and ordered him to attack Tadatsune in concert with the governors of other eastern provinces. He proceeded to his post in 1031 and commenced preparations for attack, whereupon Tadatsune, fearing Yorinobu's great prestige and doubtless impressed by the determination of the Court, offered no resistance but went directly to Yorinobu's headquarters and surrendered. He was sent to the capital as a prisoner, but died of sickness on the way. His head was cut off and despatched to the city for display.

This sudden end to Tadatsune's rising shows how great a reputation Yorinobu and other Minamoto leaders now enjoyed. Yorinobu himself, in his report to the Iwashimizu Hachiman Shrine of the War God worshipped by the Minamoto, said: "Without beating of drums or waving of banners, without loosing an arrow, or even tightening our bowstrings, we gained a victory." This was as much as to hint at the power of the Minamoto name, and the dependence of the ruling house upon the leaders of the clan.

The causes of Tadatsune's rising are clear enough. As far back as 797 edicts were issued with the intention of preventing high provincial officers from settling in the country at the end of their term and establishing settlements which grew in size as their families increased and soon were acting in a most arbitrary fashion, "threatening and browbeating the local officials, oppressing the farmers, interfering with the crops," and generally assuming lordship in their region. It was in such a way that the Taira branch to which Tadatsune belonged had established itself on the Soma estate and in surrounding territory. Following the family tradition Tadatsune exerted himself to extend the authority of his house. Yorinobu, in his report to the Throne of 1031, stated that Tadatsune had been rampant in the three eastern provinces of Kazusa, Shimosa, and Awa for some time before 1028, so that by the date of his surrender in 1031 he had been ravaging these provinces for more than four years. There is no doubt that more damage was done there by Tadatsune than by Masakado in his revolt nearly one hundred years before.

In a contemporary diary, under the date 1034, a prominent minister of state records that he has received a call from the then Governor of Kazusa, just up from his province, and he gives an account of what the Governor told him. After the surrender of Tadatsune, he reported, conditions had improved in the region and officers of the central government were no longer disregarded. The province which had suffered most from Tadatsune's depredations was his own province of Kazusa. It had been subjected to continuous requisitions by Tadatsune and by Naokata's expedition so that hardly a grain of food remained. When the last governor, appointed just after the surrender, went over the registers he found that only about 150 acres were under cultivation. These figures were checked from other returns and found accurate. The total of rice land in the province was officially recorded as about 65,000 acres. There was nothing to match this damage. Masakado had laid waste great stretches of country, but Tadatsune had done more harm.

Another contemporary writing, referring to the year 1032, reports that in the provinces overrun by Tadatsune there was danger of starvation, "a pitiful sight for people from the city." In Kazusa women and children were dying for want of food and shelter. The three provinces were like dead countries. Great effort would be needed to revive them. Fortunately, we learn, by the end of the following year fugitive peasants were beginning to return, and more land was being brought back to tillage.

It is interesting that Tadatsune and his sons were pardoned. His sons could carry on the name, thanks no doubt to the good offices of Yorinobu. They were the ancestors of leading families who became important feudal magnates in later periods.

Yorinobu's bloodless victory did much to raise him and his clan even higher in public esteem than heretofore, and his reputation was of advantage to his son Yoriyoshi, who as a youth had learned lessons in the art of war by accompanying his father on his campaigns. It was Yoriyoshi and his son Yoshiiye who were to carry on the name of Minamoto as leaders of the military class upon which the Throne depended for protection. They were jointly the heroes of a severe and protracted campaign against rebellious chieftains in northern Japan, a campaign that began in 1051 and lasted (with pauses) for twelve years. This is given in subsequent historical accounts the somewhat misleading name of the Early Nine Years War; and it was followed at an interval of more than twenty years by the so-called Later Three Years War. Both wars call for some description.

4. Wars in the North

(a) The Early Nine Years War

In the province of Mutsu there was, in addition to a governor, a military commander-in-chief responsible for the safety of the province and the superintendence of the aborigines, that is to say the "pacified" Ainu people. This office dated from the ninth century, when the Ainu had been subdued and were living more or less peacefully under Japanese rule. The holder of this post was always a member of the Abe family. In 1050 it was a warrior named Abe Yoritoki, who paid no attention to the orders of the Governor of the province, and levied taxes or confiscated property at will. The Governor, unable to enforce his authority, send word to the capital, and Yoriyoshi was now appointed both governor and commander-in-chief of the whole province, with orders to suppress Abe.

The campaign against the Abe family lasted for nine years, or allowing for pauses, twelve years. Minamoto Yoriyoshi with his son Yoshiiye, then a boy of fifteen, opened up an attack, but Yoritoki, taking advantage of a general amnesty, chose to make peace. Later, however, the

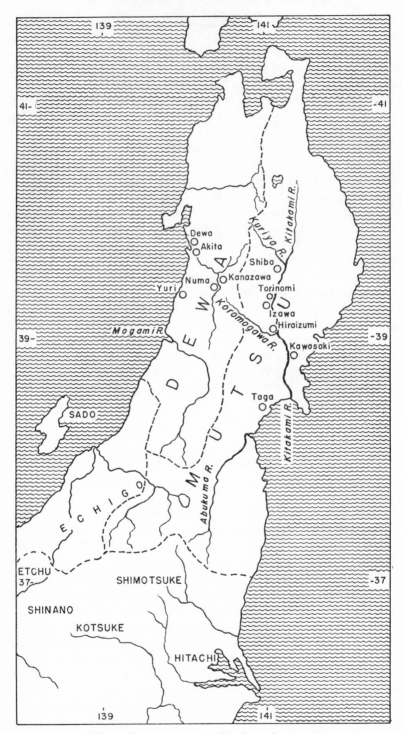

The northern provinces in the eleventh century

attack was renewed by Yoriyoshi. The fighting was very severe, owing to the nature of the terrain, the climate, and the ferocity of Abe's men. In 1057 Yoritoki was killed, but his son, Sadato, a mighty man, continued to resist. At the end of that year, while holding an entrenched position, he was attacked by Yoriyoshi with a small force of picked men. The assault failed; Yoriyoshi retreated and was pursued by Sadato in a blinding snowstorm. The Minamoto force was cut to pieces and only a few mounted officers and men escaped, Yoriyoshi and his son being among them. For a long time the government forces were unsuccessful, being handicapped by difficulties of transport, shortage of food, and inclement weather. Yoriyoshi's commission was nonetheless renewed, and he got together a new force. With this force he advanced upon the stockade and earthworks at a place on the banks of the Kuriyagawa to which Sadato had retired under pressure from several thousand fresh troops brought from the neighbouring province of Dewa by its governor, who was a member of the Kiyowara family. Sadato's resistance was stubborn, even women and children helping to defend the stockade. At last Yoshiiye set fire to it, having first diverted its water supply. There was bitter and deadly fighting for two days, until at length Sadato capitulated. This was in 1062.

In the earliest accounts of this campaign the young Yoshiiye figures as a brilliant warrior displaying "a godlike military prowess." The barbarians trembled at his name and he was called Hachiman Tarō, the firstborn of the God of War. He is thus one of the founders of the fighting tradition of his clan, worshipped almost as a divine ancestor.

Early in 1063 Yoshiiye arrived in the capital carrying the heads of Sadato and others. They were presented by two mounted officers and an escort of twenty foot-soldiers in full armour. In the following year (1064) Yoshiiye returned in triumph to Kyoto with his captives, including sons of Yoritoki, whom he treated as trustworthy attendants.

(b) The Later Three Years War

More than twenty years later, after leaders of the Kiyowara family, which had come to the aid of Yoriyoshi in his last campaign against Sadato, had built up a sorry record of misrule in the province of Mutsu, it became necessary or expedient for the Minamoto to subdue them. This task fell to Yoshiiye, who reduced the much ramified Kiyowara family to subjection in a campaign known to later chroniclers in Japan as the Later Three Years War. This also is a misleading description, for the fighting lasted from 1083 to 1087, the term of three years being arrived at by deducting periods of truce.

This war arose from a long-standing quarrel between branches of the Kiyowara house whose interests clashed, partly because of their relationships by marriage to other clans. It is not necessary to enter into details of these internecine troubles, since the result of their continuous disturbance of the peace was to make determined intervention necessary. Yoshiiye was appointed Governor of Mutsu in 1083. He had no commission from the Court to command an expedition against the Kiyowara, but part of his function was to keep order in the northern provinces. He therefore tried by peaceable means to bring an end to the fighting (in Dewa as well as Mutsu) between or among the Kiyowara leaders Masahira, Iyehira, and Narihira. His efforts, though at first not unsuccessful, did not prevent all outbreaks of violence, and at last he was obliged to intervene with his own troops. In the winter of 1086 he attacked the Numa stockade, where Iyehira was entrenched. His force was unable to reduce the enemy's strong position, but lay before it suffering from intense cold for some months, losing many men by frost and hunger, until ultimately it was obliged to withdraw.

At this point Iyehira's uncle Takahira appeared with a large force of his own, and the two marched together to the Kanazawa stockade, where they remained as a threat to Yoshiiye, who was angered by this combination against himself, and saw that he must make a great effort to retrieve his position. After long delays and inactive periods he got together a large force and, with the help of his younger brother, Yoshimitsu, who hurried north from Kyoto and brought useful reinforcements with him, laid siege to the Kanazawa position. Help was also given by Fujiwara Kiyohira, who was later to become supreme in Mutsu and Dewa. After several months—from August to November, 1087—the Kiyowara were defeated, both Iyehira and Takahira being killed while trying to escape from the stockade, to which they had set fire. The hardships suffered by both sides were terrible and Yoshiiye had great difficulty in keeping up the spirits of his men. It was thanks to his great qualities as a leader that discipline was preserved.

(c) Minamoto leadership

It was in such desperate fighting over wild, inhospitable country against a stubborn enemy in a harsh climate that the Minamoto leaders gained most valuable experience during nearly half a century. More than that, the hazards of the struggle taught their fighting men the hard lessons of obedience and discipline. During those long-drawn-out campaigns, when a man's life depended upon the alertness of his comrades and all shared equally in hardships and dangers, there naturally developed a strong bond of mutual trust between leaders and followers. It was here that the warrior's code of behaviour was formed and tested, for although Yoriyoshi commanded the best and most practised of the Bandō Bushi, the Eastern Warriors, he had no easy victories. The Minamoto paid dear for their knowledge of the arts of war, since it was from their reverses that they gained it: but it was worth the price.

Accounts of the Three Years War help to clarify the relationship between a great warrior and his followers at this time. There can be no doubt that, although a tradition of loyal service was well established during the bitter fighting in the north, the question of material reward for such service was of great importance. According to later historians of this episode, including even the author of the majestic *Nihongaishi*, Minamoto Yoshiiye complained that, since no grants were made by the Court, he had to reward his followers out of his own resources. But this rests upon a misunderstanding of Yoshiiye's position. The Court, no doubt for selfish reasons, did not regard the suppression of the Kiyowara family as a national affair, but rather as the private business of the Minamoto. The Kiyowara were disorderly, but they were not rebels. Yoshiiye does not appear to have expected help from the national treasury. He could well afford, from the profits of his manors in the east, to reward the fighting men who followed him. Every great warrior at this time was under an obligation to reward the men who had risked their lives in his service, and here we have already the germ of feudal institutions. It remained for one of the descendants of Yoshiiye to bring those early forms into maturity when a highly developed feudal society dominated the political scene at the end of the twelfth century.

The classic account of Yoriyoshi's campaigns in the north is the *Mutsu Waki*, a narrative originally compiled from provincial reports and oral descriptions not long after the events which it describes. In its present form it seems to be the work of a much later scholar who dressed it up for literary effect, but good judges think that, so far as concerns the bare facts, it is reliable.

Its author quotes freely from Chinese books, and praises the exploits of Minamoto leaders as surpassing anything recorded in antiquity. His account is interesting rather as fixing a pattern for military romances than as reporting skirmishes and battles, for its language is extremely ornamental and the feats of arms which it relates are scarcely credible. But it must have helped to inculcate certain ideals which were thenceforward to influence, if not to dictate, the conduct of members of the military caste. It is noticeable, for instance, that among the actions singled out for especial praise are examples of self-sacrifice for the sake of a leader, of disregard for death when it is required by fidelity. Thus: "The General returned and made the rounds of the camp to comfort the wounded. They all said: 'We shall give our bodies to repay our debt. We shall make light of our lives, and for our leader's sake perish without regret.'" Here we can hear an echo of the chant of the warriors in Yamato days: "Our bodies shall steep in the water or bleach on the ground." This is a literary flourish.

Some of the Minamoto who served at Court had elegant tastes, and perhaps those whose accomplishments were more literary than warlike played some part in writing or encouraging the early military romances (*gunki*), thus helping to shape the warrior's code. One cannot help feeling that although it was formed on the battlefield, it was dressed up by men of letters.

It might be supposed that after these hard campaigns the Minamoto were by now supreme in northern Japan. Certainly their warlike reputation was high, but there was another powerful clan dominating the two provinces of Mutsu and Dewa. In subduing the Kiyowara in 1087 Yoshiiye had been assisted by a Fujiwara named Kiyohira, who had been adopted into the Kiyowara family. That family had succeeded to the Abe estates in Mutsu, and this Fujiwara had been named High Sheriff (Ōryōshi) of Mutsu and Dewa, as well as Commander-in-Chief. By the time of his death in 1128 he had built up a considerable autonomy, almost a kingdom, more extensive than any other domain in the country. In 1095 he built a stronghold at a place called Hiraizumi, with a monastery and dwelling houses which he hoped would form a city rivalling Kyoto as a centre of culture. He was so powerful that he ranked with the Taira and the Minamoto in defensive if not offensive strength, and in some respects was even stronger than they were, because of dissensions within and between the other clans, and because of his own almost unassailable strategic position. But his very remoteness made it practically impossible for him to play any important role in national affairs.

Though the material wealth of the Minamoto was not commensurate with their military prestige, which was extremely high after the victories of Yoshiiye, in many parts of the country landowners commended their property to Yoshiiye in return for protection. Thus a large number of warriors became adherents of the Minamoto family in a kind of vassalage, while more and more manors came into their hands. Often fighting men of other families, who had fought under Minamoto captains, out of loyalty and gratitude would consign their property to their former leaders. The Court was alarmed by this tendency, and in 1091 an edict was issued which forbade farmers throughout the country to commend their lands to Yoshiiye, and declared that his retainers should not enter the capital with him. This was shortly after Yoshiiye's resounding victory in the Three Years War, and it seems that the Court was jealous of his successes. While he was fighting desperately in the north, he received no help or encouragement from the Crown and no reward. The cloistered Emperor Shirakawa was at this time in power. He was opposed to violence, fantastically devout, and no doubt suspicious of the Minamoto. But Yoshiiye returned to Kyoto, where he and his comrades resumed their military posts in command of Palace Guards and the Sovereign's Escorts. They also played a bold and effective part in suppressing the outrages of the armed monks who infested and plagued the city (as related in Chapter XI). They refused to be intimidated by the cry of sacrilege that the blackmailers raised when their sacred car was threatened, for the Minamoto swordsmen at this time had no scruples about drawing blood. In 1095 they killed several leaders of a monkish rabble in the street, and a decade or so later some companies of hard-bitten warriors under Minamoto command put to flight several thousand of these sacerdotal bandits. It is in accounts of these conflicts that we begin to hear other Minamoto names that are often to recur in this chronicle of war, such as Mitsukuni, Yoshichika, and Tameyoshi.

While the Minamoto were thus gaining in prestige if not in political favour, the Taira were far behind them. But their position also began to improve, perhaps because they were more astute in matters of politics. They had broad domains in the western provinces, and official posts, especially in such places as Iga, Hyōgo, and Sanuki, in regions south and west of the capital and along the shores of the Inland Sea. By contrast to the Minamoto, who were used to land fighting and understood combat between mounted men, the Taira were accustomed to coastal areas and sea fighting, so that in maritime districts they were influential. To such advantages as these were added certain mistakes made by Minamoto leaders. The misbehaviour of Yoshichika, Yoshiiye's eldest son, was a stroke of good fortune for the Taira. Yoshichika had been banished to Sanuki for an offence against the Court but escaped to Izumo, where he fomented a rising which was put down by a Taira general, Masamori, in 1108. This gave credit to the Taira family, and improved their reputation at Kyoto. Masamori's son Tadamori was the main architect of the Taira fortunes. His strategy was simple enough. He took the side of the Court in any matter which involved the Minamoto, whose rise in public esteem was displeasing to the abdicated Emperor Shirakawa. He also rendered valuable service by putting down revolts and piracy in the Inland Sea region in the year 1129. He was succeeded by Taira Kiyomori, one of the leading figures in Japanese history, who virtually governed the country for a spell of twenty years, with powers comparable to those which the great Fujiwara Regents had usurped. The Taira had now outstripped the Minamoto in influence.

5. *The Taira Ascendancy*

Although it is convenient to describe the events of the years following the abortive Hōgen Insurrection of 1156 in terms of a conflict between the two great military houses, it should not be supposed that this was the real issue at stake. What was taking place during the last half of the twelfth century was a transfer of power from the Court and nobility to the landowning classes, a new society residing in the provinces and basing its claims upon the possession of manors and the control of armed forces. During this process the two clans were on different sides as regards allegiance to the sovereigns, but in fact their interests were almost identical, if they could have agreed to share the available land and labour. But that was not to be, for such moderation did not accord with the spirit of the age, in so far as it was expressed by the warriors. There is much to be said for their courage and their loyalty; but whatever the chronicles may relate in praise of their virtues, there can be no doubt that the growth of the new society was accompanied by actions dictated not by the mind but by the passions of jealousy, anger, pride, rapacity, and cruelty.

Upon the defeat of Yorinaga's party in 1156 the punishments inflicted upon the rebels were merciless. Tameyoshi, Chieftain of the Minamoto clan, was condemned to death, and his son Yoshitomo was ordered to kill him. Yoshitomo having refused this dreadful task, a Minamoto officer, saying that it would be a disgrace for one of his clan to be killed by a Taira, despatched Tameyoshi, who made no effort to resist. The officer then took his own life in expiation. Some fifty of the unfortunate Emperor Sutoku's supporters were killed in cold blood. There had until then been no capital punishment for nearly three hundred and fifty years for offences committed by courtiers or officials, although according to the codes treason and similar crimes were punishable by death. It was a Fujiwara, a clever and unscrupulous man who had taken holy orders but held office as a Counsellor of State, one Shinzei, who pressed for the death penalty in all cases. He was the head of the successful faction at Court, and persuaded the Emperor to embark on a number of administrative measures designed to restore the authority of the Crown.

Shinzei (his lay name was Fujiwara Michinori) was friendly to Kiyomori, and Kiyomori found that his close relationship with a nobleman of such distinction was a useful asset. The two had tastes in common and both were interested in Chinese affairs and Chinese trade. Shinzei is recorded as having improved the finances of the Court, which were in low water, by methods not above suspicion. There was an opposition party, who disliked Shinzei and wished to control the Emperor themselves. This was headed by another Fujiwara, a not very capable young man named Nobuyori. He was joined by the discontented Yoshitomo, who hated Shinzei. Kiyomori, now Chieftain of the Taira, was in high favour at Court, and had been promoted in rank, while his sons were admitted to the Palace on an intimate footing. The stage was set for action; for the reigning Emperor (Nijō) took the advice of Shinzei and the abdicated Emperor (Go-Shirakawa) favoured Nobuyori.

Early in 1160 Kiyomori set off with his family on a private pilgrimage to Kumano. This gave Yoshitomo and Nobuyori an opportunity to raise a force to carry out their designs for a change of government. But they did not take full and prompt advantage of Kiyomori's absence; and indeed some historians suggest that Kiyomori by leaving the capital was laying a trap for them. However that may be, the events of the next few days provide one of the most exciting chapters in the history of Japan, full of colour and movement and plot and counterplot, escapes and pursuits, feats of arms, arson, murder, suicides, and other violent deaths. This is the Heiji Rising (so called from the era-name Heiji, which means Times of Peace) of 1159. It is celebrated in military romance and in a magnificent picture-scroll (*emakimono*) called the *Heiji Monogatari* (see Plate 12).

For a while things went well with the conspirators, since they were able to get together rapidly a force of about five hundred well-armed and experienced soldiers who on January 19, 1160, attacked the mansion of the ex-Emperor, seized his person, killed many members of his household, set fire to the building, and carried him off to one of the libraries in the precincts of the Great Palace, while the Emperor Nijō was taken from his apartments and confined in the Kurodo chamber under strict guard. The monk-counsellor Shinzei's house was next attacked and burned down, its inmates being slaughtered except for Shinzei himself, who escaped only to be captured and decapitated a few days later. Now Nobuyori began to take over the government. He had himself appointed Chancellor by the Emperor, who approved of this and other measures under duress. It seemed as if the bold stroke of Nobuyori's party had succeeded, but he still had enemies at Court who encouraged the Emperor to resist and to fall in with plans for his escape.

Meanwhile the military preparations of the Minamoto were not as thorough as they should have been, and after Kiyomori had returned to the capital they hesitated and made no decisive move. They seem to have underestimated the strength of the Taira warriors, for although Yoshihira (Yoshitomo's eldest son) had brought troops from Kamakura, Nobuyori thought it unnecessary to attack Kiyomori, who thus was given time to lay his own plans in secret. Kiyomori for his part had been alarmed at the strength of the Minamoto force, and made some peaceful proposals to Nobuyori. On returning to the capital Kiyomori and his son Shigemori, with a very small force, took up a defensive position in their family headquarters, the mansions in the Rokuhara district of Kyoto, and there they were reinforced by Taira warriors and also by a large number of courtiers and officials who were hostile to Nobuyori.

On January 29, in the Great Palace, the Emperor had been much encouraged by a bold Fujiwara who had rebuked Nobuyori in full council and in the presence of all his partisans. A few days later the Emperor, disguised as a lady-in-waiting, was smuggled out of the Palace with the Empress, and taken to the Rokuhara mansion; and at the same time the ex-Emperor, with Taira assistance, of course, escaped from the place where he had been imprisoned by Nobuyori. This was at night on February 4, and the next morning, though Nobuyori lost his nerve, Yoshitomo prepared to defend the Great Inner Palace against an attack which the Taira were bound to deliver. The defenders were doing very well until the Taira drew a number of Minamoto men off by a feigned retreat, thus allowing others to rush the gates and presently to drive the Minamoto force out of the Great Palace. The Minamoto then were obliged to attack the Rokuhara. They failed, and had to retreat, meeting with resistance from the armed monks of Hiyeizan (the Buddhist establishments on Mount Hiyei), whom in the past they had so severely trounced. Yoshitomo told his men to scatter, since there was no prospect of making a stand until fresh troops could be raised.

One of the dramatic features of this campaign, which the chroniclers are fond of describing, is the struggle of Yoshitomo and his sons Yoshihira, Tomonaga, and Yoritomo to make their way through snowstorms in wild country, pressing on to the east to collect a new force. The youngest son, Tomonaga, a boy of fifteen who had been wounded in the fight on Mount Hiyei, could not keep up, and the two older brothers went on ahead. Yoshitomo killed him at his own request, to save him from falling into the hands of an enemy; and shortly after that Yoshitomo himself was slain by a treacherous retainer. Yoshihira, hearing of his father's death, returned to the capital in the hope of assassinating a Taira leader in revenge; but he also was betrayed and, after a heroic fight against overwhelming numbers, was overcome and delivered to the enemy, who had him decapitated on the public execution ground— a cruel insult.

Thus ended, though only for a brief period, the conflict between the two great clans, after some thirty days of courage and cowardice, of plot and counterplot, of bloody murder, of disgusting treachery and barbaric cruelty—all the unsavoury ingredients of military romance. But the conflict was not in essence or in purpose a struggle for supremacy between the two clans. They were the instruments by which a political revolution was carried out, and it will have been noticed that neither in the rising of 1156 nor in that of 1160 were any large numbers of troops engaged. The Hōgen affair was over in a few days; the Heiji fighting involved only a few thousand men in all, and it was strictly local in its extent, consisting almost entirely of attacks upon buildings and street fighting.

Nor was the political revolution one which the chief actors had intended. The Fujiwara antagonists, Nobuyori and Shinzei, who were responsible for the outbreak, were competing for political control over the sovereign; they had no thought of transferring power from a civilian aristocracy to the chieftain of a military house. This transfer of power, as it turned out, made a struggle between the two clans inevitable, but it arose not as a considered policy adopted for a clear revolutionary purpose, but rather out of the spirit of rivalry and revenge that is bred by war. The trend of the times had already long been against the old bureaucracy administered from the capital, and by the year 1100 was moving already toward a transfer of authority from the city to the country, where the real foundations of wealth and strength were now established. The Hōgen and Heiji risings were merely incidents which accelerated this trend by violent means. They did not create it.

The rivalry between the two clans is nonetheless an important part of Japanese history, for it was in their strife that the new military society developed its economic foundations and its standard of behaviour. It is therefore appropriate at this point to examine in some detail the rise of the Taira house, as illustrating the progress of military leaders from a position of subordination to a complete ascendancy over the civil power.

It should not be supposed that the warrior clans were homogeneous, each comprised of men of one mind and purpose. It cannot be said that the Minamoto stood for one principle and the Taira for another; indeed, Minamoto and Taira landowners lived side by side in amity throughout the eastern provinces, and their chief concern was to preserve their property rather than to risk it by supporting their respective clans in political quarrels. The growth of the warrior class in numbers and in the extent of their landed property made it difficult to preserve the old unity within clans or even within great households. There was no longer a true community of interest between branches of a clan settled in different localities or between members of a family who, owing to a rule of primogeniture, did not share equally in its wealth. Yet in one sense all members of the rising military class had an interest or an ambition in common, for they all wished to preserve their lands, to avoid taxation, and to override if not to destroy the civil authority which desired to use but also to restrain their military power. It is possible that the prosperity of the military class as a whole would have been most easily achieved by a combination between the two great clans. But this was not to be, for it would have meant a simple sharing of existing landed property which neither side would in practice have tolerated, even if there had been enough to go round.

When Taira Kiyomori succeeded to the leadership of his clan in 1153 he was a vigorous man of thirty-five. His father, Tadamori, had raised the reputation of his family to a very high point, so that Kiyomori could meet with the greatest Court nobles on terms of equality. He soon gained the ear of the former Emperor Go-Shirakawa, who needed some support and could no longer depend upon his Fujiwara favourites, all of whom had either perished or disappeared during the recent convulsions. Kiyomori also took care to make friends with Minamoto Yorimasa, a good soldier and a good scholar, who had not taken sides with his kinsman Yoshitomo in the defence of the Palace.

By contrast the position of the Minamoto clan, the Seiwa Genji, seemed extremely weak. In the risings of 1156 and 1160 its great captains had been killed in battle or put to death, and of the family of its late chieftain Yoshitomo there remained only three young boys (Yoritomo, Noriyori, and Yoshitsune), whose lives Kiyomori unaccountably spared. Or perhaps not so unaccountably, since in 1160 these children, living in obscurity, offered no threat and the Taira clan under Kiyomori's guidance was supreme. Its supremacy needs explanation, for it was not very long since the Minamoto had kept the Taira within bounds. We have already noticed the turning of the tide after the successes of Taira Masamori in 1108, when he put down the rebellious Minamoto Yoshichika. This was perhaps the first step towards the favour of the Throne, for Masamori was welcomed on his return to the capital and promoted in rank. Contemporary records describe his entry into the city in 1108:

"To-day Tamba no Kami Masamori brought the head of Minamoto Yoshichika to the capital . . . it was impaled upon a pike and carried by five serving men. Right and left of them were forty or fifty foot soldiers carrying weapons and wearing full armour. These were followed by Masamori and about one hundred retainers, their swords and spears flashing in the sunshine, bowmen and horsemen in column stationed along the route. . . . Crowds of sightseers of all degrees came, with their carriages and horses. All the population of the city, men and women, seemed to fill the streets and all were in a state of frenzied excitement."

There can be no doubt that this incident, and others of its kind, brought the exploits of the Taira to public notice, and because Japanese crowds adore a spectacle the military must have risen in popular esteem.

Not many years after these events Masamori again entered the capital in triumph. This time he led a hundred chosen warriors of his clan, men celebrated on the seacoasts of western and southern Japan, who were escorting a troop carrying the heads of criminals whom he had captured. These were pirates and bandits who had caused great trouble to the provincial authorities, and for his services Masamori was further promoted in rank and commended by the sovereign. The proceedings were said to have "astonished the eyes and ears of the people."

Such promotions of a military officer were exceptional, but the success of Masamori's son Tadamori was even more remarkable. Indeed Tadamori's triumphs may be said to have completed the rise of the Taira as a military and a political force, thus preparing the way for the great Kiyomori, who slipped into a position of the highest authority without especial effort on his own part.

Tadamori was a first-class soldier, who besides his successes in suppressing brigandage (which was rife) dealt promptly and severely with the riotous monastic troops of the Tendai and other sects. His character and exploits give us an excellent idea of the kind of man who rose to great influence during this period of confusion, when the bureaucratic regime was gradually disintegrating. It is worth while therefore, at the cost of a little repetition, to describe some of his methods and achievements.

In his military capacity he was conspicuously successful in dealing with pirates in western Japan, along the littoral of the Inland Sea. He was able to keep on good terms with some of them, through his retainers and associates in those parts, and though he was prepared to attack them when he thought it expedient, at times he would cover up their depredations to his own great profit. One of his offices, granted as a favour, was that of bailiff or steward of the western estates of the cloistered Emperor. One account relates how in this capacity he went down to Hizen to inspect the imperial manors, and while on that journey visited the port of Hakata in Chikuzen, where he did some profitable business with merchants from Sung China.

It was not an accident that made Tadamori agent for the suppression of piracy under the Emperor Sutoku in 1135. The chief interest of the Taira in the west had always been in coastal regions, and in fact the pirates were none other than local gentry whose manors went down to the shore. When they were subdued or came to terms with the officers of the Crown they became, if they were not already offshoots of the clan, its vassals and retainers in a quasi-feudal relationship. It was because of Tadamori's successes in this sphere that he was made governor of various western provinces in succession (Bizen, Mimasaka, Harima, and others) and during his terms of office was able to extend the Taira influence all along the Inland Sea. He really had the trust of the Court, as is clear from entries in contemporary diaries, where (for instance) he is described as enjoying the favour of the ex-Emperor Shirakawa, whose personal bodyguard and confidant he had become after his early warlike feats.

Besides being a first-class military leader he was politically astute and farsighted, and knew far better than his Minamoto rivals how to get on in the world. But he was not above trickery when it would further his own private ends. Thus in 1136 he made a great impression in the metropolis by sending through the streets as captives under a strong escort some seventy persons whom he described as pirates. It was a fine spectacle, but in fact the alleged pirates were persons of some standing in the western provinces who would not submit to his orders. On one occasion at least he forged imperial warrants to cover his misdeeds.

The evidence for this forgery is interesting and throws some light upon the attitude of the officials of the old regime towards the upstart military. It occurs in the diary of a highly placed courtier,[4] who records that he received a letter from a Counsellor (Sochi-chūnagon) of the Kyūshū military government (Chinzei-fu), asking him to come secretly for an interview. The Counsellor related that, on the arrival of a Chinese vessel, the Japanese officials were examining its cargo when Tada-

---

[4] Minamoto Moritoki. His diary, generally known as *Chōshū-ki*, is a valuable historical source.

mori, Governor of Bizen, produced a paper which, he said, was an order from the cloistered Emperor ruling that Chinese vessels entering harbours in Kyūshū were not subject to official examination but came within the jurisdiction of the Kanzaki manor in Bizen, that is to say within Taira jurisdiction. The two officials agreed that this was extremely dishonest conduct on the part of Tadamori, which must be reported to the cloistered Emperor. It was unspeakable behaviour, and this kind of thing meant the ruin of Japan. People in His Sacred Majesty's service seemed to be behaving like monkeys and dogs!

Probably Tadamori's most notable achievement was outside the military sphere, for he made a successful effort to commend himself to the Court aristocracy not as a mere soldier but as a cultivated man, at home in high society. This was, in his view, a most important part of a policy by which he aimed to increase both the prestige and the power of his own clan, for it must be remembered that the inner circles of Court life, the great nobles closely related to the Imperial House, were not disposed to regard even the most successful generals as their social equals. They were inclined to despise military men as lacking in refinement and sensibility. It was only when they wanted a financial favour that they would consent to meet with warrior chieftains on something like an equal footing. Even such celebrated generals as Minamoto Yorinobu and Yorimitsu were treated in a disdainful way by Fujiwara noblemen who depended upon them for protection and support.

It seems that in the eleventh century the warriors were not yet fully conscious of their own strength, but were dazzled by the prestige of the Throne and readily submitted to a moral ascendancy which, despite its unsubstantial basis, was assumed and enjoyed by the Court nobility and the high officers of state. Their lowly place was in part at least due to a defective education—more specifically, to their ignorance of classical learning and the canons of taste, which disqualified them from entry into exclusive circles and from holding high civil appointments. Some warriors at length became aware of their inferiority in these fields of endeavour, and for reasons of pride as well as policy strove to elevate and assimilate their own standards of taste and behaviour to those of the members of noble families. This was true in particular of the Ise Heishi, that branch of the Taira clan which, belonging to the home provinces, was in close touch with the capital. It was the forebears of Kiyomori who first followed this path to social distinction by cultivating the arts; and it is characteristic of the traditional sentiment of their country that they owed their success in this enterprise to the approval of their social superiors, which they had gained by turning out good poetry and carefully following the rules of decorum. In thus remedying the shortcomings of their class the Taira not only improved their social standing but also increased their political influence.

The astute Tadamori was remarkably fortunate in his political life. Through his connexions in the provinces he was able to amass great wealth, a passport to the favours of the great. He was generous in his expenditure, and usually ready to help deserving causes. He contributed lavishly to pious undertakings in which the Throne took an interest, he took part in poetry contests, and he even performed in ritual dances at certain shrines—a rather unusual role for the head of a fighting clan, but it attracted most favourable attention to the warrior class. In addition to these accomplishments he was experienced in all the arts of a courtier. He knew how to make himself agreeable and useful, so that he gained the favour of one emperor after another, receiving handsome rewards in rank and privilege. He was careful, it should be added, to keep on good terms with influential Court ladies, and contemporary memoirs contain frequent reference to his popularity among them.

CHAPTER XIII

KIYOMORI

1. *His Character and Methods*

TADAMORI died at the age of fifty-eight in the year 1153. His place was taken by Kiyomori, whose exploits in defeating the Minamoto during the Heiji uprising of 1160 have already been described.

The exact date of his birth and the name of his mother are not precisely known, but he is thought to have been born in 1118, the son of a younger sister of the Lady Gion (Gion no Nyōgo). That lady (who lived near the Gion shrine) was a prominent figure at the Court of the abdicated Shirakawa, whose favourite mistress she was for many years. Her name appears frequently in the memoirs of the years about 1100, her lavish expenditure upon pious works and costly Buddhist services being especially recorded. Whether suggestions about her intimate relations with this notable or that are true or false, it is likely that Tadamori and the young Kiyomori owed much to her influence and that of her younger sister.

There were rumours that Kiyomori had royal blood from his father. His true paternity is not known, but he was recognized as a kinsman in some degree of Tadamori, so that his position as he grew up was hopeful, thanks to Tadamori's favour at Court. He received rapid promotion in rank, and by 1146 was made Governor of Aki. In that province was situated the celebrated Itsukushima shrine (on the island of Miyajima) a place of worship inseparable from the fortunes of the Taira clan. The faith of Kiyomori in the Itsukushima cult was remarkable, but it seems probable that his interest was not entirely religious. His frequent pilgrimages to this great family shrine gave him useful opportunities to survey and guide his numerous undertakings at points along the Inland Sea, notably certain transactions with Chinese traders in which Tadamori had made good profits. These were occasions when he could keep in touch with his associates among the leading families in western Japan, such as those piratical friends whom Tadamori had made use of and protected. Kiyomori was more temperate than Tadamori, but he was able to do a lucrative business, because of the influence of the Taira clan in that region. Whatever may be said against his politics, Kiyomori must be given credit for certain constructive work. Like Tadamori he saw the importance of seaborne trade; he built a harbour at Hyōgo, in the lee of the cape called Wada Misaki, while generally developing navigation through the Inland Sea, dredging channels, improving anchorages, and otherwise facilitating transport and commerce. No doubt his object was personal gain, but his perspective was wide.

There are differences of opinion among Japanese historians as to the character of Kiyomori, as might be expected, since great or unusual men generally display inconsistencies in their behaviour which cannot be reconciled with a simple estimate. What emerges pretty clearly from all accounts, however, is a picture of a strong-willed, stubborn, short-tempered man who could, when he chose, keep his anger under control and generally in his social intercourse behaved in a tactful, considerate, and even gentle manner. Such contradictions are not abnormal, and perhaps his fits of rage can be accounted for by ill health, since he is known to have suffered from grave illnesses. He was described by the ex-Emperor Go-Shirakawa as unsuited to be a guardian of the Throne, because he was irritable and had not patience enough to give proper thought to problems put to him for solution. This was no doubt true, but it must be added that great strength of character, quick decision, and ruthless determination were not qualities which appealed to the Court nobles of the Heian age, who preferred long discourse and frequent compromise.

It may be that the estimates of Kiyomori to be found in Court memoirs are not without prejudice against a member of the warrior class. Yet as a man of taste and breeding he conformed to the standards of Court society, where he was generally regarded as endowed with exceptional talents. Such distinguished persons as Fujiwara Michinori (the ill-fated Shinzei of the Heiji rising) were pleased to associate with him, no doubt finding also some material advantages in his friendship. Perhaps he, Kiyomori, was led astray by the glamour of Court society, in which he took part despite his origin as a soldier's son; and he became a conservative instead of making or introducing a new age, as he was fitted to do by his unusual gifts. It has been suggested that a serious illness which laid him low in 1168 caused a change in his character and a decline in his powers. He cannot be regarded as one of the greatest men in Japanese history, but he was a very important figure in a crucial phase of political development.

Although men like Kiyomori, and Michinaga before him, had a most intimate knowledge of Court life and were well aware of the very human failings of the sovereigns whom they served and manipulated, they were nevertheless deeply under the influence of the mystic properties of the occupant of the throne, the traditional "virtue" of the hereditary sovereign. They could not without trepidation pursue policies which ran entirely counter to the interest of the Imperial House, although they might ill-treat its individual members. In point of fact it is probable that Kiyomori really wished to do away with the system of cloister government and restore a limited authority to the reigning monarch, since he could then revert to a dictatorship like that of the Fujiwara Regents. He might perhaps have led the way to a reformed and modified dictatorship based upon the consent of the sovereign in which he, the chieftain of a military house with great influence in the provinces, as a Great Minister exercising plenary powers could have brought about some measure of agrarian reform. But after his illness he probably did not wish to undertake so burdensome an office or face the hostility that it would have entailed; and he remained immersed in the business of the old regime, with all its pleasures and privileges. Thus, while he was the leader of a new party with a new cause, he ended in fact as reactionary as Yorinaga and the other leaders of the attempt to restore the Fujiwara dictatorship in the rising of 1156. Once he felt free from the fear that a war of revenge would be started by the defeated Minamoto, he addressed himself to the task of guarding against any threat which the Fujiwara might offer.

The relationship between the Fujiwara and the Taira as it developed under Kiyomori's guidance provides some interesting evidence about the temper of the times. Although the military power at their disposal would have enabled the Taira to capture and retain most of the important offices in the government, they used their strength prudently at first and did not come into open conflict with the Fujiwara. Kiyomori preferred to resort to the matrimonial strategy which the Fujiwara had so successfully used, by marrying his daughters to young men who would presently inherit the highest offices. Thus Fujiwara Motozane while Regent (1158–66) took a daughter of Kiyomori to wife, and in general the Taira followed a policy of envelopment or containment, leaving to the Fujiwara the high posts that had become hereditary in their family, while reserving to the chieftain of the Taira clan the ultimate right of decision.

Although the great nobles were obliged to accept this situation, they continued to regard the Taira as upstarts, refusing to admit to themselves that the age had brought about a disturbance of the old order, under which they had prospered, and a redistribution of power. Some of them passively resisted the approaches of the Taira, finding excuses for not giving their daughters in marriage and in other ways keeping at a distance persons whom they regarded as inferior. Sometimes, though rarely, even more active resistance was offered by Fujiwara pride to Taira arrogance.

Perhaps the best example is the familiar story of the Regent Motofusa's clash with Kiyomori's son Shigemori. Motofusa had succeeded his brother Motozane as Regent in 1166. He was a capable young man, whom Kiyomori disliked and whom he managed to deprive of his authority as Chieftain of the Fujiwara clan and therefore custodian of property which Kiyomori coveted. It may be imagined that Motofusa hated the Taira in general, and with good cause, though as a rule he had to keep his temper. But one day in the summer of 1170 there was a collision between the retinue of Motofusa, who was on his way to a service at the Hōjōji which the cloistered Emperor was to attend, and a young grandson of Kiyomori, who had been to a music lesson and was on his way back to the city in a light carriage. He refused to make way for the Regent, whose followers thereupon smashed his carriage and humiliated him.

On his return to his palace the Regent sent a responsible officer with attendants to explain the incident to Shigemori, the boy's father, but Shigemori would not receive him. Later in the month reprisals were planned by the Taira. The Regent was expected to attend a mass for the great Michinaga's soul at the Hōjōji, and he was to be attacked on that occasion. The plan came to the ears of the Regent, and a clash was averted. But the Taira did not forget the incident. More than three months later a body of Shigemori's followers attacked the Regent's procession on the way to a solemn Court ceremony. Motofusa was not harmed but members of his mounted escort were dragged from their horses, beaten, and humiliated. It was such conduct as this, arising from their arrogance, that turned feeling against the Taira in the capital. This particular incident and other instances of tactless if not contemptuous treatment brought about a close relationship between the Regent and the cloistered Emperor Go-Shirakawa, and led to the Shishigatani plot and subsequent conspiracies or risings against the rule of Kiyomori, which must presently be described.

But in his armed strength Kiyomori had the answer to all complaints from civilian quarters, until some military force could be brought against him; and his hold on the monarchy grew firmer as he followed the matrimonial practices of the Fujiwara. He had some trouble with the Emperor Go-Shirakawa, who had abdicated in 1158 but still dominated his successor, a youth who reigned as the Emperor Nijō for a few years and was followed by his baby boy Rokujō in 1165. This child was quickly deposed by his grandfather, who then placed on the throne his own favourite son, the eight-year-old Emperor Takakura. Now Kiyomori's position was most favourable, for the mother of Takakura was a sister-in-law of Kiyomori himself, and Go-Shirakawa was at this juncture, if not friendly, at least not actively hostile to the head of the Taira clan. Had it occurred to Kiyomori to seek an excuse for exercising sovereign power, he might have urged that the Emperor Go-Shirakawa was incapable. Described by Shinzei as "a dark [that is to say, unenlightened] ruler, without parallel in the history of China and Japan," he was said by another contemporary to be one who "did not know black from white."

Kiyomori's progress was now most rapid. By 1167 he was Chancellor of the Realm, and promoted to the junior grade of the first rank, above which no subject could rise in his lifetime. The fact that such exceptional, almost unprecedented honours were granted to a military man of modest origin (by Court standards) is therefore significant. It is also of more than purely genealogical interest, for when Kiyomori resigned the office of Chancellor, which he held for only a few months as a symbol of his power, he was granted very extensive manors in the western provinces. Shortly afterwards, in 1168, he fell ill, and fearing a miserable future life he took the tonsure. The ex-Emperor Go-Shira-kawa followed his example, but not for the same reason. He preferred to live in seclusion since he could not control Kiyomori, who ruled for the next twelve years through the young Emperor Takakura.

In 1178 when the Empress was delivered of a male child the position was exactly as it had been at the height of the Fujiwara Regency. The heir to the throne was an infant, a grandson of Kiyomori, the effective head of the state. This infant, as the Emperor Antoku, was to perish in the downfall of the house of Taira before many years were past.

2. The Shishigatani Affair

Either his illness or an abnormal pride thereafter drove Kiyomori to a course of action that raised almost every party or faction in the state against him. He had offended the abdicated Emperor Go-Shirakawa, infuriated and humiliated the Fujiwara, and aroused the hatred of many persons prominent at Court or in public office by placing his sons in important posts. As was to be expected, plots and intrigues against him were frequent, and there grew up a feeling hostile not only to Kiyomori but to the whole Taira clan. The most celebrated of these intrigues is known as the Shishigatani Affair from the situation in a solitary valley of a country house at which the conspirators used to meet. The ring-leaders were not men of importance and the conspiracy was not of a kind to succeed against the forces at Kiyomori's disposal; significantly enough, however, it was known to Go-Shirakawa. It was divulged by a spy to Kiyomori, who at once punished the conspirators, rebuked Go-Shirakawa in harsh terms, seized a number of Fujiwara manors in the west, and dismissed from office the Fujiwara Regent of the day together with a score or two of high officials, most of whom were re-placed by men of his own family, which was very numerous—he had four brothers, eleven sons, and eight daughters. The daughters, as we have seen, made most useful matrimonial connexions. The younger sons were given provincial posts where they could contribute to Taira influence.

For various reasons, mostly prudential, Kiyomori had transferred his residence soon after his triumph in the Heiji disturbance of 1160 to a seacoast town called Fukuwara, on the site of the modern city of Hyōgo. He was, as we have noted, interested in the development of shipping routes through the Inland Sea, and he made improvements in the harbour of Fukuwara as well as building himself a fine palace there. Having retired from his office of Chancellor he deliberately kept away from the capital and its ceremonial and social entanglements, visiting his palace in the Rokuhara quarter only at rare intervals. But he had a special intelligence service, as well as a useful spy in the enemy camp in the person of Tada Yukitsuna, a Minamoto official of only moderate standing, who chose to attach himself to Kiyomori as a means of promoting his own fortunes. It was largely thanks to him that Kiyomori learned of the Shishigatani plot.

Kiyomori's vengeance upon those implicated in the Fujiwara plot was merciless. One of the conspirators, a monk named Saikō, confessed under torture and was executed. This breach of the holy law made a most unfavourable impression and created (especially in monastic circles) a mounting animosity against the Taira house, to such a point that deaths among officials in 1179 were ascribed to Saikō's vengeful ghost. Another cause of feeling hostile to the Taira was the outrageous conduct of Taira members of the Board for Promotions and Dismissals, who used their vote to get rid of rivals from other families. This might leave the field clear for Taira candidates, but it gave rise to bitter feelings in the lower ranks.

In the earlier days of their rising fortunes the Taira leaders had been circumspect. They appear to have wished not so much to destroy existing institutions as to control them. Thus they made no consistent effort to drive the erstwhile Fujiwara leaders out of office or to destroy the Regency or the system of cloister government. Backed by force and faced by no united opposition in a society averse to violence, they could afford to neglect or at most to manipulate their not very dangerous rivals. But by Kiyomori's day ambition had outrun discretion, and he in his sickness lost his touch in handling affairs. He vacillated and made blunders which hastened, if they did not cause, the downfall of his clan. It was not, however, the plots of his enemies at Court which he had most cause to fear, for the old nobility was no longer resolute or powerful, while the new men who served the sovereign or the abdicated rulers were for the most part inexperienced or of only moderate capacity. The real dangers that confronted the Taira clan were the military strength of the Buddhist monasteries and, in the background but steadily reviving, the determination of the Minamoto clansmen to take revenge for their fall.

3. *The Monastic Armies*

In normal times (if there are such) Kiyomori would have had no scruples in dealing with the Buddhist monasteries, for their military strength was not of the dimensions or character to give pause to a resolute leader. On balance the Buddhist Church, as represented by its militant members, was ill-disposed to the Taira, as it would be to any determined secular authority. Consequently Kiyomori's relations with the great monasteries are a matter of some historical interest.

The growth of the monastic armies is a remarkable feature of mediaeval life in Japan. As we have seen in Chapter XI, the conduct of the
armed monks was by no means laudable. It was nevertheless a factor
of considerable importance in the confused political situation that developed at the capital, particularly during the period of cloister government, from about 1080 to 1180. The threats and demonstrations of
armed strength to which monasteries from time to time resorted embarrassed the Taira leaders, who often found themselves torn between
a desire to crush the monasteries by sheer force and a dread of the
spiritual powers whose instruments the unholy rabble claimed to be.
Religious beliefs and superstitions were dominating features in the life
of the imperial city at that time, and the power of the armed monks to
create fear and tension in the minds of statesmen was out of all proportion to their true importance.

An understanding of the political situation during the twelfth century depends partly upon a knowledge of the influence that was exerted
by the great religious foundations. It is therefore useful at this point
to interrupt the narrative of events during the dictatorship of Kiyomori
by a somewhat detailed description of the activities of the Buddhist
Church.

The origins of these bodies of armed men are not clear, but it seems
probable that the leading religious establishments from an early date
recruited guards to protect their manors against local warriors. Such
men were doubtless chosen for their strength and courage, and were
not as a rule ordained monks, but had a standing something like that
of servitors and lay brothers in a monastic order in Christian countries.
As the great monasteries grew in influence they recruited such men in
increasing numbers in all kinds of secular occupations, and among these
there developed in course of time regular bands of men armed for the
purpose of defence. These bands were known as *sōhei*, or soldier-
monks. It was forces of this nature that, getting out of hand and beyond
the control of their superiors, caused and multiplied much of the disorder that afflicted the capital from the last decades of the tenth century. The presence of a large body of armed monks was noted at the
Kōfukuji as early as 968, but there was no important demonstration in
the city until 981, when soldiers from the Enryakuji marched through
the streets to underline their requests to the Court.

Later the monasteries developed a practice of taking with them on
their visits a sacred car, supposed to harbour a divine presence, or some
sacred emblem of a similar character, so that any attack upon them or
resistance to them by the secular authority could be condemned as
sacrilege. This form of pressure created an awkward situation for the
cloistered emperor, the usual target of their claims, for he had volun-
tarily taken holy orders, and therefore owed them sympathy and support. Here was a powerful weapon in the hands of unscrupulous monks,

and it was frequently used. Sometimes, when the Court was slow to grant requests, the monks would return to their cells or dormitories, leaving the sacred emblem unguarded in the street. This was not a retreat, but a form of blackmail, for it signified that the angry deity would remain there, to the peril of the Court, until his custodians could be induced to come and fetch him. The first recorded visit of this nature was paid in 1082 by monks from the Kumano shrine, a place of pilgrimage greatly favoured and revered by the nobility. Thereafter until about 1180 the monasteries played an important though destructive part in national affairs. Most troublesome of all was the Enryakuji, which was of great size and had a numerous army. It was in all senses in a commanding position. It overlooked the capital, it was the headquarters of the powerful Tendai sect, and it was traditionally credited with the duty and power to protect the imperial city from evil influences.

Very large numbers of soldier-monks took part in the ecclesiastical conflicts, which often resulted in bloodshed and great destruction of property by fire, because setting fire to the sacred edifices of one's enemy was a favourite method of warfare. Some description of a collision between the Enryakuji and the Onjōji may serve to give an idea of the general character of these monastic disorders. It arose from a dispute about the leadership of the Tendai sect, each monastery claiming that its abbot should be appointed Tendai Zasu (chief abbot).

The Emperor Go-Suzaku having appointed the Onjōji candidate, the Enryakuji protested by collecting some three thousand men and despatching them to the mansion of the Fujiwara Regent, Yorimichi, where they made a great uproar and could not be pacified. The Regent summoned warriors to suppress the riot, but he could not gain the Enryakuji's consent to the proposed appointment and at last the Enryakuji abbot had to be nominated by the Court. Thereupon the Onjōji monks broke away from the Enryakuji, and this created a new problem, for the right of ordination traditionally belonged to the Enryakuji and could not be shared with any other religious body. The Court was pressed to grant a separate right of ordination to the Onjōji, but the Enryakuji protested most violently and in the end the Onjōji had to depend for the ordination of its clergy upon the Tōdaiji at Nara.

Feeling between the two Tendai monasteries was thus much embittered. There was constant bickering between them, and finally, in May 1081, they came to open warfare. The clash arose out of a trifling incident. Onjōji troops had roughly handled an Imperial Messenger on his way to represent the Throne at a ceremony in one of the shrines under the protection of the Enryakuji. The "mountain monks" (as they were called from the position of their monastery on the summit of Mount Hiyei) rushed down to attack the Onjōji men. Some thousands of them took part in this affair, and they ended by destroying the whole of the Onjōji by fire. The loss was terrible. Some 20,000 rolls of scriptures were burned, and of the few treasures that were saved most were seized by the soldier-monks of the Enryakuji.

It will be noticed that at an early stage in this quarrel the government intervened by the use of its own troops, though not to much effect. On a later occasion, in 1113, when the issue was a dispute between a northern (Kyoto) monastery, Kiyomizu-dera, and a southern (Nara) monastery, the Kōfukuji, the Court was again involved, since the cause of discontent was the appointment to Kiyomizu of an abbot who had entered holy orders at the Enryakuji. Kiyomizu was by tradition a branch or subsidiary (*betsu-in*) of the Kōfukuji, which was the family church of the Fujiwara; so that a deputation of fifty monks and shrine wardens hurried to the Fujiwara college in the capital and strongly protested. They said that they would not withdraw until their demands were satisfied, and after three days the cloistered Emperor Shirakawa was obliged to give way. This further enraged the Enryakuji monks, who now marched in force to attack Kiyomizu and destroyed all the dwelling places in its precincts. Relations between the two bodies were thereafter most inflammable, and a little later in the year a great congregation of mountain monks joined with armed priests from the Hiyoshi shrine—the two contingents together numbering some two thousand— and carrying the sacred car of Gion rushed violently down to the city. There they reached the palace of the cloistered Emperor and demanded that Jikkaku, the superintendent of the monks of the Kōfukuji, be sent into exile.

The reasons for this action were trivial and need not be described; but it is to be noted that although Shirakawa-In ordered the Regent to rebuke the rioters, they paid no attention to him. They even forced their way to the main entrance of his palace, and it became necessary to place the gateway under a strong guard commanded by Minamoto and Taira officers, including Mitsukuni, Tameyoshi, and Tadamori, all men of high military reputation. It would not have been at all difficult for the warrior chiefs to put the armed monks to flight, but the Court and the ministers were afraid to take really strong measures. Such were their superstitious fears that they gave way to the pressure of the Enryakuji crowd, and the unfortunate Jikkaku was exiled. The Court nobles were afraid of the rabble, and frankly said that the best policy was to give way to the monks. But it was never possible to satisfy both parties to these wretched disputes. When the Kōfukuji monks heard what had happened they arose in anger, and the strife between the two monasteries was bitterly resumed.

Now the frightened and irresolute Court was at last obliged to take action in order to prevent a further outburst of fighting. This it was able to do without using much force, for (as might be expected) the unruly monks quickly gave way before a firm threat of chastisement. It proved sufficient to send a small force under Taira and Minamoto officers to the south, in the direction of Nara, to hold the Kōfukuji monks and their partisans in check. Still the Emperor and his courtiers were greatly alarmed, for it seemed all too likely to them that an immense host would presently approach the palace, carrying its sacred cars and sacred emblems. The courtiers assembled round His Majesty to protect him, and the Inner Palace was closely guarded. Such precautions were unnecessary. It soon became known to them that Minamoto Tameyoshi, a young soldier of nineteen, with a few dozen horse, had routed the mob, which turned and fled as far as Uji and there, pursued by Taira and Minamoto warriors, left its sacred emblems by the roadside and scuttled back to its several haunts in Nara.

It is clear that the military capacity of these monastic armies was not very great. Some of their leaders were experienced men, and there were a few very formidable fighters, armed with the deadly *naginata*, a kind of halberd with a curved blade and a long shaft which in experienced hands would keep an ordinary swordsman at a distance. Most of the soldier-monks, however, were in reality neither monks nor soldiers, but a rabble relying for their successes upon the fears of the Court. It would have been easy to deal with them as a military problem, but their religious character presented a serious obstacle to drastic measures; and thus, though they were not in reality dangerous, they were a great nuisance to established authority.

It does not appear, on a superficial study, that these monastic armies present any analogy to the forces commanded in the religious wars of Europe by princes of the Church in armour. The sōhei seem to have been moved by a kind of mass emotion, and not as a rule by directions from the high ecclesiastical authorities of their sects. Indeed at times they acted precipitately and against the wishes of their bishops or abbots. From the fact that in contemporary Japanese records they are usually referred to by a term which signifies a mass or crowd, or more politely a congregation, they may be thought of as controlled by a mob spirit and—only too often—by a desire for loot.

With regard to the power of the Enryakuji in these sectarian struggles, it must be remembered that the relations of the Tendai sect with the Court went back to the earliest days of the Heian capital, for it was the great teacher Saichō who founded the first chapel on Mount Hiyei during the reign of Kammu. It was difficult for the Emperor or his ministers to take sides against the Enryakuji in the face of such a long tradition, and no doubt there were some occasions when its ambitious prelates were not very strongly against the action taken by their armed followers, and did nothing to check them. These demonstrations certainly presented a knotty problem to the government, for a belief that the gods might be offended by punishment of their worshippers was shared by most nobles at Court and by some—perhaps most—of the warrior chieftains and their men. It is here that the attitude of Kiyomori towards the monasteries assumes some importance. He was not the man to submit meekly to opposition, but he seems to have taken care to avoid offending the Enryakuji, and there are even signs that he tried to make use of some of its high clergy for his own purposes.

There is a well-known incident which, beside throwing light on the manners of the age, illustrates Kiyomori's attitude towards the monasteries. In the year 1147 a score or so of his warriors were escorting a company of dancers to the festival of the Gion shrine, where they were to give a performance as an offering from him. When they arrived at the entrance they were roughly refused admission because they were carrying arms. Angry words were followed by blows, and one of the shrine attendants was wounded. Since the Gion shrine was a subsidiary of the Hiyeizan monasteries, the "Mountain" at once complained to the Court, blaming Kiyomori and his father Tadamori for the offence. They were declared guilty, swallowed their pride, and paid a small fine, though the monks had asked for their banishment. Kiyomori appears to have decided to make friends with the Tendai Zasu, whose name was Myōun and who had at one time given him certain religious instruction. Kiyomori himself was very devout, given to religious exercises and lavish in his contributions to the Church.

A few years later, in 1177, infuriated by outrageous behaviour on the part of the Tendai monks, the cloistered Go-Shirakawa one day ordered the arrest of Myōun and decreed that he be banished. Thereupon the monks attacked and dispersed the officers escorting Myōun into exile, rescued him, and took him back to Hiyeizan. The now indignant and enraged Emperor wished to send a punitive force against the monastery, but was dissuaded, this time not by timid courtiers, but by the military leaders, including Kiyomori. Apparently Kiyomori had been persuaded by Myōun that it would be mistaken policy to threaten the great monastery. Certainly on more than one occasion the Taira leaders, though under great provocation, abstained from taking sides against the Enryakuji.

By 1178, when once more Kiyomori refused to intervene on the Emperor's behalf against more than usually offensive conduct by the monks, he was doubtless feeling some anxiety about the Taira position, and did not wish to have his warriors involved in fighting religious battles when he might have to deal with revolts such as those planned by the Shishigatani conspirators in 1177. He needed his troops for major political purposes, as when he marched them into the capital at the end of 1179. The monks were troublesome and annoying, but they offered no serious political threat; and if at any time they seemed dangerous they could be easily disposed of by a force of his hard-bitten warriors. Meanwhile it was well to prepare for emergencies by keeping on fairly friendly terms with the Enryakuji, which unlike the southern monasteries leaned to the Taira side when the Minamoto partisans sought their support. As for the real military strength of the monasteries, all that need be said is that in 1180, when the monks of the Kōfukuji and Tōdaiji were suspected of assisting the Minamoto cause, Kiyomori's warriors had no difficulty in defeating them and burning their buildings to the ground. Even that (as we shall see) was possibly a mistake, since the use of good troops for this purpose kept them from being used against Minamoto risings to the east.

4. *Kiyomori and His Antagonists*

In 1177 the Shishigatani Affair had ended in the discomfiture of Go-Shirakawa and the triumph of Kiyomori, but it did not do away with their mutual animosity. Both were difficult men, and neither seems to have considered the possibility of settling their differences to their joint advantage. They came into collision again at the end of 1179, when for a second time Kiyomori, backed by great military force, checked the designs of the cloistered Emperor and thereby struck a hard if not fatal blow at the system of dual sovereignty which had raised Go-Shira-kawa to his great position.

Midway through December 1179 Kiyomori at the head of several thousand men marched from Fukuwara into the capital, to the con-sternation of the people and the alarm of the Court nobility. The reasons for this demonstration were various, but it was designed in the first place to show strong disapproval of Go-Shirakawa's rash action in confiscating (with some colour of legality) certain property left by Kiyomori's son Shigemori and daughter Mori-ko, who had both died earlier in 1179. Kiyomori's reprisals were drastic. He had the cloistered Emperor put into close confinement in a detached palace, and he decreed that a large number of high officers of state be banished or degraded or dismissed from posts in which they had worked against Taira interests.

The young Emperor Takakura, perhaps warned by this treatment of his father, abdicated early in 1180 in favour of his son Antoku, then only two years old, in whom Kiyomori placed all his trust and hopes. Despite his successful exercise of power, Kiyomori seems to have felt that the tide was turning against him. He was living in an uneasy age, full of misfortunes and portents of evil. Some of the diaries of the time—the closing days of 1179—are filled with melancholy reflections and grim forebodings. Kiyomori himself, soon to be stricken with the torments of a mortal disease, as the darkness gathered could find no comfort except in the fact that his little grandson was to succeed to the throne and perpetuate the Taira greatness. There is a curious entry in the diary of a Fujiwara nobleman serving at Court at this time, in which he describes a visit paid by the child to Kiyomori's palace one day in December 1179, when he was still the Crown Prince. Kiyomori fondled him all day long, but he grew fractious. To amuse him the old man moistened his finger and pushed it through the paper of a sliding screen (*shōji*). The child copied his grandfather by wetting his own finger and poking a hole. This gave great pleasure to Kiyomori, who burst into tears and gave orders that the now so precious screen was to be carefully preserved in a strong-room. By contrast to this nursery tale, the description of the little prince's journey to and from Kiyomori's palace gives a picture of the dangers by which he was surrounded. Strong guards of warriors were placed at all crossroads, entrance from either side was forbidden, screens were put up, and heavily armoured men lined the route. Altogether some six hundred mounted men and "clouds of followers" were at their posts, apart from the royal escort of cavalry.

The day before these happenings Kiyomori had presented to the Court a set of the block-printed Sung edition of the celebrated Chinese encyclopaedia, the *Taihei Gyōran* (*T'ai-ping Yü-lan*), in over three hundred volumes, which he had obtained in his commerce with Chinese merchants, for he was, as we have noticed, much interested in trade with the mainland of Asia. After he had "entered religion" he paid special attention to sacred writings and to religious art in general, and made many gifts to monasteries, including a present to the Kōfukuji of a complete Tripitaka, also from China, said to have been obtained at very great cost by Shigemori. One result of the traffic of the Taira with China was to increase the importance of seaport towns in western Japan. Hiroshima in particular was favoured by an improvement of its harbour facilities that had been undertaken at the instance of Kiyomori.

His favourite stopping place in his official travels along the Inland Sea was Miyajima, not far from Hiroshima, for on that lovely island was a shrine called Itsukushima Jinja devoted to the worship of goddesses to whom Kiyomori owed thanks, he felt, for his success in life. It was by origin a very "pure" Shintō shrine, from which all Buddhist influences were in theory at least eliminated and where no births or deaths were allowed to cause pollution (in later times, however, Buddhist observances were added to Shintō ritual). Its treasures include the celebrated Heike Nōkyō, or "Sutras dedicated by the House of Taira." These consist of thirty-two scrolls, on which the Lotus and other sutras have been copied by Kiyomori, his sons, and other members of the family, each completing the writing of one scroll. Each scroll is lavishly decorated and illustrated in colour, with free use of gold, and the fittings of the rolls are masterpieces of design and ornament. This rich offering was made to the shrine as a prayer for the success of the Taira in this life and the next.

Kiyomori lavished great wealth upon Itsukushima, and he liked to show the place to his friends and colleagues, or even to royal personages, though this offended the great monasteries. After Antoku's enthronement, when the monks heard that Kiyomori planned to take the abdicated Takakura on a pilgrimage to worship his own tutelary deities, their fury knew no bounds.

To invite the hostility of such powerful bodies at this juncture was an unfortunate blunder, for the Taira were already losing friends or supporters in other quarters. The waning of their prestige and the gathering clouds that seemed to overhang the unhappy city were perfectly apparent to Kiyomori, and he came to feel that the future of the Taira depended upon the frail child Antoku, since their authority derived from their family link with the reigning sovereign. Yet the auspices were most unfavourable, or so the enemies of the Taira argued, for at his accession ceremony there had been several untoward incidents, notably the abrupt entrance of a madman, uttering crazy announcements, into the room where the new sovereign was taking his symbolic meal with departed predecessors. Such happenings were bound to heighten superstitious fears, to depress the allies and encourage the enemies of the Taira.

Among those enemies, of course, the most dangerous were the leading Minamoto warriors and their followers, who were secretly striving to restore the strength of their clan with the aim of avenging the disgrace put upon them by Kiyomori. Sympathy with their purposes was felt in many quarters. It was invoked in particular by the treatment of Yoshitomo, the leader of the clan, who had been executed as "a traitor and a robber," his head kept on show in a Taira gaol. There were at Court a few Minamoto men of high rank who were trusted by the Taira because they were polished men of letters, known and liked for their social accomplishments and not for their military exploits. Moreover a number of Minamoto women served as ladies-in-waiting at the Palace or maids of honour to great personages, and they also kept the warriors of the clan informed of the trend of affairs in the capital.

The most important Minamoto figure in the confidence of Kiyomori was Yorimasa, a poet of some distinction who at the end of his active military career kept out of politics by serving in positions that did not oblige him to take sides. He had for a long time been trusted and favoured by Kiyomori and had risen to high official rank (the third class) by 1179, when he decided to retire and enter religion, having reached the age of seventy-five. He had been a comrade of Yoshitomo in the fighting of 1156, when Kiyomori, then Governor of Aki, had joined in the night attack that put an end to the revolt of Yorinaga. In 1160, when Kiyomori overthrew the Minamoto during the Heiji war, Yorimasa had remained aloof, leaning apparently to the Taira side, and thereby ensured a Taira victory. It was not surprising that Kiyomori should place full trust in him and regard him as an important pillar of the Taira edifice of power.

Yet discreet and silent as he seemed, he was a warrior wearing Court robes, and it seems certain that by 1179 he had long been secretly hoping to bring about the downfall of the clan that had dragged his own ancestors in the dust. Kiyomori knew that there was a strong tide of envy and hatred running against his clan, and he maintained an alert army of spies and informers. But he seems never to have suspected Yorimasa, for in recommending his promotion to the third rank in 1178 he said that, although most of the Minamoto were rebels and traitors, Yorimasa alone was honest and upright. Yet in May 1180 Yorimasa sent out an appeal to Minamoto leaders in the east and north, and also to the monasteries which Kiyomori had offended, calling upon them to join in a great rising against the Taira.

Somehow Kiyomori became aware of this plot, but without learning who were the ringleaders. With his usual promptitude he led several thousand men into the city, shut up Go-Shirakawa in still closer confinement, and gave orders for the arrest of Prince Mochihito, one of Go-Shirakawa's sons, who was involved in the conspiracy as Yorimasa's candidate for the throne and in whose name the call to arms was issued. Then followed one of the most dramatic episodes in Japanese history. Mochihito took refuge in Miidera, a beautifully situated monastery near Ōtsu on Lake Biwa. The armed monks of Miidera, owing to quarrels with other sects, could not rely upon other monastic troops to help them, so that Mochihito was obliged to push on. In company with Yorimasa and protected by a few hundred men he left Miidera and passed south to Uji, a small town on the Uji River, at that point spanned by a famous bridge. There they stopped to rest, not far from the Fujiwara villa called Byōdō-in, which had been converted into a monastery used by the Miidera fraternity. They were on the way to Nara and had crossed the bridge, part of which Yorimasa had destroyed as a precaution, when the vanguard of a great Taira force overtook them, but on the other bank of the river. After many horsemen had been lost by drowning, some Taira warriors managed to cross the stream and reach the open space between its further bank and the front of the Byōdō-in. There a desperate struggle ensued, and as more and more of the main body of the Taira army found a way to ford the river, Yorimasa, concerned for the safety of the Prince, tried to escape with him. But he was struck by an arrow, and urged the Prince on, while scarcely able to move himself. He knew what fate awaited him if caught alive, and with the proper deliberation committed harakiri in the precincts of the one-time home of Fujiwara luxury and pride. There could scarcely have been a more tragic contrast than was afforded by this bloody scene enacted at Byōdō-in in front of the Phoenix Hall, a structure with such an airy grace that it seems to be rising to escape from earthly sorrows. The Prince was soon captured and killed.

It may be easily imagined what a startling effect these events had in the city, where rumours flew fast and there were misgivings on all sides. There is a record of events at this time in the diary of the Regent

Kanezane, and an abridged extract from his already laconic report will serve to give a picture of the uneasy life of the nobility as Taira leaders strove to stem the tide that flowed against them. The dates refer to the month of June 1180, "ninth" being June 4:

＊

"*Ninth*. Fine weather. I attended at Her Majesty's palace, returning at night, in company with Lord Kanefusa. He said that last night Tomomori [after Shigemori's death the favourite son of Kiyomori] was desperately ill, and seemed to be raving mad.

"*Tenth*. This morning the Prime Minister [Kiyomori] came to the City, which is crowded with soldiery to the alarm of the populace.

"*Eleventh*. Fine weather. In the afternoon Butsugon [a Buddhist abbot] came to call. In the evening I attended at the Palace and returned late.

"*Twelfth*. Fine weather, but it became very dark after the hour of the monkey [4 P.M.], though there was no rain. Tomomori is recovering. Yesterday the Prime Minister left the City.

"*Thirteenth*. It is rumoured that the Cloistered Emperor [Go-Shirakawa] is coming to reside in the City.

"*Fourteenth*. Rain, and uncertain weather. I was summoned to the Palace by Her Majesty, and returned at once, about 10 P.M. The Toba Cloister has made a progress to the mansion of the Keeper of the Palace Treasury. He rode in a state carriage with a close escort of three hundred mounted warriors.

"I have been suffering from a cold lately and my cough has grown worse. I feel very wretched.

"*Fifteenth*. Fine weather. His Majesty the new In [i.e., the abdicated Takakura][1] inspected his Imperial stable and picked out a horse which he sent by one of his attendants to the Regent. Towards evening the whole city was in a tumult. It was rumoured that the armed monks of the Hiyeizan monasteries were about to descend upon the city. This was false. This evening it was rumoured that the Takakura Prince [i.e., Prince Mochihito, second son of the abdicated Emperor] was to be banished.

"Apart from this all kinds of rumours were spread about from this quarter and that, but for the most part they were not to be trusted.

"Since earlier this evening my cough has grown worse and I am feverish.

"*Sixteenth*. The sentence of exile of Sanjō-In was as follows: Minamoto Mochimitsu [original name Mochihito] is deprived of his title and condemned to distant exile. He is to leave the Home Provinces at once . . .

---

[1] It will be remembered that there were often two or even three abdicated emperors living at the same time. See the account of the "cloister" system in Chapter X.

"It is rumoured that before the Police Commissioners reached his house last night the Prince had secretly escaped, and gone to Miidera, where the monks could protect him and where, it was expected, they would combine with the Tendai monks to raise a revolt. When news of the Prince's flight reached the authorities [i.e., the Taira leaders] the mansion of his mother was surrounded by warriors and searched. . . . What stupid conduct! The safety of our country now rests with the will of the Great Gods of Ise, Hachiman and Kasuga."

*

The subsequent entries, of the seventeenth day onwards, deal with the news of the pursuit of Mochihito and Yorimasa as it was purveyed in the capital. They give an interesting picture of the life of a great nobleman in a high office, who depended mainly upon rumour for his knowledge of what the Taira leaders were doing. He hears only at third hand that an Emperor is to move from his palace and that a Royal Prince is to be banished. From time to time he refers to the military in uncomplimentary language, in one passage observing: "In general, words fail to describe the baseness of the warriors."

For several days after the disappearance of the Prince Mochihito there was much going and coming at Court. Rumours were flying fast until, on the twenty-first day (June 16, 1180), Kanezane records that the Prince is definitely known to be at the Miidera monastery (Onjōji), where on the nineteenth he had rebuffed officers sent to bring him back to the capital. During these days Kanezane is not able to attend to his duties, since he is in a period of abstention (monoimi, or taboo); but friends call upon him at his house to discuss the rumours and to speculate what line the monks will take or how the Taira leaders will deal with the situation. He hears that troops will be sent under Taira command, and he is told that the Taira general Munemori and his warriors fear a mass rising of the armed monks and are preparing to leave the city with their household goods. A later rumour says that the Emperor and the retired Emperor (Antoku and the cloistered Takakura) are to be taken to Fukuwara by Kiyomori as virtual prisoners.

He deplores the disasters and dangers of the epoch, but on the twenty-fourth day notes in his diary with relief that his wife has had an auspicious dream, and that a certain learned monk, a practitioner of astrology, has reported that on the strength of the omens he can assure Kanezane that he will enjoy success.

Early in the morning of the twenty-sixth day a messenger came to tell him that the Prince and Yorimasa had been pursued and attacked. He went to the Palace before noon, where he was questioned by the In (Takakura), who seems to have been more concerned about property than about the fate of Mochihito. His Majesty suggested that since the monks of Miidera and the Kōfukiji were provoking rebellion their manors should be confiscated. Kanezane replied that this was a matter for careful study, and suggested that the Minister of the Left be sent for. That night news was brought to the In by a messenger from Munemori, telling him that the rebels had been destroyed at the Byōdō-in, after desperate fighting.

This victory Kanezane ascribed to the Imperial Virtue, but he also gave credit to the good karma of the great leader Kiyomori. Later in the day the discussion at the Palace was resumed. The Minister of the Left came in, followed presently by Taira Shigehira and Koremori, fresh from the battle. Shigehira was by favour admitted, though wearing armour, and he gave an account of the fighting. The death of Mochihito was confirmed, but there seems still to have been some doubt, since only a decapitated body had been found and it could not be properly identified without the head.[2]

Some hours later the In returned to the question of the monastic estates. Kanezane replied that they should not be confiscated, since it would be unjust to punish a monastery because some monks were evil men. It would be right to punish the bad monks. The In sent word that the matter would be decided on the following day, and that Kanezane was to attend the council. Accordingly at the appointed hour he presented himself at the Palace, wearing everyday dress. This turned out to be wrong, because there was some special ceremony in the government offices that day, of which Kanezane had not been told. His colleagues were in full Court dress, and he therefore privately made his apologies, asking whether he should withdraw, since it would take him some time to return to his house and change his costume. The In, however, excused him and told him to stay.

Much discussion then ensued as to the correct procedure, since Kanezane was loth to take his seat without further command from His Majesty. He had withdrawn to a distance and thus did not know exactly what had happened. But he was informed by the Minister of the Left that he had put the question to all those present and that they must all express their opinions and come to a decision about the treatment of the offending monasteries. Thereupon, according to custom, the junior officials stated their views first. The gist of the opinions expressed was as follows:

The Counsellor Michitaka opened by condemning both Miidera and the Kōfukuji. He recommended the despatch of government troops to attack the Kōfukuji and to carry out the confiscation of its manors and subsidiaries. The ringleaders of the Miidera monks should be identified and summoned. To these proposals the Counsellor Fujiwara Sanemune agreed so far as concerned Miidera, but thought that in regard to the

---

[2] This difficulty no doubt accounts for the care taken by generals to examine the heads of reputed notables killed in battle. Note the analogy in:

"The next news is: I have to London sent
The heads of Salisbury, Spencer, Blunt, and Kent."
(*Richard the Second*, V. vi)

Kōfukuji it would be enough to summon the ringleaders before taking drastic action. It would be wrong to wipe out the whole sect.

To these proposals eight officers of middling rank agreed, but Fujiwara Takasuye, Deputy Grand Counsellor, an influential noble, agreed with Michitaka that strict measures should be taken against the Kōfukuji as well. This monastery, a Fujiwara foundation, had humiliated a messenger from the Chieftain of the Fujiwara clan (Uji no Chōja) and had been in general insulting and rebellious. Its monks were guilty of grave offences. The Police Commissioners agreed that orders should be issued to control them. A punitive force should be sent to the monastery without delay, for it was not a holy place but a military stronghold. Better to act quickly upon foolish advice than to move slowly according to the dictates of wisdom, said Takasuye.

With these sage counsels Kanezane agreed, saying that certainly the crimes of the rebellious monks deserved punishment by hanging or decapitation. But, he added, we must first have the facts ascertained under a decree of His Sacred Majesty (the In). "For if we send troops the shrines and monasteries will all be reduced to ashes, and this must mean the extinction of the whole sect." This interesting statement suggests that Kanezane's piety was real, that he was concerned to protect the Buddhist establishment, and especially the Kōfukuji.

Kanezane went on to say that the Court would set a desirable precedent by getting full information about the real state of affairs before thinking of an armed attack. If this were done, His Majesty would show that he was careful not to act as an enemy of religion. At least let the Court follow the reasonable policy of finding out whether the rebel was being harboured by the monastery.

"It is certain," Kanezane continued, "that not all the clergy are in support of the rising, and in any case it would be prudent to despatch forthwith a messenger who could be back in the capital by tomorrow morning with a true report. On that His Majesty can decide whether or not to issue an order to chastise the monastery."

The Minister of the Left agreed with Kanezane, and though there was more talk nothing of significance was added. After a pause Takasuye, the Acting Grand Counsellor (Gon-Dainagon), said that His Majesty privately wished a decision to be reached, after an exchange of opinions, on the precise terms of any chastisement order that might have to be issued. "Some of the clergy," added Takasuye, "have assured us that the militant monks are out of control. It would therefore be foolish to send a messenger. Whom should we send? How would he get there?"

After some discussion it appeared that the rebellious monks were now quiet. They were no longer blocking the roads and refusing to receive emissaries from the capital. But Takasuye insisted that they had rebelled, and that there could be no two opinions about how to deal with rebels. When Kanezane strongly objected that the facts must be ascertained before any positive action was taken against the monastery, Takasuye tried to keep His Majesty (who was behind a screen at the far end of the council chamber) in ignorance of Kanezane's opinion.

Kanezane grew angry at this point, because he was a man of high standards and despised Takasuye as an incompetent and reckless official. He said firmly: "Even if there is no doubt whatever that the Prince is alive and taking refuge in the Nara monastery, it would still be proper for His Majesty to order a detailed enquiry. To order the Prince's arrest blindly without finding out whether he is there or not would be the height of folly. And suppose we were to wipe out the Hossō sect, what good would that do?"[3]

The Minister of the Left agreed fully with Kanezane and Takasuye looked black. Then Yukitaka, an officer of the private cabinet (Kurando), went to the Throne and reported the course of the deliberations. He came back to the place where the counsellors were waiting, and said: "Let us all remain here in attendance for a while. The Chieftain of the Fujiwara has just heard from Nara that the Prince has been killed. There are still some points to clear up and enquiries are being made."

At this point the Minister of the Left looked at Kanezane and laughed, for the previous discussion was shown to have been futile. Takasuye had nothing to say, and Yukitaka went back to the presence, leaving the rest of the group waiting. He did not return until some hours later, when he reported the decision of the Throne as follows:

"As regards Onjōji [Miidera] there shall be an official order to interrogate the bad monks who are now in custody, so as to identify the ringleaders.

"As to Kōfukuji the recommendation of the two Ministers [the Minister of the Left and Kanezane] is accepted. We shall send an emissary to obtain particulars of the revolt and to enquire about Mochimitsu [Prince Mochihito]. Troops will be sent if circumstances warrant."

In further entries Kanezane records his pleasure at the outcome of the council and rejoices at the triumph of the Law, by which he means the Buddhist religion. But a few days later he notes that the Taira leaders mean to escort the Emperor and the In to their Fukuwara quarters. It is this that he describes as the work of demons, and he adds that it is an unhappy fate (his karma) to have been born in an age when such things can come to pass.

These extracts throw a clear light upon political conditions of the day. It is the year 1180. The titular Emperor is an infant, the cloistered Emperor a sickly man who reigns but does not govern. Officials at Court go through elaborate forms of devising and executing policy, and the chief concern of the sovereign at this crucial moment is the disposal

[3] The Kōfukuji represented the Hossō sect, which had been brought from China to Japan about A.D. 650 by the patriarch Dōshō.

of such land as may fall to be confiscated. Meanwhile the Taira leaders do not trouble to keep the Court informed of what is taking place. They proceed with their own arbitrary acts. But they have aroused great hostility, and they are soon to pay the price of tyranny.

5. *Kiyomori's Death. The Taira Retreat*

Shortly after Kiyomori had suppressed the rising of Yorimasa, which he saw as an expression of widespread antagonism to himself and his clan, it was announced by his spy and confidant Kunitsuna that on the third day of the following lunar month (June 1180) the Emperor would transfer his residence to Fukuwara. The officials at the capital, who were obliged to move also, found the plan "unspeakable," but it was carried out—on the second instead of the third day. Whether Kiyomori contemplated a permanent transfer of the capital is not clear, but certainly provision was made for the transfer of certain government offices from Kyoto to Fukuwara, where there were a number of villas which had been built for Taira notables. His immediate object seems to have been to get the royal family under his close charge, so as to forestall any risk of their capture by a hostile party, either the now resurgent Minamoto leaders or the monastic armies, which he had begun greatly to fear.

The procession took place as it had been announced. It was led by Kiyomori himself in a palanquin, followed by the ladies of his household and then by three carriages, with their escorts, occupied by the reigning Emperor and the first and second cloistered Emperors. Then came the Fujiwara Regent, next Munemori, the son of Kiyomori, and then other notables. They passed between two lines of mounted warriors stirrup-to-stirrup, to the number of several thousand. On arrival at Fukuwara their Majesties were lodged in the Taira mansions that had been prepared for their use while a new palace was being built. It looked as if the royal family might settle down in this place. Some of them had already visited Kiyomori a few years before, and he had given them monster entertainments at which (so one account says) "the guests drank innumerable cups of wine and there was wild dancing and the consorts and princesses wore costumes of unspeakable beauty."

But Fukuwara was not always gay. Its seaside climate was altogether too rough, cold, and damp for the delicate health of aristocrats who thought that any place more than a mile or two from the capital was outlandish and dangerous. Moreover the young Emperor Takakura was sickly; and it was his poor health, combined with other reasons, that brought about the return of the Court to the old capital some six months after the move to Fukuwara. Whatever its real motive Kiyomori's plan had failed, and he was obliged to return to his Rokuhara headquarters in order to keep a close watch on events. He returned with great reluctance, if we may judge from a record which says that the decision to leave Fukuwara was reached only after a quarrel between him and his sons. The courtiers, of course, were delighted to return, and as they neared their destination they could not restrain their tears of joy. The happy occasion was celebrated by the great poet Teika, who in his work *Meigetsu-ki* relates that during the Court's absence from Kyoto the palaces and other buildings had fallen into disrepair and presented a melancholy picture.

Kiyomori had cherished some such plan as a transfer of the capital for a long time. After the incident of the confiscated manors, when Go-Shirakawa had acted without consulting him, he had sent his son Shigehira to Court to say on his behalf:

"This poor monk [Kiyomori] has been cast aside and now cannot refrain from anxiety about the present state of the government. . . . He feels that his services are no longer needed and therefore he begs for leave of absence, so that he may retire to a remote place and lead a life of solitude.

"He wishes to take with him Their Highnesses the Consort and the Crown Prince."

This was at the end of 1179. The Consort was his daughter Toku-ko and the Crown Prince was her son, later to be the child Emperor Antoku.

Such mock humility and such arrogant claims not only offended Fujiwara nobles close to the Throne and a large number of lesser Court officials, but also angered the more unruly elements in the great monasteries. They began to show signs of restless discontent, and as we have seen, in the third month of 1180 (not long after Takakura's abdication) the monks of Miidera rose. It was rumoured that they were conspiring with the Tendai fraternities on Mount Hiyei and the Nara monasteries to seize the persons of the two cloistered Emperors so as to remove them from Kiyomori's grasp. It was to forestall such action by his enemies that Kiyomori brought Go-Shirakawa from Toba-den and kept him under close guard, and from that it was not a far step to keeping the whole Court under his own eyes and in a place that was not easy of access, like Fukuwara.

The closing years of the twelfth century, and in particular the decade from 1175 to 1185, are often described in contemporary works as a time of hardship, trouble, and anxiety about the future. For such misfortunes it was not unnatural that the rulers of the country should be judged responsible, and it thus came about that the Taira leaders were blamed for the nation's sufferings. No doubt this ill repute contributed to the downfall of the proud Taira warlords, which was by 1185 to become complete. Celestial portents noted in the diaries of the time seemed to confirm the predictions of soothsayers and astrologers, and there was much before the very eyes of the populace, in a city ravaged by fire, plague, and neglect, to encourage pessimism and mistrust. But whether it was the fault of the Taira, or, as seems likely, the inevitable collapse of an obsolete system of government, is a matter for speculation.

Though the misfortunes of the late Heian period are of earlier origin than the rise of the Taira clan, the last years of their power saw an awful accumulation of disasters. Whatever its cause, the failure of the regime was plainly attested by the frequency of robbery, arson, and murder in the very heart of the imperial city, offences which the armed forces of the Taira were unable to suppress. The government did resort to drastic measures, arresting and punishing criminals with ferocity; but the results were not good. The condition of the city was lamentable. It has been described in a celebrated work called *Hōjō-ki*, which is the notebook of a not very unworldly recluse living in a small hut in one of its suburbs. His name was Kamo Chōmei. His work contains, as well as an obviously first-hand description of Fukuwara, a striking account of material conditions in the capital in the years from 1177 to 1182. It is a dreadful tale of storms, earthquakes, conflagrations, plagues, starvation, and cold, when infants could be seen clinging to the breasts of their dead mothers and shivering men stole images of the Buddha for firewood and corpses remained unburied. In the city proper, excluding the suburbs, over forty-two thousand corpses lying in the street were counted in two months. It was a world of pollution, and famine struck not only the capital city, but also all the surrounding provinces and the western seats of Taira power.

These grim happenings, it should be remembered, were only a culminating phase in a procession of calamities that had begun long before. Apart from the destruction and damage caused by the fighting in the Heiji rising of 1160, the capital city was frequently visited by disaster, sometimes the work of man and sometimes a convulsion of nature. The *Hōjō-ki* contains, for example, a most vivid description of the great fire of 1177: "The fire fanned out as the shifting wind spread it, first in one direction and then another. Houses far away from the conflagration were enveloped in the smoke, while the area near by was a sea of flames. . . . The ashes were blown up into the sky . . . and the flames seemed to fly over two or three streets at a time. . . . Sixteen mansions belonging to the nobility were burnt, not to speak of innumerable other houses. In all about a third of the capital was destroyed. Several thousand men and women lost their lives, as well as countless horses and oxen. . . ."

The downfall of the Taira clan seems in the light of such ominous events to have an element of tragic inevitability—partly, perhaps, because most of the accounts we have of the struggle between the clans were written by men who lived in the capital and played some part in public life, so that they saw the errors and misfortunes of the Taira most clearly, while learning only of Minamoto successes. Nevertheless the story of the last days of the Taira, as it is related to subsequent generations, is the true Japanese epic, and it is significant that its keynote is the impermanence of glory.

The personal tragedy of the proud Kiyomori is a kind of miniature version of the history of the society in which he flourished, for it passes from buoyant youth to bright maturity and then to crisis, illness, failing judgment, and a painful death.

Not long after the return of the courtiers from Fukuwara to the capital city—where, despite their pleasure at finding themselves once more in accustomed surroundings, they soon perceived the growing aura of decay and misery—Kiyomori fell sick of a mortal disease. But not before he had made perhaps the worst blunder in his career by attacking and burning the monasteries (Tōdaiji and Kōfukuji) whose soldiery he feared, thus adding to the numbers of his certain enemies an army which might have been induced to side with him or at least to remain aloof from the reckoning with the Minamoto that by now was inevitable. It was in the early spring of 1181 that he took to his bed. The most reliable diary of the time reports on March 13, 1181, that the Zemmon (Kiyomori) is suffering from a high fever, and all contemporary accounts agree in describing him as suffering torments, crimson in the face, and "burning like fire." But he seems to have rallied shortly before his death, for we find it recorded on March 21 that he had died on that day, but had talked to Go-Shirakawa in the morning and expressed his views very vigorously. He had described the monk Enjitsu as a rebel and the cause of the nation's troubles, saying "After my death let all things be done in consultation with my son Munemori." The cloistered Emperor's reply was obscure, and Kiyomori displayed great wrath. He sent for his confidant Yukitaka and said: "After my death everything in the Empire is to be settled in accordance with what the late Dictator [himself] has laid down. There is to be no argument."

In reporting these things the writer adds: "Alas! The cloistered Emperor's real feelings are hostile to Munemori, and this indeed will be the ruin of the state."

Some months after Kiyomori's death Munemori is reported to have divulged several other last wishes of his father. According to this account, the dying Kiyomori roused himself to adjure his sons and grandsons never to let the body of Yoritomo be given burial but to make sure that his bones should always lie bleaching above ground. He also ordered that his own remains be buried at a monastery in the province of Harima where simple and infrequent prayers were to be said for him, but no prayers at the capital. Finally, his descendants were not to remain in the home provinces but to return to the east and remain there as settlers for good.

Kiyomori's favourite son Shigemori having died—some said of grief at his father's stubborn and misguided treatment of his opponents— affairs of state were left in the hands of Munemori, who was the least gifted of his children, and quite incapable of dealing with the crafty Go-Shirakawa. But even the greatest talent would not have saved the Taira house from disaster. Their cause was already lost, and the death of Kiyomori gave rise to little sorrow or regret.

Opinions differ as to the ability of Kiyomori; some historians even dismiss him as stupid and incompetent. But he was evidently an exceptional man, of very strong character, ruthless and stubborn. His political judgment can be called in question, for he showed no skill in the handling of the admittedly difficult Go-Shirakawa In, and in general he made more enemies than friends. He came of a warrior house, and his early training was such as to qualify him for practical administration rather than Court intrigue. In his conduct of affairs after his elevation to the highest office, his answer to all objections was a threat of force, and his success as a dictator can be ascribed to the thousands of armed men at his call rather than to any unusual gift of wisdom or even cunning. The fact is that he was at the head of his clan at a moment propitious for him in Japanese history, when none but forcible measures could solve the problems that crowded upon him.

He had to deal with a fantastically difficult situation at Court, with ambitious clerics and turbulent monks, with a generally indifferent if not hostile aristocracy, and with a discontented populace in the metropolis. By contrast the situation in the provinces was one of prosperity, or at least it afforded hope to the landed gentry, whose fortunes were rising, especially in the east, where the Minamoto clan were recovering from their defeat.

It is not easy to say what contemporary opinion of Kiyomori was like at the time of his death; but he seems to have been roundly hated in many quarters, and it was rumoured that at his obsequies the sound of wild dancing and singing could be heard from a nearby mansion, where (it was supposed) his death was being joyfully celebrated. This may not be true, but there is an ironical short verse[4] by a Court poet of the time, which says that the sleeves of the mourners must have been wet, if not with tears, at least with the spring rain that fell incessantly on the evening of his funeral.

Perhaps the most interesting feature of Kiyomori's life, from the point of view of political history, is the fact that despite his armed power he felt it necessary to obtain a cloistered Emperor's consent to his measures. It is true that he generally used pressure rather than persuasion, but the fact remains that thanks to long tradition the occupant of the Throne, however weak, was in a commanding position, which the abdicated sovereigns shared. The semblance of imperial prerogative was always preserved.

[4] The verse runs as follows:

> Harusame mo
> Otsuru namida mo
> Hima nakute
> To ni mo kaku ni mo
> Nururu sode ka na!

CHAPTER XIV

THE GEMPEI WAR

WHILE, for whatever reasons or causes, the fortunes of the Taira were thus declining, the Minamoto were regaining strength and cohesion in the east, and planning revenge for the humiliation which their leaders had suffered at the hands of Kiyomori. They were, of course, inspired by self-interest, and by a natural desire to regain the property that had been wrested from them. But some, though not all, of them were also moved by a strong feeling of loyalty to Yoritomo, who had been spared as a boy by Kiyomori and was now the acknowledged leader of their clan, inheriting the position of his father Yoshitomo.

Kiyomori lived to see Taira troops fall back before Yoritomo's men; and after his death the position of the Taira began to grow rapidly worse. In September 1180 Yoritomo at the head of a small body of men had crossed the Hakone Pass from Izu, where he had been living as an exile with a guardian appointed by Kiyomori. News of his movements reached the capital in a report of September 24, which said: "The son of the late Yoshitomo, Hyōe no Suke [Captain of the Guards] Yoritomo, has raised a volunteer force and is plundering the province of Izu. The Eastern Provinces are in an uproar." On the following day an edict was issued, appointing a commander-in-chief to suppress "the rebel Yoritomo and his following" and ordering all men in the east capable of bearing arms to join the attack.

Meanwhile attempts were made to improve the defences of the capital, but with no success. The garrison, if it may be so called, consisted of the Taira warriors in Kiyomori's service and their followers, and these were to be reinforced by able-bodied men called up by the ordinary nobility from their country estates. This order of mobilization was unpopular in the city among all classes, who had already seen far too much bloodshed and destruction for their peace of mind. Apart from the seasoned warriors serving the Taira leaders in the city, the troops available were of poor quality. At first, however, they had the advantage numerically, and Yoritimo, on his first attempt to move westward with only a few men, was checked by a superior force under a Taira captain. He was compelled to retreat and find safety for a time in the Hakone mountains. This engagement, fought on September 14, 1180, while Kiyomori was still alive, was a small-scale affair, but it is celebrated in Japanese history as the battle of Ishibashiyama, largely because it expressed the bold and offensive spirit of the eastern warrior.

The accompanying chart shows the relationships of the members of the Minamoto clan who played a leading part in the campaigns that followed Yoritomo's first attack at Ishibashiyama. It will be clear that

Important Dates in the Gempei War*
(Lunar Calendar)

1180

iv.9. Prince Mochihito issues order to destroy the Taira
viii.17. Yoritomo defeats Taira no Kanetaka
viii.23. Yoritomo loses battle of Ishibashiyama
ix.7. Yoshinaka raises troops
x.20. Taira retreat at Fujikawa
xi.7. New Taira force ordered east

1181

i.20. Taira defeat Yukiiye in Mino
Intercal. ii.4. Kiyomori dies
Intercal. ii.15. Taira no Shigehira leaves to subdue east
iii.10. Taira defeat Yukiiye at Sunomatagawa
viii.14. Order issued for pacification of Hokurikudō
ix.4. Yoshinaka defeats Taira in Echizen

1182

Famine. Virtual armistice

1183

iii. Yoshinaka and Yoritomo reach an understanding
v.11. Yoshinaka defeats Taira at Tonamiyama
vii.21. Yoshinaka threatens Kyoto
vii.25. Taira flee west
xi. Yoshinaka defeated by Taira at Mizushima

1184

i.20. Yoshinaka killed at Awazu in Ōmi
ii.7. Ichinotani
viii.8. Noriyori leaves Kamakura

1185

ii.19. Yashima
iii.24. Dannoura. The Minamoto victory

* Gen stands for Genji (Minamoto family), and Hei stands for Heike (Taira house). The compound is pronounced Gempei.

Yukiiye was an uncle and Yoshinaka a cousin of the three brothers, Yoritomo, Noriyori, and Yoshitsune.

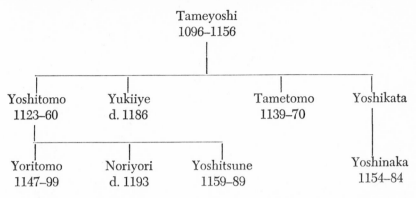

Although the Minamoto had been described in the edicts issued from the capital as bandits and rebels, or perhaps for that very reason, Yoritomo claimed that he was commissioned by Prince Mochihito to chastise the Taira. It was no doubt true that when Yorimasa sent out an appeal to Minamoto leaders in the east in May 1180, he called upon them in the name of the Prince, who (it will be recalled) was a son of the Emperor Go-Shirakawa. In any event, it is clear that Yoritomo and his party were anxious to be regarded as legitimate supporters of the Throne and not as mere revolutionaries. When Yoritomo rode up to the Hakone mountains to assemble his force of a few hundred men at Ishibashiyama, he took care to give a colour of legality to his raid by fixing to his banner a paper claiming to be an order from the Prince to punish enemies of the state. It will be seen later that even when he was carried on the full tide of success Yoritomo continued to profess that he was acting on behalf of His Imperial Majesty.

This preliminary skirmish to the great struggle that was to follow ended in Yoritomo's retreat and escape, and since he spent the next six months in raising a new army it appeared to the Taira as a success to their own arms. But subsequent news was not so encouraging. By November Yoritomo had raised a very considerable force, and had advanced into Suruga, where he encamped on the left bank of the Fuji-kawa. On November 10, 1180, the Taira levies that had been hastily sent against him and stood now on the right bank were surprised by a night attack and thrown into confusion. Their commanders decided to retreat, and Yoritomo chose not to follow them but to strengthen his base for further offensive movements. This was the last encounter in 1180, since winter had come. Kiyomori died in March 1181, and fighting was not resumed until May. Shortly after his death, however, reports reached the capital saying that troops sent against Yoritomo, after having checked Yukiiye early in the year, were starving in the province of

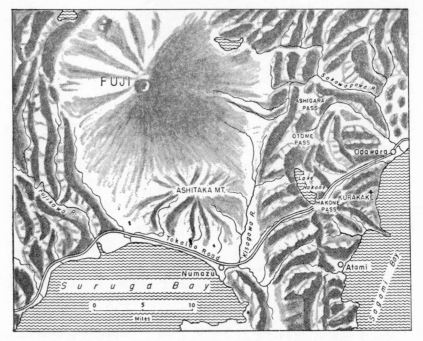

Ishibashiyama (cross), site of the opening battle in the Gempei War, 1180

Mino, while the rebel Minamoto forces in the provinces to the east of them were increasing "a thousand-fold day by day."

A council of high officials was held in Go-Shirakawa's palace on March 22, 1181, to deal with this situation. It was attended by Mune-mori and a dozen others, who listened while he presented the case to His Holiness the Cloistered Emperor. The unhappy heir to Kiyomori's legacy could only say that it was all very well for the late Dictator to decree that the Minamoto must be fought to the bitter end, but how was that to be done with indifferent troops and short supplies? Food would have to be brought in from the north and west, and how was that to be done in a time of famine? He asked for a ruling, and it was decided that a stand must be made. A new commander-in-chief was appointed, in the person of Taira Shigehira, who was said to have under him a force of 13,000 men. A report came in that he had chastised Minamoto Yukiiye in a battle on the banks of the Sunomata River in Owari; but little satisfaction was to be derived from this piece of news, for the Taira could not follow up their victory. It was now May 2, 1181, and after that there was a long pause in the fighting. All intelligence from the east showed that the Minamoto were raising more men and gaining more supporters, some of whom were Taira families settled in the Kantō.

It was at this time proposed that the whole of the Taira force should withdraw to the western provinces, taking with them the Emperor and the cloistered sovereigns, with all their courts and officers. The idea was dropped, but it was revived in 1183, after the Taira leaders had undergone most bitter trials. There was a great famine in 1182 affecting mainly the western provinces, and spirits fell in the capital, where plague as well as hunger threatened. The courtiers and the ordinary citizens were alarmed and miserable, as is clear from the diaries and memoirs of the time, which abound in such bald entries as "This is the day of the destruction of the kingdom!" and "These indeed are events deplorable beyond measure." Apart from these private calamities, the military situation grew worse and worse, mostly because of the great difficulty of finding and transporting supplies. In 1181 the government issued an order for the pacification of the northern provinces (the Hokurikudō, or Northern Land Circuit), where the Minamoto were rising; but in the autumn a Taira force which had been despatched to Echizen was defeated by Minamoto Yoshinaka, a cousin of Yoritomo with a great military reputation who had invaded Echigo during the summer and come to terms with local magnates who had fighting men at their disposal.

The famine which reached its peak in 1182 and was accompanied by epidemic sicknesses was enough to account for a pause in the fighting, and it was not until early in 1183 that Yoritomo resumed the offensive—astonishingly enough against his cousin Yoshinaka, whose strength and successes had aroused his suspicions. Yoshinaka managed to placate Yoritomo and turned his attention to a vigorous campaign against the Taira, who were making one last great effort in the north. In April and May of 1183 Taira Koremori invaded Echizen, where he succeeded in reducing Hiuchiyama and several other of Yoshinaka's strongholds and even securing some adherents in the province. But his success did not last long. Yoshinaka soon engaged him in Etchū province, and after a major battle the great Taira army was put to flight on the slopes of a mountain called Tonamiyama, which gives its name to the engagement as it is described in military annals and romances.[1]

This was a grave defeat for the Taira, especially since by all accounts they had great superiority in numbers, by some writers put at as many as forty thousand men against the Minamoto five thousand. Yoshinaka won by a clever strategy; under cover of nightfall his troops enveloped the main body of the Taira, demoralized them by a series of tactical surprises, and turned their confusion into a disastrous, headlong rout. Thousands of Taira troops were killed or wounded—one usually reliable source says more than half the total of forty thousand—and the rest threw away their weapons and armour. Yoshinaka's march to the southwest was not further impeded. Within a month or so he was threatening

[1] It is also sometimes called the battle of the Kurikara Pass.

294   THE GEMPEI WAR

the capital city from the north while Yukiiye was advancing towards it
from the east. By high summer of 1183, the outlook for the Taira was
hopeless. "In Rokuhara there was nothing but lamentation," says the
chronicler. In the words of a modern Japanese historian describing
what was being written at this time, "it all reads like the bedside diary
of a man stricken by a mortal illness."

In the late summer the cloistered Emperor Go-Shirakawa, who had
been secretly in touch with Yoritomo since Kiyomori's death, went on
a pilgrimage to Hiyeizan, where he was well protected by armed monks.
The next day the young Emperor and his consorts, with a few attendants,
left the city. There is a sad account of their movements during the
next few days in a diary known as *Kichi-ki*.[2] Under the date August 15,
1183, it records the pilgrimages of this small party to the shrines of
Kumano, Hiyoshi, and Kurama to worship their protecting deities, and
thence to a Buddhist monastery in a Kyoto suburb for the night. Theirs
was a serious pilgrimage, but Go-Shirakawa's visit to the monks of Hiyeizan was not made for religious purposes. He was escaping from the
bondage of the Taira, which he had suffered since Kiyomori put him
under close confinement. Yoshinaka was already in the adjoining province of Ōmi, only a short march from Hiyeizan, where he presently encamped. Yukiiye was also close, for he had entered the province of
Yamato. The two forces were converging upon the melancholy capital,
after brushing aside Taira resistance.

Now Munemori and other Taira captains saw that they must withdraw rapidly. The Minamoto were by this time clearly the stronger
force, and Go-Shirakawa's defection had given their cause a great moral
advantage and a colour of legitimacy. There was nothing for the Taira
to do but set fire to the Rokuhara buildings which had been the heart
of the Taira dictatorship for a generation and hasten to the west, taking
with them the young Emperor. Go-Shirakawa, for his part, took pleasure
in giving to Yoshinaka (who brought him back to the capital with an
escort of several thousand men) a mandate to join with Yukiiye in destroying Munemori and his army.

We may pause here to consider the nature of the resistance offered
by the Taira to the growing strength of the Minamoto, for quite apart
from the military interest of the Gempei War and its place in Japanese
romance and legend, it was an event of great political significance. Its
results determined the subsequent course of national life in most important respects. One has only to speculate about what would have happened had the Taira been victorious to see that the success of the warlike
eastern families and their adherents gave a special character to the institutions of mediaeval Japan and moved the political centre away from
the ancient capital and its ancient traditions.

[2] Written by a Court noble between 1171 and 1185.

Descriptions of the fighting in northern and eastern Japan from 1180 to 1183 tend to give the impression that the Taira forces were much inferior to the Minamoto in bravery and skill. This view is no doubt coloured by knowledge of the final result and due to a natural habit of ascribing success more to the wisdom of victors than to their good fortune. In view of the obstacles that the Taira had to surmount—the shortage of supplies, the long lines of communication, and the difficult terrain—their armies displayed more courage and endurance than is generally allowed. They gave a very good account of themselves at Hiuchiyama and gained many supporters among the Echizen warriors. They soundly defeated Yukiiye once, if not twice; and their first withdrawal from the Fujikawa position was not, it may be argued, a blunder but a necessary adjustment to a new situation which arose when forces belonging to a supposed ally suddenly attacked them from the rear. Their subsequent retreat was, it is true, disastrous, but the leaders in the capital did not give up. They sent new forces to the east and scored successes in 1181, and they did not hesitate to take the offensive in the distant provinces of the Hokurikudō. What is remarkable is the size of the armies which they were able to raise. It is true that the numbers given in the military romances are much swollen by their enthusiastic writers, as when the Taira force at Tonamiyama is given at 100,000, whereas more reliable documents place it at less than half that; but even the more likely figure of 40,000 is substantial.

The keynote of the military romances, especially the *Heike Monogatari,* is the fall of pride. The Taira are presented as pursued by an inescapable fate. They are doomed to defeat and disgrace because of their past arrogance, just as hubris in other chronicles of war is said to have its unhappy sequels. The literary canons demand a stress upon the failures of the loser and the virtues of the ultimate conqueror. As might be expected, however, a study of the whole campaign does not altogether bear out this stress, since it turns up many instances of shifting allegiance and mean treachery on both sides. This feature of the warfare of the times is revealed in its most unpleasing aspect by the relations between Yoshinaka and Yukiiye.

After installing the cloistered Go-Shirakawa in the capital Yoshinaka found himself in a powerful position, since he commanded the only armed force of any importance in the home provinces. Towards the end of 1183 he began secretly to prepare for an attack upon Yoritomo, whom he both feared and hated. But under pressure from the cloistered Emperor he addressed himself to the task of defeating the large Taira army which was moving westwards along the northern shore of the Inland Sea.

Meanwhile the small party headed by Munemori, which consisted of the boy Emperor Antoku, his mother, and a few attendants, had reached Kyūshū early in September and had set up a temporary Court

in the old Defence Headquarters at Dazaifu. But local revolts, instigated by Go-Shirakawa, soon drove them out of Kyūshū and obliged
them to take refuge in Shikoku at a place called Yashima,[3] where they
were in surroundings friendly to the Taira. While sending his commanders to harry the army proceeding westward under Taira Shigehira and
other Taira captains, Yoshinaka, with one eye on the position in the
capital, prepared for a descent upon Shikoku and the capture of Yashima. The force which he had sent in pursuit of Shigehira was badly
beaten at Mizushima, a point on the border of the provinces of Bizen
and Bitchū, some 120 miles west of the city. Yoshinaka, instead of taking
strong measures to repair this unfortunate blunder, hurried back to the
capital to forestall an army that was said to be on its way from Kamakura
under the command of Yoritomo's younger brother Yoshitsune. There
he plotted with Yukiiye, with the object of seizing the person of the
cloistered Emperor and setting up a government in their own northern
provinces. He even went so far as to negotiate with some of the great
Taira leaders, hoping to persuade them to attack Yoritomo, and he suggested to the powerful Fujiwara Hidehira that he should join in an
alliance against Yoritomo.

Yukiiye revealed these plans to Go-Shirakawa. His Majesty, fearful
for his own safety, managed to get word to Yoritomo, who at once ordered his brothers Yoshitsune and Noriyori to attack and destroy Yoshinaka with a large force of "myriads of men." It was put about that their
armies were escorting the year's taxes (rice and other produce) from the
eastern provinces. Yukiiye's disclosure put Yoshinaka in great jeopardy.
He seized control of the capital (December 1183) and ruled with a high
hand, while his wild mountaineers were allowed to ravage the city.
Yukiiye himself left with his own troops for the province of Harima to
attack the Taira, where he was again beaten and had to take refuge in
another province. Early in 1184 Yoshinaka attacked the Hōjōji palace
of Go-Shirakawa, set fire to the buildings, slaughtered their defenders,
and took the cloistered Emperor into custody. At this point he learned
that Yukiiye had moved into Kawachi, a province not far from the
capital, and had established himself in the fort of Ishikawa, where he
offered a threat from the south which Yoshinaka could not neglect. The
despatch of a force which Yoshinaka sent to mask this stronghold weakened his garrison in the city, and at this juncture he learned that both
Noriyori and Yoshitsune were rapidly converging upon him. He attempted to carry off the cloistered Emperor but the venture failed, and
he was obliged to risk an escape with a few followers. He got as far as
Awazu in Ōmi province, where he came up against Noriyori's vanguard
and was killed fighting early in March 1184. Much of the fighting in
this last struggle of Yoshinaka took place near the Long Bridge of Seta

[3] The modern Takamatsu.

and the Bridge of Uji, both the scene of many events famous in romantic legend. The desperate efforts of Yoshinaka to hold back the attackers by breaking down these bridges, and the forlorn hope of his foster brother Imai, who stemmed the flood of Noriyori's thousands with a handful of men, are among the most celebrated feats of arms in all the warlike chronicles of Japan.

So far, it will be noticed, the course of events was not entirely in favour of the Minamoto. The Taira had stood up well against Yoshinaka's own troops at Mizushima and had caused him great losses, while they had thrown Yukiiye back without much trouble. The intrigues and jealousies of the Minamoto captains and Yoritomo's preoccupations in the east, themselves a sign of internal strife or at best disunity among the Minamoto and their adherents, had given the Taira leaders time to recover from the panic in which they had scuttled out of Kyoto. When after some melancholy voyaging the little Court that had been driven away from Kyūshū at length arrived in the friendly port of Yashima, the bolder spirits among the Taira began to take the offensive. They had been masters of the Inland Sea for a century or so, after all, and they controlled much shipping in those waters, especially in the coastal manors which had been developed by Tomomori. It was easy for them to send men across from Yashima to the opposite shore in Bizen province, where they landed in the Kojima Bay area. This gave them a strategic control over entrances to the Inland Sea from the east, and caused anxiety in the capital, where it was thought that a great Taira army would soon advance upon the city.

Now Go-Shirakawa, concerned over this threat and anxious to regain the Imperial Regalia, sent several messages to the Taira leaders ordering them to bring the young Emperor back, with the Regalia. He gave them to understand that if they complied by the seventh day of the second month a truce could be arranged, since the Minamoto forces had been ordered not to attack before the eighth day. This was nothing but a ruse, for he had already ordered Noriyori and Yoshitsune to attack. He clearly hoped that he might at one stroke recover the Regalia and throw the Taira off their guard.

The Minamoto commanders accordingly left on March 12 (1184) in pursuit of the Taira forces, whose position at that time was not exactly known to them. They seem to have left Yashima by boat at about the time when Noriyori and Yoshitsune set out from the capital. The distance in a direct line from Yashima to Fukuwara is about sixty miles, so that the Taira force probably landed on the second day after sailing, March 14.

The Taira forces landed in Settsu at points between Fukuwara and Ichinotani, where they set about building defence works, having left the young Emperor Antoku with his guards and attendants on their ships near Wada Misaki. They were in a hopeful mood. They had recovered from their earlier defeats and (perhaps encouraged by Go-Shirakawa's message) were now preparing for a return to the capital. Their recovery had brought them fresh supporters; they had a new army and a numerous fleet that gave them command of the sea. They were back on their own ground, and the defences which they were rapidly throwing up along the shore might later be strengthened to form a protected base for future operations.

But before the works were completed Yoshitsune defeated a body of Taira troops in a preliminary encounter on the night of March 18; and then he split his force in two in preparation for the decisive engagement which he and Noriyori planned. The two forces carried out an encircling movement, one threatening the western end of the Taira position at Ichinotani, which they attacked early in the morning of March 20, the other striking at the Ikuta Woods, which formed the eastern end of the Taira line.

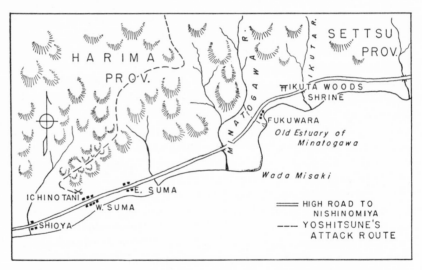

Sketch map showing the route of Yoshitsune's surprise attack upon the Taira left flank at Ichinotani, and the position of the Ikuta woods where the Taira right flank was turned and broken, March 20, 1184.

Ichinotani is a narrow strip of coast between mountains on the north and the sea on the south. It is at some points scarcely more than forty yards across, and though unsuited for any kind of manoeuvring of troops it was a seemingly impregnable position. But by a feat of daring which has been copiously celebrated in the warlike chronicles of Japan, Yoshitsune turned its situation to the advantage of the Minamoto arms. During the night before the battle he led a small force of picked men—fewer than one hundred—with their horses up through the rugged mountain terrain to the topmost ridge, which looked down upon the Taira camp. There they waited, hidden by a thick growth of bushes, from the hour of dawn until Noriyori's force pressed back the Taira from their position at Ikuta. Then, choosing their moment, Yoshitsune's cavalry rode pell-mell down the declivity, launched a furious attack on the troops manning the earthworks, and set fire to the camp.

Confused by this sudden onslaught, the Taira men could neither deploy nor retreat, being violently attacked from two directions and having the sea behind them. The Ichinotani commander Tadamori was killed and Shigehira, the general at Ikuta, was captured. Those who could escape fled by ship to Yashima.

The size of the armies engaged in this battle is uncertain. One contemporary journal says that the Taira numbered 20,000, but this seems highly improbable, since only 3,000 survivors reached Yashima and the number of prisoners taken and men killed was given by the *Azuma Kagami* as about one thousand.

It is likely that the whole Taira force engaged at Ikuta and Ichinotani amounted to little more than five thousand men. The Minamoto army was even smaller, probably not more than three thousand. If we are to believe rumours current in the capital at this time, the Minamoto force was so small that the populace were in a state of panic, fearing a great Taira attack upon the city. The exaggeration of numbers is a characteristic feature of the military romances; the *Heike Monogatari*, for example, characteristically records that the Minamoto had 70,000 men fighting in this battle—an impossible number, or at any rate an unmanageable host.

Shortly after the defeat of the Taira at Ichinotani the cloistered Go-Shirakawa called upon Shigehira, then a prisoner of war in Kyoto, to order Munemori to bring back to the capital the "former Emperor" Antoku and the Imperial Regalia. Go-Shirakawa had earlier been successful in persuading the Taira leaders to relax their military effort. This further attempt after the victory of the Minamoto shows how great an importance was attached to the Regalia.

The retreat of the Taira by sea confronted the Minamoto with a new situation, for they were not equipped to undertake an operation against the island of Shikoku. There ensued a pause in the hostilities which lasted for about six months and gave the Taira a breathing space, which they used to make good their losses in men and materials by drawing upon the resources of their lands in the central and western provinces. It was not until September 1184 that Noriyori left Kamakura with Yoritomo's commission to crush the Taira. Yoritomo was at that time occupied with major strategical decisions and the diplomatic problem of maintaining good relations with other warrior chieftains. He had for those purposes chosen Kamakura as his headquarters because of its situation, which was at the same time convenient and safe. He was busy in the east but he kept in touch with affairs in the west, orders or requests to partisans in Shikoku and Kyūshū being issued in his name. But, whether out of jealousy or fear, he delayed giving an appointment to his brother Yoshitsune.

Noriyori pushed forward, leaving Kamakura with a few hundred picked men, including some whose family names were to embellish later annals of war, notably Hōjō, Chiba, and Ashikaga. He reached the capital on October 7, 1184, and soon pushed on to the central provinces and thence towards Suō and Nagato, at the western extremity of the main island. He thus had in his rear part of the Taira army, since Munemori, the hapless son of Kiyomori, remained at Yashima with Antoku, the frail hostage to fortune given by the Taira clan, a sickly child carrying a heavy load of fate.

Noriyori soon found himself in a difficult position. If he proceeded he left in his rear the force based upon Yashima, while before him lay the Inland Sea route to the Straits of Shimonoseki, where, based upon the island of Hikoshima, stood the remainder of the Taira army under the command of Tomomori, who controlled the sea road. He could neither advance nor retreat. Moreover, since the Taira were traditionally powerful all along the way by water from Fukuwara to Shimonoseki, it was certain that their adherents or sympathizers for the most part would refuse supplies to an invading army. Noriyori was therefore in real and increasing peril, lacking food for the sustenance of his troops and boats for their transport. He appealed earnestly to Yoritomo for advice and help, but without much success; Yoritomo, himself not a very good general, gave advice, but could not offer material support. It was from a friendly magnate in Suō province that Noriyori at length obtained a supply of rice, and presently a local family came to his aid with some dozens of war junks,[4] by means of which he was able to transport his army across the straits to Bungo, where he landed in spite of some local resistance.

But he was still without enough supplies and his captains were becoming dispirited, some even urging retreat. He did not feel able to strike at Tomomori, who of course had local supporters; and his decision was perhaps governed by fear of the swift current that pours through the straits, making it difficult to control vessels in their passage from one side to the other and so giving the defenders a very real advantage. Yoritomo seems to have understood the difficulties of Noriyori's position, and treated his complaints with sympathy.

On New Year's Day of 1185 a letter from Noriyori, sent by fast courier, was brought to Yoritomo in Kamakura. (It took the courier about six weeks to reach Kamakura from the western extremity of the

---

[4] These were probably piratical craft in times of peace.

main island.) The version of this letter, and of later correspondence, given in the *Azuma Kagami* seems to be quite authentic. It throws an interesting light not only on the military situation but also on Yoritomo's character. Noriyori's message asks for the urgent despatch of ships, food, horses, and other supplies, and dwells on the difficulty of keeping his officers contented and loyal. Yoritomo replies in friendly language, saying that he is preparing to send everything required, but pointing out that the Taira people are keeping a close watch, so that it is necessary to take precautions. Should they discover the time of despatch and the route by which supplies are to be carried, the Minamoto might be disgraced forever by the loss of their own munitions of war. Noriyori must therefore be patient. Meanwhile he should make great efforts to conciliate and humour his discontented commanders and their men, while taking care in his dealings with local magnates not to offend possible allies and supporters. He reminds Noriyori that his cousin Yoshinaka came to a bad end because he had planned violence against sacred personages, and enjoins him to give constant attention to the safety of the Emperor Antoku and of the Three Treasures—the Regalia.

The tone of this and other missives shows a clear understanding of the situation in western Japan. While urging his brother to take resolute military action at the right moment, Yoritomo was careful to dwell upon the need for calm and caution, for he understood the diplomatic art. It may well be that he was pleased that Noriyori did not act without consulting him, and displeased by Yoshitsune's dash and independence. Ultimately, however, after Noriyori had spent half a year in ineffectual campaigning, Yoritomo overcame his jealous scruples and commissioned Yoshitsune to march against the Taira. This was approximately in the month of March 1185.

Making all allowance for the enthusiasm of Minamoto chroniclers, it is evident that Yoshitsune had a genius for offensive warfare. He had displayed it in his brilliant ruse at Ichinotani, and now he saw that only swift and decisive action could succeed in the situation before him. To delay and hesitate was to give the Taira comfort as well as military advantage. He reached a point on the Naniwa River in Settsu on March 20, and with characteristic energy he planned to embark for Yashima that very evening at dusk. The cloistered Emperor was afraid to be left in the capital without protection and sought to detain him, but Yoshitsune persisted in his plan. He was delayed a little by a gale of wind which destroyed many of the vessels prepared for the transport of his troops; but long before dawn on the following day, undeterred by this misfortune, he set out with only a hundred men or so in a few small craft and speeding before the gale reached the opposite shore in four hours instead of the leisurely two or three days of the regular ferryboats. Landing at Katsura in Awa province on Shikoku, his small force rode swiftly through the night and by daybreak next morning had reached a point opposite the Yashima temporary palace. The Taira, it appears, had prepared only for an attack by sea. When they saw fires, kindled purposely by Yoshitsune, ablaze in their rear they supposed that a large force was approaching by land. Without stopping to ascertain the size of the attack, they abandoned the so-called palace and took to their boats with the Emperor Antoku. Pursued to the water's edge by Yoshitsune, they stopped for a while and fought off the attackers, but their resistance had no real determination behind it and they presently fled westwards to the Straits of Shimonoseki, a distance of about two hundred miles.

Yoshitsune with his little force made no attempt to pursue them, but devoted himself to strengthening his own position in and around Yashima, so as to have a dependable base. He was soon joined by some local supporters and, more valuable, a prominent eastern warrior named Kajiwara Kagetoki who furnished a number (140?) of ships. But Yoshitsune still had a difficult problem to solve; he had two hundred miles to cover before catching up with the Taira, who were now at Dannoura in the Straits of Shimonoseki. It was a month before he made a move, and then he had the good fortune to find a very useful ally in a local official of the province of Suō, who was familiar with shipping

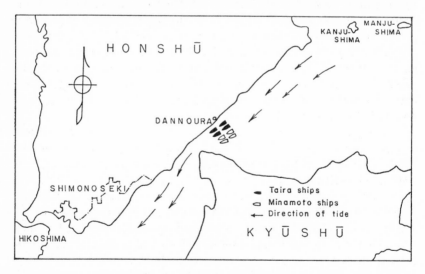

Chart illustrating the last phase of the battle of Dannoura, from 2:30 P.M. to 4 P.M.
on April 25, 1185

In the forenoon the advantage lay with the Taira fleet, which was driven towards the rocky islands of Kanju and Manju by the incoming tide. But as the tide turned, the Minamoto fleet took the offensive and, having the weather position, pressed the Taira vessels on to the shore at Dannoura, where they were either wrecked or swept out to the western channel by the tide, now running at eight knots. Yoshitsune had ordered his marksmen to shoot the Taira steersmen, neglecting other targets.

business and procured a number of vessels for him. At length Yoshitsune was able to set forth by water from Yashima to Suō. There he was joined by a member of the Miura family, one Yoshizumi, who was familiar with the currents of the straits.

The Taira were now established at Hikoshima, where Munemori and Tomomori had joined forces. They were at home on the water, and they came out boldly to meet the Minamoto, who were approaching from Ōtsu, an anchorage off the town of Chōfu—the more boldly since their retreat by land was cut off by Noriyori, and they now had no choice but to fight. After a delay of twenty-four hours (which is not accounted for) the two fleets joined battle early on April 25, 1185. The result was a total defeat of the Taira.

It is at first sight hard to understand why a sea fight should have been lost by the side which had by far the greater maritime experience. But the Taira had already lost many of their ships in action or in storms, while several chieftains in the west upon whose help they had counted had gone over to the Minamoto and put war vessels at their disposal, with trained crews. Consequently the Minamoto fleet was not much inferior in numbers and quality to that of the Taira, and although Yoshitsune had no knowledge of naval warfare he had the advantage of an acute strategic insight and a quick eye for tactical chances. Moreover the Taira fleet, according to some accounts, included a group of vessels commanded by a Shikoku warrior (named Taguchi) who in the middle of the action struck his flag and went over to the other side. Thus during the action the Minamoto may have had at their disposal as many as three hundred craft, and the Taira between four and five hundred. But these figures are mere conjectures, and are not of much importance, since the result of the battle was not due to any disparity in numbers but rather to an error in judgment on the part of the Taira commander Tomomori.

For some unaccountable reason Tomomori chose to fight in the straits, where the tide-rip is rapid and treacherous at most times, to such a degree that even modern vessels have to exercise the greatest caution there. It is possible that he hoped, by taking advantage of the morning tide, to get the weather gauge of the enemy and bear down upon them on the rapid flow, which they would have the greatest difficulty in breasting. But though the Taira ships did well, they were unsuccessful during the forenoon, and by midday the rush of the tide had turned, putting the Taira at a disadvantage. In a short time they fell into disorder and were utterly defeated. The young Emperor perished, with most of the Taira nobles, including Kiyomori's widow. This was the end of Taira resistance, and thenceforward the Minamoto family was supreme in Japan.

The causes of the failure of the Taira are not in much doubt. They are the usual causes, irresolution and incompetence. First of all was the absence of determined leadership after the death of Kiyomori. Of his sons Shigemori, who died before him, had been a man of high character but lacking strength of purpose; Tomomori had courage but only moderate ability; Munemori was weak and incompetent; Shigehira was a good soldier, but his judgment was poor. None of these men inspired trust or loyalty, and since even their most steadfast supporters had not full confidence in their capacity to lead and to conquer, it is not surprising that many waverers either remained neutral or took sides with the Minamoto on grounds of prudence. The most serious reverse suffered by the Taira because of this lack of confidence was the cloistered Go-Shirakawa's refusal to side with them. It is a curious and valuable testimony to the importance of the abdicated and cloistered sovereigns that, although the Taira had charge of the person of the young Emperor Antoku and with him of the Regalia, the very symbols of legitimacy, yet without the assent of the cloistered sovereign they could not claim full authority for their political or military action. It was in fact Minamoto generals (Yoshinaka and Yukiiye) who obtained a commission to punish the Taira from Go-Shirakawa, thus acquiring for their campaigns a certificate of legitimacy which, strange as it may appear, was important in the eyes of even the most unruly warriors.

It followed from this distribution of political support that many provincial warriors, when obliged to decide which side they should take, were inclined in favour of the power installed in the capital and approved by the cloistered sovereign. Thus at the end of 1183, when the Court moved westward after the defeat of the Taira armies in the east, the Taira leaders found that their influence in Kyūshū (and elsewhere) was not so widespread as they had supposed; and they were driven by indifference or by positive resistance to enter upon a melancholy pilgrimage from place to place until at last they had to turn back and take refuge in Yashima, only a few dozen miles across the water from the former Taira stronghold at Fukuwara. As for Taira clansmen in eastern Japan, they were by no means uniformly loyal to their ancestral house. Many thought it the part of wisdom to throw in their lot with the Minamoto. These are facts which must be borne in mind in considering the results of the defeat of the Taira armies. It did not mean the destruction of the Taira family, but only the end of Taira dominance at the capital and, of course, the seizure of the domains of those who had taken arms against the victors.

Yoshitsune's despatch announcing his victory is suitably laconic. It reads as follows:

*

"On the 24th day of last month over 840 of our war vessels put out into the Akamagaseki Channel in the province of Nagato. They were met by over 500 vessels of the Taira.[5] In the afternoon the battle ended in the defeat of the rebels.

"The former Emperor sank to the bottom of the sea.

"The following were drowned: [here a short list of Taira celebrities, including Kiyomori's widow, Nii no Ama].

"The Lady Kenreimon-In and the young prince [Antoku's mother and his younger brother] were saved.

"Prisoners: [here a short list of about twenty Taira leaders, men and women, including Munemori].

"In addition further prisoners were taken, men and women, of whom a list will be presented later.

"As to the sacred Seal, it has been found. But the Sword is lost, and a search is being made."

✻

No wonder that the great romance, the *Heike Monogatari*, opens and closes with the tolling of a bell, for its theme is the fall of the mighty.

[5] These figures are difficult to accept. Either they include the smallest craft or they are exaggerated by the compilers of the *Azuma Kagami*.

CHAPTER XV

THE EASTERN WARRIORS

1. *Yoritomo and His Adherents*

SO FAR we have examined the history of the twelfth century mainly in the light of events as they appeared to the aristocratic society at the courts of the reigning emperors and the cloistered sovereigns, without paying much attention to the hard life led by the settlers in the eastern provinces, which favoured the growth of a warlike spirit. The story of the gradual retreat of the Taira forces and their ultimate destruction has perhaps given the impression that their opponents, under the direction of Yoritomo, were a powerful and united community that could not in the long run be resisted. This is true, but only in the sense that the fortunes of the Taira were declining while those of the Minamoto were rising. At the time of the opening skirmishes in the long-drawn-out struggle between the two clans, when Yoritomo was obliged to retreat from Ishibashiyama (August 1180), the Minamoto can hardly be said to have existed as an organized body capable of devising and carrying out a policy or winning a war. Before the Taira could be displaced or destroyed it was necessary for Yoritomo, the heir to his father's position as chieftain, to establish his authority over a wide area and to build up a military force from elements contributed by warrior families who either owed some loyalty to the Minamoto or could be persuaded on grounds of self-interest to share with him the task of breaking the power of the Taira leaders. In other words, the Minamoto clan from the point of view of national politics was an idea and not a fact. It remained an idea until Yoritomo gave it a real existence by furnishing it with organized military strength, which could be exerted at his command.

It was necessary to break not only the power but also the pride of the Taira. Their pride, it may be remarked, was of a lofty order: one of Kiyomori's sons said that anybody, whether man or woman, monk or nun, who did not belong to his clan, was a nobody. Yoritomo too had intense family pride, and this no doubt was an incentive to action, since he came from a noble house—the Seiwa Genji—and his father with his two eldest brothers had been condemned to a humiliating death by Kiyomori. But for all his pride, he was first and last a hard, ambitious man, whose hunger for power was overwhelming. There is no doubt that he planned from early manhood to restore the fortunes of his house and to preside over all the warriors of the east. But for his own immediate ends he was certainly prepared to forget the past and to come to terms with the Taira, as we know from his memorial of 1181 to Go-Shirakawa.

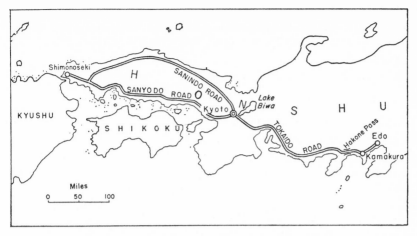

The great highroads east and west from the capital

His position early in 1180, when Prince Mochihito sent out a call to all the Minamoto warriors in the east, was by no means strong. He had lived in exile for twenty years, planning for the future but taking care not to arouse suspicions in the capital. His family home was in Izu province, and he had formed a close relationship with some of the leading landowners and warriors in that province and in Sagami. He had to proceed with caution, for there was as yet no clear division between Taira and Minamoto interests in the east, and a false step, a mistaken confidence, might reveal his intentions to Kiyomori. Many of Yoritomo's associates at this time were guided as much by self-interest as by clan loyalty. They wanted to enlarge their own domains and to extend their own influence. Consequently we find prominent among them the names of Hōjō, Miura, Chiba, and Doi, families of Taira, not Minamoto, descent. Chiba, for example, was descended from Chiba no Suke, son of the rebel Taira Tadatsune, whose pursuit in 1031 by Minamoto Yorinobu has already been related (Chapter XII).

These men and their sons gave indispensable support to Yoritomo, who could also count upon some (though by no means all) of the influential men of Minamoto stock settled in Izu and the surrounding provinces. Among his Minamoto adherents was one Sasaki Hideyoshi, who had supported Yoshitomo at the time of the Heiji revolt and then, incurring Taira displeasure, had lost his hereditary estate in Ōmi. He set out from home with the intention of appealing to his uncle, the powerful Fujiwara Hidehira, in the northern stronghold at Hiraizumi, but on the way he stopped in Sagami, where he attracted the attention of Shibuya Shigekuni, a local landholder, steward of a large manor. He stayed in this place and married the landholder's daughter, and his sons as they grew up entered the service of Yoritomo.

It was in such ways as these that a number of families in the east gradually came within the orbit of Yoritomo and thus added to the number of active Minamoto adherents. But Taira prestige was still strong, and some of Yoritomo's neighbours and acquaintances urged caution. When rumours of the rising of Prince Mochihito reached the eastern provinces, an important landholder settled in Sagami, Ōba Kagechika by name, called upon Shigekuni and warned him that Sasaki's sons should take care not to get involved in Yoritomo's designs.

For some time past, while living quietly in the province of Izu under the care of his official guardian Hōjō Tokimasa, Yoritomo had been receiving regular secret reports about political events in the capital from one Miyoshi Yasunobu, a nephew of his old nurse and at that time an official in the household of the Empress Toku-ko. He had already received news of Prince Mochihito's summons from Yukiiye, his uncle, who early in June 1180 brought him a copy of the written order (dated some three weeks before) explaining that it was to be first perused by Yoritomo himself and then sent on to other important members of the Minamoto clan. The scene is described in the opening pages of the *Azuma Kagami*. Yoritomo wore ceremonial dress and, having bowed in the direction of the Hachiman shrine,[1] respectfully opened and perused the letter.

Soon after this, news reached Yoritomo of the abortive rising in Kyoto and the death of Mochihito and Yorimasa. Miyoshi and other friends at the capital, in view of the Taira's announced intention of crushing any movement launched in response to the Prince's summons, advised Yoritomo to go into hiding for some time. Hōjō Tokimasa, his trusted counsellor, was also against hasty action. This was still in 1180, when the position of Kiyomori might well have seemed unassailable. But Yoritomo felt that it was time for him to act. He set about strengthening the Minamoto position in the east, sending a call to arms to all the clansmen whom he felt able to trust. The response was encouraging, for in many warrior households the old clan relationship of lord and vassal, master and man, still persisted, though often in secret. Their leader now decided to try his strength and the fidelity of his supporters in a preliminary encounter, choosing as the object of attack a Taira official who was making himself disliked in Izu by his arbitrary conduct. This was in August 1180.

The trial engagement proved successful and Yoritomo, reading it as an auspicious omen, felt encouraged to go further. It was only a few days afterwards that he moved with a small force of about two hundred across the border into the Hakone mountains. He took up a position at a place called Ishibashiyama, where, as we have seen, he met with a severe reverse, thanks to the intervention of Ōba Kagechika, the warrior who not long before had warned Sasaki's sons.

---

[1] The Iwashimizu Hachiman shrine is at Otokoyama, a few miles southwest of Kyoto (see map, p. 100).

Yoritomo had hoped by this bold action to persuade others to join him, but he was disappointed and in fact barely escaped with his life. His followers scattered—reluctantly and tearfully, the chronicles say—leaving him to escape without attracting attention. He reached the province of Awa about a week later, where he was met by his comrades who had eluded pursuit, Hōjō Tokimasa, Miura Yoshizumi, and others whose fortunes were now bound up with his. But neither Awa nor Shimōsa was suitable as a base, and Yoritomo decided to move. He sent word to certain well-disposed landowners, asking them to contribute armed men for his support, and went forward to meet them. By these means he got together a force of picked men, a few hundred, which included the sons of Chiba Tsunetane. The exact meeting place is not known, but it was probably the town of Chiba. Thence he moved forward to the Sumida River, where he was met by Hirotsune, a Taira warrior of the province of Kazusa, commanding a large force. There was some doubt about this chieftain's attitude, but he offered his support and later rendered valuable service. Yoritomo never fully trusted him, however, and had him assassinated later at Kamakura.

This incident, while revealing the ruthless side of Yoritomo's character, shows that he was gradually extending his authority over warriors in most if not all of the eastern provinces. It also shows that he would have failed in his ambitious designs if he had depended only upon Minamoto allies. For one thing, many of his kinsmen were unreliable friends, and he was able to deal with such opponents as the independent Minamoto notable Satake Hideyoshi only with the help of Taira Hirotsune, who brought him some 20,000 men at a crucial moment in his career, when he had only a few hundred trusted followers.

This was in the autumn of 1180. With growing confidence he now sent Hōjō Tokimasa to the powerful family of Takeda in the province of Kai with the message that he had under his flag the best warriors of the east and was about to enter the province of Suruga with them to await the Taira army. The Takeda and other families of Kai were to bring their adherents and join him. On or about October 22, he crossed the Sumida into Musashi. By this time (according to the *Azuma Kagami*) he had at his disposal over 30,000 men, including contingents from most of the leading warrior families of the east. At the end of the month he moved into Sagami, where he paid reverence to the shrine of Hachiman, the War God worshipped by his ancestors; and after a short stay at Kamakura he left orders for houses to be built there for his headquarters and started on an expedition westward, intending to join battle with the Taira army which he knew was approaching. His army crossed over the high Ashigara pass and marched on to take up a position on the left bank of the Fujikawa, a rapid stream entering the sea at Iwabuchi in Suruga and marking a strategical frontier between eastern and central Japan. Here he was joined by strong contingents from the mountainous provinces of Kai and Kōtsuke, lying to the north of Suruga, which province they had cleared of opposition.

The military and also the political position of Yoritomo had vastly improved since his defeat at Ishibashiyama. For a time, he had been in doubt about the real intentions of some of the great warlords, such as Takeda of Kai and Nitta of Kōtsuke. Their defection or even their hesitation would have changed the attitude of a number of smaller chieftains; but Yoritomo was on safe ground once those two leaders, under the persuasion of Hōjō Tokimasa, had made up their minds to accept the orders of the Minamoto and to march with them against the Taira. It was, in fact, the arrival of Takeda's force, or part of it, in the rear of the Taira that ensured a Minamoto victory in the battle that took place on November 10, 1180. Minamoto forces were to suffer some defeats thereafter, and as we have seen there was not complete loyalty and trust within the clan; but the majority of the warriors in the eastern provinces accepted the leadership of Yoritomo and together composed a military organization of great extent and power.

After the battle of Fujikawa he was prepared to move westwards in pursuit of the Taira, who fled so rapidly that their retreating army began to pour into the capital about twelve days later; but he was advised by his generals that he must first make sure of his base by pacifying or destroying certain families that either were hostile to him or at any rate wished to preserve their independence and not to take sides. One such family was that of Satake Hideyoshi, a warrior of Minamoto descent established in Hitachi, who was in touch with the Taira though not active on their behalf. Yoritomo attacked and defeated this bold chieftain, but never completely subdued him.

The Satake family descended from a brother of Yoshiiye, Yoritomo's direct forebear, and therefore they were of as good Minamoto origin as Yoritomo himself. There was another Minamoto house which was not friendly to Yoritomo, the Shida family of Hitachi, led by an uncle of Yoritomo named Yoshihiro, who had at one time planned to attack Yoritomo in Kamakura. The important Ashikaga family, also of Minamoto stock, was hostile to Yoritomo. Thus Yoritomo was faced with many difficulties. Though in general such stubborn antagonism was rare, he saw that he must firmly establish himself in the eight eastern provinces before turning his offensive strength to the destruction ·of the Taira. Within a short time his principal rivals or opponents in those provinces had come to terms. The important houses of Nitta and Satomi among others now accepted his leadership, and he was master in his own house but for the disobedience of his jealous cousin Yoshinaka. He had only to defeat the Taira to become the strongest man in the whole country, ready to turn military triumph into political mastery.

Indeed in historical retrospect the war between the clans appears less as a series of bloody encounters and romantic episodes than as a prelude to far-reaching social and political changes. The Minamoto were not content with merely transferring the political control which had once been exercised as of right by the greatest noble houses to the victorious warrior class; they went on to mould this class into an independent, highly organized society with its own laws and its own standards of behaviour. They were no longer the servants of aristocratic statesmen, but their masters.

For an understanding of the nature of this change, it is useful to go back a little and trace the main lines of development (already foreshadowed in Chapter XII) of the *buke*, the warrior families, as a social class. At one time regarded almost with contempt, they had been gradually improving their social position since the days when they were little more than husbandmen armed for self-defence or mercenaries employed by the nobility. Naturally they gained more respect as their services became more important—and in some instances indispensable—to the civilian authorities whom they obeyed and protected. Perhaps the dividing line between the subordination of military to civilian officers and the subsequent growth of a military primacy can be placed at the time of the Hōgen disturbance of 1156, when a dynastic issue was solved by military measures. The question may not have been of real importance, but it aroused violent antagonism between two parties; and the incident demonstrated very clearly to the statesmen concerned that they depended for the execution of their policies upon the support of armed men under the command of warrior chieftains.

This fact was perceived by the first great Japanese historian, the monk Jien, who (in his work *Gukanshō*, written about 1220) observed that after the Hōgen affair the power of the warrior was established because armed clashes, which had once been confined to provincial disturbances, were now taking place in the capital as a means of settling disputes between parties endeavouring to control the central government.

Of course the members of the ancient noble houses did not forthwith abandon their superior attitude. On the contrary, they took the line that warlike behaviour was barbarous, fit only for beasts. They were appalled to find that such a disgusting thing as bloodshed should sully the very home of learning and civil accomplishment. Therefore, though the result of the Hōgen dispute was determined in action, the warriors themselves were not the victors. Their warlike reputation was much enhanced, but they were not yet in a position to build a new society or to change the form and purpose of the government. Nor is there any evidence that, as a class, they had in their minds such plans or notions. The tradition of civilian supremacy persisted, and the social pride of the great families was but little diminished; so that when the Regent Motofusa, a Fujiwara of high degree, was reported to be about to marry a Taira lady, the misalliance seemed so dreadful to the great aristocrats that one of them said: "This is a mad world. There are no words for it."

But such a moral ascendancy (if it may be so called) of the civilian of high birth over the soldier of great power could not survive the growth of confidence which the warriors felt as they found that no government was secure without their support. They knew that their day was soon to come. Yet so long as one military clan was at odds with another the warrior class, being disunited, could not assert its full strength. It was therefore not until Minamoto had defeated Taira that the new military society took shape and the foundations of a new military government were laid.

2. *The First Phase of Military Rule*

Yoritomo in the first stages of erecting his edifice of power does not appear as an innovator, still less as a revolutionary. He respected, or at least professed to respect, tradition. For a few years after the flight of the Taira from the capital in August 1183, though the success of the Minamoto arms seemed then assured, he felt that he must proceed with caution. It was necessary or at any rate prudent for him, while asserting his authority in all purely military matters, to gain the approval of the Throne for any measures which he thought it necessary to introduce on other than purely military grounds.

The situation was awkward. Yoshinaka had entered the capital in the late summer of 1183 and the excesses of his rough soldiery had soon caused much distress among the citizens, while the nobles—and indeed even the cloistered Emperor Go-Shirakawa—were outraged by the confiscation of their estates. Public opinion was therefore in favour of inviting Yoritomo himself to come and restore order, and Go-Shirakawa sent a message to Kamakura, begging Yoritomo to show himself in the capital city. The invitation was despatched in August 1183 and the messenger returned some six weeks later with a memorial from Yoritomo. This reply made no mention of the invitation (though Yoritomo later explained that he thought it unwise to leave the eastern provinces, where he still had rivals and enemies who required careful handling); indeed it was couched in very respectful language, and seems to have impressed the Court by its moderation. It suggested that properties seized by the Taira clan from religious bodies or members of the royal family or great officers of state should be returned to their rightful owners. Yoritomo also proposed that members of the Taira party who had deserted to the Minamoto side—what he would describe as the loyalist side—should be spared the death penalty. He himself, he said, knew what it was to be a refugee on the losing side.

Yoritomo's memorial was in fact a rather false and unpleasant document, but it encouraged Go-Shirakawa to press him further; and after repeated appeals Yoritomo sent a force commanded by Yoshitsune and Noriyori to attack Yoshinaka. This was at the end of 1183, and in the first month of 1184 Yoshinaka was defeated and killed. He had been made Shōgun (Commander-in-chief) by the Emperor only a few days before, and according to the *Heike Monogatari*'s dramatic account of his death in battle he rode into his last fight proclaiming himself "Master of the Horse, Lord of Iyo, and General of the Rising Sun, Yoshinaka of the Minamoto."

At this point in his political gyrations the In became alarmed, and felt that he must at all costs make up to Yoritomo, since some time before he had issued an edict, at Yoshinaka's instance, ordering him to chastise Yoritomo as a rebel. His Majesty went so far as to say that if Yoritomo would not come to Kyoto he would make an imperial progress to Kamakura. This was such an unprecedented gesture that it was described by high officers of his government as madness. Go-Shirakawa was not mad, but he was not at all wise; and he was excessively addicted to intrigue and conspiracy, to what he thought were ingenious combinations, so that he was always struggling to get out of troubles of his own making.

After the victory of Ichinotani, Yoshitsune returned in triumph to Kyoto, and Go-Shirakawa might well have been satisfied with his presence there as a guarantee of tranquillity. But having suffered from Yoshinaka he naturally did not care much for generals flushed with victory; and it was perhaps on that account that he proposed to visit Kamakura. However, Yoshitsune's reputation was now very high in Court circles, and Yoritomo informed the vacillating In that he wished Yoshitsune to be given an imperial commission to subdue the Taira rebels once and for all. The In appears to have changed his mind about Yoshitsune, for he was now reluctant to send him away. He argued that the capital would be denuded of protection if Yoshitsune left, and he granted certain titles and honours to him, including the right of access to his own person.

This behaviour annoyed Yoritomo, who had already announced that it was for him, as head of the military caste, to recommend awards for good service. So far as concerned his own services to the state, of course he would leave the matter to His Majesty's choice, but he had no desire for lavish recompense. This was in reply to a hint of great honours to come, which Go-Shirakawa had felt obliged to throw out by way of making up for his commission to Yoshinaka, which he now claimed he had issued under extreme pressure.

Yoritomo was angered by Yoshitsune's popularity in the capital. He suspected or pretended to suspect that his brother's behaviour was treason to himself, for Yoshitsune, who owed loyalty to Kamakura, was attracted by the glitter of royal favour and no doubt deep in palace intrigue. Such conduct went against the unity of the warrior caste and was therefore alarming to Yoritomo, whose most urgent task was to consolidate his own authority. Indeed it was not only for fear of risings by disaffected barons that he declined the invitations of Go-Shirakawa to visit the capital. He stayed of set purpose in the centre of military power, the eastern provinces, where he occupied himself in building up piece by piece an administrative system for the control and guidance of the warriors. He sent expeditions westward against the retreating Taira, giving the supreme command to Noriyori, but he himself was looking to the future when, the Taira once destroyed, he would be in effect the ruler of the whole country.

Meanwhile Noriyori's slow pressure and Yoshitsune's brilliant tactics brought about the victory at Yashima, which was followed with unexpected speed by the ultimate downfall of the enemy at Dannoura in April 1185. News of this last battle reached Yoritomo at Kamakura on May 12, and is said to have left him speechless with surprise. On the following day he set about planning the action he should take immediately after the end of the fighting. He sent Noriyori to stay for a time in Kyūshū, where he was to take possession of all Taira manors—an order which showed that Yoritomo was already thinking of rewards for loyal vassals, knowing that property was to be the basis of his power. He ordered Yoshitsune to get hold of the missing Regalia, and to bring them with the most important prisoners back to the capital. At the same time all Kamakura vassals were strictly commanded to eschew intercourse with the Court. Any Kantō warrior who accepted an appointment or gift from the Throne was no longer regarded as loyal. He could stay where he was and serve the Court, but if he set foot east of the Kuromata River in Owari his estates would be seized and he would be executed.

It is clear from these and other acts of Yoritomo at this time that he made it a fundamental rule of the society over which he claimed to preside that its members owed obedience to him and to nobody else. On this principle he was firm in all his dealings with the Court, respectful but determined. Thus on May 27, when Yoshitsune arrived in Kyoto with his captives (from Munemori downward), Go-Shirakawa at once declared that Munemori must be put to death; but Yoritomo said No, and prayed His Majesty to send Yoshitsune with all his prisoners to Kamakura.

Yoshitsune left Kyoto early in June and could have reached Kamakura by the end of the month, but he was halted (at Sakamori stage) by Hōjō Tokimasa, who took charge of the prisoners while Yoshitsune was left at Koshigoye, a small village outside Kamakura, and told that he must not enter the town. He sent a letter to Ōye Hiromoto, swearing that he was loyal, but Yoritomo refused to see him. After Munemori and others had been interrogated by Yoritomo, they were handed back to Yoshitsune with orders that they should be taken to Kyoto. But when on the return journey the party had reached Shinowara in Ōmi province, several days' travel from Kamakura, emissaries sent by Yoritomo caught up with them and struck off the heads of Munemori and his son. The reason for this brutal act is not clear, but perhaps Yoritomo, having made his point, chose to afford Go-Shirakawa the opportunity of carrying out his original design. The heads were publicly displayed at the execution ground in Kyoto. Tokitada and the other remaining prisoners were exiled, with the exception of Shigehira, who was handed over to the monks of the Tōdaiji at their demand and killed by them in revenge for his action in setting fire to their monastery in January 1181, when almost all of the buildings of the Tōdaiji and the Kōfukuji had been destroyed by his Taira troops in revenge for the monasteries' support of Mochihito's revolt. Nor did the Minamoto vengeance end with the prisoners. At the end of the year (1185) Hōjō Tokimasa, then in Kyoto as the Shōgun's deputy, was ordered to seek out all Taira refugees. The children of Shigemori and Munemori were captured. According to one version of the *Heike Monogatari* the small children were drowned or buried alive, the older ones decapitated. Such was the dreadful cruelty allowed by the warriors' code. Kenreimon-In, Antoku's mother, was spared and spent the rest of her life in a poor nunnery at Ohara, not far from the capital.

The relations between Yoshitsune and Yoritomo meanwhile grew worse and worse. The honours which Go-Shirakawa had awarded to Yoshitsune, and Yoshitsune's enjoyment of Court life, duly reported by Ōye Hiromoto to Kamakura, had served to increase Yoritomo's suspicions and his determination to exercise firm control over his brother's movements. He would have deprived him of his command, but he was sensible enough not to lose the services of a military genius on mere grounds of private resentment. He had gone so far as to attach to Yoshitsune's force a spy in the person of Kajiwara Kagetoki, a mean, treacherous vassal who was useful in such base offices and whom Yoshitsune despised. Kagetoki's reports to Kamakura encouraged Yoritomo to believe that Yoshitsune was planning a coup against him, and it was mainly for that reason that he was denied admission to Kamakura. Yoritomo even took back a number of Taira manors that he had assigned to Yoshitsune.

In many quarters there was sympathy with Yoshitsune, though it did him little good.[2] It was a byword in the capital that he was being meanly treated, but there was no one of any consequence to stand up for him. Among his friends was the luckless Yukiiye, whose friendship was by no means advantageous, for he was generally neither trusted nor respected. After taking refuge from his pursuers in province after province, Yukiiye had ventured to emerge and to appear discreetly at the Court of Go-Shirakawa. On one such occasion he saw and no doubt conversed with Yoshitsune. These facts were duly reported to Kama-

[2] There was a kind of proverbial saying, "Hōgan hiiki no hikitaoshi," which means "Like Yoshitsune, ruined by his sympathizers."

kura, probably in highly coloured versions. Whether Yoritomo was genuinely alarmed it is not possible to say, but he did promptly (early September 1185) order one of his Minamoto supporters in the province of Ōmi, Sasaki Sadatsuna by name, to attack Yukiiye, who by himself was certainly not dangerous. It is likely that Yoritomo was using him as a bait for Yoshitsune, and as was to be expected, Yukiiye asked Yoshitsune for protection. He cunningly played upon Yoshitsune's outraged feelings and suggested that the best way to deal with their situation was to anticipate Yoritomo's action and take the offensive.

At this point certain of Go-Shirakawa's favourites (including the Minister Takashina and a Police Commissioner named Taira Tomoyasu), men who were not well thought of at Kamakura, ranged themselves on Yoshitsune's side. Before long a rumour went around that Yoshitsune planned a revolt in alliance with Yukiiye. Yoritomo found this an excellent excuse for action. He sent envoys to Kyoto instructing his representatives there to press the Court to hasten the departure of the Taira captives condemned to exile and at the same time to order Yoshitsune to attack Yukiiye. When Yoritomo's messengers reached Kyoto they called upon Yoshitsune, who feigned illness and would not receive them. They called again next day, and Yoshitsune appeared, displaying signs of suffering. He said that he could do nothing until his health was restored, and he took care that they should see marks of the moxa, which he had caused to be applied in several visible places. They were asked to report his answer to Yoritomo.

Yoritomo decided upon drastic action. After discussion with his advisers it was decided that the best course would be to take Yoshitsune unawares and kill him. Who was to be chosen for this task? Nobody seemed ready to risk an encounter with so great a champion. At length, since no warrior came forward, a renegade monk named Tosabō Shōshun offered to do the work. He left Kamakura early in November (1185) with a troop of fewer than a hundred mounted men, and arrived in Kyoto some two weeks later. He attacked Yoshitsune in his Horikawa mansion by night, and met with a very hot reception. His company of assassins was driven off with great loss and he himself was captured in flight and killed in the Rokujō river bed, a favourite spot for the execution of criminals.

As it happened, that very morning there had been a discussion at Go-Shirakawa's Court about whether an order for the punishment of Yoritomo should be issued. On the following day Yoshitsune and Yukiiye were given a commission to proceed against Yoritomo. It is not clear whether this was a serious order, or merely a gesture to placate Yoshitsune; but the Court must have known that neither of the two generals had any considerable following. Both had to make a great effort to collect adherents in the home provinces and the west, and most of the warriors approached by them had doubts about the intention of Go-Shirakawa and his advisers. Carefully watched as they were by the

agents of Kamakura, they were loth to respond to Yoshitsune's call.
Even his own soldiers showed signs of deserting, and when the cloistered
sovereign saw that there was little prospect of a successful rising against
Kamakura he became alarmed and began to think of mollifying Yoritomo in some way. But he was riding the tiger, and could not get off.
Yoshitsune and Yukiiye told him that they must go to the west to collect
new forces there. They asked for appointments which would produce
revenue for that purpose, and he gave them lucrative offices in Kyūshū
and Shikoku, together with written injunctions (*kudashibumi*) to settlers in those regions, ordering them to obey the holders of his commission.

At the end of November (1185) the two generals left Kyoto with
about two hundred horse. After beating off attacks on the way, they
reached the shore of Daimotsu, in Settsu province, and embarked for
Shikoku. A fierce storm wrecked most of their vessels, but they themselves were able to get ashore in Izumi. Here they were separated. According to the accepted legend, Yoshitsune with his mistress Shizuka
and his henchman Benkei and two other followers went to the nearby
Tennōji monastery, and then disappeared. Yukiiye also vanished, and
the two never met again.

A day or two after their departure from the capital Yoritomo had
led a large force into Suruga province, but he halted on learning that
Yoshitsune had left. His vanguard under Oyama Tomomasa and Yūki
Tomomitsu had already reached Kyoto, and it was easy for them to
persuade the terrified Go-Shirakawa to reverse his edicts and forthwith
to issue to Yoritomo an order to punish the two fugitives. Yoritomo,
having plainly shown his anger to the In, returned to Kamakura to
complete his plans for the foundation of a dominant military society
under his own direction.

He disliked, even hated, Yoshitsune, but it is difficult to believe that
he really feared him after the failure of the two discontented generals
to find support. He did however see a very useful purpose in pretending
that Yoshitsune was a dangerous rebel, for it gave him an excellent
excuse for certain political and economic measures which were necessary for his own ends. In December 1185, after consulting Ōye Hiromoto and other experts, he proclaimed the levy of a contribution of rice,
a so-called "commissariat tax" (*hyōrō-mai*), which was ostensibly to
furnish the cost of campaigns against Yoshitsune, an enemy of the state
which it was Yoritomo's duty to protect.[3]

In general Yoritomo was careful to observe the proper forms of respect and obedience in his communications to the Throne. For example,
a memorial to Go-Shirakawa In, dated December 1185, says in effect:
"I venture humbly to present to Your Majesty a statement of my views

[3] It was fixed at five measures of rice for each *tan* of rice land, and was equivalent to about two per cent of the average yield.

on the present situation, with my recommendations. I propose that a council of ten leading noblemen be appointed to consider this plan." A few months later he wrote a letter to the members of this council, expressing a hope that they would be guided in their deliberations by a sense of justice and rectitude. For some time after this he continued to request approval for military enterprises that he wished to undertake.

It is significant that he was scrupulous in observing those forms even after the issue of a commission to Yoshitsune, which had caused him intense anger. The In, fearing his revenge, had once again sent to Kamakura to say that he had acted under duress. Yoritomo in his reply brushed this aside: he was trying to bring order and peace to the country while His Majesty was concocting foolish excuses—arguing, for example, that the acts of Yoshitsune were the work of demons. So long as Yoshitsune and Yukiiye were at large, the country was in danger, he said; and he hinted that the real demon (*tengu*) of the times was the crafty and untruthful Sacred Emperor himself. It was at this point that Yoritomo decided that, without departing from the proper forms, he must take firm and positive action. After careful discussion with Hōjō Tokimasa and his adviser Ōye Hiromoto he sent Tokimasa with one thousand picked men to the capital to underline his requests to the Throne. This force arrived in the middle of December 1185. A few days later the Court, at Tokimasa's instance, reluctantly granted to Yoritomo authority to collect the above-mentioned commissariat tax on all estates, whether private or public, and to appoint stewards (*jitō*) and constables (*shugo*) in all provinces. According to Yoritomo, these almost epoch-making changes were justified by the necessity of military operations against rebels (namely Yoshitsune and Yukiiye). Supplies were needed (he said) for the punitive expedition which the In had ordered; and stewards and constables were needed to maintain peace and order in the provinces other than those of the east, which were under the control of Kamakura.

This appeal to the Throne was most displeasing to Go-Shirakawa, but he gave way out of fear. Knowing that he was helpless, he announced his consent the day after Tokimasa had made the request. By doing this he in fact surrendered the prerogative of the Throne in all matters concerning the command and employment of armed forces, for he handed to the leader of the military class effective jurisdiction in matters of land tenure and the income derived from agriculture, the vital features of a land revenue economy.

3. *Yoritomo's Relations with the Court*

The true significance of these steps taken by Yoritomo and their economic sequels may be left for later study; meanwhile we should look at the development of a purely political relationship between Yoritomo and the Court. It will have been noticed from the foregoing description that Yoritomo treated the retired and cloistered Emperor Go-Shirakawa as the sovereign whose consent must be obtained to measures proposed by Kamakura. This was a matter of common sense. As in Fujiwara days the titular emperor was not allowed by the Taira to remain long upon the throne, but was obliged or persuaded to abdicate at an early age and so to be succeeded by a young child, now by Minamoto intervention the little boy Antoku was displaced in 1184 by the young Go-Toba, then four years of age. Go-Toba in turn abdicated in 1198, when he was eighteen years old, and remained cloistered sovereign until his banishment in 1221. After that the authority of the ruling house had so diminished that questions of succession were of little importance. But until Yoritomo felt himself firmly established, the peculiarities of Go-Shirakawa and the prejudices of the Court nobles were matters of interest to him and had to be taken into account in devising his political strategy. He knew that many, perhaps most, of them were at bottom unsympathetic and even positively hostile to him. They looked upon him as an upstart, a kind of promoted police officer, and though in the long run they were powerless their intrigues could be troublesome. He saw that promotion to high offices depended upon the erratic fancies of Go-Shirakawa or the preferences of Court ladies, of whom the most redoubtable was Tango no Tsubone, the favourite mistress of His Sacred Majesty. He therefore decided that he must in his own interest somehow purge the royal entourage of possible adversaries in high places by pressing for their removal and for the appointment of men whom he could trust, if not to give him positive support, at least not to obstruct him.

At this time the Minister of the Right, Fujiwara Kanezane (the diarist quoted at length in Chapter XIII), was generally esteemed as a sensible and experienced man, with a great knowledge of precedents and a strong sense of duty. His reputation was known to Yoritomo, who decided that his own interests would best be served if he could secure the appointment of a man of such integrity as Kanezane to the highest office under the Crown. Accordingly in the spring of 1184—that is, soon after the battle of Ichinotani—he sent the In a recommendation that Kanezane be made Chieftain of the Fujiwara clan, and appointed Regent of the titular sovereign. These offices, for which Kanezane was well suited by birth and training, were then held by a young man, Fujiwara Motomichi, who was a favourite of Go-Shirakawa and was well liked by Tango no Tsubone. A powerful Regent could serve as a check upon Go-Shirakawa.

Nothing was done to meet Yoritomo's wishes, and he did not press for a reply, though news came to Kanezane that he had not abandoned his plan. This was early in the spring of 1185, and shortly after that (at the end of May) Yoshitsune entered the capital with the important

captives taken at Dannoura. The complete downfall of the Taira had
of course much strengthened Yoritomo's position, and at once the Court
began to consider the question of appropriate rewards for him. This
question, with the arguments to and fro, is discussed in Kanezane's
diary, which gives precious details of the relations between Yoritomo
and the Court, as well as the story of Yoshitsune's failure and his flight
from the ruthless pursuit of Yoritomo's agents.

The narrative which follows here is based upon Kanezane's account.
It may not be accurate in every particular, since the capital was full
of rumours and conjectures; but it has the merit of describing from
first-hand knowledge the reaction of the aristocratic society of the imperial city to the pressure of the military leaders.

The relationship between Yoritomo and Yoshitsune is a long tragedy,
beginning with Yoshitsune's dazzling successes and ending with Yoritomo's grisly triumph when he learns that his brother's head has been
taken and will be sent to Kamakura.[4] In the long history of the growth
of a dominant military caste and the formation of a warrior's code of
honour these dramatic episodes are perhaps of no great significance.
Yet they are part of the national legend and for that reason they should
be recorded here, if only as a chronicle of cruelty and breach of faith
in a society that was supposed to depend upon loyalty as well as courage, but was also built upon sordid plots and treachery. Moreover, the
unhappy relationship between these two men, in addition to its private
character, acquired a political aspect, for Yoritomo made it the osten-
sible reason for some of his most important acts of policy. It is therefore
convenient to describe the first steps in Yoritomo's gradual seizure of
power in terms of his treatment of Yoshitsune.

The first concern of the Court after the fall of the Taira was to see
to it that the captive leaders were put to death. Go-Shirakawa displayed
an unseemly haste in this matter. The captives were, as has been related,
killed on the way from Kamakura, in the province of Ōmi, and his Majesty is said to have inspected the severed heads himself. He had shortly
before this issued an Order (Insen) saying: "The former Minister
Munemori, his son Kiyomune, and General Shigehira are on the way
to the capital with Yoshitsune. It would be wrong to let them enter the
city alive. Their heads should be exposed in the province of Ōmi. The
question is whether the heads after exposure should be handed to the
Police Commission or thrown away. Yoshitsune says that Yoritomo has
directed that the orders of the In be followed."

Such were the matters that preoccupied the Holy Emperor as he
faced a tyranny no less severe than that of the vanquished Taira.

After his return to the capital from Kamakura, Yoshitsune found his

---

[4] The treatment of Yoshitsune's head throws a curious light upon the warriors
ethos. See p. 327 below.

position growing weaker and weaker as the pressure from Yoritomo increased. The issuing of a chastisement commission by the In to Yoshitsune was an act of folly, because Yoshitsune's military strength depended upon his position as Yoritomo's deputy. He had only a few personal adherents, and most of the warriors in the home provinces thought too little of his prospects to justify their taking his side against Yoritomo. Both Yoshitsune and Yukiiye with good reason mistrusted the In and his Court, and their expedition to the west was in reality a flight. Kanezane for his part was aware that the issue of a commission to Yoshitsune was a blunder, though he thought it best to let it stand, because he wanted to get the two "rebels" out of the capital as soon as possible. The city had had enough fighting and plundering in its streets, and he did not wish to invite further calamity. In his diary, after recording the shipwreck and flight of the two fugitive generals, Kanezane wrote a eulogy of Yoshitsune, but he added rather piously that perhaps his misfortunes were a punishment inflicted by Heaven for his rebellion.

A few days after news of Yoshitsune's disappearance had reached the city the demeanour of the eastern warriors who were then arriving caused great apprehension to the Court, and Go-Shirakawa began to feel very alarmed. He had good reason to fear Yoritomo's anger, for he had learned early in December (1185) that all his manors in Harima province had been confiscated by the Deputy Kajiwara. Stimulated by this news he had sent one of his ladies to the home of the Regent Motomichi to suggest that he resign in favour of Yoritomo's candidate Kanezane.

Ciphers of Minamoto Yoritomo (LEFT) *and Fujiwara* (*Kujō*) *Kanezane*

Shortly after this move by Go-Shirakawa (who was beginning to think of reigning himself), Kanezane, commenting upon the levy of commissariat rice (*hyōrō-mai*), noted in his diary that this was not merely a device for supplying troops with food, but was in fact the assumption of complete control over land. He thought it dreadful beyond words, but he knew that the Throne could not resist; and he felt that if he accepted the office of Regent he might be able to moderate the policy of Kamakura. He was no doubt encouraged in this belief by Yoritomo's suggestion that a council of ten leading nobles should be appointed as advisers to the Regent, for he interpreted this proposal as evidence of Yoritomo's desire to avoid an open breach with the Court.

Kanezane's diary contains much valuable evidence of Yoritomo's designs, and of his character as a statesman. It gives in full the text of a letter which Yoritomo sent to Kanezane at the end of 1185 and which reached him early in the New Year, 1186. In form it is a missive addressed to an official (the Uchūben Mitsunaga) for communication to Kanezane. Its more important passages are as follows:

❋

"This is for your information. A detailed discussion of the developments of the recent past would be lengthy indeed. The Taira clan, rebelling against the sovereign . . . sought only to create a disturbance. . . . Living in exile in the province of Izu, I at once formed plans for chastising the enemies of the Throne, regardless of the fact that I had not been ordered to do so. Fortunately, my efforts were not without success. Peace was restored, the enemy was crushed, and the realm was restored to the sovereign. My purposes were accomplished. As a result, there was public and private rejoicing. First, without waiting for the destruction of the Taira clan, I sent two commissioners to keep the peace by halting the brawling of warriors in the eleven provinces surrounding the capital. Moreover, because I did not think it right to issue orders as a private person, whenever I acted I obtained an order [Insen] from the Court indicating what was to be done. After the disturbances in the said provinces had for the most part been quelled, by imperial request I despatched the said commissioners to Kyūshū and Shikoku. It was not until I had received authority that I ordered them to advance.

"The properties of Harada no Tanenao, Kikuchi no Takanao, Sakai no Tanetō, and Yamaga no Hidetō are lands of persons who have been deprived of office. I thought, therefore, that manorial stewards' offices ought to be established in accordance with previous usage. Though I have stated as much, no decision has yet been reached in these, to say nothing of other cases which remain unsettled. For example, I have repeatedly said that there should be Insen to provide for the supervision of nearby provinces in order to put an end to disturbances, but a dubious situation has developed.

"The appointments of Yoshitsune as Steward of Kyūshū and Yukiiye as Steward of Shikoku were entirely contrary to my desire. Those men, relying upon one another, made plans above their station. When they left, no enemy attacked them, but the censure of Heaven is hard to evade. When they boarded their ships and cast off the moorings, they put to sea and floated on the waves, to the instant destruction of their retainers and kinsmen. This truly was beyond human endeavour; it was the will of the gods.

"Those two men have disappeared. They are fleeing furtively. Separating and making individual pleas, they will certainly create trouble in every province, manor, family, and temple. Once they are taken, we shall have peace. At present, however, it is necessary to establish stewards [jitō] in the manors of all provinces. The purpose of this action is by no means to secure personal advantage. Some of the local people, harbouring wild thoughts, will befriend the rebels, while others, joining nearby warriors, will attack on the left and right and cause untoward developments. If steps are not taken to cope with such things, there will certainly be disturbances in the future. Accordingly, stewards ought to be decided upon, without regard to whether the lands are public or private, even in the province of Iyo [the province to be governed by Kanezane]. . . . There will be nothing to prevent admonition of those who are refractory or negligent. They will exercise their authority in accordance with law. . . ."

❖

In the closing lines of the above letter, Yoritomo says to Mitsunaga, "There is another matter which I should like you to bring up at this time. I have respectfully set forth my views in a second letter. . . . This is a time when the nation's foundations are being laid. Action must be decided upon after examination of principles. . . ." Kanezane now records the contents of this further communication, which is the one dealing with the Council of Nobles.

In this second document Yoritomo proposes the dismissal, and in some cases the banishment, of high officials guilty of sympathizing with "the rebels Yoshitsune and Yukiiye"; and he respectfully puts forward names of persons to be appointed in their stead. He says that Kanezane should be appointed at once to the office of Nairan (equivalent to the Regency), while leaving the chieftainship of the Fujiwara clan to its present holder, Motomichi, a favourite of the cloistered Emperor. The letter continues with a list of provincial governorships which should be assigned to Kanezane and other members of the new council, as sources of income.

Kanezane, in noting these proposals that night, records that he told his colleague Tsunefusa, who had called upon him earlier in the evening, that he was resolved not to accept the appointment. Of late, he said, requests from the military had been followed without regard to their merits, and he did not like the idea of two great officers exercising the highest functions side by side. This could only lead to discord. Tsunefusa replied that Yoritomo's proposals, although certainly contrary to

His Majesty's wishes, could not be withstood. Kanezane insisted, arguing that precedents were all against the adoption of such new measures; but when the In was consulted he merely said that precedent did not enter into the question. Everything must be ordered as Kamakura desired. Kanezane went to Court next morning intending to protest, but he could not obtain an audience. He then asked for an interview with the Lady Tango no Tsubone, the favourite who now had a say in all state business, but she put him off with an excuse, probably (Kanezane suspected) at the instance of Go-Shirakawa, who evidently was frightened to refuse anything that Yoritomo might ask. When Kanezane pressed him for a reply, he would say nothing definite but only showed anger at being approached.

In his diary for that day Kanezane writes that "military power has steadily usurped the authority of the Throne since 1179"; that high and low in the realm are fearful of this power; and that he, Kanezane, alone has refused to flatter the usurpers or to neglect the wishes of the sovereign. Yet he did within ten days or so accept the office of Nairan and the title of Chieftain of the Clan. This was at the beginning of April 1186, when there could no longer be any doubt of the strength and determination of the military leaders; and therefore it would seem that, although ambition was no doubt a compelling force, Kanezane genuinely believed that if he could keep Yoritomo's confidence he might be able to save something of the imperial prerogative and the prestige of the nobility.

Yoritomo, apparently satisfied that he had established relations with the Court which were, if not positively friendly, at least reasonably harmonious, now gradually established his position as an adviser with a right to intervene in matters of policy. A week after Kanezane's appointment he suspended the levy of commissariat rice and sent his brother-in-law Fujiwara Yoshiyasu to Kyoto as his Deputy (Daikan) in the place of his father-in-law Hōjō Tokimasa. His relationship with Kanezane was strengthened by the marriage of Kanezane's son to Yoshiyasu's daughter.

Yoritomo's attitude towards the Court remained respectful but firm. In May 1186 he addressed a letter to the Council of Nobles saying that he had recommended the formation of a Council because he believed that government in consultation with such a body was the best kind of government. He added that the Council should examine all proposals, even his own, with a view to the best interests of the country. He was very free with such pious observations, but it is not likely that he would have been pleased by a critical examination of his own policies; his aim was rather to take a stand against the arbitrary and erratic methods of government by edict which Go-Shirakawa had followed, and he very properly wished to rid the Court of the undesirable favourites who had served the In for long past.

While paying close attention to negotiations with the Court, Yoritomo did not neglect the pursuit of his military aims. He was always on the watch for possible rivalry or insubordination. The unfortunate Yukiiye was tracked down and taken prisoner, to be killed during the early days of June 1186. Soon after this some of Yoshitsune's companions were captured, including his faithful mistress Shizuka, who though badly treated did not reveal the whereabouts of her lover, the father of her yet unborn child. He had now been a fugitive for more than a year, and Yoritomo was enraged by the failure of his spies. At his instance the Court issued a further order for the arrest and punishment of Yoshitsune and his followers.

At about this time, in order to meet the complaints of noble landowners Yoritomo made some changes in the system of estate managers or stewards (*jitō*) which he had obliged the government to approve earlier in the year. Here the concession was more apparent than real, and it is evident that it was made in order to create a general impression that he was moderate in his policies and did not wish to injure the great men at Court. Meanwhile rumours were afoot that Yoshitsune was hiding in some wild part of the hilly province of Yoshino, or in the Ninnaji monastery or in some recess of Hiyeizan. Yoritomo suspected the warlike monks of Hiyeizan, and threatened to attack them if they did not reveal the hiding place. This alarmed the Court dignitaries, who were now so anxious to please Yoritomo that they ordered monasteries and shrines to pray for Yoshitsune to show himself. He eluded his pursuers for some months longer, even visiting the capital in disguise if the legendary accounts are to be trusted; and early in the spring of 1187 he set forth from his secret haunts disguised as an itinerant monk of the fraternity of Yamabushi, with his wife and family all dressed as children. He passed through Ise and Mino on his way to the coast on the Japan Sea and then northward to seek shelter and protection under Fujiwara Hidehira, the powerful lord of Mutsu, who was now Yoritomo's only dangerous rival.

Hidehira was a descendant of those Fujiwara leaders who, beginning with Kiyohira, had built up a great and virtually independent kingdom in the northern provinces during the eleventh century, when Minamoto Yoshiiye was making war upon the rebellious Abe and Kiyowara clans. Neither the Minamoto nor the Taira had been able to subdue them, for they were disciplined, hardened fighters and their strategic position in a wide and remote mountainous region was almost impregnable. Kiyohira had been Military Governor and High Constable of Mutsu and Dewa in 1090, and was in fact at the time of his death in 1126 a great feudal lord whom none could challenge, the master of much land and many vassals. It was his son Hidehira who had received Yoshitsune as a boy of fifteen when he escaped from surveillance in the west (at Kurama-dera) in 1174. He regarded Hidehira almost as a father, and his faith was justified when he took refuge in Mutsu in 1187, for the old warrior, then over ninety years of age and near his end, charged all his sons to protect Yoshitsune and to help him to become a great commander, even the greatest in the kingdom.

Yoritomo soon learned that Yoshitsune had been welcomed by the old lord of Mutsu, and in the spring of 1188 he sent messengers requesting Yasuhira (Hidehira's successor) to put the fugitive to death. No notice was taken of this request, but Yoritomo was determined. He had here a cause and an opportunity for the satisfaction of his most urgent desires. He wanted to take revenge upon Yoshitsune on private grounds of jealousy and he wanted to destroy the power of the lords of Mutsu on public grounds of policy, since he could never complete his plan to govern the country so long as the great stronghold of the fighting Fujiwara dominated the northern marches. There at Hiraizumi they had built a monastery rivalling the richest edifices of the capital city in its rich decoration and its lavish use of gold. This was the Chūsonji, symbol of the pride of Kiyohira and his descendants.[5]

When Yoshitsune reached this stronghold he was a hunted, tragic wanderer, seeking only peace and safety. But in the accepted legend, as it is recorded in romances and stage plays, he appears always as a beloved heroic figure, in contrast to the harsh, tyrannical Yoritomo. The scenes in which Yoshitsune's faithful henchman Benkei appears are among the most applauded historical pieces, in both the popular drama and the classic Nō theatre. What the ordinary man knows of Yoshitsune's story is the bravery and loyalty of his companions in misfortune, the miserable fate that pursued him, his narrow escapes, and at last his tragic death. Much of this probably belongs to imagination rather than to history—we note again the traditional Japanese penchant for stories of tragic failure following brilliant success. Yoshitsune's story, as it has come down to us, is not unlike the ancient legend of Prince Yamato-dake, the Brave of Yamato, whose great exploits led only to a miserable end.

Having obliged the Court twice in March 1188 to order Yasuhira to arrest Yoshitsune, Yoritomo hesitated for some months before pressing for a third order, apparently because he thought that the auguries were

---

[5] I am indebted to Dr. Donald Keene for the following description of the Chūsonji, as he saw it in 1955. "It is still reached from Hiraizumi station by a horse-pulled bus, one of the last in Japan; and life seems tuned more to the trot of the horse than to the motor vehicle. The approach, through a magnificent avenue of towering cryptomerias, can have changed very little. . . . All the major artistic works have been removed to the museum, which is very well kept. In the museum are such masterpieces as the Kongōkai Dainichi Nyorai, the oldest piece of sculpture belonging to the Chūsonji, and the 'secret Buddha,' also an image of Dainichi, which probably because of its infrequent exposure still retains its original bright colouring. . . . Access to the inside of the Golden Hall is restricted. The statues, carved pillars, ceiling decorations etc. are still in good condition. . . . The privileged visitor who enters the interior is certain to be dazzled by its unforgettable beauty, the supreme example of the Japanese genius for the exquisite."

unfavourable at that time when he was engaged in building a memorial stupa to his mother. It was not until November that the order was repeated, and to this pressure Yasuhira at last yielded by attacking Yoshitsune, who at the end of the fourth intercalary month (June 15) of 1189, after killing his wife and children, committed suicide rather than surrender.

When Yasuhira sent word to Yoritomo saying that he would send the head for inspection, he was told to wait until a certain ceremony at the Hachiman shrine had been performed by Yoritomo. This was the dedication of the stupa to his mother. Owing to this filial or religious scruple the trophy was not brought to Kamakura until late in July, when it was inspected on the outskirts of the city by two of Yoritomo's highest-ranking officers, who rode out with an escort of cavalry to receive it. The head was in a black lacquer vessel, preserved in spirit (sake). Yoritomo seems not to have seen it himself; but at a later date he was to inspect the head of Yasuhira, brought to him by a traitor.

Some ten weeks after Yoshitsune's death Yoritomo set forth to attack the Fujiwara leader in the north. He had prevailed upon the In to agree to issue an order for the chastisement of Yoshitsune, but upon learning of Yoshitsune's death the Court decided that it was no longer necessary. The hesitation to consent to such an order was due in part to the opposition of some powerful nobles who were in sympathy with Yoshitsune and disliked Yoritomo. Perturbed by the Court's failure to approve his intentions but determined to continue his preparations, Yoritomo took the line that his soldiers were bound to obey his commands without awaiting imperial sanction for his campaign. It was enough for Yoritomo to announce his intentions to the Emperor, and applying this comforting doctrine he soon began to move his armies against Yasuhira. The fact that he was firm in his decision to invade the northern provinces even after Yoshitsune's death proves (if proof were needed) that his main purpose had always been the destruction of a powerful rival and not the pursuit of his hapless brother.

Three great forces converged upon the wide provinces of Mutsu and Dewa in the summer of 1189. An army from the north moved into Dewa from the Japan Sea coast, while two armies poured into Mutsu from the south, one following the Pacific coastline, the other under Yoritomo's own command making its way through the province of Shimotsuke, a Minamoto stronghold. These masses came together at a point in the centre of Mutsu, where they faced the Fujiwara vassals with such overwhelming numbers that Yasuhira could do no more than stand firm in the hope of wearing down the attack upon his stockades and other defence works. After some weeks, as Yoritomo's armies captured one position after another, it became clear that the defence was crumbling. The total number arrayed against Yasuhira's men was very great; though we need not believe the figure of over a quarter of a million given in some accounts, it was probably well above 100,000. Yasuhira was outnumbered and outfought. He could only ask for terms. He was refused, and knowing that Yoritomo intended his destruction he fled to the island of Yezo, across the straits, where he was killed by a traitor. All his vast domain fell into the hands of Yoritomo, together with much gold and silver and other riches collected by the Fujiwara chieftains during the century or more of their supremacy in the north.

Yoritomo had not expected such an easy victory. There is on record a conversation during which he discussed the campaign with Yuri Hachirō, one of Yasuhira's lieutenants who had been taken prisoner and brought to Yoritomo's headquarters. Yoritomo asked Yuri how it was that Yasuhira had been so easily overcome. He had thought that the fighting would be hard and long, but it turned out that many of Yasuhira's vassals were not loyal to him, so that, although he had 170,000 men at his command, he did not hold out for even as little as twenty days, and his whole clan was destroyed. To this Yuri replied that there had been many loyal and brave supporters of Yasuhira, but the strategy of his commanders had been mistaken. His strength was wasted because his best troops were sent to hold a number of strong points in mountainous areas while Yasuhira with older men was left to defend the castle. Moreover, Yasuhira was not so powerful as his ancestors had been. Before the Heiji rising (1159) the lord of Mutsu had been governor of fifteen provinces, but during the Heiji fighting he had lost control of all but Mutsu and Dewa, the two northern provinces. It was therefore not surprising that Yasuhira was unable to withstand the great army of Yoritomo.

The Court at Yoritomo's own request entrusted him with the administration of the conquered territories, and he appointed to each province officers who were to govern on the same lines as those laid down by Hidehira, a very capable ruler. They were to strive to conciliate the warrior families who, by their surrender, had now become vassals of Kamakura. By such measures Yoritomo designed to convert a dangerous rival into a valuable supporter, for if he could satisfy the leading houses of Mutsu and Dewa he could count upon very substantial reinforcements should he call for them in future campaigns. He need no longer fear an attack on his rear if he had to move troops to the western regions, and so he was free to turn his attention to affairs in the capital city, which he could now visit at his leisure and without misgivings. His relations with the Court at this time are of special interest as indications of his attitude towards the imperial government.

He had left Kamakura at the head of his troops on September 2, 1189, and less than two months later (in a letter dated October 19) he reported in detail to the Court the successful issue of his campaign. On the following day a messenger from Yoshiyasu, his Deputy in Kyoto, brought to him an imperial order for the chastisement of Yasuhira. This was dated September 2, the very day of Yoritomo's departure from

Kamakura, and even that date was false, for the order was written a week later. Upon receiving it Yoritomo, victorious though he was, sent word to the capital indicating, or perhaps only pretending, that he feared he had incurred the In's displeasure by making war without an imperial commission. He continued scrupulously to keep the Court informed of all his actions and duly reported his return to Kamakura from the fighting front early in December 1189. The Court, far from showing displeasure, praised him for his rapid pacification of the northern provinces. This was a disingenuous attitude, since the one thing that Yasuhira had desired was peace, and not war. But the In and his advisers knew that it would be of no advantage to them to rebuke Yoritomo, and they made it clear that they anxiously awaited his arrival in Kyoto on a visit which he had purposely delayed.

There can be no doubt that although he had a genuine respect for the Throne and had no desire to destroy the monarchy as an institution he was determined to deal with the Court on a footing of equality in matters of administration throughout the country. His intention was to put an end to palace intrigue, or at least to insist upon the appointment to high office of responsible men who would not tolerate such favourites and cronies as had flattered and influenced Go-Shirakawa. Even before the revolt of Yoshitsune he had recommended the appointment of Kanezane in place of the Regent Motomichi; and it is clear that despite the In's special liking for Motomichi, Kanezane's position in the government was already firmly established before the final triumph in Mutsu. Early in 1189 Kanezane's daughter in the true Fujiwara tradition had become the First Consort (Chūgū) of the reigning Emperor, then a child.

After his return to Kamakura in the last month of 1189, Yoritomo spent a full year consolidating his position, taking steps to reward his vassals and in other ways to ensure their fidelity. He paid particular attention to the development of certain administrative and judicial organs which were designed to confirm and increase his control over the military class as a whole. It was not until he felt his position to be unassailable that he proceeded to the capital. There he arrived during the first week of December 1190, and took up his residence in the newly prepared mansion at Rokuhara, the former headquarters of the Taira warriors. His arrival naturally excited the greatest interest, and according to Kanezane's diary the citizens went in crowds to watch the Minamoto procession as it marched in. The In himself was said to have been among the spectators. Two days later Kanezane went to the Palace at night to get the latest news. He records that Yoritomo paid his first calls during the day, going first to the In's residence and next to the palace of the Emperor Go-Toba, then ten years of age. The entry in the diary for that day continues with an account of Kanezane's interview with Yoritomo, in the following words:

"I talked to the Minister Yoritomo in the Oni no Ma [one of the pal-

ace apartments]. . . . Tonight he was given the office of Grand Counsellor [Dainagon]. During my interview with him the Minister Yoritomo said, 'An oracle from Hachiman told me to serve the sovereign
wholeheartedly and guard the hundred princes. . . . Therefore I must
serve the present ruler with all my heart. Since, however, the Hō-ō
[cloistered Emperor] now conducts the government of the realm, my
first allegiance is to him. The Son of Heaven [titular Emperor] is like a
crown prince. After the life span of the cloistered Emperor has been
completed, my allegiance must go to the Emperor. . . . The Emperor is
a child, and you too have many years ahead of you. If I am fortunate,
why should not the government be simple and honest? For the present,
since it is necessary to serve the cloistered Emperor unstintingly, nothing can be done.' The sentiments he revealed were exceedingly profound. . . ."

This statment of Yoritomo's attitude towards the monarchy and his
reason for allegiance to Go-Shirakawa In are of particular interest. At
this date Kanezane seems not yet to have decided upon full collaboration
with Yoritomo. He was aware that the government in Kyoto was largely
in the hands of incompetent if not immoral men, and he knew that
drastic remedies were needed. But he could not believe that a dominant
military class under the rule of Yoritomo was likely to cure the sickness
of the state. His views are set forth in a memorial which he presented
to Go-Shirakawa at the beginning of 1192. In that document the following passage occurs:

"Peace and disorder in the state are like sickness. A sudden illness,
promptly cured, may have no after-effects, whereas an ailment which
lasts for years, imperceptibly weakening the patient, may be beyond
the reach of prayers for recovery. It is the same with the government
of the realm. Though plunderers enter and fill the country with violence, through diligent punitive efforts it is possible to drive them off
after a time, and things return to normal. The eyes and ears of high and
low in this generation have seen and heard this. The revolts of the Taira
family and Kurō [Yoshitsune], the disturbances created by Yoshinaka
and Yukiiye—all were thus. Since Yoritomo's valour is such that it is
impossible to resist his arms, all is peaceful. But little by little the country has weakened and men have grown false. As a result of this, the
multitude are destitute; because of that, the Four Seas are destroyed.
The deterioration of annual and special Shintō and Buddhist observances grows greater day by day; the devastation of provinces and manors
of the home and outer provinces grows worse year by year. During the
six or seven years which have passed since I was raised to power, the
lapse of public functions and the decline of the provinces have been as
though heaven were replaced by earth. In such circumstances, the total
ruin of the state is near at hand. The spirits of the imperial ancestors
lament because of this. Though we long for simplicity and honesty,
they are beyond our reach. . . . What but our sovereign's benevolent

virtue can raise up the dying realm? What but our Emperor's august fortune can moisten the parched lands within the seas?"

A few days after this memorial reached Go-Shirakawa, then lying ill and unable to transact business, he began to suffer increasing pain, and his sickness grew worse and worse until he died at the age of sixty-six in the spring of 1192. Kanezane, recording the death in his diary, said that Go-Shirakawa had governed for more than thirty years with clemency; that his character was magnanimous and his devotion to Buddhism of the highest order. But having expressed these proper obituary sentiments Kanezane added: "The only thing to regret is that His Majesty forgot the ancient usages of the periods of Engi and Tenryaku." By this he meant that the late sovereign had departed from the precedents set in earlier reigns, when simplicity and frugality were respected and the law obeyed. Go-Shirakawa was not a wise ruler. His was a rule of shifts and expedients and indeed, despite his enthusiasm for religious exercises and his favours to the Church, he was not a man of high principle. Nevertheless he was a remarkable and interesting, if not admirable, character. Something of his quality appears in the well-known portrait of the Myōhō-In monastery in Kyoto (see Plate 11).[6] Perhaps he cannot be blamed for his erratic behaviour, seeing that he had to deal with military leaders and cunning was the only weapon with which he could meet force.

After the In's death his favourites lost their influence, while that of Kanezane rapidly increased until he became little less than all-powerful at Court. He cannot in his heart have welcomed the great changes that had taken place with the rise of Yoritomo, but he had the good sense to compromise with the new force rather than try to resist it. During Go-Shirakawa's lifetime Yoritomo never could obtain the imperial commission as Sei-i Tai Shōgun (Generalissimo) which he ardently desired both for its prestige and for its practical advantages to a military leader. But after Go-Shirakawa's death Kanezane was able to dictate to the youthful Go-Toba, and with very little delay the appointment was procured. Kanezane sent special messengers to the Kamakura headquarters with the good news and a paper of appointment, which they handed to Yoritomo's Deputy in a solemn ceremony in August 1192.

Thus Yoritomo in both rank and office had reached the height of his ambition. His strength was now such that Kanezane could do little more than ease the impact of the Shōgun's orders upon the life of the old aristocracy. The centre of real power had been shifted from Kyoto to Kamakura, where a new system of government was in preparation. The capital city remained the source of honours and the seat of national ceremony and ritual, while in Kamakura, under the direction of Yoritomo and his advisers, a feudal state was being swiftly organized.

[6] This is now in the Uyeno Museum. It is in poor condition. The Chōkōdo portrait, which is much later (early seventeenth century), gives Go-Shirakawa a crafty look, perhaps in accordance with a long tradition.

The administrative organ which Yoritomo had developed in Kamakura came to be known as the Bakufu, a term which strictly speaking means the field headquarters of a general in time of war (see p. 348). This description of Yoritomo's government remained appropriate in time of peace, because its most important function was to promote the welfare and secure the obedience of the warrior class.

Once Yoritomo had received his appointment as Shōgun relations between the Court and the Bakufu became almost harmonious. There was some underground opposition in the capital, but thanks to the influence of Kanezane and to the immaturity of the Emperor, there was no serious breach of any kind and Kamakura policies, cautiously worked out, met with no effective opposition. Kanezane had his enemies at Court, but after Go-Shirakawa's death he was able to deal with them. With Yoritomo's support he had now reached the summit of his ambition. He was the most powerful civil officer in the realm. His wealth increased, and his relatives and friends were appointed to high and lucrative posts, where they could be counted upon to work on his behalf in furthering plans which he had concerted with Yoritomo. Both men were satisfied. Kanezane's great dedication service at the Kōfukuji, the Fujiwara monastery, in 1193, when prayers were offered for the good fortune of the clan of which he was Chieftain, was a memorable occasion in his career.

Yoritomo, for his part, could now afford to relax his precautions against mutiny, and enjoy hunting, sight-seeing, and entertainments provided by his vassals, while not neglecting pious exercises. Thus calm and peace prevailed in Kyoto and Kamakura.

But Yoritomo was a restless, ruthless, suspicious man. In 1193 he had his half-brother Noriyori killed on a trumped-up charge of conspiracy. In 1194 he ordered or agreed to the execution of all the male members of the family of Yasuda Yoshisada, who had been one of the bravest and most loyal supporters of the Minamoto. This, like other cruel punishments, was inflicted because of false charges made by the deplorable Kagetoki, whose delations Yoritomo was always willing to credit. While responsible for such evil deeds, the Shōgun made great professions of religious faith. He had contributed lavishly to the rebuilding of the Tōdaiji (destroyed by fire in the civil wars), and indeed the Bakufu since its early days had spent funds which it could scarcely afford upon building and furnishing chapels and shrines, not so much on grounds of piety as for the purpose of gaining the approval of believers, and perhaps their political support.[7]

---

[7] As to cruelty, the student of English history will not need to be reminded that Henry VIII never hesitated to dispose of rivals or opponents by judicial or straightforward murder; while the use of the rack was common practice in his day and later. Henry is said to have sent to the executioner two queens, several ministers of state, and a number of bishops, abbots, monks, and ordinary citizens. His purpose was to get rid of members of the nobility or other persons in whom royal blood ran.

It was largely in pursuit of such aims that, when the new Tōdaiji was near completion, Yoritomo declared his intention to be present at the great dedication service which was to take place in 1195. He left Kamakura in March of that year and proceeded first to Kyoto, where he stayed in the now enlarged Rokuhara mansion, in the warm, blossomy springtime of the home provinces. This second visit was not like the first, the triumphal entry of 1190. It was a visit of courtesy, paid to the sovereign by an acknowledged dictator, with diplomatic intent. Yoritomo had with him his wife, Masa-ko, his son Yoriiye, and a modest though glittering escort of warriors. Crowds assembled outside the Rokuhara buildings, and it was clear that the populace and the nobility were impressed by the Shōgun's power and eager to catch sight of him.

A week later the great ceremony took place at Nara in the Tōdaiji. It was attended by the Emperor and all the great nobles and officers of state, and was an occasion of solemn splendour. The Shōgun with his company was there, and he was no longer a shadowy figure to the people of the west, but a real personage, whose commands must be respected, if not always obeyed. Perhaps this ceremony marked a turning point in the development of political institutions in Japan.

On returning from Nara to the capital Yoritomo settled down in his Rokuhara mansion for several weeks, which he spent in a leisurely manner. He saw all the celebrated sights of the region, met a number of people of all kinds, and strove by his amiability to make a good impression upon Kyoto society. He even went out of his way to pay respects to such formidable ladies as Senyōmon-In and Tango no Tsubone, both of whom were known to have intrigued against him. During his stay he had frequent audiences at the Palace, which sometimes lasted deep into the night. The matters discussed were various, but we know from one good contemporary source that the allocation of manors and the appointment or dismissal of stewards were among the leading topics, these being questions which naturally exercised the Emperor's mind, since there was little left to him but the revenue of his estates and those of his family and his favourites.

This genial weather was not to last. There was always an underground current in the capital, flowing against the warlords and what the aristocrats at Court thought was the usurpation of imperial power. As a rule the advisers of the Throne were none too competent, but it happened in the years following the Taira defeat that an extremely clever and determined statesman, one Minamoto Michichika, brought up in the tradition of hostility to the Fujiwara, and especially to the Kujō house, caused much distress to Kanezane by his intrigues and his influence at Court. We need not enter into details of his plans and methods. It is enough to say that at the end of 1196, a year after Yoritomo's visit to the capital, a palace revolution took place, under Michichika's guidance. Kanezane and his supporters were removed from office and Michichika's nominees were appointed in their place. The purpose of this coup was of course to diminish Bakufu influence at Court and to give a strong impetus to the restoration movement. Michichika's success brought an end to the supremacy of the Kujō branch of the Fujiwara clan, and Kanezane disappeared from public life. He died in 1207.

News of Michichika's movement was slow to reach Kamakura, owing to the death in 1197 of Yoritomo's brother-in-law Fujiwara Yoshiyasu, who had for years been his observer in Kyoto. In 1198, without any reference to the Bakufu, Michichika arranged that the younger brother of the Emperor Go-Toba should be declared Heir Apparent, and this demonstration of independence caused Yoritomo some anxiety. He took no immediate step, though he let it be known that he would pay the Court another visit very soon. But he died in 1199 and the subsequent political confusion in Kamakura gave much encouragement and useful opportunities to the restoration movement in the capital, where Michichika could now exercise his talents free from fear of decisive action by the Bakufu, which now had no acknowledged leader. Consequently Michichika enjoyed success in resisting or rather disregarding the wishes of Kamakura. At times it must have appeared to him and his party that their prospects of restoring the power of the Throne were bright. But neither his nor any other restoration movement had any true prospect of success, because they were not inspired by genuine loyalty but by hostility towards rival families, whereas the feudal autocracy, out of common sense rather than virtue, was saved from collapse by its acceptance of feudal discipline.

4. The Character of Yoritomo

In quantity there is no lack of material upon which to base an estimate of Yoritomo's character, but it is hard to reach a critical view in matters of detail, since the best source, the *Azuma Kagami*, has a certain leaning in favour of the Hōjō family and there is no other document to serve as correcting evidence.

It is certain, however, that Yoritomo was a truly great man, one of the greatest in Japanese history, perhaps the greatest of all if one takes into account the difficulty of his tasks and the measure of his achievements. Like all great men he displayed surprising variations in his behaviour, so that it is difficult to say of him with confidence that he had such-and-such virtues and such-and-such faults. Certainly as he is presented in the *Azuma Kagami* his personality is unpleasing, but his firmness of purpose and his careful planning call for admiration. Judged by the results he achieved, he certainly can be described as the founder of a coherent system of feudal government which, despite civil wars and other obstacles, lasted without fundamental change for centuries.

He was not a mere warlord fighting for victory over rival clans. He was in a true sense a revolutionary leader, determined to alter the constitution of the state. When he made war on the Taira he was not only attacking a rival but seeking to wrest from Kiyomori that control over the Imperial House which the Taira family, following upon the Fujiwara, was so ruthlessly exercising. How far ahead he saw we cannot tell, but it is clear that as a young man in exile he had thought long and carefully about his own future and that of the Minamoto clan. When he raised the standard of revolt at Ishibashiyama in 1180 he already had certain purposes in his mind, but he lost that first skirmish and in his precarious position he can scarcely have formed any but the most general plans for the future. He had yet to build up his strength, but he soon acquired a position as leader, owing less to his chieftainship of the Minamoto clan than to the recognition by important warriors of his gifts, notably his iron determination and his ability to devise and organize a proper course of action at difficult junctures. He had courage and dash where they were needed, but he took himself and his task very seriously and usually made no move without forethought.

As he gathered adherents in the latter part of the year 1180 he saw the need not only for careful organization of his growing military force but also for settling the relationship between himself as leader and those warrior chieftains who had declared themselves on his side. He established a base at Kamakura which was administrative rather than strategic, and it became his headquarters and his permanent place of residence. He had hardly recovered from his failure at Ishibashiyama when he carried out this design, and thereafter he steadily developed an administrative system which (beginning with the Samurai-dokoro, an office for the protection as well as the discipline of his fighting men) gradually developed into a complex organization for both war and peace.

His foresight was remarkable, but so was his practical good sense in setting up machinery to match his own expanding power. By the end of 1184, when the Taira armies were in flight and Minamoto troops under Noriyori were unable to overtake them for lack of food and transport, Yoritomo kept calm and had such confidence in his own capacity that he was able to encourage Noriyori with good advice. Here he showed wisdom and restraint when he might have given way to an impulsive anger, for we know from good sources that he was given at times to outbursts of rage. In general he had great self-control, being confident that difficulties could be overcome and disputes adjusted by well-considered action. He had a cold, almost inhuman, faith in principles and rules. The greatest warrior chieftain of Japan, he displayed that characteristic of Japanese political habits before and after his time, a firm reliance upon the efficacy of law and order under a closely organized government.

Although the cumulative effect of Yoritomo's actions was to bring about revolutionary changes in the nature of government in Japan, and although in fact he founded a military autocracy to which the Throne was subservient, he was by no means of a revolutionary temper. He was on the contrary conservative in sentiment and taste, appealing constantly to ancient custom and established precedent. He had no reforming zeal, only a pragmatic interest in good government, which to his mind was firm government. He made no attempt to deprive the Imperial House of its prestige or of its traditional powers. Indeed out of caution and prudence he did much to protect the Court against the intrusion of his more unruly vassals, and he endeavoured to purge it of some of its corrupt elements. If one were to estimate the position of the Court nobles and high officers of the Crown after the defeat of the Taira, it would be fair to say that they were better off than they had been under the despotic Kiyomori. They had gained in security what they had lost in nominal power.

In regard to Yoritomo's relations with the Court, it should be remembered that until he began his revolt at the age of thirty-three he had not led the ordinary warrior's life. His early childhood had been spent in or near the capital, and his immediate forebears had been great Minamoto captains serving the Crown. His was a fine pedigree: Yoshiiye (1041–1108), Yoshichika (d. 1117), Tameyoshi (1096–1156), Yoshitomo (1123–60), Yoritomo (1147–99). But despite their warlike occupation, members of this branch of the Minamoto had been familiar with Court life, and Yoritomo's own father had taken the side of the Emperor Go-Shirakawa in the Hōgen rising of 1156. Thus Yoritomo by upbringing had certain aristocratic connexions which help to account for his attitude towards the Court, which was firm but respectful. He seems to have had a feeling for forms and precedents that distinguished him from the country-bred gentry of whom the warrior society mostly consisted.

Though for such reasons as these he was loth to destroy traditional practices, he never hesitated to adjust them to his own purposes. Perhaps the wisest decision he ever made was to make use of the talents of capable men who had held important posts in the imperial government. He revealed his belief in skilled administration when he appointed men like Ōye Hiromoto to high offices in Kamakura. From them he learned much about the arts of ruling, and it was probably on their advice that he interested himself in the development of courts of law sworn to dispense impartial justice. Altogether, though he may not have had any definite plans in his early years at Kamakura, he had already in mind principles of administration which he developed and applied with great thoroughness during the remainder of his life.

The edifice of power which he built during his short existence—he died at fifty-two, less than fifteen years after the end of the civil war—

was truly remarkable. It was strong and durable, and his authority extended over the whole country. In the east it was absolute; in other regions of Japan it was limited, but strong enough to prevent the rise of any effective rival.

As a ruler he was thoughtful, even in some respects original; he was painstaking and he was successful in almost every enterprise. It is true that he had a good foundation to build upon, since most of the warriors in the east were antagonistic to the Kyoto government on account of its incompetence and its subordination to Kiyomori's tyranny and were willing to follow a strong lead. But of the three great military rulers of Japan, it was Yoritomo who excelled in achievement. He was a builder who broke new ground and he prepared the way for the mature feudal order which arose centuries later out of the labours of Hideyoshi and Iyeyasu.

His principles as a leader were strict and he was quick to punish disloyalty or disobedience. One of his most important achievements was his success in converting the simple loyalties of the clansmen into a regulated system of behaviour governing the relations between members of the warrior class, their duties and their privileges. He displayed great wisdom when, instead of taking vengeance upon defeated enemies (as was the practice of the day, which he frequently followed), he chose to accept some of them as vassals if he was convinced that they were men of honour. He thought of himself as chieftain of the Minamoto, but he also had a wider vision, for when he became Shōgun (if not before) he regarded himself as the feudal overlord not only of the eastern provinces but of the whole country. It was therefore to his interest to conciliate as many warriors as possible from houses other than his own.

He had a strong sense of duty and he liked to find moral justification for his acts, since this increased his reputation for fair dealing. But in other respects his moral standards were not praiseworthy.

He was religious in so far as he thought it necessary to worship the unseen powers. He was lavish in his gifts to monasteries and shrines, and he constantly encouraged Buddhist rites and ceremonies while not neglecting important Shintō observances. His attitude towards the established religious institutions was no doubt governed by a desire to gain their political support, but he was to all appearances very devout, always carrying a rosary and often attending long and solemn services in which his vassals were obliged to take part. He seems not to have belonged to any particular sect, though on more than one occasion he professed belief in the Lotus Sutra. Like many members of his class, indeed like many of his contemporaries, he was perhaps more superstitious than devout.

His personal morality was not consistent with the faith which he professed. He had little regard for human life and his sexual life was promiscuous. But here he was not exceptional, for all members of his class were sworn in the name of loyalty to disobey the Buddhist commandment not to kill, and most of them followed the belief expressed in a well-known saying, "The hero is addicted to carnal pleasures" ("Eiyū iro wo konomu").

A general view of Yoritomo's character would show that his most admirable qualities were those of a statesman. At his best he displayed far-sighted judgment, calm, and patience. He was able to sacrifice the present for the future. Although he was in many respects a reformer he took no reckless steps merely for the sake of change, but was conservative in his policies. Most of the changes which he introduced in methods of government were revivals or adaptations of older practices. He was gifted by nature with a rare political sense, nourished no doubt by concentrated thought during his fallow years of exile. He was not a military genius, though he raised and commanded great armies. He was a man of thought rather than a man of feeling. He can scarcely be described as a man of action, though he knew how to make others act and was crafty in his handling of subordinates, from his leading vassals the great barons down to the simple warriors.

His nature was hard. He was ruthless and cruel, as is shown in his treatment of his half-brother Yoshitsune and the many death sentences he pronounced against men of his own flesh and blood as well as warriors whom he supposed to stand in his way. The history of his rise to power includes many sickening tales of murder. He had great self-control as a rule. He was brave enough as a soldier, and is said to have been a good bowman. But he was not a man of high courage, for he dreaded his rivals. Perhaps it is unfair to cite his relations with his wife as evidence of a cowardly streak; but it is interesting to recall that on one occasion when his secret meetings with a mistress came to the knowledge of the strong-minded and fearless Masa-ko, Yoritomo thought it prudent to stay away from Kamakura for a little while rather than face her anger. It must be admitted that the lady's anger was terrible. She obliged Yoritomo to order the execution of a retainer who had killed her son-in-law at Yoritomo's command.

Although Yoritomo is beyond doubt one of the greatest men in Japanese history, as a person he is not attractive. There is nothing noble about him, nothing on a heroic scale save his insatiable thirst for power. The famous Jingō-ji portrait seems to depict his character faithfully, for it shows him as powerful, determined, satisfied, and withdrawn. An impressive figure, but grim and humourless.

CHAPTER XVI

THE FEUDAL STATE

1. *The Origins of Feudalism in Japan*

THE WORD feudalism has been sadly misused in recent years, for apart from signifying a form of government developed in mediaeval times it has come to mean almost any kind of social habit or economic practice of which the user disapproves. Strictly speaking, feudalism is not a system of government but a sort of land distribution and land tenure from which (especially in a country with an almost exclusively agrarian economy) a particular social structure arises. Nor is feudalism something deliberately created by the rulers of a country in which it develops, for in truth it is the result not of constructive planning but rather of measures taken to preserve order and to protect property where the current system of government is breaking down. Neither King John's barons nor Go-Shirakawa's warlords knew that they were exponents of feudalism. They knew only that they had to devise a system of mutual obligations to save an existing society from collapse. Certainly they had their own interests at heart, but in so far as their policy stood for order and prevented disorder it was a stage in the evolution of more advanced political forms.

In that it conforms to such a pattern Japanese feudalism is not essentially different from European feudalism. At first sight the resemblances between the two are more apparent than the differences. The likeness in terminology is especially striking, for in Japanese there are terms which correspond very closely to such words in the vocabulary of European feudalism as villa and mansus, mancipii, beneficium, honores, and commendatio. There are also analogies in the processes by which feudal institutions developed in Europe and in Japan.

In one respect, however, Japanese feudalism is peculiar. In Gaul, Germany, and Britain the evolution of society from native elements was both interrupted and altered by the intrusion of a powerful foreign element, namely the civilization of Rome, so that European feudalism owes much to Roman ideas. Similarly Chinese civilization had an immense effect upon Japanese life, but there the analogy ends, for it was not the kind of effect—the almost complete Romanization of the people—that was brought about by the Roman conquest of Gaul. Japanese feudalism seems to owe nothing to Chinese influence. On the contrary it might be explained as in many respects a reaction against foreign influence, in that it developed out of a failure of borrowed institutions. In other words, whereas the Taikwa reform had attempted to impose upon Japan a highly regulated and uniform government, the feudal system was a natural growth developed in isolation, subject to no foreign pressure, following no foreign example. It is indeed surprising that such similar results as Japanese and European feudalism should have appeared in such different environments. But on the whole the Japanese system expresses the national temper, and therefore both its external forms and its internal character are in some important respects distinct. As one Japanese writer[1] observes: "The national life under feudalism was a kind of reaction against foreign culture and an assertion of native habits and ideas. The system in Japan may seem irrational and immature in comparison with the European development of sovereign power, parliament, and capitalism, but it must be regarded as on the whole a logical and beneficial phase of growth."

The basis of any feudal system is the ownership or possession of land, and Japanese feudalism arises from a special type of private ownership known as the shō or shōen (described in Chapters VI and VIII). This is analogous to the European manor in so far as both enjoyed certain rights and immunities which in principle belonged to the sovereign as head of the state. Like the European manor, it goes back to pre-feudal times. The term shō originally (in the seventh century if not earlier) denoted the land, usually rice land, owned by a nobleman or a great religious body; just as in England the manor is one of the oldest social institutions, much more ancient than the feudal system which superimposed upon it the conception of the knight's fee, the honores for which a landholder did homage to the Crown. It must therefore be understood that the mature feudalism of Japan comes not from the development of the shō but from its breakdown, by the conversion of a complex of rights and immunities into the complete ownership of land. In the words of the Japanese writer quoted above, the shō is the mother of feudalism, but the birth of feudalism involves the death of its parent.

The process by which the development of the shō, itself an illegal growth, brought about a transfer of authority from the central government to the provincial landed gentry has been described. Here it is sufficient to recall that the class of provincial and local landholders was almost identical with the leading element of the warrior class by the time the great military families, the Minamoto and Taira, had in turn enjoyed a measure of political influence—let us say the time when Kiyomori was at the summit of his power, from about 1160. By then members of the Taira clan not only held many and valuable manors in every province but also appointed stewards to other manors, with the intention of extending Taira control over large areas of agricultural land. They also appointed commissioners (bugyō) in both eastern and western provinces so as to control those members of the warrior class who

[1] Itō Tasaburō, in his Nihon Hōkenseido-shi.

did not readily submit to their discipline. According to the *Heike Monogatari* thirty out of sixty-six provinces were dominated by Taira governors and landowners, while Taira notables were the lords of five hundred manors.

In these cases the manorial rights which they exercised tended in the aggregate to approximate to full ownership, and it was this process of conversion, organized on a grand scale and in a determined manner by Yoritomo and his advisers, which made thirteenth-century Japan into a feudal state.

2. Yoritomo's Land Policy

It will be recalled that Yoritomo, as soon as he felt confident of his strength, had in 1185 induced the government reluctantly to grant to him authority to appoint stewards (*jitō*) and constables (*shugo*) in all provinces. Here as elsewhere, it should be noted, Yoritomo was not a true innovator. He preferred to take established forms or systems and adapt them to his own purposes, being careful not to depart too abruptly from precedent. Thus the stewardship of manors was an office that had been used by Kiyomori to spread his influence throughout the country. The Taira leaders did not directly challenge ultimate domanial rights, which might belong to great nobles or even to the Crown; but the effective administration of each manor and the disposal of its product was in Taira hands. Something of this kind was in the mind of Yoshitsune when he asked Go-Shirakawa in 1185 to grant to Yukiiye and himself stewardships in Shikoku and Kyūshū as a source of revenue to enable them to raise troops in the west. Stewards held lucrative posts and they carried considerable political influence in the region around the estates which they managed.

The appointment of constables is not directly related to Yoritomo's land policy, but it is convenient to mention it here, since it was the business of the constables to keep order in the provinces and watch the behaviour of warriors residing on their estates in country districts remote from Kamakura. Yoritomo had appointed constables to the provinces of Ōmi and Suruga as early as 1180, and he had put his supporters into similar posts elsewhere before the defeat of the Taira. They had nominally functions not unlike those of the Kebiishi—the Police Commissioners under the Crown—including the mobilization of local defence forces. After the Taira defeat Yoritomo temporarily refrained from making such appointments so as to create an impression of moderation; but it became plausible for him to ask sanction for new appointments in 1185 after the Court had commissioned him to chastise Yoshitsune. Kamakura nominees were then sent to twenty-six provinces, while in the six eastern provinces no appointments were made because they were under the direct control of Yoritomo. This difference shows that constables were intended to represent Yoritomo's military strength. It followed naturally that in serious disputes about land the constable was likely to intervene on behalf of stewards appointed by Kamakura and not, as a rule, to respect the interests of the ultimate lord of a manor, who might be a great Court noble or an ecclesiastical body.

This request of Yoritomo's was granted by the Court with the greatest reluctance. What he had asked for was something much more valuable than the power over domanial lands which Kiyomori had assumed as a member of the government. His purpose was nothing less than to obtain imperial authorization to appoint his own followers to the posts of police commissioner (constable) or fiscal agent (steward), not as representatives of the central government but as vassals of the lord of Kamakura, who secured for them these offices of power and profit in reward for military services. These vassals owed, and knew that they owed, the benefits of their offices to Yoritomo as fiefs granted to them by an overlord. Here was the institutional beginning of the feudal rule of Japan, since by agreeing to these appointments the Crown delegated to the servants of Yoritomo the most important public functions, those concerned with the enforcement of law and the collection of revenue.

It should be borne in mind that when Yoritomo in December 1185 asked the Court for permission to appoint his own vassals as constables and stewards throughout the country, he made no distinction between public and private ownership of land. In his memorial he used the phrase *shōkō wo ronsezu*, which means "whether private manors [*shō*] or public domains [*kō*]." It is a curious fact that the petition presented to the Court on December 22, 1185, was granted on the following day. The cloistered Emperor and his nobles had staved off many exacting demands, yet when they made this concession without protest they signed away essential prerogatives of the Crown, which were not to be recovered for nearly seven hundred years. There can be no doubt that Go-Shirakawa was thoroughly frightened. He had already been in danger from Yoshinaka and other military men, and now Yoritomo's armies were on the move while Tokimasa's vanguard was standing ready in the capital.

In practice Yoritomo did not extend his power of appointment to all private and public domains. The Crown retained a considerable range of jurisdiction in certain places, and even in those regions where Yoritomo's vassals held appointments the fiscal and other rights of the central government were, for some time at least, not disregarded. It is difficult to ascertain exact figures, but it seems that Kamakura refrained from placing stewards in manors belonging to the reigning family and the great Court nobles in as many as half the provinces, and that where stewards were appointed they did not levy full taxation upon such properties or collected only modest fees. Thus the blow to the Court was perhaps softened by Yoritomo's moderation; moreover, his sudden and drastic action in exercising these rights was, as we have seen, not without precedent. Not only had Kiyomori taken similar arbitrary steps in his day, but Yoritomo when he was still a refugee had not hesitated to assume rights which belonged to the Crown. In 1180, when he first took arms against the Taira, he issued orders to residents in a domain over which he had no proprietary rights, and thereafter he repeatedly issued charters from his headquarters at Kamakura granting or confirming tenure of lands both private and public. In general he assumed and exercised in the eastern provinces the powers of a viceroy, giving orders to public officials and regulating as an overlord the affairs of his kinsmen and supporters, whom he regarded and treated as vassals owing duty and deserving recompense.

All acts of this nature were encroachments upon the powers of the Throne, as well as in many instances infringements of the rights of private landlords; but so long as his usurpations were limited to the eastern provinces it could be argued that he was only continuing the work of his ancestors, who had been military governors, public administrators, and managers of great estates in that region for several generations. For a time, while the Court could command the loyalty of Taira forces in the east, Yoritomo's irregularities could be checked; but as the Taira armies fell back early in 1181 the east (with some minor exceptions) fell under the control of Minamoto vassals. The Court could no longer repress Yoritomo and was indeed inclined to conciliate him.

Thereafter it made no effort to prevent Yoritomo from exercising sovereign rights in the east. Here he applied himself to his main task, the consolidation of his power, by bringing great and small warriors under vassalage, by invoking their loyalty to the Minamoto house, and by confirming or granting to them tenure of land and other rights and privileges. In this he had great success, for even in the early days of his rising, after September 1180, he was joined by warriors with thousands of men. During the period of the undeclared armistice after the Taira moved away in the spring of 1181, he became the real master of the eastern provinces, thanks to his growing military strength and to his control of land, some of which he obtained by illegal methods such as confiscating the properties of domanial lords residing in the capital. Thus by the end of 1185, when he applied for permission to appoint constables and stewards throughout the realm, he was already firmly established in the east, and as for the rest of the country his military strength was such that the Court could refuse him nothing. The Court was frightened; yet it was also moved by some feeling of gratitude, or at least of relief, upon being freed from the ruinous attentions of the Taira and, almost as gratifying, from the exactions of such generals as Yoshinaka and Yoshitsune. These are circumstances not to be overlooked in accounting for the successes of Yoritomo.

If those successes are to be described in material terms, there can be no doubt that the real source of his power was the substantial control of rights in land throughout the realm. It would have been possible for him to dominate the Court, to insist upon such high offices as had been held by Michinaga and Kiyomori. But he was not tempted by Court life. He regarded himself as a chieftain of warriors, not as a minister of the Crown. He knew that his power rested not upon the favours of the sovereign but upon the contentment of his vassals, their satisfaction with the land which they held. It is therefore not surprising that Yoritomo kept the Court at arm's length, and stayed away from its influence in his home at Kamakura, the proper seat of feudal government, where his ancestor Yoriyoshi had founded the shrine of the War God and where it was now his chief task to organize his vassals. There is no doubt that he thought of their loyalty as based upon tradition, to be sure, but subsisting ultimately upon the benefits of property. His organization was directed mainly to a just combination of discipline and protection of the warriors who recognized him as their overlord. It is therefore not surprising that one of the most important features was its judicial machinery for settling disputes about the tenure of land—no longer only in the east, but now throughout the country. Most scrupulous attention was paid to the examination of charters and instruments of sale or lease, and the tribunals of the Bakufu strove to give impartial decisions between litigants, without respect for rank. In general they succeeded in gaining the confidence of the vassals in the justice of the courts.

It may be useful at this point to indicate the kind of rights and duties which were usually at stake in suits about land. We have seen that the Japanese manor (shō) was an area of farm land (mostly rice land) owned by a noble personage or a religious body. It was either partly or wholly exempt from public taxation. The persons dwelling in those manors were usually in some degree also exempt from public jurisdiction (that is to say from entry by officers of the provincial or local government), and the tendency of such immune estates was to grow in size by the accretion or absorption of further land or people legally in the public domain.

With the expansion of the area under cultivation there naturally took place an increase in the number of tenants, and of these most belonged to that class of warrior-farmer which had come into being largely because the metropolitan government was unable to keep order in the provinces.

These warriors, ranging from a small family living and working on the land to a wealthier household employing farm workers and enjoying rights in large cultivable areas, tended to form groups under leaders of proven courage and ability, and it was in this way that binding relations of lord and vassal arose. These expanded so much that small bands and parties which had naturally come together for protection or, at times, for aggression, coalesced into larger bodies consisting of lord and vassal and rear-vassal bound together by common interest and a tradition of fidelity. Of such larger bodies the best example was the warrior society owing allegiance to Yoritomo as chieftain of the Minamoto clan.

The members of this society in all its grades depended upon land for their subsistence, since there was no other form of wealth. But because of the previous history of land tenure in Japan the warriors did not as a rule enjoy full ownership of land, but only rights in land of varying kinds not amounting to full ownership, or rights to certain offices of profit under the local government or under great manorial lords. Because of these peculiar conditions the typical warrior was not solely the vassal of a military leader, but was also the servant of a public or private landlord, to whom he had to render either some form of official service or the payment of a fixed proportion of the produce of land which he controlled.

In a society of this nature, over which the central government was unable to exert full power, such means of support needed the protection of some great personage. Should the warrior's rights appertain to a part or parts of a manor belonging to a nobleman with influence at Court, that fact would usually assure him against invasion of his rights by the civil authority or by other landholders. But for protection against armed attack he needed rather than a good legal claim the support of a powerful warrior; and such support he could obtain by becoming the vassal of a strong chieftain, who in return for an oath of loyalty would confirm the rights of the vassal and even, if it seemed advantageous, confer further rights upon him. One such right was the right to the management of a manor, the so-called Steward's Office (Jitō-shiki), which had a counterpart among the honores of European manors; this was a most lucrative office in some estates. Other rights, perhaps less lucrative but nevertheless valuable, were the right to the whole of the produce of a certain area of land, or to a share with others in such rights, or to a fixed proportion of the crop of specified fields.

Since the possible combinations of rights and obligations in respect of land under such a system were obviously very many, conflicts of interest and disputes between interested parties were sure to be frequent. To these the feudal government was bound to pay close attention, and it is no exaggeration to say that its most important and most difficult function was the firm and just execution of its land policy.

3. *The Organization of Feudal Government*

In the earliest phase of his effort to mobilize his clansmen, Yoritomo, when he was still technically a rebel, made seizures and grants of land that were arbitrary and illegal. Most of these transactions were recorded in written instruments, because that was a custom of long standing; and as far as possible he followed the usual forms in documents by which he granted, confirmed, or modified rights in cultivated land. But there is no sign in his acts during those years, from 1180 to 1183, of any care to follow set principles or rules in the treatment of warriors and their fiefs. He acted as emergency required in the completion of his great enterprise, the building up of a strong and obedient society of warriors.

After 1183, favoured by the fortunes of war, he began to plan more carefully with the intention of developing a valid feudal law out of the multiple precedents he had created by his interference with the national law based upon the constitution of 645. This interference was to continue, but it was to be regulated; and although in practice it involved a very considerable erosion of the powers of the Throne, in principle the feudal chieftain never claimed independence of the imperial rule. Yoritomo's purpose, regardless of its consequences in other spheres, was to create a strong system of vassalage which he and his successors were to administer with strict justice. The chieftain of the Minamoto clan was to be the ruler of the eastern provinces, the leader of all warriors wherever situated, and at the same time the guardian of the Throne and the protector of the state. For these reasons Yoritomo was careful to limit his relations with the aristocratic Court to formal interchanges. He was firm in his determination to make Kamakura the permanent seat of feudal government. His vassals were strictly forbidden to enter Court society or to take any office from the Crown without his approval; and he himself would accept no appointment or title other than that of Commander-in-Chief (Sei-i Tai-Shōgun), apart from honorary military ranks. He would permit his vassals to accept nomination as provincial governor, but only in eastern provinces over which he claimed authority. He himself accepted governorships of Izu and Sagami, but those were provinces which he already controlled.

As we have seen, the name given to Yoritomo's organization in Kamakura was "the Bakufu," a Chinese term originally applied to the headquarters of the Commander of the Imperial Guard. The exact date when this appellation was first applied to Yoritomo's headquarters at Kamakura is doubtful; it may have been in 1190, when he was designated Commander of the Right Division of the Guard. As early as 1180, however, there was an office which, however rudimentary, functioned in control of military affairs. This office, which Yoritomo set up upon settling in Kamakura, was known as the Samurai-dokoro or Service Room. Originally designating a room in the residence of a great noble where servants waited on call, this term gradually came to mean a guard room for soldiers on duty, and later an office where all affairs of the military were dealt with—their privileges, their obligations, their property, their ranks or dignities, and their treatment in general.

A peculiar feature of feudal society in Japan, which has no very close parallel in European feudal practice, was the close control of the lord over the personal life of the vassal. It extended to details of the conduct of the vassal and members of his family, their marriages, friendships, pastimes, and expenditure. The purpose of this supervision was to ensure that no ties of duty or sentiment should stand in the way of sacrifices on behalf of the overlord, should they be demanded. It was one of the functions of the Samurai-dokoro to organize this kind of surveillance over the lives of the feudal nobility and gentry, for the purpose of testing their behaviour as well as providing for their welfare.

The Samurai-dokoro at Kamakura came into prominence in 1181, when Yoritomo, hearing of the Taira plan to attack the eastern and northern provinces, ordered its director (*bettō*) Wada Yoshimori to summon all vassals to arms. In wartime the Samurai-dokoro was a kind of headquarters staff, with the difference that its senior members went to the fighting front with the armies. They were supposed to encourage and reward the troops and to advise the commanders, but no doubt their chief purpose was to keep an eye on ambitious generals. Wada, it will be remembered, was with Noriyori and Kajiwara with Yoshitsune in the final campaign against the Taira, and played an important part as a leader at Dannoura.

In the situation of Yoritomo at the outbreak of the civil war the Samurai-dokoro was obviously a most necessary and important establishment, since his purpose was to raise a great army consisting of warrior chiefs with their followers, men who would give him their trust and be entirely under his orders. In other words his aim was to bring all individual warriors under one single discipline and so to strengthen their unity as a class. Further, for the settlement of the many problems that arose as military government developed it was necessary to find men skilled in the conduct of official business. For this purpose he summoned from the capital two experienced men, hereditary scholars and administrators, Nakawara (Ōye) Hiromoto and Miyoshi Yoshinobu, establishing them at Kamakura as advisers.

The office over which these men presided was called the Kumonjo, a name corresponding to Secretariat, and it was established in November 1184. This was Yoritomo's highest administrative organ. At the same time, no doubt on the advice of the experts from Kyoto, a judicial body named the Monchūjo was created to enquire into disputes between vassals, thus performing the functions of former judicial officers of the Crown and also of the private manorial courts which had come into being with the growing complexity of manorial rights and obligations. Much later, when Yoritomo's position was firmly established, having returned from a visit to the capital where (as we have noted) he was treated with deference and offered high military titles, he changed the title of the Kumonjo to Mandokoro, which was the usual description of the household office of a great nobleman, where his private and some-times his public business was transacted. Here there is a curious item of history which seems trivial but explains Yoritomo's view of his own function. When he first accepted and then declined the office of U-Konoye Taishō in December 1190 he kept the title of that office, regarding himself as head of the household of the Commander of the Right Division of the Guard (Udaishō-ke) on the ground that his an-cestors had served in such a capacity. He could thus with propriety establish a Mandokoro like that of, say, the head of the Fujiwara clan. This he did in January 1191, and for a long time after that he was styled Udaishō-ke. The purpose of the change from Kumonjo to Mandokoro was no doubt to emphasize the personal character of Yoritomo's rela-tionship with his vassals, and to distinguish his secretariat from govern-ment offices in the capital by marking its independence.

When Yoritomo returned from his visit to the capital at the end of 1190, he had made up his mind on the future organization of the Bakufu and on the persons to be appointed to its more important offices. The Kumonjo had been under the charge of Ōye Hiromoto, with the style of Shikken or Director, presiding over a board of councillors; and when the change to Mandokoro was made in the new year 1191 Hiromoto remained in his post. He was succeeded in 1203 by Hōjō Tokimasa, and thereafter the office of Shikken was held by members of the Hōjō family, who were thus de facto heads of the feudal government.

These three offices together (Samurai-dokoro, Mandokoro, and Mon-chūjo) formed one organ for carrying out military government, and once the necessary appointments had been made the Bakufu was in full operation. Despite the military connotation of the term Bakufu, Yori-tomo's administration was conducted on civil rather than military lines, following for the most part precedents of government under the noble heads of ministries in the capital. Indeed, as the power of the Bakufu increased and extended over the whole country, he rarely exceeded in form and function the methods of managing household retainers and property that were traditionally used by private individuals of great wealth and distinction. The Bakufu was in essential respects not dif-ferent from the Fujiwara Mandokoro.

This is a point which needs some elaboration, since it helps to explain the nature of feudal government in Japan. It was in Kamakura that the feudal tradition was established. The Kamakura government in its essential features was similar to the household office of a great noble-man. In fact it was a copy, more or less deliberate, of that arrangement, which was of respectable origin, since rules for the conduct of such an office are laid down in the Taihō code, under the heading of the Law of Households. The management of the household of the chieftain of a great clan such as the Fujiwara required organization on a grand scale as soon as the wealth of the clan began to exceed that of the royal family. Consequently the Fujiwara Mandokoro was comparable to the Chancellor's Office (Dajōkan) of the central government, which in fact if not in name it gradually superseded.

The Fujiwara Mandokoro had a large staff, presided over by a director and including senior officials of high Court rank. In its business a strict official procedure was followed. Here the parallel with the organization of the government of the Crown was very close. There was even a Kurando-dokoro, corresponding to the extra-legal body of that name which exercised great power in the royal palace.

The abdicated emperors also, when they began to take an active part in government, resorted to these private methods by setting up an office which resembled the household office of a nobleman. This was the In's Office (Inshi, or In no Tsukasa) which usually had great authority, at times issuing orders and rules overriding the decisions of the central government. Its staff was privately, not officially, appointed and consisted of the cloistered sovereign's favourites, his stewards and chamberlains, and occasionally attendants of even lower rank. It was a family affair, not a disciplined government office; but it had great power.

Thus by the end of the Heian era private organs were in charge of almost all important administrative functions, exercising real authority while the constitutional organs created by the codes began to wither away. Before long things came to such a pass that most public functions were performed by organs that were private in origin. This trend seems to be characteristic of the institutional growth of Japan, where the tribal spirit refuses to submit to regulation. It is a feature of Japanese history which should not be overlooked by students of political notions and practices.

To sum up, here was no question of a carefully thought out political theory but rather a series of political afterthoughts. Arrangements were made on severely practical lines to suit conditions of time and place. Their purpose was to control and lead the vassals of the Minamoto, and what came with or after that was secondary. It is in the nature and treatment of the vassals that we find the true character of the feudal administration.

The authority of the Bakufu depended upon the allegiance of the Shōgun's vassals and upon his grant to them of benefits in reward for their service. These were the fundamental conditions of feudal society. In its early phases in Japan the relation between lord and vassal had a strong personal character. When a warrior applied for the status of direct vassal of the Shōgun he was ceremoniously received by Yoritomo, and upon swearing loyalty he was accepted as a member of the clan of which Yoritomo was Chieftain. But in course of time, as the number of vassals increased, his deputies in many parts of the country, for instance, the Daikan at Kyoto and the constables of distant provinces, were authorized after investigation to forward written recommendations to Kamakura. In no case, however, could the status of direct vassal be acquired by a person, however meritorious, who had not the rank of samurai.

The bond between the Shōgun and his direct vassals, being the very essence of the feudal system, could not be easily loosened. Only in the event of most grave offences would the Bakufu cease to give its protection to the life and property of a vassal; and for the same reason it was quick to prevent any infraction of a vassal's rights by third parties.

The word for vassal in the vocabulary of Japanese feudalism is *kenin,* which means house-man, house being used here in the sense of a family. Thus a vassal was, in the early days of Kamakura, a member of the Minamoto family who owed the clan chieftain a family loyalty as well as a warrior's duty. To be a house-man, a kenin, was a most valuable privilege, very sparingly granted and very jealously preserved. Though it was at first confined to those who were true kinsmen of Yoritomo, as time went on and Yoritomo's authority grew firmer and spread wider he saw fit to invite warriors who had been his allies, and even some who had been his enemies, to become his vassals; and here, though the relation between lord and vassal was contractual, it tended to acquire at the higher levels a certain quality of kinship, especially after a careful policy of matrimonial alliances had created true family ties. In time there were at least as many vassals of Taira origin as of Minamoto descent.

A good impression of the status of a kenin can be gained from certain documents of the twelfth century. The word kenin in the old codes meant little more than a household servant, but the honorific term go-kenin stood for members of an exclusive caste. The policy of Yoritomo and his successors was to strengthen this comparatively limited class of warriors by giving special attention to their economic interests. At the same time they would deprive of kenin status any person whose behaviour was in their view subversive of feudal discipline. The chronicles of the early Kamakura period record many instances of warriors who, having served the Bakufu well, applied for the rank of kenin but were not allowed it. Even the direct retainers of kenin could not become kenin themselves, though they might be loyal servants and owners of considerable property in their own right. The kenin, in other words, formed a feudal aristocracy or minor nobility, to which admittance was strictly limited.

Similarly the status of a fighting man, a samurai, was rigidly defined, and difficult to acquire. A fighting man who was a follower of a kenin could not become a samurai without official permission from the Shōgun, even when he had performed valuable military service. In one case recorded in the *Azuma Kagami* a prominent kenin, a member of the Hōjō family, wished to promote one of his trusted followers to the rank of samurai, but was refused by the Shōgun, who said: "If you make a samurai of this man who is not a samurai, then one day he will

forget his origin, and try to become a kenin. This cannot be permitted."
It will be seen that in the early feudal days the word samurai did not
stand for any fighting man, but only for a definite rank. Below the
samurai were various grades of follower or attendant (*zusa*). These
were usually foot soldiers wearing light body armour, whereas the
samurai were mounted, wore heavier armour, and carried pennants or
other heraldic insignia.

Of classes below the samurai and his followers in the Kamakura
period we know very little. The lowest class of the population consisted
as heretofore of the workers on the land and of certain guilds of unskilled
labourers. The rigid class distinctions which had been traditionally
observed, and in general recognized by the Taihō legislation, were not
formally abolished but tended to be relaxed and even to disappear in
some cases. The guilds were not strictly maintained, and in course of
time workers on the land in certain estates acquired rights which, though
not of great value in themselves, gave security of tenure and a somewhat improved status, because the demand for farm workers usually
exceeded the supply. Here we see early stages in the development of
a peasant class, consisting of small cultivators who have prescriptive
rights, amounting to ownership, in the soil they till.

Less numerous than the peasant landholders but of great importance
was the class of skilled workers in crafts ancillary to agriculture and
industrial workers in general, such as smiths, carpenters, masons,
weavers, and metalworkers of all kinds. We do not know much about
their standard of living, but there is good evidence of a rapid improvement in metallurgy and other industrial techniques during the twelfth
century, stimulated no doubt by increased production of food and by the
demands of trade with China.

Domestic demand was also increased by the peace which followed
the Gempei War. The prosperous vassals of Kamakura and the wealthy
nobles of Kyoto encouraged the building of new houses and sacred
edifices, which it was usual to decorate in a costly fashion. Architects,
painters, and sculptors found their way to Kamakura from 1185 onwards,
so that the once simple feudal society tended to become more varied
in its composition. Artists were not high in social rank, but they were
treated with respect, as were men of letters and religious leaders.

Perhaps the most interesting phenomenon in the social life of the
middle ages was the position of the Buddhist clergy. To become a monk
was almost the only way for a youth of humble origin to rise in the
social scale. He could obtain a good education, his holy calling protected him against bodily danger, and if he was promoted in ecclesiastical rank he could mix on equal terms with men in high places.

All the people so far mentioned come within the category of "good
people" (ryōmin), that is to say freemen, in contrast to the "base people"
(semmin). These "base people" include servants and slaves and certain workers in despised occupations such as butchers, leather workers,

and others who handle slaughtered animals and thus offend against the Buddhist rule not to take life.

By the eleventh century the distinction between free and unfree people was breaking down, partly by reason of intermarriages. The appellations of "slave" and "servant" were not entirely dropped but the semmin themselves, though in law the property of their masters, gained a certain de facto independence—notably during the early Kamakura period, when there was much movement and some economic growth which added to their value. They came to be treated not as chattels but as if there were a contractual relationship between master and man. This may not have made their material condition much better, but it was a step towards emancipation.

This slow improvement in the life of the semmin should not however be regarded as a substantial reform effected in the Kamakura period. The lower orders continued to be subjected to a harsh and oppressive rule, and it was still quite possible for a free person to sell or pledge his slaves. But this kind of transaction was discouraged if not positively forbidden in places under direct jurisdiction of the Bakafu or its vassals, especially when it concerned a member of a "free" household. Some light is thrown upon the attitude of the feudal authorities by the action which they took in the winter of 1232–33, when they were striving to moderate the effect of year after year of famine and plague. As an emergency measure the sale and purchase of human beings (not only slaves) was permitted, so that distressed families could raise funds for necessities. This was only reluctantly allowed, and when the emergency was past an edict was issued (1239) withdrawing the permission and ordering the release of persons already sold.

To revert to the higher grades of feudal society, it will have been seen from the foregoing account of the position of kenin and samurai that the control of vassals by the Minamoto overlord was in its essence private, and was not regarded as a concern of the Throne. Yoritomo always contended that loyalty to himself was loyalty to the Throne, and he would not tolerate any direct relation of service to the Throne by his vassals. This aspect of the government of the warrior class is well illustrated in the circumstances of Yoritomo's campaign against Fujiwara Yasuhira. Yoritomo reported to the Court his intention to chastise Yasuhira for protecting Yoshitsune. He was told that in a time of difficulty there should be no fighting. This ruling embarrassed him, and he asked a leading vassal for advice. He was advised that when the country was at war it was not necessary to obtain the sovereign's sanction for any particular military action. This was an evasive answer, since Yoritomo had not at that time been made Shōgun; but there was a further argument, that Yasuhira's family had been vassals of the Minamoto for generations and therefore could be punished for disobedience without asking for the Court's approval. This view was approved (ex post facto) in an imperial order, and accordingly when Yasuhira was killed his head was not sent to the capital for the sovereign's inspection, because he was a private enemy and not a rebel against the Crown. If the sovereign had regarded Yasuhira as a rebel, he would have given Yoritomo a commission as general with a sword of office (*settō*) to be returned when his task was accomplished. But when Yoritomo was made Sei-i Tai-Shōgun in 1192 he was appointed for life; and thereafter the leader of the warriors was always given the office of Shōgun.[2]

There has been argument among Japanese historians as to whether for the full control of the warrior class it was necessary for Yoritomo to become Commander-in-Chief. The point does not seem to be one of great importance, for we know from reliable sources that Yoritomo ardently desired the office of Sei-i Tai-Shōgun, and was disappointed by Go-Shirakawa's refusal to grant it. His urgent requests to Kanezane for help in obtaining the highest military appointment from the Court produced to his chagrin only empty titles. It was not until after Go-Shirakawa's death that he obtained the coveted office, thanks not to imperial favour but to the influence of Kanezane, whose contribution to the institutional growth of feudalism in Japan was of signal importance.

The written orders issued by the Kamakura Mandokoro in form resembled those called *kudashibumi* which were addressed by great nobles in Kyoto to their inferiors. In substance, however, they differed because the Kamakura government, in its early days at least, was not entangled in the bureaucratic circumlocutions and complexities that had almost choked the central administration. Kamakura was then inspired by a desire for simple and practical methods of conducting the affairs of the warrior class—a soldierly simplicity, one might say. But this early phase was not of very long duration, for the problems with which the feudal rulers had to deal grew in number and in difficulty as the unity achieved in war gave way to the dissensions and rivalries of peace. Most of the arguments among vassals had to do with property and rank, although the adjustment of relations with the Court at Kyoto also gave rise to differences of opinion within the Bakufu. Despite this discontent, however, changes took place only gradually at first, so that a description of the system of government developed soon after Yoritomo received his appointment as Shōgun in August 1192 holds good for some decades to follow.

The first step was the conversion of the earlier Mandokoro into the Shōgun-ke Mandokoro, or Household Office of the Commander-in-Chief. By this change the Mandokoro lost its private character and became the Court or Government of the Shōgun, who as leader of the warrior class throughout Japan dealt with the Court or Government at

---

[2] Not always immediately. Yoritomo's successor had to wait three years.

Kyoto on almost equal terms in all matters concerning the rights and duties of that class.

This development of functions is reflected in changes in the language used by the feudal authority for its orders and acts. Thus, for example, in an order of 1185 Yoritomo describes himself by his personal name, or simply as the lord of Kamakura (Kamakura Dono), but after 1192 his orders run "The Mandokoro of the Shōgun's Household decrees . . . ," the documents being signed not by him but by one or two of his high officials.

Other and simpler forms were used in documents on matters not of great importance. These, being easier to draft and issue, tended to be more frequent as official business grew in volume. They need not be described in detail here, but it is worth noting that in their number and variety we can discern the beginning of that multiplicity of written instruments which is characteristic of the feudal regime. The rule of the sword seems to have been well supported by the rule of the pen. This is no doubt in part to be explained by the presence in Kamakura of numerous civil servants trained in the capital and addicted to forms and precedents; but a respect for letters is traditional in Far Eastern countries in all classes. It must be remembered also that where travel by road was slow and difficult it was important for the Kamakura government to send precise written instructions to the provinces, especially in the earlier period during which its authority in distant parts was not completely established.

As a rule the Bakufu sent its orders in the first place to the constables, since they were military governors in control of vassals in the areas of their respective commands. In the second place orders were, if necessary, passed to the stewards appointed by Kamakura in both manors and public domains. In this way the feudal government planned to exercise a comprehensive authority throughout the country; but in the early days of the Bakufu local organization was imperfect and some warriors were not fully reconciled to Minamoto dominance, so that neither constables nor stewards were able to use their powers to the full satisfaction of Kamakura. It was not until some decades after the founding of the Shōgun's government that its representation in the provinces became efficient and tolerably uniform.

It is convenient here to recapitulate the functions of the constables and stewards. The office of Constable had its origin in the appointment by Yoritomo of leading warriors to represent him in some of the western provinces, as part of his military measures against the Taira. With the reluctant consent of the Court this system was made permanent and applied uniformly in about half the provinces, Yoritomo himself assuming the title of Constable-General (Sō-tsuibushi). The main function of the constables was the arrest of rebels and criminals, formerly the duty of the Police Commissioners (Tsuibushi or Kebiishi). They also were empowered to summon the vassals for military service, and certain other functions were later assumed by them.

In 1185, when he was first authorized to appoint constables, Yoritomo was not powerful enough to extend this right to all provinces. He could rule the east directly, but in the west and for a time in the north he had to make concessions to local particularism. Before the campaign against Fujiwara Hidehira he was of course unable to send officers to Mutsu and Dewa, while in the home provinces, in order not to offend the imperial dignity, he left it to the Bakufu representative in the capital to oversee his vassals and the warrior class in general, without any special commission.

Apart from the Shōgun's deputy who resided in the Rokuhara quarter of Kyoto—the traditional home of the warrior chieftains on duty in the capital—there was a special commissioner for the Defense Headquarters of Kyūshū (Chinzei), who was styled Chinzei Shugo or Chinzei Bugyō or, later, Chinzei Tandai.[3] The first man to hold this post was Amano, who in 1186 was sent to Kyūshū with orders to destroy any remaining supporters of Yoshitsune. In the following year Nakawara Nobufusa was sent as a special envoy of the Bakufu, with orders to suppress and destroy all resistance in southern Kyūshū (especially in Kikaijima, where there was discontent and revolt on a not very large scale). Nakawara then became High Constable of Kyūshū, with headquarters at Dazaifu, the old seat of military government in Kyūshū. All Bakufu orders went through Dazaifu, no doubt because it was felt that independent Kyūshū warriors would not submit to the constables appointed to the ordinary provinces.

There was another special commissioner in Nagato, the extreme western province of the main island, which was regarded as of special strategic importance. In the north once Yasuhira had been crushed, Yoritomo appointed commissioners for Mutsu and Dewa, whose duty was to keep order and at the same time to watch over the interests of Minamoto vassals. On Yoritomo's instructions the former dependents of the Fujiwara were conciliated as far as possible, and invited to submit to Kamakura and to have their fiefs confirmed. Many of them accepted this offer.

The Kamakura government, as its organization proceeded, delegated a good deal of authority to its representatives in the west, who were usually styled Tandai. Both the Tandai in the capital (there were two) and the Tandai of Kyūshū presided over offices resembling those of the Kamakura government, with their own Samurai-dokoro and so forth. These offices could issue orders in their own names, without citing the authority of the Shōgun. Such orders were in recognized forms, and

[3] The term Tandai has the general sense of an Inspector or Examiner. It was used of judges at a poetry contest; of supervising monks in a seminary; and of commissioners sent by the central government to keep an eye upon local officials.

were known as Rokuhara Mikyōsho and Chinzei Mikyōsho, the word *mikyōsho* meaning a written order from a high authority.

The origin of the office of Land Steward (Jitō) is obscure, but it is mentioned in documents of about 1130 as an office of profit and it no doubt existed long before that date. The function of a steward was to manage and supervise the business of a large estate, to keep order among its residents, to see to the collection of dues and the remittal (after deducting his own allowance) of a prescribed portion of the earnings of the land to the manorial lord. A typical manor (shō) consisted of parcels of land of various kinds, such as:

Land belonging to the lord of the manor, usually a great nobleman
Land belonging to a religious body
Inherited land, called "name fields" (*myōden*), usually farmed by its owner
Land donated to the lord of the manor for protection, but occupied and farmed by its owner, usually an allotment holder or a small cultivator by whom the land had been reclaimed
Land other than rice land, such as upland fields, moors, marshes, and forests.

The distinction between ownership and possession was variable. In some cases the owner and the possessor were the same, while in others the owner was unable to retain possession. Much depended upon the rank and influence of the ultimate proprietor (known as Honke or the "house of origin"), who was represented on the spot by his agent, the steward. Sometimes the steward was sent in by the proprietor to reside in the manor; more frequently he was a local man engaged for the purpose because of his local knowledge and influence. Such men were as a rule warriors, who could exercise complete control over the workers of the shō and if need be defend their rights by armed strength against any person or authority that challenged them. Thus the manor was strictly speaking an illegal growth, but it developed upon such a scale and served the interest of so many powerful persons that the state was bound to recognize it, the more so since almost all the nobles and officials in the capital and all the great monasteries and shrines lived upon income received from manorial rights. It was for this reason that the illegal and the legal systems grew up side by side without any great conflict. There were of course disputes between the representatives of the central and provincial governments and the officials of the manors, usually concerning the fiscal and juridical powers claimed by each side; but on the whole the manor flourished while the civil authority, following a general trend, declined; and so the relative power of the manorial officers increased. In early times those officers, whether newly appointed or of long standing, began to seize rights which belonged to the lord of the manor or to other tenants in the shō; this process very soon turned into virtual confiscation, and the manors became for all practical purposes the property of the stewards and their office became hereditary. As vassals of the Minamoto they were confirmed in their dubious title to the land which they had administered, and thus it is right to say that Japanese feudalism was based upon the breakdown of the manorial system.

It would be a mistake, however, to suppose that Yoritomo went out of his way to encourage confiscation as a matter of policy. It had for a long time been usual and easy for stewards to seize rights in the manors which they superintended and they needed no encouragement, though of course they welcomed support from a powerful leader. Between the time of his rising in 1180 and the time when he asked the Court for authority to appoint stewards, a space of six crowded years, he had learned a great deal by experience and he had acquired a staff of trained administrators. It was doubtless on the advice of men like Ōye Hiromoto that he took advantage of an irregular situation and, grasping the importance of the office of steward, used his prestige as a victorious general to force the required concession from the government in Kyoto. This was a clever move, for he thus left the manorial system as a whole unchanged, and confined himself to establishing a direct connexion between the Bakufu and that part of the system which was concerned with the management of estates. The functions of the stewards whom he appointed or confirmed were not interfered with, but now those stewards could not be dismissed or transferred or otherwise commanded without the consent of Kamakura even when they were guilty of illicit acts, and so their office became hereditary.

Once the constables and stewards were installed and the administrative organs at Kamakura well established, Yoritomo was better fitted than the sovereign to govern the whole country, for the bureaucratic leaders in the capital could not count upon obedience to their rulings in the provinces. Yoritomo could count on obedience because he could apply drastic sanctions through his provincial and local officers.

He had a further advantage: he was served by some of the most talented and experienced administrators in the country, men from the families of hereditary lawyers and officials who found in Kamakura scope for their powers and a respect which had not been accorded to them in the capital, where birth was more prized than brains. Chief among them was Ōye Hiromoto, but there were others of the kind, bearing names that figure in all the chronicles, among them Miyoshi and Nakawara.

With the development of the offices over which these experienced men presided there was formed a new civil service, composed partly of officials from Kyoto and partly of men drawn from the warrior class who had a taste for secretarial work. This made an important change in the nature of feudal society, especially in Kamakura, a quiet city which usually had the air of an administrative centre and not a military capital.

Finally Yoritomo could count upon the loyalty of his clansmen and of many vassals of other families who had given him their allegiance freely. In those early days, at least, the sense of obligation and duty was well developed. In contrast to the easygoing manners of civilian society, the pristine virtues still flourished among the warriors. They had a strict code which demanded the ultimate sacrifice by the vassal for the sake of his lord. The most cynical student of the pretensions of the warrior's code as it is set forth and embellished in romantic literature is bound to admit that there was a genuine tradition of loyalty, a regard for honour, and an ideal of knightly conduct that contributed to the growth of a distinct national ethos in later ages. The habit formed under the stress of warfare influenced in varying degrees the morals of classes other than the fighting men.

4. *The Warrior's Code*

Our sources of knowledge of the growth of the code of behaviour described in modern times as Bushidō or the Way of the Warrior are principally the military chronicles and romances beginning with the *Masakado-ki*, the *Mutsu Waki*, and similar documents. These were written by monks or by lay scholars whose purpose was to tell an improving story in praise of courageous deeds; and it is extremely likely that in recording instances of bravery and self-sacrifice they helped to create a legend and to found a tradition.

When Yoritomo called upon the Minamoto warriors in 1180 he was counting upon a tradition of loyalty already formed, and his faith was justified. His claim to leadership of the clan was accepted by his enemies as well as his kinsmen. It is true that it was a fact of genealogy that could hardly be disputed, and nobody thought of challenging his position. The historical connexion between lord and follower was something that all warriors recognized; and it was in order to emphasize the continuity of this relationship that Yoritomo chose as his headquarters the small town of Kamakura, where Yoriyoshi had resided as Governor of Sagami, where his father had lived, and where the clan god was worshipped. Thereafter, as we have seen, he paid close attention to promoting the solidarity of his clan.

Since his undoubted ambition was to become the leader of all warriors, it may in a very general way be said of his policy as it developed after 1180 that he was aiming at the unity of the warrior class, without undue emphasis upon pedigree. Although he was inspired by a ruthless hunger for power, as his record fully demonstrates, it is clear from the nature and measure of his successes that the unity he sought was more in keeping with the deep-seated traditions of Japan, more suited to the times and the circumstances in which he worked and flourished, than the declining aristocratic order which he shaped to his own purposes. The system that he set up, however incomplete by exacting standards, was something more durable than a mere temporary association of enemies of the current regime; and here we encounter an aspect of Japanese history which is perhaps unique, for there can be little doubt that the degree of unity brought about by Yoritomo's efforts could be achieved only where traditional sentiment set the greatest store on loyalty. Some native historians, it is true, appear to exaggerate the part played in Japanese life by the tie between lord and vassal, leader and follower, master and man. But there can be no doubt that personal loyalty was a most important element in the system of mutual obligations out of which a mature feudal society developed during the thirteenth century.

Our chief source of knowledge about the warrior's code of behaviour as it developed in Yoritomo's own times is the classic *Azuma Kagami*, or "Mirror of the East," a remarkable work which records in chronological order the events that went into the formation of the warrior class, and the code of behaviour that was to colour if not to dominate Japanese notions of morality for centuries thereafter. It opens with a description of the raising of the first levies of the Minamoto clan by Yoritomo in the late spring of 1180, and ends with the events of the year 1266, just prior to the Mongol threat to invade Japan. The first part of this work was compiled about 1270, largely from private journals and records kept by noblemen of the old regime, and deals with a very wide range of subjects; the second part is based upon official records of the Kamakura government and furnishes valuable historical data for study of the social and economic history of Japan in the later middle age. As might be expected, the account of the growth of the new military society after 1180, and especially of the struggle between the Minamoto and the Taira, includes many enthusiastic descriptions and praises of the code of behaviour of the individual warrior. Not all these tales of chivalry are trustworthy versions of events and ideas. Nevertheless the "Mirror of the East" reflects an image of the truth, distorted perhaps but real and tangible in its essence, because the ideals of a society are part of its character even when they are rarely attained.

With these conditions in mind we may take from the *Azuma Kagami* and similar sources some instances of heroic conduct that are praised as conforming to the duty of a vassal to his overlord.

First, bearing upon the nature of the relationship between lord and vassal in early Kamakura days, there is an anecdote which illustrates the strong moral element and the relatively weak contractual element in the feudal bond. Hatakeyama Shigetada, once a Taira partisan, had submitted to Yoritomo and become his vassal. Upon being accused by an enemy of plotting treason, he was examined by an emissary from

Kamakura who requested him to declare his innocence upon oath. Hatakeyama refused, saying that Yoritomo had no right to suspect him. He was a warrior and had given his word. That was enough.

The warrior does not ask for favours from his lord. He counts upon leadership and protection, but he makes no conditions about rewards. The relation between the two parties subsists upon loyalty alone. The warrior does not question the commands of his lord, but obeys them regardless of his own life, his family, and all his private interests. In defeat he must bear in mind what he owes for past favours and must be ready to die in the cause of his lord, or in the cause of the family or clan of which he is a member. It follows that a warrior's life belongs to his lord, and he may not dispose of it to suit his own ends, or merely to preserve his own reputation. Thus a brave warrior, one Sadatoki, when in danger from a robber evaded him in what seemed a cowardly way, because he felt that he must not risk his life to satisfy his own pride, still less to protect his own property, but preserve it for the service of his lord.

Among the earliest statements of the rule that a warrior's first duty is to die for his lord is the response of wounded soldiers to the compassion of Yoriyoshi, which is recorded in the *Mutsu Waki*: "We shall give our bodies to pay our debt. For our leader's sake we will perish without regret." It is most unlikely that wounded men spoke those words, but probable that this spirit prevailed among the followers of the Minamoto chieftains in their severe campaigns in the northern wilds.[4]

Another instance of this kind is the death of Saeki Tsunenori, who mistakenly supposing that Yoriyoshi had been killed in battle sought death by plunging into the ranks of the enemy. In this he was followed by some of his own retainers, who (so the legend goes) rushed into the fight saying: "It is our duty to die, humble servingmen though we be."

Of some other courageous fighters who "faced a thousand deaths without a single thought of life" and were all slain in battle for their leader, the chronicler uses a curious phrase, "They attained the warrior's death power," which seems to mean that they had the strength to die and thus triumphed over death. This is perhaps what modern psychologists call the death wish. The historian must confine himself to reporting what the Japanese chroniclers say, only observing that their accounts of feudal society are rich in tales of violent death and record with gusto suicides by the sword. In literature if not in life blood flows very freely, and something like a cult of death accompanies the cult of the sword as the bright, keen symbol of a warrior's honour.

Yet the warrior's code is not free from inconsistencies. One of the puzzling features of feudal ethics is a flat contradiction between the rule that a warrior must not serve two masters and the practice of ac-

4 See Chapter XII, pp. 252–53.

cepting the surrender of an enemy and taking him as a vassal. There is evidently here a conflict between material interests and high-flown professions. Yoritomo was a practical man, and as a rule ready to treat a powerful enemy well if he could make an ally of him. He stood by the doctrine of loyalty because that was what he and other leaders depended upon in an unruly, violent age. On one occasion he displayed his attitude very clearly. A warrior named Ashikaga Toshitsuna had joined the Taira and opposed Yoritomo, who sent a force against him. During the fighting one of Toshitsuna's men, a certain Kawada Jirō, caught him unawares, killed him, and carried his severed head to Kamakura for Yoritomo's inspection. The assassin asked to be received as a vassal, but Yoritomo had him executed forthwith, saying that he did not want the kind of vassal who would murder his own lord. In the same way he treated a treacherous captain in the army of Fujiwara Yasuhira, the great enemy of Kamakura. This man, who owed much to Yasuhira, killed him by a disgusting trick and took his head to Yoritomo, who did not hesitate to condemn him to death for a breach of loyalty.

It is obvious that the leading warriors found it to their advantage to encourage a strict code of obedience and sacrifice, and this no doubt accounts for much of the praise given to acts which, on cold assessment, seem like a deliberate waste of valuable lives. Yet there is no doubt that all societies profit by a strict code, and some of the merits of Japanese culture can certainly be ascribed to the principles which governed the life of the flower of the warrior class and spread to other social levels.

One of the important purposes of a samurai's upbringing was to instill in him a great pride of birth, a readiness to make sacrifices for the family name. This is well illustrated by an anecdote which is worth repeating at some length for the light which it throws on Eastern chivalry.[5]

In Yoritomo's campaign against Yasuhira in the north in 1189, one of Yasuhira's followers, a samurai named Yuri Hachirō, was wounded and captured, and brought to Yoritomo's headquarters by his captor, Usami Sanemasa. There another warrior, Amano Norikage, claimed that he had captured Yuri and therefore deserved the reward which was usually granted to a man who took a distinguished prisoner. Yoritomo ordered Kajiwara Kagetoki to find out from Yuri what had happened, and Kajiwara began to interrogate Yuri in a rough way, saying, "Now, fellow, answer me plainly and truthfully. What was the colour of the armour of the warrior who captured you?"

At this Yuri burst out angrily: "Who are you? A vassal of Yoritomo? What language is this? How dare you address me in such a way! My late lord was in the direct line from the Shōgun Hidehira through three

[5] "Chivalry" is not far out as a translation of *Kyūba no michi*, "the way of the horse and the bow."

generations of commanders-in-chief of the frontier defences. Not even your Master can talk to me in such terms! As for you, I am in every way your equal. The fortune of war may make a warrior a prisoner, but there is no excuse for your behaviour as a servant of the house of the Lord of Kamakura. And I will not answer you."

Kajiwara, thus put to shame, angrily suggested to Yoritomo that the prisoner, who would say nothing but abusive words, should be tortured. But Yoritomo said that the prisoner had no doubt been offended by Kajiwara's bad manners, and that his rebuke was justified. Thereupon another warrior, the above-mentioned Hatakeyama, went to Yuri and treated him with sympathy and courtesy, saying that it was not a disgrace for a brave man to be captured. It was because Yuri was so famous a captain that Yoritomo's officers were disputing the honour of having captured him. Yuri replied that he was quite willing to talk to a man like Hatakeyama, who knew what courtesy demanded. He then described the colour of his captor's helmet and his horse; the colours were Usami's. When this was reported to Yoritomo, he said that Yuri was a good soldier and he wished to talk with him. They then discussed the reasons for Yasuhira's defeat, and Yoritomo gave orders that Yuri should be well treated.

Pride of name is intense. The warrior is always ready to recite his pedigree, whether to justify his actions or to impress his adversary. An incident related in the *Hōgen Monogatari* will serve as an example. Taira Motomori, a young officer proceeding along the road from the capital into the province of Yamato, met a detachment of the enemy proceeding towards the capital. He said to their officer that they could not pass, unless they were accompanied by a messenger bearing an order from the Imperial Court. He then named himself: "I who say this am a descendant of the Emperor Kammu in the tenth generation, grandson of the Minister of Justice Tadamori, second son of the Governor of Aki, Kiyomori. My name is Motomori, my age is seventeen."

At this there stepped forward from the opposite party a man who seemed to be of a general's rank. He said: "Though I am not a person of great importance, I am not without noble ancestry." He then proclaimed his descent from the Emperor Seiwa through nine generations of princes, and named among his ancestors Yorinobu, Governor of Yamato (this was the famous ancestor of the Minamoto warriors of the day), his grandfather, and his father, and then gave his own name in these resounding words: "Uno Shichirō Minamoto Chikaharu, long settled in Yamato province, and not having lost my name as a warrior, I have been sent for by the Minister of the Left to attend upon the new Cloistered Emperor. Since a Minamoto cannot serve two masters, even with an order from the Court I could not enter the Palace." So saying he passed on towards the capital with his company of warriors.

The young Taira captain did not feel that he could stop the Minamoto officer, who was clearly doing his duty by obeying the order of a minister, and was in no way concerned with palace intrigues. The incident shows that a warrior's duty to his clan came before his loyalty to the sovereign.

Sometimes a warrior would announce not only his pedigree, but also the feats of arms for which his ancestors were celebrated. The military romances dealing with the wars of the twelfth century record many instances of such grandiloquence on the field of battle. Though doubtless highly coloured, they may be taken to represent the panache of the fighting men of those times. One example will suffice. During the Hōgen rising Oba Kageyoshi and his third son Kagechika went forward against Tametomo, the great Minamoto champion. The son challenged him, saying: "Lord Hachiman! During the Three Years War, in the attack upon the stockade at Kanazawa, Kamakura Gongorō Kagemasa, then only sixteen years of age, went to the front of the battle, and when his left eye was pierced by an arrow through his visor he loosed a shaft in return and took his assailant. I am the youngest descendant of that Gongorō, Oba Heita Kageyoshi's son, Oba Saburō Kagechika. Come on and fight!"

Scattered through the chronicles of the twelfth and thirteenth centuries, the period during which the feudal society of Kamakura was formed and matured, there are many statements of the ideals by which a warrior should be inspired. These deserve careful examination because they usually have a simplicity of character that distinguishes them from later and more elaborate evidence about the feudal ethos.

One of the most interesting of these relatively early accounts is to be found in the story, long a favourite in the romantic literature of Japan, of the celebrated warrior Kumagae Naozane. In the battle of Ichinotani Kumagae struck down an adversary in single combat and on raising the helmet of the helpless warrior in order to discover his rank found that he was a handsome youth, a mere boy. Reminded of the loss of his own son, killed earlier in the day, he was torn by compassion; and when the youth named himself as Atsumori, a Taira nobleman, Kumagae knew that even if he spared his captive's life Atsumori would be finished off by some less merciful warrior anxious for reward. Having explained his reasons he cut off Atsumori's head, swearing that he would make amends by entering religion and spending the rest of his days in prayer for the soul of the dead youth.

So runs the popular tale. But there is another version which reveals a divergent view of the warrior's duty, and does not make a tragic hero of Kumagae. When he made his intention to forsake the world known to a certain monk he received in reply a letter rebuking him in these words: "A man born in a house of warriors and brought up to bear arms must not feel grief at taking life. It is the duty of a warrior always to bear the fact of death in mind." This somewhat surprising view of a devout Buddhist is explained by his argument that a warrior should not go back on his vows by seeking peace of mind in religious exercises. He must carry out his lifelong obligation by killing himself.

Another well-known anecdote bearing upon the duty of a warrior to accept death is told of Yoshitomo, the father of Yoritomo. When during the Heiji rising of 1159 he found himself in a desperate position, he wished to die fighting. He was urged by a follower, a brave man named Kamada Masajirō, to escape from the battlefield. But Yoshitomo said: "If a man who bears arms escapes from a place where he ought to die fighting, he incurs the uttermost shame."

Death is preferred to flight, and also to surrender. A vassal may accept the shame of surrender if thereby he can save his lord. Thus when Prince Mochihito was in revolt (in 1180) he was in danger of capture. The warrior Hasebe begged the Prince to escape, saying that it was his own duty as a follower to offer his life to his lord, for only in that way could he keep his good name as a warrior. So Hasebe stayed and allowed himself to be captured, in order to delay the pursuers. Then, when soldiers of low rank tried to bind him, he cried: "Stop! How dare you put rope on a samurai?" He refused under torture to say which road the Prince had taken, saying, "Do you think that a samurai can be forced to tell what he has sworn not to tell?" It will be remembered that earlier in the day Minamoto Yorimasa had urged the Prince to escape and had committed suicide near the Byōdō-in at Uji.

Perhaps the best, because the simplest, saying about the good warrior's contempt for death is one ascribed to Yoshitsune when a comrade before an attack suggested preparing a line of retreat: "If you think of saving your life, you had better not go to war at all."[6]

It should be understood that the code of behaviour known as Bushidō or the Way of the Warrior is a body of teaching developed and organized in comparatively modern times by literate samurai, notably such writers as Yamaga Sokō, whose *Shidō* is one of a number of works in which he set forth a well-articulated statement of principles for the guidance of his own class. His writings may be looked upon as the culminating point in a long sequence of efforts to build up into a coherent body of doctrine the ideas and sentiments which had inspired warriors during the period of feudal rule. Yamaga wrote during the years around 1650, and the earliest examples of a systematic approach such as he developed belong to the fourteenth century. They are of interest in the history of Japanese thought, but they all have a certain scholastic, even artificial, flavour. They do not bear that imprint of reality which distinguishes the earlier and simpler beliefs of the fighting men who, without benefit of theory, founded the feudal society of Kamakura.

The most interesting account of those beliefs is to be found in the

6 This is a somewhat free translation of the laconic "Nige-jitaku shitaran ni wa ikusa ni katsu ya?" ("How can you win if you have prepared to escape?")

"Family Instructions" (*Kakun*) of Hōjō Shigetoki, written for the guidance of his son Nagatoki who in 1247, at the age of eighteen, was appointed to the important office of Rokuhara Tandai, the Shōgun's deputy at Kyoto. Here we have not a literary statement of abstract principles but a set of practical rules for the discipline of the men under Nagatoki's command. From these it is possible to infer the views of one of the leaders of feudal society on the duties of the warrior class. The contrast between this document and the elaborate dogma of later exponents is so marked that the student cannot help wondering whether the behaviour of military men was ever influenced by so precise and specialized a code as Bushidō, a code that was not formulated until long after the feudal wars had ended, when the country was at peace and, as the Japanese saying goes, "the waves within the four seas were still." It is obvious that of all virtues it is the military virtues that cannot flourish on a battlefield of paper.

Except for the first article, which is a summary of the duty of a warrior, Shigetoki's instructions contain few general principles. They consist mainly of advice on practical questions with which a young officer is likely to be faced, of professional guidance rather than moral teaching.

The first article enjoins fear (*osore*) of Gods and Buddhas, and unquestioning obedience to lord and parent. A man must be fully aware of the relation of cause and effect (karma, or in Japanese *inga*) and must always consider the result of his actions in future generations. He must be careful in his relations with others, eschewing the company of useless people. In all things he should display a generous spirit, and deserve the praise of others. He must be firm of purpose and never show a sign of cowardice. He must be assiduous in the practice of the military arts. He must be upright in his dealings with people of all descriptions, showing sympathy to the poor and the weak. This statement is concerned with religious morality as much as with the ethics of a warrior caste. There is, here and later, no special emphasis on duty to a feudal superior, the claims of a parent being put upon the same level as the claims of a master in the secular sphere. It is possible that this language arises naturally from the fact that the writer is himself one of the two highest feudal dignitaries, and is thus concerned with telling his son how to behave as a leader, not as a follower. Throughout the forty-odd brief articles that constitute these "Instructions" Shigetoki dwells on ways in which a young leader can make a good impression upon his colleagues and his subordinates.

He pays much attention to points of etiquette in social relations, doubtless because Nagatoki had to associate with members of the Court nobility, whose standards were exacting. Questions of courage, loyalty, and obedience are not raised; they are taken for granted. Indeed manners rather than morals are dwelt upon in detail.

The first article gives, among other pieces of advice, rules for the treatment of social inferiors by a warrior of high rank. Since the Rokuhara Command was a miniature Bakufu, it was important for the Tandai to keep the young warriors in order. They were high-spirited eastern men and needed careful handling. On this matter Shigetoki could speak with authority after long years of experience in military posts in war and peace. Some of his injunctions are worth repeating here in a slightly abridged version:

*

The men under your command, whether samurai, zōshiki, or chūgen, must be carefully chosen for your service. Do not take "difficult" fellows. If men under your orders, however loyal, are wanting in intelligence, you must not trust them with important duties, but rely upon experienced older men. If you are in doubt refer to me, Shigetoki.

In dealing with subordinates do not make an obvious distinction between good and not-good. Use the same kind of language, give the same kind of treatment to all, and thus you will get the best out of the worst. But you yourself must not lose sight of the distinction between good character and bad character, between capable and incapable. You must be fair, but in practice you must not forget the difference between men who are useful and men who are not. Remember that the key to discipline is fair treatment in rewards and in punishments. But make allowance for minor misdeeds in young soldiers and others, if their conduct is usually good.

Do not be careless or negligent in the presence of subordinates, especially of older men. Thus do not spit or snuffle or lounge about on a chest with your legs dangling. This only gives men the impression that you do not care for their good opinion. Preserve your dignity. If you behave rudely, they will tell their families and gossip will spread. You must treat all servants with proper consideration and generosity, not only your own people but also those of your parents and other superiors. If you do not, they will scorn you and say to one another: "He thinks he is very important, but he doesn't amount to much."

Remember, however, that there are times when a commander must exercise his power of deciding questions of life or death. In those circumstances since human life is at stake you must give most careful thought to your action. Never kill or wound a man in anger, however great the provocation. Better get somebody else to administer the proper punishment. Decisions made in haste before your feelings are calm can only lead to remorse. Close your eyes and reflect carefully when you have a difficult decision to make.

When accusations are brought to you, always remember that there must be another side to the question. Do not merely indulge in anger. To give fair decisions is the most important thing not only in commanding soldiers but also in governing a country.

*

Following these passages about the proper attitude of an officer towards his men comes an interesting description of the different grades of warriors in the lower ranks. First come the wakatō, who might be styled subalterns. They were young samurai, a kind of junior retainer, of the same social class as the leader and therefore not difficult to handle. Their commander could allow some familiarity and could understand their point of view, but of course must not show any weakness in their regard. When an officer goes out on horseback he must be accompanied by men of lower rank, chūgen or zōshiki, on foot. But when going out at night or at other times when there was need for caution he must be accompanied by a young samurai, carrying a sword, because a man of chūgen rank was not allowed the use of a sword. Much importance was attached to the experienced warrior of the older steady kind, the equivalent of the trusted noncommissioned officer in modern armies. In general in feudal society the services of men of mature years are thought to be of special value, and the advice of "elders" is frequently sought. A Council of Elders is a common adjunct to administrative bodies, great and small.

Shigetoki's "Instructions" are not logically arranged by subject, but the foregoing paragraphs contain the more important statements about the duty of a warrior. There is no special emphasis on duty to a feudal lord, probably because the purpose of the work is to advise a high feudal dignitary on his obligations as a leader of men. But there are some interesting references to proper behaviour in intercourse with social superiors in general. Thus he explains how to behave when a person of rank sends you a present of a horse. You should not merely summon a groom and tell him to lead the animal away. You should yourself take hold of the bridle and then order a servant to take it. Or if the giver is a person of no special consequence to whom you have no obligation, you need not go so far in showing respect, but may order one of your young samurai of good family to come forward and take the horse to a stable.

There are other suggestions of a similar nature, simple practical advice on social matters, such as one's place at table, or the tone of one's conversation; and there are some very matter-of-fact rules on intercourse with women. But the key to all these admonitions is furnished by a simple rule: "The warrior must always bear in mind his moral duty. A good heart and the faith of a warrior are like the two wheels of a carriage." The faith, the moral duty of a warrior, which is called *giri*, is described as "even at the cost of your life and your family, holding to the good, not yielding to the strong"; "this deep faith is what makes the warrior."

Apart from these broad principles most of the instructions which Shigetoki gives to his sons in the "Instructions" are practical rules of conduct for a gentleman. They include his duty to his parents, his superiors, his inferiors, his wife and children. But taken together with brief general observations on moral duty they seem faithfully to depict the character of a leading member of the feudal elite.

Certain differences between the standards of conduct of the Japanese samurai and the European knight or chevalier arise from differences in the relationship between lord and vassal. In Europe the vassal was not necessarily a knight, but in Japan nearly all vassals were samurai; and there were no plural allegiances as there sometimes were in Europe.

The attributes of chivalry and *yumiya no michi* are not all the same. There is naturally much in common between the two types of feudal society, since they arose from similar origins and responded to similar needs. Thus the feudal lord in Europe would not promise protection to his vassals unless he could with certainty depend upon their loyalty, so that the honour of the warrior is at the heart of the whole system. The Japanese samurai and the European knight each owed obedience to his superiors, and to each the principles of fidelity (fides) were of overriding importance. But there was a difference in the nature of the bond between lord and vassal. In Europe it was in essence contractual. In Japan the samurai owed absolute and unconditional duty to his lord, without claim to recompense and irrespective of other claims upon his service and even upon his life.

The idea that a vassal must not expect reward is not an invention of Japanese feudalism. In Yorinaga's *Taiki* (1153) he gives advice to his sons in these words: "You should not expect reward from your lord in gratitude for your services." Yorinaga was a Fujiwara nobleman, and not a member of one of the military houses. Evidently this view of a vassal's position is traditional, and it was accepted by the warriors as proper and natural. The vassal expected protection from his overlord, in the sense that he held his fief as a vassal, so that he was secure in his tenure of his estate. But his duty to his lord came before all personal obligations whether to his family or his friends or to any other person or institution, even the Throne and the Church.

This was the nature, or rather the ideal, of the warrior's code of behaviour. In some respects it resembles the ideal of Western chivalry, but it demands greater sacrifices by the warrior for his lord than the sworn fealty of the knight. The contrast in one particular is very marked: the moral principles of the warrior do not include any special duty towards women. The military virtues might include pity and compassion, but these sentiments were not especially directed towards women, no doubt because there was in Japan no religious cult of womanhood comparable to that which played so great a part in both pagan and Christian beliefs in Europe.

Something should be said here about the treatment of prisoners of war. According to the ideals of the warrior caste, a man should never surrender, but must die fighting. This view, if strictly held, meant that no consideration was due to a prisoner, since he had no right to be alive. But there were of course many circumstances in which a brave man might be captured. He might be unconscious from wounds, or he might be trapped and overwhelmed before he could take his own life. Thus in practice the question of how to treat prisoners of war did arise. In the fighting against the Mongol invaders in 1274 and 1281 all captives were slaughtered indiscriminately. During the frequent civil conflicts of the twelfth and thirteenth centuries there appears to have been no rule of merciful conduct towards prisoners, and the military romances contain many stories of wounded men killed by their comrades to prevent their being captured alive by the enemy.

There is an interesting anecdote in the *Azuma Kagami* which throws some light on this question. It runs as follows: Yoritomo attacked and defeated the Satake family in 1180, seizing their lands and sharing them out among his vassals. Yoritomo hated these rivals, who were of good Minamoto lineage, and he was not above resorting to treachery. He bribed a disaffected relative of the Satake chieftain and so obtained access to the Satake stronghold. After the fighting a number of captives were brought before him, and he seemed disposed to have them killed. But a youth among them said that it would be a great error for Yoritomo to slay members of his own clan at a time when he needed support. The captives had been loyal to their own lord. Should they be put to death when they might fight against the Taira?

Yoritomo is said to have spared the prisoners, but the anecdote reveals that it would not have been thought morally wrong to kill them. This attitude appears to be in marked contrast to mediaeval and later practice in Western countries. In mediaeval Europe, to be sure, there was not much positive protection for prisoners, but there was a certain negative protection in rules of law which specified when prisoners might legitimately be killed. Thus in attacks upon fortresses all defenders might be put to the sword, because there was no place where prisoners could be confined and no spare force to guard them. Similarly in the field prisoners might be killed if they hampered the action of troops. For example, in the second Civil War in England Cromwell's general at Preston was ordered to kill his prisoners (who were more numerous than his own force) if the enemy attacked; and a similar order was given by Henry V at Agincourt.

These examples suggest that the killing of prisoners was subject to certain rules in Europe, whereas in Japan it seems to have been the custom. There was no practice of ransom in Japan, but it was usual to reward a warrior who captured an enemy of high rank or great prowess. This practice helps to explain the decapitation of prisoners, since it was easy to produce a severed head as evidence when claiming a reward.

Hōjō Regents in the Thirteenth Century

	TERM OF OFFICE		TERM OF OFFICE
Tokimasa	1203–1205	Nagatoki	1256–1264
Yoshitoki	1205–1224	Masamura	1264–1268
Yasutoki	1224–1242	Tokimune	1268–1284
Tsunetoki	1242–1246	Sadatoki	1284–1301
Tokiyori	1246–1256		

The Hōjō family were of Kammu Taira stock, descended from a vice-governor of Izu whose family settled at Hōjō, in that province. Tokimasa was always referred to by the Court as Taira no Tokimasa, and his daughter as Taira Masa-ko.

Titular and Cloistered Emperors after Go-Shirakawa's Death in 1192

	TITULAR		CLOISTERED
	Succeeded	Abdicated	
Go-Toba	1184	1198	
Tsuchimikado	1198	1210	Go-Toba
Juntoku	1210	1221	Go-Toba
Chūkyō (Kanenari) *	1221	1221	Go-Toba
Go-Horikawa	1221	1232	Go-Takakura, 1221–23
Shijō	1232	1242	Go-Horikawa, 1232–34
Go-Saga	1242	1246	
Go-Fukakusa	1246	1259	Go-Saga
Kameyama	1259	1274	Go-Saga (to 1272)
Go-Uda	1274	1287	Kameyama

* Kanenari reigned for seventy days, and was then deposed. It was only in modern times that he was included in the official list of sovereigns, and given the name of Chūkyō.

CHAPTER XVII

THE HŌJŌ REGENTS

1. *Yoritomo's Death*

YORITOMO died in 1199 at the early age of fifty-two, having been thrown from his horse while returning in state from a public ceremony. He had a strong feeling for correct and regulated behaviour, and there is a certain symbolic propriety in the circumstances of his death when performing a public duty.

There was no question of a great political change. It was taken for granted that the Bakufu must be preserved. The administrative system which Yoritomo had founded proved its value after his death. The organs of which it was composed had grown out of experience. Being practical and efficient, they were of a kind to ensure continuity. Yoritomo's eldest son Yoriiye, then a youth of seventeen, succeeded to his father's offices as Constable-General and Steward-General, but he was not at once appointed Shōgun, since the Throne (or more correctly the cloistered Emperor) deliberately delayed investing him with the title in order to stress the prerogative of the Imperial House. The delay was not disapproved in Kamakura, for neither Yoriiye's mother, Masa-ko, nor the leading members of the Bakufu felt confident of the boy's character or ability to govern. Both were anxious not to risk any interference with the existing structure of the warrior society or its relationship with the ancient nobility.

Accordingly a provisional government was quickly established, in the form of a council which was presided over by Yoritomo's former guardian and adviser, Masa-ko's father Hōjō Tokimasa. Its members were the leading warrior chieftains, mostly Yoritomo's former generals, such as Miura and Wada, together with three leading jurists from Kyoto, Ōye Hiromoto, Miyoshi Yoshinobu, and Nakahara Chikayoshi, men who had chosen to leave the service of the Court and put their talents at the disposal of the feudal leaders. This was a new and important element in the ruling class at Kamakura, where one might have expected clerks and lawyers not to be in high esteem.

The new council was by no means a unanimous body. Quarrels among its military members were so frequent that the civilian members had to spend much time and effort on preserving some sort of harmony. One of the unruly barons was Kajiwara Kagetoki, already known for his greed and treachery. He became so intolerable that he was attacked and killed by his colleagues, but his riddance did not bring about harmony in the council. Tokimasa had great trouble keeping it from falling apart. One reason for this state of affairs was the character of Yoriiye, whose physical prowess was remarkable but whose wild and impatient temper made him quite unsuited to direct an administration which his father had carefully built up on a basis of law and justice. In the council both the hasty barons and the cautious lawyers were fearful of what would happen if Yoriiye should be allowed really to govern after his investiture as Shōgun, which took place in August 1202, in a ceremony performed at Kamakura by imperial envoys. The fact that the Court sent its officers to Kamakura instead of summoning Yoriiye to Kyoto gives an idea of the true balance of power as between the Throne and the Bakufu.[1]

Yoriiye's insufficiency and other impediments to enlightened rule were of course very clear to Hōjō Tokimasa, whose position was extremely awkward, since he had to meet opposition not only from troublesome warrior chieftains but also from his own daughter Masa-ko, who thought in terms of the family rather than the nation. In this unsatisfactory though not unusual situation a sudden grave illness of Yoriiye raised further issues. As his successor, or let us say his putative successor, there was a choice between Yoriiye's own eldest son, an infant aged three, and his younger brother Sanetomo, then eleven years of age. A division of authority was proposed, Sanetomo to be made leader of the warriors in the thirty-eight provinces west of the barrier (at Ōsaka in Ōmi province) and Yoriiye's son, Ichiman, to become Chieftain of the Minamoto and leader of all warriers in the twenty-eight eastern and northern provinces.

This proposed allotment was pleasing to some great vassals, including one Hiki Yoshikazu, a trusted companion of Yoritomo's. Since his daughter was Ichiman's mother, Hiki foresaw a situation in which he would be the grandsire and the guardian of an infant potentate—a position coveted by generations of Fujiwara noblemen, but not hitherto enjoyed by a Minamoto warrior.

Yet under this suggested arrangement, although Ichiman as Chieftain of the Minamoto would be the real leader of the warrior society and eligible for the office of Shōgun, his power would be limited by Sanetomo's control over the western warriors. (It should be explained that Sanetomo was the name given to Yoritomo's second son, Senman, by the Court when the Hōjō family proposed him as successor to Yoriiye, whose death they prematurely announced.) Yoriiye was murdered in 1204, while he was living in retirement some distance away from Kamakura. His assassins were allegedly sent by Tokimasa. The accompanying chart makes these somewhat complex relations clear.

---

[1] There was some plotting against the Bakufu in Kyoto in 1201, but it came to nothing, and does not appear to have been encouraged by the Court.

11

12

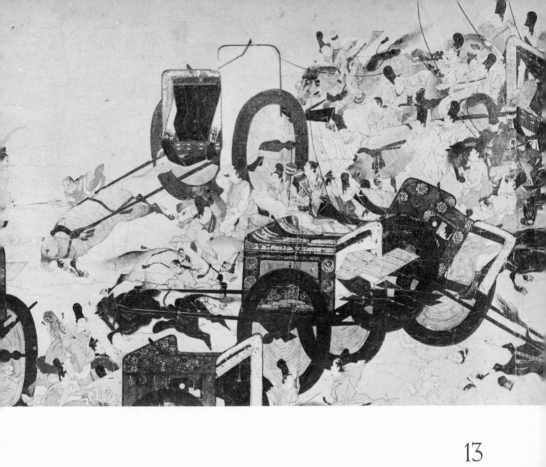

13

14

15

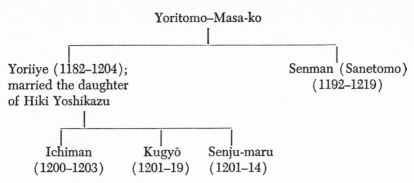

Yoritomo–Masa-ko

Yoriiye (1182–1204);
married the daughter
of Hiki Yoshikazu

Senman (Sanetomo)
(1192–1219)

Ichiman
(1200–1203)

Kugyō
(1201–19)

Senju-maru
(1201–14)

According to legend Hiki, feeling baulked by the proposal to give
Sanetomo a birthright, violently urged Yoriiye, then ill in bed, to have
Sanetomo put to death. One would suppose that, in a country where
screens were a common article of furniture, conspirators would look
behind them before making treasonable speeches. But, the story continues, Masa-ko was standing behind a screen in Yoriiye's sickroom, and
naturally she was incensed by Hiki's plan to have her own son murdered.
The indiscreet Hiki was soon after this assassinated by friends of Tokimasa; and a little later his son with other Hiki kinsmen was destroyed
by the same party, which included Yoshitoki, Yasutoki, and Wada Yoshimori, in an attack upon the palace of Ichiman, who died in the flames.

Yoriiye was so angered by this interference that he ordered two
leading warriors (Wada Yoshimori and Nitta Tadatsune) to kill Tokimasa. The former would not and the latter could not carry out this
order, and Yoriiye, ill and humiliated, was obliged to abdicate. Then
Sanetomo took his place as Chieftain of the Minamoto and was made
Shōgun before the end of 1203. Since he was a minor a Regent was
necessary, and Tokimasa was appointed to the post, newly created, of
Shikken, a title which conveys the idea of an administrator exercising
delegated powers.

Tokimasa was a wise and conscientious statesman, content to remain
behind the scenes; but he could not control certain ambitious vassals
who saw in the minority of the new Shōgun an opportunity for profitable
revolt. Nor indeed could he moderate the political activities of two
strong-minded ladies, his daughter Masa-ko and his second wife, Maki-
ko, who had their own ideas about the succession. Masa-ko wanted to
make sure that her son Sanetomo would not be displaced, while Maki-ko
strove hard to have Sanetomo put away and a very able warrior, Hiraga
Tomomasa, made Shōgun in his stead.

This difficult situation arose out of strong family feeling, for Hiraga
was Maki-ko's son-in-law, a Minamoto of good birth and a successful
fighting man. He came into prominence through his prompt action in

February 1204, when as High Constable, the Shōgun's deputy in Kyoto, he put down a rising of the Ise branch of the Taira clan. This rising furnishes an interesting sidelight on the conflict between the great clans. The romantic version of the struggle between Taira and Minamoto gives an impression that the Taira clan was completely wiped out. This is not true. There were important families of Taira origin still prospering in the east,[2] and in the west there remained some members of the Ise Heishi, the strongest element in the clan, who saw in the lack of unity at Kamakura an opportunity for revolt. Two Taira chieftains of good standing headed a rising against Minamoto power, and taking the government forces by surprise they were able to capture most of Ise and Iga provinces. In Kyoto there was naturally much alarm and some secret glee. But Hiraga was no laggard. He quickly raised a sufficient force and smashed the Ise men. This action was not important in scale, for only small forces were engaged; but it gave notice that the arm of Kamakura reached a long way to the west.

Hiraga was, like Yoritomo, a descendant of Yoriyoshi, the founder of that division of the Minamoto house called the Kawachi Genji (see table, p. 241). Yoritomo's was the senior branch deriving from Yoshiiye, the celebrated Hachiman Tarō. Hiraga's descent was from Yoshimitsu, a younger son of Yoriyoshi; and another celebrated family, the Satake, was of the same origin. Hiraga therefore might fairly claim some rights to leadership of the clan at a time when its representatives in a direct line from Yoritomo were not worthy to succeed him. Hōjō Tokimasa does not appear to have had any personal ambitions for himself or his grandsons. He was deeply concerned to preserve the administrative and judicial organs which had been created by Yoritomo under his guidance, and he would not have been reluctant to see them fall into the hands of a man of parts and suitable pedigree like Hiraga. But he thought that safety lay in perpetuating the authority of the Hōjō family, whether as trusted advisers or as appointed Regents.

With Tokimasa's knowledge, if not his actual connivance, Yoriiye was murdered in his exile in Izu province in the summer of 1204, and other obstacles were removed by equally drastic measures. But the plot thickened just as Tokimasa's agents, or those of his wife Maki-ko, were on the point of taking Sanetomo unawares and putting him to death. This was in August 1205, when Sanetomo was visiting his grandfather the Regent in his official residence. Had this plot succeeded, the whole history of Japanese feudal society in the middle ages might have taken a very different course. But the determination of another strong-willed female, Masa-ko, saved the life of her son Sanetomo, for she rescued him and quickly raised an opposition force under her brother, Hōjō Yoshitoki.

[2] It should be remembered that Tokimasa was a Taira, and that his daughter was known as Taira Masa-ko.

The Regent's Council was quickly summoned. The evidence of treasonable intent was so clear that Tokimasa was forced to resign, take the tonsure, and retire to his country house in Izu, where he lived peacefully under surveillance until his death in 1215. Hiraga was killed by troops sent to attack him in his Kyoto mansion.

It will be seen that feudal society was in turmoil at its highest levels for a few years after Yoritomo's death in 1199. But by the end of 1205 all dangerous opposition had been quelled and the leaders of the Shōgun's government could steer a smooth course. Hōjō Yoshitoki, the new Regent, remained on good terms with his sister Masa-ko, while the various administrative and judicial organs of the Bakufu served to keep most of the vassals content. Such conditions had lasted for the better part of a decade when a conspiracy against Sanetomo was discovered in the year 1213. Details of this rising need not be related here. It is sufficient to say that over one hundred warrior chieftains were found to be involved in a plot to remove Sanetomo by force and to replace him by a son of Yoriiye. It seems that the cause of this discontent was not their own treatment as vassals, but rather an anxious feeling that the existence of the Bakufu was being endangered by factional strife.

The case was investigated by the Samurai-dokoro, since that was the office concerned with the discipline of the military class; its president was Wada Yoshimori, one of Yoritomo's trusted friends. In the course of this enquiry there emerged a sharp difference between Wada and Hōjō Yoshitoki, which presently developed into open warfare. On May 24, 1213, Wada attempted to capture the mansions of Sanetomo and Yoshitoki, but by nightfall the next day forces from adjoining districts had marched into Kamakura and killed Wada with most of his adherents.

The result of this disturbance was to strengthen Yoshitoki's position. He was already Regent, having stepped into his father's shoes, and he now took Wada's place as head of the Samurai-dokoro, a key position. He was thus the most powerful man in the feudal hierarchy, and Sanetomo could assert himself only in matters of no practical importance. As holder of the office of Shōgun and as Chieftain of the Minamoto he was a necessary figurehead, and had certain ceremonial duties to perform. It was as Chieftain that in the year 1219 he proceeded to the Hachiman shrine to thank the clan god for favours granted to his family. After he had left the altar and was descending the stone steps to the entrance where his palanquin was waiting, a figure rushed out of the darkness, brandished a sword, and cut off his head. How the escort could have permitted this outrage is hard to understand. It is unlikely that tough Kamakura soldiers were so negligent or so stupid as to be unable to withstand the assassin or pursue him. Some accounts say that the vanishing figure was that of a woman. Whoever it was, there is no doubt about the real purpose of the attack. It was an attempt by Yoriiye's second son, Kugyō, then a youth in holy orders, to take revenge for having been denied what he thought was his right to succeed to the office of Shōgun.

The young man was soon disposed of by partisans of the Regent Yoshitoki, whose position was further assured by this bloodshed. The great feudal leaders never hesitated to murder such of their kinsmen as seemed to stand in their way. Just as Yoritomo had his brother Yoshi-tsune treacherously slain, so did the inheritors of Yoritomo's power see to it that all possible rivals and claimants were destroyed, irrespective of family ties or loyal intentions. If the Bakufu were to be judged by the conduct of its leaders in the early years of the thirteenth century, its record would be black indeed. But in fact it was not its leaders but its institutions that preserved the feudal order in those turbulent conditions.

In the first half of the thirteenth century the ordinary vassal, content to reside on his own land and manage his own affairs, could depend upon the impartial justice of the Shōgun's courts. If he had a grievance, he knew that he would get a careful hearing, provided that he was not suspected of connexion with parties hostile to the Regent. Thus the Bakufu, for all the treasons and stratagems of ambitious men at Kamakura, was trusted and obeyed by most of the provincial warriors, the go-kenin, in the east; and since the feudal society was on the whole competently governed, the Regency bade fair to succeed, so long as it did not depart from the principles laid down by Yoritomo and his partners in the enterprise of establishing a new order.

The most difficult problem of the Bakufu after Yoritomo's death was to find a satisfactory Shōgun as a figurehead in whose name the Regent could govern. This was a point of weakness of which the Throne did not fail to take advantage.

2. Relations between the Court and the Bakufu

Since the appointment of the Shōgun was a prerogative, indeed the most important prerogative, of the Throne, the welfare of the whole feudal society depended, despite the armed strength of the warriors, upon the good will of the reigning sovereign in Kyoto, or of the cloistered ex-emperor if he was a man of parts. We have seen how the cloistered Go-Shirakawa was able for years to manipulate affairs of state by sheer ingenuity and breathless feats of balance. Of the same kind was the use made by his successor, Go-Toba, of his peculiar position, a position that enabled him to gain political advantages without any real political strength.

Any serious disagreement within the Bakufu was welcomed by His Majesty, for it was at such critical junctures as the death of Sanetomo that he could profit by his power of appointment, playing off one faction against another to his own benefit. Go-Toba had succeeded to the throne in 1184 at the age of four, and he was still too young to abdicate and take the cloistered Emperor's place when Go-Shirakawa died in 1192. At this time the fear of Yoritomo was such that when he offered deferential advice it had to be taken as a command by the titular Emperor. Go-Toba soon learned that if he wished to enjoy some independence he must abdicate as soon as possible. This he did at the age of eighteen in 1198, being succeeded as titular sovereign by his infant son, Tsuchimikado, who was chosen as heir without any reference to Kamakura. Yoritomo was annoyed by this display of sovereignty, but he died before he could go to Kyoto and chide the Court for its boldness.

Encouraged no doubt by this success, Go-Toba continued to resist the influence of the Bakufu not by a trial of strength but by a contest of wits. He was on good terms with Sanetomo, who was old enough for his companionship and shared his taste for athletic sports and poetry; so that at times when Go-Toba took some action to which the Kamakura leaders objected, Sanetomo would intervene and cancel their orders.

The questions at issue between the Court and the Bakufu were often trivial, and would hardly be worth recording if it were not for the light which they throw upon the curious relationship between the two seats of power. The Bakufu, though conscious of overwhelming material strength, never ventured to challenge the ultimate supremacy of the Imperial House. Somehow or other a solution had to be found which, if only in form, recognized the rights of the Throne. The prestige of the Court as the fountain of honour was of such traditional importance that leaders of the warrior society did not think of denying it; indeed many of Yoritomo's vassals coveted the ranks and titles which only the Throne could confer. It was strictly laid down by Yoritomo that no member of the military class could have direct relations with the Court or receive any favours from the sovereign or his officers. He himself set an example by refusing marks of imperial favour that were pressed upon him by Go-Shirakawa. Certain nobles at the capital took an especial pleasure in persuading warriors to break these rules, notably in the years just after Yoritomo's death, while Kamakura was busy with its own troubles, and when officers of the Crown were bold enough even to arrest Bakufu representatives in the city and in manors in the country.

This state of affairs did not last long, for by 1213 or thereabouts the new Regent, Hōjō Yoshitoki, had become master of the situation in Kamakura, with the support of the indomitable Masa-ko. It is true that Sanetomo was wayward and disobedient and continued on friendly terms with Go-Toba, from whom he received honours which he coveted. Indeed, the Court being short of funds, there was much traffic in honours and titles during Sanetomo's short lifetime. But in 1219, after Sanetomo's assassination, the Bakufu was no longer willing to overlook the trifling and petty manoeuvres of Go-Toba. He had very cleverly played with the warriors for a time, but he went too far by asking for impossible favours. It was a fatal blunder.

He proposed that certain manors belonging to Kamakura kenin

should be given to one of his mistresses. To challenge or disregard a vassal's rights in landed property was a direct attack upon the feudal structure, and therefore something that the Bakufu could never tolerate. Go-Toba received a smart rebuke from Kamakura. He submitted to the scolding and appeared to have mended his ways. But he did not cease his endeavours to undermine the authority of the Bakufu by making friends of a number of military officers serving in the capital, and in this effort he had remarkable success. He knew how to exercise charm and he seems to have enjoyed matching his lively wits against the solid wisdom of the Regent's advisers. He was always on the alert to defend and enlarge the imperial prerogative, which the Bakufu hoped gradually to diminish. Thus, when Sanetomo died the Regent Yoshitoki applied to the cloistered Go-Toba to appoint one of his younger sons to succeed to the office of Shōgun. But Go-Toba saw through this scheme and refused to allow the nomination of a prince of the blood royal to serve in Kamakura, since that would give a dangerous advantage to the Bakufu in any future dispute about the succession to the throne.

The Bakufu (on the advice of Miura Yoshimura) next proposed to use the prestige of the Fujiwara family. Yoritsune, an infant son of Fujiwara Michiiye (then Minister of the Left and soon to be the chieftain of the clan) was sent to Kamakura, where he was taken into the household of Masa-ko. But Go-Toba refused to invest a two-year-old child with the title of Shōgun, and the office was perforce left vacant for several years. His Majesty did not like the idea of a family tie, or even of close friendly relations, between the Imperial House and the Shōgun's family, but thought it best for the Court to keep aloof from the Bakufu. Indeed he chose to take a positively antagonistic line, going so far as to connive at an attack upon one of the Shōgun's high officers stationed in Kyoto, Minamoto Yorinari, the constable of his palace. This was a bold step to take, since it was a challenge to manifestly superior force, but at that time Go-Toba seems to have known how far he could go without inviting reprisals. He was evidently a talented statesman, for while taking risks in his dealings with the Bakufu, he cleverly gained the admiration and support of many warriors serving in the capital, simple countrymen who were impressed by the long pedigrees and the elegant manners of the aristocrats at Court.

Perhaps where Go-Toba showed most skill and courage was in his handling of the militant Buddhist foundations, which Yoritomo had kept in order by threats, but which after his death had become turbulent again during those years when factional strife in Kamakura had weakened the authority of the Bakufu, particularly in the home provinces and generally throughout western Japan. By 1219 the old quarrels between Hiyeizan and Miidera had flared up, the Kōfukuji was once more militant, and the "mountain monks" of Enryakuji again descended

upon the capital in order to blackmail the Court. But Go-Toba, unlike
his predecessors, was not the man to be bullied by a monastic rabble.
He did what Go-Shirakawa had not dared to do. He turned loose some
of his guards against them and they were put to flight. Then, instead
of following up his triumph, he displayed his statecraft by making
friends with the monasteries and even induced them to suspend their
quarrels and unite with the Throne in resisting those feudal tyrants who
had treated them so roughly in the past.

The situation had changed since the days when the government in
Kyoto feared to invoke divine wrath if they attacked holy men. The
Minamoto were prepared to destroy any power, temporal or spiritual,
that threatened their supremacy, and the militant sects of Kyoto and
Nara had a further reason for wishing to thwart the eastern warlords.
In the early years of the thirteenth century new Buddhist sects had
arisen in Japan, the soft Amidists and the hard adherents of the Zen
school, both of whom had challenged the teaching of the older sects and
found many believers and sympathizers among the leaders as well as
the rank and file of military society. Consequently it appeared to Go-
Toba that if he could bring about an alliance between the monastic
troops and certain chieftains in western Japan, he might take the Bakufu
unawares and reassert the power of the Imperial House.

Some of his advisers warned him against such a risky enterprise, but
he had the support of most of the leading Court nobles, of important
Buddhist dignitaries, and of the wardens of the great Shintō shrines; and
in addition to such military preparations as he could make he engaged
in a continuous round of pilgrimages and religious services to appeal
for divine assistance.[3] But he had no very dependable military forces
to call upon, and he miscalculated the strength of the Bakufu.

There were, it was true, a number of chieftains in the west who had
no reason to like the Minamoto. There were disappointed warriors,
aggrieved landowners, bitter survivors of the Taira, who might take the
field. It was a bold and hazardous plan, but it might succeed if the
leaders in Kamakura were not united. Go-Toba took the risk. In May
1221 he had decided upon certain matters of succession without consulting Kamakura. Early in June he summoned all the eastern warriors
in Kyoto to a great festival, and nearly all of them attended, so great
was his popularity among them. But one important officer stayed away,
and by his absence revealed his loyalty to the Bakufu. He was attacked
and killed, and Saionji Kintsune, grandfather of the infant Shōgun designate and close to the Bakufu, was put under house arrest because he
knew what was about to happen. On June 6 the Court denounced Hōjō
Yoshitoki as an outlaw, and on June 9 the whole of eastern Japan was
solemnly declared to be in a state of rebellion.

[3] In the fifth month the Court called upon the great monasteries to perform
services (with esoteric rites) praying for the surrender of the Bakufu.

But Saionji had managed to send word to Kamakura by relays of fast messengers, so that on the same day, June 9, Yoshitoki learned how matters stood. He knew from another source (Miura Yoshimura) that Go-Toba hoped to suborn some of the strongest Minamoto vassals, especially Miura himself. But Miura remained loyal. Since he was the only chieftain in the east who might be a match for the Hōjō military strength, Yoshitoki felt safe in his own territory; and his other colleagues declared their intention to stand by him, in defence of the Bakufu. The first plan of the council of war was to close the passes of Ashigara and Hakone by which an enemy would attack from the west. But this was manifestly no plan for the leader of the warrior class to follow, and it was soon decided that all available fighting men in eastern and northern Japan should be mobilized and sent against the imperial forces.

It is interesting to note that it was the civilian Ōye Hiromoto who, with Masa-ko, insisted that the Bakufu must not stand on the defensive, but must attack without delay and in great force.

As in the campaign of 1184, three armies advanced to the attack, one by the central mountain provinces, one from the north, down by the Echizen passes, and the third, a striking force of cavalry, along the coastal road, the Tōkaidō. This last was led by Yasutoki, Yoshitoki's eldest son, who left Kamakura on June 13.

Accounts of this campaign describe episodes at strategic points familiar in the military history of Japan, such as Tonamiyama, the scene of one of the great battles in the Gempei War; the Uji River; and the bridge at Seta, where once Yoshinaka tried and failed to hold the onslaught of men from Kamakura. Here again the defending forces were to be thrown back and the river crossed, and soon Yasutoki's horsemen were to stream into the capital, just as Yoshitsune's cavalry had poured in over thirty years before.

The imperial levies were mostly inexperienced and had little fighting spirit. Many of them fled from their positions in Ōmi and Mino provinces without any attempt at resistance before the rapid advance of the Bakufu armies. Go-Toba's field commanders were outfought, and some escaped or surrendered even before the arrival of the force which was to come by way of Echizen but was delayed by strong resistance from warriors in the northern provinces not yet reconciled to the Minamoto. In fact it was those fighting men alone who gave the Bakufu forces any serious trouble.

When news of the early defeat of his army reached Go-Toba at the end of June, he left the city with a small company and proceeded to Hiyeizan, where he summoned the Chief Abbot of the Tendai and asked for the aid of monastic troops. This was declined on the score of weakness, and the party returned to the capital. Go-Toba was ill and dispirited, but decided to try a last stand at Uji and Seta with such stragglers and reserves as could be mustered. This was on July 3, and on

July 5 the combined Bakufu forces under Yasutoki delivered a frontal attack along the river line from Seta to Uji. Here the remnants of the imperial army stood firm. They were in a strong position, for the Uji River was a difficult obstacle, and they held up the enemy's advance by stubborn fighting for many hours. But at length by a great effort and with heavy losses Yasutoki's whole force got across the river late in the afternoon, and destroyed or scattered the defending force. Before dark Seta was captured and its defenders killed. The way to Kyoto was open.

Yasutoki's cavalry scouts rode into the city at once, but the formal entry of the victor was fixed for the following day, July 6. The number of Kamakura troops at his immediate disposal was probably about 50,000, his own cavalry numbering less than 10,000. When news came of the collapse of the defence at Uji and Seta, the palace of Go-Toba was filled with alarm. He had sent his family to take refuge in places on the western outskirts of the city, but he himself remained. He sent a messenger to meet Yasutoki with a rescript (Insen) stating that the present situation was due not to his own fault but to the designs of rebellious subjects. The edict calling for the chastisement of the Regent Yoshitoki was to be withdrawn, and henceforward such announcements would be issued as the Bakufu desired. In return the Bakufu commander was requested to keep his troops under strict discipline when they entered the city.

Yasutoki's formal entry took place as arranged on July 6. The city was in a distressed condition. Retreating troops had set fire to many buildings and the place was "like a cauldron." The messenger from Go-Toba went forward to meet Yasutoki as he rode in, and stated his mission. Yasutoki dismounted, and listened respectfully while the document was read aloud. He at once gave orders to guard the Imperial Palace, and his men quickly rounded up most of the fugitive soldiers who were prowling about the city. On the following day Yasutoki and his uncle Tokifusa took up residence in the Rokuhara mansions, and since there was so much urgent business to transact they established two headquarters, north and south, for the conduct of military government. Bakufu troops closed in on the Palace, and the Court was obliged to issue orders for the arrest and punishment of officers of the imperial army who had escaped and were in hiding. Firm measures were taken to restore order, by severe treatment of marauding soldiers of both armies. A few days after the surrender the Echizen army arrived, so that the imperial city was now occupied or menaced by perhaps as many as 100,000 experienced fighting men from the east. The Court was now entirely subservient to the Bakufu.

Thus ended what is known to historians as Jōkyū no Hen, or the Jōkyū Disturbance, after the era name of Jōkyū, 1219–21. Contrary to the expectation of some of its leaders, the Bakufu gained an easy victory, and from results alone it might be argued that Go-Toba had engaged in a hopeless venture. But in several parts of the country there was a degree of hostility to the Bakufu which, with good fortune and better timing, might have been used to persuade Kamakura to come to terms. Although in general the Minamoto vassals were loyal, in the east certain warrior families were dissatisfied with the conduct of affairs at Kamakura, the quarrels which left responsible posts vacant, and the gradual ousting of old, dependable leaders. Had Go-Toba been more prudent, such important persons or groups might have chosen to take part in a movement to reform the Bakufu by removing some of its leaders. Certainly if Miura had chosen to go over to Go-Toba's side the history of the relations between the Throne and the Bakufu would have followed a very different line, and might even have ended in a qualified restoration of the imperial power.

These are mere speculations, it is true. But the fact that there was a possibility of thwarting the Bakufu shows that loyalty to the imperial cause had not been destroyed by the weakness of the sovereigns and the strength of the warriors. After this experience of revolt the Bakufu was obliged to reconsider its policies. It had to pay attention to two cardinal features, namely its future relations with the Court and its future treatment of its vassals—matters which hitherto had not been thoroughly or consistently decided.

The first was not difficult, since it was necessary to treat the imperial party justly but harshly and without any sign of weakness. The second was (in principle, at least) an easy problem, since it was a question of treating the vassals generously in the matter of grants of land, so as to ensure their continued loyalty.

When Yasutoki, as commander-in-chief of the Bakufu forces, had received the submission of the ex-Emperor, at first no serious step was taken by way of punishment; but after careful debate in Kamakura it was decided to banish Go-Toba and Juntoku. In addition the ex-Emperor Tsuchimikado and the infant Emperor Kanenari, though not concerned in the rising, were removed to distant provinces, but not confined. This treatment of the reigning house was severe, but not excessive by the standards of the time. What was more important than scolding or humiliating the ruling princes was teaching their advisers a lesson. Yasutoki was instructed to seize and execute the four generals who had taken arms against him, and to put to death the Court nobles who had been ringleaders in the plot against the Bakufu. These men were sent to Kamakura under guard, but most of them were killed on the way.

Such wayside killings were not in accord with orders from the Bakufu, but they had the advantage from Yasutoki's point of view of not exciting the strong partisan feelings which would have been aroused if the executions had taken place in or near the capital. In general the Regent and his colleagues did not engage in a wanton persecution of their former enemies once they had disposed of the half-dozen or so of chief conspirators. On prudential grounds they treated most of the offenders leniently, because they felt that to punish merely for the sake of vengeance would injure rather than promote their reputation in the west, where it was their desire to gain support.

More important to them than ridding themselves of enemies was the confiscation of their enemies' estates. Here was a timely stroke of good fortune for the leaders of the military class, since it was by gifts of land that the Shōgun could best reward his loyal vassals and, even more urgent, attract to his service the most influential families in those parts of the country where Bakufu influence had hitherto been weak. These confiscated manors were of great value, since they numbered about three thousand and were for the most part very extensive properties which had belonged to the richest Court nobles. Hence the confiscation of lands served a double purpose. It increased the strength of the adherents of the Bakufu while it impoverished the noble families, thus reducing if not destroying their political importance.

It did not require much political wisdom on the part of the Regent and his council to foresee that after the wars there would be many land-hungry vassals with growing families. It was indeed an axiom of feudal government that its stability depended upon the well-being of the men-at-arms of all ranks. It was following these principles that the highest officers of the Bakufu paid close attention to all matters regarding the tenure of land. The confiscated estates were carefully assigned to vassals who had to be rewarded or propitiated. As a rule such vassals were appointed stewards of the manors, rather than outright owners; but stewardships now carried rights which amounted to ownership, and which were treated as hereditary.

Once the great manors in central and western Japan had come into the hands of vassals of the Shōgun, the danger of such risings as those stimulated by Go-Toba almost disappeared. The leaders of the feudal society could now concentrate upon strengthening its position, and it is to their credit that they saw to the stability of their administration by taking care that it was efficient and impartial. Under them, for the first time in centuries, or it might be claimed for the first time in history, Japan was governed in accordance with law. To be sure, it was not a benign law, since the purpose of government was to ensure the well-being and therefore the loyalty of a limited class, that is to say the warrior class that accepted the overlordship of the Shōgun. But within that class equal justice was dispensed to the great landholders and the small tenant alike. Indeed it is an interesting feature of the rule of the early Hōjō Regents that as individuals they lived frugal and modest lives. The country as a whole was at peace. Some strict precautions were taken in Kyoto to forestall any antagonistic movement at Court; and there was a minor disturbance in the east when the Regent Hōjō Yoshitoki died in 1224. But throughout the land there was no really dangerous opposition to the Bakufu. There were local plots and minor risings, but they were not part of a concerted movement and were suppressed with little difficulty, largely because the Throne no longer provided a rallying point, and because the holders of great fiefs in the west knew that revolt would endanger their own positions and their handsome revenues.

Thus it may be said that from about 1225 (the year of the death of Masa-ko, when some lingering conspiracies were exposed and crushed) Japan was a unified state under competent and honest government. This happy posture of affairs lasted for the better part of a century—a very long time in the history of any country.

3. *The Summit of Feudal Power*

With the departure of Go-Toba, the cloistered Emperor who had harassed the Bakufu for many years, relations between Kamakura and the capital became almost genial; not that the Court was truly reconciled to defeat, but simply because it was too weak to resist the demands of the Shōgun's officers and had to make a virtue of compliance.

The Bakufu for its part tried to put an end to the bribery and corruption which had disgraced Court life. It would not tolerate the sale of titles and offices of the Crown, and at the same time it kept its hands off the legitimate revenues of the Imperial House, though it must be admitted that its view of legitimacy did not always agree with that of the sovereign and his nobles.

One of the most interesting aspects of the relationship between the Bakufu and the Court after Go-Toba's deposition in 1221 was the policy adopted by the Bakufu in regard to the institution of Insei, or Cloister Government. The line it took is somewhat surprising at first sight, since it might well be supposed that the strength of the feudal autocracy was so overwhelming, the weakness of the Throne so undeniable, as to make this a convenient opportunity for putting an end to an anomalous situation. But far from abolishing cloistered rule, Kamakura took an opposite view, and decided to perpetuate it. The question was carefully debated in the Regent's Council, and it was decided that it was now for the Bakufu to select the next cloistered emperor.

After long discussion their choice fell upon a prince close to the direct imperial line. This was Morisada Shinnō, the second son of the Emperor Takakura. He was at the time living in seclusion in a monastery, having entered religion no doubt to escape the dangers of royal descent. His three sons had been sent to live with Buddhist prelates, and thus he had cut himself off from all secular concerns. But his lineage, position, and character made him a most suitable figure to further the designs of the Bakufu, and he was made cloistered emperor, with the title Go-Takakura In, on July 28, 1221. The table makes his position clear; the dates are reign dates.

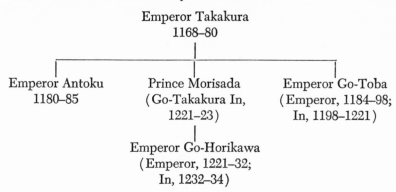

Emperor Takakura
1168–80

Emperor Antoku   Prince Morisada   Emperor Go-Toba
1180–85   (Go-Takakura In,   (Emperor, 1184–98;
    1221–23)   In, 1198–1221)

Emperor Go-Horikawa
(Emperor, 1221–32;
In, 1232–34)

It had hitherto been the custom for a reigning emperor to abdicate and, having entered religion, to assume the title and functions of the In. But the Bakufu reversed this rule when it claimed the right to nominate as cloistered emperor a prince who had never occupied the throne. To lay down qualifications in this way was equivalent to taking powers to name the titular emperor as well, for following precedent the titular emperor must be a son of the cloistered emperor. Accordingly Prince Shigehito, the third son of Go-Takakura In, was named to ascend the throne as the Emperor Go-Horikawa, at the end of the year 1221.

This rather complicated piece of constitutional history may be simplified by saying that, while preserving the usual forms of respect for the Imperial House, Kamakura now gave orders to the Court even in matters of the closest concern to the imperial family; and the Court was obedient.

Not content with the right to determine succession to the throne, the Bakufu at this time insisted upon being consulted on the appointment of a Regent (Sesshō) and in general made it clear that approval would not be given to persons whose political views were unfavourable to the feudal regime.

Thus it will be seen that very little real power was left to the Court. The Hōjō Regents were in fact supreme throughout the country. In addition to their political power they had a useful weapon in their control over land, exercised through their constables and stewards. They had so far respected the property rights of the imperial family, but when Go-Toba went into exile all his property was confiscated. It consisted of numerous and extensive manors, of great value in the aggregate. It was now in the gift of the Bakufu, and was offered to the new In, Go-Takakura. It was made clear to him, however, that any of these manors could be withdrawn should they be needed for the purposes of the Bakufu.

Yoshitoki, the second of the Hōjō Regents, died in 1224, and was succeeded by Yasutoki, whose reputation was very high because of his successes in both military and political affairs.

CHAPTER XVIII

ADMINISTRATIVE REFORMS AND RELATIONS WITH THE COURT

1. *The Distribution of Land, 1221–23*

AFTER the occupation of the capital by a great expeditionary force the first task of Yasutoki and Tokifusa was to send the troops back to the east and north to be disbanded, retaining only enough men to keep order among the now chastened citizens. The strength of the three armies has been estimated at 190,000; and though this seems excessive it was in any case a considerable number. They began to leave Kyoto towards the end of July and reached their various destinations a month or so later.

The maintenance of so many men in the field had been costly. Part of the expense had been met by vassals who contributed men and supplies, but the ultimate responsibility lay with the Kamakura government, to whose call they had responded. The first and most important task of the Bakufu now was to reward vassals for their services. Grants were made out of Bakufu resources in some cases, notably to Tokifusa and his commanders, who had borne the brunt of the fighting; and gifts of land were offered to the great shrines of Ise and Hachiman, in recognition of divine support. But the allocation of rewards to other claimants was not easily or rapidly accomplished. The Bakufu had at its disposal for sharing out among the vassals the three thousand estates which Yasutoki had confiscated from the generals and nobles whom he had overcome. But the particulars of these properties had not been accurately recorded, nor had the claims of the vassals been carefully scrutinized. It followed that there arose many and protracted disputes as to the justice of claims and awards, and much time was taken up by the strict investigation upon which the Bakufu assessors insisted.

It was not until the middle of 1223 that the outstanding claims were with but few exceptions examined and settled. The impartiality of the Bakufu courts was generally recognized, and the vassals were on the whole content. Many of them had good grounds to be satisfied, for the awards of the Bakufu were generous. The stewards, as we have noticed, obtained rights in land which were equivalent to hereditary ownership. Their incomes were much higher than those of the stewards appointed before the settlement of 1223, partly because the confiscated manors with rights in which they were now rewarded had belonged to wealthy and important nobles or religious foundations. These were treated by the Bakufu as enemy property and very often the rights of the original lords of the manor (*ryōke*) were completely disregarded, although the announced intention of Yasutoki had been to seize not the original manorial rights but only that proportion of the total revenue of the manor which was due to stewards and other functionaries.

Here again the Bakufu displayed a certain impartiality, for when suits were brought in the Kamakura courts by aggrieved noble landlords or religious bodies decisions were frequently given against the stewards whom the Bakufu had appointed. In 1223, for instance, the Shōgun's officers in the home provinces and in western Japan were ordered to investigate and report upon alleged misfeasance by newly appointed stewards, and to apply any necessary corrections. In the same year a decree was issued fixing the proportion of the crop to be taken by the stewards at the yield of one acre of arable land out of eleven acres; and similar regulations were applied to the revenue from forest land and pasture.

Although these measures gave some protection to the original holders of manorial rights, the revenue of the "new" stewards remained at a higher level than that of the previous occupants of their posts.[1] Since the new stewards were appointed to manors in which the Bakufu had acquired absolute rights as war booty, complaints were naturally frequent. To meet the costs of the campaign the Bakufu had levied a rice tax (hyōrō-mai); and after the victory stewards had collected this in a forcible and illegal manner. A flood of protests reached the law courts and Kamakura felt constrained to take notice of them. With but little delay stringent orders were issued against these practices, and in the seventh month of 1223 with the Bakufu's approval the Kyoto government issued an edict to all provinces forbidding oppressive acts by warriors in the estates of monasteries and shrines. These measures were effective and the excesses of the stewards, if not brought to an end, were at least moderated.

The evil reputations of the stewards for illegal and rapacious conduct is a commonplace in the literature of the time. It is well revealed in a satirical verse attributed to Mongaku Shōnin, a prominent Buddhist dignitary celebrated for his plain speaking. It runs:

Yo no naka ni	If in this world
Jitō nusubito	Stewards and Robbers
Nakariseba	Did not exist
Hito no kokoro wa	The hearts of men
Nodokekaramashi.	Would be at peace.

There was also current at this time the saying "Naku ko to jitō ni wa katenu," which means that there is no way of controlling a crying child or a steward.

Supplementing this attempt to improve the behaviour of stewards

---

[1] The term "new stewards" (Shinpo Jitō) was officially used.

the Bakufu addressed new orders to the constables, defining their functions more precisely than before. There had been frequent abuses of their powers by vassals appointed to this important office, and such offenders were restrained by strictly limiting their jurisdiction. They were forbidden to enter public domains for the arrest of delinquents, and they were ordered not to make arrests in private domains (shōen) without first notifying the stewards.

It will be seen from these instances that the Shōgun's deputies in the capital had many problems to cope with. The Rokuhara Headquarters had in the first place important military duties to perform, but when the armies withdrew they were left with the task of keeping order in the home provinces and, while treating the Emperor with all forms of respect, impressing upon the Court the power and determination of the Bakufu. They did not wish to resort to force, but they had to be firm. They could not afford the risk which had been taken in 1221, when the constable representing Kamakura at Court had been so friendly that he joined the imperial party in its conspiracy.

Consequently it was decided in Kamakura that the Shōgun, or rather the Regent, should be represented in the capital by a high military officer with extensive powers, who would be able to impress the Court with his authority, keep a watch for signs of plotting and act promptly to put down subversion in its early stages. Apart from the general grounds of policy upon which this decision was based, there was an urgent practical reason for keeping a strong Bakufu organization, almost a full garrison, in Kyoto. The city after the surrender was filled with anxiety; the citizens were in a state of constant alarm caused by marauders from the defeated army and other disturbers of the peace, robbers, incendiaries, and assassins. It was such conditions that decided the Bakufu to maintain a permanent delegation in Kyoto, responsible not only for surveillance of the Court but also for keeping the peace in the metropolitan area. Thus the Rokuhara Headquarters had almost plenary powers, and the choice of suitable commanding officers was a matter of great concern to the leaders in Kamakura. In fact this appointment was one of the most important and valuable in the gift of the Bakufu, and it is not surprising that after it had been held—it was a dual post at that time—by Hōjō Yasutoki and Hōjō Tokifusa, it became a monopoly of the Hōjō family. From their day it became the practice, if not the rule, to appoint to the office of Regent in Kamakura a member of the Hōjō family who had served as commanding officer at the Rokuhara Headquarters. The jurisdiction of this officer—he was subsequently styled the Tandai or Inspector—was by no means confined to the capital and its environs; it covered all the provinces westward from and including Mikawa. It was as if the organization of the Bakufu had been duplicated, giving to the Tandai full control in all but matters of the highest national importance, upon which it was understood that the Bakufu must be consulted. Orders from Kamakura were not issued direct to persons or offices within the Tandai's jurisdiction, but communicated to him and passed on in his name.

It will be seen that the organization of the Bakufu now extended throughout the whole country. It is true that its jurisdiction was not universal, and in principle applied only to vassals; but it was on a much greater scale than the simple system by which Yoritomo had regulated his administration of the society of warriors over which he presided.

The manner in which the Bakufu's authority was extended after the Jōkyū Disturbance is shown by its land policy. The ownership of land had undergone such great changes after the fighting that for the proper exercise of its administrative power it needed a clear and exact record of the situation and tenure of all farm land throughout the country. Consequently, during the years 1222 and 1223 a land survey was undertaken in all provinces. The particulars required included the area of cultivable land, the names of the domanial lord, the steward and the tenants of each manor, and evidence of title. It is not clear when the enquiry was completed but it appears to have been carried out in a thorough and accurate manner, so that not long after 1223 the Bakufu had at its disposal reliable land registers, as a necessary basis for the control of an agrarian economy upon which its rule depended.

2. Hōjō Yasutoki as Regent, 1224–42

Under the direction of Hōjō Yoshitoki as Regent (Shikken) the Kamakura government, having solved the chief problems arising immediately from Go-Toba's plot, was able to turn its attention to long-range planning. It had made good progress by the beginning of 1224, when Yoshitoki was taken with a sudden illness; he died at the age of sixty-two on July 2 of that year. He was a hard man, and unpopular, but he had the qualities needed for guiding the Bakufu through a difficult period and his power of decision was valuable in emergencies.

His son Yasutoki, who had been stationed in Rokuhara since the end of the fighting, was at once summoned to Kamakura, where he arrived about two weeks later, followed shortly by Tokifusa. These two were promptly appointed co-regents on the advice of Masa-ko and Ōye Hiromoto, now the only influential survivors from the days of the foundation of the Kamakura government in 1185. In practice this dual arrangement was not followed. Tokifusa preferred to take second place. He was Yasutoki's uncle, but he belonged to a junior branch of the family, so that the two collaborated smoothly and Tokifusa did little more than countersign Yasutoki's orders.

To replace these two men at the Rokuhara Headquarters Yasutoki's son Tokiuji and Tokifusa's son Tokimori were appointed as Tandai in August 1224, and proceeded forthwith to their post. The authority of the Bakufu had been so enlarged and strengthened under Yoshitoki's rule that his death left an unexpected gap, and it was feared that hostile forces might think this a propitious moment for a sudden uprising. A careful watch was kept on the capital but no suspicious signs were visible. In Kamakura, however, there was a subversive movement, led by a member of the Iga family, who had hopes of succeeding Yoshitoki on grounds of kinship. This came to nothing, and indeed so strong and so firmly seated was Yasutoki that the incident would be scarcely worth mentioning were it not of interest because Iga knew that he had no chance of success without the support of the powerful Miura family. He approached Yoshimura, the head of the Miura house, just as Go-Toba's emissaries had done a few years before. Yasutoki was careful to take no premature action; he was content to keep an eye upon Iga. Masa-ko, however, who scorned indirect methods, went without escort to Yoshimura's house to ascertain what was in his mind. She challenged him to say whether he was for the rebels or for the peace of Kamakura.

Yoshimura went to see Yasutoki the next day and declared that the Miura family were friends of the Hōjō family. The conspiracy therefore collapsed and the conspirators were severely punished. Since there had been no overt act of rebellion, no death penalty was declared and (partly no doubt because of family connexions) the punishments were limited to dismissal from office, confiscation of property, or banishment. The Hōjō were not so ruthless in dealing with their enemies as Yoritomo had chosen to be at times. Yasutoki's position was thus firmly established, and he could proceed with his task of conducting and improving the administration of the feudal state, meanwhile strengthening the position of the Hōjō Regents.

He was now the most powerful man in the country, though (according to some chroniclers) he was under the influence of the indomitable Masa-ko until her death, in August 1225, at the age of sixty-nine. Her old colleague Ōye Hiromoto had died a month before in his seventy-eighth year. It is interesting to reflect that the two figures who contributed most to completing the edifice of military rule begun by Yoritomo were a woman of strong character and a civilian scholar. Masa-ko's strength lay in her unbreakable will and her determination to preserve the legacy of Yoritomo. Ōye Hiromoto was renowned for his learning, a man of vast knowledge and capacious memory whom the warriors looked upon as a living encyclopaedia. His keen judgment was respected by his colleagues, who knew it to be cold and impartial. Like Masa-ko he must have been lacking in tender emotions, for it was said of both of them that they were never known to shed a tear.

Their influence in their later years tended to be conservative. They were both bold in emergency, but they were reluctant to make changes in the system which had developed under their guidance. With their demise the way was open for Yasutoki to introduce reforms. The simple machinery of the last days of the twelfth century was not suitable to the conditions which had arisen after the Jōkyū revolt. The power of the Bakufu reached throughout the whole country and in one way or another affected the whole people. The plain institutions that had sufficed to deal with the affairs of the Minamoto clan were not suited to government on a national scale. Instead of a system that had grown up almost haphazard in response to day-to-day needs it was necessary—or it was thought necessary by Yasutoki—to introduce a carefully designed and properly articulated administration.

His first step was to display his intention to make changes by replacing most of the leading officials of the Bakufu by new men with new functions. As an earnest of an impartial spirit he granted pardons to some of his recent enemies and made a point of consulting persons of different views on problems of government. At the same time he summoned all the executive officials (bugyō) in the administration to a meeting at which he made it clear that he, the Regent, was in absolute control of their functions. He obliged them to swear that they would be loyal in the performance of their duties, and in this way he gave notice to the vassals that he would protect their interests in return for their obedience. To symbolize the internal reform of the Bakufu he moved it into new quarters. At the end of the year 1225 (or more accurately on January 20, 1226) he installed there the young boy who was to be the next Shōgun and he announced the formation of a Council of State. This was an important move, since it foreshadowed the future development of feudal rule.

After the death of Yoritomo and when Yoriiye was installed as Shōgun the Hōjō family (of which Tokimasa was then the senior member) had perceived that the personal rule of Yoritomo's descendants could not be depended upon. They decided that the Shōgun's powers must be reduced, and that the affairs of the Bakufu must henceforth be directed by a committee or council of elders. This change inevitably brought about or favoured a concentration of power in the hands of the Hōjō family through its leader Tokimasa and his descendants. The great prestige of Masa-ko, herself a Hōjō by birth, and the successes of Yoshitoki and Yasutoki in reducing the Throne to comparative impotence had added to the confidence of the warrior class in the leadership of the Hōjō family. The family, for its part, did its best to gain favour by conciliatory treatment of its opponents. Thus by the time of Yasutoki's succession to the office of Regent the reputation of his family was so high that their right to direct the Shōgun's government was scarcely questioned, and thereafter Hōjō Regents were the true feudal overlords until the end of the thirteenth century, most of them displaying great talent as administrators.

But Yasutoki himself had the good sense not to assume dictatorial powers. He continued to consult experienced men and he formed an advisory body to take cognisance of all important business and to stand behind the Regent, who was to be the chief executive of the feudal government. This body was called the Hyōjōshū, a term which may be translated as Council of State. In form it was a deliberative assembly to advise the Shōgun, but in fact it was an organ of government, since its decisions could not be ignored by the Regent. Its first members included great feudatories like Miura, members of the most important warrior families, and experienced administrators like Nakahara. Their number was eleven, and their first meeting took place in January 1226.

The changes brought about by the formation of this new body were significant. It was not a mere addition to existing bodies, since it soon replaced the offices which had been devised by Ōye Hiromoto and Miyoshi Yasunobu—the Mandokoro and the Monchūjo—or at least reduced them to plain executive departments. The introduction of this new method of reaching political decisions shows much wisdom on the part of Yasutoki, since it limited his own power as well as that of the Shōgun. It was for its day a very advanced measure.

While it was intended to deprive the Shōgun of all but ceremonial functions, the prestige of his office had still to be maintained, since it was to the Shōgun that the Throne had delegated powers, and it was in the name of the Shōgun that the Regent acted. The boy Mitora, the Shōgun presumptive, had been brought to Kamakura as a child of two. He was now eight years old, and concurrently with the reorganization of the Bakufu it was felt appropriate to define his position, since he had not yet been formally invested by the Throne. At its first meeting, therefore, the Council of State declared the establishment of a number of *Ban* or watches, which were supposed to perform certain duties on behalf of the Shōgun. The Ō-Ban, or Great Watch, was of fairly long standing, being the establishment of Bakufu troops (mostly from the east) that served in the capital for fixed periods in rotation for the protection of the Court. It was one of the duties of the constable in Kyoto to recruit men for this service and to keep a roster for calling them up. The Ō-Ban now established in Kamakura was the counterpart of the one in Kyoto, since it was recruited in fifteen western provinces as a guard for the Shōgun. It may be regarded as symbolizing the interrelation of the Court and the Bakufu on approximately equal terms.

The young Mitora assumed his manly garment at the age of eight in January 1226. This was announced to the Court, and a month later, after being given the necessary ranks and titles of nobility, he was proclaimed Shōgun with the name of Yoritsune. Then, to give an air of continuing Minamoto leadership of the warriors, it was decided by the Bakufu that he must marry a girl of Minamoto stock. In 1230, when he had reached the age of thirteen he was married to a daughter of Yoriiye, then in her twenty-eighth year. He had become a puppet of the Hōjō Regents.

This was a matrimonial alliance between the Minamoto and the

Fujiwara, not between the Minamoto and the imperial family. Relations with the Court were still cool, partly because conditions in Kyoto were disturbed but also because there were several underground movements against the Bakufu of which the Court was not ignorant. The new Rokuhara leaders had only just been installed, and they found that the city had not recovered from the lawlessness which followed upon the Jōkyū fighting. Robbery, violence, and arson were rife, and not even the Palace buildings or the most sacred edifices were safe from thieves. The efforts of the Rokuhara officers to suppress these offences were not entirely successful, for the reason that the breaches of the peace were not all due to common criminals and disorderly characters. The most dangerous offenders and the most difficult to handle were the monastic establishments of Hiyeizan and Nara. A few political risings that took place in 1226 were put down without much trouble. They were not looked upon seriously by the Bakufu, and it is probable that the turbulent monks would have been punished and order soon restored in the capital and the surrounding provinces, had it not been for a series of calamities that visited the whole country for several years in succession after 1225.

Once again, as had happened fifty years before, drought was followed by famine, famine by smallpox, and after diseases came storms, earthquakes, and floods, and such inclement and unseasonable weather that there were hard frosts in summer and even snowfalls in some places used to burning sun. To propitiate or advise the powers that regulate these climatic disasters the professors of Yin-Yang recommended changes of the era name. Five times between 1221 and 1232 such changes were made, but without effect; and the year 1229, given the encouraging name of Kangi or Full Rejoicing, was the most disastrous of all.

One beneficial result of these misfortunes was the impression which they made upon the mind of the Regent Yasutoki, and his subsequent attention to economic problems. It is true that the disasters were overwhelming and his efforts had little success; but he saw that with power Kamakura had undertaken more than responsibility for the Minamoto vassals. In July 1230 he announced an Act of Grace, a kind of moratorium by which the payment of debts and similar obligations was suspended. The price of rice was fixed by imperial order soon after this, and early in 1231 edicts restricting expenditures were issued, while tax rice was distributed to the poor in some provinces. But 1231 was a dreadful year of famine and disease. Robbery by violence was so frequent in the capital and its suburbs that the Bakufu instructed Rokuhara to take most drastic steps to restore order and allay distress. Similar instructions were sent to constables and stewards throughout the country. Taxes were remitted and other measures of relief were tried, but they were not enough to cope with the natural calamities by which the people were overwhelmed.

From 1232 onwards conditions began to improve, although the sequels of hunger and pestilence were visible for long afterwards. It was of course the poor peasants and town workers that suffered most; but the Bakufu could already detect discontent among the vassals, who had begun to find it difficult to maintain the standard of life to which they had become accustomed in the years of peace. Some of them were in debt, and many found that the yields from their land, reduced by years of poor harvest, were not sufficient to support their growing households.

These difficulties were not yet acute, but they were important enough to cause the Bakufu to pay close attention to the condition of the land-owning class when they were considering new legislation which was proposed in the year 1232. They had a firm belief in justice as between members of that class, and they were anxious that in difficult times aggrieved vassals should feel that they could depend upon an impartial hearing of complaints.

3. Feudal Legislation. The Jōei Formulary, 1232

The year 1232 was given the era name Jōei, and the draft code which was on August 27 of that year submitted to and adopted by the Council of State was later known as the Jōei Shikimoku or Jōei Formulary. It was not strictly speaking a code, but rather a digest or a set of judges' rules. It had not been the practice in Japan to promulgate laws for the people to study. It was assumed that general principles were known and that these were transgressed by offenders at their own risk. What was needed therefore was a set of rules and definitions in plain language for the guidance of the Shōgun's Court (Monchūjo) and the provincial constables and magistrates, whose business it was to watch over the conduct of the vassals. This document was originally entitled *Go Seibai Shikimoku*, or "Formulary for the Shōgun's Decision of Suits."

The Formulary is written in fairly clear language, though it bears some mark of the hands of the hereditary jurists who took part in compiling it. From its concluding passages (which constitute what in a similar document in English would be called a Preamble) it is clear that the Bakufu wished it to be regarded as a pledge to the vassals that impartial justice would be dispensed by the Shōgun's judicial officers. The undertaking takes the form of an oath by which the members of the Council swear:

> That they will not be influenced by ties of relationship or by personal dislikes or prejudices, but will give judgment without fear or favour in accordance with reason.

That their decisions will be the decisions of the Council as a whole, with no single member to have responsibility or credit for its findings, which shall be anonymous.

This oath is taken in the name of Buddhist and Shintō divinities. It says: "If in the slightest particular we depart from these principles, then may . . . all the Gods of the sixty and more provinces of Japan, and especially the deities of Izu, Hakone, and Mishima, the great Bodhisattva Hachiman, Temmangu, and Jizai-Tenjin, punish us and all our families with the punishments of the Gods and Buddhas."

This resounding oath is subscribed by Hōjō Yasutoki, Hōjō Tokifusa, and the eleven members of the Council.

The text of the Formulary is brief, comprising fifty-one articles of only moderate length. The main features of this remarkable document may be summarized as follows:

(1) The first two articles deal with the upkeep of shrines and monasteries and with religious observances.

(2) The next four articles deal with the functions of constables and stewards. The importance of these officers as guardians of the peace is insisted upon, it being affirmed that they are the provincial and district representatives of the military power of the Shōgun. At the same time these articles state in definite terms that the Shōgun's officers must not encroach upon the rights of others, whether of other vassals or of landholders and officials who derive their rights from the old system. The new constables are positively enjoined not to interfere in matters outside their specified functions. Provincial governors and manorial lords (ryōke) holding their estates from the Crown are outside the jurisdiction of the Kantō authorities. Similarly with the rights and immunities of religious bodies, in so far as they are derived from Crown grants.

(3) Next come two articles dealing with the tenure of fiefs by vassals, matters of succession, and related questions. These again do not in principle interfere with the rights of persons outside the military class. But there is an important exception. In certain cases a rule of prescription is invoked. Rights in land which have been held for twenty years remain the property of their holder, despite flaws in his title. This means, for example, that where a holder has obtained property by confiscation he is confirmed in his tenure if the land has been held by him continuously for twenty years. Since the Formulary was brought into force in 1232, the critical date was 1212, so that all rights acquired between 1186 (when the stewards were first appointed by Yoritomo) and 1212 were free from challenge. This clause is of especial interest and importance because in many cases Yoritomo did not grant new estates to his vassals, but only confirmed them in their present holdings, thus offering protection in return for service.

(4) The next important group of articles deals with punishable

offences. They concern for the most part only members of the warrior
class. There is no legislation for the common people, who with a few
exceptions are left to the jurisdiction of constables and stewards, or of
manorial lords, or, when they reside in public domains, of the provincial
and district governors appointed by the Crown.

The chief offenses set forth are treason, killing and maiming, banditry, piracy, forgery, abusive language, and assault. These last two,
though seemingly not serious, were seriously regarded by the feudal
leaders because they were likely to lead to vendettas and other dangerous breaches of the peace. The punishments laid down for abusive language as well as actual bodily harm are very drastic, and include the
loss of status as a vassal in extreme cases. They show the strong purpose of the Bakufu to preserve feudal discipline—to control as well as to
protect the vassals. Much attention is paid to false charges, slander, and
attempts to coerce judges by improper influence. These clauses again
show the importance attached by the Bakufu to the preservation of
order and the impartial administration of justice. Rules are given for
the determination of joint or separate responsibility as between husband and wife, parent and child.

(5) Perhaps the most interesting articles from a historical rather
than a legal point of view are those dealing with the treatment of persons who fought against the Minamoto in the Jōkyū revolt of 1221. They
are on the whole not ungenerous to former enemies so long as it can be
shown that they were not turncoats. Allowance is made for the demands
of loyalty or of filial duty. Even persons who had received grants
from the Shōgun and yet took arms against him are let off lightly if they
escaped punishment at the time, and only a portion of their property
is confiscated, "because the time for severity has gone by."

It will be noticed that the provisions just cited display a lenient atti-
tude towards the rights of persons not direct vassals of the Shōgun.
This forgiving spirit indicates a change in the outlook of the Bakufu.
The hard core of the warrior class was the Kantō Bushi, the eastern
warriors. They formed the solid group of fighting men upon whom
Yoritomo depended. But after Yoritomo's death, as the power of the
Throne waned and the policy of the Bakufu came to be directed by the
Hōjō Regents, it became a matter of importance to spread its favours,
and consequently its authority, beyond the narrow limits of the Minamoto clan and to bring within the vassalage of the Shōgun all warriors
throughout the country upon whose obedience the Bakufu could count,
and indeed even some who were not warriors but members of the Court
nobility willing to swear allegiance. Thus the Hōjō Regents appear to
be much less rigid, much more conciliatory, than Yoritomo, though he
also allowed some "outside" warriors to become vassals and was liberal
in his attitude towards women's right to own property.

There is no systematic arrangement of the articles. In addition to the provisions already mentioned there are miscellaneous rules dealing with judicial procedure, with testament and succession and with the disposal of fiefs which, through inheritance or marriage, fall into the hands of nobles or other persons not subject to the same jurisdiction as vassals.

The Formulary, as well as being an interesting legal monument, affords useful evidence of the attitude of the new feudal rulers towards problems of government. Prefixed to the main body of the text there is a short paragraph which gives an insight into their frame of mind. It says: "With regard to lawsuits which have already been decided, here-after there will be no revision of verdicts given, irrespective of right or wrong." This means that the feudal rulers are not going to be troubled by legal subtleties or by arguments about theory or principle. They will administer rough justice, prompt and practical, making their own prece-dents. In other documents of this period there is frequent use of the term *dōri*, which (as is clear from the contexts) means what is reason-able, rational, sensible. This is not the dōri of philosophers that stands for some abstract principle which they profess. It is the common sense of plain men.

The character and purpose of the Formulary are illuminated in cer-tain explanations given by Yasutoki when he communicated copies of the Formulary to the Rokuhara Tandai (at that time Shigetoki) for his official use. Yasutoki explained that the document, which set forth "various matters upon which the courts would give their judgments" ("seibai subeki jōjō no koto"), was not a code of law but merely a list. When it was drafted its authors had wished to give it an imposing title; but this was thought excessive and it was described only as a Formulary (*shikimoku*). People might criticize it, asking upon what ideas it was based; but it had no special basis except in so far as it was compiled in accordance with reason (dōri). Unless some standard of this kind was adopted, judgments might be given in accordance not with straight or crooked, right or wrong, but rather with the strength or weakness of parties to a suit. "Therefore in deciding upon the procedure to adopt we were influenced by a desire for impartial verdicts without discrimi-nation between high and low."

This remarkable letter, so simple in its language and so striking in its ideas, goes on to say that although the national law is embodied in the ancient codes and rules (the ritsuryō and kyakushiki; see Chapter VI), not one man in a thousand knows about these. To punish persons for offences under laws which they do not know gives rise to great hardship, and therefore "we have written this Formulary in such a way that even the most illiterate fellows can understand its meaning. The old laws are like complicated Chinese characters; the new laws are like the simple syllabary [kana]."

In an earlier letter to Shigetoki, written when the draft was near completion and about to be put before the Council of State, Yasutoki says that in Yoritomo's day offences were judged and disputes settled not according to written laws and regulations, but on moral principles. The natural way for the people to obtain peace and security, he continues, is "for the man to be loyal to his master, the child to observe filial piety, the wife to obey her husband, and all in their hearts to spurn the crooked and follow the straight. It was with these things in mind that the Formulary was compiled. Some people in the capital may laugh at this as the work of eastern barbarians. But these are the principles that we wish you to follow."

These letters of Yasutoki confirm certain conclusions which are suggested by a study of the text of the Formulary. It is clear that the feudal leaders regarded the early codes as obsolete, or at any rate not satisfying the needs of a feudal society. There is here a definite rejection of the Chinese influence that inspired the legislation of the Taihō period and successive additions. Thus the Jōei provisions regarding land tenure see the whole question from an entirely new point of view, and many of them are in flat contradiction of the principles laid down in the codes. One interesting feature of the feudal law is seen in the provisions allowing a woman to hold a fief or part of a fief and even, after divorce, to retain land or rights which were hers before marriage.

The Jōei laws have sometimes been styled the Jōei Customary. This is correct inasmuch as they stood for the customs of a feudal society rather than the general principles of the Taihō codes. But in some respects the Jōei Formulary runs counter to previous feudal practice. In later times the Jōei provisions were commonly described as having brought light in contrast to the obscurity of the ancient laws. This virtue was even celebrated in poetry (a long time later, it is true) by the great Bashō, who composed a verse in which he said that the fifty-one articles came like bright moonlight after darkness.[2]

Numerous additions to the Jōei Formulary were made during the Kamakura period. Of these the most important is the *Shimpen Tsuika,* or New Supplement, which is twice as long as the Formulary and contains additions made up to 1243. There is also a valuable work called *Samurai-dokoro Sata-hen,* which contains rulings of the Samurai-dokoro on cases brought before it, that is to say upon the application of the provisions of the Formulary and its supplements until the year 1286. It is indispensable for a knowledge of the attitude of the Bakufu towards the samurai and the behaviour of the military class in general.

---

[2] The text is:

> Meigetsu no izuru ya
> Gojū-ichi ka jō.

The date is 1688, and the *haiku* has a preface by Bashō's disciple Etsujin, which runs: "Benevolence comes first and good government begins with rejecting selfish desires." It is in praise of Yasutoki.

After the fall of the Hōjō Regents the Jōei Formulary remained the chief source of feudal law, and with amendments and additions it was used, if not always enforced, by subsequent feudal rulers until the nineteenth century.

4. The Bakufu and the Militant Clergy

As conditions in Kyoto improved after the catastrophic years following the Jōkyū Disturbance, it seemed as if intercourse between the Bakufu and the Court were on an easy footing and no serious troubles lay ahead. But the great monasteries of Hiyeizan and Nara began to create trouble on a large scale in the spring of 1235, destroying all early prospects of a peaceful life in the much-tried city.

The earlier history of the monastic armies has already been touched upon and need not be retraced, but there is some interest in reviewing the mutual relations of warriors and monks after the successes of the Bakufu in 1221. The Taira in their decline had treated the great monasteries roughly, whereas the Minamoto had usually taken care not to offend them. Yoritomo had gone out of his way to gain favour with the Tōdaiji of Nara, and in general as the influence of the Bakufu grew and spread, most of the great Buddhist and Shintō establishments had avoided provoking the feudal leaders. During the Jōkyū troubles the leading monasteries had been asked for help by the Court party, but had remained neutral, and therefore had not run any risk of hostile action by the Bakufu. After Jōkyū the balance of power was changed. The feudal rulers had an absolute superiority and no longer felt disposed to treat the monasteries with caution. They might not feel obliged to intervene in disputes between the religious bodies and the Crown, except for the sake of preserving order in the metropolitan area; but they would not tolerate any kind of behaviour that infringed or endangered the rights of their vassals. This change of attitude was not perceived by the monks and they were soon to pay a heavy price for their ignorance.

Their troubles began with an error of judgment committed by the parties to a dispute between two religious institutions over a question of manorial rights. In historical perspective the issue appears most trivial, but it is worth some attention as giving a picture of the rural politics of the time, and the helplessness of the Court.

In the early summer of 1235 the warden of the great Iwashimizu Hachiman shrine (which lay some fifteen miles to the southwest of Kyoto) complained to the Bakufu of intrusions upon certain manorial rights held in the province of Yamashiro by the shrine. The worship of Hachiman the War God was of special importance to the feudal leaders, and the warden pressed the Bakufu to appoint a constable in the district, who would be able to protect Iwashimizu interests. He explained that there was a dispute between the manors of the shrine and

a neighbouring manor of the Kōfukuji monastery, which was very powerful and could raise a large body of armed monks. The Bakufu listened
to his plea and appointed an officer to protect the claims of the shrine.
But before the appointment was made there had already developed an
open conflict over water rights between the two parties. The Imperial
Court requested the Rokuhara Command to send officers to examine
the case, but before they left the priests of Iwashimizu had already
clashed with the armed monks of Kōfukuji, who had set fire to buildings
in the manor belonging to the shrine and had killed some of the priests.
Thereupon the Rokuhara Command at the instance of the Court sent a
force under two senior officers (Takeda and Utsunomiya) to protect the
Iwashimizu property and to arrest the offending managers of the neighbouring Kōfukuji estate. Against this action the Kōfukuji angrily protested, but the Court procrastinated and only after some delay sent an
envoy to Iwashimizu to look into the case. The priests of Iwashimizu
were infuriated, drove away the envoy, and prepared to march in great
numbers to the capital with their sacred emblem (*shimboku*), which
was held to be inviolable and therefore protected them against forcible
measures. This move alarmed the Court more than the threats of the
Kōfukuji. An imperial messenger was hurriedly sent to pacify the Iwashimizu shrine, to which a manor in the province of Iga was presented
as a bribe and peace offering. Then a few days later a further gift was
made of manorial rights in the province of Inaba.

This support of Iwashimizu by the Court aroused great antagonism
among the soldier-monks of the Kōfukuji, and the outlook was not hopeful. While this quarrel was brewing the Mountain Sects (Hiyeizan)
arose and caused great alarm in the capital. The cause of the disturbance was the conduct of a certain Sasaki Takanobu. He was a son of
Sasaki Nobutsuna, a warrior of high rank then constable in Ōmi province. In his father's absence Takanobu, who was steward of a manor
in that province, impressed certain priests for the national labour tax.
He thereby clashed with the priests of Hiyoshi, one of the most important Shintō shrines in the country, and in the conflict a priest was
killed by one of Takanobu's men. The Hiyeizan monks denounced him
to the Court in July 1235. As usual the Court gave a vague reply, and the
monks escorting the sacred car of the Hiyoshi shrine marched towards
Kyoto. Hearing this the Court hastily ordered the Rokuhara authorities
to prevent the car from entering the city. A Rokuhara force was sent to
meet the procession outside the city limits, and in the fighting that
ensued men on both sides were killed and wounded. The monks saw
that they were in a dangerous position and retreated, leaving the sacred
car in the precincts of the Gion shrine. They at once appealed to the
Court, demanding punishment for those who had committed the grave
offence of killing or wounding monks and others dedicated to a religious
life.

The Court had always been frightened of the Mountain Sects, and as usual its response was weak and evasive. It gave way to these demands, and ordered the Bakufu captains to punish Takanobu and the assailants who had laid hands on the shrine priests. In September the Court issued an order banishing Takanobu, and at the same time it sent a Buddhist prelate to the Enryakuji to pacify the monks there. Some weeks later the sacred car was removed from the Gion shrine and taken back to its seat in the Hiyoshi shrine. The troubles seemed to be over.

But the Bakufu was not satisfied. A vassal of some standing had been punished for doing his duty as a fighting man. There was good reason to suppose that the Hiyeizan monks were not guiltless. Accordingly, while accepting the orders of the Court, the Bakufu instructed Rokuhara to give strict orders to the Mountain Sects to report the names of offenders among the monks and to hand over the ringleaders who had moved the sacred car and so instigated hostilities. In response to this challenge the Chief Abbot of the Tendai (who was a Prince of the Blood) accepted responsibility and resigned his office at the end of the year. The situation became tense. The Enryakuji made no further move, and the Bakufu was patient for a while. In March of the following year (1236) the Bakufu pressed for the surrender of the ringleaders, but to no effect. The order was repeated some months later, but still no response came from the monastery. The Bakufu then brought strong pressure to bear on the Chief Abbot, and the situation became so dangerous that the Court tried to make peace, but with no success.

On September 7, 1236, Rokuhara proposed to put to the question a certain monk whom they regarded as the chief instigator of the troubles. A party of warriors went to Sakamoto, at the foot of the mountain, but were stopped from going up by an angry crowd who closed all the monastery buildings against them, having again moved the sacred car. Now the Court was aghast, seeing no end to this dispute but violent suppression of the monks by the warriors. The Court then offered a pardon to the monks and informed the Bakufu. But the Bakufu would not give way.

Meanwhile the Kōfukuji affair had reached a serious point. The monks, in order to intimidate the Iwashimizu priests, had set out for the capital in December 1235, bearing their sacred emblem and calling for the punishment of officials of the Inaba estates given to the shrine by the Crown. Again the Court took fright, and ordered Rokuhara to dismantle the bridge at Uji so as to keep the monks from crossing on their way towards Kyoto. Messengers were sent from the Palace to placate the rioters, but to no effect. They were checked at Uji by a strong force sent against them, and were obliged to withdraw, leaving their sacred emblem in the Byōdō-in, a chapel of the Miidera. Since the Kōfukuji was the family monastery of the Fujiwara family, the Fujiwara nobles, from the Kampaku Michiiye downwards, were in an awkward position. They stayed at home behind closed gates, and thus when the New Year (1236) came the usual ceremonies could not be performed at the Palace. The capital was empty and silent.

While holding the bridge at Uji the Rokuhara Command had sent an urgent message to the Bakufu, pointing out the danger of the situation. The Bakufu then sent a strong letter of instruction to the Kōfukuji charging the monks to return the sacred emblem to its proper seat. To this order they paid no attention, and the Bakufu, which had so far displayed a commendable patience, at last hardened its attitude. It brought strong pressure to bear upon the monastery and also tried bribery and spying on the Hiyeizan monks in order to weaken their resistance. At last the Council of State sent one of its leading generals, Gotō Mototsune, to parley. On March 22, 1236, he advanced to the Kizu River, where, after making a demonstration of force, he so upbraided and threatened the monks that they withdrew with the sacred emblem, which they installed in its home.

Even now the Kōfukuji monks had not really given way. The Bakufu leaders were aware of this and took further and stronger measures. They appointed a constable to keep strict watch over the Iwashimizu domains, and awaited a move by the monks, who shortly showed signs of resistance. At the end of August 1236 they prepared the sacred emblem for procession, collected weapons, repaired their outer walls, and stood on the defensive.

Once more the Bakufu sent Gotō to Kyoto, where in September 1236 he mobilized the vassals of the Great Watch and moved upon the Kōfukuji. From close to its boundaries he issued a stern warning, to which the monks did not respond. The next move of the Bakufu was to confiscate the Kōfukuji manors and to appoint new stewards to them, while surrounding the precincts of the monastery and cutting it off from all access by road. A constable was appointed to Yamato province, so that permanent pressure could be maintained. This was an important move, since hitherto owing to the prestige and wealth of the Kōfukuji it had been the custom not to appoint governors or high police officials to Yamato.

The stubborn monks were at last powerless. On November 16 they broke through the walls, emerged, and dispersed; and by the end of December they had returned the sacred emblem to its seat, and submitted to the Bakufu. Shortly after these events the Council of State in Kamakura decided that the constable and the new stewards could be withdrawn from Yamato. Their firm action had borne fruit; thereafter the religious establishments that had for so long bullied and blackmailed the Court did not venture to offend the feudal leaders.

One of the effects of the prolonged recalcitrance of the monks was to delay the state visit of the young Shōgun to Kyoto. The air was cleared by the end of 1237. The reputation of the Bakufu was never higher, thanks to its handling of the monks and its assistance to the Throne in its embarrassment, so that a friendly welcome was assured when it was proposed that Yoritsune should proceed to the capital early in 1238.

Great preparations were made. New buildings were put up to accommodate the Shōgun and a numerous suite, which included the Regent Yasutoki. To meet the cost of the lavish entertainment which was planned the Bakufu levied a tax on the vassals in every province. Strict precautions were taken to ensure the safety of the Shōgun and the notables who took part in the splendid ceremonies and festivities, which went on week after week. Such measures were thought to be necessary, for the streets were still infested by robbers and beggars and even by the delinquent sons of noblemen, who took pleasure in riotous behaviour.

The Shōgun was honoured by the Throne with the traditional ranks and titles, being made a Grand Councillor, Director of the Police Commission, and Commander of the Right Division of the Guards. Many meetings took place between the Regent Yasutoki and the leading men at Court, with whom political matters were discussed. The visit lasted about nine months; the Shōgun did not return to Kamakura until early December of 1238. He was seen off at Kyoto by a distinguished gathering which included all the great nobles of the capital, led by Saionji and Kujō, who were both in such close touch with the Bakufu that they might be described as agents of its policy.

One of the most interesting and at times puzzling features of the political history of Japan is the great importance which the Bakufu attached to its relations with the Imperial Court. Once the coup d'état of Go-Toba had failed and the ascendancy of the feudal leaders had been amply recognized by the ministers in Kyoto, it would seem at first sight as if the Bakufu had only to keep on formally correct terms with the Throne, paying no heed to palace appointments and edicts which could not be enforced without the approval and support of the Regent in Kamakura or his provincial representatives, including the powerful Tandai of Rokuhara. But in practice the attitude of the Bakufu was still one of respect for the prerogative of the Throne; and the Regents, conscious as they were of their superior strength, never ceased to observe the outward forms of respect and allegiance, while keeping a very strict watch upon the ebb and flow of political sentiment among the leading figures at Court and in those monasteries with which the Court had intimate relations.

This seeming anomaly needs some explanation. It arose, no doubt, from that long tradition of moral ascendancy which was the true source of the authority of the Imperial House. The sovereign was a symbol of power, but so sacred in character that all material functions were habitually delegated[3] to great servants of the Crown, whether Ministers of State or Fujiwara Regents or, in later times, the chieftains of warrior clans. It was upon this kind of delegation that the Kamakura Bakufu depended for its legitimacy; and the fact that Yoritomo and his successors felt legitimacy to be essential is perhaps the most notable aspect of the new feudal order. Certainly Yoritomo, even in the pride of victory, did not venture to think of himself as independent; and it seems that the Kamakura Bakufu never reached a state of complete confidence in its power to rule the whole country. It may be said to have moved step by step in that direction; but the Jōei Formulary contains several articles showing—what other evidence confirms—that in the middle of the thirteenth century there remained large areas of jurisdiction and economic control in which the Shōgun's officers had no power to interfere. Further, as we have seen, the Rokuhara commanders in the capital were obliged in some circumstances to obey the orders of a timid and vacillating Court for which they can have had no true respect. This point is well illustrated by the police and military action taken by Bakufu forces at the request of the Court against the insurgent monks of the Kōfukuji.

The *Azuma Kagami,* where it deals with events after the Jōkyū Disturbance, gives an impression of great strength in Kamakura as against great weakness in Kyoto. But perhaps such annals give too favourable a picture of the stability of the feudal government. Its leaders had good reason to fear some dissension and strain within the feudal order, and they were of course well aware of antagonism, sometimes barely concealed, among the greater vassals. Yoritomo, Tokimasa, and Yoshitoki were on the whole cautious men, and it may be that they thought it possible for a successful, or at least very troublesome, revolt against their rule to be planned in Kyoto in concert with discontented vassals in the east as well as in the west. To keep a garrison in the capital under the command of a deputy of the Shōgun with all but plenary powers was a natural precaution, for which there was ample precedent. But the Bakufu went much farther than this. They took the closest interest in Palace affairs, down to minute details, and they insisted upon the last word in the choice of candidates for all high positions, while claiming and exercising the right to be consulted upon, or more correctly to determine, the abdication and succession of emperors.

Despite this commanding position they felt it necessary to have their own friends at Court. Yoritomo, walking warily after his triumph in 1185, had profited by the advice and support of Kujō Kanezane;[4] and

----

[3] The Tokugawa Shōguns five centuries later in reports to the Throne used the phrase "Go inin ni makase," which means "in accordance with the powers delegated."

[4] Kanezane was the head of the Kujō branch of the Fujiwara. See below, p. 406, and Chapter XIX, p. 416, fn. 3.

after the Jōkyū affair Yasutoki paid close attention to the choice of men for such high offices as Sesshō and Kampaku and Chancellor. When the cloistered sovereigns Go-Toba and Juntoku had been exiled in most melancholy conditions, and when princes and nobles who had taken part in Go-Toba's conspiracy had left the capital under duress, and when the city was occupied by Bakufu forces, it would seem an excess of caution to insist upon the appointment of the Bakufu's own candidates to important posts in the imperial government. Whoever was in office was bound to execute the orders of the Bakufu, however reluctantly; while the open appointment of men who were known to be agents of Kamakura was likely to cause jealousy and opposition in Kyoto.

This however was not the view taken by the Council of State. Its members first of all wished to reward Saionji Kintsune for his services. He had been their eyes and ears in the capital at the time of the Jōkyū coup, and had become Chancellor in 1222. In that capacity and by virtue of his relations with the Bakufu he was all-powerful at Court. He was able to dictate to the Board of Appointments at its periodical meetings, and thus could make sure that persons acceptable to Kamakura were selected for key positions. Such irregular conduct enraged many of the nobles, but they were helpless. Kintsune's influence, with strong backing from Rokuhara, grew so rapidly that by 1225 nearly all important positions at Court were filled by members of the Saionji family. In addition to his high ministerial office Kintsune cleverly seized the valuable post of chief secretary (*bettō*) of the cloistered Emperor's cabinet, a post both influential and lucrative, since it included the administration of the In's great estates and entitled its occupant to emoluments drawn from their revenues.

Titular and Cloistered Emperors, 1198–1242

CLOISTERED (INSEI)		TITULAR	
Go-Toba	1198–1221	Tsuchimikado	1198–1210
Go-Takakura	1221–1223	Juntoku	1210–1221
Go-Horikawa	1232–1234	Chūkyō	1221 (3 months)
		Go-Horikawa	1221–1232
		Shijō	1232–1242

Regents of the Crown, 1206–1242

SESSHŌ		KAMPAKU	
Konoye Iyezane	1206–1207	Konoye Iyezane	1207–1221
Konoye Iyezane	1221–1223	Kujō Michiiye	1221
Kujō Yorimichi	1232–1235	Konoye Iyezane	1223–1228
Kujō Michiiye	1235–1237	Kujō Michiiye	1228–1231
Konoye Kanetsune	1237–1242	Kujō Yorizane	1231–1232
		Konoye Kanetsune	1242 (3 months)

Loaded with honours and treasure, Kintsune spent great sums upon extravagant entertainments and costly villas and gardens. He is said to have considered himself a more successful statesman, a more lavish spender, than even the great Michinaga, who had the highest opinion of his own merits. Kintsune thus outstripped in power and reputation his colleague Kujō Michiiye, who had been Kampaku in 1221 but was relieved of his office after the Jōkyū Disturbance. Michiiye, however, was not regarded as in any way dangerous; and since he was the father of the Shōgun Yoritsune as well as being related by marriage to Kintsune, with whom he was on good terms, it was not long before he was reinstated as Kampaku (1228–31) and restored to his former importance. The two great families thus came to dominate the political stage in Kyoto, the Saionji being the more active and the Kujō (as one of the Sekke, or families qualified to furnish Regents) the more distinguished. Michiiye followed Fujiwara precedent by arranging a match between the Emperor (Go-Horikawa) and his daughter, who became Consort (Chūgū) in 1230. By such policies Michiiye planned a permanent link between the Kujō family and the Throne. In 1231 a son was born and declared heir-apparent. Michiiye had achieved his purpose, and though he thought it seemly to resign the office of Regent he continued to be the most powerful and the most splendid nobleman at Court. In the following year, 1232, on the ground that His Majesty was not in good health and could not bear the strain of the calamities of the last few years (the famines and plagues of 1225–31), it was thought fitting that he should abdicate. This he did at the end of the year, becoming the cloistered Go-Horikawa, while his two-year-old son, Michiiye's grandson, ascended the throne and reigned from 1232 to 1242 as the Emperor Shijō.

The power of the Kujō family seemed to have reached a dizzy height, since its members could decide who should occupy the throne, who should rule from the cloister, and who should fill the great offices of state. But in fact for every move they made both Kujō and Saionji had to secure the approval of the Council of State in Kamakura. They were little more than gorgeous puppets of the Hōjō Regents; and before long they and their families suffered from mortal illnesses and other misfortunes, which the superstitious citizens readily ascribed to the vengeful feelings of the deposed Go-Toba and Juntoku, then languishing in exile.

It is clear that from a purely practical point of view the Bakufu could safely have dispensed with the assistance of men like Saionji and Kujō, since in any crucial situation the Court was weak and helpless. Even to deal with a rabble of disorderly monks the great ministers of the Crown had been obliged to call upon the warriors; and after Go-Toba's downfall there was little likelihood of any plot escaping the knowledge of Rokuhara spies, and still less of successful resistance to the armed force which the Bakufu could rapidly mobilize in the west.

Yet the Bakufu evidently did not consider its relationship with the Court in a purely matter-of-fact way. It was guided in its attitude by a number of considerations that together made it the part of prudence, in the judgment of successive feudal leaders, to treat the Throne with respect and as far as possible to use persuasion rather than force in pursuit of their aims. Possibly the most cogent reason for this policy was the reluctance of the feudal leaders to engage in further military undertakings. They were deeply interested in the organization of the new feudal order, in perfecting its administration and ensuring obedience to its laws. They did not want to see this task interrupted by mobilizing vassals who would expect generous rewards which the Bakufu could not afford. In their opinion it was simpler and safer to depend upon an alliance with great nobles of ancient lineage closely connected with the Imperial House, who would be willing to carry out Bakufu policy in return for Bakufu support of their private ambitions.

These material reasons alone are not enough to explain the close and continuous interest of the Bakufu in the affairs of the Court. There can be no doubt that the military leaders, from Yoritomo to the Hōjō Regents, and indeed the warrior class in general, believed in the hereditary supremacy of the reigning family, and were strongly influenced by the prestige and the mystic power of the Throne. This attitude was not inconsistent with a quite ruthless treatment of individual sovereigns and princes who hindered the Bakufu policy; for the power of the Emperor lay not in his action or his capacity but in his position. Of almost any Japanese sovereign it could be said—with a twist, it is true—capax imperii nisi imperasset. It was those who tried to govern that met with the greatest difficulties.

When the Emperor Shijō died suddenly in February 1242 a serious dispute arose. The line of Go-Horikawa was extinct and there was a good case for the succession of Prince Kunihito, a son of Tsuchimikado, who was the eldest son of Go-Toba. But there was also strong support for the claim of a son of Tsuchimikado's younger brother, Juntoku. This young man, named Tadanari, was favoured by Kujō Michiiye (who was his maternal grandfather) and also by Saionji Kintsune. But these two important personages were much beholden to the Bakufu and dared not take any positive action without the consent of Yasutoki. Both parties sent messengers to Kamakura asking for Bakufu support, but while they were travelling to Kamakura two members of the Council of State were on their way to the capital, with orders to insist upon the claim of Tsuchimikado's son. They had been told in confidence by Yasutoki that if Tadanari were put on the throne he would be deposed.

Yasutoki took a strong line here, chiefly because Tadanari's father, the exiled Juntoku, was well known to be hostile to Kamakura. The situation was curious, for here we see the Court not merely accepting orders from the Bakufu but seeking its decision in a matter of sovereign rights. The Prince Kunihito duly succeeeded to the throne as the Emperor Go-Saga, in April 1242. His reign was brief, for he abdicated in 1246, but he retained actual power until his death in 1272. His relations with the Bakufu were distinguished by a rare degree of mutual trust. The Court and the Bakufu seem at last to have reached a satisfactory division of functions. The officers of the Bakufu did not encroach upon the jurisdiction of the Crown in public lands or interfere with the still very extensive rights of private landowners who were not vassals. Both the imperial family and the great nobles possessed rich estates, especially in central and western Japan. Decisions upon military matters, upon the prevention of civil disorder, and upon the administration of all land held by vassals, were entirely in the hands of the feudal leaders. On questions of national importance it was the practice of the Bakufu to go through a formal procedure of consulting the Throne and where necessary requesting the government in Kyoto to issue appropriate commands. The situation of the sovereign was not unlike that of a modern constitutional monarch, in that he took no step without the approval of his political advisers—in this case the Regent and the Council of State at Kamakura.

This dual system of government in Japan was strictly speaking irregular and anomalous. But it worked very well from 1221 (when Go-Toba was deposed) until the end of the thirteenth century; and for this success the chief credit is due to the prudence and good sense of the Hōjō Regents, in particular Yasutoki (1224–42), Tokiyori (1246–56), Tokimune (1268–84), and Sadatoki (1284–1301). It is an interesting demonstration of the national habit of firm and well-organized government that a society of quarrelsome warriors should have produced a line of extremely capable administrators who combined a strong sense of justice with power to enforce discipline.

CHAPTER XIX

THE HŌJŌ REGENTS, 1242-84

1. *Internal Problems of the Bakufu, 1242-52*

WHILE the relations of the Bakufu with the Court were harmonious and even friendly after the accession of Go-Saga, the Hōjō Regency was not without its internal troubles. Yasutoki died in 1242 and his successor Tsunetoki (his grandson) was faced with two problems that needed early solution.

One was to find a suitable successor to the Shōgun Yoritsune, whom the Bakufu wished to depose. The other was to ensure the stability of the Regency at a time when it might be challenged because it was in the hands of a yet untried member of the Hōjō family.

The problem of finding a successor to Yoritsune was not difficult. As a temporary solution at least, the obvious course was to request the Throne to appoint Yoritsugu, his infant son, to replace him. This was done rather suddenly, before concerted opposition could develop, by sending a special messenger to the capital. He left Kamakura on May 29, 1244, and returned with the necessary edict dated June 6, appointing Yoritsugu to succeed his father, who was treated as having abdicated. The messenger was allowed only seven days for the distance (about 300 miles) between Kamakura and Kyoto and the same for the return, which must have been the most rapid travel possible at that time.

Yoritsugu was promptly affianced to a younger sister of Tsunetoki. Yoritsune remained in Kamakura, living in seclusion and taking holy orders to show that he had no more secular ambitions. In April 1246 Tsunetoki fell ill of a mortal disease and was succeeded by his younger brother Tokiyori. The new Regent had to cope with a menacing situation. Yoritsune had been Shōgun for nearly twenty years and had made many friends in Kamakura, some of whom were young nobles from Kyoto, others—a considerable following—members of leading feudal families who had taken service under him or frequented his Court. These people resented the Hōjō Regent's arbitrary action, and when Tokiyori took over, the situation was tense.

The reasons for forcing the resignation are not quite clear. The *Azuma Kagami* explains that it was demanded by celestial portents. That may be so; but it seems more likely that the Bakufu did not like Yoritsune's friends and suspected his family, for his father Michiiye, the Kampaku, had immense influence at Court and was a man of boundless ambition. It is probable that the Bakufu desired on grounds of high policy to install a Shōgun of tender age, open to the influence of the

Regent and without familiar friends or partisans in Kamakura. There was in the eastern provinces a small but influential group of vassals hostile to the Hōjō Regents, among them being the Nagoshi brothers, who were themselves members of the Hōjō family. They were on intimate terms with Yoritsune, and while not actively opposing the Regents they harboured somewhat disloyal sentiments, which were shared or at least not condemned by certain members of the Council of State, men of such high reputation as Gotō Mototsuna, Chiba Hidetane, and the President of the Monchūjo, Miyoshi Yasumochi. More dangerous to the Hōjō, however, was the positive antagonism of the powerful Miura family, who for some time past had been envious and suspicious of the Regents.

All these things were of course clear to Tokiyori, and he was particularly anxious to prevent the so-to-speak domestic affairs of the Bakufu from becoming a political issue at Court, where Yoritsune's father could make trouble. He therefore sent orders to the Rokuhara Command to keep a strict lookout, to watch for signs of conspiracy, and to be prepared for emergencies. Meanwhile there were signs of trouble nearer home, for during the spring of 1246 vassals and retainers from the countryside began to show themselves in Kamakura and to take sides in disputes and brawls between the supporters of Yoritsune and the loyal followers of Tokiyori.

Tokiyori took preventive steps by posting strong detachments of warriors in the city streets, with orders to keep in check the active adherents of Yoritsune and so to break up subversive movements before they grew dangerous. On July 10 in the middle of the night a clash took place which on enquiry led to discovery of a plot to assassinate the Hōjō Regent, in which his own uncle Mitsutoki was involved. Tokiyori withdrew to his mansion, which was strongly defended by the flower of Kamakura warriors, and stood in readiness. At this point Yoritsune sent an envoy to Tokiyori with excuses and conciliatory messages. But

Regents from Tokimasa to Tokimune

	BIRTH–DEATH	TERM OF REGENCY		BIRTH–DEATH	TERM OF REGENCY
Tokimasa	1138–1215	1203–1205	Tokiyori	1227–1263	1246–1256
Yoshitoki	1163–1224	1205–1224	Nagatoki	1229–1264	1256–1264
Yasutoki	1183–1242	1224–1242	Masamura	1205–1273	1264–1268
Tsunetoki	1214–1246	1242–1246	Tokimune	1251–1284	1268–1284

*

Each Regent ("Shikken") had a colleague or deputy, called "Renshō" or co-signatory, who was nominally co-equal with the Shikken, but in practice usually did little more than countersign state papers and deal with the routine of administration.

Tokiyori was not willing to lose this prime opportunity of dealing firmly with confessed conspirators. He sent the envoy back to Yoritsune and summoned his uncle Hōjō Mitsutoki, who shaved his head and came to confess his guilt.

Shortly after these events Tokiyori was secretly told of a move by one of the Miura family which made their attitude clear. Doubling his precautions he swiftly arranged a meeting with Miura leaders, hoping to pin them down to some agreement. He dismissed Gotō, Chiba, and others from their seats on the Council of State, and he was merciful to Mitsutoki, whom he deprived of all his offices and sent to Izu to live quietly on his home farm, under the eye of Kamakura.

As for the Shōgun Yoritsune, though he may have been only a puppet of those ambitious men, his conduct could not be overlooked. Tokiyori could not obtain proof of his complicity, but it was decided to send him back to Kyoto. Yoritsune was entertained by Tokiyori before he left and was paid full ceremonial honours on his departure with an imposing escort. He reached Kyoto in September 1246 and was installed in the Rokuhara mansion by Shigetoki, the Tandai.

Tokiyori's handling of Yoritsune was quick and successful but it was necessary to take precautions against a renewal of his friends' activities, and for this purpose the Bakufu had to withdraw their support of Michiiye and the Kujō family in general. There was no great difficulty here since the rival noble houses would welcome his downfall. What was more urgently needed was a settlement with the Miura family, which, though at one time friendly, had for some years been ill-disposed towards the Hōjō family.

It would be sufficient for the purpose of a general description of Tokiyori's policy to say that he found means of destroying this powerful rival; but the story is worth telling in some detail because it illuminates certain aspects of the feudal scene during the Hōjō Regency, and it contains all the proper ingredients of an internecine tragedy.

Tokiyori had no convincing evidence that the Miura intended to attack him. Moreover the Hōjō family owed a debt of gratitude to the Miura for help given during the Jōkyū Disturbance. Thus there was an uneasy peace between the two great houses. Tokiyori hesitated to take the offensive, partly because he had some hope of ending the discord by tactful handling, partly because the Miura clan had much greater fiefs and therefore more direct adherents than the Hōjō family, whose leaders had deliberately refrained from taking confiscated lands after the Jōkyū affair.

Yasumura, the head of the Miura family, was a member of the Council of State and a signatory of the Jōei Formulary. He had rendered good service and given good advice. But—alas for that unity and anonymity which its founders had sworn to preserve—sharp differences of opinion within the Council gave rise to ill-feeling between Yasumura and members of the Adachi family, which being related to the Hōjō leaders by marriage began to gain influence that Yasumura lost. Since Yoritomo's day members of the Adachi family had frequently been entrusted with important missions,[1] and this with other circumstances of a similar nature caused tension between the two clans, which was heightened by the anger of Yasumura's younger brother Mitsumura when the Shōgun Yoritsune was sent off to Kyoto in 1246. Mitsumura had been on terms of close friendship with the young Shōgun for a long time, and was therefore naturally suspected of complicity in plots against the Regent.

It should be remembered that from the point of view of the Miura family, which was as powerful in numbers as the Hōjō and of equally good birth, the Hōjō had no greater claim than they to rule the vassals. The Hōjō had been able to assume special powers because Masa-ko, the widow of the Minamoto chieftain, had given indispensable support to Tokimasa, for the sake of her sons by Yoritomo. The breach between the two families was therefore not easy to heal, and Tokiyori's difficulties seemed to be Miura's opportunities. In this uneasy situation Tokiyori remained on the alert but took no action. He seems to have been waiting for some overt act by the Miura family, which would justify reprisals on a large scale. But Yasumura continued to attend meetings of the Council and gave no opening to Tokiyori.

On the surface relations were smooth and peaceful. But in May 1247 there suddenly appeared in Kamakura an aged monk, Kakuchi by name, who made his way to Tokiyori's mansion. This was an old warrior, Adachi Kagemori, who had been living a life of retirement on Mount Kōya for the past twenty years. He was Tokiyori's maternal grandfather, and his meditations had been disturbed by news from Kamakura. He had come east to consult with Tokiyori as to the best means of dealing with the Miura family.

Meanwhile relations between the two houses seemed to be growing friendly. Tokiyori had even arranged to adopt Yasumura's second son and (on account of a family bereavement) had visited the Miura mansion on July 1; but having discerned signs of warlike preparation he hurried back to his own headquarters and sent a strong rebuke to Yasumura, who at once made excuses. Spies sent out on the following day reported that arms were being brought to the Miura residence from their manors in nearby provinces; and from that moment Kamakura was in an uproar. Tokiyori ordered Yasumura to send his men and their equipment back to their homes, and third parties tried to make peace.

[1] An Adachi had on Yoritomo's order murdered Shizuka's child by Yoshitsune. An Adachi as well as a Miura had been an original member of the Council established by Tokimasa after Yoritomo's death; and an Adachi had been sent to Kyoto in 1242 to prevent a son of Juntoku from inheriting the crown.

Yasumura showed signs of weakness and swore that he had no designs against the Hōjō family.

At this point Adachi Kagemori protested that a reconciliation could not be permanent; one or the other must be destroyed, he said, and therefore the Hōjō must strike at once and trust in Heaven. On July 8 he ordered his son Yoshikage and other Adachi warriors to attack the Miura stronghold. The assault was made according to a prearranged plan and it resulted in the complete defeat of the Miura. Yasumura and the leading warriors of his clan withdrew to the Hokkedō, a monastery founded by Yoritomo, and there they held out for some time until, unable to resist the continuing onslaughts of Hōjō forces, they committed suicide. The scene of five hundred warriors dying together by their own hand in those holy precincts is impossible to describe and difficult to imagine; but it was in the tradition of their class.

The Hōjō family was now supreme in the east and the Hōjō Regents had no rivals to fear. Kagemori went back to his monastery and resumed his religious exercises, no doubt with a good conscience, until his death about a year later.

By removing the only real threat to their supremacy the Hōjō family had brought their Regency to a high pitch of strength and capacity to govern. Tokiyori, reporting his successes to the Rokuhara deputies, ordered them to seek out and capture any remnants of hostile forces to be found in the home provinces, while in the east similar measures were taken against such scattered adherents of the Miura as were still at large. Miura estates were confiscated and part of their property was transferred to monasteries and shrines as a thank-offering for the victory of the Regent's men. The Tandai Shigetoki was summoned to Kamakura and appointed to assist the Regent, who was now free from anxiety and could address himself earnestly to organizing the Bakufu for speedy handling of its business. In 1249 he formed a special standing committee designed to promote full investigation by the Council of State of suits or appeals brought to it for judgment; and this body proved so useful that it became a permanent part of the feudal administration, known as the Hikitsuke-shū.[2]

2. Tokiyori's Attitude towards the Court

It is characteristic of the Hōjō Regents that they constantly endeavoured to improve the civil administration of the Bakufu while not neglecting its military requirements. Most of them seem to have inherited an acute political sense, and in Tokiyori this quality was highly developed. It is shown clearly in his handling of the delicate problem

[2] It consisted of five members of the Mandokoro under the chairmanship of one of three members of the Council of State, who served in rotation. Hikitsuke means a coadjutor.

of relationship with the Court, which needed firm but careful treatment after the dismissal of the Shōgun Yoritsune.

There was no great difficulty in reducing the influence of Yoritsune's father Michiiye, since his successes had created envy and opposition. As a result of strong hints conveyed by the Tandai Shigetoki to Go-Saga in the summer of 1246, and after some going and coming between Roku-hara and the In's office, Michiiye retired; and at the suggestion of Kama-kura, Go-Saga agreed to accept a member of the Saionji family as a liai-son officer or "mouthpiece" of the Bakufu (Kantō mōshitsugi). Thus the responsibility for harmonious intercourse between the Court and the Bakufu was taken out of the hands of the Kujō family. This arrange-ment had one curious sequel: at the request of the Bakufu, the Court formed a special tribunal within the In's cabinet for the decision of miscellaneous claims, on the model of similar tribunals in Kamakura. This tribunal met regularly, and its successful working testified to a new spirit of cooperation between the civil and military elements in political life.

Credit for this satisfactory condition is due in a large measure to the character of the cloistered Go-Saga, whose genuine desire for friend-ship with the Bakufu was wisely reciprocated by Tokiyori. The decline of the Kujō influence and the rise of the house of Konoye with Bakufu support combined to remove the danger of serious antagonism in high Court circles, especially since the important Saionji family could also be counted upon to side with the feudal party in any dispute about policy.

In 1247 the Council of State in Kamakura after careful secret debate declared in favour of an attitude of special respect to the Throne and voted for a generous policy in financial matters. Envoys sent to Kyoto to announce these intentions were received in audience by Go-Saga and explained to him that the Bakufu proposed certain Acts of Grace for the remission of debts and wished to offer to His Majesty a number of valuable manors. Go-Saga accepted those offers and in return under-took to make certain changes in the organization of cloister govern-ment.

Now that Tokiyori was satisfied that the atmosphere in Kyoto was really friendly he turned his attention to the crucial issue for the Bakufu, the selection of a new Shōgun not from one of the great noble families but from the imperial family itself. On March 2, 1251, he wrote to Yoshizane, the former Kampaku, who was on bad terms with Michiiye, suggesting that the position of the young Shōgun Yoritsugu was very unsafe. At the end of the year it was rumoured in Kamakura that a plot against the Bakufu had been discovered. The Bakufu acted promptly, arresting a certain monk and his accomplices. According to one account they revealed under examination that the author of the plot was Yori-tsune, the retired Shōgun. Suspicion then naturally fell upon Yoritsune's

father, Michiiye; and the Kujō family received a severe admonishment
from the Throne. Whether these accusations were true or not—and the
evidence was poor—the upshot was that the Hōjō Regent found in them
a welcome and plausible excuse for dismissing the young Shōgun Yoritsugu, as he had hinted to Yoshizane.

It was then proposed by Tokiyori that the next Shōgun should be
an imperial prince, and the Bakufu then forthwith prayed the cloistered
Go-Saga to allow his son Prince Munetaka to proceed to Kamakura and
take up the office. The mission conveying the prayer of the Bakufu
reached Kyoto towards the end of March. Its message was considered
by the In and his council, and after a delay of some fifteen days it was
agreed that the Prince should go to Kamakura. Accordingly he proceeded first to the Rokuhara Headquarters and after a short stay there
he left for the east with an imposing military escort and a large company
of nobles and warriors of high rank. He was installed as Shōgun on the
day of his arrival (April 23, 1252), and a new residence was provided
for him.

For some time past the Bakufu had discussed the arguments for and
against the appointment of an imperial prince to the office of Shōgun.
They had already (at the instance of Masa-ko) proposed it to Go-Toba
in 1221 when it was suggested that he should send one of his sons to
Kamakura; but Go-Toba suspected their motives and declined. The
view of those who favoured this plan was that it would permanently
ease relations between the Court and the Bakufu. But those who opposed it feared that the Bakufu intended gradually to merge Kyoto
and Kamakura by some such device as claiming a son of the Shōgun
as heir to the imperial Throne, or otherwise fusing the military and civil
elements in the state. A few members of the feudal aristocracy even
feared that once a dynasty of princely Shōguns was established, the
Imperial House would swallow the feudal society by its prestige, which
would raise it above those internecine disputes, those treasonable plots
against the feudal rulers that had disturbed the country since Yoritomo's
death. Such an end to the power of the Bakufu must often have been
envisaged and desired by the great nobles of Kyoto, the Five Houses
(Go-Sekke), who were almost hereditary dictators and regents; and
although it was still hidden in a distant future, the end of the feudal
autocracy was in fact ultimately brought about by the union of military
and civil authority under the Crown.[3]

---

[3] The Go-Sekke or Five Regency Houses were the five families qualified by
tradition to hold the office of Regent (Sesshō) or Dictator (Kampaku). The leaders of the Fujiwara clan had held this office from the time of Yoshifusa (858–72)
to the time of Tadamichi (1141–50). Upon Tadamichi's death his sons Motozane
and Motofusa in turn succeeded him as Regent, but their younger brother Kanezane
was not allowed to follow. He was, however, a capable man and a useful ally of
Yoritomo, who resented the monopoly of a Fujiwara clique and brought pressure
to bear upon the Court to ensure Kanezane's appointment (1185). The claimants

But in 1250, when Tokiyori had caused or contributed to the downfall of the Kujō family and had broken the monopoly of the Five Houses, the initiative in affairs of state was permanently with the Bakufu and not with the great nobles about the Throne, and still less with dissident groups within the feudal order. Thus the appointment of an imperial prince to the office of Shōgun was in its day a triumph for the Bakufu. Its later effects, however, were scarcely such as had been expected by Tokiyori and his colleagues. Though he had undoubtedly gained a political victory, he had not foreseen the remarkable social influence that was to be exerted by the aristocratic tradition of Kyoto life as it was transplanted in Kamakura.

3. *The Later Regents, 1256–84*

Relations between the Court and the Bakufu continued to be amicable after the Emperor Go-Saga, upon abdication, was succeeded in 1246 by Go-Fukakusa, who in his turn was succeeded by Kameyama in 1259. Go-Saga, though abdicated, remained in power until his death in 1272, and it was he who decided who should inherit the crown according to a rule which he laid down and which was to cause much strife in a later period of Japanese history. We need not discuss this matter here, for the troubles were yet to come.

The ten years or more from the appointment of Prince Munetaka as Shōgun (in 1252) were the years when the Hōjō Regents were at the very summit of their power. The Shōgun was the nominal head of the Bakufu, just as the titular sovereign was the nominal head of the imperial government; but the Hōjō Regent was the real ruler in Kamakura, as the cloistered Emperor was the real ruler in Kyoto.

There was an even further development of the system of delegated rule in Kamakura, since in course of time the Regent came to require a deputy, to whom the active business of administration was entrusted.

---

to the office of Sesshō thus formed two branch families descended from Tadamichi, as follows:

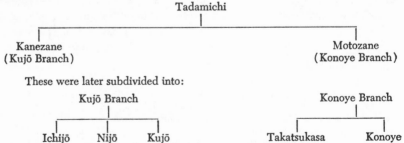

thus giving five houses qualified to furnish a Sesshō or Kampaku.

These changes were brought about mainly by the Bakufu, in order to reduce the power of any single house. The Saionji family, though never one of the Sekke, was favoured by Tokiyori as a counterbalance to the Sekke.

Originally this deputy, ranking with but after the Shikken, though he nominally had plenary powers, in practice only countersigned the orders of the Shikken. Thus Tokiyori had the assistance of Shigetoki, and when Shigetoki retired in 1256 his place as deputy was filled by his younger half-brother Masamura. Later in that year Tokiyori retired on grounds of health and entered religion in the Saimyōji monastery, his office being inherited by his son Tokimune. But Tokimune at that date was an infant, and Shigetoki's son Nagatoki, a member of the Council of State, was appointed his guardian and Regent until 1264, when he was followed by Masamura, and then in 1268 by Tokimune, the direct heir of Tokiyori. Despite all these changes, during the years between 1256 and his death in 1263 Tokiyori continued to exercise full authority in matters of policy while living in the Saimyōji monastery, just as the cloistered sovereigns in Kyoto ruled from their monastic retirement.

For all their brilliant successes the Hōjō Regents seem never to have reached complete confidence in their ability to control the Court. They continued to fear the intangible strength of the imperial ancestry and the pride of the ancient nobility. They sought to make still stronger the bond that tied the Shōgun to the Bakufu. So far they had been content to see that a new Shōgun should marry a daughter of one of the Hōjō leaders. But the position was changed when an imperial prince was made Shōgun. It was then necessary for him to marry a girl from one of the great families next to the Throne; and in 1260 a daughter of Konoye Kanetsune was brought to Kamakura and married to the Shōgun Munetaka. This was after Tokiyori's retirement, but it was he who arranged the match.

As if to punish the pride of the lords of Kamakura, from the time of Tokiyori's retirement in 1256 the eastern region was visited by one calamity after another. There was a succession of earthquake shocks for a month in 1257, doing great damage. Then followed violent storms and floods in 1258, which caused a shortage of food, and then a plague in 1259. These disasters threw a great burden upon the Bakufu, who began to find that economic problems were even more intractable than the dynastic questions that had taken up their attention for so long. This new difficulty had to be faced by new leaders, for Shigetoki died in retirement in 1261, and Tokiyori died in the Saimyōji in 1263. Both these men had deserved well of their countrymen for their capable and honest conduct of affairs. Contemporary chronicles show that their loss was the cause of great grief among the vassals, some of whom are said to have turned in their sorrow to the consolations of religion and lived a monastic life—a step which was forbidden to the kenin unless the Chieftain's permission was obtained.

The Hōjō family was prolific, and its members were as a rule men of good brains and strong bodies. Tokimasa lived to a ripe old age, and so did his vigorous daughter and many others of the name. But Tokiyori seems to have inherited a constitutional weakness, since he died in his thirty-seventh year, and his eldest son Tokimune in his thirty-third. Tokiyori, after his successful struggle with the Miura family in 1247, was unable to cope single-handed with the mass of business which his task as Regent imposed upon him, and he was obliged to send for Shigetoki, then in Kyoto as Tandai, who gave him invaluable help.

It had been intended to arrange a visit to Kyoto by the Shōgun, but the calamities of the years 1257 to 1259 had diverted the attention of the Kamakura government to the work of relief, and the Shōgun's journey had to be postponed. The deaths of Tokiyori and Shigetoki thus occurred at a difficult moment, and the situation was worsened by the retirement of Nagatoki in 1264, not long after Tokiyori's death. By that time the Shōgun had been thirteen years in Kamakura without returning to Kyoto to pay the visit to his parents that filial piety demanded. The Hōjō leaders saw that he had a grievance and, on what grounds it is not clear, began to suspect that he was plotting mischief, much as Yoritsune was thought to have done in similar circumstances. In 1266 the Shōgun fell ill and was attended by a Buddhist prelate named Ryōki, whose presence seemed to bring about a strain in the relations of the Shōgun with the Bakufu. The Shōgun's consort was reputed to be on intimate terms with the prelate, and the Shōgun was said to be in close consultation with Go-Saga in Kyoto. These facts or rumours are supposed to have alarmed the Bakufu, and accordingly on July 15 a secret meeting of members of the Council of State was held in Tokimune's residence, at which Masamura, the seventh Regent, presided. It was attended also by other Hōjō relatives, including Adachi Yasumori.

Evidence was produced to show that the Shōgun was concerned in a plot against the Regent. When Ryōki was looked for he had vanished; and assuming that there was danger of a coup d'état Tokimune, on the 19th, suddenly removed the Shōgun's wife to a vassal's house and took her child under his own roof. Strong detachments of troops were posted throughout the city, and all persons in the Shōgun's service were ordered to keep away from his palace. Tokimune then stopped all movement of private warriors in and near the city, and swiftly seized the person of the Shōgun, who was sent back to Kyoto a few days later.

By that time messengers were approaching Kyoto with news of the designs attributed to the Shōgun. Go-Saga, much perturbed, despatched envoys to Rokuhara and Kamakura, while from Kamakura there went as representatives of the Bakufu Nikaidō Yukitada and others, whose mission was to request the Court to appoint the Imperial Prince Koreyasu as Shōgun in place of Munetaka. The appointment was duly made on August 19. That is all we know, for the full story of this incident has not been told.[4] There is no evidence to show the reason for the Bakufu's

[4] The *Azuma Kagami* comes to an end just before the appointment of Prince Koreyasu as Shōgun.

action, but it is doubtful whether they believed that there was a dangerous plot. It was fear of conspiracy rather than knowledge of disloyalty on the part of Munetaka that decided them to remove him. They appear to have had some feeling of regret, for a month or two later they released him from the Rokuhara house and sent members of the Council of State to Kyoto with an offer of valuable estates. They also asked Go-Saga to take Munetaka back into his family.

It is a measure of the dominance of the Bakufu over the Imperial House that Go-Saga should have felt obliged to disown his son in order to placate the feudal autocrats.

These things happened in the year 1266, which may be taken as the highest point of political power reached by the Hōjō Regents.

Ciphers of (LEFT) the Emperor Go-Toba, dethroned 1221; (CENTRE) Hōjō Tokimune, Regent during the Mongol invasion, 1274–81; (RIGHT) the Emperor Go-Daigo, ca. 1320.

In domestic politics no events of importance occurred during the next few years. Masamura handed the Regency to Tokimune in 1268. In that year, Khubilai, the great Khan of the Mongols, then established as Emperor in Peking, sent an envoy to Japan with an invitation to its ruler to become his vassal. This was couched in threatening language, and was in fact an ultimatum.

The sequels of this threat need full description, since they include an invasion of Japan. But first it is necessary to complete our account of domestic conditions in Japan, and then to examine the intercourse between China and Japan during the Kamakura period, prior to the Mongol invasion.

4. The Social Life of Kamakura

Prince Munetaka was only ten years of age when he was installed as sixth Shōgun in 1252. Since he was the elder brother of the then titular Emperor, his illustrious origin gave great prestige to the office which he held. The Hōjō Regent was not disturbed by any fears that this young prince would exert political influence in Kamakura. Here he was not mistaken, for even if Munetaka did in 1266 make a feeble attempt to assert independence this was easily dealt with by the Bakufu, who promptly deposed him and sent him back to Kyoto, where for a time he was confined in the Rokuhara mansion.

But while the Hōjō Regents could at will appoint and dismiss the princely Shōguns—they did the same to Munetaka's son, the seventh Shōgun, who went to Kamakura as an infant and was sent back as soon as he had grown to manhood—the social influence of Kyoto upon the leaders of feudal society was something which Tokiyori and his successors did not foresee and could not prevent. The great days of hard fighting and simple living began to recede into the past as the Hōjō Regents disposed of their rivals, made friends with the Court, and devoted their great energies to civil rather than military affairs. Peaceful life in Kamakura became a life of ease, and brought with it temptations that were hard to resist. The younger members of the leading feudal families were impressed by the manners and accomplishments of the Kyoto nobles who came to Kamakura in the Shōgun's service or to visit friends. They began to follow the aristocratic lead in matters of taste and fashion, to take an interest in learning, and in general to submit to the standards of Kyoto, to prefer what was subtle to what was plain. They were neglecting the austere and frugal principles which had guided the founders of the feudal order.

Fear of the seductions of an aristocratic society, the more insidious because it was exclusive, had moved Yoritomo to forbid social intercourse between warriors serving in Kyoto and the Court nobility. He thought with some reason that the Taira leaders had been weakened by their social ambitions, and perhaps he remembered that Yoshitomo had been snubbed when he proposed that his daughter should be married to the son of a Fujiwara statesman. He wished to prevent his own vassals from falling into the same errors.

The early Hōjō Regents had been aware of these departures from tradition in a general way. Most of them, and in particular Tokiyori, had set an example of plain living and hard work. But even as soon as 1210, not a dozen years after the death of Yoritomo, the favourites of Sanetomo were not earnest soldiers but young courtiers interested in elegance rather than the more sober virtues. In spite of the rule laid down by Yoritomo that his warriors should have none but strictly formal dealings with the Imperial Court, Sanetomo remained on friendly terms with the cloistered Go-Toba, to whom he sent his verses for approval. Go-Toba enjoyed teasing the Bakufu by keeping up this friendship, which lasted until Sanetomo's death in 1219. After Go-Toba's humiliation in 1221 the Kamakura leaders were not in a mood to encourage advances by the Kyoto aristocrats, but friendly intercourse began to grow again as soon as the air cleared on the arrival of Prince Munetaka in 1252.

One reason for the spread of the social influence of the capital was the frequency of marriages between members of the nobility and members of the upper ranks of feudal society. The object of such matches was often political, but they naturally led to closer private relationship between the two classes. The Bakufu had some misgivings about these family connexions, and there is a hint of this attitude in clauses of the Jōei Formulary which lay down conditions to be fulfilled before the Bakufu can sanction the marriage of a vassal or his heir to a member of a Kyoto family. One of the results of such marriages which the Bakufu wished to guard against was the transfer of a vassal's property to a person outside the feudal order of society and a consequent loss of revenue.

But a large degree of fusion between the two societies in their higher ranks was bound to arise once an imperial prince was appointed to the office of Shōgun. Posts at his Court were attractive, and a large number of young people, men and women, left the capital for Kamakura to serve in his household or his secretariat. Thus within a few years the number of Kyoto people living in Kamakura had much increased, and they had made a mark on Kamakura life in its material aspects—furnishings, clothing, pastimes—and also in its standard of taste and its modes of enjoyment. In 1254, according to the *Azuma Kagami*, Hōjō Tokiyori at an entertainment given by the Shōgun called upon the young samurai to engage in manly sports, saying that they had forgotten their family tradition and turned their attention to accomplishments foreign to their calling. Summoned to wrestling and archery, some of them sneaked away and others flatly refused to take part.

Such anecdotes are not sufficient to prove that the martial spirit was declining. Indeed it is easy to exaggerate the difference between the two societies, and to assume a contrast betwen cultured, elegant Kyoto and ignorant, rough Kamakura. Of course Kamakura life was not so uncouth as the Kyoto exquisites pretended. Fine scholars and learned clerics lived and worked there, as well as great artists and excellent craftsmen, many of whom had been trained in the home provinces but had been attracted by the opportunities offered by the vigorous growth of Kamakura. Yoritomo had made a point of bringing scholars to the eastern provinces to aid him in setting up his Bakufu; and soon after that, since peaceful times were in prospect, artists and men of letters found wealthy patrons among the feudal notables and in the monasteries and shrines which were then being built or enlarged or beautified in response to new demands. Thus the Eifukuji, the Shōchōjūin, and other monasteries founded at about this time sent to Nara and Kyoto for painters and sculptors, among whom was Jōchō, the greatest sculptor of the age. This was as early as 1185; and a few years later we find Fujiwara artists from the capital at work upon mural paintings in those buildings.

Another way in which Kamakura was exposed to the cultural influence of Kyoto was the friendly intercourse between the courtiers and the warriors who were stationed in the capital and its environs for a turn of garrison duty—the Great Watch, which was one of the most important functions of the Shōgun's men. The effect of such intimacy was to give to Kamakura life an increasing metropolitan colour, though in many important ways the culture of the eastern provinces preserved a distinct character.

But it must not be supposed that meanwhile Kyoto life remained unchanged. It was not the life of the days of the Fujiwara dictators. For one thing, the city had expanded and developed in the natural course of events; for another, the growing power of the warriors had shaken the assurance of the Court nobility time after time since the defeat of the Taira and the rise of the Minamoto. The truth is that Kyoto changed almost as much as Kamakura, and a flat distinction between military and civilian standards is misleading. Apart from the far-reaching political sequels of the Jōkyū Disturbance (1221), which brought about an intermingling of classes and habits, many causes were operating to change the national life as a whole, affecting the two societies in very much the same way.

Owing to the geographical situation of Japan, a student following the course of Japanese history is liable to think of it as proceeding in isolation, little affected by foreign influences; but it is important to remember that the rule of the Southern Sung dynasty of China (1127 to 1276) corresponds in point of time to the rise of the military class in Japan and then the most prosperous period of the Kamakura Shōgunate.[5] During that period there was a very lively commercial intercourse between the two countries, and there was also an important intellectual influence exerted by contemporary Chinese thought upon Japan, especially in the field of philosophy. The whole of Japan was affected by these currents, which did not discriminate between Kyoto and Kamakura; and it is fair to say that they tended to diminish regional differences. The effects of an increasing foreign trade deserve separate treatment, but the developments in intellectual life, and especially in religious thought, which took place in Japan during the period in which the feudal autocracy was growing to maturity, have a direct bearing upon our present theme—the nature of Japanese society during the period of the Hōjō Regency.

5. Intercourse with China

It is an interesting feature of the influence of Chinese culture upon Japanese life that it was promoted, or at least conveyed, by commercial exchanges between the two countries. Trade with China, it will be re-

[5] The *Hsin Yüan Shih* says that in 1277 Japan sent merchants with gold to exchange for iron and copper coins. It was on this occasion that the Japanese first heard of the fall of the Sung—or more correctly the fall of Hangchow, where the Sung Emperor was captured.

called, was continuous and increasing before the establishment of the Bakufu. There was no strictly official intercourse between the two governments for several hundred years after 894, but in the middle of the twelfth century Taira Kiyomori was sending "tribute" to the Sung Court and receiving "gifts" in exchange, while the Japanese Court sent "private" letters to the Sung Court, receiving "private" replies.

After 1192, when the Shōgun was installed in Kamakura, his officers and the great landlords, especially those in western Japan, continued to trade with the mainland, and there was a lively exchange of goods in which the principal items were:

Imports from China	Exports to China
silk	gold
brocades	mercury
perfumes	fans
incense	lacquer ware
sandalwood	screens
porcelain	swords
copper coins	timber

A large proportion of these cargoes was carried in Chinese vessels, since the Japanese were less advanced in shipbuilding than the Sung Chinese. But in general the increase of overseas trade encouraged the development of harbours in western Japan, especially at Munakata in Chikuzen and Bōnotsu in Satsuma. The Chinese vessels frequently carried as passengers Zen monks invited to teach in Japan, and they would bring scarce commodities such as tea, incense, and fine porcelain. Tea had been known in Japan since about 800, but its real adoption dates from about 1200, after it had been imported and recommended by the celebrated Japanese Zen monk Eisai in 1191. The Shōgun Sanetomo is said to have taken tea to counteract the effect of strong liquor.

This foreign trade, together with an increased domestic demand for luxuries encouraged by relatively peaceful conditions after the great civil war, led to a general expansion of internal exchanges and an enrichment of life in feudal society. The feudal leaders, who were coming under the influence of the Court in matters of fashion, began to buy costly swords, armour, robes of ceremony, personal ornaments, and household furnishings, so that in some areas of the national economy money and credit tended to displace the previous habit of barter and the complicated business of transferring fractional rights in land which had hitherto served the purpose of a currency. It was a rapidly growing need for coins of small denominations that brought about an export of copper coins from China to Japan.

The comparative ease with which monetary transactions could be completed and the simplicity of credit arrangements expressed in terms of a metallic currency contributed to a rapid increase in domestic trade. It also made it too easy for imprudent samurai to get into debt.

The nature of the objects of trade, especially the articles of luxury, testifies to a growing advance in Japanese industrial methods. The swords made in Japan were much praised in China, and so were the screens, fans, lacquered chests, and other work of accomplished craftsmen. It is clear that iron smelting and forging had reached a high point, and from the exports of gold and mercury we can infer an advance in mining processes. In other words, although the Kamakura Shōgunate was built upon a foundation of warlike prowess, the arts of peace increasingly flourished between 1185 and the end of the Kamakura regime. Painting and sculpture expressed the character of the age in realistic treatment and high technical skill. Its literature also tended to depart from former standards and to take on a somewhat matter-of-fact and didactic habit, nevertheless revelling in the romantic aspects of war while paying due respect to the Buddhist belief that glory is transient.

Such general statements about literary and artistic trends are perhaps deceptive, since they depend upon the accidents of taste; but there can be no doubt that in the history of Japanese civilization in the middle ages the most interesting feature is the growth in the early thirteenth century of new religious sects which reject the subtle and high-flown doctrines of the older schools and concentrate upon what is simple and direct. Here we can discern a reaction against the metropolitan culture in which borrowed elements were predominant, and a step in the development of a truly national culture. This movement was favoured by the political changes that accompanied the rise of the warrior class. This is not to say that Chinese intellectual influence was rejected. On the contrary it was eagerly sought, but with a new discrimination.

The change is visible in the gradual substitution of the feudal law for the codes which had been in force, but with diminishing authority, during the five centuries between the Taikwa reforms and the Jōei Formulary of 1232. More complicated, and more striking, is the history of new Buddhist sects in Japan which, while owing their earliest forms to the great Tendai and Shingon schools, were less directly derived from Chinese Buddhism and more congenial to the native temperament.

6. Religious Trends

The most remarkable religious trend in the early feudal period in Japan was the spread of popular beliefs, which has been briefly described (Chapter XI). Growing out of the cult of Amida, the Pure Land (Jōdo) sect, although it had its counterpart in China, developed on characteristically Japanese lines and was eagerly joined by men and women of all classes and occupations. Its simple teaching had an appeal to the aristocratic society of the capital, as we have seen from the examples of Murasaki Shikibu, writer of the *Tale of Genji*, and Fujiwara Yorinaga, a learned man and a great figure in the political scene of his day. The poor and the wretched throughout the country welcomed its consoling message, and even a number of eastern warriors submitted to its influence.

It is at first sight surprising that a soft, emotional creed like that of the Pure Land sects should have appealed to strong-minded members of the military class. But it must be remembered that the Pure Land teaching was of fairly long standing in Japan. It had matured in an age of strife and calamity, when older forms of Buddhism had fallen in popular esteem, partly because of the gross misconduct of monks in the ancient foundations of Nara and Kyoto, partly because the spirit of the times required a simple faith that would overcome the current pessimism. The gospel of the early evangelists, Eshin (942–1017) and in particular Hōnen (1173–1212), had been clear and comforting to the people of the capital and for that reason had spread rapidly in the nearer provinces. Its later growth was marked by even greater simplicity, reducing the doctrine to its very essence, to reliance upon a single act of faith. All complexities and doubts were swept away and there remained only a complete trust in Amida Buddha, not unlike the unquestioning trust of a vassal in his overlord. To put it more plainly, the simple and direct statement of religious truth was likely to be congenial to the simple and direct temperament of the average military man.

Moreover, because the new sects did not depend upon elaborate ritual and costly ornament, they had a popular character in keeping with the tendency of the age to break down some of the rigid divisions of caste. Eshin, who may be looked upon as the founder of Pure Land Buddhism in Japan, said in clear words that he wished his teaching to be understood by all classes of people, monks and laymen, men of high and low degree. Hōnen went further, for when at the instance of the old sects he was sent into exile for his unorthodoxy, he said that it had always been his purpose to go to remote places and urge the workers in the fields to adopt his faith. But although the Pure Land doctrine gained some adherents among the eastern warriors,[6] it was not at first attractive to those who prided themselves upon self-reliance and courage. The provinces under direct Kamakura rule were well-governed and on the whole prosperous. Conditions of life were not so wretched as to produce that mood of despair which had moved early converts in the western region. It was not until after the Jōkyū Disturbance that the simpler warriors began to listen to the gospel of Shinran (1173–

6 Yoritomo's widow Masa-ko was a devout follower of Hōnen Shōnin, and in her later life was known as Ama-Shōgun (the Nun-Shōgun).

1262), a brilliant evangelist who founded what he called the True Jōdo (Jōdo Shinshū). His tenets were so plain and direct, his leadership so firm, that he was followed by many of the lesser vassals and their retainers. Yet this was not the kind of doctrine to attract the flower of the ruling class, men of positive character and some intellectual pretensions. They turned for preference to the Zen school, which cannot be described as popular or easy of comprehension.

The forms of Japanese Buddhism which grew in influence during the middle ages arose from a natural reaction against the difficult teaching of the older sects. They may thus reasonably be described as protestant in character. The Pure Land doctrine developed from earlier Amidism on extremely simple lines, reducing religion only to faith and the utterance of a formula. It therefore had a popular appeal which was lacking in Tendai and Shingon. The Zen sect, it is true, was not a popular sect, since it depends upon intellectual effort and deep meditation; but it was against scriptures and ritual and was in that sense simple and direct, so that it might be described as popular among a certain kind of warrior, especially in the eastern provinces. Nor were these two doctrines unorthodox, since they were both rooted in an older Buddhism that had long flourished in Japan.

This is not strictly true of the sect known as the Lotus or Hokke sect, which, though based upon the canonical scriptures, was of truly Japanese origin. It was founded by a Japanese teacher and it was hostile to all other forms of Buddhism. It was militant and intolerant, and therefore exceptional in a country where the common religious tradition was tolerant to the point of indifference. It could have grown up only in Japan of the thirteenth century and only in the eastern provinces, where the feudal establishment was nearly at the summit of its power and the people were prepared to listen to a new gospel.

The Hokke evangelist, a remarkable man called Nichiren, protested against all other forms of Buddhism in Japan, held that the truth was to be found only in the Lotus Sutra, and called upon believers to strengthen their faith by repeated utterance of the formula "Namu-myōhō-renge-kyō," meaning Homage to the Wonderful Law of the Lotus Sutra. Nichiren's doctrine presents in a highly dogmatic form a feature common to the new types of Buddhism which developed during the twelfth and thirteenth centuries: they had in varying degrees a certain messianic character. In some respects their beliefs resembled those current in Western countries, where it was supposed that the last days of the Christian religion had come and that men must await the advent of a Saviour. The idea of Mappō or the End of the Holy Law (already mentioned in Chapter X) coloured religious sentiment in Japan from the eleventh century onward, and it doubtless had something to do with the growth of new sects. Some historians describe a prevailing mood of pessimism in this age and are inclined to suggest that it was the spread of the concept of a degenerate era that brought about the rise of the new sects. There is no very good evidence for this view. It is true that there was much misery in the capital, as a result of misgovernment and epidemics of sickness. But such conditions were by no means unusual. In the rest of the country, and especially in the eastern provinces, where the warrior clans were growing stronger day by day, there was a mood of confidence and a vigorous creative spirit among the leaders.

It would seem mistaken, therefore, to attach too much importance to the prophecy of a last degenerate phase of religion. It was a symptom rather than a cause of the desire for new and comforting creeds, and their appearance at this stage of Japanese history is of singular interest in the history of religion. There is a curious resemblance between the feelings expressed by men like Hōnen—that the days were degenerate and a new faith must replace the old—and the apocalyptic vision of St. John, according to which a period of dreadful misery would be brought to an end by a Messiah. The parallel is not exact, for the idea of a Messiah is not a central theme in Buddhism, as it is in Christianity. But in the early Buddhist canon there is mention of a Buddha of the future, whose advent will bring the dark age to an end and restore the true faith. The Buddha is Maitreya, who is to come as a saviour.

It is the apocalyptic character of his teaching that distinguishes Nichiren, the founder of the most original of the popular sects, the Hokke or Lotus. Nichiren's doctrine, or rather its cardinal feature, is that the Lotus Sutra is to be the means by which the period of the end of the Law is to give place to a new age of faith; and he, Nichiren, was himself a bodhisattva reborn to preach the truth, whose coming was clearly foretold in the twelfth and thirteenth chapters of the scripture that gave the sect its name—Hokke meaning the Lotus Flower and Hokke-kyō being the title by which the sutra was known in Japan.[7]

The life of Nichiren and the growth of the Hokke sect are important features in Japanese history, if only as introducing into religion an entirely new spirit of intolerance and of national pride. Unlike most of the great religious leaders of his country, Nichiren was a man of the eastern provinces, born in Awa, the son of a fisherman. His contribution to the

[7] Although the resemblance between the vision of St. John the Divine and Nichiren's apocalypse is striking, the points of difference deserve some notice. St. John wrote his Revelation while in exile on Patmos, at a time when Christianity was undergoing severe persecution, and it was he who made the prophecy of the final defeat of the evil powers.

Nichiren, by contrast, cited prophetic passages from the ancient scriptures and proclaimed that he himself was the saviour whose coming had been foretold. He repeated the prophecy (ascribed to the Buddha) of the three millenia of the Holy Law, during which religion was gradually to decline to the Last Days. But he did not assume the existence of an active enemy of the Law, unless it were the leader of an opposing sect. There is in his picture nothing to correspond to John's vision of "the dragon, the old serpent which is the Devil," whom an angel bound with a great chain for a thousand years.

national life not only was strongly coloured with patriotic fervour but displayed also an independent, one might say offensive, temper, redolent of the character of the eastern warriors.

The purely spiritual part of his teaching does not depart in substance from traditional Buddhism. Its special feature is its insistence upon the perfection of the Lotus, the vehicle by which Buddhism is to be unified and peace obtained. But though he preached and wrote energetically about peace, he was a most quarrelsome and intractable saint—he said himself that he was the most intractable man in Japan—who used violent language to condemn the leaders of other sects. His polemic language is rich in such terms as liar, fiend, and devil. Nor was he sparing in invective when censuring the government in Kamakura. Indeed in his early days as an evangelist (about 1260) he aroused such animosity that he was banished for a time, and when he was released in 1263 he returned and plunged into political strife with his usual fearless energy. The Amidists, whom he had bitterly attacked, conspired against him; and when he exasperated the high officers of the Regency by asserting that they had bungled their response to the Mongol threat, they took prompt steps against him. He had accused them of lack of foresight and courage. They retorted by seizing him and putting him on trial for treason. He was condemned to death, but he was released on the execution ground by some unexplained stroke of fortune, which he of course described as a miracle. He was sent into exile during the winter of 1271 to the bleak island of Sado. There he lived and studied and meditated for three years, completing his system and reaching the conviction that he himself was the predestined saviour.

He was released in 1274 and returned to Kamakura where he had friends among the fighting men, who admired his courage. This was on the eve of the first Mongol invasion. The Bakufu made conciliatory proposals to him, but he never gave way. Until his death in a mountain retreat in 1282 he insisted that the government must condemn and suppress all heresies and unite Japan under his Church.

Nichiren is the most remarkable figure in his country's religious history, and he is certainly among the first dozen of her great men. There was something in his crusading spirit that attracted the warriors even against their will, while the gentler side of his nature, which appears in his relations with his humblest followers, accounts for the number of his converts among the people.

He was a learned if eccentric man. He wrote his treatises and tracts in a fine and vigorous prose which it is a pleasure to read even today for its literary excellence.

Western historians of late have been inclined to assume that the growth of nationalism is a Western phenomenon. But there are grounds for thinking that the germ of Japanese nationalism can be found in Nichiren's writings, such as the *Risshō Ankoku Ron*, "On the Establishment of Righteousness and the Safety of the Country." This work, while calling attention to the national peril, proclaimed that only the adoption of his own tenets could save the state. But he did not think only in national terms; a feature of special interest in his thought is his universalism, something new in Japan. He believed that the Truth should be propagated all over the world and he had visions of a Universal Church with—a final touch of nationalism—its Holy See in Japan.

All these—the new Amidism, Zen, and the Lotus doctrine of Nichiren—show Japanese Buddhism in its most creative and original phase. They are obviously natural expressions of a new feeling in Japan, which find a parallel in new systems of government, in a changing social structure, and in a general reaction against the formal aspects of Kyoto life. It is not an accident that all three, while differing among themselves, found favour in the eastern provinces.

It is an interesting feature of the religious history of Japan that most of the leaders of the Bakufu, and in particular the Hōjō Regents, took a great interest in religion and sought the company of prelates of distinction. Tokiyori in particular paid deference to Myōe and Eizon, both great ecclesiastics who had no desire to live in worldly surroundings and only under pressure consented to spend some time in Kamakura.

Apart from their admiration for the characters of the Zen masters, the leading warriors were attracted by the Zen doctrine. It had a strong appeal because it depended not upon elaborate argument but upon inner enlightenment and conviction. In its pristine form it was not institutional. It had no scriptures, no sacred buildings, no ritual, but only a strict self-discipline and the practice of meditation. For a thoughtful warrior, whose life always bordered on death, there was an attraction, even a persuasion, in the belief that truth comes like the flash of a sword as it cuts through the problem of existence. Any line of religious thought that helped a man to understand the nature of being without arduous literary studies was likely to attract the kind of warrior who felt that the greatest moments in life were the moments when death was nearest.

That Zen monks held a special position in Kamakura is shown in an interesting way by an article (No. 40) in the Jōei Formulary of 1232. It lays down punishments for an offence something like simony. Members of the Buddhist or Shintō clergy holding a benefice within the "see" of Kamakura are forbidden under pain of dismissal to approach the Imperial Court at Kyoto with a request for preferment, but there is a proviso which says that if a Zen monk should make such a request he is only to be gently admonished by an older member of his order.

The Zen patriarch Dōgen and his successors, who spread their teaching among the ruling classes in Japan during the thirteenth century, made a strong impression upon the Hōjō Regents by their high character and their wisdom. Dōgen, who had been a disciple of the Chinese master Ju-ching, returned to Japan in 1227, and in obedience to his master's advice kept aloof from princes and nobles. He settled in a remote mountain province and founded there a small chapel, later to become a splendid monastery, the Eiheiji; but he was urged by Tokiyori to visit Kamakura and this he reluctantly did in 1247. He refused to stay, though Tokiyori offered him valuable estates for the maintenance of a monastic dwelling. He presently returned to his mountain retreat, vowing that not even an edict from the Throne would persuade him to leave it again. He died there in 1253. He is regarded as the founder of the Sōtō (Ts'ao T'ung) sect of Zen in Japan, and although he was not an evangelist but preferred seclusion and self-discipline, his character inspired many neophytes and he was one of the real patriarchs of Zen Buddhism in Japan.

A monk whose qualities made a great impression upon Tokiyori and other members of the Hōjō family was Eizon (1201–90). On a visit to Kamakura in 1263 he preached to great crowds and confirmed thousands of people, monks as well as laymen, in the faith. Tokiyori was humble in his presence and tried in vain to keep him in Kamakura.

There can be no doubt that the influence of the Zen masters upon the leaders of feudal society was very great. Men like Yasutoki and Tokiyori became ardent disciples and their example was followed by several warriors of high rank. In fact it might be said that Zen became fashionable in Kamakura and thereby lost some of its early purity. But generally speaking the leading exponents of Zen Buddhism were men of great attainments. Their strong characters, their independent minds, and their direct speech were much to the taste of the feudal élite. To what extent they influenced the judgment of men like Tokiyori in political matters it is not easy to tell; but it is clear that eminent Zen monks were from time to time consulted on questions of government and of relations with China by the Regents and their high officials.

Here we encounter an interesting social phenomenon, since most of the monks who rose to eminence at this time were men of relatively humble birth. Dōgen, it is true, was of aristocratic birth. Myōe, a Zen monk admired by Hōjō Yasutoki, was of samurai family, but of a low grade. The great Hōnen was of similar origin. It has been suggested that the popular character of the Buddhism of the late Heian and Kamakura periods was due to the modest social level of its preachers. But since all the new varieties of Buddhist teaching that flourished from the twelfth century onwards were forms of protest or reaction against the older schools, or were of a revivalist character, it was natural that they should be propounded not by highly placed clerics but by men of a reforming spirit speaking to the widest possible audience. It was thus that they had, or acquired, a more popular appeal than the early sects, which were closely connected with the Court or depended largely upon noble patrons.

Tokiyori's connexion with Zen Buddhism is important in the history of the school in Japan, for his interest began with the arrival in Kamakura of a Chinese monk named Dōryū who crossed to Japan in 1246 and soon afterwards made his way to Kyoto and thence to Kamakura. He was invited in 1253 to become the abbot of the monastery which Tokiyori had built, the Kenchōji—later to become one of the most celebrated in the country.[8] Even more intimate was Kotsuan (Wu-an), who arrived in Kyoto as a refugee from China in 1260 and was pressed by the Regent to move to the Kenchōji. Tokiyori sat at his feet and thanks to his teaching is said to have at length reached the sudden enlightenment which he had sought for twenty years. He had formally entered religion in 1256. He died in 1263, wearing the stole (*kesa*) and kneeling motionless in the posture of meditation called Zazen.

His son Tokimune was instructed from early youth by Dōryū, and is said to have become an adept under Daikyū (1215–89), who at the time of the first Mongol invasion gave him the famous problem (*kōan*) called Joshu's Mu, which he was able to solve—thereby releasing his mind to deal calmly with grave issues of war and peace.[9] Tokiyori's own accomplishment was known to Zen monks in China. The master Mugaku learned of it and was on his way to Japan when he was captured by Mongol soldiers. According to the legend they were about to put him to death, but he so impressed them by his unperturbed bearing and his calm recital of a scriptural text that he was released. He reached Japan after the death of Dōryū and lived in the Kenchōji as its abbot, a post of great dignity to which he was invited by Tokimune.

[8] It is still one of the five leading Zen monasteries in Kamakura.

[9] I may be permitted a personal note here, as I have a special interest in Daikyū. He went to Japan in 1270 and stayed first at the Kenchōji. He died in Kamakura in 1289, much revered. He and Kotsuan held such high places in the esteem of the Hōjō leaders that when Tokiyori's son, the Regent Morotoki, built the Jōchiji about 1288 they were made co-founders. The Jōchiji gained in importance because of this connexion with Morotoki and his family; but it was also a seat of learning which attracted several holy men from China. In the year 1330 a Chinese monk named Bon Jikusen was sent to the Jōchiji by Hōjō Takatoki, and he became abbot in 1334. About six hundred years later I asked the then abbot, the revered Asahina Sōgen, to lease to me a piece of land within the precincts, where I could build a country retreat. He consented, and I was granted a generous space on the hilltop where (as his poems show) Bon Jikusen had built his meditation hut. It was a delightful situation and it seemed somehow to harbour the presence of that holy poetical man with an eye for landscape. I wondered whether I was a suitable occupant of such a hallowed spot and I asked the Abbot Sōgen (today Abbot of the Enkakuji) whether it was really in order to lease this Church land to a foreigner. "Why," he replied, "certainly it is. There were foreigners here from the date of the foundation, and for all I know you may be one of them—perhaps Bon Jikusen himself." I thought that this was an example of his charming courtesy. But it was more than that, for in 1941, when our two countries were on the verge of war, he wrote a preface to a little history of the Jōchiji, in which he said: "Thinking of the people who now reside within these precincts I often say to myself that they may well be reincarnations of founders of this monastery or of its early occupants. And this to me is especially true of Bon Jikusen and the foreigner who now lives where he once had his dwelling place."

There can be no doubt that the Hōjō family had strong and genuine religious feelings, reflected in their conduct of both private and public affairs, which was marked by a rare integrity and a certain selfless devotion. They surely inspired later ideals of good government which, although from time to time neglected, retained an influence in the Japanese tradition of a ruler's duty.

It will be recalled that Hōjō Shigetoki,[10] who had been the Shōgun's deputy in Kyoto from 1230 to 1247 and then returned to Kamakura, wrote at about that date a letter of guidance to his son concerning the duties of a warrior in an important office. This was a brief practical treatise, a rule of behaviour for a gentleman rather than a set of moral precepts. But there is extant a later document written by Shigetoki towards the end of his life, between 1256 and 1261, while he was living in retreat. It is known as the Gokuraku-ji Letter (*Gokuraku-ji Dono no on-shōsoku*) from the name of the monastery in whose precincts he had built a small villa. It is not a compendium of useful worldly wisdom (of which he had a good store) but a kind of testament in which, in the light of his own religious experience, he sets forth his views of a man's moral duty for the benefit of his descendants.

It is an extremely interesting document of about one hundred paragraphs of no great length, each dealing with a separate topic. It is of particular interest as evidence of the religious sentiments of a member of the ruling class in Kamakura towards the end of a life which had been full of secular activity. It may be described as a statement of moral duty in terms of religious principles, and is therefore not strictly speaking a rule of conduct for warriors; but it certainly gives a reliable picture of the ideals of behaviour to which the leaders of feudal society desired to conform.

It opens with a short preface, in which Shigetoki says that it may seem a foolish thing to leave advice for his descendants, but the bond between parent and child is something of deep significance, being part of a long sequence of relationships through past, present, and future

[10] The following table shows the relationship of Shigetoki to the Regents. The numbers in brackets show the order of appointment as Regent.

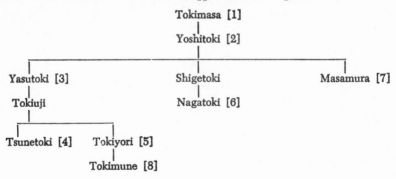

that cannot be disregarded. He then goes on to discuss the evanescent nature of human life, like a dream within a dream, like dawn on the heels of darkness, like flowers that fade as they open to the breeze. How are the young to face the hazards of this mutable world? It is in the hope of giving them guidance that he has set down his thoughts, which he urges them to study so that they may know how to face life's problems.

He is here expressing a view of life common among men of his kind, for while dwelling upon the evanescence of the pains and pleasures of the individual he stresses the permanence of the family. He is not merely stating the importance of the family as a social institution but is expressing that deep-seated feeling of continuity, in family life and in the national life, to which Japanese history so freely testifies.

He first enjoins worship of Gods and Buddhas morning and evening, saying that the Gods gain in power from the worship of men, and that the destinies of men are shaped by the blessing (*megumi*) of the Gods. When a man prays he must ask the Gods and the Buddhas for an upright heart (*shōjiki no kokoro*) in this life, for if in this life he is beloved by his fellow men then in the life to come he will surely enter the Western Paradise.

Throughout this document Shigetoki freely uses the phrase "Gods and Buddhas," but apart from this respectful notice of the indigenous deities the whole trend of his argument is Buddhist in sentiment. There is hardly any trace of the influence of Confucianism, there is one quotation from Lao-tzu, and everything else is the result of his own meditations in his monastic retreat. He shows the influence of Amidist teachings, probably those of Hōnen Shōnin, and his view of human life is strongly coloured by the doctrine of Karma, as indeed was all popular religious thought in his day and for centuries to follow.

The separate injunctions that follow his opening words do not keep to any logical order, though they deal with problems of behaviour as they were likely to be presented to his descendants during their careers. He begins with duty to superiors, whether feudal leaders or parents or men in holy orders; and here he lays down a religious basis for loyalty. His exact words are interesting: "You must not think of the good of others. You must think only of your lord, without regard for your own life or anything which is yours. Remember that if your lord is neglectful and gives no thought to you, nevertheless you will earn the protection of Gods and Buddhas." That is to say, loyalty is a religious duty.

Reverence is due to holy men and to the Buddhist scriptures. "To revile the scriptures is to disobey the profound mysterious wishes of the Lord Buddha.[11] Make sure that you and your family, even the little children, are not guilty of irreverence."

[11] This is something like the sin of blasphemy. It is regarded even in the Amidist sects as unforgivable. Shigetoki was a devout Amidist, and bitterly hostile to the Lotus sect of Nichiren.

As part of the theme of loyalty the document dwells upon filial piety. "When your parents speak, listen carefully and with a calm spirit. . . . Their minds are in the past, they do not understand what is said, they dislike what is enjoyable, they enjoy what is disagreeable. But old people are like this, and when your parents talk you should listen with compassion and not with annoyance. Their past is long; their future is brief. Remember that they will soon be silent, and do what they say. If you do not, when they are gone you will be sorry for your neglect and wish many times that you had done as they wished."

The respect due to parents should be given also to all other old persons. "Behave to younger persons as if they were your brothers, and treat children as if they were young members of your own family. When they make mistakes be indulgent, and not harsh."

Throughout his admonitions Shigetoki builds up a picture of a well-bred man of high rank. He must be tolerant and understanding, self-confident but not self-assertive, always conscious of the transience of earthly joys and sorrows, dignified but modest in his relations with equals, sympathetic and generous in his dealings with inferiors.

This model of behaviour is at first sight somewhat surprising, since it does not correspond to the character ascribed to the conventional type of warrior, brave and strong but proud and ruthless. Shigetoki in his declining years had no doubt become more pious and gentle than in his prime, but he was setting forth an attainable ideal in these words to his descendants. What he has to say is therefore of peculiar interest as evidence of contemporary moral and social standards in the ruling class of Kamakura. The following further extracts show the views of a distinguished feudal leader on life and society in the thirteenth century, while the regime of the Hōjō Regents was, to all appearances, prosperous and stable.

There is an interesting short essay on tolerance. "Bear in mind that there can be wrong in right and right in wrong. As an example of wrong in right suppose that *you* are right in a matter where your life is not in danger while another is wrong and *his* life is in danger. If you insist upon your stand, your insistence may be a case of wrong in right. Again, there may equally be right in wrong. Thus although a man may have done a thousand wrongs for which he stands to lose his life, yet it may be right for you to save him by keeping silence. That would be a case of right in wrong. If you take this to heart, and spare others, people who see and hear what you do will be impressed, and those whom you save will rejoice indeed. Or if they do not approve, still your merciful acts will have been pleasing to Gods and Buddhas, and you will have acquired merit in this world and the next."

On modesty and moderation there are some wise observations. A man should be always inclined to listen to the advice of others. The instructions of the Sages are above all precious. Even if you cannot read the scriptures and the classics, you should have them expounded to you by men of learning. Without such knowledge you will be ignorant and narrow-minded. All display is to be avoided. Your dress should always be clean and decent, but never ostentatious. Your horse should be of moderate size, and your sword not excessively long. Everything should be in accordance with your station: your house, your possessions, your behaviour. Excesses of any kind are disagreeable to others and in the long run they are to your disadvantage, for they will be against you in your next life. (This is a reference to Karma, since an offence in this existence must be expiated in the next.)

As to relationships with other people, an important part in the life of a man in a high position is his dealing with persons of lower standing. A rigid class system is assumed by Shigetoki, but within its limits he enjoins kindness and considerate behaviour. "When you are angry do not punish your servants. Wait until you are calm, and think of their past service as well as their present error. If you act upon an angry impulse, you may have cause for repentance." In several contexts what we should describe as a Christian spirit of forgiveness is strongly advised. "It is right to requite enmity with kindness, to return good for evil" ("On wo motte ada wo hōzuru").

On a somewhat lower moral plane are certain practical counsels to be borne in mind in daily social intercourse. "Be circumspect in your speech about others. Remember that Heaven has eyes and walls have ears. If you are passing by a house where there has been a bereavement, be very careful not to laugh loudly. All men have the same causes for grief, and we should grieve together." No man is an Island.

Considerate treatment of subordinates and social inferiors is a matter of principle. "When you are on horseback give warning to people by the roadside, however humble they may be. To do harm to those of low grade is especially reprehensible."

All living things deserve consideration. "Do not wantonly take the life of a creature that to you seems useless. You should know that the lowest insect clings to life as strongly as a man. You should not take life, but you should save it, though at the cost of your own." This care for living things is of course Buddhist in essence, and so is the following version of the golden rule:

"It is wrong to be kind to those who treat you well and unkind to those who treat you badly. Animals like dogs wag their tails when they are petted and bark when they are ill-treated. But it is not worth while to be a man if as well as being good to the good you are bad to the bad. If you are good to the bad, then the bad may reform. And even if they do not, the Gods and Buddhas will rejoice at your good deeds and you will be rewarded in your next existence. Try always to improve your karma by returning good for evil."

In general Shigetoki endeavours to inculcate a Buddhist view of life and a Buddhist rule of morality. These are some of his views upon religion:

"In a man's breast there is a lotus flower upon which a Buddha is seated." That is, every man has a Buddha nature which can expand as a lotus blooms, if he lives the right life.

"When you rise, with your ablutions of the body you must also cleanse the spirit by prayer to the Buddha. You must fast and observe the regular days of abstention, when the gods descend from Heaven and record good and evil deeds. A man who reveres the Law of Buddha and keeps an upright heart not only leads a good life in the present but also goes to Heaven. And when a parent is good the child is also rewarded, by the grace of Gods and Buddhas."

"Some sutras say that a woman cannot become a Buddha, but this is not true. Women have deep feelings, and when they have declared faith in the Buddha [Amida] and begged for rebirth there is no doubt that they can enter Paradise."

"All relations with other people spring from some past act, however trivial. To drink from the same stream as another, to touch with your sleeve the sleeve of another, even these acts are determined by some relationship in another life." ("Sode no furiawase dani mo tashō no en"—a common aphorism.)

The theme of Karma runs through the whole document. It is regarded as the key to all the problems of life, its joys and sorrows.

Some points of civil (as distinct from religious) duty are worth noting separately, because they seem to illustrate a characteristic attitude of the Hōjō leaders towards their task of government. Their belief in impartial justice is well displayed by what Shigetoki says about lawsuits:

"Claims and suits brought before you for judgment should be investigated and decided with the greatest care.

"Remember that the defendant is in a difficult position [because it is easy to make an accusation and hard to disprove it]. Therefore you should always listen carefully to the defendant's case.

"Do not show favour to persons of high rank. If a highly placed person is in the wrong, then he has broken the law, and you should not hesitate to find against him.

"In a court of law do not look upon the weak as persons to be impressed or frightened by your power. Make sure that they are not alarmed, listen to all they have to say, and give a fair judgment."

In his discussions of offences he makes it clear that mere punishment should not be the chief aim of a judge. He even says that in many cases the punishment of evildoers should be left to the Gods and Buddhas. Thus: "When something has been stolen from you and it is not an indispensable article, do not reveal your loss, for that may cause

the robber to lose his life. Remember that he will be punished in the
next existence. He cannot escape. The wicked criminal destroys himself."

Throughout the document there are frequent admonitions to lead a
simple life, to eschew display, and to be moderate in all things. Frugality was a character of the great Hōjō Regents, as was a high sense of
duty. Altogether the standards of conduct among the leaders of the
military class under their rule give an impression like that of the Roman
gravitas.

That there was a strong strain of ability in the Hōjō family is very
clear. Indeed most of the founders of the feudal state, the associates of
Yoritomo, were gifted men, and intermarriage among their families no
doubt served to perpetuate their qualities. It was only the direct descendants of Yoritomo himself who failed.

CHAPTER XX

RELATIONS WITH THE ASIATIC MAINLAND

1. *The Rise of Mongol Power*

WHILE Japan was developing as an orderly state under strong and capable government, political conditions in the eastern regions of the Asiatic mainland were rapidly deteriorating. China under the Sung dynasty from 960 to 1120 was a united empire, the home of a great civilization in which intellectual and artistic pursuits flourished and an important philosophical renaissance took place. But it was politically weak because it was subject to constant attack by barbarian invaders from the north—Tartars at first and later Mongols, whom the Chinese tried to buy off without success. By 1120 Tartars of the Golden Horde had advanced beyond the northern marches and had occupied Chinese territory as far south as the Yangtse River. The Tartars were eventually overcome and displaced by Mongols, who established their own dynasty in northern China from about 1230 and in 1264 transferred their capital to the city later known as Peking. Thereafter the Sung dynasty ruled only the southern part of China. It was with the Sung provinces that Japan maintained relations, which, though not official, were tolerably close and friendly as between peoples, and allowed of important cultural and mercantile exchanges.

The passengers and cargoes passing between the two countries were usually carried in Chinese vessels, for the Japanese were not successful shipbuilders or navigators. Japanese governments seem to have been afraid of getting involved in too close a relationship with China. Or, for that matter, with Japan's other neighbours: for example, although Japanese pirates at times descended upon the coast of Korea, the Japanese Court was reluctant to meet overtures made by the kingdom of Kōryö, which by the eleventh century had come to include the whole of the Korean peninsula and part of Manchuria.

It was characteristic of the good sense of the Hōjō Regents that when in 1227 the government of Korea[1] sent an envoy to Japan to protest against piratical raids, the Regent Yasutoki decided that the complaint was well-founded and at once ordered the pirates to be arrested and put to death. The Kamakura government, as well as the Court at Kyoto, was at that time far too preoccupied with domestic affairs—with the control of the great vassals and the internal development of the coun-

[1] The Kingdom of Kōryö or Kōrai is usually in English known as Korea, and that name is used for convenience here.

try—to risk hostilities with Korea over a relatively trifling matter. The kingdom of Korea was itself in an awkward situation; it was harassed by invaders from the north, first by Tartars who had poured into the Liaotung Peninsula and southern Manchuria soon after A.D. 1200 and then by Mongols who had pursued the Tartars and crossed the Yalu in great numbers in 1231 and 1238.

By 1259, Khubilai, the Great Khan of the Mongols, had become Emperor of China, and in 1264 (as we have noticed) he established his capital at Peking. The kingdom of Korea could no longer keep its independence, and was obliged to submit to Mongol suzerainty. It was now a weak and unhappy state, impoverished by its desperate resistance. Its very weakness was dangerous, since any great power that established itself in China tended to expand into Manchuria and Korea and thus to threaten Japan. Throughout Far Eastern history the peninsula had been a region of great strategic importance. Its occupation by a great Mongol army was plainly menacing to the Japanese islands, of which the nearest was only about one hundred miles from the southern tip of Korea. Fortunately this stretch of water had been sufficient for some centuries to preserve Japan from foreign domination; and now, because the Mongols were ignorant of seafaring matters, they could invade Japan only by making use of Korean ships and sailors. The Koreans were already exhausted by their long struggle against the Mongols, so that they were not willing collaborators. Yet they could scarcely withstand Mongol demands if they were pressed.

The Bakufu were well aware that the situation was full of danger. They had some spies in Korea, and certain Koreans who were not under direct Mongol orders were sympathetic enough to send useful information from time to time. Already in 1266 Khubilai had despatched two envoys to Japan with a letter which commanded the Japanese to submit under pain of invasion. The Mongol envoys were accompanied by Korean officers, but they did not get far from the Korean shore. They were brought back under stress of weather by their Korean companions, who were glad to find an excuse for giving up the mission. Khubilai was angered by this delay, and sent another expedition which reached Dazaifu at the beginning of 1268, with the same message.

This caused great alarm at Court; the Bakufu, however, though well knowing that the situation was grave, decided to take no notice of the Mongol threat and to send the envoy back empty-handed. They had now a fair general knowledge of the recent events on the mainland and of the ambitions of Khubilai. They knew that the Koreans were in a far more uncomfortable position than themselves, were indeed helpless. The Japanese had the protection of an insular situation and the advantage of a highly trained warrior class whose pride would make them redoubtable antagonists for even the fiercest barbarian soldiery.

The handling of the critical situation in which Japan now found itself provides an interesting commentary on the relations between the Court and the Bakufu. The Mongol envoys of 1268 handed the Khan's letters (which were addressed to the "King of Japan") to the Bakufu representative at Dazaifu, whose title was Chinzei Bugyō, or Defence Commissioner for the West. He was requested to transmit them to the Government of Japan. He forwarded them posthaste to Kamakura, where they were examined by the Bakufu and sent to the Court at Kyoto. The Bakufu knew that the Court was not competent to make a decision; but as a matter of form the Emperor or the In had to be consulted.

At Kyoto the threatening language of the Mongol letters caused alarm near to panic, and the Court was deeply grieved by the contemptuous way in which the Emperor was described as "the king of a little country." Plans to celebrate the jubilee of the abdicated Emperor Go-Saga[2] were hastily dropped. Messengers were sent to the great shrines to carry tidings to the national deities, and day after day councils were held in the Palace or at the In's Court to determine what action should be taken. But nothing was decided except that the draft of a letter in reply to the Great Khan was agreed upon, and sent to the Bakufu for scrutiny and transmission.

It was a poor document. While rejecting the Mongol demands it left the way open for some kind of compromise, and it warned, or at least apprised, Khubilai of the great age and the divine character of the dynasty ruling over the Land of the Gods. The Bakufu dismissed this reply as useless and sent the Mongol envoys away empty-handed, without even an acknowledgment of their communications. The Regent and his colleagues were of course fully aware of the gravity of the situation, but they kept calm. There could be no question of negotiation, still less of any kind of surrender, by the leaders of a warrior society, whose hereditary function was to protect the state against its enemies. They took a firm line and prepared to meet an attack which all their information led them to expect, perhaps even within a few months. They strengthened the coastal defence forces and ordered the western vassals then living in Kamakura to return to their fiefs.

In Kamakura the Regent Masamura was succeeded on April 18, 1268, by Tokimune, the direct heir of Tokiyori. A vigorous youth of eighteen, he was deemed to have reached manhood. He was suited by birth and character to represent and lead the warrior class. Masamura, a man of sixty, now took Tokimune's former place as co-signatory (Renshō) and devoted his great talents and experience to planning the strategy of defence, as chief-of-staff in the Bakufu.

From the time the Mongols first contemplated invading Japan they

[2] Go-Saga had succeeded to the throne in 1242 and abdicated in 1246. He was well-disposed towards Kamakura and trusted by the Bakufu. Not perhaps of great attainments, he was a man of sense and character whose friendly relations with the feudal leaders were of great value in the critical times of the Mongol threat.

had intended to make use of Korean soldiers and Korean ships. The Koreans, as we have seen, were helpless, broken by the Mongol armies which were now occupying their country. Some authorities on the history of this period state that, as a diplomatic move intended to curry favour with the Great Khan, the Korean government had suggested to him the invasion of Japan. This seems unlikely. There was no doubt in Korea a faction which saw advantage in collaboration with the victors, but in general the Koreans must have wished ardently for peace and recovery, not for prolonged warfare. They had no particular sympathy with Japan, but their relations with the Japanese government had somewhat improved in recent years, thanks to the prudence of the Bakufu in dealing with their complaints against Japanese pirates. The patriotic Koreans knew that to take part in a campaign against Japan would bring them no advantage, and might well bring them great losses. It was to their interest that the invasion should not take place. The best they could do was to warn the Japanese of an impending attack, and this they did when upon the orders of the Mongols they conveyed a third message from Khubilai in September 1271.[3]

Following their usual procedure, the Bakufu reported this to the Throne and at the same time sent to the vassals the orders framed by Tokimune. In 1272 all constables and stewards in the Western Defence Region (Chinzei) of Kyūshū were commanded to see to the strengthening of defences. Vassals belonging to Kyūshū who were then residing in Kamakura were all ordered to return to their fiefs. All kenin of the western and central provinces were also ordered to move gradually westward and to assist in the protection of Kyūshū. Meanwhile the Court devoted itself to continuous religious exercises, praying for the safety of the realm in a great Ninnō service[4] and otherwise invoking the aid of the divine powers.

Following upon the Korean mission of 1271, a Mongol ambassador landed at Imazu in the province of Chikuzen in October 1272 and began to urge the Dazaifu Defence Headquarters to arrange an audience with the Japanese sovereign at which he would present his letters. He met with no success. He then demanded that a copy of his message be sent to the Court, setting a date not later than two months thereafter for a reply. This was in substance an ultimatum. It was communicated by Dazaifu to the Bakufu, and thence passed to the Court. The Court was inclined to compromise by a reply on the lines of its previous draft, which had hinted at pourparlers; but the Bakufu would not agree, and ordered Dazaifu to expel the Mongol ambassador. This was equivalent

[3] There appear to have been other letters between 1268 and the invasion of 1274, but their contents are not on record.

[4] This service included readings from the Ninnō Kyō, or Sutra of the Benevolent King, which treats of the duties of monarchs and the protection of states. It was a regular part of Court ceremonial from 800 or thereabouts.

to a declaration of war by Japan. The retired Emperor Go-Saga had already made a pilgrimage to the Iwashimizu shrine to pray to the great national deities. Now in growing despondence he fell ill. He died on March 18, 1272, having been the de facto sovereign since his abdication in 1246, and a firm friend of the Bakufu.

2. The First Mongol Invasion, 1274

The repeated missions sent to Japan by or on behalf of the Mongols were attempts to induce the Japanese to submit without resistance; but Khubilai had determined to invade Japan as soon as he learned of the failure of the mission of 1268. He had ordered the King of Korea to build warships and to collect a large army. But the Koreans were so short of men and supplies that they could not comply, and when in 1273 a few thousand Mongol soldiers appeared as an advance guard of the invasion force they found that they could not live on the country and were obliged to send back to China for provisions. After a year's delay, during which the total rice crop was increased by ploughing new fields, the Mongol army was able to put to sea in November 1274. It was not a large force for such a great task, being composed of 15,000 Mongol and Chinese troops in addition to the advance guard just mentioned, and 8,000 Korean troops of poor quality. About 7,000 Korean sailors together with Chinese seamen formed the crews of the invasion fleet, which was composed of about three hundred large vessels and four or five hundred small craft.[5]

The islands of Tsushima and Iki were captured without much difficulty, their brave but small Japanese garrisons slaughtered after bitter resistance. The fleet then made a southeasterly turn towards the coast of Kyūshū, detaching ships to attack Hirado and other points while the main body entered the bay of Hakozaki, where they anchored on November 18. On the following day they landed at Hakata, the port at the head of the bay, sheltered by the Shiga spit. They seized also a number of small towns or villages along the shore. Not far inland was Dazaifu, the ancient seat of the administrative capital of Kyūshū and also the headquarters of the Western Defence Commissioner, who represented the Bakufu and commanded the permanent defence force.

News of the capture of Tsushima reached Dazaifu quickly and was passed at once to Rokuhara, while an alarm was sent to all warriors in the Dazaifu command, that is to say in all provinces of Kyūshū. On the day of the Mongol arrival off Hakata the summons had reached most parts of Kyūshū, and the warriors hastened to respond. At that time the chief obstacle to transport in Kyūshū was the Chikugo River, and this

[5] Higher figures are given in some sources, but these appear to be most probable. For an event of such crucial importance this invasion was very scantily reported. There is little exact evidence on the nature and extent of the fighting.

was at once bridged by pontoons, so that forces marching north from the southern provinces (Satsuma, Ōsumi, and Hyūga) were able to advance to Hakata without delay. At this time the Dazai[6] Shōni Tsunetsugu was in command of the whole area, and the defence of Hakozaki was entrusted to the Satsuma warrior Shimazu Hisatsune.

On November 19 an enemy force landed at Imazu, and under cover of dawn on the next day delivered an attack, with support from the ships, upon the town of Hakata. The whole of the Kyūshū force under Tsunetsugu's command rushed to meet this attack soon after daybreak. The fighting was desperate. The advantage lay with the battle-seasoned Mongols, who were trained to fight in close formation, whereas it was the habit of the Japanese warrior to engage in single combat with fighting men of his own rank. It was over fifty years since the last large-scale engagements had taken place in Japan, and that was during the rising of Go-Toba's adherents in 1221, when the Court party could not match the practised warriors of Kamakura. Thus at the time of the Mongol attack there was no Japanese general who had experience of commanding, still less manoeuvring, a large army in the field. The Mongols had the further advantage of weapons that were effective at long range, such as powerful crossbows and engines for throwing heavy missiles and combustible material.

Against these handicaps the resistance of the Japanese was ineffective, and it was only their courage which enabled them to hold out until nightfall, when they withdrew behind some ancient earthworks at Mizuki, a few miles inland. The outlook for the following day was grim. It looked as if the whole Kyūshū force would have to fight until near annihilation, so as to give time for the arrival of reinforcements which then were approaching from the central and eastern provinces. Despite their failure at Hakata, however, the Japanese were by no means defeated, since given time they could overwhelm the Mongols by superior numbers. As it turned out, such desperate measures were not needed, since, luckily for the Kyūshū men, that night as they lay exhausted and drenched in their dyke a great storm threatened and the weather-wise Korean pilots pressed the Mongol generals to reembark their army, lest

---

[6] The Dazai-fu was a regional government established by the Taihō codes for the administration of a special area comprising the provinces of Kyūshū and the islands of Tsushima and Iki. This area, while remote from the capital, was important for defence and was therefore placed under the rule of a high officer with something like vice-regal powers, both civil and military. Ranking next to him were officers styled Daini and Shōni, titles which may be translated as Senior and Junior Assistant. The post of Shōni became hereditary in a minor branch of the Fujiwara named Muto, which in course of time began to use the title as a surname. When Yoritomo came into power he sent his own Western Defence Commissioner (Chinzei Bugyō) to perform the military functions of the Dazai-fu, which thereafter lost its main purpose and survived only as a name. But as the Shōni family had acquired great influence in Kyūshū its head was usually given important military posts in the defence area.

they should find themselves isolated on shore, their ships on the rocks and all possibility of retreat cut off.

It was at this point possible for the Japanese, taking advantage of wind and rain, to deliver a night attack over ground which they knew well and in conditions where hand-to-hand fighting would be most deadly. The Mongol leaders saw this added danger, and a general re-embarkation was ordered and begun. Whether in fact the Japanese commander did contemplate a night attack is not known. It seems improbable, since when the Mongols covered their withdrawal by setting fire to Hakata and villages along the shore he made no attempt to leave the ditch at Mizuki and cut off the invader's rearguard. Shōni's men were exhausted, and probably not fit for night fighting in a gale of wind and rain. Fortunately for them, when daylight came they saw the last stragglers of the enemy fleet making out of the bay. One vessel at least ran aground on the Shiga spit, and many more sank in the open sea during the tempest—according to some accounts two hundred vessels were lost. Korean records say that 13,000 men of the invading force lost their lives during this expedition, many, perhaps most of them, by drowning. The invasion had failed, and the remnants of the Mongol force made their way back to Korea in disorder and distress.

The news of the landing on November 19 reached Kyoto and then Kamakura towards the end of the month. The Bakufu had naturally been very anxious, fearing that the Mongols would outnumber the Kyūshū vassals. They sent an urgent summons to Kyūshū on December 1, mobilizing all warriors and promising to make no distinctions between Minamoto vassals and others in deciding rewards for good service. All landholders in the region were thus mobilized for defensive operations.

Attention was also paid to the improvement of defences in the western part of the main island, and efforts were made to strengthen all garrisons; but these were only emergency measures, for the time was short, distances were long, and not all the warriors were ready for active service.

The Court could do little but pray to the gods for victory, send messengers to the tombs of imperial ancestors, and suspend all customary festivals. When news of the failure of the enemy attack reached the capital there was intense rejoicing and deep, vociferous gratitude for divine help.

Thus Japan appeared to be saved. But Khubilai thought that the failure of his generals was due to storm alone—an idea which the generals were careful not to contradict—and he at once sent another mission ordering the "King of Japan" to present himself at Peking to do homage. Nothing that he could have said would have more infuriated the Bakufu than this insult. They expected a further attack and made ready to meet it.

3. The Second Mongol Invasion, 1281

In preparation for a renewed attack the Bakufu now made long-range plans for defence. In 1275 they ordered the three provinces of Suwo, Aki, and Bingo (which border upon the Inland Sea at the western end of the main island) to be jointly responsible with Nagato province for the defence of the Nagato channel and adjacent waters. In Kyūshū a number of new defence posts were established at strategic points, including Hakata, the port where the main assault of the Mongols had been delivered in 1274. A roster of vassals for garrison duty at these posts was established, and steps were taken to ensure obedience to this call in the future. At the time of the first invasion certain vassals had evaded the summons under one pretence or another. Now it was proclaimed that failure to give a loyal response would be treated as a crime and severely punished.

In Kyoto early in 1275 the Emperor Kameyama proceeded in state to the Iwashimizu shrine and prayed for the safety of the country. Messengers were sent to other great shrines imploring the gods to drive away and disperse the foreign enemy. Throughout Japan appeals were made to national and local deities, and special orders were sent to the Bakufu to see to the rebuilding of the Hakozaki shrine destroyed by the invaders. In general the Shintō faith flourished in this time of national danger, thriving upon gratitude for past protection and anticipation of further divine aid. The great Buddhist foundations were not behind-hand in their prayers, but the rise in popular favour of the ancient cult is especially to be noted.

Although the Mongols were determined to attack again, time was needed for preparation, so that the Japanese were given a breathing spell. They knew that Khubilai was using an immense force for the subjugation of the Sung rulers in southern China, and they were certainly aware of conditions in Korea, which were such that the use of Korean manpower for warlike purposes would be difficult if not quite impossible until the people had recovered from the effects of the defeat in 1274. They were on the verge of famine, because all the previous year's crops had been consumed, and the forthcoming harvest would be wretched. Only a few fields had been cultivated, by old men and children, while the able-bodied adults had been drafted for shipbuilding or for fighting and many thousands of them had perished in the campaign. On these grounds the King of Korea appealed to the Great Khan, urging him to give up his plan to conquer Japan. But it was impossible to persuade Khubilai to change his mind. He repeated his demands and his envoys were sent to Japan in May 1275, landing this time at Murotsu in Nagato province. They were taken to Kamakura, and there they were executed in October, by order of stern and intractable warrior chiefs determined to show no trace of weakness.

This gesture expressed a determination to meet the Mongol assault

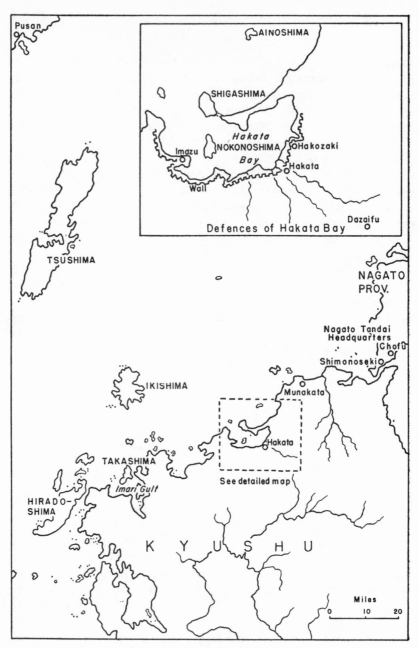

Pusan

AINOSHIMA

SHIGASHIMA

Hakata
NOKONOSHIMA
Bay

Imazu

OHakozaki

Hakata

Wall

Dazaifu

Defences of Hakata Bay

TSUSHIMA

NAGATO
PROV.

Nagato Tandai
Headquarters

Chofū

Shimonoseki

Munakata

IKISHIMA

Hakata

TAKASHIMA

See detailed map

Imari Gulf

HIRADO-
SHIMA

K Y U S H U

Miles
0   10   20

The coast of Kyūshū attacked by Mongols, 1274 and 1281

with a strong and well-planned resistance. The Bakufu now devoted all possible efforts to improving the western defences. Vassals in the western defence area were excused from the Great Watch, that is to say the regular turn of garrison duty in the home provinces. A rule of personal economy was adopted by both the Court nobility and the feudal leaders, so that the national wealth could be directed into channels serving the enlargement of military resources. Men who had rendered distinguished service in the fighting of 1274 were encouraged by ample rewards. Officers of high rank were appointed to strategic outposts, so as to stimulate warlike ardour among the remoter vassals, members of the Hōjō family being sent as special military commissioners to Kyūshū and the province of Nagato. The chief purpose of all such appointments was to supervise the movement of troops and at the same time to inspire confidence in the warriors, who would know that the eye of Kamakura was upon them.

On reviewing the situation during the period of grace which was afforded to them by the preoccupation of Khubilai in other theatres of war, the Bakufu leaders even considered taking the offensive. One of the reasons for sending high officers from Kamakura to the western maritime provinces was to survey the possibility of a naval attack upon enemy bases and ships; and by the end of 1275 orders were sent to those provinces to build or prepare warships and to recruit crews for training. Early in 1276 the Kyūshū Defence Commissioner was instructed to assemble in Hakata all persons volunteering to join an overseas expedition. There was an immediate response to this appeal. Kyūshū warriors came forward in great numbers, offering themselves and their families and their property for the service of their country. But upon reflection the Bakufu decided that the national resources would not support both an offensive and a defensive strategy, and the project of a naval expedition against Korean ports was abandoned. The naval preparations made were confined to the building and equipment of small and easily handled warships, to be manned by fighting men most of whom had good experience in piratical raids. These vessels were intended to engage the invading ships not abroad but in home waters, by boarding them and when possible setting fire to them. In the event these small craft proved extremely useful, especially in harassing large ships trying to manoeuvre out of difficult situations.

Apart from this kind of attack it was decided to concentrate the whole military strength of the nation upon building up a powerful system of defence. Of this the most important material feature was the construction of a stone wall from east of the Shiga spit along the shore of Hakozaki Bay and further to Imazu. The purpose of this wall was to hinder if not to prevent a landing in force by the enemy, and to make it difficult for troops upon landing to take up positions in massed formation.

This plan had one disadvantage. It was certain to come to the knowledge of the invaders and cause them to look for other landing places along the coast, from which they could turn Japanese positions behind the wall. It was therefore necessary for the Japanese commander to have at his disposal reserves which he could throw into action against enemy forces moving in from points beyond the extremities of the wall. In other words, the defence line must be prolonged in both directions from the ends of the wall, and would need to be manned by a powerful army. Consequently Japan's resources in material as well as manpower were bound to be strained to the limit.

The task of the Bakufu was a heavy one, a severe test not only of its ability but also of its authority over the warrior class. Fortunately for Japan the Mongol attack was delayed until 1281, which was late enough to allow completion of the wall—it took five years, by impressed labour—and the training of reliable garrisons. Meanwhile the Koreans were in a sad condition, for they were under strong pressure to prepare for a further great expedition against the Japanese. In 1279 their helpless King received orders from Khubilai in Peking to build a new fleet of one thousand vessels, find crews for them, and raise a land force of 20,000 men. A Mongol army of 50,000 would presently march to the east coast of Korea to await embarkation, and of course to terrify the people there and live at their cost. This was in numbers nearly double the invasion force of 1274, but Khubilai had even greater plans. He set up a special "Office for the Chastisement of Japan," to supervise the whole undertaking and reconcile its various parts. By subduing the Sung rulers of southern China he had become master of all their shipping, and this he decided to use in the subjection of Japan. It was an imposing fleet of vessels great and small, and it was to embark an army of 100,000 men, nearly all Chinese from the defeated Sung armies.

Meanwhile the King of Korea, hoping to receive better treatment by coming forward with an offer to help, had taken courage and gone to Changan-nor (Tsinan) to propose to the Khan that Korea should play a leading part in the invasion, supplying 900 ships, 15,000 seamen, pilots, etc., 10,000 fighting troops, and large quantities of provisions, equipment, and weapons. He wished to take the supreme command himself, or to preside over the Chastisement Office. The 15,000 seamen would man 300 ships, the remainder to be furnished by the Mongols with crews, presumably Chinese.

The King put his position plainly to Khubilai, and made certain conditions, one of which was the appointment of a Korean, Admiral Kim, to command the invasion fleet. Khubilai, it seems, was not displeased, but said that a much larger force must be employed. The Mongol records of 1281 say: "In August last year the King of Korea came to Changan-nor and was received in audience by the Great Khan. In consultation with the king and the generals the plan of attack was agreed upon. Ships carrying 40,000 Mongol, Korean, and North China troops were to rendezvous off the island of Iki with a fleet[7] carrying 100,000 South China troops, and thence to proceed to crush Japan."

The order to attack was given by Khubilai on the fourth day of the new year, 1281.

The Korean fleet was ready to put to sea in the spring of 1281, but the unwieldy Chinese armada was, it seems, delayed by the difficulties of manning and provisioning so great a number of ships. The Korean commanders, no doubt under Mongol pressure, tested their strength by an attack upon Tsushima. The island was much better prepared than in 1274, and the Mongol force was so severely handled that it withdrew and returned to its base at Masampo, where an epidemic of sickness prevented a further attempt. The ships did not put to sea againt until early summer, when the scouts of the Chinese fleet reported that its advanced squadrons were approaching the island of Iki from the south. On June 10 the Korean fleet, unwilling to await the arrival of the main body of the Chinese fleet, reduced Iki and then steered for the Chikuzen coast where they landed on June 23 at several points between Munakata and Hakozaki Bay, seizing in particular the strategically important Shiga spit, which the Japanese were obliged to keep under constant assault since it was north of the end of the wall and therefore on the right flank of the Japanese defenders.

The Japanese troops at the other end of the wall, near the town of Imazu, were equally exposed to a turning movement by any considerable force that might be landed in northern Hizen province. This weakness was evidently well known to the Mongol leaders, and the Chinese fleet from the south lost no time in capturing Hirado and other points, where great numbers of Chinese troops were disembarked. Details of these actions are not on record, but there is no doubt that the Japanese defence along the whole length of the wall, and for a time at both ends (that is from Imazu to the west and along the Shiga spit to the northeast), was so strong and effective that at some points the Kyūshū warriors were able to move from the defensive to a counterattack in which they maintained a steady pressure against the enemy, especially those who had held the Shiga spit in force. At this time also the small vessels built for attack did great service in cutting out slow and heavy enemy warships and transports. These raids were led by warriors descended from captains who had helped Yoshitsune in sea fights from Yashima to Dannoura in 1185.

How long the Japanese could have kept up this desperate and stubborn fighting we cannot tell; but it is clear that from June 23 to August 14, a space of over seven weeks, the long line from Munakata well into Hizen province was firmly held. If occasional breaks were made they were swiftly repaired, and the invaders never gained the upper

---

[7] In the records this fleet is described as the Kiangnam Fleet, because it was assembled south (*nan*, or *nam*) of the Yangtse-kiang estuary in former Southern Sung waters. The place was Chüanchow, in Fukien province.

hand in combat. The Chinese troops certainly had no great stomach for the fight. For one thing, they had no reason to be loyal to their masters, the very Mongols whom they had been opposing not long before they sailed from the Fukien coast. And even had they been filled with martial spirit it is doubtful whether they would have been a match for the finest Japanese fighting men, to whom valour was a religion.

But it was not fighting qualities that had the last word, for the elements now spoke in a loud voice. The month of August usually brings typhoon weather to the waters surrounding Japan, especially to the southwest. In 1281, as the invaders might have foreseen, a great hurricane arose and beat with violence upon the shores of Kyūshū for two days. It came to be known in Japanese annals as the Kamikaze or Divine Wind, for it blew the enemy fleet to perdition. This was on the fifteenth and sixteenth days of August.

How great the enemy losses were is not clear. Most accounts agree that the Korean shipmasters, scenting danger, managed to get most of their vessels away from the shore before the tempest reached its height; but even so they are said to have lost on their flight more than one-third of the Korean and Mongol troops that they were carrying. As for the southern fleet from China, the greater part of which was operating in the Gulf of Imari in Hizen, it was there exposed to the full power of an on-shore hurricane. When the escaping vessels in desperation made for open water, many of them were caught by tide and wind and helplessly jammed together in the narrows. Of those that got out to sea many if not most foundered in the storm. The total loss of life must have been enormous. The Chinese ships had carried perhaps as many as 100,000 men, and certainly far more than half of these were drowned or slaughtered before they could embark. The main body of this Chinese armada had entered the Gulf of Imari soon after making its landfall. It had put ashore strong forces at several points along the coast of Hizen, and a numerous contingent occupied the island of Takashima, which lies at the entrance to the gulf. Most of these men were unable to reach their ships, and thousands were killed or taken prisoner by Kyūshū warriors who attacked here and elsewhere before the storm abated.[8]

The victory was complete. Khubilai wished to make a third attempt, but his Mongol warriors were unwilling and his Korean puppets worn out. By 1286 he was so deeply committed on the mainland that Japan was no longer in immediate danger and the Bakufu had time to devote to domestic problems, which were numerous and grave.

[8] It is not possible to estimate the number of ships lost. The records do not distinguish between large ships and subsidiary craft. The fleet mustered in southern China is said to have consisted of 3,500 vessels, but this figure must include ships and boats of all kinds and sizes. The number of really big ships may not have been more than one-tenth of this figure.

CHAPTER XXI

JAPAN AFTER THE MONGOL INVASIONS

1. *The Economic Consequences*

NEWS of the second repulse of the Mongols reached the Court on September 23, 1281, and was quickly transmitted to Kamakura. The retired Emperor Kameyama proceeded in state to the Iwashimizu shrine, where the victory was celebrated by a reading of passages from the whole Buddhist canon.

The success of the Japanese arms was beyond all expectations, and although the Court and the Bakufu were very willing to echo the clergy in thanks to the divine powers for saving the country, there can be no doubt that the direct cause of victory was the courage and discipline of a military class which had been formed and nourished by Yoritomo and his successors. In later days fervent loyalists were to blame the warriors for misfortunes that overtook the reigning dynasty, but it is safe to say that had Go-Toba in 1221—or any other sovereign during the twelfth or thirteenth centuries—succeeded in restoring power to the Throne, there would have been no dynasty left to protect after 1281, for there would have been no army numerous enough or warlike enough to beat off the Mongol attacks. The development of a well-organized feudal state was therefore most fortunately timed for Japan, and much credit is due to the leaders who built it up, from Yoritomo to the Hōjō Regents, in particular Tokiyori and Tokimune.

But the Kamakura Bakufu had to pay a heavy price for saving the country. The mobilization of a great force, and its maintenance in the field, strained the resources of the country, and placed a great burden of responsibility upon the military leaders. The repulse of the invaders did not bring the responsibility of the Bakufu to an end, for they felt obliged to continue upon a war footing for several years. Shortly after receiving news of the victory in 1281 they sent an officer of high rank to supervise further defence works in Harima province, at the eastern entrance to the Inland Sea. The warriors in the Western Circuit (San-yōdō) were placed under his command, while in Kyūshū Shōni and other defence commissioners were ordered to prevent Kyūshū vassals from leaving their fiefs and to ensure that all stewards and other officials were constantly prepared for hostilities. All seagoing vessels were to be carefully examined, and in general strict measures were to be taken to prevent the escape of prisoners of war. Thus Kyūshū remained on the alert, as if a state of war were still in effect.

This was a reasonable line for the Bakufu to take. No military command could afford to relax precautions so long as the threat of invasions remained. For some years the danger of a third Mongol attack was real enough to make it prudent if not essential for the Bakufu to continue to strengthen defence works and to keep the vassals mobilized. News of these continued precautions reached the Koreans. They were already alarmed by the sorties and raids led by Japanese warrior chieftains flushed with their recent successes, who gained pleasure and some profit from descending upon the Korean coast. The Korean officials even feared a large-scale landing, and asked the Mongols to send troops to reinforce their own defences. The King of Korea now went so far as to press the Mongols to attack Japan once more, and he offered to build 150 warships for that purpose. The Mongols fell in with this design, and proceeded to construct more ships, using timber from the Yalu region.

News of these activities reached Japan and confirmed the Bakufu in their resolution to maintain their defences at a high pitch. In 1282 Hōjō Tokisada was sent to Chikuzen to strengthen the line of protection, and he set up his headquarters near Hakata. Meanwhile the Mongols were making preparations. They set up an invasion headquarters and ordered Korea to prepare a base for supplies, with a great store of provisions. It was decided to mount the invasion in the fall of 1283. News of this intention came to the ears of the Japanese in June of that year, and a special emissary was sent to Harima to see to the coastal defences of the home provinces, where an enemy raid might endanger the capital city and the Imperial Court. All Kyūshū warriors were put on the alert by Tokisada at Hakata and every available man was called to active duty.[1]

Towards the end of the year the attack was expected at any time. But it did not come, for reasons of which the Japanese were not aware. They had intelligence reports from Korea, but they knew nothing of conditions elsewhere in the great Mongol empire that stretched across Asia and most of Europe, and could not foretell that the grand strategy of its rulers would now leave Japan undisturbed. Consequently the Bakufu continued their precautions, and a large number of the vassals were kept on defence duty until 1294, when Khubilai died and his successor Timur thought it wise to reduce the commitments of his empire in the north. Already in 1286 the Koreans had been told by Khubilai to cease building ships, but it is doubtful whether the Japanese heard of this; and even after Khubilai's death, when Buddhist monks crossed over from China and described the situation there, the Bakufu dared not take the risk of full demobilization. Precautions were continued for another decade, though on a diminishing scale.

---

[1] When some soldiers were at this time arrested for brawling in Kyoto, the Bakufu asked the civil authorities to release them, on the ground that not a single able-bodied man could be spared.

Thus Japan maintained a state of readiness for more than twenty years. This long-continued expenditure of men and materials, together with the need to reward the warriors for good service, placed an almost unbearable strain upon the resources of the Bakufu; and such conditions could not fail to nourish grievances and create animosity against the Hōjō leaders. Those men, moreover, were fatigued by the burdens they had borne in planning and guiding the defence of the nation. Masamura, half-brother of Yasutoki, had been a faithful supporter of successive Hōjō Regents since 1224, and had done excellent work as chief of the headquarters staff under Tokimune. He died in 1273 and was succeeded by Yoshimasa, who resigned and entered religion in 1276. There was a shortage of experienced leaders, and the Regent Tokimune was left for a time single-handed in Kamakura, to supervise both civil and military affairs in a critical period. A co-signatory was appointed in 1283, but the amount of business which the Regent had to transact was still excessive. When in the following year (1284) Tokimune fell ill and died at the age of thirty-four, the country suffered a most serious loss, for Tokimune during his term of office as Regent had faced with courage and good sense the all but insoluble problems presented by the Mongol threat. His power of calm and bold decision is said to have grown under the influence of his Zen master Mugaku Sogen.[2]

When the news of Tokimune's death reached Kyoto the Court was much grieved and alarmed for the future, since there was no man of talent and character worthy to succeed him. The office of Regent fell to his son Sadatoki, then only fourteen years of age. This was a time when a very strong hand was needed for the control, or let us say the guidance, of the warrior class. The Hōjō clan as a whole was losing its solidarity, for both in Kamakura and in the remoter provinces there were Hōjō cousins who had of late been ready to plot against Tokimune himself. Now, with a youngster in the Regent's seat, such men were dangerous, and they had not much difficulty in finding in Kamakura big men, leaders of great feudal houses, who were greedy for power.

So long as the danger of invasions was real and imminent the vassals remained loyal in action if not in spirit. But there was one important matter in which not only their ambitions but also their fortunes were involved. During the two national emergencies of 1274 and 1281 the warrior chieftains in general, and the loyal vassals, the go-kenin, in particular, had spent their substance lavishly. Year after year they had maintained large forces in the field at their own expense, and many of them were now in trouble. They felt that the country owed them generous compensation, and they looked to the Bakufu for reward.

The Bakufu, for its part, had been obliged in the cause of national defence to consume most of its resources, so that there was little left

---

[2] Mugaku was a Chinese monk who had fled to Japan as a refugee from Mongol rule in southern China. In 1279 he was invited to Kamakura, where he founded (1282) the great Enkakuji—to this day the leading Zen monastery in eastern Japan.

with which the needy warriors could be compensated. The aggrieved feelings of many of the leading vassals, some of whom were in real distress, easily grew into animosity directed against the Bakufu. Thus the very foundations of the feudal edifice were weakened, since the Bakufu depended for its success, indeed for its very existence, upon the loyalty of the vassals.

The warrior chieftains, it should be noted, not only claimed compensation for their expenditure, but also desired rewards for their loyal service. They felt that they had saved the country. Nor were they alone in claiming rewards. The great shrines and monasteries which had prayed for victory in both campaigns were strong in their asseverations that it was their efforts that had persuaded the divine powers, the Gods and Buddhas, to destroy the enemy host on two occasions.

Thus the Bakufu was in a most awkward predicament. The Shōgun, speaking through the Regent, might as a matter of feudal discipline oblige the vassals—the go-kenin in particular—to wait patiently for their rewards. But there were some whose need was very urgent, and it was hard for the feudal overlords to deny them relief. More pressing, though not always more deserving, were the claims of those warriors who did not owe fealty to the Minamoto house, but had taken part in the campaigns out of patriotic duty. They could not be silenced by orders from Kamakura.

From the point of view of the Bakufu the most urgent of all claims were those of the religious establishments. They owed no allegiance to the military chieftains; but the greater monasteries and shrines had much influence at Court and throughout the country—the Hōjō rulers themselves were devout Buddhists and at the same time worshippers of the national deities. Indeed since Yoritomo's day the leaders of the feudal society had usually been lavish in their gifts and endowments to the churches. Moreover popular feeling would support the claims of religion, because it was generally felt that what had saved the country was the intercession of the clergy.

Thus the Bakufu could not help recognizing the claims of the religious bodies, and felt obliged to give them preference. But the new Regent Sadatoki, who succeeded Tokimune in 1284, found himself in an uncomfortable position, for there was hardly anything to distribute. The sources of reward had dried up; for a decade or more the country had been consuming more than it produced. Hitherto, after civil wars or riots, it had been easy for the victors to reward their partisans, since they could hand over to deserving claimants the estates of the vanquished. But after the Mongol invasions there was no booty to share out or newly created wealth with which to recompense the vassals. In 1284 a few valuable manorial rights were granted to certain shrines, but such offices of profit were very scarce and only a few claims could be satisfied.

The pressure upon the Bakufu was strong and persistent. To it we

Takezaki with comrades boards a Mongol war junk. He is shown at the left cutting the throat of an enemy. Taken from a printed version of the picture-scroll relating his exploits.

owe one of the most valuable sources of information about the fighting during the first Mongol attack. It is the text of the celebrated picture-scroll (known as Mōko Shūrai Emakimono) which illustrates the account of his battle experiences written by a warrior named Takezaki in support of his claim. His was a deserving case, and so were many others. But the Bakufu had nothing left for them beyond a few fields newly broken by the plough and some confiscated fiefs of no great value. Since these were clearly not enough to satisfy any important claimants, the Bakufu resorted to desperate shifts, such as dividing up a stewardship (jitō-shiki) and granting shares to several applicants for reward, or obliging them to draw lots for compensation. They even sought for flaws in the titles of some loyal landowners, and confiscated property which they then awarded to stubborn claimants. In extreme cases manors were taken from Court nobles, and even from the Crown, usually under pretence of defective title.

When such expedients were exhausted the Kamakura courts were ordered to refuse to hear further complaints. Petitioners from Kyūshū—warriors of the western defence area who had borne the brunt of the battles—were told to apply to the chief constables, Shōni, Ōtomo, Shimazu, and Shibuya, who represented the Shōgun in a capacity similar to that of the Rokuhara deputies. This device merely shifted the burden from the shoulders of the Bakufu. Vassals were forbidden to appeal in person to Kamakura or to the Rokuhara courts of enquiry. This was in August 1286, about five years after the second invasion, and the cases dragged on for several years more with little prospect of solution.

In 1294 the Bakufu, having reviewed the situation and concluded that there was no other way of bringing the intolerable disputes to an end, made a desperate decision. They chose to ride on their prestige and risk their authority by decreeing that no further rewards would be granted for services during the two campaigns of 1274 and 1281. To declare the rejection of all suits brought before the Shōgun's courts in respect of events prior to April 1284 was an action that by its sudden and arbitrary character was certain to astound and offend the vassals concerned. They had trusted in the justice of the Bakufu, not without reason in the light of the reputation of the Hōjō leaders for fair dealing and a respect for law. Now they were surprised, hurt, and angry, yet they did not mutiny. It speaks well for the discipline of the warrior class as a whole that they did not immediately rise against the Regents. Indeed the landowners in Kyūshū still carried out their duties on a war footing. They kept defence works in repair and maintained armed forces at key points—services for which the poor cultivators doubtless paid in increased taxes.

It was not until after the death of Khubilai in 1294 that the Japanese government felt that the danger of invasion was past. As late as 1293 the Bakufu had sent to the western provinces a special defence commissioner, charged with full superintendence of defence measures against an attack expected that year.

Even as late as 1299, when the Mongols (knowing the esteem in which Zen monks were held in Japan) sent a very distinguished Chinese churchman to make a friendly approach, the Bakufu remained suspicious. They took the emissary to Izu, where he was well treated but detained. He became naturalized and reached high ecclesiastical rank. Kyūshū remained on the alert for several years more.

It would be a mistake to ascribe the decline of the Hōjō Regents only to the discontent of unrewarded vassals. There were other, more remote, causes at work since long before the Mongol invasions and gradually undermining the authority of the Bakufu. As early as 1232, when the Jōei Formulary was issued, the economic foundations of the Minamoto vassalage had already begun to show signs of strain which it was hoped this legislation would relieve. Some of its articles attempted to arrest a process which the Bakufu regarded as dangerous to the feudal order, namely the transfer of fiefs held by vassals to persons or institutions not fully within the jurisdiction of the feudal government.

Many vassals and retainers were obliged to raise money by mortgaging or selling their property. Such transactions naturally weakened the bond between the overlord and the warriors, since rights belonging to a fief could be exercised by members of a different class, such as merchants or money-lenders. These embarrassments were not, however, a sign that the national economy as a whole was in difficulties. On the contrary, it had steadily expanded after the end of the Gempei

War in 1185, thanks to the opportunity for peaceful enterprise conferred upon the people at large by Yoritomo's victory and the firmly based government which he and his successors established. It might indeed be truthfully said that much of the lawmaking of the thirteenth century was designed to protect the vassals against the pressure of a rapidly developing internal trade and the growth of a mercantile class whose interests were at variance with those of warriors living upon revenues from landed estates.

The reasons for the expansion of the total economy were numerous. The increasing demand of the wealthier vassals for goods of all kinds stimulated production throughout the country at the very time the development of trade with China was increasing the output of goods for export as well as home consumption. Although this foreign commerce was partly a natural outgrowth of the friendly relations between Japan and South China (which the Zen monks of both countries did much to promote), it was primarily a sequel of the great improvements in shipbuilding and navigation which took place under the Sung dynasty during the thirteenth century, before it submitted to Mongol onslaughts. These circumstances coincided with, or helped to produce, a rapid increase of technical skills and of mercantile organization in Japan. There was a steady Chinese demand for certain Japanese commodities, while the Japanese imported large quantities of copper coins from China, partly for industrial use but mostly (as we have seen) for currency to facilitate domestic exchanges. It happened also that towards the end of the twelfth century rich deposits of gold were discovered in northern Japan, and some of this wealth was applied to the purchase of Chinese goods.

These developments, though they might profit certain warrior families whose fiefs were conveniently situated in coastal provinces, were unfavourable to most of the vassals, who lived on fixed incomes based on the sale of rice or other agricultural produce, so that the general expansion of trade placed them at a disadvantage. As might be expected, the price level of most commodities rose more than the price of agricultural produce. Some warriors found a way to adjust their standard of living to the new conditions; the rest became indebted to the new mercantile class, most commonly to brokers and money-lenders who exacted a high return for their services.

It followed that many vassals found themselves in growing financial distress and could see no way out but mortgaging their land. It was to protect them—the warriors as a class—that the Bakufu at frequent intervals after 1232 issued edicts known as *tokusei* (acts of grace) by which they decreed maximum rates of interest or the partial cancellation of debts. These measures were common during the three or four decades preceding the Mongol invasions, so that the difficulties of the warriors at that time cannot be related to their contributions to defence. It is true, however, that the expansion of the total economy was checked by the diversion of effort to military purposes for nearly two decades from about 1274. By the closing years of the thirteenth century the feudal establishment was really endangered by the distress into which many important vassals had fallen. Their condition is well illustrated by the Act of Grace of 1297, which was designed to stave off their financial ruin.

Its provisions were drastic. It reaffirmed and strengthened previous orders limiting the transfer of fiefs to persons outside the jurisdiction of the Bakufu. Not only did it prohibit all sales, but it ordered fiefs which had already been sold to be returned to their original owners unless the sale had official approval. It also cancelled all personal loans, with certain exceptions where pledges were held by the lender. Such sweeping changes naturally caused alarm among merchants and money-lenders, leading to a succession of lawsuits and a multiplicity of devices for evading the law. Before long the new rules proved unworkable, and the government was brought to recognize that the interests of the feudal society could best be served by improving rather than by attacking the system of credit. Changes were therefore made less than a year after the issue of the Act of Grace of 1297, in the hope of easing the situation of the lenders. But nothing could bring about a real improvement in the position of the warriors, for their incomes were fixed, their families were growing, and their expenditures continued to increase. Indeed, a condition of indebtedness, if not of insolvency, became endemic among the warriors.

Despite the failure of the acts of grace during the thirteenth century, they were to be frequently resorted to during the following century, out of despair rather than hope, and with no greater success. Those issued by the Bakufu brought no advantage to the insolvent samurai in general, and since such measures favoured debtors as against creditors they were resented by many members of the warrior class who had been prudent or fortunate enough to improve their fortunes and had lent money to others. In short the acts of grace were only confessions of failure on the part of the Kamakura government. This failure was a prelude to a deterioration in the standards of probity which had distinguished the great Regents, and led eventually to the downfall of the Bakufu.

Though it would be a mistake to attribute the decline of the Hōjō Regents to economic causes, the ultimate collapse of their rule is clearly in some way connected with the insolvency of the Kamakura government. Their failure cannot be put down to incompetent conduct of the nation's affairs, for their financial troubles began under the austere regime of men like Tokiyori, who were honest and capable. Nor can it be said that their policies were injurious to the economy of the nation, since (as we have observed) there was a marked expansion in the total amount of goods produced and commodities exchanged throughout the country until the last ten years or so of the thirteenth century.

The nation at large had therefore no cause to desire the overthrow of the Kamakura government. On the contrary, as prosperity increased it was enjoyed by a growing class of merchants, bankers, landholders cultivating their farms for profit, retail traders, and the numerous workers they employed as bailiffs, stewards, accountants, and clerks. These people resisted the efforts of the Bakufu to protect the vassals against their creditors, but they did not want to disturb the established order.

The position of the Kamakura government at the end of the thirteenth century thus affords an interesting example of what appears to be a general rule, that even the most efficient and trustworthy government is in danger if it is impoverished. Every remedial step which it takes to balance income and expenditure offends more members of the prosperous class than it pleases, and points the way to antagonism, if not to revolt. It cannot be said that financial embarrassment was a cause of the sickness that attacked the Bakufu after the second Mongol invasion, but it certainly was a symptom. It gave to the enemies and rivals of the Hōjō family a plausible excuse for encouraging opposition to the Regents. To fan a grievance is an easy way to inflame feelings against a government in power.

The only measure by which the Bakufu might have recovered its authority was to increase taxation so as to spread equally the burden of defense expenditure. But this was something that the later Regents had not the courage to try, even if it occurred to them.

2. The Decline of the Hōjō Regents

Little is known of the course of events at Kamakura in the decade or so following the Mongol retreat in 1284; but it seems that the quality of the chiefs of the Hōjō clan must have fallen off after the death of Tokimune. He was a capable man of strong character, and on his premature death was succeeded as Regent by his young son of fourteen, Sadatoki, an unfortunate choice in a critical time. Though there is not much on record about Sadatoki, it is clear that neither he nor any of his advisers was strong enough to hold the more ambitious warriors in check. There were long-standing rivalries even within the Hōjō clan, and a lapse of loyalty to the Regents even amongst the highest officers. Within a decade of the invasions the Regency was at the beginning of what later proved to be a steep decline.

That there was strong latent opposition to the Hōjō is apparent in the chronicles of a generation or more before the Mongol attacks. The Miura family, envious of the power of the Adachi family, had planned a revolt in 1246 and had been party to a conspiracy to murder the Regent Tokiyori. It is true that their rising was promptly suppressed, because the Hōjō rule was still quick and firm; but while the course of government ran smooth on the surface there were undercurrents of rivalry and envy throughout the warrior class. As the authority of the Regents spread over the country, their deputies in the capital and the distant western provinces came to exercise ever wider powers and tended to resent the control of Kamakura. In extreme cases they conspired against the Regent of the day. As early as 1272 one of the Rokuhara deputies (Tandai) had been put to death for plotting against Tokimune, and shortly after the second Mongol attack another Tandai, Tokikuni, was executed for a similar offence.

Even the once anonymous and unanimous decisions of the high court at Kamakura were giving way to dissension as the quality of Hōjō leadership deteriorated. By Sadatoki's day the resolute firmness of the earlier Regents had vanished. Sadatoki himself was capable enough, but he did not inherit the high sense of duty of his father Tokimune, who wore himself out by his exertions; nor did he display the earnest character of his talented grandfather Tokiyori. He was willing, it seems, to entrust the more fatiguing tasks of government to his advisers, who for the most part were vigorous but not righteous men.

He was only a boy when he became Regent (1284), and for the critical decade which followed he was directed by two particularly self-seeking counsellors, Yasumori, the head of the Adachi family, and Yoritsuna, a Taira who held a high administrative post. These two were bitter rivals, and both deservedly came to a violent end. Adachi, accused by Yoritsuna of plotting to become Shōgun on the ground of kinship with the Minamoto chieftain, was destroyed with many members of his family in 1285, just as the Miura family had been destroyed at the instance of an Adachi in 1247. It was Yoritsuna's tale-bearing that brought about the fall of the Adachi, and he in his turn was killed with his chief followers in 1293. He had been accused of designs to displace the Regent, and even a suspicion of such treachery was enough to ensure his death at the hands of the Hōjō leaders.

At this point Sadatoki, now twenty-four years old, took charge and performed the functions of Regent himself until 1301, when he decided to enter religion. A young Hōjō cousin, Morotoki, succeeded him as titular Regent, though it seems that Sadatoki continued to make decisions upon important matters until his death in 1311. His son Takatoki (born in 1303) was schooled for the succession by guardians whom Sadatoki trusted, so that during the years of his childhood the Regency was in the hands of base intriguers. The prestige of the Hōjō had sadly fallen, the office of Regent was debased by its temporary occupants, and it is clear that when Takatoki was formally installed in 1316 the great days of Kamakura were over. The leading vassals no longer felt loyalty or respect for the Hōjō Regency. Not all of them were aggrieved by the lack of reward for military service against the Mongols; this was a complaint of the Kyūshū warriors in particular. On all sides, however, antagonism to the Hōjō leaders was growing, largely because it was apparent that the Bakufu had lost its administrative skill and its judicial integrity. There is no doubt that among the causes of discontent was the failure of the Shōgun's courts to dispense impartial justice.

Plots against the Regents were discovered from time to time during the first two decades of the fourteenth century, but somehow the Hōjō family remained in power, their momentum being still stronger than any concerted opposition. It is one of the usual ironies of history that what caused their destruction was not a rising of angry feudal lords but a quarrel at Court about succession to the throne—a quarrel, moreover, that resulted from the testament of the retired Emperor Go-Saga, who had always been a faithful friend and supporter of the Hōjō Regents of his day.

Go-Saga reigned from 1242 to 1246 and was in power as retired Emperor until his death in 1272, so that his life included the years when Yasutoki, Tokiyori, and Tokimune controlled the Bakufu. He was the most valuable friend of the Hōjō leaders during their most prosperous days, when relations between Kyoto and Kamakura had never been so harmonious. Yet he unwittingly struck them a blow which was many years later to prove mortal. After the briefest of reigns he had abdicated in favour of his son Go-Fukakusa, who reigned from 1246 to 1259 and then abdicated in favour of his younger brother, Kameyama. Kameyama was titular sovereign from 1259 to 1274. There was apparent amity but concealed discord between the two brothers, though while Go-Saga was alive his authority was such that no succession troubles could come out into the open. His favourite son was Kameyama, and it was to secure the succession to Kameyama that Go-Fukakusa was obliged to abdicate and thus to become the junior (and powerless) cloistered sovereign.

So for the time being the succession was determined beyond argument and the choice had the approval of the Bakufu. It should be remembered that the succession was governed by no absolute rule of primogeniture but primarily, if not entirely, by the choice of the senior abdicated emperor. Custom, however, pointed to the older brother and his descendants. Therefore Go-Fukakusa was naturally aggrieved and his disappointment was shared by numerous supporters at Court. Though no dispute was possible during Go-Saga's lifetime, when he died the argument broke out with great heat. He had left a will to be opened after the first period of mourning on the forty-ninth day from his death. The contents of this document were as alarming to one side as they were pleasing to the other.

3. The Issue of Legitimacy

Whatever may have been Go-Saga's true feelings about the succession, his will stated very clearly his wishes regarding the property which as retired Emperor he had inherited and increased. This was a matter of political importance, because the accumulated wealth of successive retired emperors had for a long time been the chief prize in dynastic rivalries. Indeed the succession disputes of the period cannot be understood without some knowledge of their true motives.

The imperial office, that is to say the position of the titular emperor, was an empty dignity which no ambitious prince would covet. The reigning sovereign had neither power nor wealth, and was a mere prisoner of ceremonial. It was only because to ascend the throne was a necessary step to the position of retired or cloistered emperor that the position of reigning emperor was an object of strife.³ The retired emperor had at his disposal great estates, and the funds which he drew from these sources not only gave him an advantageous position as compared with the reigning emperor but also attracted to his service the most active nobles and officials. It was for this reason that factional strife in Kyoto was so strong. The stakes were high in terms of political spoils.

The value of the property changing hands upon the demise of a cloistered sovereign is hard to assess in exact terms, but it is safe to say that the estates falling to a senior retired emperor were always of great extent and produced a rich income, which at times might include a good share of the tax revenue of a whole province. Some idea of the importance of these properties may be gained from the history of the celebrated Chōkōdō domain. This was the rich endowment of a chapel (the Chōkōdō) founded by Go-Shirakawa, who at the point of death bequeathed it to his favourite consort. She in turn conveyed it to the cloistered Emperor Go-Saga, charging him to pass it on to his son, Go-Fukakusa. In his will Go-Saga left the greater part of his property to his younger son, Kameyama, though he did not neglect Go-Fukakusa, who received a fair legacy in addition to the Chōkōdō domain.

In the succession disputes which followed Go-Saga's death in 1272, Kameyama's supporters argued that it was in compensation for not being chosen as head of the line of succession that Go-Fukakusa was granted the Chōkōdō domain. This is not true, since Go-Saga had no choice. But the fact that possession of this domain could be thought of as equivalent to a throne gives a measure of the value of the In's estates.

The nature of Go-Saga's testament has been misunderstood by some

---

³ The difference is expressed by a special term which was used to identify the senior retired emperor. He was called Jisei no Kimi or Jiten no Kimi, which means the ruler of the country. One might say that the titular emperor reigned, the retired emperor ruled, and the Bakufu governed.

"Senior" in this context does not mean senior in age, but in authority. At times the newly abdicated emperor might displace the current Jisei no Kimi, though junior in years. It should be added that the term "retired emperor" is more inclusive than the term "cloistered emperor," since not all emperors who abdicated took orders. Entering a monastery was often a convenient way of avoiding burdensome duties, but it was not a formal prerequisite to the wielding of power.

students of Japanese history, who have supposed that in it Go-Saga laid down a definite rule by which the succession was to alternate between the lines of the two sons, Kameyama and Go-Fukakusa. This is not correct, for although the will contained very detailed provisions for the disposal of the property of the In (the active cloistered emperor), it was silent on the burning question of succession to the throne. It is not surprising that a dispute, or rather a series of disputes, should have arisen in which each side claimed to know what the deceased Go-Saga's intentions had been.

The evidence is not decisive, yet it seems fair to say that he expressed no choice, even by implication. It is true that he showed a special affection for Kameyama, but he was careful not to commit himself on the question of succession. His will contained a sort of codicil saying that the legatees must obey his instructions and not quarrel about the bequests he had made. In a special rescript addressed to the Bakufu he left the choice of emperor and retired emperor entirely to the decision of Kamakura, partly no doubt in gratitude for his own nomination in 1242 and partly because he knew that in any serious dispute the Bakufu would have the last word.

The Bakufu were embarrassed by this task, and enquired whether the late Go-Saga had expressed any preference. They were told by Ōmiya-In, his consort and a daughter of the powerful Saionji Saneuji,[4] that His Majesty favoured the line of the younger son, Kameyama. But there was no written evidence in support of this statement, and the Fukakusa party would not accept the Kameyama party's argument. They denied that Go-Saga had displayed a preference for Kameyama, and pointed out that his legacies included documents about poetry and football which were bequeathed to Kameyama, while serious political papers were left to Go-Fukakusa.

Harassed by other and more imminent troubles, the Bakufu did not want to take sides. But it was in fact impossible for them to remain neutral, since the opposition of Go-Fukakusa's partisans to the choice of Kameyama was bound to be strong and far-reaching. There was much more at stake than the issue of loyalty. Go-Fukakusa's party had looked forward to the enjoyment of power and emoluments. Their disappointment was intense, and neither he nor they could accept defeat without a struggle. He himself, while not openly complaining, was grieved by his father's choice. The more fortunate Kameyama at first entered with enthusiasm upon his duties as the reigning sovereign, but soon fell into a state of melancholy, and in 1274, at the age of twenty-six, he suddenly abdicated, surrendering the throne to his son, who became the Emperor Go-Uda. Go-Fukakusa had supposed that it was his son who would be chosen, not Kameyama's.

---

[4] Chancellor in 1246.

Thus began a conflict between the two lines which was to influence the course of history for a century or more. These dynastic manoeuvres and intrigues may seem to be outside the main stream of historical events, but in fact they cannot be neglected. Indeed the details of the struggle between the two factions make a fascinating story, full of curious and surprising elements. They are of considerable psychological as well as historical interest, because they illustrate certain singular aspects of the Japanese tradition of sovereignty. Only a brief summary can be given here, to explain the line of cleavage between the two contending parties.

The conflict stirred up passions and divided the whole country into factions. It was idle for the Bakufu to try to keep a balance between the two angry hostile parties, and the feudal society was deeply involved, since many discontented vassals were eager for motives of pride or profit to take sides in a great dispute which the Bakufu would have preferred to solve by diplomatic measures. In 1275, when Kameyama, having surrendered the throne to his son Go-Uda, assumed the position of retired Emperor and exercised its fullest powers, the injured Go-Fukakusa, in his state of deep pessimism, resigned all his titles, ranks, and privileges and wished his followers to join him in entering religion. In distress Kameyama asked the Bakufu for advice, and Go-Fukakusa also referred his case to the judgment of Kamakura.

The Bakufu was by no means pleased to receive these appeals. At this juncture its leaders wanted nothing so much as to be free from Court problems, for these were times when the menace of invasion was causing them great anxiety. But they were impressed by the difficulty of the situation as it was described to them, and after a close debate in council they reached a decision in favour of Go-Fukakusa, holding that his was the true line of succession and regretting that he could not now expect to become the senior retired sovereign. They suggested a compromise which, by a complicated arrangement of adoption and abdication, allowed Go-Uda to retire in favour of a son of Go-Fukakusa named Fushimi, who became titular Emperor in 1288—a date at which the Bakufu was still preoccupied with fears of a third invasion.

There were now, it will be seen, two main lines of succession to the throne, descending from Go-Fukakusa and Kameyama, respectively.[5] There was no strict rule of succession; the choice of a crown prince depended largely upon the affection of the emperor and then the agreement of the Bakufu. It was therefore to be expcted that any arrangement by which succession was to alternate between two lines would lead only to perennial quarrels; and indeed when Fushimi abdicated

[5] They were known as the Jimyō-in line, after a monastery to which Go-Fukakusa retired in 1259, and the Daikaku-ji line, from the monastery in which Kameyama and his descendants lived from 1276.

More convenient is the practice, which is adopted below, of referring to the Go-Fukakusa line as the senior and the Kameyama line as the junior dynasty.

in 1298 a series of disputes began which ended in a civil war some thirty years later.[6]

In the year 1318, following upon no fewer than five controversial accessions in the thirty-odd years after Kameyama's abdication, there came the turn of the Kameyama or junior line, and the throne fell to the Emperor Go-Daigo. This may have been in accordance with the wishes of Go-Saga, but there was a new circumstance here of great significance. Go-Daigo, unlike his five predecessors, was not a young boy, but a man of over thirty. He had no intention of abdicating as if he were a child-emperor, and in this he had the backing of his father, Go-Uda, who was happy in his lucrative retirement and would have strongly resisted any plan to surrender the throne to a member of the Go-Fukakusa or senior line.

This was the critical point in the development of a dynastic strife which was to embroil the Bakufu to its own peril; for when Go-Daigo, pressed by the Hōjō Regent, refused to abdicate and designated his own son as heir-apparent in 1326, there was a clash, and Kamakura insisted upon a son of Go-Fushimi. Here the Bakufu made a fatal blunder, a blunder that men like Tokiyori and Tokimune would hardly have made. What the Bakufu was suggesting was a continuation of the system of cloister government, which Go-Daigo had in effect repudiated by his refusal to abdicate and his determination to rule. It was clear not only to Go-Daigo's friends and supporters but also to any sensible statesman that the practice, or rather a vague approval, of alternation between the two lines must be abandoned. Already there were two bitterly antagonistic factions at Court, and there were even signs that each of these might split into two separate lines. To prevent such ridiculous situations it was clear that alternation between the two lines must be brought to an end. The question of legitimacy must be settled once and for all; and this meant that the Hōjō Regents must be somehow overthrown or at least deprived of power to dictate to the Throne. If this had been only a Court affair, a matter of palace intrigue, it might have been tolerated for a time by Kamakura. But the Bakufu was in the hands of a group of men of low character, and the Regent Takatoki, its titular leader under the Shōgun, was scarcely sane. His judgment was poor, his conduct erratic. He indulged in extremes of luxury and debauch, offending many of the greater vassals. He had retired in 1326, after handing over part of his functions to certain unworthy deputies. The Court at Kyoto was by no means displeased to learn of this degradation of feudal government, and Go-Daigo's followers were thereby encouraged to plan revolt.

In central and western Japan there were many landholders of good

[6] To describe here these complicated and contentious matters would be to interrupt the general narrative of political events to which this chapter is devoted. A summary of the main features of the succession question, with appropriate genealogical data, is given in Appendix IV.

standing who owed no duty to Kamakura, and there were members of noble Kyoto families—including descendants of the Taira—who were ready to take risks on Go-Daigo's behalf. Besides these there were certain vassals in the east who had come to envy and even to despise the Hōjō Regents.

Such men were on the lookout for a cause which they could support in opposition to the Hōjō leaders. The succession dispute offered an excellent opportunity, for the Bakufu had to take a line. Go-Daigo had knowledge of a plot against the Bakufu as early as 1324, he was at loggerheads with the military representatives in 1326, and for the next few years he was privy to other conspiracies, even if he had no direct part in them.

In May 1331 one of his confidants revealed his designs to Kamakura, and it was then that Takatoki became alarmed. He sent orders to have the known conspirators arrested and taken to Kamakura for questioning. Meanwhile Go-Daigo's activities had to be checked, and for that purpose a demonstration was made by sending to Kyoto a trusted officer (Nikaidō) with a force of 3,000 men. Go-Daigo temporized, but when he learned that the Bakufu intended to force him to abdicate in favour of a prince of the Go-Fukakusa line he saw that the time for decision had come. He knew that the Rokuhara Command would use force against him if he were stubborn, and he made up his mind to escape and set up his Court at a distance from the capital, beyond easy reach of Nikaidō's men.

He left the palace secretly by night, carrying with him the imperial seal, one of the three sacred treasures of the Regalia. This was in September 1331. He took refuge in a monastery on Mount Kasagi, which had been fortified and was now held by a small garrison. Valuable allies came to his help, notably a warrior named Kusunoki Masashige, who owed no allegiance to the Bakufu. But the force which Rokuhara brought against Kasagi was too strong to be held off, and the garrison was crushed after some weeks of stubborn fighting. Go-Daigo was captured and was banished to the island of Oki in 1332. A prince chosen by the Bakufu was placed on the throne. He was a prince of the senior line, and this was the beginning of a dynastic struggle in which the contending parties resorted to armed force, nominally to settle the question of legitimacy but in fact to decide which group or league of warrior chieftains should succeed to the power of the Hōjō Regents.

Go-Daigo succeeded in escaping from Oki in the spring of 1333. He had supporters in western Japan and after some temporary successes there he was able to return to Kyoto in June 1333, thanks to the defection of Ashikaga Takauji, the head of a powerful warrior family of Minamoto (Seiwa Genji) descent. Takauji had been sent against Go-Daigo by Kamakura, in command of a large army, but he suddenly changed his purpose, and instead of moving west towards the province of Hōki, where Go-Daigo was collecting adherents, he turned back and attacked Kyoto. There he had no great difficulty in crushing the resistance of the small Hōjō garrison in its Rokuhara base.

The Hōjō leaders were now in a difficult position, and throughout the eastern provinces there were risings against them under the leadership of disaffected warriors. An army raised by Nitta Yoshisada, a devoted loyalist, had so pressed the reserves hurriedly collected by the Hōjō that Kamakura was taken without much difficulty, and in the first few days of July it was in flames.

It seemed as if Go-Daigo were firmly seated upon the throne. But he was the victim of his own lack of political wisdom and of the ambitions of the Ashikaga family. Early in the year 1334 he announced his intentions. He decreed a change in the era name, to signify a change in the nature of the government of the country. The new era was to be called Kemmu, and it was to be devoted to the task of restoring direct imperial rule. But by the beginning of the year 1336 the Kemmu Restoration had failed and he had fled the capital to escape from the attacks of Takauji, who had again turned his coat and now supported an emperor of his own choice. Thus there were two lines and two Courts, whose rivalry led to civil strife for more than fifty years.

The failure of the restoration movement and the outbreak of a war of succession are properly to be regarded as the opening of a new phase of Japanese history.

APPENDIXES

AN EARLY CHINESE NOTICE OF ENVOYS FROM JAPAN[1]

The following is the relevant passage in the record cited in Chapter III, page 42.

". . . Then Bu [i.e., Yūryaku] came to the throne. Signing himself King of Wa, generalissimo who maintains peace in the East, Commanding with Battle Axe all military affairs in the seven countries of Wa, Paikche, Silla, Imna, Kara, Chin-han and Mok-han, in 478 he sent an envoy bearing a memorial reading as follows: 'Our land is remote and distant. Its domains lie far out in the ocean. From days of old our forebears have clad themselves in armor and helmet and gone across the hills and waters, sparing no time for rest.' "

The memorial goes on to describe Japanese campaigns in Japan and in Korea. The Emperor of Japan complains that when the Japanese wished to travel to China by way of Korea, the state of Koguryö stopped them. He therefore must attack this enemy kingdom, and asks the Emperor of China to approve his intentions and to appoint him as supreme commander of the campaign. The seven countries are Japan and the greater part of Korea. The Emperor of China issued an edict accordingly.

THE HEIAN CAPITAL AND THE PALACES

As will be seen from the accompanying diagram, the city (which followed closely the plan of the Chinese capital at Ch'ang-an under the Sui dynasty) was a great rectangle, divided at regular intervals by parallel streets crossing from north to south and from east to west. In the north centre was a walled area, the Daidairi or Great Enclosure, which contained the Imperial Palace and the offices of the government. The dimensions of the city as planned were about 2½ miles E.–W. and 3½ miles N.–S. But the western section of the city never flourished, and it gradually fell into disuse and then decay. The diagram shows only the eastern section.

The main wide streets running east and west were called jō or avenues and were known by numbers, from Ichijō, First Avenue, to Kujō, Ninth Avenue. Between the avenues there were other wide streets called ōji, and between these ran parallel narrow streets, one, two, or three in number, called kōji, which may be described as lanes. The wide streets varied in breadth from 80 to 100 feet, except for Nijō, which was 170 feet across.

The wide streets running north and south were of similar breadth, again

---

[1] This is an extract from an "Account of the Eastern and Southern Barbarians" in the *History of the Liu Sung Dynasty*, compiled about 513. [Translation of Tsunoda and De Bary.]

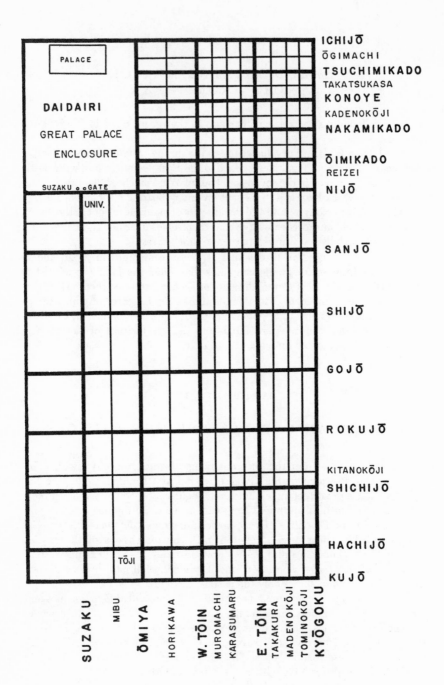

with one exception: Suzaku-ōji, which led from the southern boundary of the city to the main gate of the Great Enclosure, was 280 feet wide.

It will be seen that the position of a building could be described by stating the intersection of streets to which it was nearest. Thus the Fujiwara college (Kangaku-in) was at the intersection of Sanjō and Mibu; and the Police Commission (Kebiishi-chō) was west of the intersection of Konoye and Horikawa.

The symmetry of the original plan was soon spoiled. Apart from the decay of the western half, the city suffered time after time from earthquakes and— what was far more frequent and disastrous—great conflagrations. The fire of Angen (1177) destroyed many of the public buildings and countless dwellings, from the mansions of the nobility to the houses of the poor. It was called by the citizens, with characteristic wry humour, Tarō, or Big Brother, in contrast to the less dreadful Jirō, or Little Brother, which followed it. There were serious fires in 1180 and 1182; and then in 1188 came "the great fire of Bunji," in which most of the buildings in the Great Enclosure were destroyed, but not the Palace. There was some destruction by fire in 1221–22 and again in 1228, when the Palace, already damaged, was rendered uninhabitable.

Some historians think that the fire of 1177 put a finishing touch to the decline of the old Heian culture by destroying tens or hundreds of thousands of priceless books and documents and badly damaging great institutions like the University. The long civil strife no doubt prevented recovery, and once the Kamakura Bakufu was established in power the traditional standards of scholarship and elegance were hard to maintain. It was difficult, moreover, to maintain a Court in the seclusion of the Great Enclosure, since the sovereign was often obliged to live outside in what was called a detached palace—nominally only a temporary residence but often occupied for long periods.

A good example of such a palace is the Kanin palace, which stood at the intersection of Nijō and Higashi-Tōin. It was a large mansion with spacious grounds, which had often been lent to members of the Imperial House by Fujiwara statesmen to whom it belonged. It was burned or otherwise damaged from time to time, but was occupied at intervals from 1068 to 1184, when Go-Toba moved in after his coronation ceremonies in the Imperial Palace. Yoritomo had it rebuilt in 1187 after a severe earthquake. It was the ordinary residence of the sovereign until 1209, when it was destroyed by fire. It was again rebuilt and reoccupied in 1213. By the Jōkyū period (1220) it had developed into a miniature Imperial Palace, with the proper ceremonial halls and pavilions as well as the usual apartments.

There were several other temporary or detached palaces outside the Great Enclosure, some occupied by the reigning sovereign and some by abdicated monarchs or princes of the royal blood. Such palaces were often styled Sato-Dairi, the word *sato* meaning a person's native place. A wife visiting her parents is usually said to return to her sato; and this term was applied to residences outside the Enclosure, especially when a pregnant empress returned for her confinement to the home of her Fujiwara parents. Often the mother, and at times the father, stayed for long periods in the Sato-Dairi. Thus the Higashi Sanjō-In was used for Fujiwara daughters who were about to give birth to an heir to the throne. It was here that in 991 the Empress Akiko gave birth to the future Emperor Ichijō; and she herself was given the title of Higashi Sanjō-In.

Other names of streets recur constantly in Japanese historical records, to identify sometimes a palace, sometimes a person with whom it is associated. Among the most frequently mentioned are the Reizei Madenokōji Dairi, the Nijō Tominokōji Dairi, the Takakura Dono, the Saga-In or Daikakuji, and the Jimyō-In. Ichijō, Nijō, Sanjō, Kujō, and Tōin are the names of aristocratic families as well as the names of streets.

The Rokuhara headquarters of the Bakufu deputies (Tandai) in the capital lay in a strategically good position slightly to the east of the eastern limit of the city, across the Kamo River, extending north and south from the level of Gojō to the level of Shichijō, that is for about 700 yards.

The district called Muromachi lay north and west of the intersection of Shichijō and Higashi-Tōin.

An important topographical feature of the capital is its situation on a gentle slope, between two converging rivers, the Katsura and the Kamo. Streams or canals ran down the middle of several of the wide roads from north to south.

Kyoto was not a walled city. Its population about A.D. 1200 was probably not more than 100,000.

Very full particulars of the buildings and their history are given in *Kyoto, the Old Capital of Japan*, by R. Ponsonby-Fane (Kyoto, 1956).

APPENDIX III

A NOTE ON HIGHER EDUCATION, 700–1000

It seems appropriate to amplify the references to education in Chapter VI by some account of the University and its curriculum. The word "university" is perhaps misleading, since the Daigaku was not a school for all kinds of knowledge, but primarily, if not exclusively, a Confucian college. A service in honour of Confucius was held twice a year, the cost of offerings being met from official funds.

The subjects prescribed by law were, in order of importance, the Confucian Classics, History, Literature (composition), and Law; but changes in the nature of Japanese society during the eighth century were reflected in changes in the curriculum.

There appears to have been a government college in the seventh century, but we know little of its character until the early eighth century. At that time its declared purpose was to educate the sons of the nobility in the Chinese classics, and entry was confined to the sons of persons of the fifth rank and upwards, with a few special exceptions, chiefly for the sons of professional scholars.

The chief function of the Daigaku was to prepare young men for official careers. Discipline was severe and students were examined at frequent intervals, those who did badly being dismissed. Those who did well in their final examination were eligible for the civil service examination, at which they could qualify for degrees according to their capacity. The successful candidates were graded as follows:

First: Shūsai, for "Exceptional Talent," combining knowledge with ability to reason, to understand the nature of things.

Second: Myōkyō, for "Learning in the Classics," showing a good knowledge of two classical books, ability to read and expound them, and familiarity with the principal commentaries.

Third: Shinshi (Ch. Chin-shih), for showing a good knowledge of the principles of government (administration), and ability to recite passages from the great anthologies of Chinese literature, such as *Monzen* (*Wen-hsüan*) and *Jiga* (*Erh-ya*).

Fourth: Myōbō, "Learned in the Law," for showing a knowledge of the administrative and penal codes and commentaries thereon.

Fifth: San, for ability to calculate.

Most candidates tried for the first class, but success was rare. The records show that only sixty-five students took this degree in the years from 704 to 937, by which date the Daigaku had fallen into a decline.

In its early years instruction at the Daigaku paid most attention to the Confucian classics and less to law and literature. The inducements to attend the University in the first half of the eighth century were not great, since the important posts were given to the sons of great nobles in preference to students who obtained the highest degrees. In the year 739 age restrictions were removed in order to encourage entry, and by 750 the total enrollment is said to have exceeded capacity, though some scholars question this.

Subsequently—later in the eighth century—there was a change. Enthusiasm for the Confucian classics waned, and interest shifted to Chinese literature, both ancient and contemporary, and especially to Chinese poetry, to such a degree that a special department of Literature was formed and the Professor of Literature became the most important teacher, with the highest rank. Study of the law also attracted more students than heretofore, largely because both law and literature now afforded some prospect of good official posts. At this time also provision was made for the admission of a few sons of commoners. But since their parents were for the most part poor men, the question of their subsistence arose. Some special land was set aside to provide scholarship funds, but during the ninth century, as the influence of the University declined, funds for scholarships were not forthcoming. The tenth century saw a shrinkage in the size and importance of the Daigaku, which it is not easy to explain. It cannot be said that it was due to a loss of respect for learning. It may be attributed to the fact that preferment in official life began to go by favour of the great families, especially the Fujiwara. Furthermore the so-called "Shigaku" or Private Schools, which were founded by the great families, tended to compete with the Daigaku.

Some say that these private schools were not teaching establishments but only residential colleges, but they must in some degree have competed with the University. After the tenth century the family schools (like the Kangaku-in of the Fujiwara, the Shōgaku-in of the Ariwara, and the Gakkan-in of the Tachibana) also tended to decline in importance, and to lose their revenue, probably because local magnates confiscated the manors from which it was derived.

But perhaps the most interesting feature of the system of examinations is the importance attached to literary style. It often happened that a man with no great wisdom or knowledge of the classics was given a good place if he could compose well in Chinese. This is actually provided for in one paragraph of the code, which says "Those who are not proficient in reasoned exposition may be put forward for a degree if they are good at writing"—that is, if they can compose in good classical style. There can be no doubt that in the early Heian period this emphasis upon literary gifts affected the selection of candidates for top degrees and caused neglect of other qualifications for an official career. Even to be a good poet was at times a strong claim for promotion to high office.

A well-known passage on university education in the *Tale of Genji* gives a useful indication of the attitude of the Court aristocracy towards scholars and scholarship. It is in the chapter called "Otome," where there is a description of the ceremony at which Genji's son Yugiri is given a school-name before his admission to the University. Most of the princes and courtiers who attended this function thought that education was not necessary for young men of high birth, and they found the manners and appearance and speech of the professors very comic. But Genji was determined that his son should have a good education, remembering his own shortcomings as a youth. After Yugiri had shown proficiency in his examination the University began to attract other young men from the most aristocratic families; and before long it was quite usual for the holders of high office to be men who had taken a degree.

APPENDIX IV

DETAILS OF THE SUCCESSION DISPUTE, 1272–1318

1. *Narrative*

For students interested in the legitimacy problem which arose after the death of Go-Saga in 1272, the following account provides some particulars that were omitted from the narrative in Chapter XXI in order not to overload it with detail.

The true origin of the succession dispute was not, as is sometimes supposed, the will which Go-Saga made in 1272, but an earlier step taken in 1259, when he obliged his son Go-Fukakusa, then titular Emperor, to abdicate at the age of fifteen and to give place to a younger brother, Kameyama, then ten years old.

During Go-Saga's lifetime there was no open quarrel between the two brothers, who seemed to remain on good terms. But their respective adherents, whose fortunes were at stake, began to make trouble soon after Go-Saga's death, when his widow (Ōmiya-In) advised the Bakufu of his last wishes. If her account is to be believed, Go-Saga desired that the crown should go to a son of Kameyama, and that accordingly Kameyama should become the chief retired Emperor, the de facto ruler or Jisei no Kimi.

There are extant reliable documents to show that Ōmiya-In's version was wrong. Go-Saga left the choice of a successor to the Bakufu, well knowing that no candidate could succeed without the approval of Kamakura. Any prudent sovereign would bear in mind the fate of Go-Toba. Under the later Hōjō regime and especially during the life of Go-Saga, when intercourse between Kyoto and Kamakura was most friendly, the Regents had been careful to avoid the appearance of pressure upon the Court in matters of succession. Accordingly, upon Go-Saga's death their deputy in Kyoto confined himself to enquiring what the late sovereign's wish had been. When told that he had chosen Kameyama to succeed as Jisei no Kimi the Bakufu expressed respectful approval, without disclosing any preference. The position was now as follows:

1. Go-Saga (1220–72)
Titular: 1242–46
Retired: 1246–72

2. Go-Fukakusa (1243–1304)
Titular: 1246–59
Retired: 1259–1304

3. Kameyama (1249–1305)
Titular: 1259–74
Retired: 1274–1305

Since Kameyama was to succeed Go-Saga as the chief retired Emperor, this was a second rebuff to the elder son, Go-Fukakusa. He had been obliged to abdicate in 1259 in favour of Kameyama and now he was superseded by Kameyama in the most powerful position, which enabled its holder to name his own son as titular emperor.

Kameyama chose his son, the Prince Yohito, who was enthroned at the age of seven as the Emperor Go-Uda. There was some delay before the enthronement, which took place in 1274, two years after the death of Go-Saga—two years in which there was much going and coming between Kamakura and Kyoto, and much argument, not to say conspiracy, in both places. From the point of view of practical politics the decision of the Bakufu was reasonable, since it was probably what Go-Saga would have wished; and no doubt in the minds of the warriors there was not much to choose between the numerous princelings who might have been named. Indeed as an expression of paternal solicitude the claim of Kameyama was natural enough, for he had become a father at the age of fourteen and continued to beget children year by year for several decades.

But when Kameyama succeeded to all the profits and pleasures of chief retired Emperor, the supporters of the senior line then represented by Fukakusa were incensed, some out of sheer loyalty and many out of disappointment at losing their prospects of lucrative office. Go-Fukakusa in distress prepared to enter the religious life, being loth to struggle against his brother and the Bakufu. The Hōjō leaders, meanwhile, felt some sympathy for Go-Fukakusa, and tried to placate the senior line by approving the selection of a son of his, to succeed as titular Emperor upon the abdication of Go-Uda, which took place in 1287. This young prince was enthroned in 1288 as the Emperor Fushimi. Here was a triumph for the senior line, especially since the choice was approved, and indeed arranged, by the Bakufu. Looking ahead, the junior line now pressed for the selection of Go-Uda's first son (Prince Kuniharu) as Crown Prince, to succeed Fushimi.

I. Successors to Go-Fukakusa and Kameyama

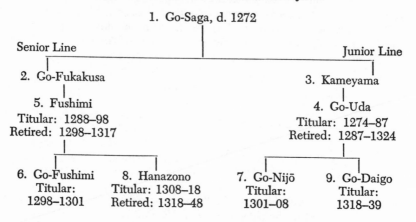

1. Go-Saga, d. 1272

Senior Line

Junior Line

2. Go-Fukakusa

3. Kameyama

5. Fushimi
Titular: 1288–98
Retired: 1298–1317

4. Go-Uda
Titular: 1274–87
Retired: 1287–1324

6. Go-Fushimi
Titular:
1298–1301

8. Hanazono
Titular: 1308–18
Retired: 1318–48

7. Go-Nijō
Titular:
1301–08

9. Go-Daigo
Titular:
1318–39

II. Accessions and Abdications in Chronological Order

LINE		BIRTH	ACCESSION	ABDICATION	DEATH
Senior	Go-Fukakusa	1243	1246	1259	1304
Junior	Kameyama	1249	1259	1274	1305
Junior	Go-Uda	1267	1274	1287	1324
Senior	Fushimi	1265	1288	1298	1317
Senior	Go-Fushimi	1288	1298	1301	1336
Junior	Go-Nijō	1285	1301	—	1308
Senior	Hanazono	1297	1308	1318	1348
Junior	Go-Daigo	1287	1318	—	1339

The periods of retirement given above are not necessarily the same as the periods during which retired emperors were in power as rulers (Jisei no Kimi). Thus, although Go-Fukakusa was in retirement from 1259 to 1304, his father Go-Saga remained the chief retired Emperor until his death in 1272, and was succeeded in that capacity by Kameyama from 1274 to 1287. Fushimi's succession to the throne in 1288 gave his father Go-Fukakusa a spell until 1301. Next came Go-Uda, from 1301 to 1308, while his son Go-Nijō was titular sovereign. It was of course the alternation of junior and senior lines that brought about these frequent changes.

The result was an open clash, for at this juncture the senior line proposed as Crown Prince a son of Fushimi, Atsuhito, whom Fushimi upon abdication was to nominate as titular Emperor. The junior line was not only dissatisfied, it was angry and alarmed. An appeal was made to the Bakufu on behalf of Go-Uda's son, supported by Kameyama, who continued to act as if he were chief retired Emperor until his death in 1305. Kameyama, in view of his birth and his prestige, might have obtained some support from the Bakufu but for a curious incident. Early in 1290 a warrior named Asawara with other armed men broke into the inner apartments of the Palace and reached the bedchamber of the Emperor Fushimi. Their attempt upon his life failed; he had been warned and escaped. It was suspected that Kameyama was somehow implicated, but His Majesty wrote in his own hand a letter to the Regent denying all knowledge of the plot, and the matter was dropped.

The further development of the succession problem is best studied in the light of the tables opposite. A striking feature of the dynastic picture as it is shown in these tables is the fact that most of the sovereigns acceded in childhood or very early youth and abdicated after brief reigns. The reason is clear. The titular emperors had no power; they only gave to their abdicated seniors a claim to power and wealth which were the privileges of the chief retired emperor. Since abdication was so frequent, there were usually several retired emperors living in Kyoto. At one time there were five.

The Emperor Fushimi remained on the throne for ten years, which brought him to the age of thirty-three. It was time for a change by current standards, and accordingly in 1298 Fushimi retired and was followed by his son Atsuhito, who was enthroned in that year as Go-Fushimi.

By this choice the senior line had provided two emperors without interruption by the junior line. Next, it will be noted, the Bakufu favoured the junior line by "recommending" as Crown Prince the young Kuniharu, who was Go-Uda's first son. In other words, whether purposely or not, the Bakufu was creating a precedent of alternation between the two lines. After the death of Go-Saga the Bakufu had ostensibly remained neutral or disinterested in the rivalry between the two lines, only intervening under pressure from one side or the other. But the Bakufu held the key to all problems, and it was essential for Kyoto and Kamakura to be in touch. The function of go-between was performed by Saionji Sanekane, who was known as the "Kantō Mōshitsugi," or the "mouthpiece" of the Hōjō Regent in dealings with the Court. His part in the succession disputes was therefore very important, and he certainly influenced the decisions of the Bakufu. By his mediation, it appears, a temporary solution was reached when Go-Nijō became titular Emperor. The younger brother of the retired Go-Fushimi was named Crown Prince, presently to succeed as the Emperor Hanazono. Thus the order of succession was as follows:

Titular Emperor	Junior Line	Senior Line
1298–1301	—	Go-Fushimi (Atsuhito)
1301–1308	Go-Nijō (Kuniharu)	—
1308–1318	—	Hanazono

Alternation was a reasonable solution so long as both lines agreed and kept their agreements. But neither was satisfied; each wanted to be the sole legitimate line. In 1317 the Bakufu attempted a compromise. At that time the designated Crown Prince (Takaharu) was thirty years old. In accordance with current notions it was thought proper that, being of the junior line, he should now without delay succeed as titular sovereign, following the abdication of Hanazono. This proposal commended itself to the Bakufu, who sent a mission from Kamakura suggesting its adoption.

There was a good deal of argument to and fro before the succession of Takaharu, as the Emperor Go-Daigo, was approved. It was finally accepted subject to two conditions: first, that the Crown Prince should be Kuninaga, a son of Go-Nijō and therefore of the junior line; second, that he must be followed by a prince of the senior line, Kazuhito, the heir of Go-Fushimi.

This indicates that Go-Fushimi (who as elder brother of the titular Emperor Hanazono was chief retired Emperor from 1313 to 1318) agreed to the succession of Go-Daigo on condition that thereafter alternation should be adopted as a fixed rule. It also appears that at first the Bakufu did not approve of the proposal that there should be two junior line emperors in sequence, namely Go-Daigo and Kuninaga. It seems probable that the merit of the arrangement from the point of view of the Bakufu was that it confined the succession to the lines of Go-Nijō and Go-Fushimi, thus excluding the descendants of Go-Daigo and Hanazono.

The arrangement reached is known as the Bunpo Wadan[1] or Compromise of 1317. At that time the most powerful member of the imperial family was the former Emperor Go-Uda, of the junior line. It is possible that he foresaw great trouble if there should be not only a breach between senior and junior lines, but also a split within each line, since that would more than double the difficulty to be overcome. Perhaps he agreed to the Compromise of 1317 because he felt that it was better than a continuing argument. If those were his hopes, he was disappointed. Within months after the signing of the Compromise the senior line had split into two factions, and no sooner had Go-Daigo ascended the throne than the same kind of split occurred in the junior line. The situation was ridiculous. The Compromise had not only failed; it had made the position worse instead of better.

It was naturally unwelcome to the Emperor Go-Daigo, for by its terms he could not hope for one of his many sons to succeed. Nor could he hope to stay long on the throne himself if the Compromise remained valid, since there was bound to be strong pressure on him to abdicate from the supporters of Prince Kuninaga, the son of Go-Nijō. Go-Daigo, being a man of character, was determined to settle the rule of succession beyond argument, and his decision led him inevitably into plots against the Bakufu. But since his father Go-Uda was still powerful, he took no active steps against the Bakufu until after 1321, when Go-Uda relinquished his powers.

In the year 1321, which was an auspicious conjunction in the sexagenary cycle, the prospects for change or reform were deemed hopeful by the soothsayers. "All things had to be renewed" at this point, and therefore the ex-Emperor Go-Fushimi addressed a special prayer to the Iwashimizu shrine. The text has been preserved. He begged for the immediate designation of Kazuhito, his son, as Crown Prince. Upon his making the same appeal to Kamakura, Go-Uda sent messengers to Kamakura to plead the cause of the junior line, as represented by his son Go-Daigo, who wished to designate his own

[1] Bunpo is the era name for 1317–18.

child Takanaga as Crown Prince. He reaffirmed this wish when Kuninaga died in 1326.

To this the Bakufu would not agree; they insisted upon the appointment of Kazuhito in accordance with the Compromise of 1317. This in turn was unacceptable to Go-Daigo, who had certain advantages in dealing with the Bakufu. He was not a child, but a grown man. He was determined not to abdicate, and he intended to govern. Finally, he had the advice of some very capable Court officials of high standing, notably the so-called Three Fusas, Madenōkoji Nobufusa, Kitabatake Chikafusa, and Yoshida Sadafusa.

Nobufusa was chief of the In's Cabinet (Inchō no bettō) under the cloistered Go-Uda, and the author of certain administrative reforms by which he hoped to improve the Kyoto government at a time when the Kamakura government was losing its old integrity. The measures he favoured were sure to make enemies—among other things he boldly proposed to confine official appointments to men of intelligence and good character. He wanted to purify the law courts and to put an end to abuses in shrines and monasteries. So high were his aims that he even proposed to put an end to the interference of Court ladies in affairs of state. He died without accomplishing these admirable purposes, for he was already aged and infirm when Go-Daigo assumed power. But he had served the junior line well. It was he who went to Kamakura as messenger for Go-Uda when the Compromise of 1317 was reached.

Kitabatake Chikafusa is a more celebrated figure in the history of Japan. He was a scholar and a fighting man of the Murakami Genji clan. He held strong views on legitimacy of succession, about which he wrote an important treatise; and he served Go-Daigo well with his sword as well as his pen.

Yoshida Sadafusa (1274–1338) was a Kyoto nobleman, a Fujiwara, and a trusted adviser to Go-Daigo. He visited Kamakura frequently as an emissary trying to reconcile the Court and the Bakufu; but in 1331 he revealed Go-Daigo's plans to the Hōjō administration and later went over to the service of the senior line.

Although Go-Daigo never achieved his ambitious purposes but died at his Court in the hills of Yoshino in 1339, he did by his stand in 1321 bring an end to the system of cloister government which had been the cause of long dynastic strife.

It should be added here that the succession was somewhat complicated by the need to appoint an imperial prince as Shōgun. It will be seen from the accompanying chart that no Shōgun was taken from the junior line—probably because the senior line was in favour at Kamakura during the years from 1289 to 1301.

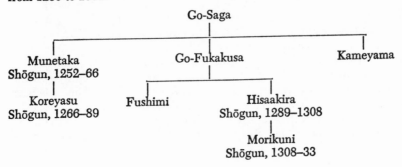

2. *Analysis*

It will be seen from the foregoing summary description that in treating questions of succession after the death of Go-Saga the Bakufu did not follow any clear dynastic principle. They were influenced by pragmatic considerations. They were uneasy about their own situation, suspicious of the Court, and aware that they had lost the confidence or the loyalty of many of their vassals. They wished to avoid any step that might lead to open conflict between the two lines, because in such a struggle powerful warrior chieftains were likely to take sides and might turn their weapons against the Kamakura government. They had several warnings of plots against themselves and they were conscious of their own weakness, which was to be openly revealed in 1320 by the failure of their forces to suppress a rebellious vassal in the province of Mutsu.

Their main purpose in dealing with both junior and senior lines was to avoid an outbreak, and for that reason they had tried to satisfy both sides without consistent support for either. They depended upon the advice of their spokesman in the capital, Saionji Sanekane, an extremely able and influential nobleman. Sanekane was useful to the Kamakura leaders because like them he had no real preference among the contending sovereigns and their offspring. His true aim was to restore and improve the fortunes of his own family. To that end it was important to cultivate the friendship of Kamakura while strengthening his own position at Court through the marriage of Saionji girls to members of the imperial family. He already had close relationship with the sovereign house. One of his aunts was a consort of the Emperor Go-Saga and the mother of both Go-Fukakusa and Kameyama. A sister was consort of Kameyama and three daughters were married to future occupants of the throne. His granddaughter Yasu-ko became the wife of Go-Fushimi.

At first he seems to have been in favour of the senior line. For example, in the choice of a Crown Prince to succeed Fushimi he recommended Fushimi's own son, as against a candidate of the junior line strongly supported by Go-Uda. It is said that he withdrew his support from the junior line because his sister was slighted by the Emperor Kameyama. However that may be, he was very powerful at Court, and was loaded with honours.

In 1291 he was appointed Chancellor (Dajō-Daijin) and raised to the highest possible rank. But the situation seemed difficult and he begged to be allowed to resign. The wind was shifting. He saw that under a surface of brotherly affection between Kameyama and Go-Fukakusa there was an irreconcilable hostility, leading their followers into dangerous intrigue and plots. The arguments of the junior line had begun to gain a hearing in Kamakura, partly because Sanekane began to change his mind. The immediate reason for the change was the conduct of the advisers of the Emperor Fushimi, notably one Fujiwara Tamekane, who was a descendant of the celebrated poet Teika and himself the leader of a progressive school. This crafty politician was a favourite at Court and his advice was welcomed by Fushimi. He began to rival Sanekane, but he made many enemies, some of whom accused him of treason. Whether these charges were true or false, they caused the Bakufu to mistrust the senior line. Sanekane thought it prudent to stand aside. He entered the religious life in 1299 and was succeeded by his son Kimpira, who took over the duties of Kantō Mōshitsugi. The expected succession of Fushimi's son took place in 1298 as arranged, and Kimpira's daughter Yasu-ko was sent to the palace, later to become the consort of the new Emperor, Go-Fushimi.

The retired Go-Fukakusa died in 1304, and shortly after that the retired Kameyama fell ill. He had to some extent profited by the suspicion which fell upon the senior line, and since the chief retired Emperor (Jisei no Kimi) was now of the junior line the outlook was favourable. He had welcomed the support of Saionji Kimpira, and was proud and joyful when Kimpira's sister, his second consort, gave birth to a son in 1303. The son was made an imperial prince, styled Tsuneaki Shinnō, and Kameyama at once told Go-Uda that Tsuneaki must be named Crown Prince instead of Go-Uda's son, Takaharu, who had already been designated. Kimpira could not agree to this change, and found himself once more close to the senior line. In 1306 (after Kameyama's death) Kimpira's daughter Yasu-ko was married to Go-Fushimi and duly presented him with a son. When Hanazono succeeded to the throne, Kimpira was an important friend of the senior line. As much for his daughter's services as his own, he was rewarded by promotion to the office of Minister of the Left. He entered the religious life in 1309 and died a few years later. His father Sanekane resumed his duties as spokesman for Kamakura, and found himself in opposition to Tamekane, the favourite of the retired Fushimi.

The dynastic quarrel had grown fiercer after the death of Go-Fukakusa and Kameyama. Each side accused the other of treachery, but on the whole the junior line had the advantage of good relations with the Bakufu and public opinion seemed to be moving against the senior line. Go-Fushimi was alarmed and warned his father. But Tamekane continued to prosper and Sanekane decided that he must act. It is not clear what steps were taken, but soon strong rumours were circulating against the senior line, and it was hinted that the abdicated Fushimi was plotting against the Bakufu. Such defamatory tales were convenient to Sanekane, for when they reached Kamakura rapid steps were taken. Tamekane was arrested and banished early in 1315. Fushimi was accused of complicity, and the Bakufu were on the point of severe measures against him when (in October 1315) he wrote a solemn declaration denying all knowledge of the alleged conspiracy and protesting his constant desire to work in harmony with the Regent.

The matter was dropped, but suspicion still clung to the senior line. The junior line profited, for within a year or two it was time for Hanazono to abdicate. He was succeeded by Takaharu, who became the Emperor Go-Daigo in 1318, and whose rule was the prelude to a long war of succession.

It is not easy to draw any precise inferences from the facts just recited. Perhaps the most interesting point to emerge is the utter lack of any rule of succession. In view of the importance attached in later Japanese history to the principles of legitimacy laid down by Kitabatake and others (notably the Jinnō Shōtō Ki of 1339), it is surprising to find that, in the critical period from the death of Go-Saga in 1272 to the accession of Go-Daigo in 1318, the choice of an heir to the throne was usually determined by a reigning or an abdicated sovereign not on grounds of primogeniture or indeed of any accepted precedent, but out of paternal affection or under the pressure of courtiers anxious to share the spoils of power.

It is true that no choice of a successor to the throne was effective unless it was approved by the Bakufu. But the decisions of the Bakufu were uncertain and even irrational, being governed by temporary circumstance. Perhaps the most significant example of a lack of fixed principle in the matter of inheritance is the split in the junior line which followed the designation of Go-Uda's son Takaharu as Crown Prince. Shortly after this nomination, which was the result of long deliberation and had the approval of the Bakufu, the philoprogenitive Kameyama, Go-Uda's father, was presented by his most recent consort with a son, for whom he claimed the right of succession in place of Takaharu. The claim was dismissed by the Bakufu, but that it should have been made shows the lack of a rule or principle, and a high disregard for primogeniture.

In these and other cases the Bakufu was quite unsystematic. Its attitude depended upon the advice of Saionji and its decisions were based upon suspicion or caution, not upon custom or precedent. Its chief concern was to keep a balance between rival lines and so to avoid civil disturbance. The leaders in Kamakura no longer had the resolution which had enabled their predecessors to suppress the insubordinate Go-Toba in 1221. It might even be said that the Hōjō Regency was destroyed by its own vacillation.

BIBLIOGRAPHICAL NOTE

For the Western student standard histories by leading Japanese scholars are indispensable. Of these I have depended mainly upon Kuroita's *Kokushi no Kenkyū* and Kurita's *Sōgō Nihonshi Kenkyū*. In addition to such modern works the foreign student should, I think, acquaint himself with the *Dokushi Yoron* of Arai Hakuseki (1657–1725). It gives the views of one of the greatest scholars of Japan (himself versed in feudal administration) upon crucial questions in his country's history, notably the conflict between the Crown and the Bakufu.

Of the histories in series published in recent years, the volumes of *Sōgō Nihonshi Taikei* will be found most useful, especially for their full references to sources. Other series should also be consulted, e.g., the volumes on Japan in the *Sekai Rekishi Taikei*.

For special periods and aspects of Japanese history I have found the following works most useful:

> Tsuda Sōkichi, *Nihon Jōdaishi no Kenkyū*
> Ikeuchi Hiroshi, *Nihon Jōdaishi no Ichi-kenkyū*
> ᵂatsuji Tetsurō, *Nihon Rinri Shisō-shi*
> ₌raoka Maretsugu, *Nihon Shisōshi no Kenkyū*, Vol. I

These deal mostly with ancient history. For later periods the following works are important:

Nara-Heian Jidai (in "Shin Nihon Rekishi" series, 1953). Collected essays.

Endō and Watanabe, *Nihon Chūsei-shi*. An admirable compendium on mediaeval studies.

Akiyama Kenzō, *Nihon Chūsei-shi*. A standard work.

Ito Tasaburō, *Nihon Hōkenseido-shi*. Excellent.

Ryū Susumu, *Kamakura Bakufu no Seiji*. Authoritative on feudal government.

Maki Kenji, *Nihon Hōseishi Gairon*. An introduction to legal history.

Miura Kaneyuki, *Nihon Hōseishi*. A standard work on the development of law in Japan.

Ōmori Kingorō, *Buke Jidai no Kenkyū*. A classic study of the growth of the warrior class, amply documented. 3 vols.

Joüon de Longrais, *Age de Kamakura*. *Sources; archives*. Valuable for the study of feudal institutions and forms, and a useful aid to the reading of documents.

Reischauer and Yamagiwa, *Translations from Early Japanese Literature*. Contains much interesting material and useful annotations.

Ikeuchi Hiroshi, *Genkō no Shin-kenkyū*. The fullest and most reliable account of the Mongol invasions of Japan.

Source Materials

Apart from the ancient records (*Kojiki* and *Nihongi*), classical belleslettres (*Genji Monogatari, Makura no Sōshi,* etc.), and the romantic war chronicles (like the *Heike Monogatari*), which are all essential but must be

486 BIBLIOGRAPHICAL NOTE

used with caution, the following basic materials have been drawn upon in the preparation of this volume:

Shoku Nihongi. Eighth-century edicts.
Nara Ibun. A collection of Nara documents (ed. Takeuchi Rizō).
Heian Ibun. A collection of Heian documents (ed. Takeuchi Rizō).

LEGAL HISTORY

For the plan, drafts, and text of *Jōei Shikimoku*, see Buke section of Gun-sho Ruijū. Additions to the Jōei code are in *Shimpen Tsuika*, in Zoku-Gunsho-Ruijū.

POPULATION STATISTICS

The best survey is in *Nihon Jinkō-shi*, by Honjō Eijirō, but for early and mediaeval periods the figures quoted are only wild guesses. The most likely estimate is one ascribed to Nichiren, who puts the total at 4,589,659, and adds that all these will go to Hell if they do not follow his teaching. For the end of the thirteenth century five million is probably not far out.

DIARIES

See list on p. 165. The most important of these is *Gyokuyō* (玉葉), the diary of the Regent Kujō Kanezane.

The diary known as *Kichiki* (吉記) or *Kikki* is the journal of a colleague of Kanezane, Fujiwara Tsunefusa (1143–1200). It covers the rise and fall of the Taira and the early phases of the Bakufu. In some points it supplements Kanezane's entries.

The celebrated *Meigetsuki* (明月記), which is intermittent from 1180 to 1236, is an important primary source for mediaeval history. Its value is due in part to the poet Teika's intimacy with the Kujō and Saionji families. Teika was the teacher of the young Shōgun Sanetomo, and knew what was going on in Kamakura. He was a good observer, with political as well as poetical insight, and provides good evidence for the last days of the Taira and the first fifty years of the Bakufu.

The *Entairyaku* (園太暦), the journal of Tōin Kinkata (1291–1360), a Minister of State under Go-Daigo, contains entries from 1311, but the extant portion includes no useful entries for the years before 1334, when Go-Daigo was in Yoshino.

Of the Imperial Diaries (*Shinki,* 宸記), the most important is the diary of the Emperor Hanazono. It provides information about life at Court and events in the capital while he was on the throne and after his abdication. The surviving portions cover the years 1310 to 1332. It is not easy to read, but it is a very interesting human document as well as a source for political and religious history. It ranks in scope and importance with the later *Kambun Gyoki* (看聞御記), the journal of the Emperor Sukō for the years 1416–48.

CHRONICLES AND HISTORICAL COMPILATIONS

Of the chronicles by far the most important is the *Azuma Kagami*, the most comprehensive source for the history of the development of feudalism in Japan. The first part was compiled about 1270, mainly from journals and records kept by noblemen of the Heian regime. It deals with matters which came to their private knowledge or their official notice. The second part is based upon official records of the Kamakura government. It contains valuable material for the study of social and economic growth, and if used with care is a useful guide to the ethos of the warrior caste. It displays a certain bias in favour of the Hōjō family.

I have had the advantage of reading an excellent dissertation by Dr. Minoru Shinoda, entitled "The Founding of the Kamakura Shogunate, 1180–1185," completed at Columbia University in 1957. It is based mainly on the *Azuma Kagami.*

The *Eiga Monogatari* is a romantic story of Michinaga's grandeur. It covers the greater part of the eleventh century, during which most of it was written, though extant versions may contain later additions. It is valuable as a description of luxurious Court society in the days of the Fujiwara dictators.

The *Ōkagami* describes the rise of the Fujiwara leaders from 850 to 1025, the summit of Michinaga's power. Its treatment is more critical than that of the *Eiga Monogatari,* and it pays attention to political intrigue behind the scenes. It was written late in the eleventh century.

The *Heike Monogatari,* despite its exaggerations and its obvious bias, is essential for the study of mediaeval Japan. Dozens of versions of this romantic tale exist. Internal evidence suggests that a basic version was written between 1190 and 1221.

The *Gukanshō* (愚管抄) is one of the great historical works of Japan. It records the national history from early times to the Jōkyū era. It is the first attempt to interpret as well as to narrate the course of events. Its world-view is coloured by the pessimist "mappō" concept, and it treats of the feudal period as an age of decline. It is ascribed to the monk Jien. He attempts (he says) "to enlighten people who find it hard to understand the vicissitudes of life." It is thought to have been written about 1220.

The *Jinnō Shōtōki* (神皇正統記) is the "history of the true line of descent of the divine emperors" by Kitabatake Chikafusa. By contrast with the *Gukanshō* this is an optimistic work, its writer being a man of great energy and strong convictions, a firm believer in the Shintō religion.

The *Hyakurenshō* (百錬抄) is a work of the late Kamakura period, written before 1304. It is an uncritical mixture of quotations from diaries and statements based upon the writer's direct knowledge. It covers the years from 967 to 1259 and deals mainly with Court life.

The *Zokushi Gushō* (續史愚抄) is a compilation by an eighteenth-century scholar of materials describing conditions in Kyoto in the late middle age. In the Kokushi Taikei edition it has an index.

The *Kojidan* (古事談), written in a curious style and mixing fact with fable, is the work of Minamoto Akikane, who put it together not long before 1215. It draws freely upon previous works. It consists of supernatural tales, Buddhist legend, and biographies of great men.

The *Kōdanshō* (江談抄) is a similar work, part of which is by Ōye Masafusa. It is used by the writer of the *Kojidan.*

The above list is by no means complete, but it includes the principal basic works consulted during the preparation of this volume, except for the writings of religious leaders like Nichiren and Shinran, which are essential for an understanding of mass psychology in the thirteenth century.

INDEX

Yedo, 6
Yin-Yang, 70, 212 ff.
Yodo River, 99
Yōmeimon-In, empress of Go-Su-zaku, 197
Yorinaga, *see under* Fujiwara
Yoritomo, *see under* Minamoto
Yoritsugu, Shōgun, 409, 415
Yoritsune, Shōgun: appointed (1227), 392; visit to Kyoto, 402–3; deposed (1244), 407–9; plots of his friends, 410–11; sent back to Kyoto, 411
Yoru Kampaku ("Night Regent"), 205
Yoshida Sadafusa, 481

Yoshi-ko, Empress Dowager, 175
Yoshitsune, *see under* Minamoto
Yosobito ("outsider," nobleman un-qualified for post of Regent), 156
Yūki Tomomitsu, 317
Yuri Hachirō, 381
Yūryaku, Emperor, 41, 43

Z

Zemmon, Buddhist appellation of Kiyomori, 287
Zen monks from China, 431
Zen teaching, 429
Zōshiki (rank of foot soldier), 367
Zuryō (deputy governor), 172, 205
Zusa (soldiers), 351

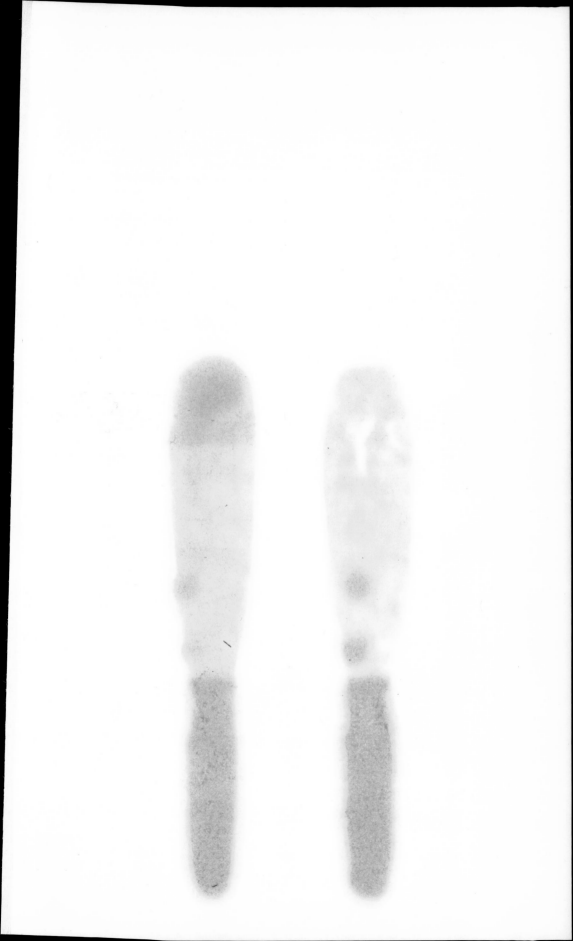